PENGUIN BOOKS

THE ORIGINS OF SEX

'A revelation . . . The book is not simply a finely crafted work of history, but a study that will reshape the way its readers understand the most intimate level of their lives. It may even bring some sanity to modern debates about sexuality' Diarmaid MacCulloch

'An enthralling history of changing ideas about sexual freedom and desire . . . inspiring as well as provocative' Sarah Bakewell, *Independent*

'The depth of detailed historical research is as eye-catching as the breadth and topicality of Dabhoiwala's argument . . . this is more than just exemplary history; it is timely and important work' Ian Kelly, *The Times*

'Dabhoiwala's balanced and responsible study takes a fascinating subject seriously without being po-faced, and in doing so, holds up a mirror to our own contradictory times' Lesley McDowell, *Independent on Sunday*

'Impressive . . . erudite . . . packed with information and peppered with fascinating examples. It will delight students of social and sexual history, and anyone interested in the history of ideas' Julie Peakman, *The Times Literary Supplement*

'Forget the '60s; sex started far earlier . . . Rich, crisply written and impressively well-researched . . . engrossing' Michael Dirda, *Washington Post*

'Exceptionally good . . . Dabhoiwala assembles a huge mass of information . . . his book has many lessons for us' Brian Morton, *Sunday Herald*

An 'exhilarating, ground-breaking book . . . the whole narrative is peppered with surprising revelations . . . a meticulously researched, rigorously argued study . . . Its epic scope . . . brings universal truths into sharp focus . . . This is a lucid and stimulating book that challenges many of our assumptions about sex' Matthew Green, *History Today*

'An informative, wide-ranging book that is also compellingly readable . . . He has done a wonderful job . . . Dabhoiwala has to tread a difficult path through a more or less limitless field, and he manages it with great care and unselfconscious aplomb' John Barrell, *Guardian*

'Fascinating . . . incorporates everything . . . an impressively illustrated argument, both literally and figura[tively]' *BBC History M[agazine]*

'A deep [and] astonishingly wide-rang[ing] fascinates throughout' Atte Jong[erius]

ABOUT THE AUTHOR

Faramerz Dabhoiwala was born in England, grew up in Amsterdam, and was educated at York and Oxford. He is the Senior Fellow in History at Exeter College, Oxford, a Fellow of the Royal Historical Society, and the father of two children. This is his first book.

FARAMERZ
DABHOIWALA

The Origins of Sex
A History of the First Sexual Revolution

PENGUIN BOOKS

PENGUIN BOOKS

Published by the Penguin Group
Penguin Books Ltd, 80 Strand, London WC2R ORL, England
Penguin Group (USA) Inc., 375 Hudson Street, New York, New York 10014, USA
Penguin Group (Canada), 90 Eglinton Avenue East, Suite 700, Toronto, Ontario, Canada M4P 2Y3
(a division of Pearson Penguin Canada Inc.)
Penguin Ireland, 25 St Stephen's Green, Dublin 2, Ireland (a division of Penguin Books Ltd)
Penguin Group (Australia), 707 Collins Street, Melbourne, Victoria 3008, Australia
(a division of Pearson Australia Group Pty Ltd)
Penguin Books India Pvt Ltd, 11 Community Centre, Panchsheel Park, New Delhi – 110 017, India
Penguin Group (NZ), 67 Apollo Drive, Rosedale, Auckland 0632, New Zealand
(a division of Pearson New Zealand Ltd)
Penguin Books (South Africa) (Pty) Ltd, Block D, Rosebank Office Park,
181 Jan Smuts Avenue, Parktown North, Gauteng 2193, South Africa

Penguin Books Ltd, Registered Offices: 80 Strand, London WC2R ORL, England

www.penguin.com

First published by Allen Lane 2012
Published in Penguin Books 2013

005

Copyright © Faramerz Dabhoiwala, 2012

Typeset by Jouve (UK), Milton Keynes
Printed in Great Britain by Clays Ltd, St Ives plc

A CIP catalogue record for this book is available from the British Library

ISBN: 978-0-241-95596-3

www.greenpenguin.co.uk

MIX
Paper from
responsible sources
FSC www.fsc.org FSC™ C018179

Penguin Books is committed to a sustainable
future for our business, our readers and our planet.
This book is made from Forest Stewardship
Council™ certified paper.

TO

JOCELYN
ZOË
AND
JO

WITH ALL MY LOVE

Contents

Acknowledgements

I should never have aspired to become a historian, nor persevered with this book, without the example and encouragement of several outstanding scholars and friends. I recall with gratitude the support of Ian Archer, Peter Biller, Jan Blokker, Michael Braddick, Robin Briggs, Marilyn Butler, Robert Darnton, Rees Davies, Anthony Fletcher, Clive Holmes, Joanna Innes, Ian Kershaw, Paul Langford, Diarmaid MacCulloch, David Parrott, Hanna Pickard, Lyndal Roper, Paul Slack, Robert Shoemaker, Lawrence Stone, Keith Thomas, Simon Walker, David Wootton, and Keith Wrightson. I am especially thankful for the unceasing kindness of Martin Ingram, who supervised my early researches, and of John Maddicott and Christina de Bellaigue, who have each helped me in innumerable ways.

I am profoundly obliged to the institutions that have sustained me at Oxford: the Faculty of History, All Souls College, and, most of all, Exeter College. I must acknowledge as well the support of the Lewis Walpole Library at Yale University and of the Arts and Humanities Research Board of the United Kingdom. And I rejoice in the vigilance and good humour of my publisher, Stuart Proffitt.

How very much I am indebted on particular points to the scholarship of others will, I hope, be evident from the notes. The book also owes an enormous amount to the intellectual stimulus of my students at Oxford, and to the benevolent interest of many colleagues across the world – historians, literary critics, lawyers, philosophers, and others – who have helped me discuss my ideas, supplied me with valuable references, and read drafts of the text. I am deeply grateful to them all.

The dedication records my happiest, most important obligation of all, to my three favourite readers.

Prologue: The Culture of Discipline

We could start anywhere in the British Isles, on any date almost from the dawn of recorded history to the later seventeenth century. But let's pick Westminster, on the bank of the Thames. It is Tuesday, 10 March 1612. If we hurry into the town's courthouse, we shall find its magistrates in session, dealing with a routine criminal case. An unmarried man and woman have been arrested and brought before them. They are accused of having had sex together. The woman confesses. The man denies it. It does not take long to decide their fate. They are put on trial before a jury of men, interrogated, and found guilty. Their punishment reflects the heinousness of their crime: not only did they have sex, they have brought into the world a bastard child. For this, Susan Perry and Robert Watson are to be cut off from their homes, their friends, their families, their livelihoods – to be forever expelled from the society in which they live. The judges order them to be taken directly

> to the prison of the Gatehouse; and both of them to be stripped naked from the waist upwards; and so tied to the cart's tail and to be whipped from the Gatehouse in Westminster unto Temple Bar; and then and there to be presently banished from the city.

What happened to their baby is not recorded.[1]

Sexual intercourse is a universal human practice. Yet sex also has a history. How we think about it, what meanings we invest in it, how we treat it as a society – all these things differ greatly across time and place. For most of western history the public punishment of men and women like Robert Watson and Susan Perry was a normal event. Sometimes they were treated more harshly, sometimes less, but all sex outside marriage was illegal, and the church, the state, and ordinary people devoted huge efforts to suppressing and punishing it. It seemed obvious that illicit relations angered God, prevented salvation, damaged personal relations, and undermined social order. Nobody seriously disagreed with this, even if men and women regularly gave way to temptation and had to be flogged, imprisoned, fined, and shamed, in order to remind them. Though the details varied from place to place, every European society promoted the ideal of sexual discipline and punished people for consensual non-marital sex. So did their colonial off-shoots, in North America and elsewhere. This was a central feature of Christian civilization, one that had steadily grown in importance since the early middle ages. In Britain alone by the early seventeenth century, thousands of men and women suffered the consequences every year. Sometimes, as we shall see, they were even put to death.

Nowadays we regard such practices with repugnance. We associate them with the Taliban, with Sharia law, with people far away and alien in outlook. Yet until quite recently, until the Enlightenment, our own culture was like this too. This was one of the main differences between the pre-modern and the modern world. The emergence of modern attitudes to sex in the later seventeenth and eighteenth centuries therefore constituted a great revolution. The aim of this book is to explain how it came about.

The subject is immense, yet it is never studied – worse still, its existence is barely acknowledged. More than thirty years ago, Sir Keith Thomas and the late Lawrence Stone, its first major English historians, recognized that the period between 1660 and 1800 marked a momentous watershed, 'a great secular change in sexual attitudes and sexual behaviour', the birth of the modern mind-set. But its origins remained unexplained. Since then, the history of sex, though increasingly popular, has also become ever more narrowly specialized. Academic historians now know more and more about past ideals of femininity and masculinity, about attitudes to the body, and about other esoteric subjects. Some are fascinated by the minute exploration of particular texts and ideas. Others concentrate on one or two individuals and their sexual experiences. This intense focus on the trees, rather than the wood, has produced a wealth of brilliant in-depth studies and theoretical insights. I have learned immensely from this work, and drawn upon it gratefully. However, it also seems to me to have overlooked the world-changing cultural shift that was so obvious to earlier, bolder scholars.[2]

This book seeks to describe that central transformation, and to connect it to the major political, intellectual, and social trends of the period. The history of sex is usually treated as part of the history of private life, or of bodily experience. Yet that is itself a consequence of the Enlightenment's conception of it as an essentially personal matter. My concern, by contrast, is not primarily to enter into the bedrooms and between the sheets of the past. It is to recover the history of sex as a central public preoccupation, and to demonstrate that how people in the past thought about and dealt with it was shaped by the most profound intellectual and social currents of their time. The Civil War and the execution of Charles I in 1649, the revolution of 1688, the growth of religious division, the expansion of urban society, the rise of the novel – all these developments, and many others, were intertwined with the dramatic changes in sexual culture that took place over the seventeenth and eighteenth centuries. Indeed, my general aim has been to show that the sexual revolution was a central part of the European and North American Enlightenment: it helped create a wholly new model of western civilization, whose principles of individual privacy, equality, and freedom remain distinctive to this day.

Compared with the Enlightenment in France, Germany, or Italy, that of the English-speaking world proceeded with so little fuss that, amazingly, historians still debate whether it can be said to have existed at all. This book takes a broad view of what the Enlightenment was – not merely a set of self-conscious philosophical debates amongst intellectuals, but a series of social and intellectual changes, across society, which altered almost everyone's conceptions of religion, truth, nature, and morality. The sexual revolution demonstrates how far and how quickly enlightened ways of thinking spread, and what important effects they had on popular attitudes and behaviour.

That does not mean they affected everyone equally, or favourably. As we shall see, though in the long term the ideals of sexual freedom were to become much more broadly accepted, in the short term their advance, like that of other kinds of liberty, primarily benefited a minority of white, heterosexual, propertied men. I have tried to indicate some of the sexual revolution's most obvious contradictions and disparities, especially for women. I hope that my analysis will provoke other scholars to explore further its varied implications for women and men, for same-sex relations, for different social classes and groups, and in other western societies.

The book's argument is not just about new ways of thinking but also about changing ways of living. It attempts to show how people's beliefs were affected by social circumstances, and how new forms of commerce, communication, and social organization transformed the perception, and the experience, of sex. Traditionally, most of the population had always lived in small, slow, rural communities in which social and moral conformity was easy to enforce. Life in big cities was different, in its scale and anonymity, the increasingly fast-paced circulation of news and ideas, and the sheer availability of sexual adventure. It placed the enforcement of sexual discipline under growing pressure. The first place to experience these changes was London, so that is where our attention will be focused.

This was the period in which London grew to be the largest metropolis in the world. For English-speaking people across the globe it was the epicentre of political power, of literature and culture, and of new ideas. Modern urban lifestyles and attitudes, new social, intellectual, and sexual trends: all were first created there, yet their effects were to be felt everywhere. What happened in London was eventually to shape the treatment of sexual issues nationally and internationally, across the British Empire – from Edinburgh to Brighton, from Dublin to New York, from Delhi to Melbourne. By the middle of the nineteenth century, the majority of the British population lived in towns, and by the end of this book we shall be in the recognizably familiar environment of Victorian and twentieth-century urban life. But the story begins in a very different world.

THE MEDIEVAL BACKGROUND

The further back in time we go, the more fragmentary the record becomes. Most of it has been lost, and what survives is often sparse and abbreviated, so that we can gain only intermittent glimpses of the law in action. Yet its general thrust is clear: the principle that illicit sex was a public crime was asserted with increasing vigour from the early middle ages onwards.

Indeed, since the dawn of history every civilization had prescribed severe laws against at least some kinds of sexual immorality. The oldest surviving legal codes (c. 2100–1700 BCE), drawn up by the kings of Babylon, made adultery punishable by death, and most other near eastern and classical cultures also treated it as a serious offence: this was the view taken by the Assyrians, the ancient Egyptians, the Jews, the Greeks, and, to some extent, the Romans. The main concern of such laws was usually to uphold the honour and property rights of fathers, husbands, and higher-status groups. The same outlook underpinned the justice of the Germanic tribes that settled across western Europe and the British Isles in the final years of the Roman Empire: the Franks, the Goths, the Saxons, the Jutes, and others. Thus the earliest English law codes, which date from this time, evoke a society where women were bought and sold, and lived constantly under the guardianship of men. Even in cases of consensual sex, its system of justice was mainly concerned with the compensation one man should pay to another for unlawful copulation with his female chattel. The laws of Ethelbert (c. 602), the Anglo-Saxon king of Kent, stipulate the different fines payable 'if a man takes a widow who does not belong to him'; for lying with servants or slave women of different classes; and for adultery with the wife of another freeman – in which case, as well as a heavy fine, the offender was 'to obtain another wife with his own money, and bring her to the other's home'. However, illicit sex was also, increasingly, abhorred for its own sake, and liable to harsh personal punishment. The code of Alfred the Great (c. 893) made it lawful for any man to kill another if he found him 'with his wedded wife, within closed doors or under the same blanket, or with his legitimate daughter or his legitimate sister, or with his mother'. That of King Cnut (c. 1020–23) forbade married men even from fornicating with their own slaves, and ordered that adulteresses should be publicly disgraced, lose their goods, and have their ears and noses cut off.[1]

This severity matched the attitude of the Christian church, and its growing status within European society during the early middle ages.

Though Jesus is not recorded as having said much on the subject, he evidently did not condone adultery or promiscuity, and the later leaders of his religion developed increasingly restrictive doctrines of sexual morality. In doing so, they drew upon many earlier teachings, so that the outcome was, as one scholar puts it, 'a complex assemblage of pagan and Jewish purity regulations, linked with primitive beliefs about the relationship between sex and the holy, joined to Stoic teachings about sexual ethics, and bound together by a patchwork of [new] doctrinal theories'. The Stoics, one of the most influential strands of Graeco-Roman philosophy, had generally distrusted sex as a low and dangerously corrupting pleasure. The same suspicion of sex as brutish and defiling ran through the Hebrew scriptures. Though the Old Testament lauded marriage as a socially and religiously indispensable institution, and sometimes (notably in the Song of Songs) celebrates marital eroticism, its overriding message was that sexual relations were unclean. Even between a husband and wife, sex was to be strictly limited in its timing, place, and purpose (only for procreation, not for pleasure), and had always to be followed by ritual purification, to wash away the dirtiness of the deed. The horror of pollution was evoked even more strongly by other forms of sex. God's instructions on this score were detailed and unequivocal. 'Thou shalt not commit adultery' was the seventh of his Ten Commandments, and every adulterer and adulteress, he had ordered, 'shall surely be put to death'. The same fate was to be imposed upon anyone guilty of incest or bestiality, as upon men who had sex with each other: all such people defiled themselves and the community. If the daughter of a priest were to fornicate, she should be burned alive. If a man lay with a menstruating woman, 'both of them shall be cut off from among their people'. If any man should lie with a betrothed maid, God's will was that 'ye shall bring them both out unto the gate of that city, and ye shall stone them with stones that they die' – 'so thou shalt put away evil from among you'.[2]

Christian teachings incorporated this basic outlook and went further still. Jewish law had been fairly tolerant of fornication between unmarried men and women, of men using Gentile prostitutes, and of concubines – indeed, as the Bible recorded, the ancient Hebrews had often had multiple wives. In its earliest centuries, Christianity too seems to have tolerated concubinage. More generally, however, the leaders of the new religion interpreted God's commands as forbidding any sex at all outside marriage: that way lay hell-fire and damnation. Many of them were so repelled by sexual relations that they saw even marriage as a less pure and desirable state than complete celibacy. Already in Christianity's earliest surviving texts this message is spelled out by St Paul, the dominant figure of the early church. 'It is good for a man not to touch a woman', he explained to the Christian community at Corinth around the middle of the first century, for even within marriage, sex seduced one's mind and body away from its highest purpose of communing with God. Paul himself was pure, single, and abstinent, and that was the holiest state. 'I would that all men were even as I myself,' he wrote, and maids and widows too: 'it is good for them if they abide even as I. But if they cannot contain [their lusts], let them marry: for it is better to marry than to burn' (I Corinthians 7.1–40; see Romans 1 for his condemnation of same-sex relations). In other words, marriage was but a regrettable indulgence to those who were too weak to bridle their bodily urges.

In the centuries that followed, the leading authorities of the church (most of whom were themselves celibate men) developed further this essentially negative view of sex. The ascetic ideal of abstinence, particularly for the clergy but also for lay men and women, was ever more strongly stressed; whilst a huge body of teaching grew up in support of the notion that bodily desire was inherently shameful and sinful. The most powerful exponent of this view was St Augustine (354–430), bishop of the town of Hippo on the north African coast: probably no other person has had a more profound and lasting impact on western Christian attitudes towards sexuality. In his youth this would have seemed unlikely. Whilst building a career as a clever young academic, in north Africa and then in Italy, he lived for many years with his unmarried lover and their illegitimate son, and was far more attracted to Manichaeism than to mainstream Christianity. Even when, as he famously recalled in his *Confessions*, he had begun to see the error of his ways, his prayer to God had been 'grant me chastity and self-control – but please not yet': for he was still full of 'lust which I was more anxious to satisfy than to snuff out'. Yet, as in the case of countless later critics of sensuality, it was precisely his experience of the force of human passion that led him, once converted and dedicated to a celibate life, to inveigh so vehemently against its foul, debilitating temptations. Ultimately, Augustine came to see lust as the most dangerous of all human drives. Like many other medieval theologians, he argued that it was a direct consequence of the Fall – sexual feelings were not a good at all but a punishment inflicted by God upon Adam and Eve and their descendants, an indelible marker of their sinful, corrupted state. After all, lust had an unparalleled power to overwhelm reason and human will: when aroused, men and women could not even control the stirrings of their own genitals. Worse still, no one could ever be sure of having conquered it for good, irrespective of their most strenuous efforts. In old age, almost forty years after becoming celibate, having dedicated his life to the mortification of desire, Augustine summed up his own experience in a letter to another bishop, Atticus of Constantinople. To restrain 'this concupiscence of the flesh', he complained, was a life-long battle for everyone, whether virgin, married, or widowed:

For it intrudes where it is not needed and tempts the hearts of faithful and holy people with its untimely and even wicked desire. Even if we do not give in to these restless impulses of it by any sign of consent but rather fight against them, we would nonetheless, out of a holier desire, want them not to exist in us at all, if that were possible.

But it was not possible. As long as humankind remained in its fallen state, sexual procreation itself passed on the evil from generation to generation: 'the guilt of this sin is contracted by birth'. Even in marriage, men and women had to be constantly on their guard against sinning through immoderate, unchaste, or unprocreative sex. For every Christian, throughout their life, sexual discipline was a fundamental, inescapable necessity.[3]

These were the doctrines that the church sought to instil in its followers everywhere that the new religion spread. In England, the earliest surviving handbooks for the Anglo-Saxon clergy (dating from the seventh to the eleventh century) describe in graphic detail the many different sexual sins, solitary, heterosexual, and homosexual, that laypeople and priests might commit, and the penalties for each of them – months or years of fasting, flogging, divorce, loss of clerical office.[4] The propagation of Christian moral standards had an increasingly notice-able effect on lay attitudes. Under pressure from the clergy, the aristocratic custom of taking concubines gradually declined, and the church's definition of monogamy slowly gained ground.[5]

The high middle ages saw a considerable acceleration in the theory and practice of sexual discipline. Between the eleventh and the thir-teenth centuries, the western church greatly expanded its power in this sphere, in line with its growing social and intellectual dominance. Across Europe, ecclesiastical laws relating to sex and marriage were elaborated, standardized, and tightened up, for clergy and laypeople, kings and peasants alike. This was, for example, the point at which the leaders of the church began a concerted and increasingly success-ful campaign to enforce celibacy on all priests and to banish clerical marriage. The establishment of the church's own permanent courts from about 1100 onwards likewise transformed the punishment of sexual offences amongst the population at large. From being primar-ily a matter of private confession and ad hoc jurisdiction, it now became the concern of an increasingly powerful system of public inquisition. Finally, the rise of towns and cities led to the addition of new civic penalties against adultery, fornication, and prostitution, alongside the older structures of royal, manorial, and ecclesiastical justice.[6]

By the later middle ages, extra-marital sex had come to be continu-ally policed by a dense network of jurisdictions. Sexual and marital cases dominated the business of the English church courts: already in the later thirteenth century, they account for between 60 and 90 per cent of all litigation for which records survive, and most later fifteenth-and early sixteenth-century evidence reveals the same overwhelming focus on combating adultery, fornication, and prostitution. The penalties imposed varied by time and place. In fourteenth-century Rochester, men and women were sometimes sent on pilgrimages to atone for their sins, ordered to give alms to the poor, or allowed to commute their sentence into a fine. The most common penance was to be beaten, publicly and repeatedly, around the parish church and the market-place, as the entire community looked on.[7] The same crimes were also punished by town courts. In Coventry in 1439, the magis-trates ordered that William Powlet, a cap-maker, should be publicly paraded through town in an open cart together with his lover, 'in example of punishment of sin', and that henceforth all fornicators should be treated in the same way. In London, Bristol, and Gloucester, they constructed a special public 'cage' in the main market-place, in which to imprison and display prostitutes, adulterers, and lecherous priests; elsewhere, cucking-stools were used to punish whores. From at least the late fourteenth century, special campaigns against sexual offenders were a regular occurrence in London, on top of the more routine policing of unchastity. There also became established elaborate rituals of civic punishment for convicted whores, bawds, and adulterers. Serious offenders were taken on a long public procession through the city, dressed in symbolically degrading clothes and accompanied by the raucous clanging of pans and basins. Sometimes they would also be whipped, put in the pillory, have their hair shaved off, or be banished from the city.[8]

The frequency with which these punishments were imposed throughout the later middle ages points to the persistence of sex outside marriage. Both in medieval literature and in daily life, illicit love and mercenary sex were often discussed in a more matter-of-fact way, implying that they might not always be culpable. Many people believed that fornication was not a serious offence, reported a twelfth-century bishop of Exeter; and though in 1287 the idea that it was wholly blameless was formally classified as a heresy, it persisted. It was especially accepted that young people fell in love, and that they might sometimes fool around. As the leaders of the early Tudor church were to complain in the 1540s, 'among many, it is counted no sin at all, but rather a pastime, a dalliance, and but a touch of youth: not rebuked, but winked at: not punished, but laughed at'.[9]

There were also obvious limits and inconsistencies in official attitudes to sexual discipline.[10] Unmarried cohabitation, both amongst the clergy and the laity, was commonplace until the high middle ages, and endured right up to the Reformation. The criminalization of fornication was further complicated by the church's own law of marriage, which was codified in the twelfth century (and not altered in England until the Marriage Act of 1753). All that it required for an unbreakable wedlock was that a marriageable man and woman exchanged vows in words of the present tense (and if they did so in words of the future tense, a single act of intercourse would create a legal union). In theory the legitimation of sex therefore required only the consent of the couple themselves, without the need for any priest, witnesses, or ceremony. In practice the church tried, with increasing success, to discourage and penalize all forms of quick, irregular, and clandestine marriage: already by the later middle ages the norm was a wedding that was advertised publicly, long in advance, and solemnized by a priest in the parish church, in front of the local community.[11] Yet the idea never completely died out that, ultimately, it was for a couple themselves to decide whether or not they were married in the sight of God (as we shall see in Chapter 2). Finally, public prostitution was tolerated, and in the later middle ages increasingly sanctioned, as a necessary evil. Given that in practice it was impossible to restrain the lusts of unmarried laymen and clerics, so the argument ran, it was better to allow brothels than to provoke seduction, rape, adultery, and worse. As a popular medieval analogy had it, 'remove the sewer, and you will fill the palace with a stench ... take away whores from the world, and you will fill it with sodomy'.[12]

All the same, the main trend over time was towards ever-tighter control and punishment of non-marital sex, by secular and ecclesiastical authorities alike. It is also evident that, over the course of the middle ages, the gap between Christian precepts and popular attitudes had steadily narrowed. Though people might quibble about the limits of sexual discipline, or resent its imposition on them personally, its effects were ubiquitous, and its necessity was taken for granted.

REFORMED MORALITY

In fact, by the early sixteenth century the main public criticism was that existing practice was far too lenient. This was a major complaint of the Protestant movement, which began around 1500 as a campaign to purify the church from within, but pretty soon developed into a cataclysmic struggle for truth that tore apart the unity of western Christendom. By the later sixteenth century, the western world (including its growing overseas colonies) was to be bitterly and permanently divided along religious lines – between Catholics and Protestants, and between different varieties of Protestantism. What Protestants had in common was a belief that the Catholic church's doctrines and practice had become corrupt and worldly. Their ambition was to rediscover what God really demanded of Christians, and to order their own societies accordingly: not just in terms of religious worship, but in every sphere of life. Rather than the accumulated dogma of the church and its popes and priests, their chief basis for this was to be the direct inspiration of the word of God: the text of the Bible.

Sex was central to the Reformation's reshaping of the world. To Protestant eyes, the Catholic church's whole attitude to sexual morality seemed pathetically lax and dishonest. Its priests were lecherous parasites: the ideal of clerical celibacy was no more than a joke. Ecclesiastical courts were not nearly fierce enough in pursuing sexual offenders and punishing their mortal sins. Particularly scandalous was the toleration of prostitution. As far as the reformers were concerned, overt vice was, if anything, more dangerous than secret liaisons: the open sight of whores and brothels set a terrible example to young people, tempted men and women into sin, and was especially provoking to God. What is more, by allowing and regulating sexual trade, the Catholic church – the Whore of Babylon – was literally maintaining itself on the proceeds of fornication and adultery. 'Oh *Rome*!', ran the conventional Protestant denunciation, 'the courtesan keeps open shop, pays yearly rent to his Holiness's treasury, and takes a license for her trade'.[1] Meanwhile, as the morals of the people were left to decay, the church itself grew rich on the proceeds of fines, indulgences, and the other tricks it imposed on its hapless flock. In short, there was a direct connection between the spiritual and sexual corruption of the papacy and its followers. This proved to be an extremely powerful polemical connection, which Protestants were to exploit ever afterwards.[2]

Instead of such wickedness, Protestants advanced a purer, more rigorous morality. The Catholic aspiration to celibacy was jettisoned as unrealistic and counter-productive. For all men, including priests, marriage was henceforth to be the only appropriate outlet for sexual desire. On the other hand, God's many pronouncements against whoredom were to be taken even more seriously: all sex outside marriage should be severely punished. That adulterers ought to be put to death was the ideal of Luther, Zwingli, Bucer, Bullinger, and other leading reformers.[3] The consequence was that wherever the Reformation succeeded it was followed by self-conscious efforts to tighten moral discipline: the closure of brothels, the expulsion of prostitutes, and the introduction of harsher punishments for adultery and fornication. In response to the Protestant challenge, more rigorous sexual policing equally became a feature of the Catholic Counter-Reformation. Throughout the western world, the period saw an intensification of Christian propaganda, and action, against fornication, adultery, prostitution, and sodomy.[4]

England was no exception. It is unclear why, but already in the later middle ages its mores seem to have been less permissive than those of continental Christendom. Very few towns appear to have allowed licensed brothels; and there is no evidence at all of religious foundations to assist penitent prostitutes, which were popular elsewhere in western Europe.[5] Throughout the sixteenth century there were many attempts to enact harsher national laws against sexual offenders. A statute of 1534 made 'buggery', whether with another person or an animal, punishable by death. Another, in 1576, empowered justices of the peace to punish the parents of any infant born out of wedlock.* Meanwhile, many churchmen and parliamentarians worked towards still greater discipline. In 1552, a wholesale revision of canon law led by Archbishop Cranmer recommended that adulterers should suffer life imprisonment or exile (though stoning to death, the commissioners noted wistfully, had been 'by our godly forefathers [the] punishment specially designed for it').[6] At the very least, whores, fornicators, and adulterers ought to be seared with hot irons on their cheeks or foreheads, suggested the writer Philip Stubbes, so that 'honest and chaste Christians might be discerned from the adulterous children of Satan'. Many others urged that adultery should be a capital crime. The official Tudor homily against whoredom, which from 1547 was regularly recited in every parish church across the land, noted approvingly that

---

* 25 Henry VIII c. 6; 18 Elizabeth c. 3. The latter law was probably intended to apply only where the bastard child was likely to require financial support from the parish. When the legislation was updated in 1610 the new statute made this explicit: henceforth the mothers of bastards who were a charge on the parish were to be imprisoned at hard labour for a year (7 James I c. 4). They were often also whipped.

many foreign and heathen nations of the past and present executed sexual sinners, just as God had commanded in the Bible. As a result, every English man and woman of the period would have known that, for example, 'among the Turks ... they that be taken in adultery, both man and woman, are stoned straightaway to death, without mercy'.[7] The effects of this growing disapproval can be seen even amongst the highest ranks. Many medieval and early sixteenth-century noblemen had owned their bastards, or openly kept mistresses. After the Reformation, however, such behaviour was to become more controversial – by the early seventeenth century, aristocratic immorality provoked growing unease about the degeneration of the ruling classes.[8]

From the later sixteenth century onwards, in line with this hardening of attitudes, local church courts stepped up their efforts against sex before marriage, illicit pregnancies, bastardy, and related matters.[9] So did the governors of towns and cities. In Southampton and Norwich in the 1550s, notorious whores were expelled from the city, on pain of being whipped and branded in the face if they dared return. In Rye, fornicators were forced to wear special yellow and green collars around their necks. Elsewhere, they were flogged, carted, or put in the stocks. Especially elaborate rituals were devised at Bury St Edmunds in the later 1570s. On Sundays, sexual offenders were paraded to the public whipping-post. The women had their hair cut off. Then they were all tied up and left for a whole day and night, at the mercy of the elements and the contempt of their community. Finally, on the following market day, they were publicly whipped, 'receiving thirty stripes well laid on till the blood come'.[10]

The impetus for this growing severity came partly from religious zeal: the most enthusiastic punishers of whoredom were often the most evangelical Protestants, who sought the ever-further purification of society ('Puritans', as they came to be called in England). It also reflected mounting social pressures. The sixteenth century was a period of unprecedented population growth and economic upheaval. By the reign of Elizabeth I (1558–1603) this was resulting in considerable hardship, overpopulation, and pressure on local resources. The increasingly virulent spread of syphilis from the end of the fifteenth century onwards provoked growing anxiety, especially in towns.

Against this background, the social problems caused by sexual immorality – crime, disease, bastardy, impoverishment – came to be ever more acutely felt. The sharpening of measures against adultery and fornication can, therefore, be seen as part of a broader late-Tudor attempt to combat impoverishment and social disorder, through the foundation of new kinds of prisons and workhouses, a wholly new system of poor relief, and a crack-down on other kinds of anti-social behaviour, such as drunkenness, vagrancy, and begging. Taken together, this amounted to a significant expansion of governmental intervention in economic and social problems.

London was the epicentre of Protestant enthusiasm, of civic and central power, and of novel initiatives. From the early sixteenth century onwards, in line with the advance of Protestantism and of syphilis, immorality was treated with renewed hostility. Already in 1506 the licensed brothels of Southwark were temporarily shut down; in 1546 they were abolished for good. A succession of evangelical lord mayors and aldermen launched their own crusades against sexual offenders – not just ordering prostitutes to be carted, pilloried, flogged, banished, and dragged through the Thames, but using the secular law to pursue fornicators and adulterers systematically as well. When Rowland Hill, Lord Mayor in 1550, instigated the carting of notable citizens for unchastity, several of them 'told him that it was not right to be so severe, and said that it would cost him dear when he finished his office, but he did not cease on that account, although many men would have paid large sums of money to be saved from disgrace'.[11]

Particularly important was the foundation in the 1550s of an entirely new kind of penal institution, Bridewell, to deal with the City's sexual miscreants, beggars, vagrants, and other petty criminals. This building on the western border of the City, originally one of Henry VIII's palaces, was the first English 'house of correction': a place to which offenders were summarily committed, not just for a sharp whipping, but for weeks of incarceration and hard labour, in order to instil in them the fear of God and the habit of industry. It was a model that was eventually to be adopted by every other city and county in England (the name 'bridewell' likewise became a generic term for any house of correction). Its foundation had an immediate effect on the punishment of sexual offences in London. This single institution alone punished hundreds of unchaste men and women per year – in addition to the large numbers that must have been dealt with by the capital's parish officers and church courts, its neighbourhood ward meetings, its livery companies and other corporate bodies, and its justices of the peace. By the end of the sixteenth century, sexual immorality was probably being policed with greater vigour in London than it had ever been before.

POWER AND PUNISHMENT

The orthodox ideals of the church and state continually came up against attitudes that were more tolerant of illicit sex. These alternative views are, however, not easy to recover in detail. Because they were neither respectable nor very fully developed, they were rarely written down at length. In poetry and fiction, love was endlessly celebrated, but sexual passion more often implied than directly described. Yet the basic idea that sex was fun, and that men and women desired it, indeed required it, was relayed in countless jokes, chapbooks, and other forms of popular communication. The ballad 'A Remedy for the Green Sickness' (c. 1670), for example, took its cue from the popular seventeenth-century idea that it was unhealthy for women to remain virgins for too long:

> A handsome buxom lass
> lay panting in her bed
> she looked as green as grass
> and mournfully she said
> 'Except I have some lusty lad
> to ease me of my pain
> I cannot live
> I sigh and grieve
> my life now I disdain.'

Around the same time, an anonymous English writer, translating an erotic French text, set down an unusually lengthy description of how a seventeenth-century woman might, in more explicit language, have experienced and described the throes of passion with her lover:

At last we had both of us a mind to ease our selves; therefore he lay flat on the bed with his tarse [i.e. penis] upright, pulled me upon him, and I my self stuck it into my cunt, wagging my arse. And saying 'I fuck thee, my dear', he bid me mind my business, and follow my fucking, holding his tongue all this while in my mouth, and calling me 'my life, my soul, my dear fucking rogue', and holding his hands on my buttocks, [until] at last the sweet pleasure approaching made us ply one another with might and main, till at last it came, to the incredible satisfaction of each party.[1]

The unmediated voices of real women are much harder to recover. Even within marriage, it is rare before the eighteenth century to find female correspondence that alludes even as vaguely to sexual passion as the reply that the Wiltshire gentlewoman Maria Thynne wrote around 1607 to a now lost letter from her husband Thomas, far away from her in London. Their union was an extraordinary one. They had encountered each other for the first time one evening in May 1594, at a party in a Buckinghamshire tavern. She had come there from Queen Elizabeth's court, he from Oxford, where he was studying. They were both only sixteen. Yet that very day they were secretly married, and spent their first night together. Their families were bitter, powerful enemies, and Thomas's parents did all they could to undo the marriage: but their love was strong. Their story may well have inspired William Shakespeare, shortly afterwards, to set down his play *Romeo and Juliet* (c. 1595-6). Here is Maria, by now aged about twenty-seven, a few years after she and Thomas were finally able to start living together:

My best beloved Thomken, and my best little Sirrah,

Know that I have not, nor will not forget how you made my modest blood flush up into my bashful cheek at your first letter. Thou threatened sound payment, and I sound repayment, so as when we meet, there will be pay, and repay, which will pass and repass, *allgiges vltes fregnan tolles*, thou knowest my mind, though thou dost not understand me.*

. . .

---

* The deliberately distorted Latin phrase means something like 'you will collect frequently: you will rise up'.

Being as mad as a pilchard and as proud as a piece of Aragon ling, I salute thy best beloved self with the return of thine own wish in thy last letter, and so once more fare ever well, my best and sweetest Thomken, and many thousand times more than these 1 000 000 000 000 000 000 000 000 00 for thy kind wanton letters.

Thine and only all thine

Maria[2]

By contrast, the unhappily married Lady Sarah Cowper noted in 1701 that she had lived with her husband for over thirty-five years, and had conceived four children by him, 'without knowing what it is to have an unchaste thought or sensual pleasure'. This was as much a boast about her virtuous attitude to sex as a complaint about her relationship. Given how disreputable unchaste speech and behaviour were, it was usually only women who made their living from sex (or from the sexual exploitation of others) who spoke more positively about it, at least in ways that have left traces in the historical record. To get a young relative of hers to sleep with men, for example, a bawd called Margery in early seventeenth-century Glastonbury encouraged her 'that she had a good cunt and bid her make use thereto for if she did not she would do her self wrong, for if ground were not tilled and manured it would be overgrown with thorns and briars'. 'Don't lay niggling on me so,' the experienced adulteress Susannah Cooke chided one of her lovers, equally directly, as they lay in bed, 'mount and let me have as it should be.' (So he did.)[3]

Contemporary opinions about sexual desire, and especially about its lawfulness outside marriage, were overwhelmingly articulated by men (or through them, in their capacity as scribes and authors). When such views were expressed publicly it was normally in facetious form – in 1631, for example, the king's printer Robert Barker got into terrible trouble when his employees produced an edition of the Bible in which the word 'not' was omitted from the seventh commandment. (That this was no innocent typo can be seen from the rendering in another verse of 'God's greatnesse' as 'God's great asse'.) More usually, however, they were uttered privately – especially in response to the threat of punishment. When Miles Horne and Elizabeth Powell were arrested and brought to Bridewell in May 1576 for having sex in a Southwark tavern, for example, they responded simply 'that they were so minded and being about it were taken afore they were done'. A peasant in early seventeenth-century Somerset was equally matter-of-fact upon being surprised in the act with his lover and being told 'that they must look to be punished for what they had done'. 'Did you never see a cow bulled before?' he retorted. When a married Essex clergyman was accused in 1636 of kissing another woman, he defended himself with a similar analogy: 'change of pasture made fat calves, and a bit abroad was worth two at home'. As one humble Londoner in 1632 summed up the general notion echoed in all these fragments, 'fornication was not sin at all if both parties are agreed'. Even outside of marriage, a bit of sex between a consenting man and woman could be treated as an innocent, natural pleasure.[4]

The most common justification of all was that the couple intended to marry. 'The restraints upon sexual activity', observes a historian of the period, 'crumbled once marriage was in sight.' We mainly know what lovers said to each other about this from cases where, in fact, the courtship later foundered and they were prosecuted for fornication or bastardy – but often, evidently, couples had sex following a promise of marriage, whereas at other times they (or at least one of them) believed they would marry if the woman fell pregnant. Dorothy Cornish's lover, for example,

took note at the second time he had carnal copulation with her in his table book at which time the birth of the child would be, and that she should take no care – if she should prove with child he would marry her.

When Miliard Davies, of Plaitford in Wiltshire, bore Christopher Vincent's child in 1602, she likewise told a court that

in regard the said Christopher and she were both born in one parish and neighbours' children, and she had at his persuasion and request yielded unto him to be carnally known, she was in good hope that he would have married her.[5]

Against this backdrop it is easy to see the limits of sexual policing. After all, this was not a society in which the sexes were rigidly segregated. Most people stayed single until, in their mid or late twenties, they had accumulated the skills and savings needed to get married and set up an independent household. In many areas of social and

1. Rembrandt, *The Bed* (1646): a rare contemporary illustration of a couple making love, composed around the time that the artist began an illicit relationship with his maid, Hendrickje Stoffels.

economic life, moreover, men and women mingled freely – working, socializing, and courting each other secretly or openly. That was the case even in rural parishes, but it was especially true in London, which was a world of its own, teeming with opportunities for illicit meetings and sexual encounters: brothels, street-walkers, taverns, hostelries, churches, playhouses, fairs, markets, and streets, all swarming with strangers.[6]

Countless adulterers, fornicators, prostitutes and sodomites must therefore have gone undetected. Many others escaped public penalty. Historians also like to point out the obvious biases of the system. Women were more liable to be punished than men. Wealthy and powerful people were much less likely to suffer than their inferiors: even after the Reformation, plenty of aristocrats and gentlemen had bastards without having to worry about prosecution. (In 1593, in fact, Members of Parliament rejected whipping as a punishment for men who had conceived bastards, specifically for fear that it 'might chance upon gentlemen or men of quality, whom it were not fit to put to such a shame'.)[7] Sometimes the law was abused, and often its workings were inefficient. All these limitations are significant (and similar caveats would apply to the study of most other crimes and judicial systems, throughout history), for they reflect how power was distributed within society: between men and women, between the rich and the poor, and between different forms of intellectual and social authority.

Yet they should not distract us from the simplest fact of all: sexual policing was an integral part of pre-modern society. Its workings symbolized the central values of the culture. By almost any standard, its enforcement of external discipline was remarkably successful. From the early middle ages to the dawn of the seventeenth century it slowly imposed ever-stricter standards of behaviour. Both its theory and practice had a profound impact upon the minds and lives of the entire population.

Indeed, sexual policing was not merely some top-down, external imposition. It certainly had the power of the church and state behind it. But it was brought to life by popular participation, and broad concurrence with its principles. Everyone had a part in it – even watchmen, constables and churchwardens were but ordinary male householders taking their turn to hold a particular office in the community. Nobody got paid for this. There was no separate, professional police force. This was a system of grass-roots self-regulation, of communities policing themselves and upholding collective standards of behaviour. Because of this, and because solid evidence was often lacking in cases of suspected immorality, its judgements mainly reflected the consensus of respectable opinion.[8]

The basis for most church court proceedings was thus not hard fact but a 'common fame' or 'repute' of immorality. Such phrases implied public notoriety and agreement, rather than merely private suspicions. Even public opinions were not of equal weight: they were judged by the reputation of those who held them. A common fame amongst respectable citizens was a serious matter; but one spread 'by the nude and sole accusation of some naughty woman who confesseth her own naughtiness', as a contemporary handbook explained, was in fact not 'a fame, but rather a false rumour'. Similarly, the usual method of establishing guilt and innocence in the church courts was not a trial of evidence but a process of public 'compurgation', which tested the views of the whole community. If the accused could produce a specified number of honest neighbours to swear publicly that the suspicion was unfounded, and if no one else came forward to contradict them convincingly, the charge was dropped: otherwise the common fame was held to be true. Between the later middle ages and the early seventeenth century, compurgation appears to have become an increasingly onerous test to pass, perhaps reflecting tightening attitudes to sexual offenders. By the 1610s and 1620s, in one of the best-documented cases, the archdeaconry of Salisbury, almost half the defendants in a sample of over 200 failed to purge themselves and were convicted.[9]

Civic justice was based on similar assessments of credit, reputation, and fame, and in practice there was no great divide between the sexual jurisdiction of the church and that of secular magistrates. Under common law, men and women suspected of sexual misconduct could be arrested and summarily committed to the nearest house of correction, to be whipped if necessary and set to hard labour for a few days or weeks. If they were householders they would be required to post bail (in other words, find respectable members of the community to vouch for them) and appear before a court. Such punishments were commonly inflicted not just for evident 'evil behaviour' or an obvious breach of the peace, but equally, as in the church courts, on the grounds of 'evil fame', 'name' or 'report' of immorality, or of 'suspicious' behaviour.[10]

Given this outlook, even the appearance or attempt of unchastity could be as fatal as its actual commission. In May 1555, when the London court of aldermen found that an apprentice had propositioned his master's wife, they ordered him to be immediately taken out, stripped naked to the waist 'at the outer door of this hall, and so to be led from thence to the post of reformation in Cheapside and there be well beaten till his body bleed and then to be led from thence tied at a cart's tail', to be processed ignominiously through the city and then symbolically dumped outside it. For couples to consort privately if not married could be equally dangerous. Countless men and women were prosecuted merely for inappropriately 'keeping company' with another's spouse, whilst the diary of Samuel Pepys provides a casual glimpse of the kind of routine moral policing that his society took for granted. Coming back home with his wife and friends after dinner late one evening in August 1666, his coach was stopped at the entrance to the City, and its occupants cross-examined 'whether we were husbands and wives'. It almost goes without saying that any woman walking alone after dark was liable to be arrested (or harassed) on suspicion of immorality.[11]

Underpinning this unceasing watchfulness was the continual indoctrination of the ideals of monogamy and chastity. That lust was a dangerous and shameful passion, that fornication was evil, and adultery criminal – these were doctrines drummed into every man, woman, and child, throughout their life, in speech and print, from every conceivable direction. Most people internalized them profoundly, even when they sometimes acted in contrary ways. We can see this in the books people read, the letters they wrote, the education they received, the sermons they listened to, the slanders and libels they hurled at one another, the contempt they manifested towards sexual transgression of all kinds. The gentry and aristocracy were not immune from this; nor, even, were kings and queens. For, in the words that every adult and child regularly heard recited in church, whoredom was a 'filthy, stinking, and abominable ... sin ... not lawful neither in king nor subject, neither in common officer nor private person ... in no man nor woman, of whatsoever degree or age they be'.[12]

Public punishment was therefore only the sharpest manifestation of the more general culture of sexual discipline. When legal proceedings were brought, their aim was often as much to put pressure on an individual to reform as it was to secure a conviction. There were also countless instances where discipline was successfully exercised outside the courts – adultery nipped in the bud, fornicators admonished, brothels suppressed – by parents, pastors, friends, families, neighbours, and employers. We glimpse this hinterland whenever the language of litigation reveals that legal proceedings had been a last resort, or that a punishment was being imposed not for a single infraction but for recalcitrance in the face of previous efforts. Thus, a woman might be prosecuted for unmarried cohabitation and fornication because 'notwithstanding you have been often gravely and seriously advised either by words of mouth or letters to desist from such your filthy and lascivious life and conversation, yet you have rejected the said advice'.[13]

More vivid still is the abundant evidence, from cities, towns, and villages everywhere in sixteenth- and seventeenth-century England, of the ways in which whores and adulterers were publicly ridiculed and humiliated by their neighbours and by the community at large. When Ann George was caught one summer's afternoon having sex with a soldier in a barn, 'the neighbouring people took and ducked her in a mill stream, saying that if she was hot they would cool her'. In the winter of 1605, when it was rumoured around Evesham in Worcestershire that George Hawkins, a local landowner, had fathered a bastard child, more elaborate measures were taken. As a well-off gentleman and a leading officer in the law courts, he was well placed to head off any serious legal trouble for such a fault; but he could not avoid the open criticism of his subordinates. One day in December, a group of them met at Edward Freme's inn, the Swan, and decided to take action. None of them could write, so they shared their story with three travelling salesmen from Coventry, who set it down on paper for them. Together they composed a song in ridicule of Hawkins, his whore, and their bastard, complete with scurrilous pictures of the shameful trio, and set about publicizing it to maximum effect. One of the salesmen, Lancelot Ratsey, dashed off a stack of duplicates, and also reproduced the whole thing on a public wall. They pinned the sheets all over the Swan, and performed the ballad for the other customers there. Over the next few weeks they did the same thing all over town and into the surrounding countryside: distributing copies to all the local pubs, posting them up on doors, walls, and posts everywhere, and going about singing the ballad of Squire Hawkins and his whore. This is how it went, evidently referring to the pictures (now lost) that were drawn above:

> 'I can no more':
> This is the whore,
> Of cowardly George Hawkins.
> He got [her] with child,
> In a place most wild,
> Which for to name it is a shame.
> Yet for your satisfaction,
> I will make relation,
> It was in a privy,
> A place most filthy,
> As gent[lemen] you may judge.
> Yet nothing too bad,
> For a knave and a drab,
> And so they pray go trudge.
>
> This is the bastard,
> With his father the dastard,
> George Hawkins highte he so [i.e. he is called].
> In all this shire,
> There is not a squire,
> More like a knave I trowe [i.e. believe].
> O cursed seed,
> My heart doth bleed,
> To think how thou was born.
> To the whore thy mother,
> And the knave thy father,
> An everlasting scorn.[14]

In short, this was a culture in which self-discipline in all spheres of life was prized as the ultimate mark of civilization, and unchastity mocked, not just for fun but as a pre-eminent sign of weakness. The fundamental principle of conventional ethics was that men and women were personally responsible for their actions, no matter how powerful the temptation. Only beasts and savages gave 'unrestrained liberty' to 'the cravings of nature' – civilized Christians were rather 'to bring under the flesh; bring nature under the government of reason, and, in short bring the body under the command of the soul'.[15] The mental and physical government of fleshly appetites was the very foundation of the whole culture of discipline. For all the practical ways in which sexual discipline was limited, there was no coherent or respectable alternative ideology of sexual liberty, no way of conceiving of a society without moral policing. Even Pepys's private diary, the boldest pre-eighteenth-century account of sexual adventure, is thus shot through with a much deeper consciousness of guilt and shame than most of its later counterparts would ever be.

Why did people think this way? Why was sexual discipline presumed to be so fundamental to the social order? If, reader, you happen to be a member of the Iranian or Saudi Arabian moral police, which even today enforce a similar ethos, you can probably guess the answers. Otherwise, read on.

THE FOUNDATIONS OF SEXUAL DISCIPLINE

In truth this was an over-determined matter, for many different patterns of thought underpinned sexual discipline and were invoked in its justification. The most basic was the patriarchal principle that every woman was the property of her father or husband, so that it was a kind of theft for any stranger to have sex with her, and a grave affront to her relatives. Indeed, fantasized the aristocrat Margaret Cavendish in 1662, in an honourable family any woman so defiled deserved to be put to death straightaway by her own kinsmen,

for the impurity, immodesty, dishonesty, and dishonour of unchastity, which was an offence to the Gods, a reproach to her life, a disgrace to her race, a dishonour to her kindred, and an infamy to her family.[1]

Illicit sex also invaded property rights more concretely: gifts between lovers, payments to prostitutes, and the conception of bastard children all threatened the possessions and inheritance of others. In addition, whoredom spread venereal disease, heartache, and discord within families. It provoked crime and disorder, and led inevitably to other sins: drunkenness, theft, lying, cheating, infanticide, murder. In all these ways it destroyed individuals and wrecked social order. Its prohibition and punishment was consequently a matter of great public importance.

This way of thinking made perfect sense because, in general, people took for granted that the external regulation of many areas of personal life was essential to the public good. In economic and social terms, society was not made up of autonomous individuals, but of households and families. (Indeed, for a young man to be 'masterless', or a woman to live 'at her own hand', was inherently suspicious, even criminal.)[2] Parents and employers were meant to oversee the morals of their children and servants, just as friends, neighbours, and relations felt responsible, as a matter of course, for watching over each other's way of life. These basic attitudes prevailed at every social level, but they weighed most heavily on the weaker members of society – on women more than on men of equivalent status; on the poor and unrespectable more than on their superiors. Indeed, because every community was ultimately responsible for the maintenance of its inhabitants, poor couples were sometimes barred altogether from marrying by their richer neighbours, or forced to live apart. The Elizabethan poor laws, which taxed the wealthy of each parish according to the needs of its indigents, led to the increasingly callous treatment of men and women who might be potential burdens, or breeders of pauper children. In 1570, for example, the leading parishioners of Adlington in Kent were so 'sore against' the proposed marriage of Alice Cheeseman that they prevented the reading of the banns and 'threatened Alice to expel her out of the parish' if she defied their 'hindrance'. When Anthony Adams of Stockton in Worcestershire sought to bring his new bride, 'an honest young woman', to live with him in his home parish in 1618, the locals were 'not willing he should bring her into the parish saying they would breed up a charge among them' – she was compelled to dwell elsewhere. In late-Elizabethan Terling (Essex), the labourer Robert Johnson lived and had a child with Elizabeth Whitland, and 'would have married her if the inhabitants would have suffered him': but they did not. Over a decade later, in the same parish, another labourer complained that he had tried to marry his lover more than a year before. The banns had been called in church, but 'the parish would not suffer them to marry' – and now were prosecuting the couple for fornication and unmarried cohabitation. By the later seventeenth century such practices were common enough across England to attract repeated discussion. 'It is an ill custom in many country parishes,' observed the writer Carew Reynell in 1674, 'where they, as much as they can, hinder poor people from marrying'. '"Oh," say the churchwardens,' noted the merchant Sir Dudley North, '"they will have more children than they can keep, and so increase the charge of the parish."'[3]

Throughout the sixteenth and seventeenth centuries this fear of rampant bastardy, as a source of social disorder, moral pollution, and communal impoverishment, underpinned the condemnation of sexual licence, at both a national and a local level. Hence in 1606, when the chief inhabitants of Castle Combe in Wiltshire noticed just one unmarried pregnancy, they immediately drew up a petition to the local magistrates urging that the woman be severely punished, for her

filthy act of whoredom . . . by the which licentious life of hers not only God's wrath may be poured down upon us inhabitants of the town, but also her evil example may so greatly corrupt others that great and extraordinary charge for the maintenance of baseborn children may be imposed upon us.

In reality, of course, the real hardship fell upon any pregnant single woman. She would lose her employment, and expect to be expelled from her lodgings: to harbour a bastard-bearer was a crime. If she went into labour, as Margaret Wheeler did in 1616, at the point of her most awful agonies, 'in great pain and travail and almost beyond the hope of life', she would normally be interrogated by her midwives and neighbours, refused all help by them, and threatened with death and damnation – sometimes for hours on end, sometimes as she actually lay dying – unless she truthfully confessed the name of the bastard's father.[4]

Unwanted pregnancy was therefore also the most serious worry for couples engaged in illicit sex. Some evidently tried to prevent pregnancy, or took herbs and potions to induce abortion, but the basic biology of conception was not properly understood until the nineteenth century, and there were no widely available or reliable methods of contraception. The risks of fornication were immeasurably greater for any woman than for a man, because she alone bore the life-threatening dangers of pregnancy and childbirth, the automatic responsibility for any infant, and the almost impossible task of physically concealing her shame and avoiding harsh punishment. As one poor early seventeenth-century maidservant told her would-be lover,

No, truly you shall not lie with me till we be married for you see how many do falsify their promises . . . I am but a servant and if your friends should not consent to our marriage we are undone.

If a woman was already married she was safe from punishment for bastardy, for no child she conceived could be illegitimate. Yet even in such cases comparable worries preoccupied illicit lovers. As the testimony of one married Somerset woman in the mid-1650s reveals, even the most amoral, irreligious seducer could not deny the force of this perennial concern:

Roger did then solicit her . . . to be dishonest with him and then better to persuade her so to do thereunto he told her that if she had any child by him he would give it means to maintain it. And then there was no punishment for any man . . . but only in this life which was none at all so long as he would allow means to maintain the child: after this life there was no punishment because there was neither heaven nor hell.[5]

On similar, economic grounds, when paupers had children out of wedlock they could be taken away from them. At the end of the seventeenth century, Daniel Taylor and Sarah Ellis lived with their three children in the East End parish of St Botolph Aldgate in London. In December 1700, some time after the death of Sarah Ellis, the churchwardens and overseers of the poor suddenly decided that the remaining members of the family constituted an unacceptable burden to the rate-payers of the parish. Daniel Taylor was interviewed by two justices of the peace and 'confessed', in their words, 'that he was never married to the said Sarah Ellis but only cohabited with her as man and wife and that all the said children are bastards'. Two of his children, William and Sarah, were consequently taken from their father and sent to the neighbouring parish of St Mary Whitechapel, where they had been born; on the same grounds the third, Elizabeth, was separated from the rest of the family and sent west to St Botolph Bishopsgate. Ultimately, the right to have sex, and to form a family, was regulated by the community.*

In addition to all these worldly considerations, there were obvious religious imperatives for sexual discipline. Unchastity had to be penalized because, as the Bible showed, it was highly offensive to God. Those who broke his commandments were risking their salvation, but their sins also reflected upon the wider community, even if hidden from sight. As the chronicler Thomas Walsingham noted of Londoners during a popular campaign against adulterers in the early 1380s,

they expressed their fears that the entire commonalty would be destroyed by such sins committed in secret when God punished them. For that reason, they wished to cleanse this stain from the city so that it might not fall to ruin or the sword, or be swallowed when the earth opened up.[6]

More than 200 years later those citizens of Castle Combe who took fright at a single bastard-bearer were acting on the same principle. If any community tolerated such insults to the Almighty, his wrath would punish them all. Ultimately, such divine retribution could bring down entire cities and lands, as it had wiped out Sodom and Gomorrah (e.g. Genesis 18–19; Deuteronomy 29 and 32; Jeremiah 23; Jude 1). That is why, to ward off God's vengeful providence, families, parishes, cities, and whole nations were anxious to hunt down and cast out the unclean from their midst. The purer their community, the more favourably the Almighty would treat them.

For the same reason there had always been a powerful parallel between the enforcement of sexual and of religious purity. In premodern society, religious diversity was an essentially alien, undesirable concept. Both before and after the Reformation, there had always

---

* The churchwardens of St Mary Whitechapel and St Botolph Bishopsgate subsequently appealed against these orders, and the children were passed back again – such brutal shipping of children and adults back and forth whilst parish officers wrangled about their legal place of settlement was not uncommon under the poor law: London Metropolitan Archives, CLA/047/LJ/13/1700 (City Sessions Papers, Dec. 1700).

been only one church. Everyone was obliged to belong to it, and to assent to the same religious beliefs – the penalty for propounding heterodox views was, ultimately, death. It was axiomatic that belief and worship were not issues that could safely be left to individual judgement.[7] As in sexual matters, the correct forms were prescribed by law; adherence to them was enforced; deviations were punishable. The means of enforcement were also strikingly similar. Until the outbreak of the Civil War in 1642, religious and sexual conformity were both policed by the church courts; and after the Restoration in 1660 the secular mechanisms employed to persecute religious dissenters were the same as those used to punish sexual offenders.

In both cases, religious and sexual, punishment was believed to be an effective means of reforming souls and preserving social cohesion. It worked in four main ways. In the first place, ritual punishment assuaged the community's anger and expunged the pollution from its midst. Secondly, it deterred others. Thirdly, it forced the offender to stop the criminal behaviour. Finally, it could also help bring about a real change of heart. A major aim of sexual policing was always to induce penitence and reconciliation between sinners and those they had offended. If combined with education and persuasion, the imposition of suffering was held to be an effective means of opening people's minds to the error of their ways. Those inflicting it liked to think of themselves as benevolent doctors, bringing spiritual lunatics back to sanity, using corporal methods to purge diseases from the soul. What matter that it did not always work? 'Is medicine to be neglected, because some men's plague is incurable?'[8] Indeed, as moralists never tired of pointing out, the punishment of sinners and apostates was an act of profound charity – 'the greatest mercy imaginable', as the prison chaplain Edmund Cressy put it in 1675. For what was a little shame and pain on earth in comparison with the horrible, everlasting torment that would otherwise await them in hell?[9]

In consequence there was a close intellectual association between sexual and spiritual discipline. As St Augustine had said, heresy and adultery were the same kind of crime: people claimed only to be following their hearts, but they were still guilty.[10] More generally, there was believed to be a direct connection between moral and spiritual deviance. Throughout history, noted the popular preacher William

Clagett, 'doctrines that give liberty to lust' had been used 'to draw men off from the truth' and lead them into religious error. After apostasy itself, remarked a preacher, the second greatest sin of all was 'uncleanness, the natural consequent of the love of error'.[11]

This connection between sexual and spiritual impurity had an immense pedigree. Just as the Bible described spiritual enlightenment as marriage with Christ, so in the Old Testament God himself had described idolatry as going 'a whoring', and committing 'whoredom' against him.[12] It was also clear from scripture (e.g. I Corinthians 7.5) and from countless later teachings that the immense pleasure that could be derived from sex was but a snare of Satan's, the thing that made it the most dangerous sin of all. It was a Christian commonplace that anyone who succumbed to this impure appetite, even just once, risked developing a fatal addiction to it. As one clergyman warned his readers: 'You must know yourself very little, if you can suppose, that in such a situation, you shall retain your scruples. No, Sir, lust indulged will not be reasoned with. A fiercer affection the mind of man knows not'. Indeed, whereas other crimes were liable to provoke subsequent remorse, in this case the opposite was true: 'the reflection on sins of uncleanness revives the pleasure, and makes repentance of them exceeding difficult' – 'it is like a deep ditch, and a narrow pit, which it is almost impossible to get out of'.[13] That sexual and spiritual deviance went hand in hand was further established by the endless practical examples of false prophets and sects, throughout history and into the present, who had encouraged vice. Catholics, Presbyterians, Anabaptists, atheists, Muslims, pagans, heathens and heretics: all were said to tend to lechery. (And most of these groups were themselves just as keen on using the charge of doctrinal and moral impurity against others.)[14]

At the root of this way of thinking lay the presumption that it was folly to leave religion and morality to personal interpretation. People might hold views sincerely, even passionately, and still be dangerously mistaken. As one learned writer enumerated, '1. The heart of man is deceitful and desperately wicked; and what will it not do, if it may do what it will? 2. When men know that they are liable to no restraint, it will let loose their lusts, and make them worse.'[15] By comparison with the inherent corruption of human nature, the powers of reason and conscience were weak, and the forces of error and evil lay everywhere in wait to ensnare and corrupt them. Reason was 'a false weapon' against sin, explained the physician Richard Capel, for it was the devil's tool. 'We lose all if once we begin to enter into disputation with such an old Sophister and crafty fox as Satan is . . . our reason is corrupt, and on his side, and it will betray us into his hands'. As for conscience, in unregenerate men it was but blind and helpless as a guide. Even in the most virtuous persons, 'it is in part defiled and corrupt and imperfect, and therefore it is mistaken and cannot be our rule, and it is our sin, to set our conscience in [place] of the Word of God'.[16]

These ideas were ubiquitous in popular religious teaching. They are brought vividly to life in John Bunyan's wonderful allegory *The Holy War* (1682), which depicted the continual struggle between the forces of God and the devil for the 'town' of 'Mansoul'. The devil first takes possession by denouncing God's moral laws as 'unreasonable, intricate, and intolerable', and promising greater freedom and knowledge. After debauching and deranging Mansoul's conscience, he destroys all 'doctrines of morals', and replaces them with a general 'liberty' (especially to 'the lusts of the flesh') for everybody to do as they please, without 'law, statute, or judgment of mine to fright you'. As lord mayor he installs the bestial Lord Lustings; amongst his aldermen are Mr Swearing, Mr Whoreing, and Mr Atheism. Even after the town is retaken by the Lord Emanuel, evil forces remain within, waiting for a new opportunity, led by 'The Lord Fornication' and 'The Lord Adultery'. The moral was that only the guidance of sound doctrine and superior teachers could lead people safely to salvation.[17]*

It also followed that safeguarding the spiritual welfare of the people had to be a paramount aim of government. Plato and Aristotle seem to have regarded extra-marital sex as a dangerously corrupting pleasure, and most pre-modern commentators eagerly agreed with them.[18] 'Even as the soul is the worthier part of man,' explained Richard Hooker, one of the most influential theologians of the sixteenth century, 'so human societies are much more to care for that which tendeth properly unto the soul's estate than for such temporal things as this

* Cf. 1 Peter 2.11: 'abstain from fleshly lusts, which war against the soul'.

life doth stand in need of'. In a godly commonwealth, said the seventeenth-century religious leader and writer Richard Baxter, 'the honour and pleasing of God, and the salvation of the people are the principal ends, and their corporal welfare but subordinate to these'. Punishing unchaste persons, for their own good and that of the community, was a Christian and a public duty, incumbent upon all members of society.[19]

The culture of sexual discipline was therefore not only sustained by strongly held beliefs about the dangers of immorality. It also rested on central political, philosophical, and psychological presumptions about the purpose of government, the nature of human beings, the ethics of belief, and the imperfection of innate understanding. So long had the practice of discipline persisted, so closely was it intertwined with the fabric of social life, so deep were its intellectual foundations, that no one in 1600 could possibly have envisaged its abolition.

Yet its decline and fall were just around the corner. Initially, the Reformation led to a tightening of sexual regulation; but it also shattered the unity of European Christendom. In the course of the seventeenth century the growth of religious division was to destroy everything.

I

The Decline and Fall of Public Punishment

[Magistrates should prosecute] common whoremongers, and common whores; for (by good opinion) adultery and bawdry is an offence temporal, as well as spiritual, and is against the peace of the land . . . a constable [may seek out and arrest] a man and a woman [committing] adultery or fornication together.
Michael Dalton, *The Countrey Justice* (1618), 160

For the suppressing of the abominable and crying sins of incest, adultery and fornication, wherewith this land is much defiled, and Almighty God highly displeased; be it enacted . . . That in case any married woman shall . . . be carnally known by any man (other than her husband) . . . as well the man as the woman . . . shall suffer death.
An Act for Suppressing the Detestable Sins of Incest, Adultery and Fornication (1650)

The apprehension of . . . prostitutes, cannot be justified by any existing law.
Second Report from the Committee on the State of the Police of the Metropolis, Parliamentary Papers (1817), vii. 463

The sexual revolution began with the collapse of public discipline. This was partly the result of increasing social pressures. Before the seventeenth century, 90 per cent of the population lived in the countryside, and, except for London, there were no large cities in England. The traditional methods of moral policing had evolved in small

2. This huge bird's eye view, by the great printmaker Wenceslaus Hollar,

shows the tremendous expansion of London's West End by the early 1660s.

communities where everybody knew, and kept a close watch on, one another. In the countryside this was slow to change: even towards the end of the eighteenth century there were still rural parishes where the church courts continued to punish unchastity in the old-fashioned way. Things were different in towns, especially in London. At the end of the middle ages only about 40,000 people lived there, but by 1660 there were already 400,000; by 1800 there would be over a million. This extraordinary explosion created new kinds of social pressures and new ways of living, and placed the conventional machinery of sexual discipline under impossible strain.

The deeper cause, however, was not primarily social or legal, but theological. Religious conflict, which arose from the slow, incomplete English Reformation, was the most potent intellectual and political force in seventeenth-century England. By 1700 it had brought about changes that would have seemed unthinkable a century earlier: civil war, regicide, the abolition of the monarchy and the Church of England, freedom of religion. It was also to destroy the system of public sexual discipline.

THE DRIVE TOWARDS PERFECTION

The most important difference between Catholic and Reformed attitudes to sex was the Protestant aspiration to perfection. The traditional Catholic view had been that fleshly lusts were reprehensible but inevitable: to restrain them completely might be impossible, or counter-productive. The enforcement of sexual discipline was accordingly balanced by a certain amount of toleration of organized prostitution and of clerical concubines. In contrast, the Protestant tendency was to believe that unchastity truly could be banished from the world, or at least that Christians had a duty to eradicate it as thoroughly as possible. As Archbishop Cranmer's model eccelesiastical law of 1552 put it, 'fornication and unbridled lusts of every kind are to be checked with great severity of punishment, so that they may eventually be uprooted from the kingdom'.[1] Out of this difference came a greater demand for both personal and external discipline.

We have already noted the immediate impact that the Reformation had on the punishment of immorality. The steady tightening of attitudes continued in the decades after 1600, in England as elsewhere across Europe. Particularly striking was the church courts' attack on what had hitherto been the most widely condoned type of illicit sex, that between couples who were betrothed but not yet formally married. Previously, such cases had been punished only incidentally. But in the early seventeenth century prenuptial fornication came to be targeted with unprecedented rigour. In many jurisdictions across the country (York, Oxford, Leicester, Canterbury, Essex, and others) the number of prosecutions increased sharply. In Wiltshire, for example, only a handful of such cases were brought each year before the later 1590s, but by the 1610s and 1620s, the annual average had shot up to at least fifty (plus many more cases now hard to enumerate from the surviving records). Perhaps a fifth of all brides were pregnant when they married, suggesting that many couples started having sex during courtship. Over time, however, there was a noticeable drop in the proportion who came to the altar pregnant – and thus, we can infer, in the actual practice of pre-marital sex. There was a similar pattern in cases of ordinary fornication and of bastardy: more prosecutions, fewer illegitimate births, a real change in popular behaviour and attitudes. Indeed, the aspirations of ecclesiastical discipline were ever more ambitious. When in 1604 the Church of England's canon law was revised for the first time since the Reformation, it stipulated that its courts were to proceed against not only adultery and fornication, but also 'any other uncleanness and wickedness of life'. In literature, politics, and daily life, too, there is considerable evidence for the internalization of the church's moral teachings, and for popular hostility towards unchastity. It is clear that the principle that sex was only permissible within marriage was being upheld, and internalized, with increasing force.[2]

It is equally telling that in the early seventeenth century the church's most powerful court, High Commission, was repeatedly used to punish members of the gentry and aristocracy for adultery and other sexual crimes. Some of these suits may have been motivated at least in part by power-struggles within the political elite, but they nevertheless illustrate the extent to which, by this time, even the sexual failings of the most elevated men and women could be treated as public crimes.

In 1634, Sir Alexander Cave was ordered to do penance in his parish church, pay the huge sum of £500, and be jailed until he could find bail, all for having persisted in adultery with Amy Roe despite previous admonishments. In the same year, Thomas Cotton and Dorothy Thornton of Lichfield were sentenced to do penance in both their parish church and the local cathedral, fined £500 and sent to prison for their adultery: in the winter of 1639 they were still there. For multiple adulteries Thomas Hesketh Esq. of Rufford in Lancashire was fined £1,000 plus costs, and ordered to do penance in the cathedrals of York and Chester, as well as in his local parish church: he too was committed to prison until he could post an extremely large bail. Sir Robert Howard, son of the Earl of Suffolk, and Frances, Lady Purbeck, the sister-in-law of the Duke of Buckingham, had long lived together adulterously in the depths of Shropshire. When they travelled to London in the spring of 1635, the king himself ordered the Archbishop of Canterbury to take action against them for their shameless behaviour. They were both immediately arrested and incarcerated. He was fined £3,000 and kept in prison for weeks; she was ordered to do public penance in church, like any other adulteress, barefoot and clad in a white sheet.*[3] The same attitude is abundantly illustrated by the mass of informal, popular attacks on unchastity in high places that survives from the period. In political libels, lampoons, satires, and other forms of writing and action, upper-class immorality is almost inevitably the object of sharp disapproval, reflecting the growing grip of Protestant attitudes to sin, social order, and divine vengeance.[4]

The other main effect of the Reformation was, however, a growing divergence of opinion amongst Protestants about the limits of sexual regulation. Pretty much everyone who expressed a public opinion agreed that unchastity ought to be treated more severely. This was a particular complaint of the Puritans. The existing punishments were 'so small and slight', Queen Elizabeth was admonished in 1585, that 'God must therefore be angry with Your Majesty'. It was scandalous, grumbled the Norfolk minister William Yonger in 1617, that 'so

---

* To avoid this fate she escaped from prison disguised as a man, ran away to Paris and, when the High Commission pursued her even there, converted to Catholicism and entered a nunnery (though before long she fell out with the nuns and departed again).

renowned and famous a church as this of England, should have no sharper censure for adultery than a white sheet'.[5] But there was no consensus on exactly how to tackle it.

The problem had been debated since the earliest days of the break with Rome. Evangelical Protestants were not the only voices in favour of greater severity. In the early sixteenth century many Catholic humanists had felt the same way, and in 1586 adultery was briefly made a capital offence in Rome itself, by the vigorous but short-lived Pope Sixtus V (1585–90). But Puritans were certainly the most zealous campaigners against immorality across the English-speaking world. In general they took the most rigidly limited view of appropriate sexual behaviour. Even intercourse between a husband and wife was commonly viewed as breaking God's law if the woman was pregnant or menstruating – John Cotton's 1636 model law code for Massachusetts and New Haven made the latter a capital offence. In general, because of their fundamentalist belief in the Bible's commandments, many Puritans wanted to reintroduce the death penalty for adultery and other serious sexual crimes. This was not a backward-looking but a radical, progressive aim: it would bring England in line with the most advanced Protestant communities of the modern world. Scots, Genevans, Germans, Bohemians: there were many contemporary precedents for such severity. (So zealously did the burgesses of Dundee pursue sexual offenders that in 1589 they decided to build an entirely new prison just for adulterers and fornicators.)[6] This on-going debate was one of the inspirations for Shakespeare's topical play *Measure for Measure* (c. 1604), whose plot turns on illicit sex, betrothal, and the possibility of capital punishment for unchastity.

By contrast the practice of the English church courts seemed to most Puritans wholly inadequate. Their 'toyish censures' (as a Puritan manifesto of 1572 put it) did nothing to reduce immorality; the main point of their proceedings seemed to be to milk people for legal fees. This evangelical distaste deepened as, from the end of the sixteenth century onwards, ecclesiastical law was increasingly used by the establishment of the Church of England to prosecute Puritan ministers and laypeople for religious nonconformity (such as refusal to use the sign of the cross, to follow the prescribed Prayer Book, or to kneel at communion). Not only were the church courts corrupt and ineffective, it now seemed, they also unjustly persecuted godly men and women for following their consciences. As the religious divisions between English Protestants sharpened over the course of the later sixteenth and seventeenth centuries, this perception, unfair though it was in many respects, hardened into a polemical commonplace. By the 1630s, when Charles I and his archbishop, William Laud, launched an especially unyielding campaign to enforce religious uniformity, it had undermined the church courts' moral authority in the eyes of many Puritan observers.[7]

As a result, there was a sustained effort by radical Protestants to shift the responsibility for moral policing into the civil sphere. Bills for the stricter punishment of sexual offences were introduced in almost every parliament of the early seventeenth century: in 1601, 1604, 1606–7, 1614, 1621, 1626, 1628, and 1629.[8] An Act of 1610 made unmarried mothers liable to at least a year's imprisonment if their bastards were likely to need parish support. In 1624, growing paranoia about the supposed tide of bastard-bearing and infanticide led to another extraordinarily punitive statute, which presumed the guilt (and execution) of any unwed woman who concealed the birth of an infant later found dead, even if she swore on oath that it had been still-born, or had died naturally.[9] Meanwhile, wherever zealous evangelicals gained control of village and town governments they tightened up local discipline, to noticeable effect. In Dorchester, which became the most Puritan town in England, there was a dramatic decline in pre- and extra-marital sex in the decades leading up to the Civil War.[10] The same spirit animated the tens of thousands of Puritans who, over the same period, emigrated to North America to found a New Jerusalem there. In the early seventeenth century, all the colonies of New England enacted harsh laws against unchastity: banishment, imprisonment, severe public flogging, the wearing of scarlet letters and other shaming garments for the rest of one's life. Many of them, affirming with the founders of New Haven that 'the Scriptures do hold forth a perfect rule' of government, followed the Old Testament and made adultery punishable by death.[11]

In practice, executions were rare. Given the difficulty of obtaining proof, New England couples were often convicted of a lesser offence (such as 'lascivious, gross, and foul actions tending to adultery'), and punished by fine, flogging, and public shaming.[12] Yet the severity of the capital law was symbolically important. To abominate and expunge sexual pollution as thoroughly as possible was, in the eyes of radical Protestants, essential to the building of a better world, the honouring of God, and the creation of a perfect society.* So pervasive was this ideology in godly communities that even those who paid with their life for defying it could not escape its hold over their minds and actions. When the Massachusetts settler James Britton fell ill in the winter of 1644, he became gripped by a 'fearful horror of conscience' that this was God's punishment on him for his past unchastities. So he publicly confessed his sins. Amongst other things, he claimed once, after a night of heavy drinking with some companions, to have tried (but failed) to have sex with a young bride from a good family, Mary Latham. Though she now lived far away, in Plymouth colony, the magistrates there were alerted. She was found, arrested, and brought back, across the icy landscape, to stand trial in Boston. When, despite her denial that they had actually had sex, she was convicted of adultery, she broke down, confessed it was true, 'proved very penitent, and had deep apprehension of the foulness of her sin ... and was willing to die in satisfaction to justice'. On 21 March, a fortnight after her trial, she was taken to the public scaffold. Britton was executed alongside her; he, too, 'died very penitently'. In the shadow of the gallows Mary Latham addressed the assembled crowds, exhorting other young women to be warned by her example, and again proclaiming her abhorrence and penitence for her terrible crime against God and society. Then she was hanged by the neck until dead. She was eighteen years old.[13]

TRIUMPH AND FAILURE

These piecemeal, local and colonial attempts to create a brave new world, dedicated to God and purified of sin, were in the 1640s and 1650s suddenly played out on a national scale. Within English society,

* This is why in Scotland those guilty of incest, sodomy, and bestiality, the most abominable crimes of all, were sometimes beheaded or burned at the stake, rather than 'only hanged': George Mackenzie, *The Laws and Customes of Scotland* (1678), 160–62.

Puritans had always been only a minority, albeit one with dispropor-
tionate influence. The Civil War of the 1640s, which culminated in the
execution of Charles I in 1649 and the establishment of a republic,
gave them supreme power.

The escalating struggle between royalists and parliamentarians was
fundamentally, though never exclusively, a war of religion – it came
about because each side was passionately committed to a particular
vision of God's will on earth, and believed that its opponents were
dedicated to destroying it. Puritans were terrified that the king's religious policies, at home and abroad, threatened to roll back the
Reformation and reintroduce popery, the ultimate threat to English
liberties as well as to their eternal salvation. The king and his supporters in turn feared and persecuted Puritans because they believed them
to be dangerously subversive radicals, whose principles and actions
undermined the stability of the church and the authority of the monarchy.

The king's uncompromising policy proved to be self-defeating. By
1640 Charles had been humiliated by his Scottish subjects, who had
risen up in national rebellion against his attempts to impose changes
of doctrine and worship on their own church. The Scottish army
invaded and occupied the north of England; within months, Ireland
too was engulfed in bloodshed, this time by a Catholic uprising that
massacred thousands of Protestants and seemed to confirm the worst
Puritan fears about the king's dubious religious motives. Even before
the outbreak of war in England, Charles was forced into making
heavy concessions; and his ultimate defeat in 1648 seemed, to his
most zealous opponents, the clearest possible sign that God actively
supported their cause and had destined them to sweep away the corrupt old order and establish His kingdom on earth.

The church courts were one of the earliest casualties of this conflict.
Within a few weeks of the opening of the Long Parliament, the
'root and branch' petition of December 1640, which set out Puritan
demands for reform, complained of a 'great increase and frequency of
whoredoms and adulteries' as a direct result of corrupt ecclesiastical
justice. In July 1641, the court of High Commission was duly abolished, and with it all ecclesiastical powers of punishment. In their
place, the House of Commons ordered a new statute to be drawn up

against sexual offences. As with much other legislation during the war years, its passage was a long drawn-out affair, but it gained new impetus from the spring of 1649 – after the army had excluded all but the most hard-line MPs, and forced through the execution of the king, the abolition of the monarchy and the House of Lords, and the proclamation of a Commonwealth. On 10 May 1650, alongside a slew of other measures for moral reform, the purged Parliament finally passed the Act 'for suppressing the detestable sins of incest, adultery, and fornication'. Adultery and incest became capital crimes. Brothel-keepers would be whipped, branded on the forehead with a capital B, and imprisoned for three years; if they reoffended they would suffer death. Fornicators were to be jailed for three months, and possibly (the wording is ambiguous) they too were to be executed for a second offence. A copy of the Act was sent to every parish in England, to announce the dawn of this new sexual regime.[1]

This seemed a great triumph. Finally, after more than a century of determined campaigning, the strictest possible laws had been put in place to enforce sexual discipline. Many other revolutionary social, religious, and constitutional developments took place or were contemplated around the same time. The prospect of creating an entirely new society, led by God's chosen people and dedicated to His honour, was discernibly in the air. Throughout the 1650s, successive regimes of the unstable English republic repeatedly exhorted their subjects to moral reform: the extirpation of uncleanness and of other sins took on an urgent significance for men who truly believed that they were the instruments of a daily unfolding divine mission. Puritan magistrates likewise felt empowered to pursue sexual offenders with fresh zeal. Within a few weeks of the passage of the Act, Oliver Cromwell's own brother-in-law, the energetic army officer John Disbrowe, presided over the trial and execution of an adulteress at Taunton. Though the criminal records of the period are very incomplete, it is certain that other men and women were hanged, too (as they were also in Scotland). When Susan Bounty was convicted of adultery in Devon in 1654, she pleaded for mercy on the grounds of her pregnancy. So she was allowed to carry her baby to term. Shortly after she gave birth to it and held it in her arms, her child was taken from her, and she was carried to the gallows. After her execution, the tiny infant was sent forty miles across country, to her widower, Richard, for him to look after and bring up.[2]

More generally, however, the practical impact of the Act was muted. Its wording included so many provisos that conviction was almost impossible unless unimpeachable witnesses actually caught a couple in the act of sex. Circumstantial evidence, no matter how strong, was not enough. Husbands and wives were prohibited from testifying against one another; and so, even, were guilty couples – the confession of one party could not be used as evidence against the other. Thus, when in London in 1651 Susan Ward's husband brought home his mistress and had sex 'with her whilst his wife was in the bed with them', the Adultery Act was no use to her. Nor was it to Robert Pegg in 1655, when he came home late one night to find his wife in bed and her lover hurriedly pulling on his breeches. Nor could it help the parish officers who entered the bawdy-house of Priscilla Fotheringham in March 1652 to find her 'sitting between two Dutchmen with her breasts naked to the waist and without stockings, drinking and singing in a very uncivil manner'. Given the extraordinary standards of proof required, it is not surprising that there were not many formal trials under the Act, and still fewer convictions. In Middlesex, which included most of London's suburbs, at least forty men and women were indicted for adultery in the course of the 1650s, many of them notorious for their loose living, but only one was found guilty. (A few more were tried instead, or in addition, for bigamy, which was also a capital crime, and easier to prove.)[3]

Instead, the main effect of the new regime was a surge of lesser prosecutions and punishments. In Middlesex, instead of being tried by jury, hundreds of suspected adulterers were instead bound over by magistrates – in other words, forced to end their alleged relationship, find respectable citizens to post bail for their good behaviour, and appear in court to answer for their future conduct. Presentments for brothel-keeping continued to be made in the court of King's Bench, without any obvious reference to the new law. In many counties there was a notable rise in prosecutions for fornication and bastardy: in Devon, at the height of Disbrowe's campaign against immorality in 1655, they accounted for over 30 per cent of all criminal prosecutions.[4]

Much of this activity relied not on the Adultery Act, but on the older bastardy statutes (which, though technically incompatible, remained in force), on common law, and on the discretionary power that zealous magistrates had traditionally wielded against sexual misconduct – even if this contradicted the letter of the new statute. Just as in the old days, many offenders were evidently admonished informally first, and only proceeded against if incorrigible. Similarly, when, in February 1652, Elizabeth Ratcliffe, who had borne a bastard child, was tried under the Act for fornication, she was set free because, though convicted by her own confession, she was 'very penitent for her fault'. Elizabeth Goodheart was put on trial for her life, with a watertight case against her: she had given birth to twins who were evidently not her husband's children, and had confessed to adultery with two different men. Yet she, too, 'being heartily sorry for her fault', was pardoned by the London bench of magistrates.[5]

Judicial discretion could also go the other way. In Middlesex during the 1650s several men and women acquitted of adultery were nevertheless sent to the house of correction, or imprisoned until they could post bail for their good behaviour. The parliamentary army was even more peremptory in its justice. In 1642, it went to extraordinary lengths to show its displeasure against a single 'whore which had followed our camp from London': she was 'first led about the city, then set in the pillory, after in the cage, then ducked in a river, and at the last banished the city'. After winning the battle of Naseby in 1645, its troops turned with a vengeance on the defeated royalists' female camp followers. About a hundred of them, who were Irish, were simply killed; and every Englishwoman was slashed across the face to disfigure her for ever. Many parliamentary soldiers themselves, and their paramours, were court-martialled for immorality: at Leith in Scotland in the winter of 1651, for example, one couple was sentenced

to be ducked twice at a high tide, and then whipped at cart's tail and receive 39 stripes on the naked back from the main guard at Leith to Edinburgh port . . . and then both turned forth of the town at several [i.e. different] ports.

During 1655 and 1656, military rule was temporarily introduced across the whole of England. At the same time, the republic was keen to strengthen its plantations in the West Indies. So, in the spring of

1656, troops of soldiers were sent in to raid London's streets and taverns. They kidnapped over a thousand 'women of loose life', imprisoned them on three specially commissioned ships, and transported them forcibly across the world, to populate Barbados. The Adultery Act had been hedged around by procedural safeguards because of widespread concern that it not be used unfairly against respectable men and women. But harlots did not have the same rights.[6]

Ultimately, therefore, the passage of the Act was a pyrrhic victory. The reign of the Puritans clearly inhibited sexual licence: the number of children born out of wedlock seems to have dropped to an all-time low in the 1650s. Yet the Act's impact was mainly symbolic: most policing did not rely on it, and in the longer term the Puritan experiment was fatally counter-productive. The abolition of the church courts turned out to be disastrous. It created a huge gap in sexual policing which was only slowly and partially filled by the expansion of secular mechanisms. More generally, it destroyed a system of discipline that, for all its weaknesses, had proved to be broadly in step with popular sentiments – replacing it with one whose principles appealed only to a small, zealous minority, and whose severity proved to be unenforceable.[7]

In 1660 the monarchy and the Church of England were restored, and the Adultery Act abolished. Yet the effects of the mid-century cataclysm were impossible to reverse. Even before the Civil War, the capital's rapid expansion had begun to affect moral policing.[8] The crucial additional problem now was that of widening religious division. The 1640s and 1650s had seen a large increase not just in disaffection from the old national church, but in differences between Puritans. In the absence of censorship, and without the enforcement of religious uniformity, a great diversity of churches and sects had sprung up. The restored Church of England was determined to reverse this: religious nonconformity once more became a crime, alternative religious meetings were banned, and the church courts spent much of their time prosecuting people for religious dissent. Yet in cities this proved an impossible task: nonconformity was by now too widespread, and too entrenched. It also fatally compromised the church courts' claim to be exercising universal moral and spiritual discipline.

In some small rural communities the church courts managed to re-establish their jurisdiction over sexual offences, and continued to exercise it even through the eighteenth century: but in London and in other major towns this proved largely impossible.[9]

Though the machinery of discipline had been severely weakened, sexual immorality remained a major target of secular policing. During the decades of the Restoration, there were close to a thousand prosecutions in London each year for sexual offences: a considerable number in its own right, and a sizeable proportion of all criminal litigation across the city. Most of this concerned overt prostitution, the traditional focus of secular policing. As in the 1650s, however, it also remained quite common for men and women to be prosecuted for illicit pre- and extra-marital relations. Compared with the early seventeenth century, when the church courts had been fully active, the numbers punished were inevitably much reduced. Nevertheless, adultery and fornication plainly remained within the scope of the law, and there was plenty of enthusiasm for keeping them there.[10] In the decades after 1660 the Scots and the colonists of New England reaffirmed their harsh statutes against extra-marital sex, as did many European states.[11] In England, too, there were periodic calls during the reigns of Charles II and James II for parliament to ensure the stricter execution of existing laws, to draft new statutes against uncleanness, or to reinstate the death penalty for adultery.[12]

Yet the attack on vice was no longer led from above. Though the Interregnum Puritans had been exceptional in their zeal, all previous monarchs and leaders of the church had supported the sexual disciplining of the populace. Now, Charles II did not even pay lip-service to it. (We shall see why in the next chapter.) His attitude was condemned much more than it was celebrated. As early as 1668, the first major political riots of his reign symbolically took the form of attacks by religious nonconformists on London's brothels. It was sexual immorality that the government should be zealously repressing, they argued, not religious dissenters. In the propaganda war that followed, the king's critics lashed out at his own indiscipline and the debauchery of his court. These were not just central themes of opposition criticism. Frustration and anxiety about royal frivolity was equally widespread, though usually concealed, amongst prominent courtiers and clergymen. In the eyes of orthodox Christians, the court's bad example undermined popular respect and, worse still, risked the wrath of God. Sexual licence was the route to irreligion, social anarchy, and political disaster. It was imperative, they thought, to rein it in and to reform.[13] In 1688, they got their chance.

GOD'S REVOLUTION

The Glorious Revolution of 1688, in which the Catholic James II was overthrown by the invasion of his son-in-law, the Dutch Protestant prince William of Orange, was widely perceived by English Protestants as a divine intervention. It was God's way of giving England one last chance to reject sin, irreligion, and ill government. In response, the Revolution provoked a fervent movement for moral and spiritual reform, which lasted well into the next century – the national campaign for 'reformation of manners'. The new monarchs backed it enthusiastically, for it contrasted their godliness with the immorality of their predecessors, and justified the expensive wars against Catholic France upon which they embarked.[1] So did countless politicians, clergymen, magistrates, writers, activists, and ordinary people. From the moment that William and Mary were proclaimed there were spontaneous efforts across the country to crack down on immoral behaviour.

The stricter punishment of illicit sex was central to the campaign from its very beginning. One obvious hope was that new laws might now be passed. As the lawyer George Meriton put it, the existing sanctions against sexual immorality were laughably 'gentle and easy'. If vice was to be restrained, agreed John Bellers, the Quaker philanthropist, 'less than parliament authority will not do it'.[2] Even before William and Mary had assumed the throne they came under pressure to take up this cause.[3] In February 1690, the new king duly went on the offensive, in an open letter issued to every parish in the land. Exhorting clergymen and churchwardens to assist towards 'a general reformation of the lives and manners of all our subjects', he commanded the immediate prosecution in the church courts of all sexual offenders, but only as 'there is as yet no sufficient provision by any statute-law for the punishing of adultery and fornication.'[4]

Serious attempts were made throughout the 1690s to remedy this lack. In 1690, a group of reform-minded bishops and judges put together a draft bill that would have reinstated the death penalty for adultery, and imprisonment for fornication, and also have improved on some of the weaknesses of the 1650 Act. To make convictions easier, the standard of proof was lowered: guilt was to be presumed whenever an unmarried couple 'shall be found in bed, or in any such posture of nakedness'. Prostitution was now treated as a separate offence, and tackled systematically – sexual trade was becoming an increasingly intractable problem in London, as the capital expanded exponentially and older forms of communal oversight lost their grip. In an effort to regain the initiative, the draft bill ordered that 'common strumpets' were to be flushed out through regular searches in every parish, and summarily punished as vagrants. Keepers of taverns and ale-houses would be banned from admitting suspicious women after dark. Procurers and brothel-keepers were to be fined, pilloried, and if necessary banished overseas.[5]

Similar concerns over the spread of prostitution informed a 1698 bill against whoring and other vices, which not only would have made adultery and fornication punishable by branding, transportation or hanging, but also sought to clamp down on sexual rendezvous in places such as hackney coaches.[6] Finally, in 1699, following a concerted public campaign by bishops and reformers, there was considerable momentum towards the passage of another bill, which proposed that adultery and fornication be tried as misdemeanors and punished by fine.[7]

The desire to strengthen the law against prostitution, adultery and fornication was widely felt amongst moral reformers – even after 1700 the hope remained that 'it would be possible to get a new bill through the House against immorality'. These abortive bills formed part of a broader resurgence of political efforts against vice, which resulted in proposed and actual legislation against blasphemy, profanity, gambling, and duelling.[8] There were also encouraging developments in New England and in neighbouring countries. In Holland, a movement for 'further reformation', including the stricter repression of adultery, fornication, and prostitution, had been gathering pace throughout the seventeenth century, and in Scotland the revolution had been followed by a notable drive against 'filthiness, adulteries, and other abominations'. Fresh Scottish statutes in 1690, 1693, 1695, 1696, and 1701 encouraged action against immorality, and the 'strict and vigorous execution' of capital punishment upon notorious adulterers.[9] In England a majority of MPs voted to give the 1699 bill a second reading, and ultimately it was foiled only by repeated adjournments. Yet only a zealous minority thought the passage of a new statute essential. As one sceptical politician put it, 'those that would not take the Old and New Testament for a rule of life would never be reformed by an act of parliament'.[10]

In the absence of new legislation, moral reformers stepped up the use of existing, common-law sanctions, not just against prostitution but against all unchastity. In the early 1690s about a hundred prosecutions for adultery and fornication were brought in London every year. In Bristol, similarly, reforming magistrates ordered constables to draw up lists of persons 'supposed to live lewdly' with one another, or 'in whoredom', and took steps to flush out secret whores. As the campaign for reformation constantly advised its supporters, 'adultery, etc., and all acts of bawdry, are breaches of the peace . . . for which an indictment will lie'.[11]

Some later commentators took the same line. Although they were but imperfect weapons compared with the death penalty, urged one of George II's bishops, fines and shaming punishments 'ought more strictly and impartially to be inflicted' upon adulterers. Throughout the eighteenth century, zealous magistrates continued to maintain that men and women discovered in whoredom should be charged: for 'acts of lewdness were always punishable at the common law'.[12] Yet by then, as we shall see in the next chapter, the intellectual consensus was steadily moving in the opposite direction. The failure to enshrine the principle in legislation further hastened its demise. Already by 1703 the number of prosecutions brought in London had halved, compared with a decade earlier. In the years that followed, the notion that adultery and fornication were public crimes gradually faded away. By 1730 few men and women appealed to it, most magistrates no longer recognized the procedure, and it had become, as the editor of the State Trials put it, the 'general opinion' that such matters were beyond the reach of the criminal law. Even in Scotland, the same trend was clearly visible. The last English prosecution for adultery as a public crime appears to have taken place in 1746.[13]

SOCIETIES OF VIRTUE

The campaign against prostitution was much more successful, in all sorts of ways. Some godly magistrates waged war on sin more or less single-handedly, in the spirit of earlier Puritan magistrates. The mayor of Deal in 1703, Thomas Powell, plastered his town with royal proclamations against vice and went around personally admonishing and punishing swearers, Sabbath-breakers, and other offenders against decency. 'I took up a common prostitute, whose conduct was very offensive,' he wrote in his diary,

brought her to the whipping-post – being about mid-market, where was present some hundreds of people – I caused her to have twelve lashes; and at every third lash I parleyed with her and bid her tell all the women of the like calling wheresoever she came that the Mayor of Deal would serve them as he had served her, if they came to Deal and committed such wicked deeds as she had done.

In most places, however, moral reformers banded together to form dedicated societies for the prosecution of public drunkards, swearers, gamblers, Sabbath-breakers, adulterers, and fornicators.[1]

By the early eighteenth century, scores of such societies for reformation of manners had been founded across the British Isles, the North American colonies, and continental Europe. There were rural and county-wide associations in Bedfordshire, Buckinghamshire, Cheshire, Gloucestershire, Kent, Monmouthshire, Staffordshire, Pembrokeshire, and the Isle of Wight; they also existed in many small towns, including Alnwick, Bangor, Tamworth, Kendal, Carlisle, Kidderminster, Lyme Regis, Shepton Mallet, and Longbridge Deverill in Wiltshire (where there was a society of 'zealous and able' elderly people). But they were most prominent in larger cities, where vice and disorder were most prevalent. By 1699 societies for reformation were at work in Coventry, Chester, Gloucester, Hull, Leicester, Liverpool, Newcastle, Nottingham, and Shrewsbury; others were active or in prospect at

Bristol, Derby, Canterbury, Leeds, Norwich, Northampton, Portsmouth, Reading, Wigan, Warrington, and York; and outside England in Dublin, Edinburgh, Boston, Jamaica, Belgium, Germany, Holland, Switzerland, Sweden, and Denmark.[2]

London was the movement's birthplace and its centre.[3] Here the primary target was sexual licence. One of its earliest leaders was the Reverend Dr Thomas Tenison, a man entirely unafraid of adultery and fornication. In 1687, he had attended Nell Gwyn on her deathbed and encouraged her penitence. After the revolution, he preached before the queen against lust and uncleanness, reproved the new king for keeping a mistress, and, when made Archbishop of Canterbury, became a tireless promoter of moral reform. It was also Tenison who, as rector of St Martin in the Fields in the West End, had first encouraged the campaign against vice. Soon after the coronation of William and Mary, in the summer of 1689, his parish mounted a petition against local bawdy houses; a few weeks later, a group of local magistrates began to clear the neighbourhood of prostitutes. In the City, the new Whig Lord Mayor likewise cracked down on the 'most dissolute and infamous practice, for men and women in the evening to wander about the streets and impudently solicit others to wickedness'. Shortly after these initiatives in the City and the West End, a group of churchwardens, constables, and other householders in the East End ('the Tower Hamlets') combined together to form a society specifically for 'the suppression of publick bawdy-houses'. They resolved to raise money amongst themselves; to employ lawyers to prosecute all keepers and frequenters of brothels; and to organize a network of local 'stewards', who would supervise the police officers of their neighbourhood and organize the collection and disbursement of money. Within a few months, hoping to inspire others, they published a manifesto.[4]

By 1700 there were well over a dozen different groups in the capital with the object of prosecuting vice. Nevertheless, the original Tower Hamlets society dominated the campaign against prostitution, expanding and reorganizing itself into the main, city-wide organization for detecting 'houses of lewdness and bawdry and persons that haunt them, in order to their legal prosecution, conviction and punishment.' It was also the first to publish an annual account of its achievements. Every year from 1694 to 1707, until the numbers grew too large, the society produced a 'Black Roll' or 'Black List', which displayed, in exact alphabetical order, the name and crime of every sexual offender it had brought to justice over the past twelve months. Thousands of these papers were distributed and posted up, as a warning to sinners and an inspiration to their enemies, far beyond the capital itself.[5]

The new campaign against unchastity concentrated primarily on street-walking and brothel-keeping: these were the crimes whose unchecked prevalence in London seemed particularly aggravating. As one magistrate explained, 'vice when it is private and retired is not attended with those provoking circumstances, as when it revels in your streets, and in your markets, and bids defiance to God and religion, in the face of open day.' Of all sexual crimes, moreover, prostitution seemed the one whose effects were most pernicious. The spread of venereal disease slaughtered innocent wives and families by the thousands; the plague of bawdy houses destroyed the peace and livelihood of honest citizens. It was here that impudent harlots

allure and tempt our sons and servants to debauchery, and consequently to embezzle and steal from us, to maintain their strumpets. Here 'tis that hirelings consume their wages, that should pay debts to tradesmen, and buy bread for children, thereby families are beggared and parishes much impoverished. Here 'tis that bodies are poxed and pockets are picked of considerable sums, the revenge of which injuries hath frequently occasioned quarrellings, fightings, bloodshed . . . routs, riots and uproars, to the great disturbance and disquietment of Their Majesties peaceable subjects.[6]

Yet the methods used against street-walkers, brothel-keepers and their clients also recalled the traditional means and ends of sexual policing. Although reprobates were flogged, carted, and set to hard labour, attempts were made to redeem less hardened offenders by reproving them, reasoning privately with them about their way of life, and distributing admonitory literature to them. The innovative use of the press to name and shame sexual offenders followed similar principles. There were also persistent hopes of reviving church discipline, even in London. The Tower Hamlets society proposed that in every parish the minister should appoint secret inspectors to spy on those

3. *The Eleventh Black List* (1706), giving the names and offences of all 830 men and women punished over the previous year by the Tower Hamlets society for reformation of manners.

persons 'most known or suspected' of debauchery. Each Sunday he would then 'in the presence of the congregation, cause the names and crimes to be distinctly read', excluding them from communion 'till they purge themselves by open confession, and visible tokens of repentance'. This was exactly what happened in Scotland, and in 1708 Queen Anne commanded every English presbytery and parish henceforth to do likewise, and 'nominate fit persons . . . to take notice of vice and immorality, and to [report] and prosecute those guilty thereof', in cooperation with secular justice. The ultimate prospect was a society in which the immoral were 'shunned by all but the unclean herd of the vicious and profane, forced to hide away in dark corners, and in continual fear of being discovered'.[7]

The immediate impact of the campaign was considerable. In 1693, the first year in which the Tower Hamlets society was fully active across the metropolis, it prosecuted several hundred men and women for promiscuity. It also managed to impose heavy fines and public whippings on almost thirty brothel-keepers in the City, a spectacular increase over Restoration levels of prosecution. All this reflected considerable support for the campaign – not just from the bench of magistrates but also from ordinary citizens, who assisted in many prosecutions, served on trial juries, and, as grand jurors, repeatedly demanded the further punishment of brothels and street-walkers.[8]

These high levels of activity were maintained for many years. Between 1700 and 1710 well over a thousand prosecutions of sexual offenders were brought by the societies almost every year. Between 1715 and 1725 the figures were even greater, at times approaching two thousand convictions annually. The consequences were particularly visible in the City, the symbolic heart of the campaign and the capital, as it was of the nation. Within a few years, both street-walking and brothel-keeping were much less in evidence. By 1709, the societies' account of proceedings against bawdy houses proudly proclaimed that they had uncovered 'but one within the City'; a few years later that there had been 'none within the City'. Even towards the very end of the campaign, the City appears to have been kept relatively free of overt vice.[9]

The consequence of their zeal was that the societies soon became responsible for the bulk of sexual policing in the capital. In 1693, the

4. A man and woman caught *in flagrante* by the night watch during a routine raid (a mid eighteenth-century version of a composition dating from the 1710s).

campaign had claimed credit for roughly a quarter of all such prosecutions, most having been brought in conventional fashion by local officers and private individuals. Within a decade the proportions had been more than reversed: by 1703, 85 per cent of all sexual convictions were due to the societies. The same was true of the prosecution of sodomites, which from the later 1690s was largely down to the societies. The campaign thus began by supplementing the existing levels of sexual policing, but ended by more or less taking over the task completely.[10]

Yet even as they came to dominate judicial activity against immorality, the societies faced mounting difficulties. The most intractable problem was simply the unceasing expansion of the metropolis. Set against this backdrop, even the seemingly impressive trend of convictions for prostitution takes on a different complexion. The ever greater number of harlots punished each year could not begin to match the overall increase in sexual vice. Just as the campaign appeared to be going from strength to strength, it had begun to be overwhelmed by its task.

FROM AMATEURS TO PROFESSIONALS

The rise and fall of the societies helped to bring about a fundamental change in the relationship between law and society. Up to this point the policing of sexual offences, as of other crimes, had been based on the principle of communal self-regulation. The offices of watchman, constable, and churchwarden were supposed to be held in rotation by the citizens of each neighbourhood, who collectively were responsible for keeping good order amongst themselves. The societies for reformation claimed to be reinvigorating such popular participation, and it is usually presumed that their campaign roused large numbers of ordinary people to act as vigilante informers against vice.[1]

In fact the active membership of the main (Tower Hamlets) society was strikingly small. Unless they happened to be parish officers, most of its supporters simply contributed a quarterly subscription. The core of the society – those who attended a monthly general meeting and stood for election to its various offices – numbered only 'about fifty persons'; and most business was dealt with by an acting committee of nine. Nor did the campaign against sexual immorality depend upon an army of lay activists, quite the contrary. The detection and prosecution of bawdy houses relied on a handful of salaried employees: usually two men, supported by sympathetic constables, sometimes with one or two additional helpers.[2] In its policing of prostitutes, too, the campaign worked mainly by encouraging existing officers and magistrates to do their duty. Its literature, bureaucracy, and network of local supervisors spurred on reform-minded constables, whilst it eased and rewarded their work with large amounts of cash. In 1694, the only year for which detailed accounts survive, the main society paid out almost £200 to its two full-time brothel-detectors and its clerk; another £80 towards prosecuting bawdy houses; and a further sum reimbursing the expenses of diligent parish officers. Even the local 'stewards' of the society were paid a commission for every subscription they raised. 'Since the process of our law is not a little chargeable', explained the chief propagandist of the campaign with a Ciceronian flourish, 'it must be allowed, that money is the sinews of this war'.[3]

The main tendency of the campaign for reformation was therefore not to set up 'a kind of voluntary police', as has been traditionally thought, nor even to 'mobiliz[e] ordinary citizens in the enforcement of the laws', as the *New Oxford History of England* describes it, but simply to increase the efficiency of existing methods of policing. The prosecution of sexual offenders had always tended to be dominated by particularly zealous justices and constables. To this, the campaign added its employment of dedicated assistants, the systematic use of blanket search warrants, and the establishment of regular petty sessions by reforming justices. Through the exploitation of these techniques even a handful of men could achieve large numbers of summary convictions. The same methods characterized the societies' efforts against other vices. As is evident from the campaign's own propaganda, most of its sympathizers were discouraged from going to law themselves by the trouble, expense, and unpopularity of informing against moral offenders.[4]

In fact it is notable that those volunteers who consistently took a more active part in the campaign tended to end up making a living from the law. The most famous of all the societies' activists was John Dent. At the outset of the campaign, he had been a devout young man of lowly origins. He joined it in 1692, after members of his prayer group decided they should be willing to inform on moral offenders. A decade later, in 1702, he was helping out against 'public lewdness' at May Fair when one of his colleagues was attacked by soldiers. Dent pulled his friend from the fray and held him, as he lay dying, in his arms. Between 1704 and 1707, we catch sight of him working as a regular informer against profanation of the Sabbath, swearing, and drunkenness. By 1709 he had been made a constable. In March of that year, he was himself killed whilst assisting in the arrest of a streetwalker. Although Dent was, as his friends eulogized, an honest, pious man, one of the pillars of 'the good fight of faith', he was clearly also something of a professional, whose life had become devoted to 'the

apprehending and prosecuting of several thousands of lewd and profligate persons [i.e. prostitutes], besides a vast number of Sabbath
breakers, profane swearers, and drunkards'.[5]

Jonathan Easden, a joiner by trade, was part of the campaign even
earlier than Dent; in fact, he helped found it. In 1690 he was one of
the signatories of the original East End manifesto against bawdy
houses; and within a few years he had developed into one of its leading activists. Yet almost from the outset his motives were publicly
impugned. He was repeatedly prosecuted for vexatious litigation,
extortion, and assault. The Middlesex bench inquired into his apparent blackmail of the keepers and clients of disorderly houses, and so
did the House of Commons. In the early 1690s he was fined, outlawed, and imprisoned in Newgate for many months; and more than
a decade later he was again convicted of fraud, fined £20, pilloried,
and sent to prison.[6]

A still fuller example of how lay activism against immorality could
shade into venality is provided by Easden's colleague Bodenham
Rewse, another linchpin of the movement in its earliest years. Rewse
appears to have started out much like John Dent: when the campaign
was launched, he was a newly married member of a religious society.
By training, like his wife Thomasine, he was an embroiderer; but he
used the movement to carve himself a successful career at the under-
side of metropolitan law enforcement. Between 1693 and 1695 he
was employed by the Tower Hamlets society as one of its detectors of
bawdy houses, earning about £75 a year in salary and expenses. This
led him to the even more lucrative business of pursuing felons. In the
later 1690s Rewse became a successful thief-taker, reaping large
rewards for the capture of Jacobite conspirators, clippers, and coin-
ers. Within a few years he had made enough money to buy himself
one of the deputy keeperships of Newgate Prison, where he remained
until his death in 1725. If Rewse had any great antipathy towards
sexual immorality when he started out, it had certainly vanished by
the turn of the century, by which time he had taken up with whores,
infected his wife with the pox, and begun physically to abuse her in
the cruellest manner.[7]

We are faced with a remarkable irony: the societies were intended
to be popular in their appeal, and their declared aim was to revive

community involvement in moral regulation. Yet their campaign had exactly the reverse effect. Despite the rhetoric of grass-roots activism, it relied mainly upon a small group of regular informers and officers. Rather than lending personal assistance, most sympathizers simply gave cash. Its main consequence was to place metropolitan policing on a more mercenary footing.

This was a development with long antecedents. Since at least the reign of Elizabeth, the growing size and complexity of life in the capital had undermined the appeal and effectiveness of the traditional system of policing, in which ordinary householders patrolled the streets and took turns serving as constables and other officers. The earliest casualty was the night watch, which already by the early seventeenth century appears in some parts of the city to have been largely made up of hired substitutes; by 1700 this practice had become so common that some neighbourhoods levied a formal tax for the purpose. The hiring of stand-in constables also steadily increased as the demands of the office became more onerous. Yet the principle of personal obligation remained intact, many householders still served in person, and the piecemeal employment of substitutes did not really improve the system's effectiveness. This was the context that spawned the methods of the reform societies – raising money by subscription, rewarding dedicated officers, and employing full-time informers. These innovations offered a radical new solution to the breakdown of amateur office-holding. Their relative success formalized the idea of law enforcement for payment, and helped accelerate the professionalization of policing.[8]

In turn, the decline of the societies coincided with a general perception that London was inadequately policed. The result was a fundamental overhaul of the system in the years around 1740. Every parish in the capital now set up a permanent, salaried night watch. Professional constables became more common. Across the city, magistrates established public offices devoted full-time to law enforcement, and everywhere their number was increased considerably. The wholesale introduction of these changes marked the end of the long-established principle that policing was a matter of civic duty, to be undertaken in person. Henceforth, the role of householders was simply to pay for the work of others; and the practice of professional patrols and business-like magistracy was to be the norm, rather than a perversion of it.[9]

The result was that, by the middle of the eighteenth century, ordinary citizens who sought to fight vice no longer went to law themselves, but instead employed others to do the job for them. Faced with the nuisance of brothels in the 1750s, the inhabitants of Covent Garden offered rewards to informers rather than take matters in their own hands. Attempting to stamp out street-walking in the 1760s, householders in St Martin's Ludgate hired a professional to clear the streets on their behalf. When broader campaigns were mounted their methods were similar. Sexual impropriety of various kinds was one of the targets of a revived London Society for Reformation of Manners which lasted from 1757 to 1766; of the national Proclamation Society founded by William Wilberforce in 1787; and of the Society for the Suppression of Vice, which came into being in 1802. In each case, the reformers raised money by subscription and encouraged constables and magistrates to put existing laws into effect. But only exceptionally did they themselves take part in policing and prosecuting offenders: such business was now largely left to hirelings and specialists.[10]

There were similar developments in other areas. Men who made a trade of prosecuting people for profit became a growing feature of criminal justice. The government itself encouraged the practice by offering substantial rewards. In addition, especially after 1750, private associations were founded across the country to encourage and fund the prosecution of poachers, thieves, and other felons: by 1800 there may have been over a thousand of these. Salary and profit were also increasingly accepted to be normal motives for urban justices of the peace: in 1792, the Middlesex Justices Act made permanent the practice of stipendiary magistrates. This growing reliance on professionals was part of a general decline in the use of the law by ordinary men and women in the decades after 1700.[11] The ideological importance of the law remained considerable; in certain respects it even increased. Yet its collective basis, and its role in everyday life, had been irrevocably diminished. The consequences were profound. The culture of legal discipline had depended for centuries on popular involvement. By 1800 this had largely disappeared.

HIERARCHY AND HYPOCRISY

An equally striking effect of the campaign for reformation was that even the prosecution of common whores and brothel-keepers became controversial. In 1700 no one thought that such criminals were beyond punishment, and the reform societies were able to proceed vigorously against them. Yet though in the short term their tactics were remarkably successful, they also created growing opposition.

The most common criticism faced by reformers after 1688 was not that moral policing was wrong, but that its practice was unfair. It was evident that only the poor suffered for their vices, critics objected, whilst the rich escaped punishment. This was an old problem, one that advocates of sexual discipline had always acknowledged and fought against. In fact, they had traditionally urged, it was *more* important to punish vice in high places than in low. What matter thy eminence and grandeur, asked a Jacobean preacher, 'shall this protect thee in evil, shall it challenge any immunity, or privilege to sin?' On the contrary, 'the greater men are in place, the more distasteful and foul are their voluptuous actions', and the more they deserved to be punished. At the end of the seventeenth century it remained axiomatic that 'the quality of the persons aggravates the crime', and that the punishing of one exalted criminal did more good, by example and influence, 'than of twenty meaner ones'. Merely to punish 'little sinners' but not 'the whore-master of quality' was hence ineffective, offensive to God, and distasteful to the world.[1] Sporadic efforts were made at the outset of the campaign to put these principles into practice.[2]

As time went on, however, most activists were content to settle for less. Whoredom and the like, acknowledged a clergyman in 1697, were patently 'not the vices only of servants, but masters; not of meaner people only, but of your equals and superiors'. In principle, moreover, all were equally culpable, 'for what is an offence against the law of God and the land in one man, is so in another'. All the same, he advised reformers, 'where it would be likely to do more hurt than good, I think you may forbear . . . sometimes the best rebuke that can be given some great men and superiors, is to let them see what is the just and deserved punishment of their own faults, by the punishment of inferiors, for the same things which they know themselves to be guilty of'. It was this attitude that provoked Daniel Defoe in 1698 to one of his earliest publications. A national reformation of manners was 'absolutely necessary', he complained, yet 'the partiality of this reforming rigor makes the real work impossible'. It was unreasonable and unjust to pursue commoners but to leave unpunished the gentry and magistracy, whose bad example was the real cause of English degeneracy. A decade later, whilst living in Scotland, Defoe withdrew for similar reasons from the main Edinburgh society for reformation, which had chosen to ignore the exposure of one of its leading members as a notorious adulterer. No real reformation, he warned bitterly, could ever be accomplished on such a hypocritical basis.[3]

Yet in the eighteenth century precisely such social selectivity came to be robustly defended. It was only proper, argued a bishop in 1731, that the reforming societies confined themselves to the lower orders, 'upon whose industry and virtue the strength and the riches of the nation so much depend'. Persons of superior rank could be left to their consciences and to higher judgement. All sexual indecency was to be condemned, agreed Sir John Fielding in 1763, but worst of all were 'low, and common bawdy-houses, where vice is rendered cheap, and consequently within the reach of the common people, who are the very stamina of the constitution'. It was more important to regulate 'public' behaviour, argued the Society for the Suppression of Vice a few decades later, than to police the 'private' conduct of the upper classes. Even though by 1800 denunciations of aristocratic depravity had become even more trenchant than they had been a century earlier, it had also come to be widely accepted that judicial campaigns had their limits. It was now the exception, rather than the expectation, that any society 'for the suppression of public lewdness' should pursue offenders of all ranks.[4]

This shift of principle helps explain why, in the course of the eighteenth century, the criticism of sexual regulation as inequitable became ever sharper, more vociferous, and more widely held. By the end of the century the social basis of policing was also obviously much narrower and more partial. Particularly contentious was the growing reliance on informers, who could claim part of the fine levied on any offender.

This had not previously been a feature of moral policing, but had a long and contentious history in other spheres. Already in the early seventeenth century, it had been widely felt that common informers acted 'for malice or private ends and never for love of justice', whilst in the reigns of Charles II and James II their growing use against dissenters became particularly controversial, as it allowed venal and unscrupulous people to profit from denouncing sincere Christians. In London between 1682 and 1686, at the high point of the state's persecution of nonconformists, thousands of men and women were arrested, fined, and imprisoned for their spiritual views. Yet this was not a sign of grass-roots enthusiasm for the strict enforcement of religious uniformity. Most of these people, left in peace by their Anglican neighbours, were instead targeted by gangs of cynical, mercenary informers.[5]*

When, just a few years later, the campaign for moral reform employed the same methods, it therefore struggled to overcome a barrage of doubt and hostility. Even its backers needed constant reassurance that informing was now God's work, 'however scandalous, and infamous, that term hath appeared in these late days, whilst some have been agents for the devil, and made it their design to ruin men, and enrich themselves'. Though informers against immorality were not supposed to accept reward money, the whiff of venality was impossible to shake off. 'It must indeed be confessed,' the societies themselves acknowledged in 1709, 'that there have been some base and wicked persons ... who have extorted money from offenders, and sometimes from honest men.' Informers against vice were honourable men, agreed the Bishop of London in 1724, and if 'an ill-designing person shall sometimes mix with them, and carry on his own private interest under colour of suppressing vice and profaneness, this is not to be wonder'd at'. Most observers, though, were less

* In 1683 the Quaker leaders George Whitehead and William Crouch complained to the Archbishop of Canterbury 'about the great sufferings of our Friends by informers ... telling him what wicked persons they were, and that many of them had forsworn themselves, and deserved to be indicted for perjury: and what a dishonour it was to their Church, to employ such agents to force people to a conformity by persecution ... To excuse them, his answer was, *There must be some crooked timber used in building a ship*': *The Christian Progress of ... George Whitehead* (1725), 500.

forgiving. The suppressing of debauchery was certainly, wrote the journalist Edward Ward, 'a most commendable undertaking'. But the whole thing was falling 'under a great disreputation' by relying on greedy informers, 'who live by filthy means, like flies upon a t[ur]d'. Even ostensible supporters of sexual policing were increasingly disillusioned by the grubby methods, and concerned that its entire foundation seemed to be biased and corrupt. The project had begun with excellent intentions, noted Jonathan Swift, but had degenerated into no more than 'a trade to enrich little knavish informers of the meanest rank, such as common constables, and broken shopkeepers'.[6]

The lecherous, hypocritical reformer thus became an instantly recognizable figure of ridicule in early eighteenth-century drama. In Mary Pix's farce *The Different Widows* (1703), the reformer Mr Drawle is a canting fool whose wife despises him. When discovered under a bed with a young woman, he is forced to confess 'that many times, when I have rebuk'd the wicked, my self have been tempted' – so that many a 'pretty white transgressor' had ended up in his bed, rather than in bridewell. George Farquhar's *The Constant Couple* (1700) featured an elderly alderman, Mr Smuggler, who boasts of his exertions against vice even as he intrigues with the disreputable Madam Lurewell. The moment she appears to give way, he reveals the truth: 'I am an old fornicator, I'm not half so religious as I seem to be. You little rogue, why I'm disguis'd as I am, our sanctity is all outside, all hypocrisy.' In another play, the archetypal 'scourge to public lewdness' is a deputy alderman, Mr Driver, who admits that 'privately I love a wench myself', and that his society for reformation blackmails whores and pickpockets.[7]

Such mockery followed in a long literary tradition of portraying Puritans and other zealots as dissembling and misguided. In the eighteenth century it gained in force and currency because the ethical objections it raised had become increasingly plausible. Not only did moral reformers openly discriminate against poorer sinners, but as time went on they ever more overtly embraced the use of mercenary agents, even of unscrupulous tactics. It was pointless not to descend to this level, argued the propagandists of the Vice Society in 1804, for 'the rat is only to be hunted to his hole by the ferret, and iniquity can

5. A humorous popular ballad (addressed to all 'Friends to Reformation') about the lechery of a supposedly upstanding dissenting clergyman.

only be tracked to its burrows, by beings like itself'. The consequence was that many critics saw little moral distinction any more between prostitutes and those who policed them. 'A modern reformer of vice,' sneered Ward in 1700, was 'a man most commonly of a very scandalous necessity who has no way left, but, pimp-like, to live upon other people's debaucheries. Every night he goes to bed he prays heartily that the world may grow more wicked, for one and the same interest serves him and the devil.' More than a hundred years later, Sydney Smith attacked the Vice Society in identical terms. 'Men, whose trade is rat-catching, love to catch rats; the bug destroyer seizes on his bug with delight; and the suppresser is gratified by finding his vice. The last soon becomes a mere tradesman like the others; none of them moralize, or lament that their respective evils should exist in the world.'[8]

CRIMES AND PUNISHMENTS

After 1688 even the summary conviction of sexual offenders was increasingly called into question. Throughout the middle ages, the sixteenth century, and the seventeenth, as we have seen, it had been common practice to punish harlots summarily for their evil life. The societies for reformation continued this practice, systematically using so-called general warrants, which empowered constables to round up anyone they suspected. Yet by the early decades of the eighteenth century it had become highly contentious.

We can see this partly in the rise of popular resistance to the arrest of street-walkers. The presence in London of ever-larger numbers of soldiers and sailors in the course of the eighteenth century meant that antagonism towards moral policing became increasingly aggressive and commonplace. In 1702, and again in 1709, reforming constables were stabbed to death in public whilst attempting to detain street-walkers. In the spring of 1711, a drive against 'loose women and their male followers' in Covent Garden was foiled when 'the constables were dreadfully maimed, and one mortally wounded, by ruffians aided by 40 soldiers of the guards, who entered into a combination to protect the women'. On another occasion in the East End, a crowd of over a thousand seamen mobbed the local magistrates and forcibly released a group of convicted prostitutes being sent to a house of correction.[1]

As well as this newly muscular popular antagonism towards moral policing, there was a growing undercurrent of unease about its legal implications. In 1709, the trial of three soldiers for the death of the reforming constable turned into a major debate about whether an officer could lawfully arrest a prostitute if she was only soliciting, rather than actually having sex. Before 1688 this would have been an inconceivable question: no one would have doubted that common whores could be summarily punished, or cared much about the legal niceties of their detention. But the actions of the societies made it for the first time a matter of serious debate how far the law should be stretched to correct the morals even of harlots and scoundrels. The tendency of legal opinion was increasingly sceptical. 'What!' exclaimed the Lord Chief Justice, Sir John Holt, in an interpretation upheld by the majority of his fellow-judges, 'must not a woman, tho' she be lewd, have the liberty to walk quietly about the streets? ... What! must not a woman of the town walk in the town streets? ... Why, a light woman hath a right of liberty as well as another to walk about the streets.' It was insupportable that 'the liberty of the subject shall depend upon the good opinion of the constable'; to arrest a woman 'upon a bare suspicion that she was lewd ... is not that against Magna Carta?' It was on similar grounds that the campaign for reformation was dealt a fatal blow in 1725, when its use of general warrants to round up suspected prostitutes was ruled by the Westminster bench of justices to be irregular and illegal.[2]

Not surprisingly, reformers believed that such legal challenges arose from opposition to the very idea of moral policing. It was obvious that many magistrates disliked informers, refused to assist the societies, or discouraged their work. Yet often such distaste concerned the methods rather than the aims of the campaign – some of the justices most vilified as enemies of reform were themselves notably active against immorality. More generally, the difficulties faced by the societies reflected deeper shifts in legal principle, which affected the treatment of all kinds of crime in the course of the eighteenth century. One crucial change was that punishment was increasingly inflicted only upon proof of specific misconduct. In earlier times, the perception of immoral demeanour had often sufficed: the law allowed men and women to be arrested if they were accounted 'lewd, idle, and disorderly' or 'of evil name and fame, generally'. Now its scope was gradually limited to particular actions, rather than a person's general character; and magistrates, judges, and parliament were concerned to define offences with greater specificity. A related development was that, as eighteenth-century statutes relied ever more upon summary jurisdiction, the powers of justices and inferior officers were increasingly subjected to scrutiny, formalized, and more clearly delimited. In this climate of greater scrupulosity, the societies' methods could seem alarmingly cavalier. When questioned by the Secretary of State James Vernon in 1698, one Presbyterian reformer conceded that they sometimes proceeded contrary 'to the received rules of law', as was 'justifiable by the prerogative of the king of heaven, whose honour ought to be vindicated by extraordinary methods'. This was the attitude that the Puritan major-generals of the 1650s had taken. Even then it had been exceptional; by the dawn of the eighteenth century it had become generally discredited.[3]

As a consequence of such trends, it gradually came to be doubted whether prostitutes were culpable at all. This did not mean that such women were no longer subjected to harassment, arrest, and incarceration: the balance of power was still heavily stacked against them.[4] Nevertheless it was a remarkable development, which reversed centuries of legal tradition and – at least in principle – gave them unprecedented rights. By the middle of the eighteenth century the idea had become firmly established that street-walking by prostitutes was not itself punishable. Around 1750, the novelist and magistrate Henry Fielding identified this as an abuse in urgent need of remedy. Though 'the law hath formerly held to be otherwise', he noted with some frustration, nowadays it was impossible to punish prostitutes just for soliciting and for their general 'indecent behaviour'. In 1770 his half-brother, Sir John Fielding, confirmed to a parliamentary committee that there was a 'great difficulty, as the law now stands, to punish those offenders, they being, as common prostitutes, scarce, if at all, within the description of any statute'. Even open soliciting, and 'prostitutes ... walking the streets and using the most obnoxious and obscene language', the Guardian Society for the Preservation of Public Morals found a generation later, had come to be beyond the reach of justice.[5]

The nineteenth century saw repeated attempts to remedy this increasingly glaring defect; but their failure shows how completely the underlying assumptions of the law had moved away from their pre-modern origins. The Vagrancy Act of 1822 briefly revived the Jacobean interpretation, by specifying that 'all common prostitutes . . . not giving a satisfactory account of themselves, shall be deemed idle and disorderly persons'; but two years later another statute restored the principle that only an actual breach of the peace was punishable. The three Contagious Diseases Acts passed in the 1860s empowered policemen in certain military districts to identify women as 'common prostitutes' and forcibly register them. Yet this system of licensing and regulating prostitution proved deeply controversial, and, following a national campaign, the acts were repealed in 1886.[6]

The final and most striking change of all was the dwindling hold of the law upon bawds and brothel-keepers. Up to the end of the seventeenth century, legal action against such offenders had remained commonplace and fairly effective. In the early 1670s there were perhaps 400 or 500 prosecutions each year across the metropolis, accounting for as much as a quarter of all criminal indictments brought at the main suburban sessions. In the 1690s, the societies for reformation stepped up the pressure further, particularly in the City, leading to the conviction of dozens of brothel-keepers every year. Yet over the first half of the eighteenth century the number of prosecutions steadily declined, and by the middle of the century the law had effectively lost its grip on the problem. In 1748, in an attempt to reinvigorate it, the energetic new high constable of Holborn, Saunders Welch, himself brought indictments against the three most notorious brothel-keepers in London: Peter Wood of 'The Star', Elizabeth Owen of 'The Crown', and Anne Everett of 'The Bunch of Grapes', all on the Strand. His own petty constables acted as witnesses. About a hundred other bawds were prosecuted in the course of the year, many of them more than once. Not one was convicted.[7]

This was all the more remarkable because it was also in the early eighteenth century that bawds and brothels came to be viewed with mounting hostility. As it became fashionable to downplay the personal culpability of individual prostitutes, the role of the wicked procurer was newly emphasized. The capital's bawdy houses were also increasingly singled out as a prime cause of robberies, burglaries, and serious lawlessness.[8] As a result, the middle decades of the eighteenth century saw redoubled efforts to stamp out the problem. In 1752, parliament passed a new 'Act for the better preventing thefts and robberies ... and punishing persons keeping disorderly houses', in order to solve the legal difficulties. It outlawed the most common defence tactics, offered large rewards, and obliged parishes to bear the costs of prosecutions. Yet its impact was negligible. In 1758, Saunders Welch, by now a magistrate, noted with dismay the Act's failure to suppress even 'the open and bare-faced bawdy houses'. That same year there were, despite his own efforts, probably no more than ten or fifteen successful actions for brothel-keeping across the whole of London, a city of some 700,000 people. In the following decade the Act proved equally useless to the new society for reformation of manners. Thus by the later eighteenth century even the application of special zeal, private largesse, and tailor-made legislation, in a sympathetic climate of opinion, could not bring about the effective repression of bawdy houses.[9]

The most obvious reason for this was expense. Already in the 1690s the various proposed acts against immorality had been concerned to remedy this. For even though the societies for reformation raised and spent huge sums on legal fees, they never had enough money to see through every case, let alone to indict all the brothels they detected. Most bawds fought back viciously, not only defending themselves tenaciously but mounting vexatious counter-prosecutions that tied up the reformers legally and crippled them financially. Other moral offences, by contrast, remained comparatively easy and inexpensive to prosecute. When the new Society for Reformation was first set up in the later 1750s, it was able to prosecute over 6,000 Sabbath-breakers, gamblers, and drunkards, and distribute over 40,000 books and broadsides, for about seventy pounds per year. Yet from the moment it joined battle against prostitution, its finances became much more precarious. Annual expenditure shot up, to between 300 and 400 pounds, at least half of which was spent fending off malicious prosecutions by the keepers of disorderly houses. It was just such a counter-suit that destroyed the new society in 1763, when the mistress of a Chancery Lane brothel used perjured evidence to win punitive damages against it.[10]

A deeper problem was therefore the rising legal expertise of hardened sexual criminals. Litigation against such people must always have been particularly difficult; but in the eighteenth century the balance seems to have shifted decisively in their favour. It was dismaying to see how easily lewd and disorderly houses brushed aside justice by 'the suborning of false witnesses, and perjuries in the open courts', complained a preacher in 1734. Compared with their opponents, bawds and their associates increasingly had deeper pockets and greater confidence in manipulating the law. An important contributory factor appears to have been the growing involvement of lawyers, whose influence is evident from around the turn of the century in several procedural challenges to the prosecution of whores and bawds.[11] By the 1730s it was not uncommon in cases of all kinds for solicitors and barristers to offer themselves for hire to offenders taken before a magistrate, put on trial, wishing to appeal, or looking to sue for damages. In Westminster, the bench repeatedly ran out of money defending constables against vexatious suits by the keepers and frequenters of disorderly houses.[12] By the middle decades of the century even ordinary street-walkers sometimes had recourse to lawyers, and by the end of the century the legal confidence of some of them was remarkable. In 1791, when one young woman was picked up by Viscount Dungarvan and the transaction between them went wrong, she promptly sued him for theft. She lost, but only after an extraordinarily long trial, lasting almost six hours. For an illiterate London prostitute to have put an aristocratic client on trial for his life over such a matter would have been inconceivable in any earlier age. (Her name was Elizabeth Weldon, alias Troughton, alias Smith. When cross-examined she spoke frankly and confidently about her life and profession. Her attorney had been recommended to her by her hairdresser.)[13]

The rising litigiousness of such experienced sexual miscreants inhibited constables and magistrates from pursuing them. It made the work of moral reformers so difficult that in the later 1730s the societies for reformation gave up on legal methods altogether, whilst others, such as the early leaders of the Vice Society, resorted to fraud and perjury themselves. Above all, it greatly reduced the willingness of ordinary men and women to take part in moral regulation. Even in the 1690s it had been common for householders to be well acquainted with the machinery of the law, and to take an active role in the policing of bawds and whores. Yet just a few decades later they had become notoriously reluctant to do so, for fear of abuse, expense, and vexatious litigation. Most respectable parishioners, already far removed from the day-to-day policing of their neighbourhoods, preferred to keep their distance from such dangerous adversaries.[14] Public discipline had come to be ever harder to enforce, even upon the most notorious and widely reviled sexual criminals.

THE END OF LEGAL DISCIPLINE

By 1750 most forms of consensual sex outside marriage had drifted beyond the reach of the law. This was a development that could not have been foreseen in 1700, let alone a hundred years earlier, for it overturned some of the longest-established moral and legal principles in English history.

Until the later nineteenth century there were sporadic attempts to re-criminalize certain forms of consensual unchastity. The idea was canvassed by successive groups of moral reformers; and legislation penalizing adultery in a variety of ways was introduced in parliament in 1771, 1779, 1800, 1809, and 1856–7.[1] The arguments put forward in its support were little different from those that had sustained punishment in earlier times: the offence was a clear breach of God's commandments; it caused grave injury to individuals and families; it disturbed the order of civil society. However, the motives and circumstances were by this time crucially different. The main object now was not necessarily to punish or even to prevent immorality, but to improve the law of divorce and to restrict private suits for 'criminal conversation'. Above all, the prospect of treating adulterers and fornicators as public criminals was no longer one with any substantial basis in current jurisdiction, which made it much more difficult to contemplate. Around 1700, the intention of legislating had been to shore up a legal practice that, although on the decline, was still current. A century later, however, the machinery of criminal justice in this sphere, vigorously active for so many hundreds of years, had fallen almost entirely into disuse.

This did not mean that unchastity was no longer policed or punished. Bawds and prostitutes remained subject to various forms of legal and semi-legal harassment and penalty. Sodomy remained a capital crime, and (as we shall see) was targeted with increasing ferocity after 1700, as it came to be defined as the quintessentially 'unnatural' kind of behaviour. For plebeian men and women, the bastardy laws continued to criminalize the bearing of children out of wedlock. Amongst the propertied classes, the gradual rise of new forms of private litigation and divorce over unchastity compensated, at least symbolically, for the falling away of public jurisdiction.[2] In America, the much stronger inheritance of Puritan ideals ensured that even in 1800 – indeed, well into the twentieth century – most states continued to treat adultery and fornication as public crimes, despite the weakening of sexual policing. More generally, as the judicial punishment of immorality declined, ever more energy was expended everywhere on the inculcation of sexual mores through education, literature, and social norms. As we shall see, even though chastity was no longer imposed by law, it remained, especially for women, a matter of overwhelming social importance.

Sexual discipline therefore encompassed many different things. But the decline and fall of public policing was nonetheless a momentous development. Since the dawn of English civilization the courts of the state and church had enforced the principle that illicit sex should not be tolerated by the community. Yet by 1800 the law had come to take a markedly different view of private and public affairs. Thus far we have followed the legal and social aspects of this transformation. As we are about to discover, it was also the consequence of the most profound intellectual earthquake ever to hit the western world: the Enlightenment.

2

The Rise of Sexual Freedom

Others say, it is true freedom to have community with all women, and to have liberty to satisfy their lusts and greedy appetites: but this is the freedom of wanton unreasonable beasts, and tends to destruction.

Gerrard Winstanley, *The Law of Freedom* (1652), 17.

God has given these natural affections and lusts to be gratified with reason, to make life sweet and agreeable. ... the gratification of carnal lust to the injury of none, is no evil; nor is the lust or desire itself.

'Gideon Archer' [i.e. Peter Annet], *Social Bliss Considered* (1749), iii, 83.

Love is free: to promise for ever to love the same woman, is not less absurd than to promise to believe the same creed ... I conceive that, from the abolition of marriage, the fit and natural arrangement of sexual connection would result.

Percy Bysshe Shelley, *Queen Mab* (1813), 147, 151

There remains [one argument] which we believe to be decisive, namely, the importance which society and the law ought to give to individual freedom of choice and action in matters of private morality ... We accordingly recommend that

homosexual behaviour between consenting adults in private
should no longer be a criminal offence.
*Report of the Committee on Homosexual Offences and
Prostitution* (1957), 24–5.

The most profound cultural development of the later sixteenth and seventeenth centuries was the spread of religious division. After decades of civil war, sectarian strife and attempts to re-establish uniformity, by force if necessary, the Toleration Act of 1689 legalized religious plurality. The reverberation of these momentous theological and political disputes gradually destroyed the theoretical foundations of sexual discipline. Sexual toleration grew out of religious toleration.

Its evolution was, in fact, a central feature of the European Enlightenment. The principle of sexual liberty engaged many seventeenth- and eighteenth-century thinkers, and epitomized the most fundamental intellectual developments of the age. What is more, although it originated in the theological and philosophical debates of a particular time and place, its influence has been felt ever since. Its emergence permanently altered how we think about sex. Even today, in very different social and intellectual circumstances, it continues to inspire new developments.

RELIGIOUS AND MORAL TOLERATION

Because the theory and practice of sexual and of religious discipline had traditionally been so closely intertwined, the growth of religious liberty in the later seventeenth century raised obvious questions about moral liberty. To most observers, however, this was a deeply unwanted development. Indeed, the orthodox view amongst advocates of toleration was that freedom of religion was wholly different from other types of freedom. It did not imply a general liberty of thought or action. Still less could it be used to justify adultery, fornication, or any other kind of licentiousness. As the Presbyterian John Shower pointed out, even

the greatest sticklers for the most unlimited toleration, as to different sentiments about matters of faith, and worship; do yet all agree, that these instances of immorality do properly come under the cognisance of the civil magistrate, as having a mighty influence upon public society, being very prejudicial to the welfare of it. So that no man can complain of persecution for his opinions, when he is punished for such gross immoralities against the laws of God and the land.[1]

This difference between spiritual and moral freedom was articulated most influentially by John Locke. There were, he maintained, two grounds on which it was reasonable to tolerate varying religious opinions. The first was that people's innermost beliefs simply could not be changed by force.

Confiscation of estate, imprisonment, torments, nothing of that nature can have any such efficacy as to make men change the inward judgement that they have framed of things ... It is only light and evidence that can work a change in men's opinions; which light can in no manner proceed from corporal sufferings, or any other outward penalties.[2]

Punishment was therefore useless.

The second fact was that the spiritual beliefs and practices of a person or a church were private matters. Their truth or error did not threaten the well-being of others, or of society as a whole; they were not, therefore, the business of civil government. Against this, Locke contrasted beliefs and practices which could not be safely allowed because they were not merely private, but impinged on the public good. Repeatedly, he raised the spectre of unbounded 'adultery, fornication, uncleanness, lasciviousness', which were not tolerable even under the guise of religious freedom. What, asked Locke rhetorically, if a congregation felt itself spiritually inspired to

lustfully pollute themselves in promiscuous uncleanness, or practise any other such heinous enormities, is the magistrate obliged to tolerate them, because they are committed in a religious assembly? I answer, no. These things are not lawful in the ordinary course of life, nor in any private house; and therefore neither are they so in the worship of God, or in any religious meeting.

It was never, he stressed, his aim to advocate 'the toleration of corrupt manners, and the debaucheries of life ... but say it is properly the magistrate's business, by punishments, to restrain and suppress them'.[3]

Given the traditional connection between spiritual and moral deviance, it was imperative to pre-empt the objection that freedom of conscience would imply a general licentiousness.

Yet this proved a tricky balancing act to sustain. Many contemporaries thought the distinction between moral and religious liberty difficult to justify. 'It is no wonder', scoffed one of Locke's earliest critics, 'that this author doth intersperse his discourse with the recommendation of love and unity, and declamation against scandalous vices of whoredom, etc. . . . these are but baits to cover the hook, and invite the licentious readers to swallow it the more greedily.' If it was right to exempt religion from public oversight and leave it to conscience, objected an Oxford don, 'perhaps other men may think it as reasonable to except some other things, which they have a kindness for. For instance: some perhaps may except arbitrary divorcing, others polygamy, others concubinacy, others simple fornication', or even incest. One had but to think back to the Interregnum to see what the fruits of religious toleration were likely to be.[4]

The example of the 1640s and 1650s was indeed a telling one. Precisely the same arguments for and against liberty of conscience had been advanced forcefully then. Most sectarians and independents had claimed that it was impossible and indefensible to coerce beliefs, and that a limited toleration would lead to greater concord between Protestants, rather than the reverse. They also took for granted that any attempt to indulge immorality should be strictly punished: liberty of conscience could not extend to ideas or practices that were contrary to divine law or social order. John Milton, the Commonwealth's most ambitious theorist of intellectual freedom, would nonetheless censor opinions defending sexual licence (as well as popery, which he believed encouraged it).[5] The 'only way to true liberty', in his opinion, was 'by innocence of life and sanctity of manners'. Even those, like William Walwyn, who were for a complete freedom of worship, extending to Muslims, heathens, and atheists, denounced the notion that this might provide 'greater liberty to be vicious'. 'Let the strictness and severity of law be multiplied tenfold against all manner of vice and enormity.' Offenders against chastity, agreed Roger Williams, the founder of Rhode Island, 'ought not to be tolerated, but suppressed'.[6]

Yet in practice the events of the Interregnum appeared to confirm traditional views about the danger of even a limited toleration. The notion that religious freedom would foster peace and union was contradicted by political instability and the willingness of godly groups to persecute each other. To hostile observers its social consequences seemed equally pernicious. Milton's own writings on divorce were held up as an example of how spiritual indulgence bred moral licentiousness; worse still were persistent reports of the supposed promiscuity of Ranters, Quakers, and other radical groups. The Levellers and Diggers similarly found their advocacy of religious and political liberty tainted by association with sexual freedom. Arresting the Leveller leader Richard Overton at his lodgings in March 1649, Lieutenant-Colonel Daniel Axtell was moved to abuse him repeatedly for practising 'community of women', and 'gave it out in the court and street, amongst the soldiers and neighbours that it was a bawdy-house, and that all the women that lived in it were whores, and that he had taken me in bed with another man's wife'.[7] These fears and smears were largely baseless,* but they stuck. After 1660, analogous associations between licentiousness, tyranny, and religious liberty (now especially for popery) remained topical and commonplace.[8]†

Locke's separation of religious and moral matters was thus disputable on the grounds of recent experience. But the truth is also that his own views on the limits of personal freedom were somewhat precarious. On the one hand, he argued forcefully that every man had a liberty to do as he pleased with his goods, his self, and his soul. Laws and punishments should not extend to 'the care of souls', any more than they should presume to protect a person's health or estate against his own 'negligence or ill-husbandry'. Just as 'nobody corrects a spendthrift for consuming his substance in taverns', so 'no man can be forced to be rich or healthful', and equally 'the care of each man's salvation belongs only to himself' – these were all private matters.[9] Yet on the other hand, Locke also maintained, along traditional lines,

* Though not entirely: see below, pp. 89–90.
† 'Set the nation free', orders the king of *Sodom*, in which the proclamation of buggery stands satirically for Charles II's Declaration of Indulgence (1672), 'Let conscience have its force of liberty': *The Works of John Wilmot, Earl of Rochester*, ed. Harold Love (1999), 305.

that it was proper and necessary to regulate personal conduct by punishing people for their vices. This was for their own good, for it brought them, as well as their society, closer to God. When faced with 'drunkenness, lasciviousness, and all sorts of debauchery', magistrates therefore

may and ought to interpose their power, and by severities . . . reduce the irregularities of men's manners into order, and bring sobriety, peaceableness, industry and honesty into fashion. This is their proper business everywhere; and for this they have a commission from God, both by the light of nature and revelation.

In short, people should be 'forced by the magistrate to live sober, honest and strict lives', for 'in men's lives lies the main obstacle to right opinions in religion'.[10]

In short, it seems that pretty much every proponent of toleration before 1700 was keenly concerned not to weaken moral discipline. On the contrary, many wished to strengthen it. Yet this position was open to obvious objections. If people could rely on conscience for their ultimate salvation, why should it not guide them in lesser issues too? If compulsion could not change people's minds about spiritual truth and error, why should it work any better against moral failings?[11] Ultimately these were problems concerning not just the limits of private conscience and coercion, but the definition of true and false knowledge, the extent of free will, and the purpose of civil society. What exactly was the relationship between private morals and the public good? How far should a government intervene in the lives of its citizens? How free was anyone to hold or reject particular beliefs? To champion them? To act upon them?

None of these final questions was new. Indeed, each of them can be said to derive from the central problem of all political thought, that of obedience and authority. Yet no serious medieval or Renaissance theorist of freedom or justice would have thought it appropriate to apply them systematically to sexual conduct. The traditional definition of personal liberty was largely a political and legal one. It was only from the later seventeenth century onwards that its potential scope came to be seen as much wider, encompassing not just spiritual but, in due course, moral freedoms too.

FREEDOM AND CONSCIENCE

There were a number of important catalysts. In the later seventeenth century, after a long period in which population expansion and shortage of resources had underpinned the tightening of attitudes towards immorality, demographic pressure levelled off and living standards started to rise: against this backdrop, fears about bastardy gradually receded.* The general ideal of personal liberty, meanwhile, was greatly enhanced by the political developments of the seventeenth and eighteenth centuries. From the English Civil War to the American Revolution and beyond, tension between governmental authority and the rights of the subject was a central political issue, and 'liberty' perhaps the most potent ideological concept of all. What limits should be placed upon personal autonomy was a question not just about private conscience, but about the whole sphere of public action. It is no surprise that by the early eighteenth century many commentators linked the apparent rise of immorality to this growing spirit of political independence. The general presumption of personal freedom had grown so strong and unbounded, observed a bishop in 1730, that it had spawned a doctrine of moral licentiousness:

Nothing is thought liberty, which does not leave men an unrestrained power of saying and doing what they please, at least in every thing relating to themselves. *Reasonable* liberty is a language they don't understand; liberty in their opinion, ceases to be so, the minute it comes under rules and limitations.[1]

A more direct influence was the passage of the Toleration Act (1689), which legalized nonconformist worship. This did not happen because the intellectual arguments for toleration had become widely accepted. On the contrary, most mainstream opinion remained critical of the idea. The new law was proposed only as a limited, regrettable, political concession, after the revolution of 1688 had deposed James II, and was meant to gain the support of religious dissenters for the new regime, not as an inherently desirable policy. (Indeed, many churchmen rapidly came to regret its passage, and

* See below, Chapter 4, 'Polygamy and Population'.

worked towards its repeal).[2] Yet in practice it soon established a more or less complete freedom of conscience, at least for nominally Protestant men and women. It also made it possible for people to avoid worship altogether, despite the letter of the law. Above all, the establishment of toleration helped to weaken the presumption that plurality in matters of faith inevitably caused social disorder. Despite the continued ferocity of religious and political divisions after the Glorious Revolution, it became increasingly common to stress that divergence of speech and belief was inevitable, and that laws should govern only actions, not thoughts. English public life thus came to be characterized by an unprecedented diversity of opinion and expression.

The question of to what extent personal freedom should extend to private actions as well as to beliefs was thrown into especially sharp focus by the campaign for reformation of manners. This also politicized the issue, so that the enforcement of sexual discipline became closely bound up with religious and party politics. For the movement was driven primarily by Whigs, and by dissenters and their sympathizers. Their method, of organizing themselves into private societies and punishing sinners through secular means, implicitly defied the Church of England's authority. It also raised again the spectre of dangerous Interregnum precedents, as 'reformation of manners' had been a Puritan slogan. For such reasons the movement provoked fierce opposition from Tories and religious conservatives.[3]

The consequence was that, after 1689, enemies of nonconformity and critics of the campaign regularly attacked dissenters and moral activists for basking in liberty yet denying it to others. Was morality not equally a matter of personal conscience? Who were they to prescribe everybody else's path to salvation? 'Why can't you be so civil to do as you would be done by, and give what you take? For is it not reasonable that people should go their own *pace* as well as their own *way* to heaven?' So what if some chose to go slowly, stopping now and again 'to drink (and it may be whore) by the way'? 'You are for punk: I am for bottle', argues a character in John Dennis's play *Gibraltar* (1705). 'As long as there is liberty of conscience abroad. Why should not every man be damned in his own way?'. 'Liberty of conscience, you know, Madam', says Octavio to Belliza in *Love's Contrivance* (1703), defending sexual freedom ('Ay, and men's con-

86

sciences are very large,' she replies). On the modern stage, observed the moralist Arthur Bedford, the Toleration Act was 'particularly applied to encourage adultery' – 'If a man can commit a sin without a scruple, they say he hath his liberty by law, and may go on.'[4]

The growing prominence of this way of thinking hence revealed political and social tensions over the limits of governmental authority, the toleration of nonconformity, and the basis of moral policing. But it also reflected deeper intellectual trends. Three in particular boosted the idea that sexual behaviour was essentially a private matter: changing conceptions of conscience, of punishment, and of moral laws.

The defence of sexual freedom on grounds of conscience grew partly out of arguments for religious indulgence. Some theorists of spiritual liberty did take the idea to its logical conclusion, and argue that one's conscience *should* be the ultimate guide in all things. This gradual elevation of personal instinct as the supreme moral arbiter was one of the most striking conceptual developments of the period.[5] Nowadays the idea that one should follow one's conscience when wrestling with ethical problems seems simple and straightforward. Already by 1750 it could be taken for granted: 'that every man should regulate his actions by his own conscience, without any regard to the opinions of the rest of the world, is one of the first precepts of moral prudence', noted Samuel Johnson. Before 1700, however, it constituted a direct repudiation of conventional thinking about the inherent corruption of humanity and the fallibility of private scruples. To make sincerity the final judge of sinfulness was to bypass the essential duty of informing one's self adequately, of seeking truth and taking responsibility for error. It unjustifiably presumed that individual men and women could judge right and wrong for themselves, without the aid of scripture, laws, or teachers. It even implied that moral norms might be relative. Of all the seditious doctrines that could poison a commonwealth, declared Thomas Hobbes in *Leviathan* (1651), the very first was 'that every private man is judge of good and evil actions', and the second, 'that whatsoever a man does against his conscience, is sin'.[6]

Yet notions like the supremacy of the 'inner spirit' over scripture and outward authority, or the actual presence of God in believers, had a long history. They grew out of medieval and continental mysticism, and were closely connected to orthodox Protestant doctrines about God's direct, unmediated influence upon his chosen people. The same was true of ideas about Christ's redemption of humankind and the banishment of all sin through spiritual perfection.

In consequence, they had had a powerful impact in the early years of the Reformation, when questions of marriage and sexuality were opened up to wide-ranging debate. From the 1520s onwards, various radical continental groups experimented with new marital and sexual arrangements, including voluntary divorce and multiple marriage. Several of the leading reformers, including Martin Luther, Martin Bucer, and Philipp Melanchthon, were willing to countenance polygamy in certain circumstances. Similar ideas circulated in England. Some late fourteenth- and early fifteenth-century Lollards had defended extra-marital sex, free love, and divorce. Amongst the Marian martyrs of the 1550s were several who apparently advocated polygamy or community of wives, as did other groups discovered in 1553 and 1572. The influential Bernardino Ochino, whom Archbishop Cranmer had brought to London in the reign of Edward VI to help advance the English Reformation, published a notoriously open-minded treatise on the issue. (In it, one character advances at length all the apparent biblical justifications in support of his desire to marry more than one wife. His opponent tries but fails to gainsay him – in the end he is forced simply to conclude that 'If you then do that to which God shall incline you, so that you are sure that you are led by Divine instigation, you shall not err.') These were not attempts to enlarge personal freedom so much as to rethink the character of sexual purity, discipline, and patriarchy – as well as compulsory polygamy, the Anabaptists of Münster accordingly instituted the death penalty for adultery, fornication, intercourse with a pregnant or menstruating spouse, female bigamy, and even for simply lusting after another man's wife.[7]

The lasting influence of these early examples was mainly negative. The association with promiscuity and the horrible example of Münster helped to taint such ideas in the eyes of most observers. Partly in response, mainstream reformers gradually came to reaffirm conventional norms of marriage and monogamy. Nonetheless, the underlying ways of thinking persisted amongst some groups on the fringes of the

Church of England.[8] For if salvation was a matter of faith alone, as orthodox Calvinism would have it, then one logical conclusion (the so-called 'antinomian' view) was that no action, however extreme, could contradict one's inner purity. In 1616 the charismatic northern preacher Roger Brereley and his congregation were in trouble for alleging, amongst other things, that 'the christian assured can never commit a gross sin'. Robert Towne, another clergyman active in Lancashire and Yorkshire in the 1630s and 1640s, was similarly committed to the view that an enlightened conscience was above the moral law laid down in scripture. Normally such propositions were to be understood in a refined theological and metaphorical sense only. To conclude from them that God's commandments were not to be obeyed was an error of 'palpable ugliness, and gross vileness', complained Towne. 'I was never guilty of lewdness', protested the Quaker leader James Nayler, 'I abhor filthiness.'[9]

Even so, they were sometimes interpreted more loosely. In the febrile atmosphere of the 1640s and 1650s, as in earlier times of spiritual ferment, they were explored with new-found enthusiasm. In 1650 the popular preacher Laurence Clarkson urged the world that, as all actions were inspired by God, nothing could be sinful if done with a clear conscience, 'though it be that act called adultery' – 'No matter what scripture, saints, or churches say'. Indeed, he implied, to be able to engage in extra-marital sex with a pure mind was a mark of spiritual liberation: 'for my part, till I acted that so called sin, I could not predominate over sin', whereas now he felt at one with all his fellow creatures.[10]

As political and religious authority broke down, the rhetoric of liberty and revelation was likewise used by adulterers, bigamists, and sexual adventurers to argue that public discipline was but 'persecution for conscience'; that it was wrong to restrict a wife to the 'bondage' of monogamy; and that when 'a man did commit adultery [this was] moved and acted by God'.[11] The parson of Langley Burrell in Wiltshire, the long-haired, music-loving antinomian Thomas Webbe, set up house with his third wife, his mistress, her husband, and several other men and women. In the early 1650s, when he publicly confessed to adultery, and was twice put on trial for it, he was said to have maintained that 'there's no heaven but women, nor no hell save marriage', that 'God requires no obedience to any scripture-commands', and that he himself 'did live above ordinances' and 'could lie with any woman except his own mother'. Observing 'a great cock pigeon' mating, so one of his companions testified, Webbe had instructed the assembled company that copulation 'was lawful for every man and woman, and that they ought to take that liberty and freedom one with the other, as those pigeons did, although they were not married the one to the other'.[12]*

Though they provoked considerable publicity, the direct spread of such spiritually inspired doctrines of sexual freedom was always extremely limited.[13] Yet in certain respects the intellectual outlook of the antinomians prefigured more general trends. In particular, their emphasis on sin as a matter primarily of personal scruple was increasingly shared by theorists of conscience in the more pluralist climate around the turn of the century. Foremost among these was the great Huguenot thinker Pierre Bayle, whose defence of spiritual freedom led him to conclude that, in the end, all moral good and evil lay simply in the intention of the actor. Nothing done in a sincere belief of its rightness could be condemned as wrong. To use one of his favourite examples, a woman who has sex with a man she erroneously believes to be her husband is not guilty of anything; in fact, she does a good thing. In following her conscience, she commits neither adultery nor sin.[14]

Theologians such as Bayle were always careful to maintain a clear distinction between immoral opinions, which were necessarily private, and immoral acts, which were not.[15] Hence the elevation of conscience did not in itself immediately promote sexual licence. Its main effect was rather to extend the scope of personal liberty to cover all moral judgements and beliefs. In turn, though, this sharpened the division between private ethics and public actions: only the latter were now to be judged by church or state.

Moreover, as it came to be presumed that people's consciences could not be compelled, the punishment of sexual transgression lost

---

* The sectarian practice of private marriage also led to predictable charges of adultery and fornication: see e.g. *Truth Cleared from Reproaches* (1654), 1–6; Laur[ence] Claxton [i.e. Clarkson], *The Lost Sheep Found* (1660), 15–17; Adrian Davies, *The Quakers in English Society 1655–1725* (2000), 39–40.

much of its traditional justification. This was the second nota..
trend. In the 1690s, at the beginning of the campaign for moral
reform, it was still widely held that punishing sinners would help
bring about their inner reformation. Within a few decades, however,
the balance had shifted towards the view that true penitence could
not be encouraged by force, only through gentler methods, such as
charity, education, and persuasion. The idea of rehabilitation through
punishment never went away completely. But the view that men and
women's ethics were essentially private and beyond legal coercion
marked a notable reduction in the scope of sexual discipline. The
main task left to the law was now only the residual one of upholding
public order. It should deal with people's outward actions, rather than
their inner consciences. Its business was only crime, not sin. It was
useless trying to reform sinners, conceded the clergyman William Bisset in 1704. 'We grant 'tis in their power to do what they will with
their own [souls] ... They may be as secretly wicked, lewd, and
worldly as they please': nobody was going to force them 'to an heavenly mind, much less to heaven against their liking'. The aim of
policing was simply to make sure that *other* people were not harmed.[16]

So the use of the law increasingly came to be seen as separate from,
and less fundamental than, the project of making people virtuous.
Punishment merely checked the effects of vice; only constructive
methods could address the causes of immorality. This separation helps
to explain why there was such an upsurge in new forms of philanthropy in early eighteenth-century England. Charities, educational
works, persuasive literature – these were now regarded as the best
ways of improving the morals of the lower classes, and vast energies
were poured into them. By the 1720s and 1730s even the propaganda
of the societies for reformation tended to highlight their various preventative and constructive 'methods of instruction, admonition, and
reproof': punishment was increasingly seen as appropriate only for
the utterly reprobate. The same shift is evident in the new ethos of
politeness that became fashionable amongst the propertied classes.
Instead of the fear of divine wrath and damnation, arguments against
adultery were now increasingly couched in terms of good manners,
civility, and conscience. The impulse to virtue was supposed to come
from within. None of the leading theorists of politeness had much

regard for punishment. 'For, tho' I am a Reformer', announced Richard Steele in the *Tatler*, 'I scorn to be an Inquisitor' – and he went on to attack the hypocrisy and futility of sexual policing.[17]

This trend was reinforced by the fading of providence. At a national and communal level, fear of God's fury had been a major justification for the public punishment of sexual sinners throughout medieval, Tudor, and early Stuart times. During the Interregnum it provided one of the grounds for the passage of the Adultery Act. In the wake of the Glorious Revolution it underpinned the urgent activism of the campaign for reformation of manners. Yet as the eighteenth century progressed, most Anglicans and moderate evangelicals came to believe that divine providence worked only 'generally', through predictable laws of cause and effect, rather than 'specially', by intervening directly to punish particular human action or inaction. This interpretation was also popular with deists and religious sceptics. 'The providence of the deity', wrote David Hume in the 1750s, 'appears not immediately in any operation, but governs every thing by those general and immutable laws, which have been established from the beginning of time.' It was 'plainly false' that God ever interceded directly: all things depended simply on 'the general laws of matter and motion'. When the idea was invoked by moral campaigners in the second half of the eighteenth century, its appeal was consequently more limited and its tone strikingly different. Providence was now usually regarded as a benign and distant force. Though the English were a nation in need of reform, they also enjoyed 'invaluable blessings', 'benign government', and 'national successes'. As a reforming sermon put it in 1765, England was 'this our sinful, while highly favoured, distinguished land'. The impetus to punish vice now tended to come less from moral panic at the prospect of imminent disaster than from a more positive desire to improve society and glorify God.[18]

There was a similar tendency to emphasize Christ's benevolence, and to presume the superiority of the Gospel over the harsh and complex doctrines of the Old Testament. Traditionally, theologians had asserted the essential compatibility of the two texts, developing sophisticated systems of exegesis to explain the apparent inconsistencies of God's word. Thus some parts of the Mosaic code (its 'moral' law, such as the Ten Commandments) were generally regarded as eternal, and some (its 'ceremonial' dietary and religious prescriptions) as no longer relevant, whilst the continuing validity of its 'judicial' laws was fiercely contested. (As John Whitgift, later Archbishop of Canterbury, noted excitedly in 1574, 'It is now debated at every table whether the magistrate be of necessity bound to the judicials of Moses'.) But now such learned and complicated reasoning became increasingly suspect as a basis for supposedly self-evident truths. Instead, even staunch defenders of sexual discipline stressed that Christian morality derived primarily from Jesus's own charitable example. In this gentler, plainer theology, the burden of sin and its rectification fell much more upon private conscience than on public justice. So rarely did God nowadays strike down whoremongers, observed a dismayed moralist in 1693, 'that we cannot but be filled with wonder and amazement, at the long-suffering patience, of that Immaculate Undefiled Being'.[19]

The fear of future punishment was likewise increasingly outweighed by optimism about God's infinite clemency. The existence of hell had always been the ultimate argument against sin. Why then, asked a clergyman in 1720, did modern Christians indulge so widely in sexual licence? It was not because people didn't believe in hell, but because they had come to think that sin and salvation were reconcilable. 'Many take refuge in the divine goodness and mercy', presuming that God would understand or except their sins; 'others flatter themselves, that though God has threatened eternal punishment to sinners, yet he reserves the power of executing his threats in his own hands, and possibly after all may not execute them'.[20] Some even argued that unchastity was so prevalent in the world only because omnipotent benevolent God permitted it: from which they concluded that 'that sin is not of that malignant nature, or mischievous consequence as 'tis reported to be.'[21]

MORAL LAWS AND MORAL TRUTHS

The most corrosive idea of all was that unchastity was not always harmful or wrong. As we have seen, this was an age-old challenge to the enforcement of sexual discipline. Yet throughout the middle ages and the Renaissance, sexual freedom had been only weakly and implicitly defended. Most of the time it had been advanced light-heartedly or privately: as a fictional trope, or in justification of particular offenders, rather than as a public doctrine derived from general principles. Furthermore, the weight of social, intellectual, and institutional authority was always heavily against it. There was certainly continued controversy about how, and to what extent, to enforce sexual discipline; but the idea that it should be wholly abandoned was never seriously mooted. From the later seventeenth century onwards, by contrast, the notion that unchastity might be harmless came to be expressed with much greater cogency and influence.

The main reason for this was that the question of how moral laws were to be defined was caught up in the greatest theological and philosophical controversies of the early Enlightenment – about the nature of truth and how to ascertain it, about the status of the Bible, and about the proper foundations of civil and ethical authority. Out of these debates there emerged, from various directions, new ideas which cast doubt upon the blanket prohibition of unchastity. Their contribution was often implicit or unintentional: neither conservative nor radical theorists of ethics and religion necessarily wished to promote sexual licence. Nevertheless, the overall effect was to place moral norms on a much more liberal and pluralist footing.

Within orthodox divinity itself there had always been plenty of potential for the rethinking of sexual rules. Though the general thrust of biblical injunctions was clear enough, the detail of their interpretation had never been straightforward. The very concept of chastity depended upon the definition of valid wedlock. It was therefore important to determine the scriptural basis for such matters as permissible degrees of consanguinity, the possibility of divorce and remarriage, and the institution of monogamy itself. Furthermore, although the official line was that the seventh commandment covered all unchaste actions, it was debatable exactly how the various biblical prohibitions of adultery, fornication, incest, whoredom, uncleanness, and lasciviousness were to be interpreted; how consistent they were with one another; and how far they conformed to the norms implied elsewhere in scripture. In addition, there was the vexed question of appropriate punishments. Many Tudor and early Stuart observers had thought that adulterers ought to be executed, as the Old Testament commanded (Leviticus 20, Deuteronomy 22), and in 1650 this policy was enshrined in the Adultery Act. Nonetheless, the more conventional view had always been that this aspect of the Mosaic law, although instructive, was no longer necessarily binding: so that 'it is free for every state to punish it either by death, or by some other grievous censure'.[1] A further complication was Christ's apparent ambivalence in confirming and even strengthening the moral law against unchastity (for example in Matthew 5 and Mark 10),* yet showing mercy towards the woman taken in adultery (John 8): did the latter imply a more lenient view of the crime, or merely his refusal to 'meddle with magistratical matters'?[2]

As had been the case before, during the Reformation and the Interregnum, the fracturing of religious uniformity towards the end of the seventeenth century gave fresh impetus to these longstanding questions. It was denied that the biblical condemnations of adultery and whoredom covered simple fornication, 'a very trivial crime in those days'. Pre-marital sex, it was argued, was 'innocent and harmless'; the Old Testament showed it 'was anciently tolerated and allowed'; it did 'no wrong to any third person, where both the parties are single'. It likewise became fashionable to invoke biblical precedents in defence of divorce, concubinage, or polygamy. Some even sought on scriptural grounds to excuse 'half-adultery' between a married and a single person.[3] In the 1690s the clergyman John Butler caused outrage by asserting at length in the church courts and in print that, in certain circumstances, it was neither adultery nor fornication to live unmarried with a woman, as he did, and to have children with her, as he also did, despite having a previous wife and children elsewhere.[4] The questioning of traditional norms was given still greater publicity by the scale and openness of debates about sexual morality in the new periodical press of the period. Arguments 'in favour of free love, even

---

* Matthew 5: 'Think not that I am come to destroy the law, or the prophets: I am not come to destroy, but to fulfil. For verily I say unto you, Till heaven and earth pass, one jot or one tittle shall in no wise pass from the law, till all be fulfilled . . . Whosoever looketh on a woman to lust after her hath committed adultery with her already in his heart.' Mark 10: 'Whosoever shall put away his wife, and marry another, committeth adultery against her. And if a woman shall put away her husband, and be married to another, she committeth adultery . . . Thou knowest the commandments: Do not commit adultery.'

without the formality of divorce', lamented Gilbert Burnet, the Bishop of Salisbury, were nowadays openly propounded, 'propagated among the crowd, and almost universally discussed'.[5]

Yet the most direct challenge to traditional ethics came not through the reinterpretation of God's word, but from the growing controversy around 1700 about its very truth and authority. The biblical basis of morality came under fire from two directions. It was argued that nothing in scripture that was contrary to reason could be accepted as true; and it was asserted that the moral laws of Christianity were not God-given but, like those of other cultures, merely human customs and inventions.

The latter idea was fuelled by the increasing awareness amongst seventeenth-century writers of the sheer scope and variety of ancient and modern societies across the world. It was particularly striking how radically diverse the sexual mores of other peoples appeared to be. There were nations 'where virgins show their secret parts openly', which permitted fornication and infanticide, or which celebrated the prostitution of brides. In other societies, 'public brothel-houses of men are kept', or beds were shared by 'ten or twelve' couples at a time. There were places where women were bought and sold, or divorced at will; peoples whose king deflowered all virgins before their marriage; still others which promoted incest, held all women in common, or valued female promiscuity. Amongst the ancient Britons, so Julius Caesar had reported, 'ten or a dozen men' had a single wife in common, and parents often lay with their own children. Among modern Muslims, it was said, a man could be revered as a 'saint . . . of very great piety and unblemish'd virtue, because he had never defiled himself with women or boys, but only with asses and mules'. The Greeks and Romans seemed to have thought nothing of sodomy: indeed, 'the divine Plato recommended it'.[6] The Bible itself illustrated that polygamy and concubinage had been perfectly acceptable to other civilizations favoured by God. Did all this not prove that sexual ethics were mutable? Why should only monogamous intercourse be permitted?

The conventional answer was that Christian morality, particularly that of the Church of England, was superior. It was 'preposterous, and vain', warned a clergyman in 1698, 'for us to shelter ourselves under the examples and customs of any ages, or persons that have been before us. We are under a better, and nobler dispensation of grace, and therefore we are tied up to stricter rules, and nobler degrees of virtue'.[7] The moral codes of heathens and savages by contrast were but 'incoherent apophthegms'. They varied so much because they had no solid foundation. 'What sort of men' after all, asked Locke contemptuously, 'were Socrates and Cato, the wisest of the Greeks and Romans? They admitted others to their bridal bed, they lent their wives to friends and made themselves abettors of another man's lust'. To send a person to the ancient philosophers for ethical guidance was to direct them 'into a wild wood of uncertainty, to an endless maze; from which they should never get out: if to the religions of the world, yet worse'. The truth was 'that 'tis too hard a thing for unassisted reason, to establish morality' effectively and comprehensively.[8] Only the 'plain commands' of divine revelation could do that, argued Locke:

To one who is once persuaded that Jesus Christ was sent by God to be a king, and a saviour of those who do believe in him; All his commands become principles: There needs no other proof for the truth of what he says, but that he said it. And then there needs no more but to read the inspired books to be instructed: All the duties of morality lie there clear, and plain, and easy to be understood.[9]

As the jurist John Selden put it, more bluntly,

I cannot fancy to my self what the Law of Nature means, but the Law of God. How should I know I ought not to steal, I ought not to commit adultery, unless some body had told me so? Surely 'tis because I have been told so? 'Tis not because I think I ought not to do them, nor because you think I ought not; if so, our minds might change. Whence then comes the restraint? From a higher power, nothing else can bind.[10]

Yet by 1700 the presumption that in ethical matters faith and obedience should trump rational understanding seemed to many people deeply questionable. It had been undermined by the spread of religious plurality: and it was also beginning to seem old-fashioned in the light of contemporary advances in natural science and metaphysics, which seemed to hold out the promise of new, scientific proofs of God's workings. The more modern view was that spiritual and moral truths ought to be established primarily on a logical, verifiable foundation. From this perspective, true belief could follow only from real understanding: nothing that was above reason could be believed. Only the laws of nature could properly oblige and explain rules of morality, a Cambridge theologian noted in 1682. Otherwise something was merely 'good or bad for a woman's reason, because it is; and this reason will serve as well to prove, that murder or adultery are good things, as that they are bad ones'.[11]

The arguments for rational judgement often overlapped with those for liberty of conscience. Both were characterized by doubts about the possibility of proof in religious matters, scepticism about the reliability of biblical texts, suspicion of clerical pretensions, trust in the essential simplicity of true religion, and confidence in the inherent capacity of ordinary men and women to interpret it. 'If the people would but take boldness to themselves and not distrust their own understandings', Walwyn had urged, they would soon reject all the spurious and self-interested complications introduced by priests, and find 'that all necessary knowledge is easy to be had, and by themselves acquirable'. Nothing that was said to follow from scripture should be believed if it went against natural reason, advised Bayle: even God's moral commands could not contradict our 'common notions of reason'. As Hume summed up this attitude in 1755, 'all the law of Moses is abolished, except so far as it is established by the law of nature'.[12]

Towards the end of the seventeenth century the terms of debate about sexual morality thus began to shift, as part of the general controversy over the compatibility of revealed and 'rational' religion. Up to this point, serious attempts to reformulate sexual norms had always been confined to re-translations and interpretations of scripture and patristic writings. As Christopher Hill once memorably described the limits of mid-seventeenth-century radicalism, 'however radical the conclusions, however heretical their theology, their escape-route from theology was theological'.[13] Yet as it gradually became intellectually unfashionable for moral prescriptions to rest primarily on revelation, greater support had to be found in what seemed intrinsically 'reasonable' or 'natural'. This opened up a much wider field of inquiry. Did the law of nature support God's commandments against fornication and adultery? Or did it permit a greater degree of sexual freedom?

NATURAL LAW AND NATURAL ETHICS

The question was complicated by disagreements over how to define natural law, and how to conceive of human understanding. Essentially, though, there were two poles of opinion. The orthodox view throughout the sixteenth and seventeenth centuries was that the law of nature was entirely consistent with the moral law laid down in the Bible. All the peoples of the earth, whether pagan, heathen, or Christian, were bound to obey it as 'the will of God and divine reason inscribed immediately by God in the hearts of all men; whereby generally they know what is good and evil'. It did not convey the religious precepts essential to salvation, and it was often obscured by the base inclinations of humankind.[1] Yet 'that which is imperfectly written in the minds of men naturally, is perfectly declared by the Law written by the finger of God in tables of stone, i.e. the Ten Commandments, and more fully opened in other parts of Scripture'. The Bible was 'the Law of Nature in the most legible characters', and the seventh commandment one of 'God's Universal Politics', which 'belong to every commonwealth in particular to enforce, and see them executed, as well as ethically to private consciences'.[2] Some godly authorities even argued that natural law, like the Old Testament, prescribed the death penalty for incest and adultery. This was a rule 'of common equity . . . according to the law or instinct of nature common to all men', insisted William Perkins; to deny its universal force, claimed Thomas Cartwright, was to 'fight against the light of nature' (all he was willing to concede was that, depending on mitigating circumstances, the *method* of execution might be made 'sharper or softer').[3]

This way of reasoning tended to be fairly partial, for it usually began with the biblical proscriptions and then sought support for them elsewhere. In the eighteenth century there were likewise many attempts to prove that monogamy and chastity were enjoined by reason and nature. Now, however, most theologians and philosophers attempted to do so more objectively, by first establishing and then referring to supposedly universal concepts such as justice, benevolence, and truth. The moral law laid down in scripture hence became only a secondary exemplification of what followed from rational

enquiry. This was the method pioneered in England by Locke, Cud-
worth, and Cumberland, amongst others, and developed further by
most moderate deist and Christian thinkers of the eighteenth century.

The conclusion that unchastity was wrong could be reached in different ways. Some were of the opinion that all acts should be judged
primarily according to their public and private effects, and that sexual
freedom always led to injury.[4] But most took the opposite view, that
there existed an absolute, natural morality, prior to God's command
or to human laws. In this scheme sexual immorality broke the law
of nature irrespective of its context or consequences. Unchastity
was intrinsically 'against reason and truth', inferred William Wollas-
ton.[5] It was undeniable, admitted Joseph Butler, that it sometimes
(even in 'some of the most shocking instances') appeared to cause
more happiness than misery – but nevertheless it was always automatically and absolutely condemned by our innate moral faculty.
Similar deductions were made by Richard Fiddes, Francis Hutcheson,
Richard Price, Joseph Priestley, Robert Malthus, and countless lesser
thinkers.[6]*

Yet the danger of a purely reasoned approach to morals was that,
even when aimed at supporting virtue, it could sometimes lead away
from conventional norms.[7] Having worked out an entirely rational
system of sexual ethics, Hutcheson found himself drawn towards the
conclusion that 'defect of offspring' would justify married men taking
concubines.[8] Other moralists, such as Adam Smith and the third Earl
of Shaftesbury, developed the classical ethos that the distinction
between permissible and impermissible sexual behaviour was essentially one of degree, involving the avoidance of overindulgence, rather
than a restriction to certain types of relationship. In the case of 'the
passion by which Nature unites the two sexes', explained Smith, 'all
strong expressions of it are upon every occasion indecent', irrespective of whether a couple be married or not. Shaftesbury, for his part,

---

* That all humans had an intrinsic attraction to chastity, reasoned Hutcheson, was
proved by the fact that libertines seduced modest women despite the availability of
prostitutes: 'Chastity it self has a powerful charm in the eyes of the dissolute, even
when they are attempting to destroy it' (*An Inquiry into the Original of Our Ideas of
Beauty and Virtue* (1725), 235; the same argument can be found in the anonymous
popular pamphlet *A Conference about Whoring* (1725), 26).

simply advised his readers that just as 'laughter provoked by titillation grows an excessive pain', so sex was pleasureable in moderation
but in 'excess ... occasions disorder and unhappiness'. Such views
were not necessarily intended to promote sexual freedom: but they
did place the definition of chastity on a looser footing than before.[9] As
we shall see in Chapter 4 ('Polygamy and Population'), a similar risk
attached to the growing vogue for considering sexual ethics from the
perspective of demographic and economic theory. It even became conventional to concede, as Malthus put it in 1803, 'that there have been
some irregular connections with women which have added to the
happiness of both parties, and have injured no one', a notion that
earlier commentators would have found inconceivable.[10]

The impact of such ethical open-mindedness gradually affected
even the highest ranks of the clergy. In the eighteenth century it
accordingly became possible for one of the leaders of the Church of
Scotland to write a treatise seriously commending 'a much more free
commerce of the sexes'. By that, the Reverend Robert Wallace meant
complete liberty for both men and women to cohabit successively
with as many partners as they liked, and an end to spurious notions
of female delicacy – for 'a woman's being enjoyed by a dozen in proper
circumstances can never render her less fit or agreeable to a thir-
teenth'.[11] Less intellectually innovative but equally striking was the
relaxed position apparently adopted by George II's Archbishop of
York, Lancelot Blackburne. 'I often dined with him,' reported Horace
Walpole,

his mistress Mrs Cruwys sat at the head of the table, and Hayter, his natural
son by another woman, and very much like him, at the bottom ... One story
I recollect, which showed how much he was a man of this world, and which
the Queen herself repeated to my father. On the King's last journey to Hano-
ver, before Lady Yarmouth [the king's mistress] came over, the Archbishop
being with her Majesty, said to her, 'Madam, I have been with your minister
Walpole, and he tells me, that you are a wise woman, and do not mind your
husband's having a mistress'.[12]

It is difficult to imagine a similar account being given of any Protestant bishop before 1700.[13] And here is another clergyman, the Reverend
Charles de Guiffardière, later to become a great favourite of George

III and his family, boasting about his latest affair and advising a young man on the irrelevance of the Bible to modern sexual ethics:

> Believe me, our hearts' morality is the only morality we have to lead us, and that disgusting mass of precepts that people no longer read, that derive from I know not what absurd principles, is made only for those gross and clumsy souls incapable of ever attaining to that delicacy of taste which enables a well-born soul to feel all that is lovable in virtue and hateful in vice, independently of the ridiculous reasons advanced by our sages ... Above all, devote yourself to women.[14]

The rise of such attitudes also illustrates the emergence of the opposite view of natural law. This was the notion that sexual *laissez-faire* was normal, and the rules of chastity artificial. The idea itself was hardly new, for the Christian view of lust as an expression of human sinfulness strongly implied it. The difference lay in the increasing valuation of carnal appetite over restraint. In its most extreme form, this approach turned on its head the orthodox connection between Christianity and morality. Radical deists and free-thinkers asserted that organized religion did not teach virtue but concealed it. God's real laws were simple and rational, not mysterious, laid down in nature not scripture. It was only priests and rulers who had imposed the complicated rituals and superstitions that prevented people from apprehending moral truth and 'natural religion' for themselves. Having spent years in 'much and serious reasonings and ponderings' about the basis of religion, wrote the Edinburgh student Thomas Aikenhead in 1697, shortly before his execution for blasphemy, it seemed to him inescapable that 'a great part of morality (if not all)' was of merely human invention. In truth, 'anything may be morally evil, and anything good also; and consequently anything may be decent or indecent, moral or immoral'.[15] Similar views became current also amongst educated Englishmen. As a young man at the Inns of Court, John Bowes, later Lord Chancellor of Ireland, was not alone in urging his friends that Christianity was but a dubious and made-up set of doctrines, and that the natural purpose of women was 'to be subservient to a man's lust'. Most of his male readers, concurred Daniel Defoe, regarded monogamy as 'a mere church imposition, a piece of priestcraft, and unreasonable'. 'If we observe the discourse of our professed debauchees', noted a philosopher in 1725, 'we shall find their vices clothed, in their imaginations, with some amiable dress of liberty, generosity, just resentment against the contrivers of artful rules to enslave men, and rob them of their pleasures.'[16]

This type of interpretation had some basis in the great seventeenth-century debates about the state of nature and the foundations of civil society. One of Hobbes's notorious exemplifications of temporal sovereignty was that, whilst adultery was forbidden by natural law, only human rules could determine what exactly this meant. How the crime was defined thus varied tremendously from culture to culture – so that 'copulation which in one city is matrimony, in another will be judged adultery'.[17] The Restoration judge Sir John Vaughan, a close friend of Hobbes, Selden, and Matthew Hale, went further still in arguing that there was no morality in nature. 'So no copulation of any man with any woman, nor an effect of that copulation by generation, can be said unnatural': it was only custom and tradition that made it so.[18] Similar conclusions could be drawn from Spinoza's moral philosophy.[19] Even Locke himself in private concluded that for a man to cohabit and have children with one or more women, without marriage, was by the law of nature an intrinsically innocent action, only rendered 'a vice of deep dye' by the rules and customs of society.[20]

During the succession crisis of the 1670s and 1680s the political implications of the idea were pursued by some supporters of Charles II's illegitimate son, the Duke of Monmouth. (Many Protestants would have preferred him to inherit the throne rather than the Catholic James, Duke of York (later James II).) The Whig lawyer William Lawrence published a lengthy collection of arguments from nature, reason, history, and divinity, to prove that all existing marital laws were but pernicious clerical inventions; that the very concept of illegitimacy contradicted divine and natural law; and that, by the same standards, sexual intercourse between unmarried persons was not fornication but the purest form of 'private marriage', to choose which 'all persons ought to be left liberty of conscience'.* It was opinions such as these

---

* Monmouth himself lived, and died, by the same principles. When, at his execution in 1685, the two bishops present on the scaffold badgered him to repent his adulterous life, even refusing him communion, he replied angrily that he cared much more for his mistress than his wife, and had been faithful to her: *ODNB*.

that were famously satirized by John Dryden in 1681, in the opening lines of his poem 'Absalom and Achitophel':

> In pious times, e'r priestcraft did begin,
> Before *polygamy* was made a sin;
> When man, on many, multiply'd his kind,
> E'r one to one was, cursedly, confined:
> When nature prompted, and no law deny'd
> Promiscuous use of concubine and bride.[21]

Further support for the idea that marriage and chastity were merely invented traditions came from the cultural relativism that was becoming increasingly fashionable in radical theological discussion. It was not hard to infer from the multiplicity of religions in the world, and their contradictory ethical precepts, that ultimately there were no objective standards of good and evil, or right and wrong behaviour. 'Virtue?' exclaims a character in one of Vanbrugh's plays, caricaturing such modish views, 'virtue alas is no more like the thing that's called so, than 'tis like vice it self. Virtue consists in goodness, honour, gratitude, sincerity, and pity; and not in peevish, snarling, straight-laced chastity'.[22] There was no inherent goodness in sexual continence, merely artifice. Even the presumption that one should not copulate in public, suggested Bayle mischievously, seemed to be based only on 'the arbitrary yoke of customs, and . . . opinion'.[23]

In the eighteenth century, fresh discoveries of the sexual freedoms apparently enjoyed by overseas civilizations lent increasing empirical support to such ideas; as did the widespread adoption of theories of societal development, in which the variation and refinement of sexual mores was often a central theme.[24] As the British Empire expanded across North America and Asia, and the great voyages of James Cook and others traversed the far east and the Pacific, the sexual customs of Native Americans, Indian tribes, and Pacific islanders were all to be catalogued with increasing fascination.* Yet already in the later sev-

---

* Though staunch upholders of conventional morality were apt to dismiss such evidence as fanciful. 'Meeting with a celebrated book, a volume of Captain Cook's voyages,' recorded John Wesley in his diary on 17 December 1773, 'I sat down to read it with huge expectation. But how was I disappointed. I observed, 1. Things absolutely incredible: A nation . . . without any sense of shame! Men and women coupling

enteenth century the same kind of anthropological approach had helped to raise the status of alternative, non-Christian moral philosophies, and advance the idea of the artificiality of virtue. The celebration of natural appetites and of divine benevolence in Epicurus and Lucretius, for example, which provided a powerful validation of sexual freedom, became increasingly influential in English writing at precisely this time.[25]

These various ways of justifying sexual liberty were enthusiastically, if not always very coherently, taken up by the sexual libertines of the Restoration (as we shall also see in the next chapter). Charles II 'could not think God would make a man miserable only for taking a little pleasure out of the way'. Sexual continence was merely the product of 'humour or vanity': no one was chaste 'out of principle'. Likewise, the whole moral philosophy of John Wilmot, Earl of Rochester, could be summed up in two maxims: that he should do nothing to injure himself, or to hurt another person. Immorality, he argued, was no offence to God, for He was too great to hate His creatures, or to punish them: 'he could not think so good a Being as the Deity would make him miserable'. Nor did he believe in hell (a sanction 'too extreme to be inflicted for sin'). Religion was no more than 'the jugglings of priests'; the Bible and its miracles were but incoherent and unbelievable stories; Christian morality was only hypocrisy, obeyed by 'the rabble world' because they knew no better. It was absurd to think that humans were fallen, that 'there should be any corruption in the nature of man', or that reason was meant to restrain our physical instincts – the only true 'rules of good and ill' were those provided by our bodily senses, the only real purpose of life, to pursue happiness. It followed that the ideas of monogamy and chastity were 'unreasonable impositions on the freedom of mankind'. On the contrary, sexual pleasure 'was to be indulged as the gratification of our natural appetites. It seemed unreasonable to imagine these were put into a man only to be restrained, or curbed to such a narrowness'.[26]

Before 1700 the association of such arguments with irreligion and debauchery made it easier for orthodox moralists to dismiss them as

together in the face of the sun, and in the sight of scores of people! . . . Hume or Voltaire might believe this: but I cannot.'

specious sophistry. They were but 'many a lame excuse'; the disingenuous fabrications of men who 'having their appetites unbridled ... are resolved to pursue them whithersoever they go; and invent the best arguments they can to defend them'; their reasoning was inevitably 'prejudiced, biased, and bribed', for 'this is the influence which adultery, fornication, and all sensual uncleanness naturally have on the mind'.[27] There was some truth to these charges. Compared with the rigour of traditional morality, early attempts to defend sexual freedom often seem sloppy and inconsistent, the product as much of social and intellectual posturing as of serious thought. As a satirist observed in 1675, the modern libertine, who 'denies there is any essential difference betwixt good and evil', pretended that he was following the doctrines of *Leviathan* – 'yet he never saw it in his life' and had no idea what Hobbes's book really was about.[28]

Yet in the early eighteenth century essentially the same views came to be articulated with much greater cogency and dispassion. Though the inference of sexual freedom remained controversial, the underlying ways of thinking about nature, reason, and custom were becoming much less contentious.[29] Both grew familiar enough to be parodied by the leading novelists of the age. Samuel Richardson's anti-hero Lovelace is taken by the logic of annual marriage and divorce, which would obviate all adultery and fornication. In Fielding's *Tom Jones*, the deist philosopher Mr Square, when exposed as a lustful fornicator, seeks to persuade the protagonist that in fact no harm has been done: 'Fitness is governed by the nature of things, and not by customs, forms, or municipal laws. Nothing is, indeed, unfit which is not unnatural.' '"Right!"' cries Jones, '"What can be more innocent than the indulgence of a natural appetite? Or what more laudable than the propagation of our species?"' Exactly, replies Mr Square.[30]

In serious writing, too, the idea was now often advanced as part of a more general philosophical scheme. Matthew Tindal's masterpiece of deist reasoning, *Christianity as Old as the Creation* (1730), ridiculed Christian sexual norms as priestly contrivances, no more appropriate to a modern state than the biblical injunctions against usury or the eating of blood. Actions could only truly be judged by their tendency to promote human felicity:

Enjoying a woman, or lusting after her, can't be said, without considering the circumstances, to be either good, or evil; that warm desire, which is implanted in human nature, can't be criminal, when perused after such a manner, as tends most to promote the happiness of the parties; and to propagate and preserve the species.[31]

The aim of Christ himself, agreed a contemporary *philosophe*, had really been to deliver mankind 'from the curse of the Laws of Moses'. He had judged adultery a harmless action, 'what all men continually commit, in thought, or deed'. Though perverted by the church, Jesus's own teachings had instead aimed to restore the laws of nature, such as were found in all happy, innocent societies where 'women, and all other things, were in common'. In fact, goodness and happiness consisted primarily in gratifying nature's appetites: 'when hungry, of food; when thirsty, of drink; when they are stimulated with the motions of concupiscence, they require coition' – it was but 'the vulgar opinion' that there was any such thing as 'good and bad morals', in sexual or in other affairs.[32]

The physician and philosopher Bernard Mandeville similarly argued in 1714 that the classification of moral good and evil in all ages was merely the imposition of cunning politicians. So-called virtue was always 'contrary to the impulse of Nature'; it was only the artificial rules of religion and society that sought to stigmatize lust as odious, to stifle its expression, to deny its force, and to ensure 'that women should linger, waste, and die, rather than relieve themselves in an unlawful manner'. Sexual freedom, urged a popular writer in 1749, was in fact one of 'the rights of human nature, and the righteous liberties of mankind ... the nature and proneness of men and women to embrace each other, is so fitted and disposed as God will have it, and gratifying the appetites and desires they have in common, tends to their common good'. So there was nothing wrong in unmarried people having sex, begetting children, and living together; in allowing public prostitution; or in permitting men and women to divorce and marry others whenever they wished. The same attitude can be found amongst the Enlightenment's early advocates of a more reasoned approach to crime and punishment. Sexual passion between the sexes, said Cesare Beccaria, was an unstoppable force of nature. Adultery sprang from 'a natural necessity'; it did not 'tend to the destruction of society'; it was pointless and pernicious to penalize it.[33]

The most ambitious synthesis to emerge out of the seventeenth- and eighteenth-century controversy about nature and morality was David Hume's interpretation of sexual mores, first presented in *A Treatise of Human Nature* (1739–40), and refined in *An Enquiry Concerning the Principles of Morals* (1751). Hume's initial view was that human beings did have an innate moral sensibility, from which derived certain natural virtues, but that chastity was not included – 'confinement of the appetite is not natural'. On the contrary, lust usually had 'a strong connection with all the agreeable emotions', whilst chastity was merely an artificial virtue, invented primarily for men to feel secure that 'their children . . . are really their own'.[34] The *Enquiry* went further, taking up the standard libertarian theme of the great diversity of sexual norms in different societies. Hume's contribution was to develop the by now conventional insight that moral distinctions were the product of custom and interest into a more systematic account of how divergent sexual codes in fact all shared a common rationality. The deeper truth was that 'the principles upon which men reason in morals are always the same; though the conclusions which they draw are often very different'. He himself, though disparaging of polygamy and divorce, shared the fashionable view that 'libertine love', or even adultery, was less odious or pernicious than, say, drunkenness.[35]

By 1750 there had thus emerged a fairly well-developed doctrine of sexual liberty – not merely a rejection of existing laws, but a new way of conceiving of the boundaries between permissible and impermissible behaviour, derived from different premises. It usually relied, implicitly or explicitly, on two main qualifications. The first was that the behaviour was natural (and, it usually followed, harmless to the individual). In reality this was, of course, not an objective but a culturally determined definition. Conduct deemed to be 'unnatural', such as sodomy or masturbation, did not meet its test,[36] but otherwise what one did with one's own body was a private matter. It is no coincidence that many of the late seventeenth- and early eighteenth-century writers who advocated greater sexual freedom also defended the right to suicide, on similar grounds of personal liberty.[37]

On the other hand, sexual liberty could evidently affect others. The second criterion was consequently that the act did not seriously harm the public good, or at the very least caused less harm than good. This was to be judged not, as in the past, against an absolute standard, but in the light of its circumstances and effects. The argument that infidelity was harmless to others as long as it was kept secret, for example, though hardly original, was increasingly discussed.[38]* It likewise came to be presumed that the sexual rules of any society derived from its collective judgement of 'public conveniency'. Because cultures, indeed individuals, differed for many legitimate reasons in their perception of 'common interest and utility', they had different sexual norms. The implication of this way of thinking was twofold. It created a much sharper division between private and public spheres of life than had been conventional in earlier times. Yet it also raised difficult questions about the exact definition and relationship of the two. The crux of the matter, as Hume rightly pointed out, was that there would always be a tension between the twin aims of modern, secular morality – the maximizing of personal pleasure, and the pursuit of social utility. In sexual affairs 'these ends are both good, and are somewhat difficult to reconcile; nor need we be surprised, if the customs of nations incline too much, sometimes to the one side, sometimes to the other'. Ultimately, and paradoxically, sexual appetite was both the basis of civilization – 'the first and original principle of human society' – and an ever-present threat to social bonds.[39]

The overall effect was nonetheless to strengthen the presumption that sex was primarily a private matter. It bolstered the view of those who engaged in unchastity, like the fourth Earl of Sandwich, that others should 'forgive my weaknesses, when they do not interfere with my conduct as a public man'. 'Public conduct' and 'private character', it could now be argued, were two 'distinct, irrelative things'.[40] The main question became where to draw the line between them. By the later eighteenth century this distinction, although never

* 'When I hear a fine gentleman talking much about his *honour* before women,' observed a mid-eighteenth-century author, 'it gives me the same impression as if I heard him say, *Ladies, you may very safely grant my request, and let me lie with you; for I assure you, I am a man of honour, and never boast of those favours*': *An Essay on Modern Gallantry* [c. 1750], 9.

unquestioned, had become a key doctrine of public policy. It remained so throughout the nineteenth and twentieth centuries, and it underpins our thinking still. Though the precise boundaries of the public and the private have constantly fluctuated, this was the chief foundation of most subsequent defences of sexual freedom. Even the most ambitious later theorists of liberty tended to maintain that immoral acts stopped being private and became culpable if they affected others. As John Stuart Mill was to conceive of it, the freedom of the individual extended absolutely to fornication – though perhaps not to trading in it, and certainly not to performing it in public. But the basic point was 'that what any persons may freely do with respect to sexual relations should be deemed to be an unimportant and purely private matter, which concerns no one but themselves'. It was his fervent hope, he recorded in 1854, that to hold men and women to public account for such things 'will one day be thought one of the superstitions and barbarisms of the infancy of the human race'.[41]

PRIVATE VICES, PUBLIC BENEFITS

The gradual separation of personal morality and public affairs around the dawn of the eighteenth century also paved the way for a still more radical challenge. This was the idea that allowing sex outside marriage could actually benefit the public good. Some sexual licence was therefore to be tolerated, even encouraged.

This notion directly contradicted the orthodox Protestant view that tolerating prostitution would not curb licentiousness but inflame it. 'If lust have the reins, and may range without control', warned a preacher in 1704, 'it will not be confined to the common cattle, but attempt the chastity of maids and matrons; and no virtue almost will be safe'. It was a great mistake, pointed out another author in 1699, to say 'that to restrain lust in a natural way, will put men on using ways unnatural', for sodomy was nowhere more 'to be found in the world as in Italy, where there are eighty thousand whores in the pope's books'.[1]

As these examples suggest, though, there appears to have been a revival of interest around 1700 in the idea of tolerating prostitution. Would it not be an improvement to set aside a place for all street-walkers to congregate every evening, as they did in Amsterdam, enquired a correspondent of the *Athenian Mercury* in 1691? The editors responded that it was 'a very unchristian maxim, to necessitate one evil, to avoid two'; but conceded that, religion aside, this was indeed 'a pretty sort of policy, and many evils would be avoided by it'. The same presumption can be glimpsed in the diary of a Scots clergyman visiting London in 1689. It was 'lest chaste women should be tempted', he noted, that 'the gay courtesans so frequent in the streets at twilight, are winked at'.[2] Over the following decades, as punishment gradually fell out of favour, the idea slowly gained respectability.

By the middle of the eighteenth century it had become a commonplace even amongst clergymen and magistrates that prostitution was inevitable, perhaps even beneficial, and there was general familiarity with its classical, medieval, and continental precedents. Amongst the ancient Greeks and Jews, wrote John Potter, the future Archbishop of Canterbury, in a best-selling account, harlots, concubines, and public brothels were everywhere openly permitted. 'The wisest of the heathen sages' encouraged youths 'to empty their lust upon those' rather than attacking honest women: no one thought such sexual liberty 'repugnant to good manners'.[3] It was neither possible nor desirable, decided the justice of the peace Saunders Welch, 'totally to suppress whoring'; prostitutes formed an essential 'waste ground', without which men might turn to sodomy. Many others concurred that without such an opportunity 'to give vent to the calls of nature', buggery, rape, and murder would inevitably ensue.[4] The idea of actually licensing prostitutes was more contentious, but it, too, gradually gained credibility. To suppress the evil, concluded the influential magistrate and social reformer Patrick Colquhoun, was 'as impossible as to resist the torrent of the tides'; better to institute 'a prudent and discreet regulation' of sexual trade, under police supervision.[5] By the middle of the nineteenth century similar measures were widely advocated, and in the 1860s the Contagious Diseases Acts put into practice a system of governmental registration and control of prostitutes.

This trend was underpinned by several practical developments. One was a growing anxiety about the apparent spread of sodomy, fuelled by the discovery in early eighteenth-century London of an extensive male homosexual subculture, complete with special houses of assignation, transvestite assemblies, and casual sex in parks and public lavatories.[6] Prostitution itself became an ever more visible and apparently intractable problem, as the capital and its night-life expanded throughout the century. Of crucial importance in its continuing rise was the massive growth of the British army and navy. The regular presence of soldiers and sailors in London and other port and garrison towns created a huge new market for casual sex, as well as mounting concern over venereal disease. Charles II had employed a standing army of perhaps 7,000 men, and a navy that, at its wartime peak, numbered up to 25,000. In the 1690s, however, the total figure for the armed forces swelled to over 115,000; by the time of the War of American Independence it had reached 190,000.[7] More generally, the notion that young men of all kinds needed sexual outlets to prevent them raping or leading astray innocent women, or resorting to unnatural practices, was part of a growing obsession over the prevalence of female seduction and mercenary marriage (as we shall examine in the next chapter).

The idea of tolerating prostitution was popularized especially by the writings of Bernard Mandeville and the controversy they caused. His treatise *The Fable of the Bees: or, Private Vices, Publick Benefits*, first published in 1714, included a spirited defence of public prostitution, or the 'necessity of sacrificing one part of womankind to preserve the other, and prevent a filthiness of a more heinous nature'. A decade later, when this passage suddenly attracted enormous attention, he fanned the debate by anonymously publishing a humorous elaboration of it, *A Modest Defence of Publick Stews*. Like his philosophy in general, these salvos were aimed directly at the societies for reformation of manners, whose methods (as we saw in the last chapter) had aroused such disquiet. 'If courtesans and strumpets were to be prosecuted with as much rigour as some silly people would have it,' asked the *Fable*, 'what locks or bars would be sufficient to preserve the honour of our wives and daughters?' Bawdy houses were as necessary as bog-houses; prostitutes were 'already tainted, and not worth keeping'; allowing such women to be fully exploited 'secures the safety of the rest'.[8]

The wit and fluency of Mandeville's thought, its unblinking opposition to conventional morality, and its tremendously wide circulation, together ensured that his advocacy of prostitution became the starting point for all further eighteenth-century discussion of the topic. Already by 1760 there had been at least half a dozen editions of the *Modest Defence*, a dozen of *The Fable* itself, several partial plagiaries of the text, and countless works of criticism and commentary. So widely was his basic philosophy disseminated that it is hard to find an eighteenth-century intellectual who did not notice it. The popular impression of his sexual ideas is equally obvious from the ubiquity of casual references in satirical literature, tracts, sermons, speeches, and popular prints.[9]

Mandeville's views owed a considerable debt to earlier thinkers, not least Pierre Bayle, whom he had probably met in his youth and whom he quoted extensively. His writing also echoed criticisms of moral policing that had long been current in facetious and popular literature. Though now pushed to its limits, his general point that virtue and morality were artificial constructions was, as we have seen, already a commonplace of radical theology and philosophy well before 1700. Indeed, if Mandeville's ideas had been more original they probably would not have attained such immediate popularity. His contribution lay rather in the way in which he was able to take a handful of fairly unsophisticated and unrespectable notions and transform them into a forceful manifesto for sexual licence – by setting them out systematically, developing their intellectual implications, and integrating them into a much broader philosophical scheme. This was not merely a challenge to orthodox sexual morality, but to received thinking about the whole relationship between personal actions and public welfare. The conventional wisdom was all wrong, Mandeville proposed gleefully: paradoxical though it might seem, private vices could actually benefit the common good. By this he did not mean that *all* vice was beneficial, only that some actions conventionally thought evil were in fact beneficial to society. In economic affairs, for example:

the sensual courtier that sets no limits to his luxury; the fickle strumpet that invents new fashions every week ... the profuse rake and lavish heir, that scatter about their money without wit or judgement ... He that gives most trouble to thousands of his neighbours, and invents the most operose manufactures is, right or wrong, the greatest friend to the society.[10]

Just as in trade and industry, so in sexual affairs: asceticism, temperance and other conventional virtues were counterproductive. In fact, human beings were driven by selfish passions, and it was the proper management rather than the repression of these that produced the most socially desirable outcomes. At a stroke, he called into question most of the remaining justifications for sexual policing.

Not surprisingly, his assertion provoked great scandal and denunciation. It was a ridiculous illogicality, spluttered a bishop, contrary 'to the experience of all ages and nations ... [which] have flourished chiefly by religion and virtue, and have proportionably decayed, and finally have been sunk and ruined, by a general luxury and dissolution of manners'. Having searched through the ancient and medieval laws against vice of the Jews, Greeks, Romans, Visigoths, Lombards, and other major civilizations, the clergyman and moral reformer John Disney was equally certain that all received wisdom was against the 'new maxim'. By the middle of the eighteenth century it had nonetheless become universally known. 'Rake to rake', chuckles Lovelace to Belford in Samuel Richardson's *Clarissa*, was it not plain that the seduction of women was 'a necessary evil'? His own actions were 'entirely within my worthy friend Mandeville's rule, that private vices are public benefits'. So notorious was the argument by the 1750s that the handbook of the Magdalen charity for penitent prostitutes felt the need to argue on its opening page for the contrary proposition, that private vices were public injuries.[11]

Such was the impact of this new way of thinking, therefore, that it helped permanently to shift the parameters of discussion. Even the last uncontested principle of sexual discipline, that public whoring was detrimental to the public good, was now called seriously into question, its advocates forced onto the defensive. Although the idea that social order and prosperity might depend on vice and unchastity was often rejected, it was also endlessly discussed. Over time, many of its tenets were assimilated and accepted into the mainstream. A typical example of their casual reiteration occurs in a 1747 obituary of Sir Thomas de Veil, the chief magistrate of Middlesex and a notorious womanizer. 'Upon the whole,' observed the *Gentleman's Magazine*, after cataloguing his sexual abuses, 'he seems to have been a remarkable instance of how far vices themselves may, with respect to the public, supply the want of private virtue'.[12]

Historians of economics have pointed out that Mandeville's

thoughts about the benefits of self-interest influenced those of later thinkers such as Adam Smith, and helped pave the way for new theories of social progress based on an ethos of consumption rather than of frugality and abstention.[13] Much the same is true of his moral views. By 1800, it had become common to argue that the proscription of all extra-marital sex created more problems than it solved. Some commentators decried as intrinsically perverse the idea that free men and women should be restricted in the 'natural right to dispose of their own persons according to their own pleasure'. The evidence of earlier ages showed only too clearly, warned a lawyer in 1785, 'what public mischief, what private conflict, what dark and atrocious crimes have proceeded from a mistaken notion of religion, inculcating a perpetual warfare with the dictates of nature'.[14] And many more people now had come to believe that a loosening of sexual mores, far from heralding national ruin, was in fact an acceptable by-product of social and commercial progress. Similar ways of thinking about the morality of luxury and consumption had been gaining ground since the early seventeenth century.[15] Yet their application to sexual ethics was a novel development, which completely reversed traditional Protestant presumptions. Instead of taking for granted that punishing vice and increasing sexual discipline contributed to the stability of a society, it proposed the opposite.

The development of sexual freedom thus also benefited from the growing purchase of new economic philosophies, with their novel outlook on morality, continence, and prosperity. The extent to which attitudes were shifting by the later eighteenth century is captured perfectly by a conversation that William Wilberforce had in the summer of 1787 with his political adversary, the fourth Earl Fitzwilliam. 'I agreed with him,' reported Fitzwilliam, 'that there was a great deal of debauchery, much looseness of behaviour, and very little religion.' 'But then I could not agree with him, that it ever would be otherwise, as long as there continued a great deal of activity, trade and riches: that the latter produced the former, and if he wished that the former should not exist, I advised him to apply the proper remedy by annihilating the latter.' Even Wilberforce himself, the most zealous moral campaigner of his time, publicly conceded the point. It had to be confessed, he wrote in 1797, 'that the commercial spirit, much as we are indebted to it, is not naturally favourable to the maintenance of the religious principle in a vigorous and lively state'.[16]

LIBERTY BOUNDED AND EXTENDED

To survey the rise of sexual liberty up to 1800 is to contemplate a momentous ideological upheaval. The conventional justification for sexual discipline had been that immoral actions, even immoral beliefs, were dangerous. They corrupted individuals and undermined the well-being of societies; it was therefore legitimate, indeed imperative, to punish them. By the end of the eighteenth century every premise of this doctrine had come to be seriously challenged. A much greater division was asserted between supposedly private and public affairs. It was successfully argued that public authorities had no business meddling in people's personal consciences, and that this extended to their moral choices. It was proposed that immoral acts, too, could be treated as private matters. It even came to be suggested that a degree of sexual licence was a good thing, a sign of social health and progress rather than of corruption and decay. In short, in place of sexual discipline were advanced the ideals of personal liberty in thought and action.

By the dawn of the nineteenth century sexual freedom was thus defended much more systematically and publicly than ever before. Behind this shift lay fundamental reinterpretations of human nature, Christian doctrine, moral philosophy, and the very purpose of mortal life. It is sometimes remarked that the Enlightenment's greatest triumph was its elevation of the pursuit of happiness as the most important aim in life. As the writer and politician Soame Jenyns saw it in 1757, God, in his 'infinite goodness' and with his 'infinite power', had made it that 'happiness is the only thing of real value in existence; neither riches, nor power, nor wisdom, nor learning, nor strength, nor beauty, nor virtue, nor religion, nor even life itself, being of any importance but as they contribute to its production'. Nothing better epitomizes the advance of this general idea than changing attitudes towards sexual pleasure. Instead of as a sin, the mark of the devil and the Fall, the joy to be derived from intercourse was now increasingly regarded as a sign of the action's essential goodness, and of God's benevolence. Sexual desire was not an unclean passion to be bridled, but a physical delight to be indulged. After all, asked the deist writer and schoolteacher Peter Annet,

> If the action be evil, why was there not another way found out of producing the human species? If it be proper to thank God for our existence, is it proper to blame the means or instruments he makes use of to accomplish the end, for which we give thanks? If it be evil to give pain to, or take away life from any of the human kind, is not the contrary a good, *viz.* to give pleasure, produce life, and maintain the production?[1]

It is true that the older fear of sex as impure and debilitating lived on, and not just in religiously devout circles. The ascetic scholar Lord Monboddo, for one, warned that sex was so enjoyable that it risked derailing the life of the mind: as James Boswell recorded, he 'would not allow a philosopher to indulge in women as a pleasure, but only as an evacuation; for he said that a man who used their embraces as a pleasure would soon have that enjoyment as a business, than which nothing could make one more despicable'. Yet even such deprecations of the power of sexual gratification testify to its raised status. By the middle of the eighteenth century, it was not just libertines who celebrated lust as the greatest passion of all, 'the most exquisite, and most exstatick pleasure' in life. As one influential thinker noted in 1785, the question of sexual freedom was of the profoundest philosophical weight: because its practical implications were considerable, but above all because 'this topic concerns the greatest, and perhaps the only real pleasures of mankind, and in that respect is the subject of greatest interest to mortal men'.[2] (Or, as John Wilkes's *Essay on Woman* had put it, more pithily, 'life can little more supply / than just a few good fucks, and then we die'.)

Despite its increasing prominence, the doctrine was far from intellectually dominant. The idea of carnal licence was incessantly deplored and attacked, and most men and women continued to respect the ideals of sexual discipline. Though it was true that all men were naturally inclined to fornicate, it was absurd and unnecessary to tolerate fornication, prostitution, or any 'irregular intercourse whatever between the sexes', thought Dr Johnson. 'I would punish it much more than is done, and so restrain it,' he told Boswell – 'Depend upon it, Sir, severe laws, steadily enforced, would be sufficient against those evils.'[3] In the second half of the eighteenth century and into the nineteenth, as we shall see in the Epilogue, there was a growing popular and evangelical reaction against overt sexual permissiveness. Indeed, Victorian and twentieth-century doctrines of sexual restraint were often derived from the same rational, progressive ideologies as their libertarian counterparts.[4] Yet although the advance of sexual liberty remained contentious, its rise did help to create a more pluralist intellectual landscape, and a growing acceptance that, for better or worse, moral norms were bound to differ, within as well as between societies.[5]

The arguments for personal freedom were also more easily applicable to some kinds of behaviour than to others. This was equally true of what we might call the libertine and the libertarian outlook: the one essentially defending promiscuity, the other concerned to liberate sexual conduct from unreasonable rules and traditions. In both cases, the justification of sex as a healthy natural activity was almost invariably restricted to heterosexual intercourse. Likewise, it was sometimes asserted that all liaisons between men and women should be free, but on the whole the principle was much more widely accepted in the case of unmarried than of married persons. It was easier to justify fornication and prostitution as essentially private transactions, whose commission did not seriously harm other people than it was to place adultery in the same category – for evidently extra-marital infidelity did often deeply upset spouses and children.*

To modern eyes the most glaring limitations were those of class and gender.[6] Although the idea of carnal liberty was articulated at all levels of society, and free unions of various kinds were to be found in many late eighteenth- and nineteenth-century working-class communities, its reasoned justification was pre-eminently associated with gentlemen and noblemen. By contrast, sexual propriety was often held up as a distinguishing feature of middle-class respectability.[7] It likewise remained axiomatic in educated circles that the morality of the labouring classes was a public matter, because the overall strength

---

* Though critics of sexual toleration were quick to point out that even common prostitutes were 'wives and daughters', whose families were affected by their actions: [George Bluet?], *An Enquiry whether a General Practice of Virtue tends to the Wealth or Poverty, Benefit or Disadvantage of a People?* (1725), 141–6.

and prosperity of the nation depended directly on it and because illegitimate births among the poor were a burden on parochial rates and resources. 'In every civilized society,' commented Adam Smith in 1776, there were to be found two different moral codes: a 'strict' one for the common people, and a 'loose' one for people of fashion. Only the latter could afford, and hence excuse in each other, the pursuit of pleasure through 'the breach of chastity, at least in one of the two sexes'. Although by the later eighteenth century the bastardy laws probably constituted the most important remaining form of public discipline over unchastity, it is therefore not surprising that gentlemanly advocates of sexual freedom tended largely to ignore them.[8]

As Smith pointed out, sexual liberty was also strongly biased in favour of men. Sometimes the doctrine was expressed in general terms; now and again (most strikingly in Aphra Behn's poetry of the 1680s) it was held to include both sexes. But mostly it was conceived explicitly as the entitlement of men freely to be able to 'use' or 'enjoy' women. There was very little public discussion specifically advocating women's rights to sexual freedom. On the contrary, the shift away from religious standards of morality, towards greater emphasis on worldly considerations, tended to strengthen the sexual double standard. Many discussions of sexual freedom acknowledged that female chastity was ultimately an artificial concept, the product of cultural and educational indoctrination: by 1740, Hume thought this 'so obvious' that it did not need explaining. Yet they nonetheless felt obliged to countenance its enforcement, on much the same practical, patriarchal grounds as traditionally employed by defenders of sexual discipline. The most basic of these was the presumption that, as Bishop Burnet had put it, 'men have a property in their wives and daughters, so that to defile the one, or corrupt the other, is an unjust and injurious thing.' The other point commonly stressed was that an unchaste woman could impose illegitimate children upon her husband, thereby undermining inheritance and paternal fidelity, whereas the reverse was impossible. 'From this trivial and anatomical observation', argued Hume, 'is derived that vast difference betwixt the education and duties of the two sexes.' As the confusion of lineage and property directly threatened the interests of civil society, female unchastity could not be regarded as a harmless or private affair.[9]

(Though 'a shorter way of explaining the matter', observed another author, would be 'that men are generally the framers and explainers of the law'.)[10]

Thus, at the same time as it was increasingly argued that sexual freedom was natural for men, renewed stress was placed, often in the same breath, on the desirability of chastity in respectable women. Even Dr Johnson, despite his general aversion to licentiousness, thought there was a 'boundless' difference between a little discreet adultery on the part of a husband, which was 'nothing', no 'very material injury' to the wife, and female infidelity, which risked undermining 'all the property in the world'.[11]

It is certainly possible to find eighteenth-century women, especially in higher circles, who exhibited a striking degree of overt sexual freedom.* There is also some evidence of how they justified their behaviour. In 1751, Frances, Lady Vane, took the extraordinary step of publishing a 50,000-word narrative of her adulterous love-life, the thinly veiled 'Memoirs of a Lady of Quality', which appeared as part of Tobias Smollett's novel *The Adventures of Peregrine Pickle*. Given that her second husband had proved a cruel and contemptible impotent, she asserted, she was free to transfer her fidelity to other men. Such engagements 'I held as sacred as any nuptial tie, and much more binding than a forced or unnatural marriage'. The only responsibility she felt to her spouse was that she should not impose another's child as heir to his estate.[12]

In the same way, one female friend of Boswell argued 'that she may indulge herself in gallantries with equal freedom as her husband does, provided she takes care not to introduce a spurious issue into his family'. His young lover Jean Home, the daughter of Lord Kames, took a similar view of their own adultery:

She was a subtle philosopher. She said, 'I love my husband as a husband, and you as a lover, each in his own sphere. I perform for him all the duties of a

* Between them, notes Barbara Taylor, Georgiana Duchess of Devonshire and her sister in the 1780s and 1790s chalked up 'two marriages, seven affairs (including two probable lesbian ones on the part of the Duchess, one of them a *ménage à trois* involving her husband), and nine children, three of them illegitimate': *Mary Wollstonecraft and the Feminist Imagination* (2003), 200.

good wife. With you I give myself up to delicious pleasures. We keep our secret. Nature has so made me that I shall never bear children. No one suffers because of our loves. My conscience does not reproach me, and I am sure that God cannot be offended by them.'

When Boswell confessed his unease at their intrigue, 'although she was affectionate and generous, she was set in her ideas. She reproached me for my weakness. What could I do? I continued my criminal amour . . .'. Jean Home was then just sixteen or seventeen years old. A decade later, her husband, Patrick Heron, divorced her for adultery with an army officer. When this affair was discovered, she declared 'that she hoped that God Almighty would not punish her for the only crime she could charge herself with, which was the gratification of those passions which he himself had implanted in her nature'.[13]

Yet despite their obvious parallels, such arguments never attained the same prominence, let alone the respectability, that was accorded to male licence. Kames himself took the conventional view that adultery in a man 'may happen occasionally, with little or no alienation of affection', but in a woman was unpardonable. After his daughter's divorce, he and Lady Kames exiled her to France and never spoke to her again.[14] In short, the notion of sexual liberty for propertied women was mainly treated with alarm or amusement, in fiction and in criticism of licentious individuals, rather than as a seriously defensible proposition. Its prevalence amongst the lower classes was likewise abhorred as a pitiable consequence of male seduction, or stigmatized as the sign of inferior moral character, a form of voluntary prostitution.[15] Meanwhile, as we shall see in the next two chapters, the sharpened presumption that female modesty, even if innate, depended heavily on instruction, as well as constant vigilance against male lust, gave rise in general to ever more restrictive, asexual codes of female behaviour.

Before 1800, sexual liberty was therefore limited in several important respects. Yet in subsequent years many of its central premises – about privacy, moral liberty, the limits of the criminal law, and the rational and cultural bases of sexual ethics – were to become commonplaces of orthodox judicial and social thought. Henceforth, it was increasingly their precise definition that was contested, rather than the presumptions themselves. Compared with the seventeenth and eighteenth centuries, it is remarkable how comparatively little the fundamentals of sexual liberty seem to have been overtly debated throughout the nineteenth and twentieth centuries, even as the doctrine gradually advanced into a position of intellectual dominance. Even the most profound Victorian critique of progressive arguments for moral freedom, James Fitzjames Stephen's *Liberty, Equality, Fraternity* (1873–4), thus typically took for granted both that 'legislation and public opinion ought in all cases whatever scrupulously to respect privacy', and that the moral standards of societies inevitably differed, and could only be based on expediency. 'It is possible,' he concluded, 'that a time may come when it may appear natural and right to punish adultery, seduction, or possibly even fornication, but the prospect is, at present, indefinitely remote, and it may be doubted whether we are moving in that direction.'[16]

As the basic idea that sex between consenting adults should be treated as private was increasingly accepted, its scope also came to be gradually extended. The most obvious consequence was that, through the nineteenth century and into the twentieth, acquiescence in male promiscuity became less and less controversial, despite recurrent criticism of it from the adherents of traditional mores. When in 1834 the bastardy laws were radically revised, the Poor Law Commissioners, invoking the laws of nature and providence, held lower-class women responsible for provoking or consenting to illicit sex, and absolved men of punishment for the consequences.[17] As far as the male sex was concerned, Charles Dickens told a foreign visitor in 1848, 'incontinence is so much the rule in England that if his own son were particularly chaste, he should be alarmed on his account, as if he could not be in good health'. The use of prostitutes by men, declared a Royal Commission in 1871, was to be regarded as no more than 'an irregular indulgence of a natural impulse'. As an internal civil service memo on the same subject concluded in 1886, it was 'an indisputable proposition that men will be immoral'.[18] The growing influence of Freudian and other avowedly scientific theories of sex in the twentieth century likewise served most immediately to validate the sex-drive of heterosexual men. Yet over time the ideal of sexual liberty also came to be appropriated by other groups.

Its overt extension to women was closely related to the rise of feminism and other ideologies of social equality. This was not a

straightforward connection. Most early feminists and their supporters, deploring the rise of male liberty, presumed that women were the
chaster sex, and aspired to improve male self-control, rather than to
grant women the same licence as men. This was the message conveyed
by almost all eighteenth-, nineteenth-, and early twentieth-century
advocates of the rights of women. In 1854, for example, John Stuart
Mill was 'anxious to leave on record' for posterity 'my deliberate
opinion that any great improvement in human lfe is not to be looked
for so long as the animal instinct of sex occupies the absurdly dispro-
portionate place it does therein'. Josephine Butler, the brilliant and
charismatic leader of the successful nationwide campaign against the
Contagious Diseases Acts (passed in 1864–9, repealed in 1886)
thought that, because of their promiscuity, venereal disease was
'almost universal' amongst males. In 1913, the suffragette Christabel
Pankhurst put the proportion at between 75 and 80 per cent of all
men; 'Votes for Women and Chastity for Men' accordingly became
the slogan of her Women's Social and Political Union. In short, the
building of a better society depended on greater rights for women and
stricter purity for both sexes.[19] It was also often argued, with some
justification, that increased sexual freedom for women would not end
men's exploitation of female sexuality. Yet alongside this dominant
stress on sexual restraint, and not always entirely in opposition to it,
there also developed, from the end of the eighteenth century onwards,
a notable feminist and communitarian interest in free love as a
means to the emancipation of women and the creation of a more just
society.

The idea took many different forms, reflecting the diverse origins
and concerns of radical and dissenting thought. The main impetus
came from a common dissatisfaction with the existing system of marriage. The notion that divorce should be freely allowed if a relationship
had broken down had been occasionally mooted ever since the Reformation.[20] Now its appeal was greatly broadened by a growing
consciousness amongst progressive thinkers of how oppressive of
women's freedom current marital laws and conventions were. Sometimes these were attacked, in language inherited from earlier deists
and free-thinkers, as the corrupt impositions of Christian priests. The
parallel between marriage and slavery was another favourite theme,

as was the idea that the obsession with female chastity only served to sustain prostitution, the great *bête noire* of nineteenth-century feminists and social reformers. Many early socialists, moreover, considered the conventional arrangement of sexual and domestic relations to be connected to, and as pernicious as, the entire organization of the capitalist economy. In consequence some radical commentators argued that couples should be able to separate and remarry as they wished, whilst others took the idea even further, proposing the wholesale abolition of marriage.

In the years before 1800, such ideas were held most notoriously by the leading radical philosophers William Godwin and Mary Wollstonecraft: first independently, then as lovers, and finally during the few months of their married life together, before her death in 1797. When they first met, he had already begun work on the first edition of his *Political Justice* (1793), which forthrightly declared that 'the institution of marriage is a system of fraud', that 'the abolition of marriage will be attended with no evils', and that both women and men should be free to engage in sexual intercourse ('a very trivial object') with whomever they liked for as long as they liked. When, the year after her death, the grief-stricken Godwin published a memoir of Wollstonecraft, it equally shocked the respectable world with its honest recounting of her affairs, her unmarried motherhood, and her open avowal of them during her life. For example (as he put it in his ponderous way),

It was about four months after her arrival at Paris in December 1792, that she entered into that species of connection for which her heart secretly panted ... [a few months later] her attachment to Mr Imlay gained a new link, by finding reason to suppose herself with child.

When she and Godwin began sleeping together, likewise,

we did not marry ... nothing can be so ridiculous upon the face of it, or so contrary to the genuine march of sentiment, as to require the overflowing of the soul to wait upon a ceremony ... Mary felt an entire conviction of the propriety of her conduct.[21]

By the 1820s, the Devon tinsmith turned editor of *The Republican*, Richard Carlile, who was later to act out his principles with the feminist Eliza Sharples, was able to put forth a series of best-selling publications in which he advocated sex for pleasure, birth control, regular intercourse for all young people, and free and equal relations between the sexes, irrespective of marriage. 'There is nothing in sexual intercourse', he explained,

that has any relation to morals, more than in eating or in drinking together . . . A true moralist sees no crime in what is natural, and will never denounce an intercourse between the sexes where no violence nor any kind of injury is inflicted . . . it is the very source of human happiness, and essential alike to health, beauty and sweetness of temper . . . A woman, that consents to live with a man for a month, for a year, or for life, without paying a fee for a priestly bond [i.e. marriage], is as virtuous as if she had been regularly married . . . if she were thus to proceed with a hundred different men, her virtue would be equally sound. It is religion, and priestly profit, and ignorance, that raises the contrary clamour.

Many of Carlile's followers and correspondents enthusiastically concurred with these sentiments. As one, an obscure vintner from Canterbury, told him,

I have long been convinced that any other law than mutual sympathy is insufficient and pernicious in the regulation of sexual intercourse. I entered seven years ago into the marriage state with these sentiments, and my continued experience has constantly tended and added to the same opinion. So far also I am an Epicurean that I think pleasure and virtue synonymous; as also, vice and pain. To excite pleasurable sensation in the world without a corresponding evil is, indeed, the height of moral rectitude in my opinion.

Amongst others who helped publicize such views were the great radical activist Francis Place and the youthful John Stuart Mill. That women and men should freely associate and disassociate themselves, on terms of equality, was also the ideal propagated, and sometimes practised, by other late eighteenth- and early nineteenth-century social, political, and religious reformers, including William Thompson and Anna Wheeler, Mill and Harriet Taylor, William Linton, Robert Owen and many Owenites, and, most famously, Percy Bysshe Shelley and Mary Wollstonecraft Godwin, the author of *Frankenstein* and only child of Mary Wollstonecraft and William Godwin.[22]

As Carlile's example shows, even female promiscuity was now occasionally championed. 'The love of variety', observed a popular author, was 'quite as natural to woman as to man': the pattern of all classical and modern societies showed that 'a certain degree of natural liberty' for both sexes was inevitable and desirable. The sexual act was 'moral, humanizing, polishing, beneficent', urged Robert Dale Owen in a best-selling tract: 'the social education of no man or woman is fully completed without it ... the pleasure derived from this instinct ... is good, proper, worth securing and enjoying'. It was unavoidable that young women would form transient and 'unlegalized connexions' – they should be offered contraception, not abuse. (The early nineteenth century was also the point at which, for the first time ever, the mass adoption of birth control was publicly advocated – as a means of limiting the population and ameliorating working-class life – by social reformers like Owen, Carlile, and Place.)[23]

In a similar vein, in the years around 1800 the poet James Lawrence, inspired by Wollstonecraft and by contemporary German debates on the nature of women, as well as by anthropological accounts of the sexual customs of other cultures, published a remarkable series of works in which he argued for the social benefits of abolishing marriage, granting complete sexual freedom to women, and introducing matrilineal descent. Both sexes, he urged, were naturally promiscuous: 'There is no greater reason in enacting that a man should love a woman tomorrow, because he may love her today, than there would be in compelling a man to dance with a woman at the next ball, because he happened to be her partner at the last.' In short, 'the happiness and liberty of mankind' depended on the sexual liberation of women: 'Let every female live perfectly uncontrolled by any man, and enjoying every freedom which the males at present enjoy; let her be visited by as many lovers as she may please, and of whatever rank they may be.'[24]

It was on such grounds that Shelley, in one of the most widely read poems of the early nineteenth century, declared enthusiastically for an end to all sexual rules: 'Love withers under constraint: its very essence is liberty ... That which will result from the abolition of marriage, will be natural and right, because choice and change will be exempted from restraint.' His sister-in-law Claire Clairmont likewise asserted that only illegitimate children ('the offspring of freedom and love') provoked real maternal affection, and fantasized that if only other 'free women' as brilliant as herself would assert themselves socially, wives across Europe would soon enough 'be scudding away from their husbands as quickly as they could'.* In the United States several early communitarian settlements experimented with new sexual models. In the late 1820s, the indomitable social reformer Frances Wright defended the practice of free love and miscegenation at her mixed-race abolitionist community in Tennessee; whilst from 1848 onwards the members of the large utopian commune at Oneida, in upstate New York, lived in 'complex marriage', whereby men and women were obliged to change sexual partners regularly.[25]

Although the following decades saw the continued advance of more restrictive ideals of female behaviour in mainstream thought, by the early twentieth century there had also developed, on both sides of the Atlantic, several outspoken organizations, journals, and coalitions of individuals advocating unmarried cohabitation, sexual liberty for women, the scientific investigation of variant sexual practices, and the use of birth control as an aid to female independence. In England they included the Legitimation League (founded in 1893), whose purpose was to influence public opinion 'in the direction of freedom in sexual relationships', and the Malthusian League (1877), several of whose members practised or preached free love. Its tireless founder, Charles Robert Drysdale, lived in unmarried happiness with his fellow-doctor and feminist Alice Vickery, and their two children. His elder brother and inspiration, George Drysdale, sold 90,000 copies of *Physical, Sexual, and Natural Religion* (1855), which uncompromisingly advocated contraception, women's rights, and the embrace of sexual pleasure. Its great aim was 'to make unmarried intercourse honourable and legitimate', for 'unmarried and unfettered love' was

---

* Though in one later unpublished fragment of a memoir, looking back on her life, she was bitterly to attack what she had by then come to regard as a masculine tyranny: 'the worshippers of free love not only preyed upon one another, but preyed equally upon their own individual selves, turning their existence into a perfect hell ... The selfishness, the treachery, and meanness, and the cruelty practised by the opponents of marriage and the misery these same opponents induced ... exceeded any amount of the same results produced by marriage': printed in Daisy Hay, *Young Romantics* (2010), 307–9.

the only true mode of sexual union; it is the one which Nature points out to us, and we may be certain, that any institution which defies the natural laws of love, as marriage does, will be found to be the cause of immense evils; ever accumulating as the world rolls on, and mankind become more free, and more enlightened in the physical and moral laws of their being.[26]

THINKING THE UNTHINKABLE

More notable still was the gradual extension of sexual liberty to homosexual acts. This was a development that would have been inconceivable to most early advocates of sexual licence, whose intention was often precisely to prevent sodomy,[1] and it remained anathema to mainstream opinion throughout the eighteenth and nineteenth centuries, and for most of the twentieth. Indeed, the legal punishment of sodomy, and its denunciation as the antithesis of normal sexual conduct, became *more* common after 1700 than it had been before: executions for sodomy took place regularly in England until the 1830s. Yet alongside the heightening of official and unofficial ostracism and repression there slowly emerged a semi-clandestine, alternative, minority pattern of argument in justification of same-sex relations.

This was not just an intellectual development. This period also saw the birth of a whole new culture of male homosexuality in London and other western European cities. The same kind of urban, pluralist environment in which the theory and practice of heterosexual freedom first developed thus also fostered the emergence of distinctively modern ways of same-sex living and thinking.[2]

Homoerotic sentiments were themselves not new. Indeed, especially between men they had long been regarded as entirely compatible with the main well-springs of English culture. Though Christianity unequivocally condemned the act of sodomy, its conception of religious commitment as love and marriage with Christ sometimes led sixteenth- and seventeenth-century men to express themselves in unabashedly sensual terms. 'Batter my heart, three personed God,' wrote John Donne in one of his *Holy Sonnets*, 'Take me to you, imprison me, for I / Except you enthral me, never shall be free, / Nor ever chaste, except you ravish me.' The New England Puritan Edward

Taylor was even more explicit in imagining his 'womb' being penetrated and impregnated by 'the spermadote' of Christ:

> O let thy lovely streams of love distill
> Upon myself and spout their spirits pure
> Into my vial, and my vessel fill
> With liveliness . . .

The huge prestige attached to classical literary models similarly gave
rise to a fair amount of same-sex imagery in Renaissance writing, as
well as to a more general familiarity with the fact that love between
men had been favoured, and commonplace, amongst the ancients.
Moreover, the ordinary pattern of social relations encouraged considerable emotional and physical intimacy between men (and indeed
between women). Even at its most intense, though, such 'homosocial'
friendship, both in fiction and in reality, was meant to be distinguished
from homosexual acts and tendencies. Like heterosexual unchastity,
but still more acutely, sodomy was traditionally interpreted as deeply
offensive to God, a terribly dangerous form of sexual and social indiscipline, whose toleration showed the inferiority and corruption of
other cultures.[3]*

It is therefore remarkable to find it being increasingly justified on
principle at around the same time, and in comparable terms, as heterosexual freedom. One line of argument was to deny that the practice
was particularly abhorrent to God. The minimal version of this was,
as the nonconformist George Duffus put it when apprehended in
1721, 'that we were all sinners': sodomites no more than other Christians. At its most developed, though, the idea went a good deal further.
Attempting to seduce the inexperienced William Minton in November 1698, Edward Rigby offered him wine, sat in his lap and kissed
him, put his tongue in his mouth and his hand in his breeches, and

---

* King James I, who was notoriously attracted to male favourites, declared in 1617 to
his privy councillors that 'he loved the Earl of Buckingham more than any other man',
and that they should not take this amiss: after all, 'Jesus had done the same as he
was doing . . . for Christ had his John and he had his George'. He also publicly advised
his heir and all his subjects that sodomy was an 'unpardonable' crime that ought
always to be punished by death: *ODNB*, George Villiers, first Duke of Buckingham;
Βασιλικόν Δῶρον (Edinburgh, 1599), 38; *Calendar of the Manuscripts of the most
Hon. the Marquis of Salisbury*, vol. 21: *1609–1612*, ed. G. Dyfnallt Owen (1970), 274.

then asked him outright 'whether he should fuck him'. When Minton expressed surprise – 'how can that be?' – Rigby replied, 'I will show you how, for it was no more than what was done in our forefathers' time: our saviour called St. John the handsome apostle for that reason . . . do you not read it in the scripture?' (see plate 1). The allusion was a striking echo of the words imputed more than a century earlier to Christopher Marlowe: 'that St John the Evangelist was bedfellow to Christ and leaned always in his bosom, that he used him as the sinners of Sodom'.[4]

Then there were the further examples of celebrated men and grand civilizations. 'Is it not what great men do?' asked Rigby confidently, 'The French King did it, the Czar of Muscovy made Alexander, a carpenter, a Prince for that purpose.' Most prestigious of all were the mores of the ancient world. By the 1740s, classical precedent had become such a well-known part of homosexual consciousness that Smollett satirized it archly in his novel *Roderick Random*. When the hero meets the uncommonly affectionate Lord Strutwell, the latter reveals his true colours to us by displaying 'an intimate knowledge of the authors of antiquity'. Plucking from his bosom a copy of the *Satyricon*, he declaims that any aversion to Petronius's 'taste in love' was

more owing to prejudice and misapprehension, than to true reason and deliberation. – The best man among the ancients is said to have entertained that passion; one of the wisest of their legislators has permitted the indulgence of it in his commonwealth; the most celebrated poets have not scrupled to avow it.[5]*

A similar mindset appears to have underlain the first extended public defence of homosexual relations in English, Thomas Cannon's *Ancient and Modern Pederasty Investigated and Exemplify'd* (1749), which, disingenuously pretending the custom was now universally 'exploded . . . and disowned', described it as 'that celebrated passion,

---

* Or, as the libertine poet and politician Sir Charles Hanbury Williams put it, in a private, humorous ode to the young, beautiful Horatio Townshend (inspired by Horace, Ode IV): 'Come to my Breast, my Lovely Boy! / Thou Source of Greek and Roman Joy! / And let my Arms entwine 'ye; / Behold my strong erected Tarse [i.e. Cock], / Display your plump, and milk-white Arse, / Young, blooming, Ligurine!': Yale Lewis Walpole Library, MS CHW 69, fol. 19 (1740).

sealed by sensualists, espoused by philosophers, enshrined by kings', and set out to 'discuss it with freedom, and the most philosophical exactness'. As Cannon pointed out in his introduction, 'every dabbler knows by his classics . . . that boy-love ever was the top refinement of most enlightened ages.'[6] Justifying the work to his anxious printers, he likewise 'made an elaborate display of learning, in which he talked of Petronius Arbiter and Aretine, and quoted other ancient writers, Greek as well as Roman'.[7]

Especially in private, homosexual freedom was also justified with growing confidence as natural, harmless, and commonplace. In the summer of 1726, shortly after a series of raids and executions for sodomy in London, William Brown, a married man, went cruising at Moorfields, a notorious pick-up spot. He recognized Thomas Newton, a well-known catamite; what he did not know was that Newton, having been detained himself, had turned to the betrayal and entrapment of others. Yet when, having steered the other man's hand into his breeches, Brown found himself surrounded, arrested, and challenged as to 'why he took such indecent liberties . . . he was not ashamed to answer, *I did it because I thought I knew him, and I think there is no crime in making what use I please of my own body*'. 'There is no harm in this, my dear', the predatory head of Wadham College, Oxford, was said to have explained at length in 1737, when his barber, bending over to shave him, 'found the Warden trying to introduce his hand into his breeches'.* 'I asked him what he meant by it?', deposed one of George Duffus's bedfellows, 'He answered, *no harm, nothing but love.*' 'He told me', reported a second, 'that I need not be troubled, or wonder at what he had done, for it was what was very common, and he had often practised it with others.'[8]

Such assertions were not unusual. 'He did frequently do and use the same practice with diverse other persons,' another man told the weaver John Jones in the early 1690s, after he had fondled him, taken him to an alehouse, and persuaded Jones 'to frig him' – he hoped they

---

* The next time he dared visit, the barber deposed, 'as soon as he came into the room, the Warden said to him, How dost do, my dear barber? It's fine weather, my dear barber. How does thy cock do, my dear barber? Let me feel it; and then went to kiss him': *A Faithful Narrative of the Proceedings in a late Affair between the Rev. Mr. John Swinton and Mr. George Baker* (1739), 18.

could do it again.[9] Thomas Rix, hanged for sodomy in 1806, recounted that his initiation into homosexual practices had happened about twenty years earlier, when he had stopped to pee one night on the way home from a Manchester pub. His drinking companion 'came up to him and took hold of his yard'; they 'used friction with each other till nature spent'; and his friend reassured Rix that 'there were many other persons who did what they had been doing'. As Cannon expressed the sentiment, homosexual lust was no different from any other kind – 'Unnatural desire is a contradiction in terms; downright nonsense. Desire is an amatory impulse of the inmost human parts: are not they, however constructed, and consequently impelling, nature?' The physical and emotional pleasures of sodomy were, if anything, greater than those of coition with women.[10]

The final inversion of conventional thinking was to suggest that the toleration of sex between men might actually have broader social benefits. This was a difficult and more abstract proposition to defend, but it evidently was discussed. Lord Strutwell explained that the practice prevented bastardy, seduction, prostitution, and venereal disease. As for being unprocreative, argued Cannon, so was sex with a pregnant woman; whilst the fact that sodomy did not cause depopulation more generally, 'all China swarming with inhabitants, yet warmly pursuing uncontrolled pederasty, beyond contradiction demonstrates'.[11]

Even harder to contemplate was the notion of sex between women. Compared with sodomy, this was a much more obscure matter. It was not in itself a criminal offence; it had never been the focus of deep theological or moral concern; the evidence of actual relationships was very limited; and its contemporary discussion was correspondingly vague and piecemeal. Yet, from the later seventeenth century onwards, perceptions of it seem to have developed in analogous ways.

By the 1740s it was possible, at least in libertine circles, to posit a straightforward equivalence between the same-sex affairs of men and of women, not just in terms of intimate friendships and natural passions, but also of their essential innocuousness. Thus, in Sir Charles Hanbury Williams's facetious verse dialogue between the politician Thomas Winnington and his lover, the Viscountess Townshend, she defends a supposed affair with Catherine Edwin as not just enjoyable but safer than sex with men: for 'when I melt in tender Kitty's lap, / I fear no children, and I dread no clap'.[12] And when, in the early years of the nineteenth century, the Yorkshire gentlewoman Anne Lister set down the first full, albeit private, justification of lesbian love in English, she drew on precisely the same intellectual resources as were deployed by advocates of other kinds of sexual freedom. Her relations with other women, she argued, would not be damned but understood and forgiven by God – 'lord have mercy on me and not justice'. In addition, she pursued the idea that sexual norms were culturally determined and unfairly oppressive of women, exploring the freer sexual customs of other religions and describing the marriage of one of her lovers as nothing more than 'legalized prostitution'. She herself had 'no priest but love'. For positive examples, classical literature provided a rich source of allusion to male and female homosexuality and androgyny, which Lister assiduously collated and interpreted, where necessary reading against its misogynist grain and into its suggestive silences to support her own presumptions. Further inspiration came from defences of male libertinism and romantic freedom, such as Byron's poetry. Finally, like all previous defenders of sexual liberty, Anne Lister laid great stress on the naturalness of her emotions and actions: 'my conduct and feelings being surely natural to me inasmuch as they were not taught, not fictitious but instinctive'.[13]

Given how strongly the public defence of same-sex relations was discouraged and repressed, it is not surprising to find such views articulated mainly in self-interested, indirect, and fragmentary forms. Their most fearless exponent, Thomas Cannon, was prosecuted and his work disappeared. He fled into exile, only to return a changed and broken man: compelled to print a penitent retraction, he spent years living in quiet retirement, writing prose and verse that reviled deists and extolled the truth of Christianity, the virtues of chastity, his yearning for 'Jesus, my bleeding only love', and his *immense* desire' for death.[14] As in the case of sexual freedom for women, the evolution of new ways of thinking about sex therefore had a dual impact. The perception and persecution of sodomy as quintessentially 'unnatural' was certainly sharpened by the heightened importance of defining 'natural' behaviour. Yet the new approaches to human nature, law, and ethics that had advanced the idea of heterosexual liberty also made it increasingly possible by the later eighteenth century to defend homosexual freedom in equivalently wide-ranging, cogent, and dispassionate terms.

The fullest evidence of this development lies in the sustained critical attention devoted to the subject, throughout his adult life, by Jeremy Bentham, the greatest reforming mind of the age. Over many hundreds of pages of notes and treatises, composed between the 1770s and the 1820s, he not only systematically considered and dismissed every conventional argument against the toleration of sodomy, but also took up the existing justifications for heterosexual liberty and argued for their logical extension to homosexual and other supposedly unnatural acts.[15]

Bentham's attack on the religious foundations of homophobia ('the supposed warrant from scripture') was two-pronged. Like many of his predecessors, he argued that the whole Judaeo-Christian obsession with chastity had been artificially imposed on society by priests and rulers, for their own pernicious ends. This 'false religion' had produced 'a labyrinth without an end' of irrational sexual prohibitions.[16] In fact, the Jews' prohibition of sodomy deserved no more respect from more advanced civilizations than their dietary or sartorial taboos, or their proscription of intercourse with a menstruating wife.[17]

On the other hand, in order to fight the enemy on its own territory, he also pushed to newly elaborate extremes the favourable reinterpretation of scriptural precedents. The inhabitants of Sodom, his reading of the Bible convinced him, had been punished not for their homosexual practices, but for imposing them by force on strangers: it was the rape and the violation of hospitality that had so offended God.[18] Furthermore, he found that the Israelites had often disregarded the Mosaic injunction against sodomy and openly tolerated homosexual behaviour. The relationship between David and Jonathan was plainly one of 'the most ardent sexual love', and there were many others like it. Such conduct was deemed natural, commonplace, and praiseworthy: sometimes it was even promoted by government. After all, did the Old Testament not refer to 'the houses of the sodomites that were by the house of the Lord' (II Kings 23.7)? Thus, 'so far from its being punished, we find receptacles for this species of gratification set up by authority and maintained at different periods in Judah'.[19] Most telling of all was the example of Jesus himself, whose real message ('sexuality not discouraged rather encouraged') had later been concealed and distorted by St Paul and his successors. Not only did Christ 'declare the utter abolition of the Mosaic law' (including the Ten Commandments), as 'but a mere human law . . . ill adapted to the welfare of society', it was clear that he viewed with 'scorn and ridicule' all forms of 'ascetic self-denial' and punishment for 'sexual irregularity': 'On this whole field, in which Moses legislates with such diversified minuteness and such impassioned asperity, Jesus is altogether silent.'[20] He was in fact 'an Epicurean', who considered no kind of sexual gratification to be sinful. He lived at a time and place where 'the practice in question [was] universally spread'. His most faithful attendant was a young male prostitute, whom he treated without any disapproval. Christ himself was not only sexually active with women such as Mary Magdalen, but likely also to 'have been a participator in the Attic taste', and to have enjoyed a sexual relationship with St John the Apostle.[21]*

Why, then, should consensual sex between men not be freely allowed in modern society? Bentham granted that, except to its practitioners, such behaviour was thought 'to the highest degree odious and disgusting'. He himself described it in his early writings as a 'miserable', 'corrupted', 'detestable', and 'perverted taste', 'a filthiness', an 'infection', a 'physical impurity', a 'preposterous propensity', a 'depraved appetite', and an 'abomination'.[22] But the fact that the custom was abhorrent to the majority of the community no more justified the punishment of sodomy than it did the killing of Jews, Moors, heretics, Anabaptists, hermaphrodites, smokers, or people who ate oysters. 'To destroy a man there should certainly be some better reason than mere dislike to his taste, let that dislike be ever so strong'.[23] The action was voluntary, and evidently pleasurable to the participants. It did not cause them any immediate injury, or disturb the peace of others. It was tolerated in other contemporary societies and had

* 'Evidence of participation not altogether wanting, though certainly not absolutely conclusive' was Bentham's ultimate verdict on the last point (Bentham MSS, clxi. 339). 'Would probably be prosecuted, if published to-day,' noted the UCL cataloguer when he came across these papers in the 1930s.

been practised by many great men in the past. So the real question ought to be, what harm did it produce?[24]

Might the habit of sodomy tend to enervate men, as was sometimes suggested, and hence reduce the strength of the state? There was no physiological evidence that it did, and history suggested the opposite. The ancient Greeks and Romans were stronger and braver than any modern nation, yet amongst them 'this propensity was universally predominant' – 'everybody practised it; nobody was ashamed of it'.[25] Did it lead to depopulation? This traditional fear, too, was disproved by the example of other societies; and by 1800 it had been replaced in any case by Malthusian concerns about overpopulation. Either way, argued Bentham, sodomy was *a priori* far less important in determining population levels than economic circumstances, voluntary celibacy, female biology, heterosexual seduction and prostitution, and other extraneous factors.[26] Finally, did sodomy infringe the rights of women, by making men indifferent to them and thus diminishing the amount of 'venereal enjoyment' that they received? Given that in all civilized countries women were permitted to gratify themselves only within marriage, the answer must be no. For the evidence appeared to show that same-sex relations were not normally permanent or exclusive: it was only persecution that tended to encourage that. Sodomy itself did not preclude or delay marriage, nor need it injure a wife any more than would heterosexual adultery.[27] In short, it was harmless, 'an imaginary crime': no more dangerous to society than the practices of scratching or of blowing one's nose, and penalized 'on no other foundation than prejudice'.[28]

It was even possible, reasoned Bentham, that the toleration of sodomy would be socially beneficial. It was likely to decrease masturbation, which, though unpunishable, appeared of all sexual acts to be 'the most incontestably pernicious ... to the health and lasting happiness of those who are led to practise it' (this was the conventional eighteenth-century view, which even Bentham was persuaded of).[29] Unlike heterosexual intercourse, sodomy did not lead to the seduction and prostitution of women, unwanted pregnancies, dangerous childbirths, abortion, infanticide, illegitimacy, or overpopulation. In fact, he came to argue with increasing conviction, it was tendentious and wrong to call the practice 'unnatural'. Lust was a natural human appetite: a taste for this particular way of gratifying it was encouraged whenever civilized nations saw fit to educate their virile young men in close proximity to one another, whilst restricting their intercourse with women.[30]

Indeed, Bentham's justification of 'irregular' sexual practices was not restricted to sodomy. On the same grounds, he came to urge the toleration of sex between women, relations between pupils and teachers, bestiality, and any sexual act between consenting adults, within or without marriage – for 'if there be one idea more ridiculous than another it is that of a legislator who, when a man and a woman are agreed about a business of this sort, thrusts himself in between them, examining situations, regulating times, and prescribing modes and postures'.[31] On the contrary, from a utilitarian point of view, the sum total of human pleasure that could be derived from sex was without compare. It was the most universal, the most easily accessible, the most intense, 'the most copious source of enjoyment', 'of all pleasures the most exquisite'; nothing, it could be mathematically demonstrated, was 'more conducive to happiness'. Were an 'all-comprehensive liberty for all modes of sexual gratification' to be established, including the toleration of contraception, abortion, infanticide, and divorce, it would be of huge, permanent benefit to humankind: 'what calculation shall compute the aggregate mass of pleasure that may be brought into existence'?[32]

It is notable that Bentham never published these proposals, though he repeatedly considered doing so.* He was intensely aware of the odium they would bring upon his philosophy and his personal

---

* When drafting some of his earliest statements on the decriminalization of sodomy, in the 1770s, Bentham envisaged them as part of a larger volume on penal law, intending that these passages should be printed in Latin and inserted only in 'some copies' of the work. Towards the end of his life, he conceived of publishing his arguments for sexual toleration at much greater length, and anonymously, as a two-part work to be called *Not Paul, but Jesus*. In 1817 he drew up a prospectus of it, addressed to the fabulously rich bisexual writer and art collector William Beckford. The first part, which he eventually published under this title in 1823, using the pseudonym 'Gamaliel Smith', was intended to undermine the authority and doctrines of St Paul as the basis of conventional, ascetic Christian morality. The second part, 'not proposed to be published till some time after the first', which was to uphold 'the liberty of [sexual] taste' on utilitarian grounds, remained unfinished and unpublished.[33]

character in a climate in which, as he himself analysed so acutely, hatred of sodomy had become a touchstone of respectability.[34] Yet 'for the sake of the interests of humanity' he also felt compelled to think them through in detail, to set them down on paper repeatedly and at great length, to share them privately with others, and to hope that all this might contribute to their eventual 'free discussion' and general acceptance: 'at any rate,' he explained, 'when I am dead mankind will be the better for it'.[35]

We can be certain, moreover, that these ideas were debated amongst his friends and in radical intellectual circles more generally. Whilst revising them in the mid-1810s, Bentham lived together with his close friends and helpers, Francis Place and James Mill, the political philosopher (as well as the latter's young son, John Stuart Mill, whose own later strictures against 'Christian morality (so called)' and its 'horror of sensuality' owe an obvious debt to Bentham). Amongst others evidently aware of Bentham's views on sodomy were such influential thinkers and activists as William Godwin, Aaron Burr, Peter Mark Roget, Etienne Dumont, and his own brother and collaborator, Samuel.[36] Already as a young man in the early 1770s, Bentham had come to know 'more than a few' heterosexuals who, like him, abhorred the irrational persecution of 'innocent' men whose sexual tastes did 'no harm to anyone'. Shortly after his death, many of the arguments he had privately elaborated were given lengthy printed utterance in the remarkable anonymous poem 'Don Leon', whose plea for the toleration of the harmless natural passions of sodomites was circulated, at first semi-clandestinely and then publicly, from the 1830s onwards.[37] Even though such views remained exceptional and objectionable, their increasing elaboration demonstrates just how potentially far-reaching the ideals of sexual freedom had become by the dawn of the nineteenth century.

ENLIGHTENED ATTITUDES

The rise of sexual freedom was not unique to England, but part of the general European Enlightenment. Because it has been so little studied, it is difficult to know to what extent its ideals had spread in other countries by the end of the eighteenth century, though it seems clear that they were advancing everywhere. It also seems likely that the precise ways in which sexual liberty was justified differed according to national context.[1] All the same, it is obvious that, as had been the case since the middle ages, English theological and philosophical ideas evolved in parallel with those on the continent, and were deeply influenced by foreign authors and examples.[2] The most extreme exponents of sexual freedom, from Adriaan Beverland to Charles Fourier, tended to come from abroad; whilst all the most influential domestic theorists of personal liberty, from Hobbes to Bentham, took their cue partly from international debates on toleration, natural law, criminal justice, and personal ethics.

It is equally clear that the advance of sexual freedom was largely a jumbled, unconscious process. It was not part of any philosophical or political programme: very few thinkers pursued it systematically. It mainly came about through the gradual diffusion of new ways of thinking, and their popular adoption, manipulation and extension. Ideas of sexual liberty could be derived from biblical as well as from militantly anti-religious foundations – just as it proved perfectly possible to use new, radically secular philosophies to uphold conventional morality. In practice, there was no necessary connection between any particular approach and any particular conclusion.[3]

The transformation of sexual attitudes by 1800 thus came about in a remarkably messy and inadvertent way, from the piecemeal and sometimes incoherent assimilation of old and new points of view. Yet is that not how most ideas spread, and how most of us in practice make sense of the world around us? It was this combination of intellectual multiplicity and more general, fundamental shifts in ways of thinking that explains why the development of sexual liberty, though never a central aim of the Enlightenment, was nonetheless one of its most pervasive effects.

It also helps to explain why, as many eighteenth-century thinkers recognized, the ultimate outcome was not a new consensus about the scope of sexual freedom, but rather a greater plurality of moral views, with irresolvable tensions between them. This was not only because of the continued appeal of the orthodox ways of thinking that had underpinned the culture of sexual discipline. It was also inherent in enlightened attitudes towards reason, nature, and society, which, in shifting the parameters of debate, had themselves raised many new questions of principle and interpretation. As the philosopher Francis Hutcheson wrote in 1725, it was easy to see why there was such a 'vast diversity of moral principles' in the world – they derived from 'different opinions of happiness, or natural good, and of the most effectual means to advance it', from disagreements over 'public good, and the means to promote it', and from varying 'opinions of the will or laws of the Deity'.[4]

In short, sexual liberty was not a string of agreed conclusions but a set of ideas amenable to many different interpretations. Where precisely was the line to be drawn between public and private acts? What were the limits of 'natural' behaviour? How should 'harm' be defined, or 'consent'? What role remained for the state in sanctioning relationships, upholding morality, preserving health, defining unacceptable behaviour, and protecting the vulnerable? And what should happen when sexual freedom conflicted with other fundamental values? Compared with the definition of a valid marriage, which had been the central issue in traditional sexual ethics, these were, and still are, much more complicated and intractable questions. As a culture, our answers keep changing; and we can never entirely agree. Often, in fact, we disagree very much: in law, philosophy, politics, and public life, these issues have provoked some of the most contentious debates of the nineteenth, twentieth, and twenty-first centuries.[5] But that is the price we pay for trying to base our moral values on reason, rather than on divine commandments.

3

The Cult of Seduction

Of women's unnatural, insatiable lust, what country, what village doth not complain?
[Robert Burton], *The Anatomy of Melancholy* (1621), 541

Why should women have more invention in love than men? It
can only be, because they have more desires, more solliciting
passions, more lust, and more of the devil.
William Wycherley, *The Country-Wife* (1675), Act IV scene 2

As a sex, women are more chaste than men ... Men are certainly more under the influence of their appetites than women.
Mary Wollstonecraft, *A Vindication of the Rights of Woman*
(1792), 281, 312

The majority of women (happily for them) are not very much
troubled with sexual feeling of any kind. What men are habit-
ually, women are only exceptionally.
William Acton, *The Functions and Disorders of the
Reproductive Organs* (4th edn, 1865), 112

Ever since the dawn of western civilization it had always been presumed that women were the more lustful sex. The most extreme,
misogynist version of this argument asserted that women's minds

were so corrupt, their wombs so ravenous, their 'amorous fire' so vor-
acious, that truly 'if they dared, all women would be whores'.[1] More
generally the idea was simply that, though lust was a universal temptation, females were mentally, morally, and bodily weaker than
males – less rational, less able to control their passions, less capable of
self-discipline. Indeed all human sin, so Christians were taught,
derived ultimately from the original weakness of Eve, the first woman:
the pollution of sex was itself but one manifestation of this. The presumption of female infirmity and lust was a commonplace of biblical,
classical, medieval, and Renaissance thought. As historians, literary
critics, and other scholars have explored at length, it was a basic
building block of the pre-modern conceptual universe.[2]

Because women's easy arousal was taken for granted, it was also
generally believed until the eighteenth century that female orgasm
was essential to pregnancy: without it, no child could be conceived.
That is why Samuel Pepys, after climaxing during sex with one of his
illicit lovers, was immediately terrified that he might have made her
come too – until the tone of her voice reassured him that she had not.
It equally explains the breathless speech of the maidservant Anna
Harrison, who in the 1690s supplemented her income through casual
sex with acquaintances. 'Pray make haste, make haste, make haste,'
she would exclaim, as a man penetrated her body, 'I am afraid you
should get me with child . . . no, no, I must take care for that, 'tis a
very troublesome thing to have a child, and no father, who owns it.'
The orthodox view was, as the devout, monogamous John Evelyn
advised a young bride in 1676, that the avoidance of female orgasm
during intercourse was 'not only impossible, but a stupidity'.[3]

By 1800, however, exactly the opposite idea had become firmly
entrenched. Now it was believed that men were much more naturally
libidinous, and liable to seduce women. Women had come to be seen
as comparatively delicate, defensive, and sexually passive, needing to
be constantly on their guard against male rapacity. Female orgasm
was no longer thought essential to procreation.

This shift was already well advanced by the middle of the eighteenth century. Most famously it was manifested in the first great
novels of the English language, which appeared in the 1740s and
1750s. As the critic Ian Watt pointed out more than fifty years ago,

the sexual ideology that these embodied was 'a historical novelty . . . in complete contradiction' to all of previous literature: they marked 'a very notable epiphany in the history of our culture'. Never before had there existed such a distinction between the irredeemable lustfulness of men and the essential asexuality of virtuous women; yet from that point forward this view of sex became 'an essential feature of our civilisation'. Henceforth, it was taken for granted that the female sex was inherently less lecherous than the male. The effects of this new presumption were, if anything, even more profound. Throughout the nineteenth and twentieth centuries, the notion of women's relative sexual passivity was fundamental to gender dynamics across the western world.[4] Its effects were ubiquitous – they still are.

SCIENTIFIC EXPLANATIONS?

The question of how this transformation came about is almost never asked.[1] Instead, historians, literary critics, philosophers, legal theorists, and other scholars routinely take it for granted, and focus instead on its consequences, often supposing that the change was the result of new scientific ideas. Particularly influential in cementing this presumption has been the work of Thomas Laqueur, whose justly celebrated *Making Sex: Body and Gender from the Greeks to Freud* (1990) dominates current historical writing on sex and gender. The book is a beautiful case-study of how medical ideas have been socially constructed throughout western history. The terms in which scientists described the body, Laqueur shows, were never neutral, but derived from evolving cultural presumptions about the nature of men and women. From classical times until the Enlightenment it was generally held that both sexes shared the same basic anatomical make-up; whilst subsequently much greater stress came to be placed, though never exclusively, on the supposedly innate physical differences between them.[2]

Professor Laqueur is acutely aware that changing presumptions about anatomy reflected more general cultural shifts, rather than scientific advances – that is part of his point. As to what these crucial 'new social and political developments' actually were, and how they related to intellectual changes, 'more detailed studies are needed'. Nevertheless, he also suggests that 'the remaking of the body' was the deepest change of all: it shaped 'the broad discursive fields that underlie competing ideologies, that define the terms of conflict, and that give meaning to various debates.' It was not '*caused*' by, but was 'itself intrinsic to',

the rise of evangelical religion, Enlightenment political theory, the development of new sorts of public spaces in the eighteenth century, Lockean ideas of marriage as a contract, the cataclysmic possibilities for social change wrought by the French revolution, postrevolutionary conservatism, postrevolutionary feminism, the factory system with its restructuring of the sexual division of labor, the rise of a free market economy in services or commodities, the birth of classes.

Little wonder that, in the absence of an alternative account, many historians nowadays simply invoke the changing medical ideas of the late seventeenth and eighteenth centuries as themselves having brought about new attitudes towards male and female sexuality.[3]

In fact the shift can only properly be explained by taking a wider view. Even by 1800, biological ideas about sexual behaviour remained far less independently influential than they were to become in the nineteenth and twentieth centuries. It is true that people did start to regard male and female bodies differently in the course of the eighteenth century, but this did not cause so much as replicate the broader cultural transformation. As we shall see, the shifting balance of ideas about the relative lustfulness of men and women was articulated earlier and with greater influence through other, more general ways of considering nature, culture, and society: in plays and novels, journalism, poetry, works of theology, philosophy, and moral commentary. This chapter will begin by describing the most obvious features of the change, and end by explaining the striking coincidence between two of the most enduring cultural innovations of the eighteenth century – the rise of the novel, and the cult of seduction.

THE RISE OF THE LIBERTINE

The first development was a growing presumption that men were inevitably rapacious. The idea that they might have strong sexual urges was, of course, not new. It was a commonplace of Christian doctrine that lust was an elemental drive, part of the fallen nature of both sexes. The rape and seduction of women had therefore always been an obvious danger. When men gave way to sinful passion, lamented the official Tudor homily, 'how many maidens be deflowered, how many wives corrupted, how many widows defiled'. 'We women', warned Dorothy Leigh in 1616, know 'that men lie in wait every where to deceive us, as the Elders did to deceive Susanna.' Already in the middle ages, churchmen had lamented the tricking of women into bed under promise of marriage. Many serious discussions of adultery likewise stressed the greater culpability of the male, for corrupting other people's wives and marriages. As one of the mid seventeenth-century leaders of the Church of Scotland acknowledged, 'the man is ordinarily the temptor'. 'If God had not restrained lust by laws', noted another leading theologian in 1673, 'it would have made the female sex most contemptible and miserable, and used worse by men than dogs are' – men would have ravished at will, or used and discarded woman after woman.[1]

In reality, too, men were more sexually aggressive. Though their pursuit of women was underpinned by presumptions about female desire and moral frailty, it is male importunity and harassment that dominate the records of daily life amongst the mass of the population. In theory there was supposed to be a clear distinction between consensual and non-consensual sex. Rape was a capital offence: no man had the right to force a woman (though within marriage, because a wife belonged to her husband, the concept was held to be meaningless). Yet the stigma of unchastity that attached even to raped women, together with the impossibility of securing a conviction without evidence of serious injury or the presence of witnesses, meant that trials for the offence were rare. The common presumption that conception was impossible without orgasm added a further horrific twist to the fate of women who had been forcibly impregnated. In 1632 a young woman of Waltham Holy Cross explained to a court that her rapist had 'used much violence to her by dragging her about the fields, and said he would kill her if she would not lie with him, and being much scared and in fear of her life she yielded unto him'. Yet as she was carrying his child it was she who was punished and made to perform public penance in church. Meanwhile, the supposition that in all cases short of rape women shared responsibility, or had little basis for complaint, legitimized a wide range of behaviour that was in reality predatory rather than consensual. As one distinguished scholar of seventeenth-century English life has concluded, 'sexual harassment, in some form, was experienced by very many women, possibly most'.[2]

Here, for example, is Samuel Pepys in February 1664, aged thirty, witnessing the abuse of a young woman and wishing himself a participant in it:

This night late, coming in my coach coming up Ludgate Hill, I saw two gallants and their footmen taking a pretty wench which I have much eyed lately ... a seller of ribbons and gloves. They seemed to drag her by some force, but the wench went and I believe had her turn served; but God forgive me, what thoughts and wishes I had of being in their place.

Later that same year, his diary records some of his earliest encounters with the pretty wife of his subordinate, William Bagwell. For over twenty-five years, he was to promote Bagwell: 'I am your friend and always have and will be so,' he wrote to the man in 1687. We do not know his wife's name: in all of Pepys's diaries and correspondence it is never mentioned. Yet from the moment he met the couple, Pepys preyed on her ruthlessly – he was still sleeping with her when his first diary ended in 1669. This is how their sexual relationship began, after several preliminary meetings in which he had begun to force himself upon her with kisses and gropings, in spite of her obvious resistance:

15 Nov. 1664 [at a tavern]: and there I did caress her and eat and drank, and many hard looks and sighs the poor wretch did give me, and I think verily was troubled at what I did; but at last, after many protestings, by degrees I did arrive at what I would, with great pleasure.

20 Dec. 1664 [at the Bagwells' house]: the poor people did get a dinner for me in their fashion – of which I also ate very well. After dinner I found occasion of sending him abroad [= away]; and then alone avec elle je tentais à faire ce que je voudrais, et contre sa force je le faisais, bien que passe à mon contentment [= alone with her I attempted to do that which I wanted, and against her resistance I achieved it: it went well, to my content].

23 Jan. 1665: . . . finding Mrs Bagwell waiting at the office after dinner, away elle [= she] and I to a cabaret where elle and I have été [= been] before; and there I had her company toute l'après-dîner [= the whole time after dinner] and had mon plein plaisir of elle [= my full pleasure of her] – but strange, to see how a woman, notwithstanding her greatest pretences of love à son mari [= to her husband] and religion, may be vaincue [= vanquished].

20 Feb. 1665: . . . it being dark, did privately enter en la maison de la femme de Bagwell [= into the house of Bagwell's wife], and there I had sa compagnie [= her company], though with a great deal of difficulty; néanmoins, enfins j'avais ma volonté d'elle [= nevertheless, in the end I had my will of her]. And being sated therewith, I walked home.

21 Feb. 1665: Up, and to the office (having a mighty pain in my forefinger of my left hand, from a strain that it received last night in struggling avec la femme que je [= with the woman whom I] mentioned yesterday).[3]

Cruder still were the importunities of countless men (Pepys himself again included) who took advantage of the vulnerability of their young, live-in servants. Only if the victimized woman became pregnant were such cases even likely to have been legally recorded; yet the resigned tone in which they were commonly recounted, and the contemporary response to them, evoke a much broader culture of sexual exploitation in the guise of patriarchal entitlement. Alice Ashmore's master, a cook, 'had the use and carnal knowledge of her' for a year, 'sometimes in his own chamber on his bed and diverse other places wheresoever he could find her alone'. When she said no, he would reply bluntly 'thou art my servant and I may do with thee what I please'; but when she fell pregnant, he denied his paternity, and she was prosecuted for bastardy at Bridewell. Whenever she entered her master's bedroom in the mornings, another servant told the Bridewell court in the same year, 1605, he 'would pull her to his bed, and there abuse her body'. Most brutally exploitative of all were the secret rape and abuse of children, sometimes apparently informed by the tragic folk-belief that having sex with a virgin girl would cure a man of venereal disease. Everywhere, even between social equals, there was always an irreducible gap between most men's sense of sexual entitlement and most women's experience of vulnerability. That is why, even in Shakespeare, with his incomparable inventiveness, the language of

sex was always dominated by the basic themes of men hunting, possessing, besieging, and conquering women.⁴ By our own standards, the
balance of power between men and women was grossly skewed, and
female agency and consent in sexual affairs highly circumscribed.

The broader concepts that our ancestors used were just as historically specific. In the eighteenth century the basic definition of
'seduction' was to induce a woman to have illicit but consensual sex.
Though both parties might be culpable for their intercourse, the
seduction itself was not a crime – even if it came about through deception, such as a false promise of marriage. Yet because male sexual
violence tended to be so trivialized, the contemporary meanings of
seduction also overlapped with behaviour that we should nowadays
view as sexual harassment, compulsion, abduction, or rape. Indeed,
this was a culture in which even rape itself was commonly treated as
a joke – on the grounds that all women secretly desired to be ravished,
and that they could never be believed when they claimed to have been
taken against their will. This was an age-old message, recycled for
amusement by early female playwrights like Mary Pix and Charlotte
Lennox, as well as in countless masculine fantasies. Like many men of
his time, for example, Henry Fielding was fascinated by sexual violence. As we shall see later in this chapter, he grappled throughout his
life with the complexities of male and female passion, seduction, and
sexual injustice. For now, though, to attune ourselves to the mind-set
that he and his contemporaries inherited, let us begin by listening
to his anonymous rendition of the famous, endlessly read advice to
lovers by the Roman poet Ovid, on what women are like, what
they really want, and how to give it to them. We men, he instructs his
readers,

are more able to command our affections, nor are our desires so furious, and
exceeding all bounds, as theirs . . . Every new amour pleases them, and they
all hanker after the lovers and husbands of other women.

. . .

Perhaps she will scratch, and say you are rude: nothwithstanding her
scratches, she will be pleased with your getting the better . . . Now when you
have proceeded to kisses [keep going] to your Journey's End! . . . The girls
may call this perhaps violence, but it is a violence agreeable to them. For they
are often desirous of being pleased against their will. For a woman taken

without her consent, notwithstanding her frowns, is often well satisfied in her heart, and your impudence is taken as a favour; whilst she who, when inclined to be ravished, hath retreated untouched, however she may affect to smile, is in reality out of humour.

Though Fielding immediately cautions his modern readers that this is Ovid's view, not his (for 'ravishing is indeed out of fashion in this age'), there are many other passages in his own work, as in the whole of the western canon of literature before and beyond the eighteenth century, that illustrate a similar outlook.[5] The line between coercion and consent is not always easy to discern. In all that follows, and especially in considering contemporary attitudes to seduction, we need to bear in mind these basic differences between our own presumptions about gender relations and those of men and women (especially men) in the past.

It will be clear that, even before the eighteenth century, the endless public repetition of platitudes about female lechery was to some extent balanced by an appreciation of male rapaciousness. Nonetheless, it was precisely because lust was acknowledged to be such a dangerous force that great value had traditionally been placed on its mastery. Because men were both intellectually and bodily superior to women, it followed that they should be better able to exercise such self-control. This strong equation of chastity with rational self-discipline was another reason why classical, medieval, and Renaissance discussions of male immorality often portrayed it as more wilful and reprehensible than the sexual lapses of women and youths, who were weaker and less mature creatures.[6] In the decades leading up to 1700, however, the age-old framework of sexual discipline began to unravel. As we have seen, its intellectual basis was increasingly eroded by arguments in favour of greater sexual liberty for men, whilst its practical force was seriously undermined by the growing complexity of urban life, the fatal weakening of the church courts, and the decline of communal moral regulation. In short, some of the most important pressures towards male sexual continence suddenly started to fall away.

The effect of these changing circumstances can be seen in the rise of libertine attitudes at the court of Charles II. As part of their self-conscious inversion of conventional values, libertines cultivated an ethos in which unbridled lechery was seen as enhancing rather than diminishing masculine distinction. The immediate reaction to this was strongly hostile, even amongst the king's most loyal supporters. Most early observers saw it in conventional terms, as the personal failing of men who lacked self-discipline and had come to be governed by their basest appetites. This perception was strengthened by fears of God's wrath, as well as by the traditional connection between debauchery and political tyranny. Even libertines themselves shared these associations between lust and degeneracy. For all its bravado about male sexual conquest, libertine writing about sex is notably obsessed with the insatiability of women and the emasculating effects of sexual excess. Here is the Earl of Rochester, imagining a dialogue between two of Charles II's mistresses ('Sodom' was a shady London neighbourhood; the last line refers to two more of the Duchess of Cleveland's many lovers):

Quoth the Duchess of Cleveland to counselor Knight,
'I'd fain have a prick, knew I how to come by 't.
I desire you'll be secret and give your advice:
Though cunt be not coy, reputation is nice.'

'To some cellar in Sodom Your Grace must retire
Where porters with black-pots sit round a coal-fire;
There open your case, and Your Grace cannot fail
Of a dozen of pricks for a dozen of ale.'

'Is 't so?' quoth the Duchess. 'Aye, by God!' quoth the whore.
'Then give me the key that unlocks the back door,
For I'd rather be fucked by porters and carmen [i.e. carters]
Than thus be abused by Churchill and Jermyn.'

Just as ruthlessly he described the king himself and another mistress, Nell Gwyn:

His sceptre and his prick are of a length;
And she may sway the one who plays with th' other . . .
Poor prince! thy prick, like thy buffoons at Court,
Will govern thee because it makes thee sport . . .
Restless he rolls about from whore to whore,

> A merry monarch, scandalous and poor ...
> This you'd believe, had I but time to tell ye
> The pains it costs to poor, laborious Nelly,
> Whilst she employs hands, fingers, mouth, and thighs,
> Ere she can raise the member she enjoys.

The effects of such corruption, it was widely feared, would infect the whole of society. As another poet criticized Charles II,

> Thy base example ruins the whole town,
> For all keep whores, from gentleman to clown.
> The issue of a wife is unlawful seed;
> And none's legitimate, but mongrel breed.
> Thou, and thy branches, have quite cross'd the strain,
> We ne'er shall see a true-bred whelp again.[7]

Yet despite such unease, because it was the ethos of such a prestigious group of men, and because it went unpunished, the visibility of Restoration libertinism also greatly strengthened the association between sexual licence and social eminence. Far beyond the court and capital, rakish ideals came to be defended as fashionable. As a Leicestershire man justified himself with chilling insouciance in the 1660s, after having raped and impregnated his maid, 'it was the fashion nowadays ... the best sort of gentlemen now in the country keep a whore in their houses'.[8]

This was the kind of increasing laxity that the movement for reformation of manners was aimed at after 1688.[9] Yet the campaign's de facto concentration on lower-class vice, together with the rise of arguments for sexual liberty, led to a significant change in attitudes towards male licence. By the early eighteenth century, as we saw in the previous chapter, it had come to be widely believed that the corruption of sexual manners was so pervasive that it could not be eradicated by trying to reform individuals one at a time, still less by force. The punishment of sexual offenders was, it now seemed, but a superficial palliative. The real problem was not that some individuals chose, or fell into, vice: it was that men in general, especially those in higher circles, lacked morality. They thought so little of it, remarked Jonathan Swift in 1709, that 'any man ... will let you know he is going to a whore, or that he has got a clap, with as much indifference as he would a piece of public news'. For a man in fashionable life to aspire to chastity, noted the *Guardian* a few years later, had 'become ridiculous'. Though fornicators and seducers still felt pangs of guilt, these had become easy to overcome. Nowadays, amongst 'men of mode', 'the restraints of shame and ignominy are broken down by the prevalence of custom'.[10]

Such pessimism can be found in the sentiments of many earlier moralists. Yet in the early eighteenth century it gained new force. The context had changed radically: both the theory and practice of sexual discipline were now, for the first time ever, seriously impaired. In addition, new ways of explaining sexual immorality were gaining ground, which undermined the basic Christian presumption that, ultimately, men and women bore personal responsibility for their moral behaviour. As part of attempts to understand the world in more empirically sophisticated ways, the balance began to shift away from its traditional focus on free will, towards modes of thinking that laid greater emphasis on the impersonal, structural forces in nature and society that appeared to compel different sexes and classes of people to behave in particular ways.

These developments, together with the rise of libertine attitudes, gradually created an immensely powerful commonplace of male entrapment and female victimization. For many centuries there had been an indestructible association between female lust and the original sin of Eve, the devil's accomplice, whose weakness and temptation of Adam into carnality had, it was said, prefigured the duplicitous wiles of women down the ages. Now, all these negative attributes came to be transposed to the sexual character of men. 'In our general pursuit of the sex,' observed Daniel Defoe as early as 1706, 'the devil generally acts the man, not the woman.' 'Every art that can be practised, every snare that can be laid for beauty and virtue', agreed Henry Fielding, was by men 'practised and laid at this day' – 'is not the basest fraud and treachery constantly used on this occasion?' Women, by contrast, 'seldom stray but when they are misled by men; by whom they are deceived, corrupted, betrayed, and often brought to destruction, both of body and soul'. 'The man,' concluded a critic flatly in 1754, 'is always the tempter and seducer.'[11]

Eve herself was no longer seen as Satan's tool but as the first seduced woman. Her fall presaged 'a general seduction of her sex; for every woman in a state of innocence at this day, is besieged with a tempter of equal craft . . . if women inherit the credulity and weakness of Eve, men are well supplied with the art and subtlety of the Devil'. Like a snake, warned a preacher, 'the seducer . . . strives to fascinate, and then destroy!' The lustful man, concurred the author of *Advice to Unmarried Women* (1791), was a ubiquitous, insidious danger, to be shunned 'as the serpent that beguiled the first of your sex'. In fact, it was generally agreed, men had not only the devil's inspiration but all his unfair advantages over their weaker, unwary prey. Like him, they were masters of insinuation and deception, intent on corrupting the guiltless virgin: 'the seducer spreads his toils, against artless unsuspecting innocence. Golden dreams, and gay delights lull her fancy and her conscience: and she thinks of nothing else, till she awakens from her sleep – and finds herself undone.' Through his male accomplices, Satan was now continually inflicting on women 'the same fatal catastrophe, that happened in Eden so many thousand years ago'.[12]

RAKES AND HARLOTS

Even attitudes towards prostitutes were radically reshaped in the decades after 1700. The traditional view of them had always been strongly unsympathetic. After all, the biblical archetype of the lustful whore, who destroyed unsuspecting men, epitomized the conventional view of women as the more lascivious, dangerous sex. Like Mary Magdalen, prostitutes could repent, but otherwise their behaviour was conceived of mainly as an extreme form of female promiscuity. Despite the long-standing argument that it was a necessary evil, for else men would commit 'adulteries, deflowering of virgins, unnatural lust, and the like', the idea that whores themselves might be the victims of male seduction, or of economic desperation, was almost invisible in serious writing before 1700. Only on the stage were prostitutes sometimes portrayed as more than wilful, greedy sinners. Even here, though, male culpability for their fate remained a very minor theme. Although prostitution was an obvious symbol for the amorality and corruption of the world, ultimately whores, like all men and women, were held to be personally responsible for their moral choices, their own sins and their own redemption. In sixteenth- and early seventeenth-century drama, women trick, seduce, and deceive men sexually as much as the reverse. The battle of the sexes, it implies, is pretty evenly balanced, and the ethical fate of individuals lies largely in their own hands and that of fate.[1]

Even at the very end of the seventeenth century, most commentators remained wedded to these presumptions. In *The Night-Walker* (1696–7), the period's most extensive discussion of prostitution, the leading journalist and bookseller John Dunton wove together supposedly true undercover stories and interviews in order to prove that most whores simply gave in to their corrupt nature. Many were first tempted to fornication 'to gratify a little itch after stolen pleasure', and, once aroused, the female libido – 'the powerful inclinations of nature' – was hard to curb. If their husbands proved inadequate, it forced women to seduce apprentices, pay strangers, or go on the town. Indeed, there was 'such a bewitchery in the sin' that many prostitutes continued in their trade 'merely to satisfy the lusts of the flesh'. Though other factors might contribute, the primary responsibility for her fate usually lay with the woman herself. In similar fashion, the paper attacked male libertinism as the personal, wilful failure of certain men to uphold correct standards of behaviour.[2]

Yet barely a dozen years later, amidst growing opposition to the societies for reformation, mainstream public opinion had moved decisively towards the opposite conception of prostitution and male rapacity. By the 1710s, it was becoming fashionable to analyse immorality primarily in terms of social pressures and structural constraints, which affected different groups in society in different ways. As the *Spectator* (1711–14), the most influential and widely read publication of the age, repeatedly articulated it, 'poor and public whores' were not independent, culpable sinners by choice, but largely innocent victims – of financial necessity, exploitation by bawds, and seduction by men of superior status. 'The compassionate case of very many', it concluded, was that they were ensnared 'without any the least suspicion, previous temptation, or admonition'. Likewise, 'wenching, and particularly the insnaring part ... the practice of deluding women' was increasingly portrayed as an established social norm, one of the central vices of the age. Bawds and libertines together were now held chiefly responsible for prostitution, their culpability contrasting starkly with that of the innocent, pitiable women whose lives they destroyed. 'Servitus crescit nova,' warned Richard Steele, quoting Horace – 'a new band of slaves is increasing'.[3]

The same attitude was also steadily more dominant in popular writing. It was evident, explained a Grub Street journalist in 1723, that prostitutes were 'ruined wretches who deserve rather our commiseration than contempt'. In fact, no 'woman's passion can be so strong as to act anything criminal in love affairs, did not the violent lust of men, and their fatal arts, blow up and kindle that fire in innocent unguarded maidens which frequently ends in their utter undoing'. The basic truth, concurred another, was that 'man's solicitation tempts them to lewdness, necessity succeeds sin, and want puts an end to shame'. This was exactly the narrative depicted in William Hogarth's famous pictorial series, *A Harlot's Progress* (1730–32), whose opening shows the very moment of entrapment already envisaged by the *Spectator* two decades earlier: 'an inn in the city', the arrival of 'a wagon out of the country', 'the most artful procuress in the town, examining a most beautiful country-girl, who had come up in the same wagon' with, in the background, the rake for whom she is being ensnared. Thereafter inevitably followed her dishonour, descent, and destruction, 'from pampered vice in the habitations of the wealthy, to distressed indigent wickedness expelled the harbours of the brothel', to her ignominious death (see illustration 21, pp. 284–9 below).[4]

By 1730, discussions of prostitution and culpability therefore tended to strike a markedly different note than had been the case up to the end of the seventeenth century. It remained a commonplace that whores were dangerous agents of corruption, who preyed on unwary young men. Yet now this presumption was increasingly balanced by the perception that they themselves were, in origin, the innocent victims of seduction by bawds and rakes, and that they continued in their way of life mainly out of economic need and social ostracism. Thus it was male rapacity, not female lust, that lay at the root of the problem.

This new idea was boosted by Mandeville's writings on prostitution,

which took for granted that male sexual passion was an unrestrain-
able natural force, and the debauching of women its inevitable
consequence. Its growing popularity was also reflected in George Lillo's *The London Merchant*, one of the earliest English tragedies about
the moral dilemmas of ordinary people. This was an instant hit when
it opened in 1731, and went on to become one of the most enduringly
successful works of the later eighteenth-century English and American stage. Its plot was taken from an old and well-known tale – that
of George Barnwell, a London apprentice led to theft, murder, and the
gallows by his prostitute lover. In every earlier setting of the story, the
temptress Sarah Millwood had been pictured as an intrinsically evil,
duplicitous whore. But in Lillo's account, for the first time, she is given
a back-story which accounts for her character. It turns out that it was
not her own inclinations but the selfish, hypocritical, predatory ways
of men that had first undone her: 'what pains will they not take, what
arts not use, to seduce us from our innocence, and make us contemptible and wicked, even in their own opinions?' She herself had once
been naive and blameless, possessed of wit and beauty: yet men had
'robbed me of them, ere I knew their worth; then left me too late, to
count their value by their loss. Another and another spoiler came, and
all my gain was poverty and reproach.' 'We are but slaves to men,' she
exclaimed bitterly; it was their own exploitation by the 'barbarous
sex' that taught women like herself to be wicked and avaricious. Once
ruined, they had no option but to maintain themselves by preying in
turn on 'the young and innocent part of the sex, who having never
injured women, apprehend no injury from them'.[5]

By mid-century the notion of the prostitute as victim had become
firmly entrenched, even in judicial circles. Faced with a pretty, seemingly demure street-walker on the morning after her arrest, the justice's
clerk Joshua Brogden looked past all the evidence of her drunken
soliciting, and focused on the real criminal: her original seducer. 'What
doth that wretch deserve, that was the destroyer of an innocent lovely
young creature?' Prostitution, complained Henry Fielding, was 'the
misery and ruin of great numbers of young, thoughtless, helpless,
poor girls, who are as often betrayed, and even forced into guilt, as
they are bribed and allured into it'. It was abundantly clear, agreed a
preacher in 1759, that most fallen women had been led astray 'by

every unjustifiable method, which cruel and brutish lust suggests to the crafty seducer'. Even amongst the most 'superlatively depraved' whores, a later expert claimed, he had been unable to find 'a single instance where the perfidy of a man was not the source of the mischief'.[6]

Innumerable later eighteenth-century fictions likewise featured the seduction, prostitution, and unhappy end of young innocent virgins. John Hawkesworth's massively popular *Adventurer* (1753–4) told of a rake who first debauches an innocent maidservant, and then, twenty years later, is about to have sex with a young whore when, horrifically, she is revealed to be his own abandoned, illegitimate daughter, entrapped by poverty, mistreatment, and an evil bawd. Dr Johnson's 'Misella' was ruined and abandoned by her own guardian. In William Dodd's *The Sisters* (1754), it is the terrible fate that threatens both Lucy and Caroline Sanson; in the end their father, too, expires of grief. In *Nature and Art* (1796), by the radical reformer Elizabeth Inchbald, a poor cottager's daughter is successively seduced, forced into prostitution, and literally sentenced to death by the same evil man, who rises from youthful libertine to callous judge. By 1800 the basic plot was so familiar, even to a provincial audience, that the whole narrative arc could be traversed in a few paragraphs. In the cheap popular pamphlet *Innocence Betrayed* (reprinted as far afield as Hull, Banbury, and Penrith) barely five pages sufficed to describe in full the tragic life of Sarah Martin, a beautiful farmer's daughter, seduced 'by one of those depraved wretches, whose favourite pursuit is to ruin female innocence', abandoned in London, 'compelled by necessity, to gain a miserable support by prostitution', and finally driven to take her own life.[7]

The same ideas were endlessly recycled in poems, pictures, and legal writing (see plate 2). Here is Thomas Holcroft's 'The Dying Prostitute' (1785), alternately addressing the compassionate reader and the treacherous, bestial libertine who had first destroyed her:

> Weep o'er the mis'ries of a wretched maid,
>> Who sacrificed to man her health and fame;
> Whose love, and truth, and trust were all repaid
>> By want and woe, disease and endless shame.

Curse not the poor lost wretch, who ev'ry ill
 That proud unfeeling man can heap sustains;
Sure she enough is cursed o'er whom his will
 Enflamed by brutal passion, boundless reigns.

. . .

That I was virtuous once, and beauteous too,
 And free from envious tongues my spotless fame:
These but torment, these but my tears renew,
 These aggravate my present guilt and shame.

. . .

Ah! Say, insidious Damon! Monster! where?
 What glory hast thou gained by my defeat?
Art thou more happy for that I'm less fair?
 Or bloom thy laurels o'er my winding-sheet?[8]

Out of this new mindset was to emerge that most enduring of modern fictional archetypes, the tart with a heart. That prostitutes were beautiful, innocent 'fallen angels' was already in the 1740s the theme of John Cleland's erotic and serious writing alike.* After 1800 it was developed by Thomas de Quincey, Charles Dickens, Dante Gabriel Rossetti, Elizabeth Gaskell, Thomas Hardy, and countless other writers and artists. Throughout the nineteenth and twentieth centuries, the whore with the heart of gold remained a staple of novels, plays, opera, film, and television.[9]

This was certainly never the only perspective. In satirical prints, the popular press, and moral tracts, two older attitudes also persisted well beyond 1800. One was a fascination with street-walkers and courtesans as self-confident entrepreneurs, able to outwit their simple cullies (see illustration 6). The other was a fear of them as loathsome and predatory threats to the health and order of society: we shall see in Chapters 4 and 5 how far even philanthropists were unable to shake off revulsion towards the objects of their charity. The self-perception of plebeian women whose lovers had abandoned them, or who had

---

* 'Those unfortunate women who live by prostitution', concurred Adam Smith in 1776, were 'the most beautiful women perhaps in the British dominions': *An Inquiry into the Nature and Causes of the Wealth of Nations*, ed. R. H. Campbell, A. S. Skinner and W. B. Todd (1976), I. xi. b. 41.

SQUIRE THOMAS JUST ARRIV'D. *Touch me not! I'm still a Maid.*

Publish'd Nov.18th 1778, by W. Humphrey.

6. In this 1778 caricature by James Gillray, a plump young countryman becomes the sexual prey of a group of confident London prostitutes: 'Touch me not! I'm still a Maid', he shrieks in terror.

sex for money, also tended to be less melodramatic than the middle-class rhetoric of male rapacity, female innocence, and prostitution. When, for example, in 1729, Winifred Lloyd, a middle-aged bawd, introduced two young, willing maidservants, Mary Macdonald and Hanna Smith, to the attractions of having a good time with her client, Mr Janssen, the women were persuaded that the whole process, far from degrading them, represented a passage into independence and adulthood. After Mary slept with the kindly squire for the first time, for the huge sum of five guineas, Mrs Lloyd 'commended [her], telling her she was now made a woman of'. With Hanna, who was only four-teen, she commiserated on the pain of sexual intercourse – 'O', she told her, 'when he first lay with me I cried out murder, but if you was forty years old it would not hurt you' – and likewise 'encouraged her saying he would make a woman of her for ever'. As the East End prostitute Anne Carter put it in 1730, what she did for a living was not the desperate resort of a ruined woman, but simply the exchange of money in return for 'the satisfaction of her body . . . according to contract'.[10]

Yet the languages of pity and of male treachery gradually infiltrated even such alternative points of view. So entrenched did they become that prostitutes and other unchaste women were increasingly known, and referred to themselves in public, simply as 'misfortunate' or 'unfor-tunate' persons.[11] The stereotype of the seduced harlot was therefore one of the most remarkable and influential cultural innovations of the eighteenth century. It overturned age-old, deeply rooted presumptions about whores; it rose to prominence with extraordinary speed; and it dominated the perception of prostitution from the middle of the eight-eenth century onwards. Throughout the nineteenth and twentieth centuries, this new way of regarding prostitutes – not as wilful, inde-pendent sexual agents, but as the victims of seduction, entrapment, and impoverishment – was to remain the overriding view of sexual trade.

FEMININE PERSPECTIVES

Changing attitudes to prostitution were only the tip of a much larger, growing concern about seduction. The basis for this was a newly dominant conception of men as inherently selfish and deceitful in love. Many of its most articulate exponents were themselves male – but the crucial reason for its increasing prominence was the rise of women as public writers, poets, actors, and philosophers, which introduced into the cultural mainstream powerful new female perspectives on courtship and lust.[1]

This was a completely unprecedented development, and one whose effects have thus far been remarkably under-appreciated. In all earlier times, women's direct intervention in public discussion had always been very limited. Beyond ordinary speech, men monopolized every medium in which male and female qualities were prescribed and reinforced – fiction, drama, poetry, sermons, journalism, education, popular writing, moral polemic, theology, and philosophy. This was why femininity had tended to be so publicly undervalued. But from the later seventeenth century onwards this began to change, in several overlapping respects.

One novelty was the advent of professional actresses on the English stage after 1660. Until this point, women had been generally barred from public performance: for them to act was seen as grossly unfeminine, and female parts were played by boys. In Italy, Spain and France, however, women had begun appearing on stage from the later sixteenth century onwards, and this fashion greatly influenced Charles II. His French mother, Queen Henrietta Maria, promoted it privately at court in the 1620s and 1630s, and he got used to it during his many years in exile on the continent during the 1650s. When he returned to England as king in 1660 and reopened the public theatres (which had been closed by the Puritans since 1642), he immediately sanctioned the practice. This transformed the treatment of female character in drama, the most prominent medium of public entertainment. Henceforth, the dramatic exploitation of actresses' sexuality tended above all to emphasize their submission to masculine conquest. Compared with Elizabethan and Jacobean plays, male lust and female helplessness were now far more sharply contrasted. Rape became a regular feature of tragic plots, even being added gratuitously to adaptations of older plays. This allowed for much titillating on-stage exploitation of sexual suffering, but also drove home the idea that even the most innocent women were defenceless in the face of male appetites. The class basis of women's domination was highlighted too. The stage rapist was invariably a man of superior status, who entrapped his victim less by brute force than through the abuse of his sexual, social, and political power.[2]

In comedy, the appearance of real women on stage stimulated the cynical scrutiny of courtship, love, and marriage that is such a notable feature of Restoration drama. For the first time, prostitutes and mistresses came to be depicted as the unhappy victims of male seduction and social dysfunction. In tragedy there was a marked shift to domestic 'she-tragedies', centred on the male victimization of women. In Nahum Tate's updating of *King Lear* (1681), Edmund kidnaps and intends to rape Cordelia. In John Banks's *Virtue Betray'd* (1682), Anne Boleyn is tricked into marrying Henry VIII, though she loves another. In Thomas Otway's endlessly read and performed *The Orphan* (1680), the evil libertine vows to treat the defenceless heroine just as 'The lusty bull ranges through all the field, / And from the herd singling his female out, / Enjoys her, and abandons her at will'. No matter that she is on her guard against the whole of his sex, 'for flattery and deceit renown'd! ... T'undo poor maids and make our ruin easie'. No matter that other men warn her:

Trust not a man; we are by nature false,
Dissembling, subtle, cruel, and unconstant:
When a man talks of love, with caution trust him;
But if he swears, he'll certainly deceive thee.

No matter that she loves and secretly marries another: it is all in vain.[3]

By the beginning of the eighteenth century these novel conceptions of feminine suffering had become staple themes of English theatre. Nicholas Rowe's *The Fair Penitent*, first acted in 1703 and incessantly revived, reprinted, and re-quoted, was based on an early seventeenth-century play about a ruthless adulteress who is killed by her outraged husband. Now, in keeping with the new sensibility, this figure was transformed into the tragic virgin Calista, who is seduced and abandoned by the heartless Lothario (such was the play's popularity that his name became proverbial). From a story about a lustful villainess it had become a cautionary tale about the wiles of libertine men, the social constraints on women, and the terrible cost of unlawful love. 'Perfidious man!' exclaims Calista's confidante, 'Man! Who makes his mirth of our undoing! / The base, professed betrayer of our sex ...

Guard me from men, / From their deceitful tongues, their vows and flatteries'. 'How hard is the condition of our sex,' Calista herself bitterly observes, 'Thro' ev'ry state of life the slaves of man.' She blames her own weakness (she fell, 'because I lov'd, and was a woman'), but as the Epilogue pointed out, the real, underlying problem was male licentiousness – 'if you wou'd e'er bring constancy in fashion, / you men must first begin the reformation'. The same transformation is visible in eighteenth-century treatments of the story of Jane Shore, the legendary mistress of Edward IV, who previously had always been portrayed as a scheming harlot. Henceforth, beginning with Rowe's own *Jane Shore* (1714), she was reinvented as a beautiful, tragic exemplar of the sexual double standard:

> Mark by what partial justice we are judged;
> Such is the fate unhappy women find,
> And such the curse entailed upon our kind,
> That man, the lawless libertine, may rove
> Free and unquestioned through the wilds of love;
> While woman, sense and nature's easy fool,
> If poor weak woman swerve from virtue's rule,
> If, strongly charmed, she leave the thorny way,
> And in the softer paths of pleasure stray;
> Ruin ensues, reproach and endless shame,
> And one false step entirely damns her fame.
> In vain with tears the loss she may deplore,
> In vain look back to what she was before,
> She sets, like stars that fall, to rise no more.[4]

As is well known, Restoration drama also included plenty of lusty female roles – adulterous wives, scheming mistresses, and mercenary whores did not suddenly vanish from the stage. Betty Frisque in John Crowne's *The Country Wit* (1676), Mrs Tricksy in Dryden's *The Kind Keeper* (1678), and Madam Tricklove in Thomas D'Urfey's *Squire Oldsapp* (1678), for example, all lived up to their names. The new archetypes emerged gradually alongside such traditional figures, rather than supplanting them overnight. Yet by the turn of the century they had grown increasingly influential. It is notable that plays like *The Orphan* and *The Fair Penitent* increased their popularity throughout the eighteenth century, whilst those that portrayed women as lustful manipulators largely fell out of fashion. Already in the 1670s and 1680s, a telling sign of shifting attitudes was the fact that libertines on stage were made to spout the traditional rhetoric of female inconstancy in ways that highlighted its artificiality. 'Find out some song to please me,' the villain Polydor orders his page in *The Orphan*, as he prepares to assault the virtue of an innocent maid,

> ... that describes,
> Women's hypocrisies, their subtle wiles,
> Betraying smiles, feigned tears, inconstancies,
> Their painted outsides, and corrupted minds,
> The sum of all their follies, and their falsehoods.

When his prey resists, he flings the same misogynist slanders at her. But we, the audience, are meant to see that all this is but cynical, manipulative bluster. For we contrast it with what is really being shown. A weak and pitiful woman is under siege from a ruthless, powerful male. As in so many other Restoration analyses of morality, the overriding message is that social life is governed by irrational customs. In the light of empirical scrutiny, it proclaims, the age-old tropes about female lustfulness and duplicity are revealed to be merely conventional, customary, artificial ways of thinking.[5]

It was not just the advent of female performers that inspired these new attitudes, but a much more general emergence, for the first time, of women as a permanent part of the world of letters.[6] As playwrights, poets, novelists, and writers of other kinds, women influenced male authors, looked to one another, and addressed themselves directly to the public. Though, to begin with, their conceptions of femininity often included conventional ideas about the fickleness of amorous women, female writers also tended, and increasingly so, to stress male rapaciousness and duplicity in love. Women dramatists, for example, were more likely to ridicule male pretension, and to explore female views at greater length. It is no accident that the first sympathetic, in-depth depictions of unhappy fallen women ever written in English came from the pen of Aphra Behn, the great pioneer in the exploration of female sexual sensibility. Particularly telling was her revision (in *The Revenge*, 1680) of John Marston's *The Dutch Courtesan*

(1605). In the original the protagonist had been a devilish whore who gets her justified comeuppance; now this character was transformed into Corina, a tragic, innocent victim. Seduced and betrayed by the man she loves, she is treated as a whore but never acts like one. When his perfidy becomes clear, her heart erupts in pain and anger:

is it true, hast thou abandon'd me? Canst thou forget our numerous blisses past, the hours we've wasted out in tales of love, and curst all interruption but of kisses, which 'twixt thy charming words I ever gave thee; when the whole live-long day we thought too short, yet blest the coming night? Hast thou forgot, false are thy vows, all perjur'd, and thy faith broken as my poor lost forsaken heart? And wou'dst thou wish me live to see this change! Cou'dst thou believe, if thou hadst hid it from the talking world, my heart cou'd not have found it out by sympathy! A foolish, unconsidering, faithless man!

In much female writing about sexual relations, the bottom line was, as the teenage poet Sarah Fyge explained in 1686, that men were always trying 'to make a prey' of chaste women. All their bluster about female lust and inconstancy was but to make women 'the scapegoat' – it was actually men who constantly pressured and ensnared women, who were insatiable in their thirst for new conquests, and shameless in their commission:

> Instead of hiding their prodigious Acts,
> They do reveal, brag of their horrid Facts;

and yet,

> you'd persuade us, that 'tis we alone
> Are guilty of all crimes and you have none,
>
> . . .
>
> And 'cause you have made whores of all you could,
> So if you dared, you'd say all women would.[7]

Even more influential in the long term was the role of women in creating the new genre of the novel, which by the middle of the eighteenth century had exploded into the most influential fictional form of all, and become a central conduit of moral and social education. (As its pre-eminent exponent explained in 1747, the 'story or amusement should be considered as little more than the vehicle to the more necessary instruction'.) Though the novel was never a stable or uniform category, more a constantly evolving hybrid of forms, the impact of this newly fashionable kind of narrative was unmistakable. Its authors made increasing claims to realism – to be portraying the lives of actual men and women, rather than of fictional characters. The genre also allowed for much more insight into the minds and feelings of its protagonists than the theatre, with its constraints of plot, time, and speech, had ever managed. Now, there was unlimited scope for the dissection of changing emotional states, internal thoughts, and subjective perceptions, which could be privately pondered by each individual reader. For all these reasons, courtship and seduction were prime novelistic subjects. From the outset, women were prominent as novelists, as readers of novels, and as their heroines. By the beginning of the nineteenth century, Jane Austen could confidently assert that, despite being denigrated as trivial, women novelists' exploration of female lives had in fact 'afforded more extensive and unaffected pleasure than those of any other literary corporation in the world': these were the literary productions 'in which the greatest powers of the mind are displayed, in which the most thorough knowledge of human nature, the happiest delineation of its varieties, the liveliest effusions of wit and humour are conveyed to the world in the best chosen language'.[8]*

The heroines of Austen's early predecessors, such as Aphra Behn, Delarivier Manley, and Eliza Haywood, had by no means all been innocent of lust. All the same, as in the case of early female dramatists, this theme was increasingly supplanted by a stress on masculine seduction, betrayal, and inconstancy, and the in-depth presentation of victimized feminine points of view. In the first episode of Manley's *New Atalantis* (1709), we see a lascivious woman sexually deceived and punished by two scheming men. The second, even more starkly, shows us a powerful aristocrat who ruthlessly plots the seduction and rape of his innocent virgin ward, and then abandons her to ruin:

the remainder of her life was one continued scene of horror, sorrow and repentance. She died a true landmark to warn all believing virgins from ship-

---

* 'For an historian', by contrast, 'great abilities . . . are not requisite', noted Samuel Johnson, 'for in historical composition, all the greatest powers of the human mind are quiescent' – 'no writer has a more easy task than the historian': *Boswell's Life of Johnson*, ed. George Birkbeck Hill and L. F. Powell, 6 vols (1934–50), i. 424–5.

wrecking their honour upon that dangerous coast of rocks, the vows and pretended passion of mankind.[9]

Ideas about the essential callousness and iniquity of male attitudes to sex also began to be expounded in depth by female thinkers and philosophers. As Mary Astell put it in 1700, with brilliant bitterness, ''tis no great matter to them if women, who were born to be their slaves, be now and then ruined for their entertainment ... It were endless to reckon up the diverse stratagems men use to catch their prey.' No woman could ever 'be too much upon her guard'. Similar views were expressed by Margaret Cavendish, Damaris Masham, and other early feminists. It was not that the arguments they put forward had been unthinkable before. We catch a glimpse of them in 1640, for example, when the popular poet John Taylor imagined women's feelings on the subject. Whores were not born but made by the treachery of men: 'who vitiated them, but you that would seem the virtuous? Or who corrupted them, but you the male crocodiles? ... It is not possible, that the world could yield any one branded with the name of a whore, but there must be a whoremaster to make her so.' It was men who were 'addicted to incontinency', women who were naturally chaste.[10] Analogous points had been developed by some medieval critics of misogyny.[11] Yet it was only from the later seventeenth century onwards that they came to be put forward publicly, at length, and in quantity, in a way that discernibly changed the broader culture of the age.

Even very ordinary women were now newly able to access and publicize similar views, as consumers and correspondents of the burgeoning periodical press. From the 1690s onwards, newspapers commonly encouraged their readers to send in questions, observations, essays, and poems for publication. Many periodicals addressed themselves specifically to women; many more presumed a mixed readership. Female attitudes, love, and courtship accordingly became massively popular journalistic themes. For a woman to venture into print had previously tended to be a controversial action. Now, as part of the broader explosion and democratization of printed media, literacy, and correspondence, female voices and concerns became a permanent, daily part of public discussion, continually and confidently speaking to a huge and growing reading public.[12]

All these social and intellectual developments (which we shall explore further in Chapter 6) are epitomized in an extraordinary letter written on 20 May 1726 by a young, heartbroken woman from London. During her husband's absence at sea, she had been seduced (perhaps raped) by an acquaintance, inveigled into an affair with him, impregnated, and finally abandoned. Desperate and heavily pregnant, she travelled a hundred miles to Kent to track him down, and sent word to him on board his ship, off the coast at Deal. When he ignored her letters, rejecting her callously as nothing but 'a common whore', she drowned herself. Within days of her suicide, her farewell letter to a friend, found in her lodgings, had been printed on the front page of the *London Journal*, to be read by thousands of men and women across the land. These were her final recorded words:

Madam,

. . .

I wish I could cease thinking. To suffer shame, I cannot; and to face my friends, or indeed the world, is to me more terrible than death. I freely forgive all the world, and even Mr L. the greatest enemy I ever met with in it . . . I own my self to blame for reposing so much confidence in him: I wish my unhappy state may be a warning to others, not to put too much trust in faithless Man.

. . .

Mr L. should not read Mr Locke's books so much and practise them so little; he inculcates the necessity of doing as we would be done by, and of shunning a lie, though to the saving a man's life. Let him think of this when he thinks of me. He cannot forget the confusion I was in when he first took the advantage of my weakness, not having strength enough to resist him: he continued on his knees, begging me to forgive him; promising all that man could say; calling God to damn him if ever he proved base to me . . . He declared he would no longer esteem me his friend but wife, though not in his power to make me so, but should own the same love and duty. O that he had always kept his word! Then I should have still been happy; but not being used to men's company, was unacquainted with such treachery . . . But I can still forgive him, and own my fault. Let no one judge too rash, that does not know the cause I had for it.

I am,

Your humble servant,

H. B.[13]

This was a completely private tragedy, amongst people so utterly obscure that not even their full names are now known to us. In no previous age would it have been conceivable for such a woman to set down a narrative of her ruin, blaming it naturally on the libidinous treachery of men, and for this intimate account of a common sexual victim to be immediately publicized to a national audience of sympathetic readers. By the early eighteenth century, however, all this was possible.

Over the course of the later seventeenth and early eighteenth century, a new view of relations between the sexes thus became increasingly dominant. Its presumption of male lustfulness owed much to the growing cultural prominence of female performers, writers, viewers, and readers. In past ages, noted Samuel Johnson in 1750, 'as the faculty of writing has been chiefly a masculine endowment, the reproach of making the world miserable has been always thrown upon the women': but now their breaking of the male monopoly on writing, and their 'stronger arguments', had overturned the ancient masculine falsehood that women were the more fickle and lecherous sex.[14] Ironically enough, the new attitude was shared by defenders as well as critics of male liberty. As a consequence it became ever more influential. Already by the 1730s it had become a commonplace that men, especially gentlemen, were constantly and cold-bloodedly out to use women – that they employed all their superior knowledge and power to outwit innocent females, whilst upholding an iniquitous double standard of morality that damned the victim rather than the seducer.

NOVEL ATTITUDES

This is why the first great novelists of the English language were so obsessed with seduction. Foremost amongst them was Samuel Richardson, whose *Pamela* (1740), *Clarissa* (1747–8), and *Sir Charles Grandison* (1753–4) were the most sensationally popular and influential fictions of the eighteenth century. His was a classic instance of the growing power of female viewpoints. For all its originality of treatment, the general approach and subject-matter of his fiction owes an obvious debt to the stream of earlier novels about heroines courted, seduced, raped, and oppressed which had flown from the pens of pioneering women writers such as Penelope Aubin, Jane Barker, Mary Davys, Eliza Haywood, and Elizabeth Rowe. A wide circle of women acquaintances, readers, and correspondents helped him; in turn, his work presented eyewitness perspectives of respectable women under threat from rapacious, superior men. These were, above all others, the books that helped establish the novel as the pre-eminent form of English literature, and the seduction narrative as its most fundamental plot. Right through the nineteenth century, it is hard to think of many serious novelists who did *not* pursue this theme.[1]

Richardson's writing was the more powerful in its social impact because it self-consciously drew on real-life examples, presented itself as documentary history, and sought to instruct its readers in matters of love, courtship, and lust. Indeed, many of its themes are adumbrated in his earlier, overtly didactic publications. Already in his first book, the *Familiar Letters*, the danger of male sexual cupidity had been a prominent subject. The bottom line, as one father bluntly counselled his daughter, was that 'men are deceitful'. 'The profligateness of the generality of young fellows of the present age,' cautioned another, brought frightening 'risks which a virtuous young woman has to encounter with.' Yet another girl was warned against the terrible danger of 'keeping company with a gentleman of a bad character', who had 'already ruin'd two, if not three, worthy tradesmen's daughters' and would undo her too – 'whatever he may promise you' in way of marriage. For libertines were ubiquitous and incorrigible. Usually they sought only sexual conquest, insinuating themselves 'by all the professions of an honourable love', before having their wicked way. The greatest threat of all was posed by men of higher status: the rake 'of superior fortune' to his prey; the master who makes a 'vile attempt' upon his servant's chastity.[2]

This last instance echoed actual cases that Richardson was familiar with. There was a particular story he had heard, of the beautiful young maidservant who 'by the time she was fifteen, engaged the attention of her lady's son, a young gentleman of free principles, who, on her lady's death, attempted, by all manner of temptations and devices, to seduce her'.* Then there were the endless examples,

---

* For a similar, real-life, case from the mid-1740s with remarkable parallels to *Pamela*, see Giles Worsley, 'The Seduction of Elizabeth Lister', *Women's History Review* 13 (2004) – it is very tempting to suppose that the protagonists must have read Richardson's novel.

privately repeated and reported in the newspapers, of women like Isabella Cranston, who in the early 1720s had been 'decoyed' into the brothel of Sarah Jolly 'under pretence of being hired into service' and was there delivered up to the libertine Colonel Francis Charteris. Or like Anne Bond at the end of the decade, who 'being out of service, and sitting at the door of the house where she lodged, a woman, who was a stranger to her, came to her, and asked her, if she wanted a place? And told her, she helped servants to places.' This woman was Elizabeth Needham, sometime neighbour of Mrs Jolly and just as notorious a brothel-keeper and bawd; and Anne Bond, too, found herself in service to Colonel Charteris. For ten days he trapped her indoors, made her sleep in his bedroom, 'offered her a purse of gold ... several times, and told her, that he would give her fine clothes and money, and a house to live in, and would also get her a husband'. Then he gave up trying to persuade her, raped her, and threw her out.[3]

Like so many contemporary commentators, Richardson evidently came to be fascinated by women's enforced seduction and entrapment into prostitution. In the *Familiar Letters* he included his own remarkable narrative of a young woman, new to London, who is tricked into a brothel under pretence of going into service with a lady. There she meets another young woman, who tearfully recounts her own entrapment, rape, and enforced prostitution:

In this dreadful situation, I have been perplexed with the hateful importunities of different men every day; and tho' I long resisted to my utmost, yet downright force never failed to overcome. Thus in a shameful round of guilt and horror, have I lingered out ten months; subject to more miseries than tongue can express.

So concerned was Richardson to drive home the reality of such scenarios that, of all the 173 letters in the volume, to this one alone he appended a postscript stressing its absolute truth: 'N.B. This shocking story is taken from the mouth of the young woman herself, who so narrowly escaped the snare of the vile procuress; and is fact in every circumstance.'[4]

In his novels, the same facts come vividly to life. His heroines are all virgins who are pursued, abducted, and under constant threat from

predatory, superior men. In *Pamela*, the lustful squire B preys on his
fifteen-year-old servant: not because he is an especially bad man but
because their entire culture acquiesces in the destruction of inferior
girls by older, richer, more powerful men. Like a bawd, his housekeeper Mrs Jewkes, 'a wicked procuress', keeps Pamela imprisoned
whilst alternately threatening and cajoling her to comply with her
master. 'Are not the two sexes made for one another? And is it not
natural for a gentleman to love a pretty woman? And suppose he can
obtain his desires, is that so bad?' 'Ruin' was a 'foolish word', she
wheedles, extolling the status of a kept mistress, 'Why ne'er a lady in
the land may live happier than you, if you will, or be more honourably used.' When Pamela resists all the same, the older woman loses
patience, beats and abuses her, encourages Mr B, and holds the girl
down for him to rape (see plate 3). 'Why, what is all this,' drawls one
of Mr B's neighbours about the heroine's predicament, 'but that the
squire our neighbour has a mind to his mother's waiting-maid? And
if he takes care she wants for nothing, I don't see any great injury will
be done her. He hurts no family by this.' (By which he means: Mr B
hurts no one who matters, no one of his own class). Even the parish
priest is resigned to the ways of the world: 'for, he said, it was too
common and fashionable a case to be withstood by a private clergyman or two'. To be the kept mistress of a great man was perfectly
honourable, 'and 'tis what all young gentlemen will do'.[5]

Richardson's masterpiece, *Clarissa*, further sharpens the archetypes
of sexual vice and virtue. In *Pamela*, the heroine's virtue and steadfast-
ness eventually redeem Mr B, who is not yet 'a very abandoned
profligate':* he refrains from ravishing her, they marry, and live happily ever after. But Richardson was evidently stung by those readers
who had found this reversal unbelievable, doubting especially that
Pamela could be as innocent as she is made out. In *Clarissa* the narrative is accordingly more single-minded, the tone much darker, the

---

* Indeed he was a useless seducer, complained one male critic: 'how sheepishly does
he act, and what blunders does he not commit?' If he'd acted with more guile and
confidence 'he would have met with less and less resistance, till at last he might have
accomplished his desires, before Miss Pamela had certainly known what he would be
at': *Critical Remarks on Sir Charles Grandison* (1754), 22–3.

ultimate blow she remains virtuous, dies like a true Christian, and so
triumphs over her worldly enemies.[6]

The impact of Richardson's portrayal of male rapacity and female
seduction was enormous – not just on English attitudes in the later
eighteenth and nineteenth centuries, but on literate culture across the
whole of the western world. It can be seen in the first great novel in
Dutch, *De historie van Mejuffrouw Sara Burgerhart* (1782), and in
countless other major writers: Rousseau, Diderot, Laclos, Goethe,
Kleist, Pushkin, even the Marquis de Sade. Susanna Rowson's *Charlotte Temple* (1791) reworked Richardson's themes in a transatlantic
setting and became a massive best-seller, by far the most popular fiction of early nineteenth-century America. Across the English-speaking
world, his novels were endlessly praised, referred to, read, and imi-
tated by other writers.[7]

Naturally, not everyone shared Richardson's exact presumptions.
Some high-spirited female novelists poked fun at the stereotype of the
all-powerful rake – though their satire equally illustrates its pervasive-
ness. Thus Sir Edward Denham, the anti-hero of Jane Austen's last,
uncompleted, novel, *Sanditon* (1817),

had read more sentimental novels than agreed with him. His fancy had been
early caught by all the impassioned, and most exceptionable parts of Richardson's; and such authors as have since appeared to tread in Richardson's
steps, so far as man's determined pursuit of woman in defiance of every feeling and convenience is concerned, had since occupied the greater part of his
literary hours, and formed his character.

173

In consequence,

Sir Edward's great object in life was to be seductive. – With such personal advantages as he knew himself to possess, and such talents as he did also give himself credit for, he regarded it as his duty. – He felt that he was formed to be a dangerous man – quite in the line of the Lovelaces ... He was armed against the highest pitch of disdain or aversion. – If she could not be won by affection, he must carry her off. He knew his business.[8]

In real life, on the other hand, rapacious men often denigrated female modesty as no more than artificial repression. 'I have my own private notions as to modesty', recorded Boswell, 'of which I would only value the *appearance*: for unless a woman has amorous heat she is a dull companion.'[9]* A similar ethos seemed to be revealed in Lord Chesterfield's private advice to his son, which caused a scandal when it was published in 1774. (In Samuel Jackson Pratt's *The Pupil of Pleasure* (1776), which satirizes Chesterfield's morality, the anti-hero Philip Sedley scoffs that 'Richardson's a child ... his Lovelace a bungler'.) When in 1813 Byron read his future wife's views on relations between the sexes, he sneered that 'she seems to have been spoiled – not as children usually are – but systematically Clarissa Harlowed into an awkward kind of correctness – with a dependence upon her own infallibility which will or may lead her into some egregious blunder' (it did, of course: marriage to him).[10]

Other currents of thought therefore continued to flow alongside the mainstream obsession with male predation. It is nonetheless remarkable how far there had developed by the middle of the eighteenth century an underlying consensus about the essential nature of male and female sexuality. To illustrate this we have only to compare Richardson's views with those of Henry Fielding, his foremost literary antagonist.

From the beginning of his career, Fielding wrote his novels in conscious opposition to those of Richardson, explicitly repudiating his

---

* It was ridiculous how obsessed everyone was with the 'fictitious merit' of female chastity, complained Shelley in 1812: in truth, seduction was a term which 'could have no meaning, in a rational society'. *The Letters of Percy Bysshe Shelley*, ed. Frederick L. Jones, 2 vols (1964), i. 323.

style, tone, and plots. In real life, too, the two authors belonged to markedly different sexual milieux. Richardson, the buttoned-up, barely educated, middle-class tradesman, surrounded himself with adoring, virtuous women, was proud of never even having *met* an unchaste one, and addressed himself at least as much to a female as a male audience. Fielding, by contrast, was an Etonian gentleman and lawyer, the son of a libertine, the near relation of powerful aristocrats and courtiers. As a young man, he lived the rakish, promiscuous exist-ence of a West End playwright; in middle age, he impregnated (and ended up marrying) his maid; towards the end of his life, as a magis-trate, he immersed himself daily in the sordid circumstances of bawdry and sexual trade. His was an upper-class, libertine, masculine world – reflected, his contemporary critics thought, in the character of his writing. Richardson himself, Samuel Johnson, and Charles Burney all deplored Fielding's 'loose life, and the profligacy of almost all his male characters. Who would venture to read one of his novels aloud to modest women? His novels are *male* amusements.'[11]

It is hardly surprising, therefore, that the two writers have long been held up as moral opposites. At first sight, Fielding's ethics do look quite different. On the surface, his work conveyed a worldly acceptance of male sexual freedom that enraged pious readers. It also featured sexually experienced women who were ardent, seductive, and dangerous to men. In his hilarious spoof, *Shamela* (1741), Pamela is revealed to be a shameless hussy, a whore and bastard-bearer, who, in league with his equally knowing servants, entraps the clueless Mr 'Booby' into matrimony. In *Joseph Andrews* (1742), Pamela's inno-cent brother is pursued by a lascivious widow, Lady Booby. The heroes of *Tom Jones* (1749) and of *Amelia* (1751) both succumb to the wiles of experienced women.

Yet, for all his levity and bawdy banter, Fielding's underlying atti-tudes towards lust and seduction were remarkably close to those of his great rival. He shared their culture's basic presumptions that, in general, men pursued women; that female innocence was constantly under threat from masculine wiles; and that fallen women were the victims of libertine seducers. As we have already seen, these were the attitudes he expressed in his journalism, and they equally per-vaded his fiction. The lasciviousness of Shamela, Lady Booby, and

Lady Bellaston (in *Tom Jones*) is an inversion, for comic effect, of the natural order – women were not naturally wanton. Moreover, though Fielding believed it was unavoidable that men should fornicate, he also made it clear that it was contemptible for them to seduce virgins, and admirable if they remained chaste or monogamous. Even in *Tom Jones*, with its rambunctious pleasure in human folly and imperfection, these rules are observed – indeed, the plot's twists and happy surprises often turn on their seeming to be flouted, before being triumphantly re-established. The flawed but humane morality that Fielding celebrates is that of Jones himself:

I am no canting hypocrite, nor do I pretend to the gift of chastity, more than my neighbours. I have been guilty with women, I own it; but am not conscious that I have ever injured any – nor would I, to procure pleasure to myself, be knowingly the cause of misery to any human being.

Against it he contrasts the vicious amorality of libertine men, who, as in Richardson, are a ubiquitous danger. They treat women as 'enemies', and have 'a regular, premeditated scheme' for their conquest. Their promises of marriage are worthless. They are guilty of 'indefensible treachery'. Like Lord Fellamar, who tries to rape Sophia Western in order to force her to marry him, they are all shadows of Lovelace.[12]

This picture is drawn most sharply in Fielding's last and darkest novel, *Amelia*. First we meet Miss Mathews, an apparently amoral femme fatale, who temporarily leads the hero astray. But then we are given her history, the explanation for her character. She herself was first undone by a handsome, villainous officer, who cynically seduced her, kept her as his mistress, and repeatedly abandoned her for other women – until, driven to rage and despair by his callousness, she finally stabs him through the heart. 'O may my fate be a warning to every woman,' she exclaims,

to keep her innocence, to resist every temptation, since she is certain to repent of the foolish bargain. May it be a warning to her to deal with mankind with care and caution; to shun the least approaches of dishonour, and never to confide too much in the honesty of a man, nor in her own strength, where she has so much at stake; let her remember she walks on a precipice, and the bottomless pit is to receive her, if she slips; nay, if she makes but one false step.[13]

Another central character, the virtuous wife of an impoverished clergyman, falls prey to a coldly calculating aristocrat, one of those serial debauchers of women who regards them as 'enemies', to be pursued and destroyed: he sleeps with them only once, for 'novelty and resistance' are what arouse him. Using his established network of pimps and 'a long, regular, premeditated design', he lures her to a masquerade, drugs, and rapes her. In doing so he infects her with venereal disease. Then her husband, the clergyman, catches it from her and realizes the truth. Insane with grief, he tries to kill himself and his wife, and expires shortly afterwards. The book's heroine herself is repeatedly pursued by insidious and experienced rakes. Her resistance proves her virtue; but also her luck in the face of overwhelming odds. Such dangers lurk everywhere, and superior men in pursuit of vice will use every means at their disposal: insinuation, flattery, wealth, bribery, their power over husbands and fathers, patronage, alcohol, drugs, masquerades, bawds, pimps, lies, and brute force.[14] Ultimately, beneath the comedy, Fielding is fundamentally preoccupied with male rapacity and female victimization.

Just as striking is the extent to which Richardson and his admirers accepted the basic premise that men were bound to take sexual liberties – the real division was that between 'moderate rakes' and incorrigible libertines. To Richardson's frustration, even his most virtuous female readers palliated the vices of men like Lovelace and Sir Hargrave Pollexfen, the libertine would-be rapist in *Grandison*. Yet he too observed this distinction. In the first draft of *Sir Charles Grandison*, the heroine is perfectly willing to marry a sexually experienced man, so long as he would give up his libertine ways – for, as she puts it, 'it may not be thought absolutely necessary perhaps to make very nice scrutinies into the past life and actions of the man to whom we have no very material objections'.[15] The same pre-marital indulgence was allowed to Mr B in *Pamela*, and to Belford, Lovelace's fellow rake in *Clarissa*. Even in Richardson, male fornication, and even seduction, were always potentially forgivable.

When, in his final novel, he tried instead to portray an entirely chaste hero, he was therefore intensely conscious of advocating an extreme view. Surely, asked one of his admirers, 'none but divines and prudes' could object to 'a moderate rake'? When consulted on how to show 'the character of a good man', Richardson's elderly friend Colley Cibber advised that a such a paragon would always be sure to cast off his mistress before proposing marriage to an honourable woman. 'When I made my objections to the mistress,' the novelist recounted, Cibber was astonished: 'A male-virgin, said he – ha, ha, ha, hah! ... and he laughed me quite out of countenance!' It was a mistake to have implied that Sir Charles Grandison 'still kept his maidenhead', agreed another otherwise sympathetic critic, 'I find it has hurt his character a good deal with the ladies'. To Richardson's dismay, even his closest confidante, Lady Bradshaigh, the novel's original promoter, took a similar view of the necessity of female complaisance with male unchastity. Surely, she argued, a man could be sexually active without becoming an irredeemably 'abandoned profligate', just 'as a man may sometimes drink a little too much without being a sot'. 'As, then, there are so few good men', she concluded, 'the girls will find it necessary to marry rakes, rather than not marry at all.'[16]*

By the middle of the eighteenth century there had become firmly established a new balance of presumptions about sex, seduction, and the natural, inevitable unchastity of men. This set of ideas was shared by men and women of widely differing backgrounds. It was especially flaunted by advocates of sexual freedom. Everywhere one looks, especially in the private writings and conversations of the period, there can be found the chillingly ruthless, misogynist celebration of gentlemanly sexual conquest – not merely for sensual enjoyment, but as the exercise of power over one's inferiors. As the fashionable radical John Gawler, publicly renowned for his wit and charm, explained privately to William Godwin, he did not sleep with women because he enjoyed sex, but simply to humiliate them: 'there is more pleasure in frigging one's self, considered merely in a sensual view ... the superior pleas-

---

* In the first letter she ever wrote to Richardson, in the midst of reading *Clarissa*, she had already (anonymously) confessed 'though I shall blush ... that if I was to die for it, I cannot help being fond of Lovelace', and fantasized about his redemption: 'a faultless husband have I made him, even without danger of a relapse' (*The Correspondence of Samuel Richardson*, ed. Anna Laetitia Barbauld, 6 vols (1804), iv. 180–81).

ure in the other case consists in outwitting a woman, taking from her what she does not like to part with.'[17] Yet the basic principles of male rapacity and female passivity were equally accepted by those who deplored male licentiousness. They saturated the literature of the period. This new way of thinking about lust and gender was to dominate nineteenth- and twentieth-century views of sexuality.

4

The New World of Men and Women

The men will complain of your reserve. They will assure you that a franker behaviour would make you more amiable. But trust me, they are not sincere when they tell you so.
John Gregory, *A Father's Legacy to his Daughters*
(2nd edn, 1774), 36

In the various nations [of the world] we find men, in gradations from brutality to considerable knowledge and civilization. I know no circumstance by which this gradation may be marked with so much accuracy and justice, as the treatment of women. It may be denominated the moral thermometer.
Letters on Love, Marriage, and Adultery (1789), 37

The extreme severity with which females, who have fallen from the path of virtue, are treated [is due to] the necessity of separating them entirely from the virtuous ... A virtuous woman ought not only to be pure in body, but in mind: she should be kept perfectly ignorant of those things.
An Address to the Guardian Society (1817), 10–11

Woman, as is well known, in a natural state – unperverted, unseduced, and healthy – seldom, if ever, makes any of those

advances, which clearly indicate sexual desire; and for this
very plain reason that she does not feel them.
[William Andrus Allcott], *The Physiology of Marriage*
(1856), 167

The revolution in attitudes towards male and female sexuality had
far-reaching consequences. Though, as we have seen, the cult of seduction seemed to lay particular blame on the supposed rapacity of
upper-class men, its most obvious effect in practice was to tighten the
social constraints on female behaviour. Intertwined with its basic
notions of gender were also complicated presumptions about class,
privilege, purity, and power. Indeed, the Enlightenment reconfiguration of masculinity and femininity gave rise to some of the thorniest
social and ethical questions of the modern sexual world. How culpable was anyone for their own actions? What broader forces moulded
human behaviour? How ought men and women to behave?

POLITENESS AND SENSIBILITY

The first theme underlying all discussions of sexuality after 1688 was
the corruption and reformation of male manners. Given that men
behaved so badly, and external regulation had largely fallen away,
how to tame their apparently natural recklessness and promiscuity
became a matter of urgent concern.

Earlier models of male honour and civility had largely ignored the
other sex, and focused on interactions between men. Women, it was
generally presumed, were inferior in virtue and self-control: it was not
from them that men should learn how to conduct themselves. In the
eighteenth century, however, this idea was increasingly turned on its
head: now it gradually became axiomatic that, in fact, women possessed a superior morality. Social intercourse with them was hence a
prime means of polishing male manners, of inculcating new ideals of
'politeness', 'sensibility', and general refinement.[1]

Most contemporary commentators traced the history of this outlook back to medieval times, asserting that the birth of chivalry had

been a key advance of western civilization. Its 'great respect and veneration for the ladies', explained John Millar's immensely popular *Origin of the Distinction of Ranks* (1779), 'has still a considerable influence upon our behaviour towards them, and has occasioned their being treated with a degree of politeness, delicacy, and attention, that was unknown to the Greeks and Romans, and perhaps to all the nations of antiquity.' But Mary Wollstonecraft was closer to the truth when she blamed 'Lewis the XIVth in particular' for the stylized conventions of male 'attention and respect' to which women in her day were subjected.[2] The immediate antecedents of this new attitude had indeed evolved in seventeenth-century France.

From the early seventeenth century onwards, several leading French thinkers had advanced the novel idea that women, far from being morally inferior, embodied all that was good and beautiful. It was also in France that arguments for the rational equality of the sexes were first widely taken up and developed, partly under the influence of Descartes's revolutionary ideas about the separation of mind and body. At the French court, in its salons, and more generally in the upper echelons of French culture, the status of cultivated women as patrons, intellectuals, and arbiters of male manners came to be considerable. As Christopher Wren noted on a visit in 1665, 'the women ... make here the language and fashions, and meddle with politics and philosophy.'[3]

Yet the translation of such ideals to England was slow and complicated. They obviously influenced the cult of platonic love at the court of Charles I; but then the Civil War intervened. In the later seventeenth century, a few English writers espoused comparable views. One of Charles II's physicians, William Ramesey, who had been educated at Montpellier, asserted that women 'differ nothing from us but in the odd instruments of generation. They are generally more witty, and quicker of spirit than men ... they are for the most part, more pitiful, more pious, faithful, merciful, chaste, beautiful, than men.' Their very beings were made of 'a more noble matter, and refined'.[4] But this was not a conventional view at the Restoration court, and in England there was no alternative culture of mixed intellectual and social salons in which such ideas could flourish.

After 1688, by contrast, the notion of female influence was taken up with enthusiasm. This was part of a general movement to replace libertine norms with better standards of behaviour in public and private life, which grew out of the campaign for reformation of manners. Just as the Glorious Revolution was supposed to have ushered in a fresh age of prosperity and political stability, so the ideal of politeness, as promoted by Addison, Steele, and other early eighteenth-century writers, epitomized a new model of refined but virtuous urban masculinity fit for the modern, commercial world. The presumption of female refinement was central to this (its French and aristocratic origins conveniently forgotten). As 'women were formed to temper mankind, and soothe them into tenderness and compassion', regular conversation with them, treating their opinions with respect, and learning from their virtues, was now promoted as a pre-eminent means of imbibing civility and becoming a true gentleman. Men's 'endeavours to please the opposite sex, polishes and refines them out of those manners which are most natural to them'; without this spur 'man would not only be an unhappy, but a rude unfinished creature'.[5]

How far men should go in pleasing and imitating women was obviously a crucial question. Some early advocates of politeness believed that male manners were better improved by sticking altogether to masculine company, but that was a minority position. 'Gallantry and ladies must have a part in everything that passes for polite in our age,' the third Earl of Shaftesbury grumbled in 1705, 'worse luck for us.' By the 1730s this had become a commonplace. 'Politeness can be no other way attained', a best-selling conduct-book book stated bluntly:

Books may furnish us with right ideas, experience may improve our judgements, but it is the acquaintance of the ladies only, which can bestow that easiness of address, whereby the fine gentleman is distinguished from the scholar, and the man of business.

'Without the company of women', agreed Swift, politeness was unsustainable: they 'never fail to lead us into the right way, and there to keep us'. There was no 'better school for manners, than the company of virtuous women', wrote Hume, 'where the mutual endeavour to please must insensibly polish the mind, where the example of the female softness and modesty must communicate itself to their admirers, and where the delicacy of that sex puts every one on his guard'.[6]

The effects of this idea were extremely wide-ranging. It was on this basis that scholars came to theorize that the whole of human civilization had developed through men's growing attention and regard for the opposite sex – if women had such an effect on modern men, then surely they must have done so in the past, too. The progressive refinement of successive ages thus came to be linked to the rising status of women through history. Just so, the relative backwardness of other cultures could be judged by their males' lack of respect for females. This analogy was already implicit in some of Addison's writings in the 1710s. It became particularly influential after 1740, as part of the general Enlightenment interest in charting the progress of human society. In the writings of many of the age's pioneering anthropologists and historians, it was axiomatic that, as William Alexander put it in 1779,

we shall almost constantly find women among savages condemned to every species of servile, or rather, of slavish drudgery; and shall as constantly find them emerging from this state, in the same proportion as we find the men emerging from ignorance and brutality, and approaching to knowledge and refinement; the rank, therefore, and condition, in which we find women in any country, mark out to us with the greatest precision, the exact point in the scale of civil society, to which the people of such country have arrived; and were their history entirely silent on every other subject, and only mentioned the manner in which they treated their women, we would, from thence, be enabled to form a tolerable judgement of the barbarity, or culture of their manners.[7]

The consequences for sexual norms were equally profound. The basic presumption that women were somehow morally superior to men was to become one of the cornerstones of late eighteenth-, nineteenth-, and twentieth-century gender relations. As Byron wrote to Annabella Milbanke in September 1813, recycling the platitude as countless other suitors must have done, 'I think the worst woman that ever existed would have made a *man* of very passable reputation – they are all better than us – and their faults such as they are must originate with ourselves'. In public, too, this notion came to be endlessly celebrated, by men and women alike. Already by the middle of the eighteenth century its growing power was clearly visible. The stereotype of the libertine reformed by the love of a good woman epitomized the presumption that promiscuity was natural, even attractive, in men, but could be cured by exposure to superior female morality. No writer grappled with this theme as persistently as Richardson. How infuriating it was, he mused privately, 'that many, very many young women . . . will admire a good man; but they will marry a bad one. – Are not rakes pretty fellows?' 'All women flatter themselves, that even the man whom they know to have been base to *others*, will not, cannot, be so to *them*.' His *Familiar Letters* accordingly warned that 'the wild assertion of a rake making a good husband, was the most dangerous opinion a young woman could imbibe'; and *Clarissa* itself was expressly written to combat 'that dangerous but too commonly received notion, *that a reformed rake makes the best husband*.'[8]

Yet paradoxically there was scarcely another author who promoted a more exalted view of the transformative power of female chastity over male rapacity. In his first novel, constant exposure to Pamela's virtue brings the libertine Mr B to feel that 'I shall not think I deserve her, till I can bring my manners, my sentiments, and my actions, to a conformity with her own'. As the novel's introduction shows, she was intended to have the same effect on her readers: 'May every headstrong libertine whose hands you reach, be reclaimed', it urged, 'and every tempted virgin who reads you, imitate the virtue, and meet the reward' of the heroine. The superior morality of Clarissa likewise transforms Lovelace's closest friend, John Belford, so that he repents, reforms, resolves to seek out and rescue all his former victims, and ends up a happy husband and father. Even the worst rakes, after exposure to the sensibility of a chaste virgin, die remorseful for their past actions. That is the fate of Sir Hargrave Pollexfen, the evil libertine in *Sir Charles Grandison*, and of Lovelace himself. In fiction, as in real life, the idea of women's moral superiority was tremendously strong.[9]

Beyond this obvious, superficial inference lay a deeper truth. In fact, the presumption that women should tame male sexuality by exhibiting their supposedly innate modesty reflected, and perpetuated, female inferiority. Most writers took this for granted, and applauded it. 'As nature has given man the superiority above woman, by endowing him with greater strength both of mind and body,' wrote Hume, 'it is his part to alleviate that superiority, as much as possible, by the generosity of his behaviour, and by a studied deference and complaisance for all her inclinations and opinions.' Do not 'let it be thought hard, that a

character so amiable and exalted should be allotted to a state of hon-
oured subordination,' commented one of George III's chaplains, for

a mind thus gentle and thus adorned exalts subordination itself into the power
of superiority and command. It carries with it the influence and irresistible force
of virtue; which is of weight to control the most boisterous passions, and by a
steady perseverance in goodness, to subdue and to win the most obdurate heart.[10]

Worse still, the new conventions of politeness exposed women to
constant sexual interest and engagement, whilst tending to absolve
men of responsibility for their supposedly natural rapacity. As novelists and commentators loved to point out, dangerous men were often
polished and attractive company: the most 'irresistible gentlemen
among us' were in fact 'your ruiners of ladies', the ones addicted to
'woman-slaughter'. Even 'delicate women', lamented Hannah More,
too often competed for 'the attentions of a popular libertine, whose
voluble small talk they admire, and whose sprightly nothings they
quote, and whom perhaps their very favour tends to prevent from
becoming a better character, because he finds himself more acceptable
as he is'. Because there was no equivalent loosening of strictures
against female unchastity, the net effect was to place most of the psychological and practical burden for correct behaviour on women. The
unchaste man, observed the actress Mary Robinson acidly,

pleads the frailty of human nature ... he urges the sovereignty of the passions, the dominion of the senses, the sanction of long established custom. He
is a man of universal gallantry; he is consequently courted and idolized by the
generality of women, though all his days and all his actions prove, that
woman is the victim of his falsehood.

Courtship between men and women, wrote Lady Mary Wortley Montagu to a suitor in 1710, was nothing but a cruel bloodsport: ''tis play
to you, but 'tis death to us'. The way things were, agreed Steele,
'females adventure all against those who have nothing to lose'; and
afterwards 'they have nothing but empty sighs, tears and reproaches
against those who reduced them to real sorrow and infamy'.* In

* Cf. *Disraeli's Reminiscences*, ed. Helen M. Swartz and Marvin Swartz (1975), 120:
'Lady Tankerville asked Lord Lyndhurst, whether he believed in Platonic Friendship?
"After, but not before" was the reply.'

short, for all the rhetoric about superior female manners disciplining male sexuality, the main consequence of new doctrines of politeness and civility was to constrain *female* behaviour.[11]

Of course, the expression of male lust was in fact no more 'natural' than the conventions of female restraint: men could simply adopt or reject libertine attitudes, consciously or unconsciously, to a greater or lesser degree. Yet over time, the presumption that women were naturally chaste, and men not, was given increasingly elaborate scientific foundations. In the early eighteenth century, theories of politeness laid particular stress, for both sexes, on the learning of correct manners. From the middle of the century onwards, however, it became more common to emphasize the expression of supposedly natural sensibilities. Building on the intellectual advances of Locke and Newton, the leading scientists and physicians of the day developed a new, dominant paradigm about the nature of human psychology, sensory perception, and the nervous system. Amongst the many media through which it was popularized, novels, with their obsessive attention to emotional states, played a leading part – Richardson, for example, drew on the expertise of his friend and doctor George Cheyne in order to describe exactly how human beings experienced feelings and events. This way of thinking now became the basis for the conviction that women inherently, bodily, ought to have more 'delicacy', 'tenderness', 'softness', 'imagination', 'sensibility', and sexual purity. It followed that the physical and psychological causes and effects of unchastity differed profoundly in the two sexes:

The consequences resulting from the infidelity of a husband and wife are very different. It is the nature of man that he may have a connexion with other women, beside his wife, and yet have a sincere affection for her; but a married woman never yet made a sacrifice of virtue without, at the same time, making a sacrifice of every sentiment of honour, decency and decorum, which are guardians of connubial felicity and domestic happiness.[12]

This growing stress on the 'naturalness' of female chastity was one crucial way in which the intellectual foundations of patriarchy were gradually reshaped. By 1700, many of the age-old justifications for female subordination had been called into question by broader political and philosophical developments. The status of biblical and

patristic writings was challenged by the rise of 'reasoned' understandings of truth. The presumption of an unchanging, divinely ordained,
paternal order was fatally undermined by the deposition of James II
and the rise of contract theories of politics and social relations. Finally,
existing social theories were challenged by novel economic and social
developments: the decline of courtly influence, the increasing pre-
eminence of urban life, and the expansion of new kinds of commerce,
communication, and social organization.

The ways in which male superiority was justified evolved accordingly. Earlier understandings of patriarchy and sexuality had been
based on an essentially theological view of the imperfection of *all*
human beings. For all their misogynistic tendencies, they had always
implied that, though women were weaker than men, they shared a
basic commonality of psychology and biology. Yet by 1800, scriptural
precedents for female subordination were no longer a conventional
starting-point; nor the theology of original sin and female weakness;
nor even classical medical theories, which had stressed that male and
female bodies, though similar, tended to differ in their balance of
'humours'. None of these ideas completely disappeared, but the ultimate foundations of gender difference were now more commonly sought
in anthropological and historical theories about the evolution and
purpose of sexual and social relations, and in supposedly unassailable
biological facts about mental and bodily differences between the sexes.

In some areas, the new kinds of reasoning allowed for greater
equality – an obvious example is the increasing (albeit piecemeal)
acceptance of women writing for the public, which in previous ages
had been treated as a fundamentally unfeminine act. In the sphere of
sexual relations, however, the opposite occurred: the division between
the supposed sexual character of men and women was sharpened. It
was still almost universally taken for granted that allowing women
greater sexual autonomy would create anarchy. In consequence, new
descriptions of human nature tended to defend this basic principle.
Often they stressed that chastity was desirable in both sexes, the route
to greatest happiness for men as well as women. On the other hand,
they also often accepted that men tended to be more promiscuous.
And almost always they found that the natural state of women was to
be chaste. As the influential moralist John Brown explained in 1765,

it was ultimately from women's obvious 'delicacy of body' and 'delicate timidity of mind' that 'the great female virtue of chastity ariseth on its strongest and most impregnable foundations'. The same basic presumption that women were inherently modest was central to the massively influential doctrines of Jean-Jacques Rousseau, the great late eighteenth-century theorist of nature and custom.[13]

This increasing naturalization of ideas about female chastity powerfully shaped subsequent models of appropriate feminine behaviour. At the same time as conversation between the sexes was increasingly held up as an essential part of civilized life, and new demands were made of women to engage socially with men, they were simultaneously constrained to show ever more elaborate outward manifestations of their supposedly superior, asexual morality. By the end of the century, feminists decried with increasing resentment what they saw as the mindless, artificial code of femininity that was created by these twin pressures. It was perverse, exclaimed Mary Hays, how men 'talk indeed of female virtue, and seem even by their laws, to consider it as the chief bond of society; yet never scruple to break this bond' with base deceit. Women were 'much degraded by mistaken notions of female excellence', complained Mary Wollstonecraft: 'woman, weak woman! Made by her education the slave of sensibility, is required, on the most trying occasions, to resist that sensibility'.* As the witty (and unmarried) historian Lucy Aikin put it:

> Ah! feigned humility to scorn allied,
> That stoops to conquer, flatters to deride!
> Learn, thoughtless woman, learn his arts to scan,
> And dread that fearful portent . . . kneeling man![14]

---

* The same point was to be made by John Stuart Mill in 1826: 'Good treatment of women . . . is one of the surest marks of high civilization. But it seems to be very little considered, in what good treatment of women consists. It does not consist in treating them as idols to be worshipped, or as trinkets to be worn for display; any more than in shutting them up like jewels in a case, removed from the light of the sun and the sight of men. In both cases, this treatment is a proof that they are valued; else why are so much pains taken about them? But in both cases they are valued exactly like beautiful trinkets; the value set upon them is quite compatible with perfect indifference to their happiness or misery.' *The Collected Works of John Stuart Mill*, ed. J. M. Robson et al., 33 vols (1963–91), xx. 45–6.

So deeply ingrained had the underlying presumptions become by 1800, however, that even Wollstonecraft herself took for granted that women *were* naturally more modest; that 'all the causes of female weakness ... branch out of one grand cause – want of chastity in men'; and that the primary need was for men to 'become more chaste and modest'. Most other feminists presumed the same. Her friend Hays, though an equally bold thinker, writer, and life-long enemy of sexual convention, thought it obvious that

modesty is innate in a greater degree in women than in men. The history of all nations, – of the human race, wild and tame, social and savage, – all, all agree in this great truth; and would delicacy permit, a thousand and a thousand arguments might be adduced to support a fact, so undeniably, so sacredly true; – so dear to the happiness of individuals and society; – so essential to domestic bliss. And, at the same time a truth, the most honorable, and flattering for the female sex; enslaved and mortified as they are, in so many other cases.[15]

That females in general were chaster than males, and that it was important they should remain so, was for her a law of reason and nature alike. Throughout the nineteenth century, and up to the very end of the twentieth century, this idea only gained in strength, until it had become almost universally accepted as a completely self-evident fact. Indeed, it was to be one of the central premises of nineteenth- and twentieth-century feminism, and a source of great moral authority for women in their claims for social and political rights. In historical terms this was ironic. The idea of women's moral superiority was originally promoted as a means of improving male manners – yet in practice it ended up strengthening the sexual double standard.

NATURE AND NURTURE

Our focus thus far has been on the emergence of new ideas about masculinity and femininity in general. The second important theme in all thinking about male promiscuity and female chastity was that of social difference. We have seen already that this was integral to ideas about masculine behaviour. Libertines were always held to prey on women of inferior status, their sexual potency confirming, rather than transgressing, other hierarchies of power. The idea that manners were shaped by environmental and social influences was equally central to ideals of politeness. It also came to be increasingly prominent in attitudes to female morality, for even the most extravagant believers in the inherent virtue of women acknowledged that modesty also had to be learned and reinforced – 'especially in this age', as William Ramesey had pointed out, 'wherein they need to be furnished with abundance of virtue, to withstand the continual assaults men make on their chastity'.[1]

Everyone could agree that morality was the product of both nature and nurture. The real questions were more complicated. What exactly was the balance between the two? What kind of education best instilled virtue? How far could it ever overcome the constraints of birth and class? Were poor women not bound to be inevitably less chaste, less perfectly feminine? Such issues had been implicit in earlier thinking about immorality, but from around 1700 they took on much greater and more explicit importance in all discussions of sexual morality, social policy, and relations between the sexes. The outcome was a much firmer association between chastity and social class than had ever existed before.

Intertwined with the new obsession with male seduction were many older commonplaces about the weakness, vanity, and inferiority of women, their sexual culpability, and the essential vileness of unchaste females. Even the idea that all women were secretly lustful (as Alexander Pope notoriously put it, that 'every woman is, at heart, a rake')[2] lived on, albeit in muted form, in facetious and erotic works. However, it now became much more common to stress that women only became sexually avaricious, if they ever did, through improper stimulation. Female lust was an essentially dormant passion. If aroused outside the proper outlet of marriage, it could range out of control, turning its possessor into an a-feminine monster: that is what happened to fallen women. Yet normally it did not motivate women as it did men. So the key question became: what made some women more vulnerable to male seduction than others?

The answer, it seemed, lay mainly in their education and environment. These were the forces that shaped every woman's moral sense – which either accentuated her feminine weakness, making her more liable to fall, or were able to counter it and bolster her virtue. Before 1700, this hadn't meant much more than imbibing religious instruction and avoiding bad company. Piety was supposed to breed modesty; whereas religious ignorance, and the wrong kinds of friends, pushed men and women down the slippery slope of vice. In the eighteenth century, however, the effects of environment came to be approached and described in much more wide-ranging terms.

The old fear that, deep down, women's passions were as strong as those of men, was now translated into ever more detailed prescriptions for the repression of feminine sexuality. As Clarissa herself warned her friend Anna Howe, women had to be more self-disciplined, or they'd end up as bad as men:

Learn, my dear, I beseech you learn, to subdue your own passions. Be the motives what they will, excess is excess. Those passions in our sex, which we take no pains to subdue, may have one and the same source with those infinitely blacker passions which we used so often to condemn in the violent and headstrong of the other sex; and which may be heightened in them only by custom, and their freer education. Let us both, my dear, ponder well this thought; look into ourselves, and fear.[3]

Yet even in prescriptive literature this was never a straightforward ideal. In reality, moreover, as the novelists of the age explored with considerable sensitivity, the new stress on female asexuality and innocence created a profound ambiguity.[4] If modesty was innate, how could it be cultivated? Was artlessness an admirable quality, the essence of modesty; or was it in fact a dangerous weakness, liable to leave girls defenceless against the wiles of the world? This was the great tension in all eighteenth-century novels about courtship, seduction, and the sexual predicament of women – the minefield through which all its heroines were compelled to tread.

Conversely, what kind of education and environment would make a woman *more* susceptible to immorality? In the sixteenth and seventeenth centuries the answer had always been a general one: people fell because they failed to control their own corrupt inclinations. In the eighteenth century this stress on personal responsibility was increasingly overlaid by an appreciation of the social forces that affected different groups in society. Daniel Defoe's *Moll Flanders* (1722) is an early example of this new approach. In most respects the description of Moll's sexual career follows an old-fashioned, universal narrative of personal sin and redemption. It is 'the devil' who tempts her ever further into wickedness, and her own weakness that makes her give way. Throughout the book, though, as elsewhere in Defoe's writing of the 1720s, there are also clear glimpses of more modern ways of thinking about the particular, structural vulnerability of poor, ill-educated women. Especially telling is the description of how Moll first loses her virginity, and sets off down the slippery slope to perdition. As in all sin, her own passions are partly to blame. She has 'the common vanity of my sex' and 'my head full of pride', which make her an easy prey. But the real forces of evil are twofold. The first is the sexual guile of upper-class men. Like Pamela after her, like countless other young, unsuspecting maidservants, she is ensnared by a wicked, experienced bachelor who knows exactly 'how to catch a woman in his net as a partridge', whilst for her part 'knowing nothing of the wickedness of the times, I had not one thought of my own safety or of my virtue about me'.[5]

The second root cause is Moll's inappropriate education, which has left her with 'a most unbounded stock of vanity and pride, and but a very little stock of virtue'. Like every orthodox author before and after him, Defoe took for granted that only a thoroughly religious upbringing and environment could safely guide men and women through life. Without such 'divine assistance', even well-intentioned persons could never 'preserve the most solemn resolutions of virtue'. Instead, Moll, who starts off as an honest, industrious orphan girl, is left deficient in virtue by being educated and habituated to a way of living above her real station in life.[6] Within a few decades, as the balance swung firmly towards structural explanations of female seduction and degradation, this had become an endlessly elaborated commonplace – one that seemed to capture the ways in which nature and nurture conspired to render some women much more vulnerable (and some men more rapacious) than others.

The increasing conviction that upbringing was more important than innate sinfulness was based on new ideas about the malleability of human nature. In particular, the immense, ever-growing authority of John Locke's theories of selfhood and custom, set out in his *Essay Concerning Human Understanding* (1689) and *Some Thoughts Concerning Education* (1693), had by the middle decades of the eighteenth century helped overturn the established Christian convention that all mortals were born intrinsically corrupted by original sin. Instead, it became conventional to observe, as Locke had, 'that of all the men we meet with, nine parts of ten are what they are, good or evil, useful or not, by their education'.[7] Differences of character were not innate, but largely learned.

This principle came to dominate the explanation of sexual mores. A prime cause of adultery, noted a critic in 1739, was obviously 'the wrong, I may say, wretched way of educating our youth: particularly our young ladies' – 'I beg you, sir, to reflect a little, how our young misses of rank and quality, and even some shopkeepers' daughters are educated'. Exposing them to frivolity, luxury, and constant social intercourse with men, as the modern fashion did, was the surest way to disaster. By the 1740s, Richardson's characters are all to be understood in similar terms. How do we explain libertinism? Like this: Mr B is so ungoverned because

his poor dear mother spoiled him at first. Nobody must speak to him or contradict him, as I have heard, when he was a child, and so he has not been used to be controlled and cannot bear the least thing that crosses his violent will.

Why are some women more easily corrupted than others? Well, Lovelace explains, Sally Martin and Polly Horton, the archetypal fallen women in *Clarissa*, were 'creatures who, brought up too high for their fortunes, and to a taste of pleasure and the public diversions, had fallen an easy prey to his seducing arts'. It was not they personally, but their parents

who were in a great measure answerable for their miscarriages, by indulging them in the fashionable follies and luxury of an age given up to those amusements and pleasures which are so apt to set people of but middle fortunes above all the useful employments of life; and to make young women an easy prey to rakes and libertines.[8]

This was to become a major theme in all analyses of seduction and prostitution. Education or aspiration above their station was the fatal weakness that made some women more susceptible to sexual danger. Sometimes, it is true, this was conceived of simply as an intrinsic female tendency. 'Was it vanity, the childish vanity of dress that so beguiled you?' a Hackney clergyman chided the fallen women of his parish in 1791,

Did you yield to the solicitation of someone superior to yourself to gratify the pride of being better dressed, supplied with money, and living at your ease? And did you expect that the same profusion which supplied you then would continue to support you in the way that your foolish heart might wish? Your own experience has shown you your mistake ... Root out therefore from your heart the very wish of dressing or aspiring beyond the state in which the providence of God hath placed you. Whenever you are enticed by those above you, whether they be your masters, your master's sons or friends, or whoever else, ruin must ensue if you have not the resolution to withstand the bribes with which your virtue is assailed.[9]

From this perspective, with its orthodox Christian emphasis on personal discipline in the face of temptation, foolish women were at least partly culpable for their own ruin. More commonly, however, the blame for faulty principles was laid at the door of parents who gave their daughters an over-refined education. That this created exactly the kind of frivolous, pleasure-loving victims most at risk of sexual danger was the standard argument in most fictional accounts – even the ultra-condensed *Innocence Betrayed* noted in passing that the father of poor, guiltless Sarah Martin had 'educated his daughter in a style rather above their situation'. The proper ideal, accordingly, was for poor girls at risk of seduction to 'be instructed, not in ornamental learning, above their stations, but in the menial offices of domestic servitude'.[10]

The idea that women were conditioned into vice, rather than personally to blame, was extended still further by more systematic thinkers. Henry Fielding's reading of history persuaded him that even the most depraved harlots of the past 'derived their iniquity rather from the general corruption which then prevailed, than from any extraordinary disparity in their own nature; and that a Livilla, a Messalina, an Agrippina or a Poppæa, might in better times have made chaste and virtuous matrons'. It was clear, he concluded, 'That if weak women go astray, / *The Age* is more at fault than they.'[11]

This line of thinking became especially popular with feminists, who developed it into a penetrating critique of female indoctrination. More women were led into unchastity, wrote Catharine Macaulay in 1790, 'by the ignorance, the prejudices, and the false craft of those by whom they are educated, than from any other cause founded either in nature or in chance'. It was perverse to educate women to be innocent and unworldly. At best this left them helpless and enervated; at worst, it distorted them into mindless, unnatural coquettes. Either way, such cultivated weakness actually increased the risks of seduction, unchastity, and prostitution. The real solution to these evils was not to lay ever-greater restraints on women, but to stop treating them as brainless sex-objects. Only when men and women were equally free to develop their natural reason would real chastity flourish, in both sexes. This was one of the principal themes of Mary Wollstonecraft's *Vindication of the Rights of Woman* (1792), as of many earlier and later attacks on the artificiality and iniquity of modern sexual roles.[12]

By the second half of the eighteenth century explanations of female sexual susceptibility thus ranged widely – but what they shared was a tendency to blame undesirable social trends, rather than innate female lust. Yet the practical effect of this new way of thinking was highly ambiguous.

At one level, it contributed to the growing perception that even fallen women retained some innocence, that their further ruin was not inevitable, and that they might rejoin society. This idea had obvious roots in orthodox Christian teaching about personal sin and redemption. It also extended St Augustine's famous argument that chastity was 'not a treasure which can be stolen without the mind's consent'. As one public writer put it in 1757, 'incontinence is not always a proof of unchastity. Many unhappy fair ones, won by soothing solicitations, have confided in false promises, and devoted their persons to an indiscreet affection, who have nevertheless retained their chastity, and been unpolluted in their minds.' 'I never was vicious so much from a depravity of nature as from a kind of habitual infamy,' argued an imprisoned prostitute in 1773. She retained the seeds of a virtuous education; she was not yet despoiled 'of every tender sensation, of every delicacy of thought, of every desirable quality necessary to render our sex amiable. And though I have suffered them to sleep, or permitted them to mix with the grosser passions, I have not totally discarded them.'[13]

This notion that, just as sexual vice was learned, it could also be unlearned, was increasingly popular with late eighteenth and nineteenth-century philanthropists (as we shall see in the next chapter). It also appealed to feminists and others who noted that the moral and worldly ruin of seduced women was essentially a matter of custom. Females were not driven to prostitution because one slip irrevocably degraded their morals, but because the world (and other women in particular) so cruelly ostracized them. No one shunned libertine men, exclaimed Mary Robinson, who had had many lovers herself – yet how unfair was the fate of most fallen women:

CUSTOM, that pliant and convenient friend to man, declares her infamous.
. . .

She has no remedy. She appeals to the feeling and reflecting part of mankind; they pity, but they do not seek to redress her; she flies to her own sex, they not only condemn, but they avoid her.

It was a 'trite and foolish observation', argued Catharine Macaulay,

that the first fault against chastity in woman has a radical power to deprave the character. But no such frail beings come out of the hands of Nature. The human mind is built of nobler materials than to be easily corrupted; and with all their disadvantages of situation and education, women seldom become entirely abandoned till they are thrown into a state of desperation, by the venomous rancour of their own sex.

However natural it might be for virtuous women to feel 'hatred, contempt, and terror' for prostitutes, agreed Mary Hays, it was wrong. Even the worst whores were ultimately the victims of 'profligate men' and 'unfortunate circumstances'. So every woman should instead 'look inward upon herself and say – If I have more purity of heart and conduct, than these unfortunate sisters, have I not more cause for thankfulness than triumph?'[14]

Yet, on the other hand, even the most sympathetic reformers tended to concede that continued promiscuity did render women 'a disgrace to their sex and to human nature'. And the more common presumption remained that a single slip irreparably polluted a woman and destroyed her virtue. William Paley, one of the most influential moralists of the later eighteenth century, was typical in his view that even a woman who had been deceitfully seduced was nonetheless turned immediately into a whore: 'As a woman collects her virtue into this point, the loss of her chastity is generally *the destruction of her moral principle*; and this consequence is to be apprehended, whether the criminal intercourse be discovered or not.' Even Bentham thought it illogical to speak of the seduction of a 'concubine' or 'common harlot'. Such women had no virtue to lose: even to rape one would not necessarily be a crime.[15] In short, alongside the elevation of female innocence, and a new sympathy for the prostitute as victim, the eighteenth century also saw a continued, and in some respects increased, contempt for immodest women.

It is easy to see why this should have been so. The falling away of judicial punishment, combined with increasing freedom for men, placed ever heavier demands on respectable women. Their self-discipline was now the key to all sexual propriety. For a woman to fail in this duty, when her entire culture depended on it, was therefore unforgivable. This was a point on which even libertines and churchmen agreed. As Lovelace scoffed, 'because we *men* cannot resist temptation, is that a reason that *women* ought not, when the whole of their education is caution and warning against our attempts?' It was not. At best a woman's unchastity showed fatal weakness, at worst it raised suspicions of lecherous complicity. Either way, her fall transformed the female into a sexual and social enemy. Fallen women stole away men; they degenerated into repulsive, unfeminine harpies; and they threatened to corrupt other women into the same way of life. For all these reasons they had to be shunned – especially by their own sex.[16]

This attitude was further sharpened by the new association between education and chastity. The fact that the working classes were especially in danger of seduction garnered them some pity and understanding. (Women 'in low life', noted Paley, were 'most exposed to solicitations of this sort'.) But in many observers their susceptibility provoked disdain rather than sympathy, as it seemed to confirm the basic point that poorer women were less refined – and hence more likely to be, or become, immoral. Women below 'the middle rank', wrote Mandeville in 1724, were not as well-instructed in modesty, and if they had but the least 'degree of beauty ... to provoke young men ... their chastity can never hold out long, but must infallibly surrender'. All women were to some extent 'guarded and defended' from lust, concurred Defoe, when he read this passage, but such 'innate modesty ... among people of condition, is always improved by education'.[17]

By 1740, this fusion of social condescension with the sexual double standard was central to the plot of *Pamela*, in which the heroine is oppressed not just by the conventions of feminine subordination, but by her immense social inferiority. The difficulty of defending chastity without offending social propriety is one of the book's chief themes. All her superiors presume that, given her twin handicaps, she must succumb to the inevitable. Yet if she does they will doubly condemn her – for her weakness and her immodesty. She was but 'painted dirt', sneers Mr B's sister, thinking Pamela has given way. 'I did indeed pity you while I thought you innocent', but now she despises her: 'Oh *Pamela, Pamela*, I am sorry for thy thus aping thy betters, and giving thyself such airs; I see thou art quite spoiled! Of a modest, innocent girl, that thou was, and humble too, thou now art fit for nothing in the world, but what I fear thou art.' Similar presumptions fuelled the many hostile reactions of 'anti-Pamela' readers like Henry Fielding, who objected to the story as inherently implausible, even subversive. From their perspective, it seemed that in any such a situation either the lower-class woman would certainly give in, or she was secretly complicit herself – either way, she was bound to be wanting in virtue and chastity. As one gentlemanly critic remarked contemptuously, Pamela was nothing more than 'a little pert minx, whom any man of common sense or address might have had on his own terms in a week or a fortnight'.[18]

It has long been appreciated that the decades around 1800 were the period in which the English middling and working classes first became visible as coherent and self-conscious groups, and in which class became the predominant way of dividing up society. It has also been shown, more recently, that ideologies of gender were central to the formation of class identity.[19] What we see in debates about morality and social structure is the reverse of this: how the growing importance of ideas about class influenced ideas about masculinity and femininity.

By Victorian times, extraordinarily elaborate hypotheses about the connection were routinely put forward. For reasons of physiology and culture alike, noted the Christian physician and feminist Elizabeth Blackwell in the 1880s, the working classes were sexually unrestrained in the same way as primitive peoples and animals: 'in the savage state, existing in wild regions of country, and in the slums of all great towns, both men and women are grossly unchaste'. To countless educated observers, the immodesty and lasciviousness of plebeian women was axiomatic.[20]

The origin of such attitudes can already be glimpsed a century earlier. 'The lower class of women', sniffed one educated writer in 1772, had no sexual inhibitions at all. They were attracted to black men, 'for reasons too brutal to mention; they would connect themselves with horses and asses, if the law permitted them'. This was an extreme view, but from the perspective of many later eighteenth-century commentators it seemed obvious that, on the whole, working women were less educated, and so less civilized, less feminine, and less virtuous. This was not their personal failing but a systematic social problem. 'London is so much the sink of vice, that the lower class of people are very much corrupted,' observed a clergyman in 1786. In consequence, 'there are few servant maids in London, or indeed in the country, but what are whores; it is perhaps an uncharitable supposition, but it is nevertheless true.' Unchastity meant nothing to common women, agreed a lawyer: 'in the lower order of the people, the force of transactions of this nature is lost, through want of possessing the nicer feelings'. Female chastity was manifestly the product of 'custom, habit, and education', rather than 'natural and inherent', noted another critic, and for that reason 'there are fewer unchaste women, even in proportion to their numbers, among those of rank and condition, than there are chaste among these of an inferior order, though the lives of the first are generally lazy and luxurious'. Dr Johnson likewise took for granted that 'the more people are taught, the more modest they are', and that therefore 'so far as I have observed, the higher the rank, the richer ladies are, they are the better instructed and more virtuous'.[21]

This was hardly an uncontested view. Boswell, for one, disagreed. 'The notion of the world, Sir', he countered, 'is, that the morals of women of quality are worse than those in lower stations.' Indeed it is obvious that the later eighteenth century also saw increasing public criticism of the supposed immorality of upper class men and women. But this was part of the same intellectual development. The main point is simply that, by the later eighteenth century, it had become conventional to think about morality in class terms, and to take for granted that different social groups had different sexual mores.[22]

The ultimate outcome of these various ways of considering nature and nurture was a profound double consciousness, which was to reach its apogee under the Victorians, and persist into the twentieth century. At one level there was established a powerful presumption of female sexual innocence and victimhood, which for many observers extended even to prostitutes. Yet at the same time the sexuality of uneducated women was often viewed with suspicion, and, even in philanthropic thought, whores were also routinely abhorred as disgusting and depraved. Thus male rapacity could be deplored, yet fallen women ostracized, and working women treated as imperfectly feminine. The balance between sympathy and disgust obviously differed from observer to observer; but few commentators escaped this kind of double-think altogether. It was the Enlightenment development of new associations between morality, education, and class that allowed it to flourish.

MARRIAGE AND MONEY

The third major theme underlying all eighteenth-century discussions of seduction was anxiety about the state of modern marriage. The problem seemed to be that, nowadays, people married only for money, or not at all. Propertied men disdained wedlock because it had become so easy to 'indulge themselves in an illicit intercourse'. Worse still, they abused the rituals of courtship in order to seduce women: sleeping with them under promise of marriage but then abandoning them. When men and women did marry, for the wrong, mercenary reasons, it led to ill-matched couples, unhappy unions, and adultery.[1]

These basic themes had first been explored at length in seventeenth-century fiction, poetry and drama. Francis Bacon's utopian fable, *New Atlantis* (1627), laments the decline of matrimony:

when men have at hand a remedy more agreeable to their corrupt will, marriage is almost expulsed. And therefore there are with you seen infinite men that marry not, but choose rather a libertine and impure single life, than to be yoked in marriage ... And when they do marry, what is marriage to them but a very bargain; wherein is sought alliance, or portion, or reputation ... and not the faithful nuptial union of man and wife, that was first instituted.

Or, as Samuel Butler put it a few decades later,

> For matrimony's but a bargain made
> To serve the turns of interest and trade;
> Not out of love or kindness, but designs,
> To settle land and tenements like fines.

Tragic plays often explored the unhappy consequences of young people forced into loveless marriage. In comedy, likewise, the contrast between spontaneous love and contrived wedlock was a popular theme.[2] As many scholars have pointed out, however, this was only ever a limited critique. It simultaneously celebrated the ideal of happy, affectionate marriage, and its force was restrained by the evident artificiality of theatrical plots and settings.

It was only after the Glorious Revolution of 1688, as part of the more general moral panic about the state of the nation, that the apparent degeneration of marriage came to be a topic of serious public discussion. Most early commentators presumed it was a recent development, but pretty soon its prevalence became a stock trope amongst social analysts. The *Tatler*, the *Guardian*, and the *Spectator* all decried it. In 1727, Daniel Defoe coined the phrase 'legal prostitution', which became a popular and enduring shorthand for the evils of loveless, arranged marriages.[3]

It was also a favourite theme of many early feminists. Most men took wives only for money, complained Mary Astell, a life-long spinster; like slaves, women were 'sold ... into mercenary hands' and tyrannized by their husbands. One of Astell's readers, Sarah Cowper, who as the rich, orphaned, daughter of a merchant had found herself trapped in marriage to an ambitious baronet, recorded bitterly in her diary that she had 'all my days lived a slave'. When her husband finally died in 1706, she reminded herself henceforth to 'lead your life in freedom and liberty, and throw not your self into slavery'. Such was the lust and calculating avarice of modern man, protested Sarah Fyge (soon herself to be forced into a loveless union), that even were 'polygamy allow'd',

> Yet all his wives would surely be abhorr'd,
> And some common *Lais* [i.e. whore] be ador'd.
> Most mortally the name of wife they hate,
> Yet they will take one as their proper fate,
> That they may have a child legitimate,
> To be their heir, if they have an estate,
> Or else to bear their names: so, for by ends,
> They take a wife, and satisfy their friends,
> Who are desirous that it should be so,
> And for that end, perhaps, estates bestow;
> Which, when possess'd is spent another way;
> The spurious issue do the right betray,
> And with their mother-strumpets are maintain'd;
> The wife and children by neglect disdain'd,
> Wretched and poor unto their friends return,
> Having got nothing, unless cause to mourn.[4]

By the middle of the eighteenth century it had become a standard subject of fiction and serious writing alike that marrying for money was a ubiquitous problem amongst the propertied classes, the root cause of endless unhappiness, seduction, prostitution, adultery, and immorality. All the leading artists and writers of the period proceed from this premise. The perversity of the marriage market was one of Richardson's main targets. In *Clarissa*, even Lovelace's evil character is blamed on it. It was only when the woman he had wanted to marry jilted him for 'a coronet' (i.e., an aristocrat) that he had turned bad, vowing to revenge himself 'upon as many of the sex as shall come into my power'.[5] Hogarth's series *Marriage à la Mode* (1745) brilliantly illustrated the same subject. In the first scene we meet the protagonists – the fatuous spendthrift earl, desperate for money; his degenerate son, already poxed from too much whoring; the rich, boorish middle-class Alderman, trading his unwilling daughter for status; and the girl herself, forced by this unnatural marriage into shameful adultery. By the end, her lover has been executed for murdering her husband, the miserable wife has poisoned herself, and her miserly, stone-hearted father strips her dying body of its jewels. The only innocent party, her newborn baby, is already crippled and diseased from inherited syphilis – symbolizing not just the fatal unhealthiness of its parents but the dangerous moral and physical corruption of the entire ruling class (see plates 6 and 7).

Why did mercenary marriage become such a fixation? The most basic reason was the increasingly sharp sense that matrimony was not a timeless, God-given institution but merely a fragile human invention. Until the Reformation, it had been a divine sacrament. By the later eighteenth century, however, it had become firmly established that the laws of marriage were merely customary and changeable: as a result, marital trends came to be scrutinized anxiously for signs of social malaise. As Dr Johnson, that great modern conservative, put it, wedlock was a wholly artificial yet socially indispensable construct, which needed all the help it could get from laws and conventions:

it is so far from being natural for a man and woman to live in a state of marriage, that we find all the motives which they have for remaining in that connection, and the restraints which civilized society imposes to prevent separation, are hardly sufficient to keep them together.[6]

There were also various more specific reasons for the growing obsession. One was that the advance of male liberty led to a real increase in fornication and seduction under promise of marriage. As Joseph Priestley put it in 1778, 'the number of women who are debauched by those who really intend to marry them at the time, is small in comparison with those who are seduced by persons who had no such intention'. We can measure this, crudely but unmistakably, in the numbers of children conceived out of wedlock. During the seventeenth century this figure had been extremely low: by 1650 only about 1 per cent of all births were illegitimate. Thereafter it increased steadily, to unprecedented levels. By 1800, about a quarter of all women who gave birth for the first time were unmarried. How many of these were the victims of calculated seduction, rather than a genuine court-ship that foundered, we shall never know (and in any case the distinction is obviously not a clear-cut one). Yet very many of these women had certainly had sex in the expectation of marriage. This was evidently a general trend: by 1800, almost 40 per cent of women who *did* marry were also already pregnant.[7]

In eighteenth-century London, the proportion of illegitimate births (and hence, we may presume, the incidence of seduction) had grown to be much higher than in the rest of the country. The few statistics we have suggest that, if anything, middling and upper-class bachelors were over-represented amongst those who impregnated and then abandoned plebeian single women. Their stories are echoed in Moll Flanders's account of how her mistress's son tricked her into having sex by acting 'as if there was no such thing as any kind of love but that which tended to matrimony', and assuring her 'that he resolv'd to marry me as soon as he came into his estate; that in the mean time, if I would grant his request, he would maintain me very honourably; and made me a thousand protestations of his sincerity and of his affection to me; and that he would never abandon me'. Only later does she realize 'that he had never spoken a word of having me for a wife after he had conquer'd me for a mistress'.[8]

Libertines in high society used the same approach. It was, for instance, the tactic of Charles Calvert, Lord Baltimore, when pursuing the attractive young widow Mary Pendarves in the later 1720s. For several years he courted her, whilst secretly sleeping with other women. Finally, he moved in for the kill, declaring his love openly and pretending that sex was a necessary prelude to a happy marriage. 'Our conversation,' Mary recalled later,

> began with common talk of news. Some marriage was named, and we both observed how little probability of happiness there was in most of the fashionable matches where interest and not inclination was consulted. At last he said he was determined never to marry, unless he was well assured of the affection of the person he married. My reply was, 'can you have stronger proof (if the person is at her own disposal) than her consenting to marry you?' He replied that was not sufficient.

The implication was obvious. (When she demurred, he walked out, leaving her broken-hearted.) So notorious was this snare by mid-century that Lady Bradshaigh thought it inexcusable for any sensible girl to be 'tempted by such an old bait as a promise of marriage'.[9]

Another reason for the mounting concern over mercenary unions was the growth of the marriage market. Matrimony had always been a matter of prudential calculation. The greater a family's estate, the more pressing their concern over its preservation, and the more likely that suitable matches would be carefully arranged by the parents and kin, rather than the children themselves. At all levels of propertied society, negotiations over money (dowries, portions, marital property, and inheritance) were a standard part of the making of marriage.[10] The theme was already being satirized on the Elizabethan stage. But these material considerations became still more prominent in the later seventeenth and early eighteenth century.

For a start, the period saw a real demographic shortage of eligible elite men, and a sharp increase in the number of upper-class sons marrying rich bourgeois daughters. In addition, matchmaking increasingly took place in larger and more public forums. Across the country, the growth of provincial towns and resorts during this period was closely linked, as one observer put it in 1732, to their providing opportunities for ladies 'to show themselves and make their market'. The competition for wealthy partners thus became much more visible. The effect was further magnified by the rise of newspapers and other media, which not only avidly reported on the business of marriage, but themselves became part of the process. By the 1740s, the location and availability of rich heiresses was so well publicized that one enterprising fortune-hunter was able to fill thirty-two densely printed pages with all the relevant details (names, addresses, stock-market holdings, and reputed wealth) of the latest crop of well-endowed single women (see illustration 7). Finally, partly no doubt in response to these social developments, the upper classes collectively tightened patriarchal control over marriage, in ways that underscored its economic purpose. A series of late seventeenth-century statutes and legal changes weakened the property-rights of wives and children; whilst the 1753 Marriage Act greatly restricted the freedom of young people to marry without the proper oversight and consent of their families. Secret (or 'clandestine') marriages, which had become hugely popular in the decades since 1660, were outlawed; all weddings had to take place in the couple's parish and be publicly announced in advance; and no man or woman under twenty-one could marry if a parent objected. Any clergyman who ignored the new law was to be treated as a felon, and sentenced to fourteen years' transportation to America (one or two did, and were).[11]

Contemporary awareness of these trends fed into a more general unease about the growing commercialization of society. It was further sharpened by the rise of the opposite ideal: that marriage should primarily be a free contract between individuals, based on personal affection. The growing appeal of this ideology was the third reason for the mounting criticism of mercenary marriages. The principle of mutual attraction had deep roots in medieval and Renaissance culture, and it was never as diametrically opposed to prudential considerations as contemporary rhetoric sometimes suggested. Nonetheless, its authority was boosted at this time by exactly the same intellectual currents that advanced the principle of sexual freedom: the elevation of private conscience, the ideals of personal liberty and the pursuit of happiness, and the presumption that, in all spheres of life, natural instincts should trump artificial customs and prudential considerations. It gained further traction from the growing visibility of female perspectives on courtship and fidelity, for critics of arranged marriage especially decried its unfairness to women.

Nowadays we take for granted that romantic attraction and individual choice should be the foundation of marriage: it is one of the distinguishing features of western society. Yet the pre-eminence of this principle is a comparatively recent development. In the eighteenth and early nineteenth centuries its political and legal strength amongst the propertied classes was still very limited. The 1753 Marriage Act directly contradicted it – by trying to make it impossible for the young and infatuated to marry against the wishes of their elders, it ranked individual happiness firmly below the material interests of the patriarchal family. As the historian David Lemmings has beautifully shown, even those parliamentarians who appealed to the ideology of love and affection in opposing the legislation were only cynically adopting its rhetoric. In fact, they were 'fortune-hunters, who wanted only to keep the marriage-market open for fellow spirits': rich

A

MASTER-KEY

TO THE

RICH LADIES TREASURY.

OR,

The WIDOWER and BATCHELOR's

DIRECTORY.

CONTAINING

An exact ALPHABETICAL LIST of the

Duchess		Ladies by Curtesie, Daugh-
Marchioness		ters of Peers.
Countess	Dowagers.	Baronets Widows.
Viscountess		Widows, *and*
Baroness		Spinsters in *Great-Britain*.

WITH

An ACCOUNT of their PLACES of ABODE, Reputed FORTUNES,
and FORTUNES they possess in the STOCKS.

By a YOUNGER BROTHER.

——— He took his Stand
Upon a Widow's Jointure Land.

HUDIBRAS.

LONDON:
Printed for J. ROBERTS in *Warwick-Lane.*

M DCC XLII.
[Price 1s.]

7. *A Master-Key to the Rich Ladies Treasury*: the single man's guide to the
upper echelons of the marriage market in 1742.

[20]

Spinſters.

Names.	Places of Abode.	Reputed Fortunes.	In the Stocks.
Miſs			
Coulthurſt –	Baſinghall-ſtreet	8,000	
Clark –	York-buildings –	10,000	1000 E. I.
Chowne –	Forſter-lane –	5,000	
De Caſtro –	Beavers Mark –	10,000	1000 E. I.
Cholmley –	Theobalds,Hertfordſh.	12,000	1000 E. I.
Clayton –	Brook-ſtreet –	15,000	
Coteſworth –	Conduit-ſtreet –	16,000	1000 E. I. 1000 B.
Coteſworth –	Hexam, Northumberl.	16,000	1000 E. I. 1000 B.
Chock –	Villars-ſtreet –	10,000	1000 E. I.
Craile –	Pall-mall –	15,000	
Cudworth –	Cecil-ſtreet –	10,000	1000 E. I.
Croſs –	Mill-bank –	15,000	
Cutler 2 –	– –	10,000 Each	1000 B. Each
Carpue –	Haymarket –	5,000	
Cox 2 –	– –	10,000 Each	1000 B. Each
Cox Jenny –	Princes-ſtrt.Stocks-Mt.	6,000	
Clerk –	Kenſington –	8,000	
Cooke 2 –	– –	10,000 Each	1000 B. Each
Craggs –	Bond-ſtreet –	20,000	
Coulſton –	– –	12,000	1000 B.
Cornwallis –	Sackvile-ſtreet –	15,000	
Cater –	– –	20,000	1000 B.
Cotton 3 –	Dover-ſtreet –	10,000 Each	
Carey –	–	12,000	1000 B.
Cock –	–	10,000	1000 B.
Collins –	– –	15,000	1000 B.
Cloſe –	–	10,000	1000 B.
Calamy 3 –	– –	8,000 Each	1000 B. Each
Carpenter –	Highgate –	7,000	
D			
Dixon –	Hackney –	20,000	1000 B. 1000 E. I. 1000 S. S.
Drake –	Cavendiſh-ſquare	20,000	
Decker –	St. James's-ſquare	30,000	1000 E. I.
Dives –	St. James's –	20,000	
Decker 3 –	Golden-ſquare –	15,000 Each	
Davis –	St. Alban's-ſtreet –	10,000	1000 E. I.
Dickens 3.	Golden-ſquare –	10,000 Each	
Derham –	Drayton, Middleſex	12,000	1000 E. I.

Spinſters

heiresses, they felt, should be fair game for everyone. Yet the attitude was certainly gaining in cultural prominence. Its appeal helps to explain the enormous upsurge in clandestine marriages that occurred in the later seventeenth and early eighteenth centuries. Its tenets became ubiquitous not just in prescriptive literature, but also in the minds of fashionable men and women. Many upper-class women, especially, appear to have internalized them, even as they navigated unions arranged for profit. All this explains why, by the 1750s, the distinction between marriage for love and for money had become so widely debated.[12]

Mercenary marriage was therefore a fascinating topic because it illuminated the tensions between passion and prudence, male and female interests, genuine courtship and cynical seduction. Moreover, for most observers its significance went far beyond the motives of the couple themselves. The perversion of marriage also raised deeper, more troubling questions about social order and deference.

As early as 1701, the writer and diplomat Sir William Temple had lamented that mercenary 'marriages contracted without affection, choice, or inclination' were leading to the physical and moral degeneration of the aristocracy and gentry. By the middle of the eighteenth century it was a commonplace of social observation that the upper ranks married less than other classes, and with less success, and that their stock was commensurately deteriorating. To many radicals and feminists this phenomenon epitomized the essential corruption of the ruling elite. Aristocrats had become hopelessly inbred, complained one opponent of the 1753 Marriage Act, and by making cross-class marriages less easy (as greater parental control would doubtless do) the new law would only worsen the problem: 'Will you confine the great people to marry merely among one another and prevent them from getting a little wholesome blood which they so much want? Will you marry disease to distemper?' 'The meaner sort and poor', observed a demographer around the same time, were generally more fertile, and 'their children are generally the most vigorous, healthy, hearty, long-lived, liable to the fewest hereditary diseases, and fit to bear the greatest fatigues'. Yet obviously their morals could not be trusted either. Ultimately, as a newspaper correspondent complained in 1752, the problem affected both ends of the social scale:

In low life, people often intermarry with no other view or regard, than the sensual gratification of a present appetite: the copulation of the mob is no better than legal or ecclesiastical fornication ... In high life, marriage is a mere trade, a bargain and sale, where both parties endeavour to cheat one another.[13]

Across society, it was feared, lust and avarice were destroying the marital and social fabric.

The final key issue was the balance of authority between parents (especially fathers) and their children (especially daughters). Evidently young couples were often cajoled into marriage by their parents, for the sake of money. This created a moral and social conundrum. So ingrained was the presumption of paternal wisdom and supremacy, so obvious its importance to the stability of families and, by extension, the order of society, that it was difficult to argue that any particular child, let alone all children, had the right to defy a father's express wishes. All the same, what *were* the proper limits of parental control? What if the parents were so misguided as to insist on an unhappy, mercenary match?

These questions were the more pressing from the later seventeenth century onwards because they had obvious political implications. Monarchy was after all a system of government based on patriarchal principles: but in the 1640s and 1650s it had been attacked and destroyed, and after 1688 it was increasingly modified by new, contractual ideas. As a result, analogies between royal, paternal, and husbandly authority were frequently drawn. This was part of the intellectual background to all debates about marriage. In various ways, therefore, the apparent growth of parental tyranny and avarice could be seen as a quintessential feature of the modern condition, and as the ultimate cause of other serious social evils: the mis-education of children, seduction, adultery, and marital misery. This was one of the central themes of *Clarissa*, and it resonated widely. 'Are not such parents answerable for any misconduct in the child they have cruelly distressed?' asked one of the novel's readers, musing on the heroine's real-life counterparts. 'I charge all woeful consequences to their account. They are more wicked, infinitely worse, than a Lovelace.'[14] It was a classic Enlightenment perspective. Once again, the explanation lay not primarily in personal wickedness or frailty, but in a structural social problem: the corruption of parental authority.

PUNISHING SEDUCTION

By the middle of the eighteenth century the spread of male sexual freedom was thus accompanied by mounting concern over its consequences. To most observers neither the resurrection of old-fashioned discipline nor the abolition of all sexual constraints seemed feasible. How, then, should male lust be channelled so as to minimize its dangers to women? This was the final major theme underlying the obsession with seduction.

The most obvious way out was to accept prostitution. As we saw in Chapter 2, it increasingly came to be taken for granted that it was desirable to set aside a class of inferior women in order to protect respectable females from danger. In consequence the theory and practice of tolerating prostitution was to become ever more central to the sexual economy of the English-speaking world from the middle of the eighteenth century onwards. By the later nineteenth century, governmental regulation of prostitutes had been enacted across the British Empire, and in many other western societies. The scale of commercial sex also expanded greatly, in line with the growth of cities, the industrial economy, the armed services, global commerce, transport, and the development of overseas colonies. Only at the end of the twentieth century was its importance to the sexual economy to diminish, following the spread of mass contraception and sexual freedom for women.

Prostitution was, though, never a universally accepted solution. Its many critics (whether Christian, liberal, radical, or feminist) were troubled by its institutionalization of male promiscuity, and by the presumption that harlots were expendable, lesser human beings. It also sat uneasily with the belief that prostitutes were themselves the victims of seduction, social ostracism, and economic hardship. In this view, far from preventing the corruption of innocent women, prostitution was actually based on it. As we shall see in the next chapter, such attitudes were to have a deep impact on eighteenth-, nineteenth-,

Cap.ᵇ Edward Rigby of Leyton in Lanci Shire

T.Murrey pinx: I.Smith fec:

Plate 1. Edward Rigby striking an unrepentant pose in 1702. This print was produced just a few months after his release from prison for attempted sodomy (see Chapter 2, 'Thinking the Unthinkable').

The **VICTIM**.
From the Original Picture by John Collet, in the possession of Carington Bowles

Printed for & Sold by CARINGTON BOWLES, *at his Map & Print Warehouse, N.º 69 in S.ᵗ Pauls Church Yard* LONDON. *Published as the Act directs.*

Plate 2. The sacrifice of young woman to the lechery of a seasoned debauchee: melodramatic prints on this subject became immensely popular in the later eighteenth century (see Chapter 3, 'Rakes and Harlots').

Plate 3. Pamela fainting, having discovered Mr B. hiding in her bedroom to ravish her. In the background is his accomplice, Mrs Jewkes. From a set of popular illustrations to Samuel Richardson's sensational and deeply influential best-seller *Pamela* (1740) (see Chapter 3, 'Novel Attitudes').

Plate 4. William Blake's life-long fascination with multiple marriage is illustrated by his 1795 print of Lamech, the first polygamist mentioned in the Bible: on the left are his two wives, Adah and Zillah (Genesis 4.19) (see Chapter 4, 'Polygamy and Population').

CLARISSE HARLOW.

Consider me Dear Lovelace by that honor,
by your humanity, by all you have Vowed;
I conjure you not to make me abhor myself
not to make me vile in my own eyes

Clarisse Harlow. Lre. 84

Je vous supplie cher Lovelace, par cet honneu
par votre humanité, par tous les Sermens q
vous m'avez faits je vous conjure de ne point n
rendre un Objet d'horreur à mes propres yeux

A Paris chez Chalton Salle, rue du Palais Marchand

Plate 5. Clarissa Harlow, her dress already ripped open by the heartless rapist Lovelace, begs
in vain for mercy. A later eighteenth-century illustration to Samuel Richardson's *Clarissa*
(1747–8), with captions in French as well as English for the benefit of the novel's innumerable
continental readers (see Chapter 3, 'Novel Attitudes').

Plate 6. William Hogarth, *Marriage à la Mode* (1745), opening scene. On the left is the syphilitic Viscount Squanderfield — ignoring his bride-to-be, who is already intriguing with one of the lawyers, Mr Silvertongue. On the right their fathers haggle over the marriage contract, interested only in the material aspects of the match.

Plate 7. *Marriage à la Mode* (1745), final scene. The miserable countess has poisoned herself upon learning of her lover's execution. As her crippled, syphilitic baby grips her lifeless face, her unfeeling, avaricious father strips the rings off her fingers (see Chapter 4, 'Marriage and Money').

Robert Dingley Esq.ʳ Treasurer to the Magdalen-House.
Done from an Original Picture presented to that Charity by M.ʳ William Hoare.

Plate 8. The patriarchal philanthropist: Robert Dingley, merchant and founder of the Magdalen Hospital for Penitent Prostitutes. On his knee, in the frontispiece to the charity's published *Account* (1761), rests one of the penitents (see Chapter 5, 'Self-interest and Sexual Interest').

Plate 9. The octagonal chapel of the London Magdalen Hospital in Blackfriars Road, which opened in 1772 and could seat 500 visitors. In the centre of the gallery, visible behind the gauze screen, are the penitents themselves (see Chapter 5, 'Self-interest and Sexual Interest').

Plate 10. The dining hall of the Lambeth Asylum for poor orphan girls (founded in 1758), the inmates in their uniforms apparently being visited by the middle-class family shown at the centre (see Chapter 5, 'Chastity and Class').

Plate 11. One of the countless consumer objects based on Hogarth's *Harlot's Progress* (1732): an expensive, hand-painted porcelain plate with an image of scene 2, produced at the Meissen porcelain works in eastern Germany around 1740 (see Chapter 6, 'The Growth of Mass Culture').

Plate 12. Emily Warren, a renowned courtesan, portrayed by Joshua Reynolds in 1781 as Thaïs, Alexander the Great's favourite prostitute (see Chapter 6, 'Sexual Celebrity').

Louise Dutchess of Portsmouth &c.

P. Lely Pinxit   A. Blooteling fecit et Ex:

Plate 13. Louise de Kéroualle, Duchess of Portsmouth: one of Charles II's most powerful
mistresses, and the object of ceaseless public interest (see Chapter 6, 'Sexual Celebrity')

The Sculpters part is done the features' hitt of Madam Gwin, No Arte can shew her Witt,

P Lely Pinxit.

G Valck Sculp d ex

Plate 14. Nell Gwyn, whose rivalry with the Duchess of Portsmouth fascinated contemporary observers (see Chapter 6, 'Sexual Celebrity').

Plate 15. James Gillray's lurid pun on the name and role of Dorothy Jordan, longtime mistress to the Duke of Clarence, later King William IV (see Chapter 6, 'Sexual Celebrity').

Plate 16. One of Joshua Reynolds's best-known and most-copied paintings of Kitty Fisher (1759): as Cleopatra, dissolving a priceless pearl in wine to impress Marc Antony (see Chapter 6, 'Self-promotion and Exploitation').

Plate 17. One of the engravings that Reynolds and Fisher commissioned immediately after the portrait's completion, to bring the image to mass public attention (see Chapter 6, 'Self-promotion and Exploitation').

Plate 18. Another of the many pictures that Kitty Fisher commissioned to enhance her celebrity (1765). As well as providing a pun on her name, the goldfish bowl reflects a crowd of people peering through the window to catch a glimpse of the famous courtesan (see Chapter 6, 'Self-promotion and Exploitation').

Plate 19. William Heath, Which is the Dirtiest (1820): the estranged Queen Caroline and King George IV, flinging filth at one another – it sticks to him, but not to her (see Chapter 6, 'Self-promotion and Exploitation').

Plate 20. A smiling Mary Anne Clarke and her printer and publisher rejoice in their enormous pay-offs, as the relieved Prince of Wales and other noblemen destroy the damning evidence of corruption and immorality that her memoirs had threatened to uncover (see Chapter 6, 'Self-promotion and Exploitation').

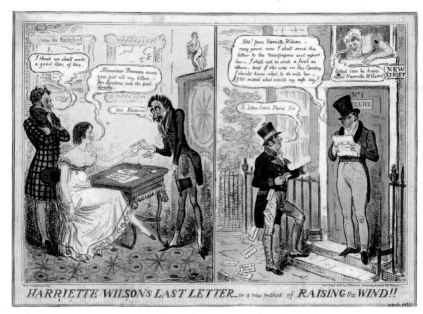

Plate 21. An 1825 satire on Harriette Wilson's practice of writing blackmailing letters to her former lovers, offering them the opportunity to buy themselves out of her memoirs (see Chapter 6, 'Self-promotion and Exploitation').

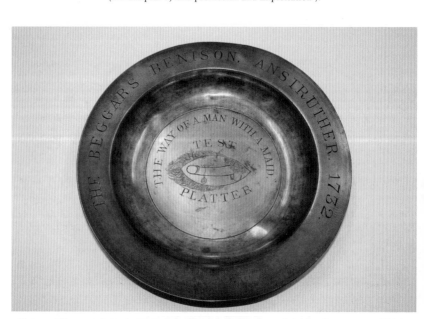

Plate 22. The central ritual object of the 'Beggar's Benison' sex club: the platter upon which its members collectively ejaculated (see Chapter 6, 'Celebrating Sex').

and twentieth-century philanthropy, social policy, feminism, and politics.

The alternative approach was to regulate male licence in new ways. From the later seventeenth century, as the jurisdiction of the church courts declined, a variety of new (or newly extended) legal procedures evolved to prosecute adulterers and fornicators. In contrast to traditional discipline, which had always in practice penalized women more than men, these actions were all predicated on the idea that women were the victims of male predation. Their essential concern was not so much to punish immorality for its own sake as to protect women, shore up the institution of marriage, and uphold the sexual property rights of fathers and husbands. A man who seduced a woman but then abandoned her could be sued for breach of promise; or, by her parent, for damages. The same patriarchal presumptions underlay the action for 'criminal conversation', whereby a husband sued his wife's lover, and obtained monetary compensation for their adultery.[1]

Yet all these were private, civil procedures. Their only remedy was money, and the aggrieved party had to go to the trouble of suing, at considerable cost, risk, and inconvenience. Few victims could afford this. In consequence, many later eighteenth- and early nineteenth-century commentators agitated for a general law against seduction. This was a crime with far worse social effects than most capital offences, noted William Paley: it was scandalous that 'the law has provided no punishment for this offence beyond a pecuniary satisfaction to the injured family'. It was absurd, another writer pointed out in 1780, that it had become less punishable for a man 'to seduce, defile, and abandon to prostitution and ruin, a *thousand women*, married or unmarried, than to *steal*, *kill*, or even *maliciously* to *maim* or *wound*, an *ox* or a *sheep*'.[2]

Many of the period's leading lawyers and legislators agreed with them. That all seducers of married women ought to suffer fine or imprisonment was a recurrent theme in the debates surrounding the adultery and divorce bills of the late eighteenth and early nineteenth centuries, and in the 1770s both Jeremy Bentham and Lord Mansfield, the lord chief justice, drafted laws against the seduction of unmarried women. This was also one of the foundations of Patrick Colquhoun's popular blueprint for wholesale social and legal reform, which decried the subversive modern 'distinction . . . between public and private crimes' – seducers should face hard labour, imprisonment, or transportation for life.[3]

More common still was the concern that those who corrupted innocent virgins should be required to take care of them. 'When a man seduces a woman,' wrote Mary Wollstonecraft, he 'should be *legally* obliged to maintain the woman and her children'. Best of all, for society and for the individuals, would be if all seducers were simply made to marry their victims. This was a very old idea. It had been the Old Testament sanction (Deuteronomy 22), and many early Protestants had supported its reintroduction.* Its principles appealed equally to many eighteenth-century sensibilities. 'Whenever a virgin is seduced of her virtue by a single man,' argued a popular author in 1753, 'it must, it ought, to be presumed, that he prevailed upon her through the promise of marriage; and therefore he should be compell'd to fulfil his contract.'[4] In countless cases this was already privately achieved, through familial and social pressure. There were also obvious public precedents, for until the reform of the Poor Law in 1834 overseers of the poor often forced the parents of illegitimate children to marry. In consequence it was not hard to contemplate extending the practice to all seduced women. This was Henry Fielding's solution when faced, as a magistrate, with a young unmarried couple taken in bed together: 'after a reprimand from the Justice, and some threats, the lad declared he was willing to make her all the reparation in his power, and to marry her immediately', and so they were. (A few years earlier Fielding had himself done the right thing and married his kitchen maid, Mary Daniel, after she fell pregnant by him.)† Even in

---

* Though not the early Stuart MP Sir Sydney Montagu, who was fond of saying 'that he that doth get a wench with child and marries her afterward it is as if a man should shit in his hat and then clap it upon his head': *The Diary of Samuel Pepys*, ed. Robert Latham and William Matthews, 11 vols (1970–83), i. 261.

† His strong views on this subject are equally evident in his anonymous translation of Ovid, composed at exactly the time that his relationship with Mary Daniel was developing. In recommending flattery and deceit, the poet had advised men that 'if a girl insists upon a promise of marriage, give it her, and bind it by many oaths: for no indictment lies for this sort of perjury'. To these lines Fielding, who nowhere else criticizes the work's morality, appended an urgent footnote: 'This is the most exceptionable passage in the whole work . . . we cannot help expressing our detestation of

cases of forcible rape, asserted Colquhoun, as long as the woman agreed, 'it would be well for society, if the same rule extended'. In nineteenth- and early twentieth-century North America exactly these principles came to be enshrined in law. In most states, seduction became a crime, but marriage was the desired outcome – both for the courts and, evidently, for most of the women who appealed to them.[5]

But what if the seducer was already married? Should the same principle apply? Bigamy had been a capital offence since 1603, yet in the eighteenth century this became a widely debated question. Many serious observers were keenly interested in polygamy as a remedy for seduction. If everyone agreed that marriage was best for women, children, and society, yet it was unreasonable to confine men to a single partner, then was this not the obvious solution? In the absence of divorce, might polygamy provide a sensible way of balancing male rapacity and sexual responsibility, indeed of bolstering marriage itself?*

POLYGAMY AND POPULATION

The arguments for and against polygamy were evidently already being widely discussed around 1700, in sermons, conversations, and private writings, as well as in print.[1] In her best-selling *New Atalantis* (1709), Delarivier Manley included several passages based on both her own marriage to a bigamist (from whom she soon parted), and the ménage of William Cowper, the leading Whig politician and Lord Chancellor, who had simultaneously kept (and had children with) two women, both claiming to be his wife. His second mistress, Manley claimed, had been persuaded by Cowper's 'learned discourse of the lawfulness of double marriages':

---

this sentiment, which appears shocking even in a heathen writer': [Henry Fielding], *Ovid's Art of Love Paraphrased* (1747), 71.

* The philosopher Francis Hutcheson thought he had an even better idea – adulterers should be divorced, but forbidden to marry 'the partner of their guilt'; instead they would be compelled 'to marriages with persons formerly infamous, and of sufficient lust for them, to prevent their corrupting others': Francis Hutcheson, *A System of Moral Philosophy*, 2 vols (1755), ii. 181.

Indeed he owned that, in all ages, women had been appropriated: that, for the benefit and distinction of children, with other necessary occurrences, polygamy had been justly denied the sex since the coldness of their constitutions, the length of time they carried their children and other incidents seemed to declare against them; but for a man who possessed an uninterrupted capacity of propagating the specie[s] and must necessarily find all the inconveniences above-mentioned in any one wife, the law of nature, as well as the custom of many nations and most religions, seemed to declare for him. The ancient Jews, who pretend to receive the law from an only god, not only indulged plurality of wives, but an unlimited use of concubinage ... The Turks and all the people of the world but the Europeans still preserved the privilege. That it was to be owned their manners in all things are less adulterated than ours, their veracity, morality, and habit of living less corrupted: that, in pretending to reform from their abuses, Europe had only refined their vices ... That, true, he condemned a promiscuous pursuit, because it was irrational and polluted, but if one or more women, whether married or not, were appropriated to one man, they were so far from transgressing, that they but fulfilled the law of nature.[2]

Amongst the mid-century thinkers who were fascinated by the idea was Samuel Richardson. In the later 1730s, he printed two editions of a long and learned book against polygamy by his friend Patrick Delany, the leading Irish scholar, who noted that the doctrine was by then 'daily defended in common conversation, and often in print, by a great variety of *plausible* arguments'.* Shortly afterwards, in the second part of *Pamela* (1741), Richardson made Mr B's supposed fondness for polygamy a central plot device. Lovelace, too, ponders the pluralism of the patriarchs, 'who had wives and concubines without number!' – no wonder the idea was nowadays so 'panted after'. By the early 1750s, when grappling with the problem of Sir Charles

* Though Delany, unsurprisingly, robustly affirmed orthodox arguments against polygamy, it is perhaps not irrelevant to his interest in the subject that his own marriage to a rich widow a few years earlier had been entirely prudential – he was already in love with none other than Mary Pendarves (whom we met earlier in this chapter), and she with him. When his first wife died in 1742, Delany quickly travelled to England, proposed, and finally was married to Mary Pendarves, more than a decade after they had first met. She was to become one of Richardson's favourite correspondents and advisers.

Grandison's simultaneous love for two different women, Richardson privately confessed that he could see no very good reason against the practice. It was obviously not against the law of nature, nor against scripture. On the contrary: both seemed to encourage it, as did almost every modern civilization. If it were to become legal in England, he mused, 'I know not my own heart, if I would give in to the allowance'; and he was pretty certain that, in general, polygamy would bring greater happiness, rather than increasing licentiousness. (Mrs Richardson's views are not recorded.)[3]

The same conclusion was eagerly and repeatedly drawn by James Boswell. When as a young man he travelled to Switzerland in 1764 to meet his hero, Rousseau, this was one of the topics upon which he most urgently sought the great man's approval. 'Morals', he explained,

appear to me an uncertain thing. For instance, I should like to have thirty women. Could I not satisfy that desire? . . . Consider: if I am rich, I can take a number of girls; I get them with child; propagation is thus increased. I give them dowries, and I marry them off to good peasants who are very happy to have them. Thus they become wives at the same age as would have been the case if they had remained virgins, and I on my side, have had the benefit of enjoying a great variety of women.

When Rousseau unexpectedly demurred, Boswell blurted out the other variations on his fantasy: 'But cannot I follow the Oriental usage?' or else 'I should like to follow the example of the old Patriarchs, worthy men whose memory I hold in respect'. Years later, long after he had married, he was still obsessively proposing the same arguments to himself, his friends, and his wife.* Around the same time, the charismatic dissenter Westley Hall, John Wesley's pupil and brother-in-law, was going about preaching that monogamy was no part of real, primitive Christianity: he also put his beliefs into practice with several women.[4]

The idea equally gained the support of more disinterested thinkers. In the early 1780s, Martin Madan, a popular evangelical preacher,

---

* For Dr Johnson's characteristically ambiguous views on the subject (bigamy was wrong; but he himself had often fantasized about keeping a seraglio), see *Boswell's Life of Johnson*, ed. George Birkbeck Hill and L. F. Powell, 6 vols (1934–50), v. 216–17.

great-nephew of Lord Chancellor Cowper, and chaplain of the Lock Hospital for diseased prostitutes, published an immense and best-selling 'Treatise on Female Ruin', advocating that 'on pain of death, or at least of perpetual imprisonment till compliance, every man who had seduced a woman, whether with or without a promise of marriage, should be obliged to wed her publicly', even if he was already married. This was, he argued, the obvious, divinely ordained solution to the twin evils of seduction and prostitution – had God not commanded that 'if a man entice a maid that is not betrothed, and lie with her, he shall surely endow her to be his wife' (Exodus 22.16)?* In response a huge popular debate erupted on the question, which rehearsed and extended all the arguments for and against polygamy that had been accumulating over the previous two centuries. Months after Madan's book first came out, the minister of a Cheshire parish, far away from London, marvelled that it was 'still the general topic of conversation, in almost every company where I go'.[5]

There were three main reasons for the subject's prominence. The most basic was that the Bible seemed to provide considerable support for men taking multiple wives. The polygamy of the patriarchs, and the absence of any clear condemnation of it in the New Testament, was a longstanding theological conundrum.[6] After the Reformation, as we saw in Chapter 2, the authority of scriptural precedent had led various early Protestants to experiment with multiple marriage. Interest in the practice was further revived in the 1650s, when it seemed that a radical refashioning of society might truly be underway. Amongst those who became convinced at that point that polygamy was 'a true form of marriage', 'lawful and honourable', and wholly approved by God, were Milton, the republican MP Henry Marten, and Hobbes's 'great acquaintance', the celebrated author and judge Francis Osborne, whose widely read writings deprecated monogamy as but the invention of 'wily priests'. In 1657, one of Osborne's friends published an English translation of Bernardino Ochino's famous defence of polygamy; the following year, the Lord Protector was publicly urged to allow multiple marriage. As Hobbes himself pointed

* Exactly the same arguments had been put forward in a letter to *The London Chronicle* of 12–14 July 1759, signed 'M. M.' – if, as seems likely, this was by Madan, he evidently spent over twenty years composing his thoughts on the subject.

out, its prohibition was purely a matter of arbitrary, human convention: 'in some places of the world, men have the liberty of many wives: in other places, such liberty is not allowed'. Even clerical opponents of polygamy sometimes conceded this. It was silly not to admit that the Bible permitted considerable licence, wrote a Cambridge professor in 1731: 'not only a plurality of wives, but a number of concubines into the bargain'.[7]

Throughout the later seventeenth and eighteenth centuries, the biblical and patristic texts continued to form part of all serious discussions of polygamy. When, in 1780, Madan made scriptural exegesis the main foundation of his argument, he self-consciously placed himself in this intellectual tradition. He was, he believed, simply completing the vital work, begun by the first Protestant reformers, of stripping away popish accretions and returning the marital practices of Christianity to God's original design. (The true message of the Old and New Testaments, he asserted, was that sexual intercourse itself created an indissoluble marriage, and that any man could be husband to multiple women; all other rites and interpretations were but later, priestly inventions). In the 1580s such detailed biblical scholarship would have been the only way of proceeding. Even in the 1680s it would have remained the most respectable approach. Madan's recourse to it in the 1780s demonstrates how central the fundamentalist reading of scripture was to the late eighteenth- and early nineteenth-century religious revival, and how powerfully it could inspire evangelicals to radical social reform. Yet by then it also lay far outside the mainstream of ordinary clerical culture, let alone of lay opinion.[8]

After 1700, in fact, interest in polygamy was mainly bound up with the general development of sexual freedom. This was the second reason for its growing prominence. Increasingly, scriptural arguments were outnumbered by other presumptions – the natural promiscuity of men; the artificiality of sexual ethics; the priestly concealment of primitive Christianity; the appeal to natural law; the example of other cultures; the patriarchal ownership of women and children. Like the evangelical urge to recover the true meaning of scripture, this approach presumed that recent marital customs were mainly of human invention, but its conclusion was the opposite – that the rules of matrimony ought to follow human policy, rather than biblical tradition. By the middle of the eighteenth century, this had become the more common view. 'Thank God!' exclaimed the Attorney General Sir Dudley Ryder in Parliament in 1753, rejecting the idea that marriage was an immutable divine institution, 'we have in this age got the better of this, as well as of a great many other superstitious opinions'. Already as young men in the 1710s, he and his friends had debated the desirability of polygamy and divorce, and presumed that 'the interest of the world', not of God, should determine such questions.[9]

The question of whether polygamy was in the national interest had previously arisen in the context of royal marriages. In the early sixteenth century, Luther, Bucer, and Melanchthon had all advised Henry VIII that it would be lawful for him simply to take Anne Boleyn as a second wife – this was apparently also the view of several authoritative Catholic theologians. Later in the 1530s, the same arguments were used to justify the actual bigamy of Philip of Hesse. Exactly the same situation recurred in the later seventeenth century, when Charles II found himself unable to conceive a legitimate heir by his queen. Amongst the various solutions seriously contemplated were divorce or polygamy. John Locke, secretary to Lord Ashley (the future first Earl of Shaftesbury), repeatedly set down for his patron the arguments for why either practice might be tolerated. In 1671, Ashley and some of the king's other close advisers sought the further authority of leading lawyers and churchmen to show that neither course contravened divine law. Four years later, the zealous MP Michael Malet, keen for the king to renounce his papist whores and beget a Protestant successor, tried to introduce a bill to allow multiple marriage, arguing that its prohibition was but a remnant of Catholic superstition.[10]

In the eighteenth century polygamy became linked to a more general political issue: the state of the nation's population. Demographic concerns had always had a general influence on thinking about sexual mores. During the high middle ages, population pressure was one reason why theologians argued that virginity was superior to marriage, even though God had commanded Adam and Eve to 'be fruitful, and multiply' (Genesis 1.28).[11] Increasing overpopulation in the later sixteenth and early seventeenth century similarly coincided with the tightening of attitudes against sexual immorality, as we saw in earlier chapters. The same correlation would again arise from the early nine-teenth century onwards: the adoption of Malthusian ideas at that point led to renewed concern over the dangers of excessive popula-tion, which in turn gave new urgency to the cause of sexual restraint. It was only the advent of mass contraception at the end of the twenti-eth century that severed this close connection between attitudes to sex and to population.

Within this longer story, the era between about 1650 and 1800 formed a crucial watershed. This was the period in which social sci-ence as we know it was born, and demographic thought (which previously had been a much vaguer and more specialized concern) first became central to social and governmental attitudes to sex. One of the earliest manifestations of this was the development of a new approach to population called 'political arithmetic'. 'Arithmetic' was short-hand for the new practice of scientifically collecting and manip-ulating large amounts of data on population, fertility, mortality, wealth, social structure, and so on. The practice was 'political' because its ultimate aim was to improve national prosperity. This revolution in demographic attitudes occurred at a time of relative demographic and economic ease, but also of continual war, economic competition, and imperial expansion.[12] As a result its impact was considerable: henceforth, every social question was subjected to such calculations. This was the final reason why polygamy became a topic of particular interest at this time.

The most basic effect of political arithmetic was namely to estab-lish that a nation's strength depended above all on the number of inhabitants – as Paley put it, 'the decay of population is the greatest evil that a state can suffer; and the improvement of it the object which ought, in all countries, to be aimed at, in preference to every other political purpose whatsoever'.[13] The paramount concern was hence to maximize fertility, and to find out which marital and sexual arrange-ments would best promote it. What was the effect of promoting celibacy, as many prosperous Catholic nations had, of tolerating pros-titution, of permitting divorce – or of encouraging polygamy, as the Turks did? Did any of these customs give other nations an advantage?

Most orthodox commentators thought not. There was already a long-standing tradition of explaining why monogamous marriage was in every way superior to other sexual practices (and its Protestant, English variant most excellent of all). Now the demographic aspects of this argument were increasingly elaborated. Fornication, adultery, celibacy, and prostitution were held to detract from population: such practices were less fertile, and their offspring less likely to be healthy and loved, than licit sex. As a popular tract put it in 1700, everyone knew that 'the beaten paths are always barren, and never productive of any fruit'; equally, 'whatever springs from an adulterous bed is rarely of long continuance'. Nor, it was generally agreed, was multiple marriage more productive, for there was no surplus of women over men in the general population, and the practice put intolerable strain on the unfortunate husbands. 'As polygamy debilitates the fathers', explained a patriotic writer, 'so it naturally creates a weak and infirm issue [and] hinders the increase of mankind'.[14]*

The increasing prominence of demographic concerns also stimulated many new practical initiatives. The growing desire to save every possible life fuelled the great mid eighteenth-century efflorescence of new charities for the health and procreation of the labouring classes – beginning with the London Foundling Hospital, which opened in 1741 to take in illegitimate and otherwise unwanted infants. This concept was not new, but had previously always been rejected by the English on grounds of morality. Its acceptability by the 1730s and 1740s owed much to the increasing primacy of political arithmetic. Mounting anxiety about the spread of seduction and the decline of marriage was equally fuelled by the new way of thinking. Many observers feared the Marriage Act would reduce marriage, and in turn the population, because it mandated expensive and cumbersome church weddings instead of the cheap, quick, clandestine weddings that had become popular amongst the poorer sorts. As a political arithmetician urged in 1750, 'people of this class should be encouraged to marry for procreation, and all hinderances removed as much as possible by the legislature'. The Act wrongly favoured wealthy

---

* Malthus, characteristically, was to argue both that polygamy, like whoring, was less productive, *and* that, in certain circumstances, it led to overpopulation and misery: T. R. Malthus, *An Essay on the Principle of Population* [edns of 1803–26], ed. Patricia James, 2 vols (1989), i. 28, 32–4, 55, 88, 92, 111; and ibid., i. 80, 90–92.

families at the expense of the public good, argued the Duke of Bedford in 1765: 'in order to save thousands, it has undone millions'.[15]

In consequence, and in emulation of other classical and modern cultures, measures to encourage wedlock and childbirth came to be widely advocated. Between 1695 and 1706, the war against France was partly financed by a special annual levy on all childless widowers and bachelors over twenty-five, graded according to status – so that, for example, an unmarried duke was fined £12 11s per year, a bishop £5 1s, and a labourer one shilling. Throughout the eighteenth century there were many further proposals to tax bachelors, debar them from public office, or otherwise pressure them into doing their public duty by becoming husbands and fathers. Single men should be heavily penalized, argued Josiah Tucker, especially the wealthiest, for 'they are the people, who set bad examples, and by their station, riches, intrigues, and address, debauch those young women at first, who afterwards become the common prostitutes of the town'. And thence, concurred a clergyman in 1782, 'this monster, prostitution, with giant-strides, proceeds to depopulate the land' – thus were every year thousands of lives ruined, marriages prevented, and children left unborn. The harm was incalculable.[16]

Yet the basic notion that population increase was good was also taken up by many advocates of greater sexual liberty. As procreation was enjoined by God, and vital to the well-being of the body politic, they argued, every act of intercourse strengthened the nation. This attitude fitted beautifully with the presumption that sex was healthy and natural, and it was part of almost every discussion in favour of sexual freedom. If fornication were freely permitted, urged a young clergyman in 1735, facetiously summarizing the arguments, the nation's wealth and population would exponentially increase, so that 'we should soon become the terror of all Europe, and the most formidable power upon the face of the globe':

Here then is an action in which both parties mean well; that is vastly pleasing while they are about it, and attended with good consequences with respect to society; it must therefore be suitable to the main scope and tenor of the Bible, agreeable to what we call reason, and worthy the dignity of our natures.[17]

Polygamy attracted serious supporters from both sides of this debate. Many commentators presumed that it would enhance the population, and was preferable to prostitution. As one author noted in 1695, whoring was 'very pernicious to the state, and hinders the great increase of people' – 'bigamy, polygamy, or any gamy is better than that'. Allowing men to take multiple wives would also prevent the horrible, depopulating infanticide of thousands of bastard children per year. Moreover, it was obviously more natural than the rigid, artificial restraint of monogamy, which was only a recent, popish imposition on one small corner of the globe – throughout the rest of the world, and in the European past, polygamy was the norm, and brought greater felicity and prosperity. As the influential politician and philosopher Henry St John, the first Viscount Bolingbroke, urged, 'It has therefore prevailed always, and it still prevails generally ... was authorized by God himself ... and provides the most effectual means for the generation and education of children' and increasing the population. In short, its 'prohibition is absurd'.[18]

It also held out the promise of balancing male freedom with social responsibility. That is why it tempted Boswell, Thomas Jefferson, and untold lesser men with fantasies of patriarchal sexual dominion. They did not consider themselves to be libertines: they cared about morality and abhorred seduction. Boswell, who slept with countless married and unmarried women, from every rank of society, nevertheless had a firm 'principle of never debauching an innocent girl'. Instead, the examples of the Old Testament patriarchs and the mighty potentates of the East seemed to provide a responsible, ethical model of how masculine freedom and power could be exercised over women without destroying them. 'Were it not better, honester, and more becoming our duty, and to prevent worse disorders', asked a modern philosopher in 1759, if men were obliged to marry, rather than abandon, all those they debauched? Would it not add 'much to the health, credit, strength, policy and increase of our species'? If multiple marriage were adopted, urged Madan, 'millions of women (especially of the lower sort) would be saved from ruin'.[19]

Polygamy was therefore often seen as a means of expanding marriage and bolstering sexual discipline, against the rising tide of upper-class male rapacity. What was 'the most common and most powerful of all moral Evils', the greatest social problem of the century, asked the followers of Emmanuel Swedenborg in 1789? It was surely not 'the attachment of one unmarried man to one free woman, and simply concubinage, which under certain regulations never ought to be forbidden in a Free State', but rather:

(1.) Adultery. (2.) The lust of variety. (3.) The lust of defloration. (4.) The lust of violation. (5.) The lust of seducing the innocent. If these five species of lasciviousness are not rooted out from a society, and especially from among men in office, both ecclesiastical and civil, and from all such as by their exalted sphere in life, should be examples to others; then that society . . . can be nothing else but a nest for vice of every kind, and an habitation for misery in every degree.[20]

The same attitude animated a female reader of Madan's work who, having 'made the causes of female ruin, a subject of her particular attention', organized a public debate 'upon the consequence of allowing in this country a plurality of wives' so as 'to prevent seduction and prostitution'. Boswell's friend, Peggy Stuart, was likewise

clear for it, because she said there were so many men who could not afford to marry that a number of women were useless; that supposing as many men as women in the world, a man who can maintain many wives or women, having them, is not depriving some other men of their share; because you deprive a man of nothing when you take what he at any rate would not have.[21]

These were the reasons why the idea of limited polygamy attracted Richardson, Madan, and other serious Christian moralists, whose chief concerns were not to advance sexual freedom but to rein in male licence, promote marriage, patriarchy, and family life, and protect 'the *weaker* sex, from the villainy, treachery, and cruelty of the *stronger*'. 'What mischiefs can result from polygamy being practised by a comparatively small number of persons', asked another of its proponents in 1786, compared with

those infinite disorders, that follow from our not compelling *every* man, who *seduced* a virgin, to *marry* her, as the Deity ordained. Is it not owing to this cause, that every city, town, village, is filled with prostitutes? Is it not owing to this that infanticide is so frequently perpetrated? Is it not owing to this that celibacy [i.e. bachelorhood] is so prevalent, since men may gratify their passions, without having the hazard of having a family to support? Is it not owing to this that the most shameful of diseases is so common? To this in great measure may be attributed, the almost general prophaneness, irreligion, debauchery, selfishness, the enemy of patriotism and every virtue: in a word, almost all the evils of society.[22]

Polygamy was thus so widely discussed by the later eighteenth century because it appealed in one way or another to so many different points of view. It illustrates the continued inspiration and fertility of biblical ideas, the influence of demographic thought, the patriarchal mind-set of most eighteenth-century men and women, and the intellectual overlap between proponents and opponents of greater sexual liberty. Exactly what different observers meant by 'polygamy' varied accordingly. When Boswell dwelled upon 'patriarchal' or 'asiatic' precedents he evidently was often fantasizing about fairly casual liaisons, but he and many others also speculated about real, life-long marriage to multiple women. It was never proposed that all men should engage in polygamy, nor that it was necessarily superior to monogamy – merely that it was 'not bad in itself', that it was not explicitly prohibited by divine or natural law, and that it might be expedient to allow it, at least to a certain 'number and quality of persons', to mitigate greater evils such as barrenness, seduction, or simply (as Boswell mused, likening himself to Philip of Hesse) if 'a man is *too many* for one woman'.[23]

Yet this spectrum of meanings also helps to explain why the idea was never widely embraced as a public policy. Countless men (and women) appear to have solaced themselves privately with the idea that their unmarried relationships resembled the natural, divinely sanctioned concubinage of other, glorious, times and places. All the same, when polygamy was proposed as a serious, publicly enforced expedient against seduction, its longstanding associations with immorality damned it in the eyes of most observers. His arguments were pure 'poison', Madan's critics told him; they contained 'many very dangerous, and pernicious tenets'; he had put forward a plan 'which, if adopted by the world, must lead to the introduction of licentiousness, and must terminate in the overthrow of every principle of social comfort'.[24] The panic about moral degeneration and social disintegration that followed the American and French Revolutions gave fresh impetus to the arguments for traditional Christian monogamy as the perfect building block of a civilized society. So did the growth of empire and of missionary activity in the course of the eighteenth and nineteenth centuries: polygamy came increasingly to be associated with backward, dark-skinned heathens, and their alien faiths. Meanwhile, the practical incentive for propertied men to develop serious arguments in its favour was lessened after 1700 by the gradual rise of parliamentary divorce, the decline of sexual regulation, the ease of informal concubinage, and the movement towards natural rather than biblical arguments for sexual freedom – for if marriage itself was essentially unnatural and unnecessary, why multiply it?

It had also long been reasoned that polygamy detracted from wifely status. With the growing appreciation of feminine perspectives on marriage, this became an increasingly important point. 'What do I care for the patriarchs!' exclaimed Lady Bradshaigh, opposing polygamy, 'If they took it into their head to be tyrants, why should we allow them to be worthy examples to imitate?' For Hume, Priestley, and, later, Wollstonecraft too, this came to be the central objection.[25]

When, in 1776, the tireless abolitionist and social reformer Granville Sharp met the celebrated Tahitian Omai, he consequently drew on many of these themes to explain that polygamy, like adultery, offended every principle of modern, enlightened ethics: the laws of nature, principles of divine justice, the rights and sensibilities of women, and the natural empathy between all human beings. 'Mr Omai,' he recounted later, was 'a *black man*, who by custom and education entertained as inveterate prejudices in favour of keeping several wives, as any Maroon or African whatsoever':

'Ohh!' says he, 'two wives – very good; three wives – very, very good.' – 'No, Mr Omai', I said, 'not so; that would be contrary to the first principle of the law of nature.' – 'First principle of the law of nature,' said he; 'what that? what that?' – '*The first principle of the law of nature*', I said, 'is, that *no man must do any thing that he would not like to be done to himself.*' . . . 'Well, Mr. Omai,' said I, 'suppose, then, that your wife loves you very much; she would not like that you should love another woman; for the women have the same passions, and feelings, and love toward the men, that we have toward the women; and we ought, therefore, to regulate our behaviour toward them by

8. Omai in his early twenties, around the time of his meeting
with Granville Sharp.

our own feelings of what we should like and expect of faithful love and duty
from them towards ourselves.'[26]

As a result, even though polygamy had come to be widely discussed,
by the end of the eighteenth century various intellectual and practical
developments also made it increasingly unacceptable. In 1795, the
law against it was reaffirmed in parliament. Shortly afterwards, the
Malthusian sea-change in attitudes towards population further undermined its general intellectual credibility. Yet even then the ideal lived
on. This was partly because, by 1800, many of its presumptions had
become part of the general language of sexual liberty. Martin Madan's
own godson, Samuel Wesley, the nephew of the Methodist leader,
grew up convinced that sexual intercourse alone was the true basis of
a valid union between two people. Though no 'stickler' for it, his god-
father's book and his own reading of the scriptures had 'confirmed
him in the lawfulness of polygamy' – once a man and woman achieved

9. Granville Sharp, who was in his early forties when he
encountered Omai. He never married.

'mental and corporal conjunction ... a marriage is perfect, without
any additional ceremony invented or enforced by priests of any
religion'. On this basis he lived openly for many years with his lover
Charlotte Martin, and conceived a child with her, in defiance of his
family's horrified disapproval. 'She is truly and properly my wife by
all the laws of God and Nature,' he wrote angrily to his mother in
1792. 'She never can be made more so, by the mercenary tricks of
divine jugglers ... [not] a million of ceremonies, repeated myriads
of times, by as many successors and imitators of Simon Magus, can
serve to make her more happy, or more honourable.' Eventually they
went through a ceremony; but subsequently Wesley set up house with
their housekeeper, Sarah Suter, with whom he then lived unmarried,
having many more children, for almost thirty years. It is clear from
the practice of several of its early nineteenth-century exponents that
free love and multiple marriage were not always far apart. As Edward

Trelawny, Byron and Shelley's friend, declared, polygamy was 'not only lawful, but meritorious'.[27]

Its influence also persisted within various radical Protestant sects, who even after 1800 continued, like their sixteenth-, seventeenth-, and eighteenth-century forebears, to apply scriptural precedents to modern circumstances. In England, those attracted to the Swedenborgian advocacy of pre- and extra-marital concubinage included the artist William Blake, who appears to have been fascinated by polygamy. Even as an elderly man, in the 1820s, he continued to preach that the scriptures showed 'there should be a community of women' (see plate 4). James Edward Hamilton, the self-styled 'Ebionite', likewise thought it obvious 'that polygamy is, even *now*, permitted by God' – only 'bigots and prejudiced persons' could fail to appreciate the clear meaning of the Bible.[28]

Above all, the idea flourished in the United States. Already by the early 1780s it is possible to find New Englanders speaking and publishing that God's word favoured polygamy. After the turn of the century, several messianic leaders on the fringes of the religious revival embraced the practice. From the 1810s onwards, in Maine and then in upstate New York, it spread amongst the followers of Jacob Cochran, who taught that monogamous marriage was incompatible with biblical teaching and the practice of the apostolic church. In the 1830s and 1840s it came to be adopted by some members of the Church of Latter Day Saints (also known as Mormons), whose early membership in New York overlapped with that of the Cochranites. From the early 1830s onwards plural marriage was privately embraced and taught by the Mormons' founder and prophet, Joseph Smith Jr, who claimed to be inspired by recurrent angelic visitations. In 1843, as the practice was spreading amongst the leaders of the church, Charlotte Haven wrote excitedly to her family about 'wonderful revelations not yet made public'. After one of the elders returned from England with a second wife, the first was

reconciled to this at first unwelcome guest in her home . . . for her husband and some others have reasoned with her that plurality of wives is taught in the Bible, that Abraham, Jacob, Solomon, David and indeed all the old prophets and good men, had several wives, and if it is all right for them, it is all right for the Latter Day Saints.

In 1852, after the community had moved to the western territory of Utah, Smith's successor Brigham Young publicly announced it as the church's official doctrine. Exactly the same arguments underpinned the Mormon revelation as had inspired their eighteenth-century pre-decessors: the model of the Old Testament patriarchs, the tenor of Christ's teachings, God's command to be fruitful and multiply, the reasoning of earlier reformers such as Luther and Milton, the conceal-ment of divine truth by 'prejudice and priestcraft', the fact that most of the world's civilizations rejected monogamy, and the basic principle of religious liberty.[29] Only in 1890, after decades of fierce military and political pressure from the Federal Government, did the church renounce the practice.

Nowadays, though polygamy remains legal and fairly widespread in many African and Asian societies, especially Islamic ones, in the west it is routinely dismissed as essentially misogynist, as the product of atavistic religious beliefs, or as both – for modern polygamists nor-mally only allow men the right to multiple wives. Yet the continued prohibition of multiple marriage between consenting men and women also sits somewhat uneasily with the fundamental principles of mod-ern, secular sexual ethics, as recent debates in the United States show. Already in the 1850s this point had been stressed by John Stuart Mill. At the height of English and American condemnation of Mormon polygamy, he chose to make it the culminating example of his famous manifesto on human liberty. It was evident, wrote Mill, that Mormon-ism was, like all religion, 'the product of palpable imposture', and marriage in general was obviously unjust to women: so that, as for polygamy, 'no one has a deeper disapprobation' of it than he himself. But that was irrelevant. The polygamists of Utah deserved exactly the same rights of religious and personal freedom as everyone else. After all, the general principle of liberty was that

as it is useful that while mankind are imperfect there should be different opinions, so it is that there should be different experiments of living; that free scope should be given to varieties of character, short of injury to others; and that the worth of different modes of life should be proved practically, when anyone thinks fit to try them.[30]

MODERN PRINCIPLES

By the end of the eighteenth century, attitudes towards male and female sexuality had been transformed. As we have seen, this reconfiguration drew on many older ideas about the nature of men and women: but it was only made possible by the emergence of new ways of thinking about human character and society. It was also triggered by two unprecedented social developments: a great expansion of sexual freedom for men, and the irreversible breakthrough of female voices into public life. Their impact on mainstream culture was profound. The growing prominence of feminine views on sex supported the perception that men, not women, were the more seductive. Yet it also fuelled public concern about the ill effects of male licentiousness, and a growing backlash against its proponents.

The practical effects of this combination can be seen everywhere in eighteenth-, nineteenth-, and twentieth-century society. It produced a huge outpouring of philanthropic energy towards the rescue and reform of fallen women, which is examined in the next chapter. It helps explain the remarkable shift in pornographic treatments of sex, which up to the later seventeenth century presumed the superior sexual capacity of women, but thereafter increasingly celebrated male agency and female passivity.[1] Its general themes came to dominate art and literature, courtship, marriage, education, and every sphere of public and private life.

The creation of this new world was one of the most ambiguous legacies of the Enlightenment. In the longer term it benefited the emancipation of women. Right up until the late twentieth century, the belief that women were morally superior to men was to be a huge spur to feminist consciousness, solidarity, activism, and claims to equality. Its main basis was the presumption that women were the chaster sex. The idea was hence one of the chief foundations of modern feminism. Yet more immediately the revolution in attitudes towards lust had a less positive impact on the lives of generations of women. Though it bolstered female unity, it did so at the cost of sharpening many social and sexual biases. As we have explored, it led directly to the tightening of constraints on female behaviour, an increasing obsession with the desexualization of women, a widening gap between male and female sexual standards, and a pervasive concern with class differences in morality. Meanwhile the main aim of the reaction against male licence was less to restrain it completely than simply to ameliorate its effects.

This is not to say that women had ever been treated equally in earlier times; nor that female sexuality had no place in Victorian culture; nor that male freedom became universal or untrammelled. Nonetheless, already by 1800 there had taken place a fundamental and irreversible change in how the sexuality of men and women was thought of, and controlled. It sowed the seeds for an increasingly powerful feminist critique of how propertied men dominated their inferiors. However, it also placed patriarchal power on a new footing, and strengthened it in ways that, as in previous ages, were internalized and perpetuated by women as well as men. These were the hypocrisies and inconsistencies, the tensions between freedom and repression, that were created by the eighteenth-century revolution, energetically elaborated by the Victorians, and inherited by our twentieth-century predecessors. They never affected everybody equally. In recent decades their intellectual and social force has gradually diminished. Yet they are with us even now.

5

The Origins of White Slavery

Keep thee from the evil woman, from the flattery of the tongue
of a strange woman ... For by means of a whorish woman a
man is brought to a piece of bread: and the adulteress will
hunt for the precious life.

The Holy Bible (1611 edn), Proverbs 6.24 and 26

Instead of condemning ... reason, argument, and the unerring
laws of nature plead strongly in behalf of the unfortunate,
seduced, and ruined woman ... Let us then with an open and
munificent hand contribute to the relief of these our distressed
fellow-creatures.

Richard Harrison, *A Sermon ... before the
Governors of the Magdalen-Charity* (1768), 11, 20

The trafficking of persons, particularly women ... for sexual
exploitation, is one of the most egregious violations of human
rights that the United Nations now confronts. It is widespread
and growing. It is rooted in social and economic conditions.

*United Nations Convention Against Transnational
Organized Crime* (2004), iv

In the eighteenth century attitudes to prostitution were transformed
for ever. The conventional Protestant view had been that common
whores were the worst sexual reprobates of all. They were given the

harshest punishments: summarily whipped, imprisoned, and set to hard labour. During the 1650s, when the Adultery Act made them liable to execution, hundreds were simply rounded up, ripped from their friends and families, and transported thousands of miles across the ocean to the West Indies, without so much as a trial.* The entire culture of sexual discipline depended on such severity. For the terrible threat that lustful, avaricious whores posed to social order was abundantly illustrated in the Bible, and deeply imprinted upon the minds of ordinary men and women. Prostitutes had no special licence, no necessary function: on the contrary. Any unchaste woman was a whore; repeated promiscuity merely deepened her sin and her monstrousness.

Long after 1800, prostitutes continued to be treated as dangerous spreaders of disease and disorder. But from the middle of the eighteenth century this perspective was increasingly matched, and often overshadowed, by the emergence of alternative attitudes to commercial sex. Whores were henceforth as likely to be regarded with sympathy as with condemnation. In the eyes of countless eighteenth-, nineteenth-, and twentieth-century thinkers and activists, prostitution exemplified the nature of masculinity and femininity in modern western society – in its sexual theory and practice, its class dynamics, and its distribution of economic and political power.

PROSTITUTION AND PHILANTHROPY

From the 1750s onwards, the rescue and rehabilitation of prostitutes became a major social concern. Huge efforts were poured into the foundation and operation of asylums, workhouses, and other charities for fallen women, girls at risk of seduction, and other actual or potential victims of male lust.

We have already noticed several of the main developments that made this possible. By the middle of the eighteenth century, as a by-product of the advance of sexual liberty for men, the scope and visibility of prostitution had increased significantly. The view that it

---

* See above, Chapter 1, 'God's Revolution'.

should be tolerated had become widely accepted. So too had the idea that prostitutes were usually the victims of seduction and abandonment. And the age-old presumption that common whores could be summarily punished for their evil-doing was gradually supplanted by the principle that, in fact, prostitution itself was not legally punishable. What remains to be explained is the rise and shape of public philanthropy towards prostitutes. Why did it become so wildly popular?

The basic ideas that prostitution might be a necessary evil, and that penitents deserved assistance, had first emerged as part of medieval Catholic doctrine. In the pre-Reformation church the cult of Mary Magdalen had been immensely popular, and in Protestant England her story lived on as a powerful parable of moral failing and redemption. 'I doubt not but we be all Magdalens in falling into sin,' wrote John Foxe in the 1560s, 'but we be not again Magdalens in knowing ourselves and in rising from sin'. The theatre of the early reformers adapted the medieval dramatizations of her life to propagate Calvinist doctrine; and hers was one of the few saints' days that continued to be marked by the Church of England. In the early seventeenth century her image remained recognizable enough to adorn street signs and to inspire verse. Indeed, depictions of the Magdalen weeping were such a popular theme in contemporary poetry that they gave rise to a new adjective, 'maudlin', to describe tearful sentiment. Later in the century, under the influence of continental examples, painted and printed images of beautiful penitents became highly fashionable. Several of Charles II's mistresses were pictured as Magdalens. By the 1740s, the genre had grown so ubiquitous as to be one of the tired and worn-out clichés attacked by Hogarth in his satirical *Battle of the Pictures* (see illustrations 10–12).[1]

This new fascination with penitents coincided with mounting dissatisfaction over the efficacy of punishment. The traditional view had been that chastisement was the best way of encouraging sexual sinners to reform. To let the 'punishment beat you home to God', they were told, was the true 'work of charity to your soule'. 'Charity expended for correcting the idle,' explained one divine, 'is better than that which gives them a present ease', for if left uncorrected they would destroy not only themselves but others too. 'Pity therefore in

10. The Duchess of Cleveland, Charles II's mistress, as 'England's Magdalen'.

11. In the later 1660s Sir Peter Lely painted Mary Davis, another of Charles II's mistresses, in the guise of the Magdalen: this engraved, mass-market version was produced some years later.

12. *Magdalena*, by Jan Griffier: a typically salacious popular mezzotint of the ostensibly religious subject.

you would be the greatest cruelty,' another preacher urged magistrates in 1698: to be truly charitable towards whores and whoremongers they should rather 'put off all bowels of compassion' and exercise 'the utmost rigour'. 'Few are committed to the house of correction,' it was conventionally believed, 'but they come out better.'[2]

By the middle of the eighteenth century, however, this had become a questionable supposition. It was, thought the businessman Jonas Hanway, merely the out-dated logic of 'lawgivers and magistrates', who believed that 'compulsive labour, or corporal correction, would either awe the wicked, and prevent iniquity; or that the actual suffering of these severities, would reform all gross enormities'. It was also increasingly difficult to reconcile with the overstretched, grubby reality of metropolitan justice. Stripping a woman naked and whipping her in public 'may, for aught I know, contribute to her modesty, and put her in a state of innocence', mused Bernard Mandeville disingenuously: but really 'flogging has a quite contrary effect'. The hero of *The London-Spy* was equally certain: if anything, 'it makes many whores . . . but it can in no measure reclaim 'em.'[3]

Such cynicism about the efficacy of punishment had a long popular history. Now, though, as we saw in Chapters 1 and 2, it took on new respectability. As early as the 1690s, even some supporters of the reformation societies acknowledged that, contrary to the traditional view, prostitutes sent to a house of correction 'do generally come out ten times worse and more impudent than they went in'. The same conclusion gradually imposed itself on lawgivers and magistrates as well. A Commons committee resolved in 1751 that there were 'great defects in, and abuses of, the houses of correction'. Henry Fielding agreed: they tended more to 'the improvement, than for the correction of debauchery'. In short, as one of his subordinates concluded despondently, after years of zealously enforcing the law, it was a 'useless severity' to punish prostitutes, for 'punishment only prevents for the time it operates, but hardly ever produced one reformation'.[4]

Alternative proposals, based on the power of religion, were first put forward around the turn of the century. Surely, argued Thomas Bray, founder of the Societies for the Propagation of the Gospel and for Promoting Christian Knowledge, if prostitutes were confined in 'a penitential hospital . . . under the government of some wise and virtuous matrons, and some aged and holy divines', they would in due course 'recover to a due fear of God, and horror of their evil ways'. Instead of mere outward punishment, they should be subjected to prayers, catechisms, 'penances and methods of mortification . . . 'til they are morally persuaded [and] become thoroughly and sincerely reformed'. His fellow missionary and philanthropist Thomas Nelson became equally convinced of the need for 'a house to receive such young women as may be convinced of their folly', where they might be restored to moral health 'by a true Christian discipline'.[5] Until general attitudes towards the culpability of whores began to soften in the 1730s and 1740s, however, such charitable views were uncommon.

Indeed, for many centuries English attitudes on this point seem to have been harsher than those in other Christian countries. During the middle ages, with the encouragement of successive popes, many convents and other institutions for repentant prostitutes had been founded across the continent, in Byzantium, Italy, Germany, France, and elsewhere. But not in England. Many more were established as part of the Catholic Counter-Reformation of the sixteenth and seventeenth centuries. Yet to English commentators these had always been illustrations of popish sexual corruption, rather than serious social projects.[6]

It was only towards the middle of the eighteenth century, as support for the idea slowly spread, that its practice in Catholic countries was increasingly referred to with approval rather than distaste. By the 1750s, many English proponents of a penitential hospital were frank in their admiration of foreign examples. The English, thought Hanway, were not on the whole as sexually 'abandoned' as, say, the Italians; but when it came to dealing with the consequences they had much to learn. 'Though we think ourselves so much wiser than many other nations, yet, in this particular, we are many years behind several of them.'[7] It was the language not just of a well-travelled individual, but of a more cosmopolitan generation. Half a century of increasing English involvement in European affairs, through trade, travel, and war, had greatly broadened the appreciation, at first or second hand, of foreign ways of doing things.

The notion of a penitential hospital also became increasingly practicable. At the beginning of the eighteenth century, innovative proposals such as those of Bray and Nelson had remained the pursuit of a pious minority, and their implementation faced widespread hostility. Like every area of public life after the Glorious Revolution, new philanthropies tended to become a battle-ground between the interests of Whigs and Tories, High Churchmen, and dissenters. Each of the main charitable initiatives of the period – corporations of the poor, workhouses, and charity schools – was undermined by such political and sectarian conflicts.[8]

From the 1730s onwards, by contrast, there emerged a new, less politicized way of organizing public philanthropy, adapted from the world of commercial speculation: a private, joint-stock company, funded by subscription and targeted at a specific problem, rather than at the poor as a whole. The spectacular success on this model of the London Foundling Hospital (chartered in 1739, opened in 1741) suddenly made practical intervention in social problems seem much easier than it had been earlier in the century. Together with the outbreak of war at the end of the 1730s (and again in the mid-1750s), it also helped to make joint-stock philanthropy fashionable, especially amongst the capital's growing business community. As political arithmetic became established as a central foundation of public policy, saving lives became an ever more urgent national priority.[9]

The Foundling was rapidly followed by the London (1740) and Middlesex (1745) Hospitals, which addressed themselves to illness and injury, and then by a multitude of more specialized projects: amongst them the so-called Lock Hospital for treating venereal disease (1747), two hospitals for the cure of smallpox, and no fewer than five 'lying-in' charities to ease the childbirth of poor women. The Magdalen House for penitent prostitutes, and the Lambeth Asylum to protect poor girls from seduction, both of which opened in London in 1758, followed the same model. So did the Dublin Magdalen Asylum, founded in 1767, and every later institution of this kind.[10]

By mid-century, attitudes towards innovative social projects had been turned on their head. From being the preserve of a minority and the outgrowth of exceptional religious zeal, public charity had become a leading expression of social and mercantile status. Amongst the founders of the Magdalen and the Lambeth Asylum there was not a

View of the MAGDALEN HOSPITAL, *in S.t George's Fields.*

13. The London Magdalen House: the first refuge for penitent prostitutes to be founded in the English-speaking world.

single clergyman. Instead, philanthropy was now an activity indulged in by a large and varied community of propertied men and women, and widely celebrated as a mark of British enlightenment. 'It is hardly possible to mention a sickness or disease,' marvelled a metropolitan preacher in 1762, 'but an asylum is readily found for the unhappy . . . indigent sufferer'. 'A general philanthropy happily abounds through the nation,' exulted others; London as a whole was 'an ornament, in its public charities especially, to human nature, and to Christianity'.[11]

The foundation of charities to rescue poor women from sexual suffering was thus one instance of a more general movement to improve the health and numbers of the labouring classes, and thereby increase national strength and prosperity. However, the prominence of sexual philanthropies also illustrates the advance of new sentiments about female innocence and culpability. The older view had always been that providing for bastards and sexual sinners would simply encourage fornication. As Defoe summarized the arguments against a Foundling Hospital in 1728, it would 'set up a nursery for lewdness, and encourage fornication . . . Who would be afraid of sinning, if they can so easily get rid of their bastards? We shall soon be over-run with

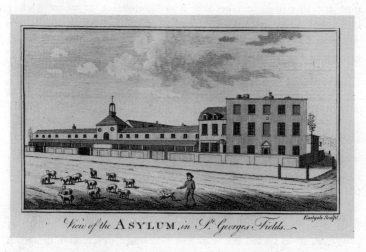

View of the ASYLUM, in S.t Georges Fields.

14. The Lambeth Asylum: poor girls deemed to be at risk of seduction were sent to live here, to be brought up as servants and apprentices.

foundlings when there is such encouragement given to whoredom.'
But by the middle of the eighteenth century, for the first time, the contrary opinion had begun to hold sway. It is true that the application of
sympathy was easier in some cases than in others. To argue, for
example, that sufferers from venereal disease were deserving victims,
rather than foul and culpable sinners, involved the early propagandists of the Lock Hospital in some revealingly defensive rhetoric.
No, they were forced to stress, diseased whores (and others 'who vol-
untarily draw this misery on themselves') were not 'improper objects';
no, they should not 'be left to rot alive'; no, they continued in their
trade, spreading disease, not willingly but only out of 'a kind of necessity'. The hospital's main problem in attracting fashionable backing
was that its practical benefits appeared to be comparatively limited.
The sheer repulsiveness of the subject did not help. At no other charity would the chaplain himself, far from rushing in to rescue souls,
frankly admit to his patients that he could not bear to stay long in the
ward, or 'converse with you in private', because of their repugnant
state.[12]

Far more appealing was the prospect of 'making *bad* women into
good ones' through a charity for penitent whores. By the 1750s support for this idea had become a commonplace of polite society.
Newspapers and pamphleteers eagerly discussed its principles and
practice. Members of Parliament spoke approvingly of it. The Archbishop of Canterbury took a keen interest. Horace Walpole joked
about turning Strawberry Hill into 'an hospital for *filles repenties*'.
The topical poet John Lockman rushed out 'The ruined Margaretta's
soliloquy, in her garret, Drury-Lane, after reading the proposal for
saving deserted and prostitute girls', to be performed to music at
Vauxhall. The less fashionable public could purchase a penny pamphlet that explained the utility of a penitential hospital. The Dowager
Duchess of Somerset, who had been the first of the 'Lady Petitioners'
for a Foundling Hospital back in 1729, again set an example by head-
ing a subscription. Many competing plans were devised. The *London
Chronicle* announced that it would defray the cost of publishing any
proposal, so as to aid the search for the most practicable design. A
large committee of luminaries set up for the same purpose included
amongst its number the uxorious actor David Garrick, so happily

married that he never so much as spent a day apart from his wife, as well as the infamous libertine John Wilkes, who revelled in sexual variety.* No other practical scheme of the period so successfully appealed to men and women of widely differing sensibilities.[13]

Its universal attraction was equally evident from the attitude of the leading authors of the day. By the 1750s Samuel Johnson had plenty of experience picking up prostitutes: though mainly, he stressed, 'for the sake of hearing their stories'. 'His younger friends now and then affected to tax him with less chast[e] intentions,' records an early biographer. 'But he would answer – "No Sir; we never proceeded to the *Opus Magnum*."' At one point Dr Johnson had himself taken direct action to save 'one of those wretched females'. He carried her home on his back, nursed her to recovery from venereal disease, and found her a respectable job: precisely the kind of charity that, it was now envisaged, a public hospital should provide.[14]

Samuel Richardson, by contrast, boasted that he'd never in his life visited a brothel, nor ever even been 'in company with a lewd woman'. Yet he was equally taken with the idea. Already in the 1740s he had advocated a 'college for Magdalens', and discussed with his confidante Lady Bradshaigh how best to help fallen women. When revising *Clarissa* in 1751, he laid new emphasis on the heroine's repentance for her forced unchastity. Miss Harlowe, a character now observed, 'hath been a *second Magdalen* in her *penitence*, and yet not so bad as a *Magdalen* in her *faults*'. Three years later, the superior sensibility of Sir Charles Grandison was revealed by his merciful response to the 'melancholy story' of his father's old mistress, the 'poor Magdalen' Mrs Oldham, who 'wept ... as a penitent' in gratitude for his goodness. Later in the novel, Richardson has Sir Charles make an impassioned speech in favour of 'An Hospital for Female Penitents', where seduced women might 'recover the path of virtue'. When the Magdalen House opened, Richardson became a generous subscriber and activist on its behalf.[15]

Even more important was the engagement of two key groups. The first were the city's leading magistrates. 'Who will not rejoice to see

* Among the Lambeth Asylum's earliest Guardians-for-Life was likewise the notorious rake Sir Francis Dashwood: *An Account of the Institution, and Proceedings of the Guardians, of the Asylum* (1761), 28.

this happy change,' exclaimed the blind justice John Fielding, 'miserable prostitutes, etc. converted into modest, decent, happy women, and useful domestic servants'. For years, wrote his colleague Saunders Welch in 1753, he had wished 'with an aching heart' that, in this age of 'hospitals for almost every human calamity', one could be provided 'whereby these unhappy fellow-creatures might be rescued from disease and misery, and instead of being a nuisance to the public, become useful to it'. In the later 1750s both men submitted detailed plans to the public and set about vigorously raising money.[16]

More helpfully still, the scheme was taken up by a group of mercantile philanthropists including Hanway, the most active and eccentric humanitarian of the eighteenth century, and his business partner Robert Dingley. These were men with wide-ranging contacts, adept at mobilizing public opinion, who already had considerable experience as the founders and governors of other joint-stock charities. Once they turned their full attention to the creation of a penitential hospital the outcome was scarcely in doubt. 'This seems to be the *only object* that has escaped us,' wrote Hanway excitedly to Dingley in 1758, as its foundation came within their sights. What a glorious prospect it was, he exulted, 'to co-operate with heaven' in turning abandoned prostitutes into happy wives and mothers – 'a work of *creation* as well as *redemption*'.[17]

Once it had been articulated and promoted in these ways, the idea of a hospital for penitents captured the popular imagination more quickly and more fully than any other charitable institution of the eighteenth century. When a subscription was first opened it reached over three thousand pounds within a few weeks – more money than other charities raised in years. Within a few months, the governors had rented and equipped a building, and on 10 August 1758 the Magdalen House in Whitechapel received its first penitents. By 1760 the number of inmates, originally restricted to fifty, had swelled to over 130; by 1769, when the hospital began constructing new accommodation in Blackfriars, over 1,500 women had passed through it. Throughout the following decades, benefactions poured in from across the English-speaking world. 'From Buckinghamshire to Barbados, from Middlesex to Madras, from Chepstow to Calcutta', men and women eagerly supported the new charity.[18]

Its success exemplified a profound and lasting shift in the treatment of sexual immorality. Henceforth, non-governmental, charitable organizations would always play a major role in social policy towards prostitution, supplementing and even sidelining the church and the state's traditional focus on policing and punishment. This was a notable expansion in the scale and ambition of collective charity. Moreover, public policy now presumed that women were not always wholly responsible for their own sexual conduct. Instead, they needed to be rescued from circumstances beyond their control. Philanthropy thus both reconceived the problem of prostitution and promised a radical new solution. 'The old method of fighting has been found so ineffectual,' urged Hanway. 'Let us try a different kind of treatment.'[19]

PENITENCE AND RESURRECTION

Philanthropy promised to deliver three kinds of benefit: spiritual, demographic, and economic. Its methods were evidently novel. But the arguments for it were strikingly similar to those that had traditionally underpinned punishment.

The most fundamental motive of both, for example, was to rescue sinners from damnation. Unlike other hospitals, boasted the supporters of the Magdalen, this one saved souls as well as bodies. It alone comforted 'the wounded mind', and relieved 'the unutterable anguish of a bleeding conscience'; it alone was 'intended to heal the soul, and not only to abate temporary pains, but to save from eternal torments'. The 'great and material point' of her confinement, every woman was reminded upon admission, was her salvation.[1]

To this end, life in the Magdalen House was dominated by private and public prayer, sermons, hymns, the reading of edifying texts, and religious instruction by the resident matron and chaplain. Fasting was 'particularly recommended'. The ultimate aim of it all was to prepare inmates for a good end. Like the death-bed conversions of egregious sinners, or the last dying confessions of convicted felons, the spiritual regime of penitent prostitutes was meant to put them in an appropriate state of readiness for paradise. Indeed, death itself was often portrayed as an imminent, happy relief. 'Future bliss' was not far away, the inmates were reassured; 'everlasting comforts' were being prepared for them in heaven; the holy angels were tuning their harps in readiness.[2]

The same note was often struck in edifying literature. When in 1770 the charity's governors published 'An authentic narrative of a Magdalen', to give the public an idea of what happened to successful penitents, it described a girl who almost immediately after her discharge had fallen ill, lost a leg to gangrene, and died. In the wildly popular *Triumphant Death of F. S., A Converted Prostitute who died April 1763, aged 26* (which by 1800 had gone through at least fourteen editions across the Empire) the heroine spends a month on her death-bed, receiving visitors, testifying to the goodness of God, and breaking into impromptu song, before she finally expires 'without the least sign of pain'. Even the inspirational picture chosen to decorate the matron's parlour at the Magdalen House depicted the 'Death of a Penitent Prostitute'.[3]

Yet penitents were meant to be resurrected in this life as well. It was sometimes suggested that the hospital itself was an earthly paradise: 'a little heaven', a 'blessed place', 'a heavenly hospitable asylum'. So great was the sanctity of the place, boasted one early account, that the mere report of it was known to have converted sinners. Other observers, like Horace Walpole and his friend, the poet Edward Jerningham, were much taken with its resemblance to a convent. 'What tho' their youth imbib'd an early stain,' declaimed the latter, in an unaccountably well-received effort of 1763, 'A second innocence they here obtain, / And nun-clad penance heals their wounded name.'[4]

The commonest metaphor was that the Magdalen House was a family. Its inmates were infants, to be sheltered from the world and brought up in order, virtue, and obedience. The directors were not to be called governors but 'Guardians' or 'Fathers'; the matron was 'a good mother to all her little family'; the penitents were treated with 'the gentleness of parental affection'. Reduced to a state of infantile helplessness, they were their parents' 'daughters of shame', their 'children of affliction'. They lived, it was happily observed, 'with the simplicity of young children'. In order to facilitate their regression and rebirth, a preference was given to younger, more malleable applicants, and every effort was made to expunge the past. A woman could take a new name. No one was permitted to inquire into her history. Contact with the outside world was minimized.[5]

Through such means the reputation of each penitent was to be wiped clean and her character reshaped. In place of idleness and vice she would imbibe habits of discipline and sobriety. Upon admission, she swore 'to behave herself decently and orderly'. Her old clothes were removed, and, if deemed 'too fine' for her station, confiscated. She was dressed instead in a plain grey uniform; admonished to maintain 'the humble, meek, and downcast look'; and nourished on simple, wholesome food. Every day followed a strict timetable of worship and hard work, whose practical purpose is neatly captured by the biblical passages on the life of Christ that were recommended for contemplation and imitation: 'His frequent performance of the duty of private prayer'; 'His humility and lowliness of mind'; 'His contentment in a low and mean condition in this world'; and so on. Re-educating prostitutes in this way enabled their rehabilitation in the world by restoring them to health and virtue, and curing for good their 'disease of the mind'. Above all it paved the way for their return to a family, the best guarantor of public and private harmony. Restoring the fabric of domestic life was a central concern of the charity's governors, who devoted considerable time and effort to reconciling penitents to their parents and friends.[6]

In its paternalism, its stress on re-education, and its desire to repair damaged social relations, the Magdalen House unwittingly echoed the ideals of sixteenth- and seventeenth-century houses of correction. The same was true of its concern with national health, although by the mid eighteenth century this had become a much more central and elaborate preoccupation than had been the case in Tudor and Stuart times. Like every major charitable institution of the mid eighteenth century, the Magdalen was intended to increase the population. Sixty per cent of the women they rescued, estimated the governors in 1759, would otherwise 'have been dead in less than two years'. In the eyes of its supporters these were invaluable lives to have saved, especially 'at a period when war is spreading so widely its terrible devastations of the human species'.[7]

Most inspiring of all was the prospect of stimulating marriage and fertility. Nothing epitomized the transformative power of philanthropy in the 1750s and 1760s as vividly as the image of barren prostitutes turned into 'the joyful mothers of children', or of orphan girls preserved from ruin, and trained up instead to be 'good wives, and mothers of a numerous issue'. 'Particular encouragement is intended for those who shall marry,' declared the promoters of the Dublin Asylum. Jonas Hanway, a life-long bachelor, was confident that 'great numbers of these converts would find good husbands'; for it was evident to him that 'all men are not equally delicate, in this instance'. 'A change of manners of this kind', conceded one early account of Magdalens mutating into eligible young brides, was 'not less strange than new'; but they would undoubtedly make 'the best of wives'. A system of cash rewards was set up to encourage the practice. The initial results were encouraging. Roughly 10 to 15 per cent of the women who completed their time in the House went on to be married. Before long, to the 'inexpressible satisfaction' of the governors, children began to be born to them.[8]

Within a few decades, though, political arithmetic was starting to move in the opposite direction. In 1798, Malthus's *Essay on the Principle of Population* codified the new orthodoxy: it was overpopulation, not underpopulation, that constituted the real threat to national prosperity. Well before then, the notion had begun to gain ground that the numbers of the labouring classes were less important than their economic discipline. The population, stated the leading economic commentator Arthur Young flatly in 1774, 'ought to be left to its own course'. The same idea was implicit in Adam Smith's hugely influential *Wealth of Nations*, published two years later. It was, concluded the secretary of the Philanthropic Society in 1789, 'a supposition not always verified by experience' that every life was worth saving or supporting.[9] Though demographic principles had been central to the foundation of mid-eighteenth-century philanthropies, by the early nineteenth century their practical application had come to seem much less straightforward.

SEX AND WORK

A more enduring argument was that charity was the best way of turning orphan girls and prostitutes into economically productive members of society. This consideration, too, had long antecedents.

Forced labour in houses of correction had been introduced in Tudor times as a means of accustoming the idle and the dissolute to economic as well as moral discipline. The general idea of improving national prosperity by systematically training up the poor and putting them to work had been around for at least as long, and had gained new momentum in the later seventeenth century.

Initially it was not easy to envisage using prostitutes in this way. In the 1690s Thomas Bray could only think that penitent whores should be 'put to work at whatsoever they are found fittest for'; whilst in 1726 it was still possible for Daniel Defoe to doubt that any fallen woman could ever reacquire habits of industry. By the middle of the eighteenth century, however, it had become a powerfully attractive proposition. 'Do but employ them,' it was now said of prostitutes, 'and you will save them.' Underlying this new optimism was the perennial hope that charitable institutions might be able to finance themselves from the labour of their inmates, perhaps even to turn a profit. It was in anticipation of 'a great increase of national wealth' through such means that the Society for the Encouragement of Arts, Manufactures and Commerce offered its gold medal in 1758 for the best plan 'to receive and employ such common prostitutes as are desirous to forsake their evil courses'.[1]

This change in attitudes arose from a new way of thinking about the connection between prostitution and work. The older view, largely unchallenged before 1700 and still easily traceable half a century later, was that women became whores because of the kind of work that they did and the dissolute habits that it bred. Maid-servants, milliners, and seamstresses were so generally exposed to temptations, opportunities and dangers, the argument ran, that many of them ended up selling their bodies as well as their skills. Nine out of ten girls apprenticed to milliners, warned an occupational survey in 1747, were 'ruined and undone: take a survey of all the common women of the town, who take their walks between Charing Cross and Fleet Ditch, and, I am persuaded, more than one half of them have been bred milliners' (see illustration 15).[2]

Implicit in this outlook was one of the most cherished presumptions of the propertied classes: that an honest living was available to any man or woman who wanted one, and that poverty was a consequence,

15. In the first scene of this satire, one milliner fondles her lover, whilst the other gets drunk. In the second, a man invites her into his bed; the final image shows the discovery of their bastard child, abandoned in the street. The motto below sums up how milliners make their living.

never a cause, of whoredom. 'Better for you to work hard and to submit to the meanest service than to make yourselves odious to God and man,' John Dunton had urged immoral women in 1696: fecklessness was no excuse for vice. A few years later, the societies for reformation of manners took to distributing free pamphlets to prostitutes, in which the same message was spelled out with uncompromising clarity. 'To such as plead that their *poverty* drives them to this accursed way of life', proclaimed the author of one such tract,

I reply,

1. There are many honest ways of providing the necessaries of life. And if they have not been bred to labour (which is their usual answer to this), yet they ought now to accustom themselves to it, rather than sell their souls to the Devil . . .
2. The real necessaries of life are easily provided; if once humility, mortification, and self-denial come to prescribe the quantity and quality of our food and raiment.
3. God has promised to *add these outward Things to such as seek his Kingdom, and the Righteousness thereof* . . . (Matthew 6. 33).
4. If the case were really as you put it, you had better starve here, than *perish* to all eternity.

It was but 'a wicked and a false pretence' for any prostitute to plead poverty, agreed another, 'it was the inordinate love of sensual pleasure, it was idleness, and an aversion to honest labour, which first corrupted their minds'.[3]

Yet the evident defensiveness of such arguments from around the turn of the century points to the emergence of alternative ideas. Thomas Bray was moved to hear 'that many of those thievish and lewd women who are committed to Newgate, as also those strolling gilts [i.e. street-walkers] which are whipped in Bridewell, do often complain with tears in their eyes, that it is for want of employment, and to get bread, that they betake themselves to or continue in that abominable course of life'. It was 'very plain', he concluded, that 'their necessities and lusts together are too violent to restrain their licentiousness'. The same unease about the distinction between enforced poverty and inherent fecklessness permeates the work of other social commentators of the period. 'We find', wrote Dunton of common whores, 'that those criminals consist generally of idle or poor persons. If there were care taken to compel the former to work, and to find out means to employ the latter, much of this lewdness might be prevented.' Many other Londoners appear to have thought the same; a few months later a new corporation of the poor began its campaign against idleness and poverty along similar lines.[4]

In the course of the eighteenth century such tentative distinctions came to be developed into an essentially new and more sophisticated view of the relationship between work and vice. This was not just because of the general shift towards structural rather than personal explanations of sexual behaviour. It also reflected an important economic trend: in the course of the eighteenth century many traditionally female branches of urban employment came to be increasingly subjected to male competition and monopoly. By the 1780s the matter was so notorious that *The Times* urged parliament to 'lay a heavy tax on shopmen in all such branches as ought to afford employment to women'; drawing attention in particular to the pernicious masculinization of perfumery, millinery, haberdashery, and linen-drapery.[5]

As a result, what was perceived to be the causal connection between whoredom and impoverishment was more or less reversed. Towards the end of the century, for example, the first sustained feminist analyses of prostitution focused upon the evils of female unemployment. The fact that 'multitudes of men' had encroached on such female avocations as selling 'linen, gauze, ribbons, and lace . . . perfumes and cosmetics . . . feathers and trinkets . . . bonnets and caps', argued Priscilla Wakefield in 1798, left no means 'of gaining a creditable livelihood to many destitute women, whom a dreadful necessity drives to the business of prostitution'. The male monopolization of employments, agreed Mary Ann Radcliffe in *The Female Advocate: or an Attempt to Recover the Rights of Women from Male Usurpation* (1799), forced women directly to 'the absolute necessity of bartering their virtue for bread'. Both of them knew from personal experience how difficult it was for women to maintain a family without the support of a husband.[6]

In the work of more radical thinkers such as Mary Hays and Mary Wollstonecraft the critique went further still, and prostitution sometimes was held up as an epitome of all female suffering. In Wollstonecraft's unfinished novel *The Wrongs of Woman*, when the protagonist hears the horrific story of a former prostitute, it makes 'her thoughts take a wider range . . . she was led to consider the oppressed state of women' more generally. Such assertions had particular force in the difficult economic climate of the 1790s. Yet by then the idea that inadequate opportunity of employment was one of the main causes of prostitution had been long established. 'Women have but few trades and fewer manufactures to employ them', it was observed in 1758: small wonder that so many ended up as whores. It was an absurd affectation, warned another writer in 1760, to refuse countenance and employment to fallen women, and suppose that they should rather 'die martyrs to chastity' than support themselves in the only way left to them.[7]

As a consequence it was commonly argued by mid eighteenth-century philanthropists that some form of employment should be provided to prostitutes, to allow them to live honestly and to harness their untapped industry for the greater good. John Fielding suggested that the Magdalen House be run as a public laundry, so as to maximize its utility. The Lambeth Asylum sought to apprentice its girls to useful trades. The further such ideas were pursued, however, the clearer it became that they could not easily succeed without putting other women out of work. 'If all the linen washed out were done here, what would become of the poor washerwomen?', asked one critical commentator, 'would it not be necessary to immediately establish an infirmary or hospital for them?' As for training up orphans and penitents to sewing, dress-making, and other such skills, that would but ruin, and drive into prostitution, the women already established in those trades.[8]

It was partly to escape this paradox that many philanthropists proposed to open up entirely new spheres of employment. It was the burgeoning market for Persian rugs, and the prospect of cornering it by producing them domestically, that first impelled Hanway to take the whole idea of a penitential hospital seriously (see illustration 16). Others suggested a lace-making enterprise, so that 'vast sums would be saved that are now sent to France and Flanders', or the manufacture by English women of 'Dresden Work, so much now the mode'. Every aspect of the scheme, agreed the economic theorist Joseph Massie, should be aimed at undermining foreign imports.[9]

An even more inviting target was the sexism of the domestic labour market. 'There are many trades, now in the hands of men,' explained Hanway, 'in which women might do as well, and some in which their natural ingenuity would enable them to carry on much better.' John Fielding drew up a list of them – 'the closing and braiding of shoes . . . the making of all sorts of slops for the use of the Navy . . . the studding of watch-cases . . . the making of wig and band-boxes'. The possibilities appeared to be limitless: pin-making, the weaving of hair for wig-makers, artificial flowers, children's toys. If the range of female

16. Jonas Hanway's early vision of life in the penitential hospital: prayer, healthy food, and useful, carpet-making, industry.

employments could be widened, it was hoped, fewer women would be forced into prostitution in the first place. In Birmingham, one writer noted, women were employed in all sorts of male occupations, such as watch-making and engraving. 'I have likewise been told,' he concluded triumphantly, 'that there is no such thing as street-walkers in Birmingham'.[10]

Yet when the Magdalen House and the Lambeth and Dublin Asylums opened, their inmates' work was conventional and the income from it minimal. Apart from an early experiment in making carpets 'after the Turkey manner', they spun wool and flax, wound silk, and sewed clothes: not at all the 'new trades for women' that had been envisaged. The Lambeth Asylum repeatedly tried to drum up trade by advertising publicly. Its girls offered to sew 'a full-trimmed shirt' for two shillings; a 'plain' one for a shilling and sixpence; or a servant's shift for only a shilling. But there was very little demand. As a consequence the charity was forced to get by on the cheap. Parts of the premises were sublet to a fish merchant. A converted stable served as its first chapel; the gardener doubled as an usher; and a blind boy of fourteen was found to play the organ during services (until 'great complaint' was made about his performance and a paid musician had to be engaged instead).[11] Once again, there proved to be a considerable mismatch between the ambitions and the immediate achievements of sexual charity.

SELF-INTEREST AND SEXUAL INTEREST

The appeal of the philanthropic approach went far beyond its promise of social improvement. Vanity, fashion, and self-interest were also important motives. Networks of family, friendship, and business, for example, were crucial to the success of every public charity. Between them, the eight men who founded the Magdalen held five directorships of the Russia Company, four of the Marine Society, and four of the Foundling Hospital; with other ties through kinship, trade, the Bank of England, and the Society for Promoting Christian Knowledge.[1]

The disadvantage of this dependence on private connections was that clashes of personality led easily to division. In 1756, for example, John Fielding had set up a scheme to supply homeless boys to the navy, only to have it hijacked by a group of merchants led by Jonas Hanway and Robert Dingley. Two years later, when the same men proposed a charity for prostitutes, he pointedly refused to join them and started a subscription of his own. This in turn provoked the expression of even deeper personal resentment by his fellow magistrate and social reformer Saunders Welch, who had risen to the bench from humble origins. For years, Welch had felt 'insulted in the grossest manner' by Fielding's snobbery. Now he struck back. Without ever mentioning him by name, he published a withering attack on Fielding's proposals, and then joined Dingley and Hanway's committee.[2] Out of these rival groups would emerge the Asylum and the Magdalen. The two projects had always been conceived of as part of the same scheme. They came to be separated not on principle but because of personal animosity.

Such unseemly squabbles provided ammunition for the view that all public charity was but a mask for selfish motives. It was easy to see, warned Dr Johnson in the aftermath of Fielding's 'ridiculous feuds', that 'open competition between different hospitals, and the animosity with which their patrons oppose one another, may prejudice weak minds against them all'. Was it not obvious, asked a sceptic in 1763, that when a magistrate neglected his real business 'while he is busied in raising money for new charities, under the pretence of suppressing vice ... his charitable zeal proceeds from finding it his private advantage, and not from a public spirit, or a design of doing good?' This was unfair, and yet it is undeniable that the greatest beneficiaries of public charities were often its employees and promoters. In *The Adventures of Ferdinand Count Fathom* (1753) by the surgeon and novelist Tobias Smollett, the hero schemes to make his fortune as a London doctor by acquiring 'interest enough to erect an hospital, lock [i.e. a venereal disease hospital], or infirmary, by the voluntary subscription of his friends; a scheme which had succeeded to a miracle, with many of the profession, who had raised themselves into notice, upon the carcases of the poor'.[3]

At sexual charities it was clergymen who showed themselves at their worst. The chaplain of St Thomas's put about rumours that the chaplain of the Magdalen 'had been excommunicated for immorality'. The chaplain of the Lock became convinced of 'unnatural wickedness being practised' at the Magdalen and forced himself on it with a formal court of inquiry. Yet financial rather than sexual irregularity was both the most dangerous and the most likely problem in the uncertain, impoverished, and competitive world of unbeneficed clerics. The Lock Hospital was obliged to dismiss successive clergymen for larceny. The preacher of the Magdalen turned out to be a swindler and a cheat: in 1777, deep in debt, he was hanged for having obtained over 4,000 pounds through a forged bill of exchange. At the Lambeth Asylum the rot went deepest of all. In March 1761 the Reverend Francis Kelly Maxwell, long in the market for such a post, managed to get himself elected chaplain of the institution, at a stipend of half a guinea per week. Within a few weeks he had engineered the sacking of the charity's secretary and added the post to his duties, thereby doubling his salary. By June, he and his family had been allotted rent-free apartments on the premises, and Maxwell had taken on the additional position of receiver of donations. As well as making himself ever more indispensable and highly paid, he began to steal from the charity. By 1770 his emoluments had swollen to 200 guineas per year, as well as free housing, heat, and light. When, in the same year, the Asylum's treasurer accused him of financial impropriety, Maxwell managed to oust him, took over the office himself, and expanded his misappropriations. Not until 1782 was he exposed and sacked.[4]

Self-interest also motivated the ordinary benefactors of any charity. It was a general truth that all organized philanthropy involved the exercise of authority over one's inferiors: what Mandeville had described in 1723 as 'one motive above all, which . . . is to be carefully conceal'd, I mean the satisfaction there is in ordering and directing'. By the second half of the century this was overtly acknowledged, even celebrated. As we have seen, it was conventional to portray the inmates of sexual charities as helpless children, and the patrons as their wise and benevolent parents. A prostitute, explained one preacher in 1759, was little different from 'a poor harmless animal . . . suffering in misery': only the intervention of a benevolent superior could save her. Her saviours, by contrast, were as angels: their beneficence outshone the sun, their endeavours were 'truly godlike', they were 'the stewards and vice-gerents of heaven'. Subscribers to the Lock Hospital received an illustrated certificate which represented the Magdalen as an attractively demure young sinner and equated the subscriber's donation with Christ-like benevolence and power.[5]

17. The Lock Hospital's subscription certificate.

This was not merely an abstract ideal. As at other types of hospital, it was presumed that any 'object' who desired the help of a charity would approach one of its benefactors in person, for him to decide her fate. 'As the list of governors will be published from time to time', explained one proposal for the Magdalen charity, 'the women will of course endeavour to be recommended by some of them'. At the Lock Hospital no one was normally admitted except upon the recommendation of a governor, and it was decreed that 'a preference be always given to those who subscribe the largest sums'. Similar rules applied at the Lambeth Asylum, where 'the Guardians present according to the priority of their subscriptions'. Such presumptions came naturally to propertied men, who valued social and sexual hierarchy and were used to the exercise of patronage and deference (see plate 8).[6]

For similar reasons, high-born support was crucial, for it created publicity and attracted the rest of polite and would-be polite society. In the second half of the eighteenth century, as ever more philanthropic institutions competed for attention, such fashionability was the key to success. In 1782 the Lambeth Asylum boasted as its patron the queen, and as its president the Prime Minister, Lord North. The Lock Hospital by contrast developed into a centre of evangelical piety, with close connections to the Wesley family and the 'genteel Methodist' circle of Selina, Countess of Huntingdon. It was whilst attending a revivalist sermon in its chapel in 1783 that the young William Wilberforce experienced the beginning of his spiritual conversion. In 1787 he was amongst the founders of its sister institution, the Lock Asylum for female penitents.[7]

The most powerfully attractive sexual charity of all was the Magdalen House. Its chapel was a public theatre of benevolence, designed to attract the favour of the great, the good, and the merely curious. Its decoration carefully combined the prominent commemoration of noble benefactions with the latest fashions in interior design ('hung with Gothic paper', noted Horace Walpole approvingly on his first visit).[8] Its centrepiece was the weekly public service by the sentimental preacher and poet William Dodd.

Dodd was young, handsome, and, at least to begin with, impoverished – the epitome of an eighteenth-century clergyman on the make. The Magdalen was his opportunity for fame and advancement, and he shamelessly exploited its sexual potential in a stream of publications, even inserting anonymous letters in the papers that purported to come from grateful penitents. In sermon, likewise, he thought nothing of addressing his audience as if they were rakes and seducers, and he their innocent, abandoned whore. 'Now see the sad end of thy triumph! – Oh look upon me, and see what cause thou hast to exult! Behold these wretched tatters, which scarcely cover my diseased limbs . . . See, my tongue cleaves to the roof of my mouth with hunger and with anguish . . . Oh see me hopeless and abandoned . . . mercy, mercy sweet father!' In 1769, when the Scottish Presbyterian Alexander Carlyle attended one of Dodd's services, he was so shocked by its indelicacy (the text was Matthew 5.28, 'whosoever looketh on a woman to lust after her') that he spoke out to the congregation, 'condemning the whole institution, as well as the exhibition of the preacher, as *contra bonos mores*, and a disgrace to a Christian city'.[9]

What lent these occasions particular frisson was the presence in

WILLIAM DODD, LL.D.

18. The Reverend Dr William Dodd: preacher,
novelist, poet, and swindler.

chapel of the penitents themselves. It was not unusual to exhibit the
objects of a charity. Tudor and Stuart hospitals for the infirm, the insane,
and the criminal had always, like their medieval predecessors, been open
to visitors. Since at least the early seventeenth century the orphans of
Christ's Hospital were every Easter paraded to a special service to sing a
'psalm of thanksgiving' to their benefactors. Charity schools employed
similar methods; and joint-stock philanthropies followed their lead. In
1763, to raise money for the Lambeth Asylum, its chaplain dragged the
girls around as many churches and chapels as would receive him, exhibiting them to the congregations. It also became common for charities to
commission special anthems, public concerts, and other entertainments
as part of their programme of fund-raising. The Lock Hospital, whose
chaplain Martin Madan was an enthusiastic amateur musician, became
especially renowned for the high standard of its music.[10]

Yet at the Magdalen the implications of such conventional methods of publicity were unusually ambiguous. It was precisely to end their public exposure that its inmates were supposed to have been withdrawn from the world. They lived in complete seclusion. 'To prevent these penitents being exposed to the public eye', a contemporary guidebook explained, all the windows of the house were covered by special shutters, 'so that there is no possibility of these once unhappy women either seeing or being seen by any person who passes by'. No woman could ordinarily leave the house, and no casual visitors were permitted. Despite this, every Sunday every penitent was put on display before a large audience of strangers, who keenly observed the inmates singing, weeping, and publicly demonstrating their contrition. Amongst the hymns they performed was one 'Against Lewdness'. It began:

> Why should you let your wand'ring eyes,
> Entice your souls to shameful sin!
> Scandal and ruin are the prize
> You take such fatal pains to win

and ended with the rousing chorus,

> Flee, sinners, flee th'unlawful bed,
> Lest vengeance send you down to dwell
> In the dark regions of the dead,
> To feed the fiercest fire in hell.

After such singing usually came one of Dodd's 'haranguing' sermons. This stirred up such emotions amongst the penitents, reported Walpole after a visit in 1760, that they 'sobbed and cried from their souls', until the onlookers, too, were moved to tears. As Dodd himself described it rhapsodically,

> When thou shalt hear their solemn prayers,
> Mix'd with deep repentant tears:
> Grateful songs and tuneful praise,
> Pious orgies, sacred lays;
> Finer pleasures which dispense
> Than the finest joys of sense:
> And each melting bosom move,
> And each liquid eye o'erflow
> With benevolence and love!

It proved to be a highly successful formula. By 1761 the crowds had grown so large that new galleries were added to the chapel and tickets issued in advance. When, on a visit to London, Carlyle tried to obtain some, having heard that it was 'much the fashion' to attend the service, he 'had difficulty to get tolerable seats for my sister and wife, the crowd of genteel people was so great'. Even after an entirely new chapel was constructed, seating 500 people (and concealing the penitents behind a screen), even after Dodd's disgrace and execution for forgery in 1777, the demand for entrance remained so insatiable that tickets for admission were traded by scalpers in the streets (see plate 9).[11]

The immense popularity of sexual charity depended only in part on its tangible effects. Its wider significance lies in what it tells us about changing philanthropic and sexual ideals, economic principles, and social practices. Yet thus far we have only briefly glimpsed life inside these new institutions. What was it like to enter the Magdalen as a penitent prostitute? To live there as an inmate? To embark on a new life afterwards?

INSIDE THE ASYLUM

Few traces have survived of life in these places before the nineteenth century. Their buildings have long vanished. All the manuscripts of the London Magdalen House have been destroyed. A single ledger is all that survives from the Lambeth Asylum. Our only way in is through the admissions books of the third main charity, the Dublin Magdalen Asylum. In these large volumes are recorded brief details about every inmate who passed through its doors. The only unmediated sign of the women themselves is their handwriting. A few signed their names confidently, but more often they struggled laboriously to spell out the letters with pen and ink, and many could manage only a small, hesitant cross. A 'mark' to show they had been present – and now the only personal remnant left of them on earth. Yet in and between the lines of the dry, bureaucratic entries, there are other fragments of their lives outside and inside the institution.[1]

Dublin was the second greatest metropolis of the Empire, a huge, thriving port and capital city. Its Magdalen Asylum was founded in 1767 by the philanthropist Lady Arbella Denny, a grand-daughter of the political arithmetician Sir William Petty, in direct imitation of the London Magdalen House. It was always much smaller than its sister institution. It raised less money and could house fewer inmates. In essentials, though, the two foundations, and later penitential houses, were alike in their regime.

We cannot see the women's faces, and nothing is recorded of their previous lives. But we can conjure up some sense of their appearance on entry, before they were stripped and changed into the Magdalen uniform that they wore throughout their time inside. What's more, we can see their names, their real names, which they also gave up for the duration of their stay, and sometimes for ever. Sarah McDowel came in under that name in November 1767 but left eighteen months later as 'Sarah Grace'; Sophia Roder went back into the world as 'Sophia Godly', in testimony of her new life. Inside the house no woman had any name at all, just a number: 'Mrs One', 'Mrs Two', 'Mrs Three', and so on. That was how the staff referred to them, and how they addressed one another.

They were all young. At the London Magdalen many were still in their early teens, and most were under twenty. In Dublin only girls under nineteen were admitted.[2] A few of them were dressed splendidly. In the summer of 1774, Harriet Rubery arrived with night-gowns, ear-rings, and 'thirteen books', but she was an exception. So was Ann Fenton in 1777, who owned the latest fiction, a decent wardrobe, and a large amount of cash – but even she could not write her name. A handful of other inmates appear to have been moderately well-off young women. Some were evidently sheltering from the shame of fornication rather than prolonged prostitution. Mary Thompson, recommended by the Bishop of Waterford himself, arrived with an ample wardrobe, a Bible, and a book of common prayer, and later had sent over still more gowns, ruffles, caps, and other clothes. Elinor Ward returned to her family after only a few months, 'in expectation of marriage'. A few, like Catherine Robinson, 'descended of a good family', and Ann Stanhope, whose people were 'creditable persons', stayed as paying boarders. Ann Clapham's father was 'so genteel that he would not allow her to take the guinea' that departing inmates were given by the charity. Ann Stanhope likewise declined the offer of money and new clothes.

More commonly, though, the women who sought admittance had few possessions – even fewer, in fact, than most workhouse paupers.[3] Most did not even own a decent pair of shoes. Many, for the sake of appearances, had come in borrowed clothes; others in rags that were so foul they had to be burned or thrown away. Their lack of decent dress testified to grim and desperate lives. No wonder that the gift of a new wardrobe was such a prominent part of the Asylum's charity. On entering, each Magdalen was given a set of plain clothes: petti-coats, shifts, aprons, caps, neckerchiefs, stays, stockings, shoes, and towels. Every woman who stayed the full term (eighteen months, or two years) left with this essential bounty. For respectable attire was vital to respectable employment. Without 'clothing to fit her for ser-vice', even the best-intentioned former inmate would struggle to maintain a virtuous life.

To such women life inside the Asylum must have been a shock. Its main purpose was relentless religious indoctrination, through com-plete seclusion from the world, private reading and instruction, collective rituals, and a rigid daily routine. Every day, and even more intensely on Sunday, there were several hours of compulsory 'private devotion and meditation', regular prayers, and a service in chapel. Twice a week they were given formal lectures about the basic tenets of Christianity, on which every woman was publicly examined. The overall behaviour of each Magdalen was monitored daily, judged, and recorded in a special book of censure. If any woman misbehaved per-sistently, the other inmates were assembled to humiliate and expel her publicly. First they collectively chanted a prayer over her, warning of 'the bitter pains of eternal death', then they all sang a special hymn on the terrors of conscience, the wrath of God, and the horrors of unchas-tity.[4] Then she was cast out. Conversely, the most penitent and devout inmates were allowed to take communion once a month. This was evidently a ritual that was seen to convey special protection upon the recipient. As her time of departure drew near, Jane Utley 'beg'd to receive the sacrament, hoping for the grace of God to enable her to live a Christian life': after a year and a half inside, she did not want to leave the Asylum without it.[5] To modern eyes the whole regime resembles that of a religious cult, intent on brainwashing its members during months of captivity. And that was precisely the idea.

All sexual philanthropy was therefore riven by a great contradiction. Its propaganda incessantly stressed that every fallen woman was essentially innocent: the poor, unwary, ignorant victim of rich, experienced, and merciless seducers. 'You know not', she begged her saviours, 'by what artifice, by what flattery, by what treacherous devices, my inexperienced, untutored, unprotected, unsuspecting youth is thus plunged into the depths of shame and sorrow'. Prostitution was 'abhorrent to the female character'; women were only forced into it by the cruelty of men and the iniquity of the double standard.[6]

Yet, at the same time, the practice of sexual charity was entirely focused on inculcating Magdalens with the deepest sense of their own guilt, in order that they might break down, repent, and be reborn as true Christians. Their entire being was corrupted and depraved, they were told: only the severest treatment could bridle their disgusting sexual incontinence. 'We are every moment,' warned one of their preachers, 'to apprehend a relapse, and to guard against it by a scrupulous caution, and regimen apparently severe. Appetites may be craving, and desires irregular; but these must be obstinately controlled.' Despite all the talk and writing and concern over the structural causes of prostitution, in the end the philanthropic solution was simply to place the entire burden back onto the individual female conscience – to inculcate women with a horror of their past crimes and a terror of their future damnation should they be weak enough to relapse and 'be entangled in your former pollutions'.[7]

The spiritual inoculation they received in the Asylum was supposed to be the main safeguard against reinfection with sin. To keep their piety alive after their return to the world, the women were sent back into it not only with clothes and a little money, but a stack of essential reading – such as a prayer book, a catechism, *The Knowledge and Practice of Christianity*, the *Happiness of the Next Life*, a *Companion to the Altar*, and *Instructions for the Sacrament*.

Apart from religious indoctrination, the main aim of life inside was to work as hard as possible. Many hours every day were spent on domestic chores and on sewing. Instilling the women with proper habits of industry was meant to help them gain employment upon their departure: domestic service and needlework were pretty much the only conceivable occupations for a young friendless woman. As time went on, its practical importance was acknowledged ever more openly. Departing women were given fewer books, and received instead a set of embroidery tools. Less time was devoted to prayers and reading, more to work.[8] Their sewing also helped the finances of the house, though never by much. But the main purpose of daily labour was ethical – hard work was supposed to demonstrate and support a virtuous character. So the overseers of the Asylum constantly worried and scolded that lack of diligence was a sign of imperfect reform, and presaged a return to evil habits. Mary Layfield's 'understanding is not very strong . . . she means to be virtuous, but she wants industry'. Susanna Cottrell took 'a long time . . . to see it was her duty to work as well as she was capable'. Arabella Carter 'seems very sensible of her past errors [yet] she has not been as industrious as she shou'd have been'. It was to be hoped that Ann Langford would 'remain virtuous', noted Lady Arbella Denny, 'but a weak understanding will expose her to many evils, and I fear she has not a just sense of the necessity of industry'.

A sizeable minority of penitents grasped their opportunity with both hands, and thrived within and beyond the Asylum. Jenny King, alias Purcell, alias Gallaher, whose multiple names suggest she was far from newly seduced, entered in October 1767. One of her hands was maimed; she had no possessions save a ragged gown and petticoat. But she had come determined to start her life over. She soon made contact with her mother, a poor, devout widow in Sligo, who was overjoyed by the 'life reviving' news that Jenny had turned her back on vice, and was desperate to see her again. Upon returning home, a year and a half later, she embraced her dying parent and resolved henceforth to 'live as becomes a penitent; who hopes, by a pious and truly Christian behaviour, to obtain a pardon from the great God of my manifold sins'.[9] Alice Sandilon proved herself 'an extraordinary good work-woman and very diligent'. Her behaviour was so good that it won her 'a very good service with an honourable family', and an early exit. Jane Holdcraft likewise 'behaved very well and went to a service that was ready for her before she left'. A decade later she had prospered and was living, happily married and industriously occupied, on a thirty-acre farm in Wexford.

Many women, however, could not endure the enforced piety and subordination. By the end of the century, over a third of those admitted to the Dublin Asylum had asked to leave, run away, been expelled, or otherwise failed to complete their course of treatment.[10] Emelia Pierce 'would not submit to the rules'. Ann Collier 'could say a great deal on the wrong side of the question' and was expelled 'for stubbornness and disobedience'; Sarah Neal for 'idleness and an ill tongue and impudence'. Even amongst those who got through and left with credit, many faced an uncertain future. Secure employment was hard to find, especially for suspect women. Some relapsed into sin, like Sarah Lucas, discharged into service but then found by her mistress in bed with a man. Or they might simply disappear. After twelve months back in the world, any woman who could testify that she had lived respectably could write in to claim a bounty of two guineas from the Asylum. It is notable that most did not. Doubtless some of these vanished penitents just wanted to leave their former life behind them, like those who went overseas. Elizabeth Gogan shipped for Maryland when, even after she had emerged from the Asylum as a well-behaved penitent, 'her friends and relations would not see her, [and] thought she had best leave the kingdom'. In numberless other cases the silence in the record probably signals a more ominous fate.

These figures were similar to those of the London Magdalen House, about half of whose early inmates (according to its published accounts) successfully completed their time and went on to respectable careers. The high failure rate is surely significant. The women who passed through these institutions were not a cross-section of ordinary prostitutes, but hand-picked recruits – many of them recently seduced girls rather than hardened whores. There were always more applicants than places: even of the volunteers, only the most promising got in. The fact that, even then, so many of them fell by the wayside is a measure of quite how demanding and uncertain the new philanthropic remedies proved to be – and of the huge gap between their obsession with personal character and the broader structural problems of female victimization, impoverishment, seduction, and prostitution.

Yet, however imperfectly and fitfully, those methods did also work. In their first few decades alone, the Lambeth Asylum and the two Magdalen houses helped transform hundreds of lives. Even women who were expelled often left determined and able to make a new beginning, convinced of the Christian truths that had been drummed into them. Margaret Clark lasted only eight months before she was ejected 'for bad behaviour being vulgar and ungovernable'. She was only just learning to read and write. All the same, 'she vowed she designed to be virtuous', promised she would find work as a servant, and wrote triumphantly from America a few months later: 'I could not have found a better Master and Mistress than I have got'. Another, perhaps the Sarah McDowel who had left as 'Sarah Grace', relapsed into unchastity following her discharge. But then she, too, found God and shipped herself to America as an indentured servant. 'Your once darling daughter', she wrote to her mother from across the globe, 'for whom you thought nothing good enough, is now a slave':

Think not I tell you this to grieve you; no, my Mother, rejoice, for it is this that must draw my soul out of the horrible pit; it was not in voluptuous pleasures I was to find my God, it was in adversity. I hope that my fate may be a warning to them to whom the beginning of my life has been a parable. Yet, Oh! For God's sake forgive my crimes, and let your prayers be night and morning offered up to the throne of mercy for me.

And then, with this reminder of the extraordinary power of religious ideals to shape the consciousness even of the most obscure eighteenth-century harlot, she vanishes forever from our sight.[11]

CHASTITY AND CLASS

We have seen how far, and with what success, sexual charities tried to reaffirm traditional Christian principles of personal responsibility for sin and redemption. The public philanthropy of the later eighteenth century also helped to develop new ideas. In particular, it undermined the idea that all acts of unchastity were inherently and equally culpable, and promoted the opposite assumption: that sexual behaviour was essentially determined by sex and class, and that poor women were much more likely to become whores.

The rise of the word 'prostitute' itself epitomized this development. Before 1700 it was not a term often used, or differentiated from general notions such as 'whore' or 'harlot'. In the course of eighteenth century it took on a much sharper definition. As the focus of public policy narrowed from whoredom in general to the problem of the unchaste poor in particular, 'prostitutes' and 'prostitution' became pre-eminent categories in the classification of immorality. The older, generic archetype of the whore was still generally invoked. Its corollary, that a single fall inevitably led down the slippery slope to disease, destitution, and death, remained a cornerstone of philanthropic argument. Yet, even in religious thinking, the traditional idea that vice and virtue were essentially the product of free personal choice was gradually eroded. In its place there now emerged, out of the desire to understand prostitution in social and scientific terms, a much more perniciously deterministic view. Superficially, this proclaimed the innocence of women trapped by forces beyond their control. In practice, however, it made much more categorical the belief that virtue and morality were neither innate human qualities nor solely the product of individual choice, but attributes closely connected to social status.

This notion of the essential moral depravity of the working class was to reach its fullest expression in the nineteenth century. 'The chastity of marriage,' wrote Peter Gaskell in 1833, 'is but little known or exercised amongst them: husband and wife sin equally, and an habitual indifference to sexual vice is generated.' This was the period in which rough and ready statistics first became a widely used tool of social observation, allowing guesswork and prejudice about the morals of the lower classes to be presented as scientific fact. 'It would be no strain on his conscience,' deposed one witness before the Factory Commission, also in 1833, 'to say that three-quarters of the girls between fourteen and twenty years of age were unchaste.' Even Friedrich Engels, surveying the condition of the working class in England in 1844, deplored the supposedly 'unbridled sexual intercourse' of industrial workers.[1]

Such casual bigotry masquerading as sociology was to become a particular feature of the study of prostitution. As early as 1800, the magistrate and political arithmetician Patrick Colquhoun estimated that there were 50,000 prostitutes in London: a figure he arrived at by simply 'including the multitudes of low females, who cohabit with labourers and others without matrimony'.* Similar assumptions underpinned the analysis of the great Victorian authority on the subject, William Acton. In the first edition of his monumental study *Prostitution* (1857), he concluded merely from their appearance that 'a third at least' of the girls he observed at a popular London dancehall must be whores. By the second edition, in 1870, there was even less doubt in his mind: they were 'of course all prostitutes'.[2]

The foundations for such views had been laid in the previous century, in the attempts of philanthropists and political arithmeticians to understand prostitution as a social phenomenon rather than a personal failing. The main question that preoccupied them was where prostitutes came from.

The simplest answer was that they were poor women, driven by hardship. 'It is notorious,' declared Joseph Massie, 'that necessity is the general cause of common prostitution,' and he went on to list the circumstances that rendered large numbers of women in London vulnerable to seduction: lack of friends, failure to find work, inability to claim settlement or poor relief. Others agreed on the symptoms but preferred to blame the increasing idleness and immorality of the labouring classes. Amongst 'women in higher life, whose parents have been careful of them', observed Hanway, a sense of honour and religion protected against unchastity, but among the common people there was no such defence. In the case of poor girls left altogether orphaned or deserted, prostitution was almost guaranteed. 'In such hopeless circumstances,' reflected a preacher in 1760, it was 'a moral certainty that the infant breast must be corrupted, must practise debauchery, even before it feels desire.'[3]

Even in normal working-class families, it was increasingly argued, education and religious principles were neglected; idleness was encouraged; parents failed their children. 'The common people,' lamented the influential economist Josiah Tucker, 'are given up to drunkenness and debauchery. The women walk the streets and spread the infection [i.e. venereal disease] till they are rotten ... the men are as bad as can be described: both sexes never working, while they have anything to spend

* On the same basis he later computed that in the kingdom as a whole there were at least 100,000 'lewd and immoral women, who live wholly or partly by prostitution': P. Colquhoun, *A Treatise on Indigence* (1806), 40.

upon their vices.' The fathers, said John Fielding, commonly died of drunkenness; the mothers sometimes sold their own daughters into prostitution. It was small wonder that the girls 'often become prosti-tutes from necessity, even before their passions can have any share in their guilt'. The young girls who entered the Lambeth Asylum were told bluntly that their removal from such corrupting surroundings was 'the means of better instruction in religion, in honesty, in sobriety, in chas-tity, in industry, in temperance, than you could possibly have received under the protection of your natural parents'. On similar grounds the charity decided in 1761, after the governors had experienced 'great inconveniences' from allowing girls to be visited by their surviving par-ents, that henceforth only orphans would be admitted. The following year all contact between the girls and visiting relatives was severely curtailed. In 1764, finally, it was 'resolved that the children's friends be not admitted to see them on any pretence whatever'. The implication was that only complete separation from their unwholesome origins could give impoverished girls a decent chance of escaping immorality and degradation (see plate 10). By the end of the century, Malthus thought it incontrovertible that poverty and the 'moral degradation of character' were inseparable: 'squalid poverty, particularly when joined with idleness, is a state the most unfavourable to chastity that can well be conceived'. It would be 'an absolute miracle' for any girl brought up in such circumstances not to succumb to unchastity.[4]

Such was the prevalence and variety of sexual trade, however, that it was not hard to advance alternative explanations. 'It seems to me a mistake to assert, that the bawdy-houses and streets are furnished with prostitutes from the children of the laborious poor,' countered Saunders Welch, whose own parents had been paupers. It was rather 'the children of those in the next sphere of life' who, educated above their station or corrupted by pretensions acquired in service, were laid wide open to ruin. It was certainly necessity that drove women to prostitute themselves, agreed William Dodd, but too often this arose 'from a mistaken neglect of their parents in their education; several of whom, while they absurdly expend much on boarding-schools, think it beneath them to have their daughters taught a trade'.[5]

The same concern with middle-class impoverishment was ubiqui-tous in literature. By the mid eighteenth century most fictional prostitutes tended to be drawn from the politer ranks. In Henry Fielding's farce *Rape upon Rape* (1730), Hilaret, pretending to be a whore, says she and her fifteen sisters in the same profession are all the daughters of a country vicar. Hogarth, too, thought this a 'common opinion'. By the following decade it had become a rhetorical commonplace 'that the greatest part of the London prostitutes are the daughters of parsons'. In *The Histories of Some of the Penitents in the Magdalen House* (1760), the first inmate to arrive is 'Emily', the orphan of an impoverished West Country clergyman, whose first seduction had occurred whilst in service to the gentry. The heroine of another widely read account 'was the daughter of a gentleman in the army, had a genteel and liberal education, but was reduced by various distresses to great poverty and want'. According to the Magdalen House's own propaganda, its archetypal inmate was 'the favourite daughter of her father, a person of decent and respectable character in life'. By the end of the eighteenth century, discussions of prostitution hence tended to define it as the behaviour forced upon two general classes of seduced women: girls from the ranks of the labouring poor, and the genteel 'daughters of poor tradesmen, or of clergymen of poor livings in the country'.[6]

In consequence it was presumed there should be at least two classes of inmates within any penitential hospital: 'those who had been of inferior families and low extraction', and 'those of a genteeler education'. More sophisticated planners like Joseph Massie stressed the need for greater subdivision. Each class was to be housed separately, in its own building; with different labour, clothing, diet, and future prospects, according to rank:

1. Women or girls who had been virtuously or genteelly educated, of which there were evident proofs in their conversation and visible traces in their demeanour.
2. Women or girls who appeared and behaved as if they had been servants in reputable families, or were evidently a degree above the meanest sort of people.
3. Women or girls who were very ignorant, rude, intractable, or audacious.
4. Women or girls whose principles of health and strength were so far vitiated or impaired as not to be restorable.[7]

When the London Magdalen House opened, it was organized along precisely such lines, with 'a superiority or preference of wards, according to the education or behaviour of the person admitted', and 'inferior persons' in the lower classes. Within each ward, one woman was appointed a 'superior' or 'presider' and the others arranged in strict hierarchy below her, according to their character and conduct. When in 1772 the hospital moved to its purpose-built premises in Blackfriars, the three 'Classes' of 'Objects' were kept incommunicado at all times, in separate buildings 'so formed that the front of each look to the back of the other'.[8]

Yet underneath this concern with social differentiation the deeper conclusion remained that poor women were bound to be less chaste. Whores of higher rank were not only better educated but inherently more 'delicate' and virtuous; and many of them, it was hoped, might be rescued whilst still high up on the slippery slope. 'The generality of the common people,' by contrast, had 'worn off a sense of shame'.

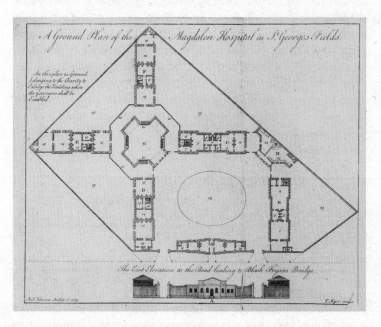

19. The new buildings of the Magdalen Hospital, with separate wings for each class of inmate.

'Delicacy' had never been inculcated in them. Their parents never protected them, so even their 'native modesty' was worn off in their youth. Their sexual morals were lax, so they fell far more easily into prostitution of the lowest kind.[9] Such condescension did not go uncontested: by the early nineteenth century it had begun to provoke a notable feminist critique. Nor was it entirely new. Nevertheless, it was henceforth expressed more blatantly, with greater pretension to empirical precision, and in terms of more exactly conceived 'classes' than ever before.*

Its impact on philanthropic practice was profound. In the short term, philanthropists came to favour higher-born, better-educated women as more amenable to reform. The governors of the Dublin Asylum keenly noted the rank and education of prospective penitents, and seem to have discriminated against 'the refuse of the people'. Though all souls were equal, exactly thirty-two of the past sixty-one inmates had been 'at least of the middle rank', the Bishop of Dromore observed proudly in 1773. In the following decade the governors of the London Magdalen shifted its purpose away from actual prostitutes, giving preference instead to young women seduced under promise of marriage, who had 'never been publicly upon the town'. The institution's success rate shot up accordingly.[10] Soon after the Magdalen House had opened, Jonas Hanway had commissioned an engraving that showed its transformative power. In the background looms the charity's chapel. Slumped on the ground we see a horrible, tattered whore, barefoot and bereft. In front of her there stands, proud yet demure, the redeemed Magdalen, dressed in her clean new clothes, hat, gloves, and shoes, her prayer-book open before her, glowing with health and promise (illustration 20). By the time the governors of the charity came to reuse this image for their propaganda in the 1770s, the ragged harlot had become an embarrassment, and was erased from the plate. A faint shadow behind the Magdalen was all that remained of her.

---

* There was a similar hardening of racial attitudes. Across the British Empire, white colonial distaste for the supposedly lax mores of other races was increasingly prominent. At home, in 1782 the governors of the Lambeth Asylum decreed that it should admit 'no negro or mulatto girl'; the following year, the Magdalen Hospital likewise barred all 'black women'. *An Account of the Institution and Proceedings of the Guardians of the Asylum* (1782), 17; H. F. B. Compston, *The Magdalen Hospital* (1917), 200; Philippa Levene (ed.), *Gender and Empire* (2004), ch. 6.

20. A proud, uniformed Magdalen inmate, contrasted with
the pitiful whore behind her (1761).

Even as the movement to rescue fallen women expanded there was, in fact, growing pessimism about the ever-growing scale of the problem, and the possibility of truly rehabilitating common whores. In the longer term, this was to be the more enduring development. From the outset, there had been doubts about the efficacy of philanthropy, and some of the enthusiasm for it had been motivated simply by the desire to suppress open prostitution. By the early nineteenth century, amidst mounting political concern over the indiscipline and disorder of the urban poor, this utilitarian approach was increasingly to the fore. It was a commonplace that ninety-nine per cent of all criminality derived 'from illicit associations with profligate women'. From this point of view, though the complete eradication of prostitution was usually thought to be impossible and undesirable, the saving of penitents and the tougher punishment of 'abandoned women' went hand in hand: the overriding concern was simply to get them off the streets.[11]

Instead of rehabilitation, asylums were therefore increasingly focused on the 'containment and quarantine' of fallen women, as much to protect society as for their own benefit. Even the London Magdalen Hospital abandoned its attempt to teach vocational skills, preferring to employ the penitents mainly as washer-women. This was to become the norm. Throughout the nineteenth and twentieth centuries, Magdalen asylums across England and Ireland operated as large-scale commercial laundries, sustained by the heavy labour of their inmates. In this respect, as in others, their economic and social bias grew ever more explicit after 1800. 'In the present day', noted the chaplain of the Magdalen Hospital in 1917, 'girls of good social antecedents are sent elsewhere' – public asylums were places for the re-education of women 'from average working-class homes'. Though it started as an alternative to punishment, institutional philanthropy thus increasingly evolved into another means of disciplining lower-class sexuality.[12]

RESCUE AND REFORMATION

The emergence of sexual philanthropies helped establish a new model for the treatment of all kinds of criminals and social misfits. Until the 1770s, most convicts were sentenced to a few weeks of hard labour, bound over, transported, or hanged. Imprisonment as such was not widely used. But the later eighteenth century saw a great movement for prison reform, which culminated in the establishment of the first modern penitentiaries. Several of its proponents had strong links to sexual charities: the word 'penitentiary' itself was most immediately adopted from such institutions. Though Magdalen hospitals were voluntary asylums, their regime and buildings nonetheless influenced the new attitude to imprisonment. Their inmates were housed in purpose-built architecture that was meant to facilitate their round-the-clock monitoring. They were segregated into different classes. They were kept under constant observation, prescribed a daily routine, and obliged to work and pray. Through incarceration for lengthy periods, followed by supervised release, they were to be disciplined, reformed, and made useful to society. Exactly these principles were to inspire the foundation of modern prisons, reformatories for youths, and systems of parole.[1]

The philanthropic approach also came to dominate attitudes towards fallen women. Prostitutes continued to be policed, punished, and disdained as depraved criminals. Nevertheless, even their harshest critics now tended to accept that the root causes of sexual trade lay in social and economic circumstances, rather than personal character. For their part, feminists saw prostitution as emblematic of all the deeper injustices of a male-dominated society. 'Asylums and Magdalens are not the proper remedies for these abuses,' wrote Mary Wollstonecraft. 'It is justice, not charity that is wanting in the world!'[2] Meanwhile, though, they too championed the plight of prostitutes. In consequence, the attraction of 'rescuing' and reforming fallen women continued to grow.

Amongst those who privately practised or advocated it before 1800 were James Boswell, Samuel Richardson, Samuel Johnson, Jeremy Bentham, Robert Holloway, John Wesley, Dorothy Ripley, and several other leading Methodists and missionaries. One reason it attracted increasing evangelical attention was that the parallels between black and white slavery were obvious. One did not have to look abroad for examples of repulsive human trade, remarked a late-Georgian advocate of rescue work. 'What are the sorrows of the enslaved negro from which the outcast prostitute of London is exempted? A seducer or ravisher has torn them both, for ever, from the abodes of their youth ... violent brutality assails their persons ... and tramples them to a level with the meanest of brute creation. Is the bosom of the unhappy girl less tender than that of the swarthy savage?' The 'slavery and misery' of prostitutes, observed another critic, was 'worse, much worse, than that of the African in the West Indies'.[3]

In the nineteenth century prostitution came to be commonly referred to as *the* 'Great Social Evil', or as 'white slavery', and the rescue of fallen women became a craze to which some of the most prominent figures in public life devoted extraordinary energies. Amongst campaigners for women's rights the oppression of prostitutes and the need to reach out to them personally became a particular article of faith. Missionary groups like the Salvation Army also made it a cornerstone of their work. The ideal was equally commonplace amongst mainstream Anglican clergymen, writers, artists, social reformers, politicians, and innumerable private citizens. By 1837, one charity alone, the Religious Tract Society, had issued over 500 million pamphlets aimed at the redemption of fallen women. At the height of his fame, Charles Dickens threw himself into the foundation and administration of a refuge for penitents, with the financial backing of the millionairess Angela Burdett-Coutts. His fellow-novelist George Gissing tried (and failed) to redeem a young prostitute by marrying her himself. William Gladstone called the issue 'the chief burden of my soul', and for decades, even whilst Prime Minister, roamed the streets at night attempting to save prostitutes. Mrs Gladstone invited penitents to tea at 10 Downing Street. By 1928, in Evelyn Waugh's brilliant satirical novel, *Decline and Fall*, white slavery and the furore surrounding it had become an easily recognizable symbol for the universal, hopeless corruption of the modern world.[4]

The movement for the sexual redemption of women therefore continued to grow in significance well beyond 1800. Many other Lock hospitals, preventative asylums, and penitential houses were soon founded at home and abroad. As early as 1816, there existed at least a dozen refuges for fallen women across Britain, as well as several in Ireland, India, and the United States. The real explosion came in the hundred years that followed. In 1860 a new periodical, the *Magdalen's Friend*, estimated that there were about two dozen 'homes' in London alone, and another forty around the country. By 1917, there were more than 400 across the English-speaking world. Alongside them there grew up a network of hundreds of voluntary associations and asylums dedicated to the sexual purity and salvation of working-class women. The saving of single mothers, observes one historian of the phenomenon, became nothing less than 'a national pursuit'. The rescue work pioneered by the Magdalen and the Lambeth Asylum thus grew into one of the most enduring obsessions of the Victorian and early twentieth-century middle classes, on both sides of the Atlantic.[5]

By the early twentieth century the scope of sexual rescue campaigns had extended worldwide. International white slavery became a major concern of governments and of the League of Nations. Even today such work continues. The notion that most prostitution is ultimately involuntary has become a commonplace of modern western thought, as well as the basis for legislation and social policy. The focus of British and American rescue groups is now often on the trafficking for sexual purposes of women in third-world countries: yet even in such cases many of their essential principles recall those first articulated in mid eighteenth-century England.

The emergence of organized philanthropy thus had a profound impact on later attitudes to sexuality. In recent years its practical effects have often come to be criticized as misguided and repressive. In Ireland, where Magdalen asylums persisted until the 1990s, the routine, long-term incarceration and economic exploitation of prostitutes and unmarried mothers is now generally regarded to have been a shameful, misogynist phenomenon.[6] The practice of sexual philanthropy certainly imposed particular ideas about class, gender, and sexual discipline upon its recipients. These days, we also tend to presume that institutionalization is not good for people, or conducive to their moral elevation. Yet we still take for granted the basic principles of sexual charity. That social and economic circumstances can leave women at risk of sexual exploitation; that in such conditions their own free will and moral consciousness are compromised; and that external intervention is justified to save them from degradation – these convictions continue to underpin legislation, public opinion, and action by governments, charities, and individuals across the globe. This is another central legacy of the first sexual revolution.

6

The Media and the Message

No person or persons whatsoever, shall at any time print or cause to be imprinted, any book or pamphlet whatsoever [without prior certification by a government censor] that there is nothing in that book or books contained, that is contrary to Christian faith . . . to good life, or good manners.

A Decree of Starre-Chamber, Concerning Printing (1637)

She has been abused in public papers, exposed in print-shops, and to wind up the whole, some wretches, mean, ignorant and venal, would impose upon the public, by daring to pretend to publish her Memoirs. She hopes to prevent the success of their endeavours, by thus publicly declaring that nothing of that sort has the slightest foundation in truth. *C. Fisher*

Advertisement by a courtesan in *The Public Advertiser*, 24 March 1759

The periodical press of Great Britain . . . is the most powerful moral machine in the world, and exercises a greater influence over the manners and opinions of civilized society than the united eloquence of the bar, the senate and the pulpit.

The Periodical Press of Great Britain (1824), 1

The origins of our modern attitudes to sex lie in the great changes that swept through western society in the later seventeenth and eighteenth centuries – the breakdown of religious authority, the dawn of the Enlightenment, the large-scale emergence of female voices into public life. The final major cause was the transformation of the universe of communication. From the later seventeenth century onwards there developed new attitudes towards privacy and publicity, new ways of shaping public opinion, and a new openness about sexual affairs.

Some of these developments have already been alluded to in previous chapters, for they were intimately intertwined with the growing complexity of urban life, the advance of new ways of thinking, and the breakdown of sexual policing. But the media revolution of the Enlightenment was so central to changing ways of living and thinking that we need now to pay it proper attention.[1] Without it, there would have been no sexual revolution.

THE GROWTH OF MASS CULTURE

In the space of a few months in 1730 and 1731, the artist William Hogarth created the most immediately popular fictional images the English-speaking world had ever seen. First, he hit upon the idea of a series of six paintings showing the life-cycle of a London prostitute: from her innocent, fresh-faced arrival in town and immediate entrapment by a rake and bawd, to her inevitable downfall, disease, and death. Hundreds of people came to his studio to admire the canvases. Then, in 1732, he sold engravings of them to over a thousand subscribers. They were an instant sensation. As his colleague George Vertue noted, in the only surviving contemporary account, they 'had the greatest subscription and public esteem that any prints ever had'. *A Harlot's Progress* 'captivated the minds of most people, persons of all ranks and conditions, from the greatest quality to the meanest'.[1]

People have been trying ever since to explain exactly why these pictures were so phenomenally, and enduringly, popular. After successfully repeating the formula in three later series, *A Rake's Progress* (1735), *Marriage à la Mode* (1745), and *Industry and Idleness* (1747), Hogarth himself came to believe that it was simply down to his genius in having hit upon a new and uniquely attractive kind of art. He had, he boasted, invented a wholly 'novel mode, *viz.* painting and engraving

21. William Hogarth, *A Harlot's Progress* (1732): Scene 1: The
entrapment of a defenceless country maid upon her arrival in London.

modern moral subjects', something never before done 'by any other
man', 'in any country or any age'.[2]

That is also essentially the view of the world's foremost authority,
Ronald Paulson, whose dazzling scholarship over many decades has
been devoted to showing that Hogarth was one of the greatest artists of
all time. Professor Paulson's main method has been to trace increasingly
complex connections between Hogarth's images and the whole of the
previous western canon of art, literature, theology, and philosophy, in
order to demonstrate the artist's astonishing erudition and sophistica-
tion. *A Harlot's Progress*, we are told, is only superficially about the
seduction and ruin of a young woman. In fact, it was intended as a scandalous parody of the New Testament, and its iconography consciously
echoed the religious imagery of Leonardo, Dürer, and other old masters –
small matter that Hogarth himself never mentioned any of this, and not
a single one of his contemporaries seems to have noticed it.[3]

Scene 2: Her innocence lost, she becomes the kept mistress
of a rich Jew, and cheats on him.

To balk at Professor Paulson's more extreme suggestions is not to
deny that Hogarth was an immensely inventive satirist (nor, of course,
that we might see things in his art that he himself did not). The contemporary impact of his work did derive partly from its originality
and richness. Yet it also had two other, more basic causes. In the first
place it encapsulated themes that, as we saw in previous chapters,
were already matters of intense public fascination. The topic of *A
Harlot's Progress* was far from original. On the contrary, as Horace
Walpole pointed out, its success was due to 'the familiarity of the subject, and the propriety of the execution'.[4] It put into an easily readable
visual narrative the growing contemporary obsession with female victimization, libertine impunity, and the uselessness of punishment,
complete with topical references to its most infamous real-life perso-
nas: the rapist rake, Colonel Francis Charteris, and his pimp; the
infamous brothel-keeper Mrs Needham; the highwayman James

Scene 3: The harlot's lodgings are raided by supporters
of the societies for reformation of manners.

Dalton; Captain Macheath, the hero of *The Beggar's Opera*; the zealous magistrate Sir John Gonson; and the prostitute Kate Hackabout,
whose name Hogarth adopted for his harlot. Over the following decades, too, the enduring popularity of Hogarth's images was as much a
consequence as a cause of the ever-greater general fixation on narratives of seduction and prostitution.[5]

The other reason the *Harlot's Progress* became so wildly popular
was that it was endlessly duplicated, quoted, adapted, and referred to
by other writers and artists. 'Every engraver set himself to copy it', as
Walpole noted, 'and thousands of imitations were dispersed all over
the kingdom'. Ironically enough these secondary versions are now
much rarer than the originals, and almost completely unknown.
Hogarth hated being plagiarized – his annoyance led directly to the
Engravers' Copyright Act of 1735. Critics likewise often disdain these
inferior productions and ignore them. At best, the flood of derivative

Scene 4: She and her maid are sent to a bridewell and set at hard labour.

copies is portrayed as illustrative of the original prints' general impact.[6]

In fact it was the other way round. It was precisely through second- and third-hand copies and allusions that Hogarth's work achieved its greatest popular impression. Only 1,240 copies of *A Harlot's Progress* were printed in 1732. They were available solely by personal subscription, and their high cost (21 shillings per set) put them well beyond the reach of ordinary people. The work's wide and lasting popularity therefore resulted largely from the indirect ripple effect of countless copies, adaptations, and quotations, which were much more widely distributed and accessible. It was these that made it so generally familiar.

This secondary dissemination took many different forms, even leaving aside innumerable passing references in poems, novels, pamphlets and newspapers. There were, first of all, the officially authorized texts and copies that Hogarth himself, and later his widow, sanctioned,

Scene 5: Senseless and impoverished, attended by
quacks, she lies dying of venereal disease.

in order to bring his work to a wider audience. These ranged from the huge sheets engraved by Giles King in 1732 to the tiny images inserted from 1768 onwards in editions of John Trusler's *Hogarth Moralized* (see illustrations 22 and 23). Then there was a vast number of unauthorized plagiaries, of every shape and size, issued and reissued throughout the century and beyond. There were large sets, 'the same size as Mr Hogarth's' but at a fraction of his price, engraved or in mezzotint, with or without verses, in black or in coloured ink. For still less money, one could buy various medium-sized plagiaries. Cheapest and most popular of all were small-format copies, available in a dazzling variety: with or without verses printed below, in black and white, in green or pink, or even in full colour. There were even plagiaries, large and small, of Giles King's own copies.[7]

It is unlikely that the purchasers of these images regarded them as inferior to the originals – indeed, the plagiaries usually provided add-

Scene 6: Her coffin, surrounded by other whores and their acolytes.

itional value through a verse explication below each scene. Anyone with a shilling or two could equally buy one of the many pamphlet versions of the story, which usually came with their own accompanying sets of small prints. In addition, there were pantomimes, operas, comedies, and other dramatic stagings of the *Harlot's Progress*, which remained popular long after 1732. The series was also reproduced, in whole or in part, in other visual media – in paintings and embroidery; on ladies' fans; on cups, saucers, and other kinds of china and pewter objects (see plate 11).[8] Finally, we can trace its popular impact through many later visual allusions. Amongst full-blown reworkings and parodies in the 1730s were *R[o]b[i]n's Progress* and *Vanella's Progress*, respectively satirizing the Prime Minister, Robert Walpole, and Anne Vane, the mistress of the Prince of Wales. Half a century later, they included *The Modern Harlot's Progress, or The Adventures of Harriet Heedless* (1780), and George Morland's *Laetitia: or Seduction* (1786), which both updated the tale and, in keeping with later eighteenth-

22. Giles King's huge sheets, with authorized copies of the scenes

from *A Harlot's Progress*, were each more than half a metre wide.

23. A miniscule facsimile of scene 1, from John Trusler and Jane
Hogarth's popular handbook, *Hogarth Moralized* (1768).

century sensibilities, gave it a happier ending.[9] Even more common
was the recycling of particular details, as images on their own or as
part of other compositions. In all these ways, Hogarth's ideas and
imagery came to be consciously and unconsciously appropriated,
reused, and disseminated, far beyond the circle of his own clients (see
illustrations 24 to 27).

Exactly the same happened to the *Rake's Progress*, whose original
prints were swamped by a flood of authorized and (especially) unauthorized copies and adaptations – some of which went so far as to add an
extra scene to the story (see illustrations 28 to 35).[10] Even the name of
the work was endlessly parroted and reappropriated: the 'rake's progress' has become a proverbial phrase. From the early eighteenth
century onwards, this general process of copying, echoing, and respond-
ing to original works was one of the chief means through which all
popular images and texts achieved their cultural impact.

The evolution of copyright did eventually come to inhibit the most
direct kinds of borrowing. The Engravers' Copyright Act of 1735 was
one reason why fewer plagiaries were produced of *Marriage à la
Mode* and *Industry and Idleness* than of Hogarth's earlier series –
though it never stopped them altogether. In the case of books, likewise,
as William St Clair has brilliantly shown, by the end of the eighteenth

century the development of copyright law directly affected what texts were likely, or not, to be widely re-printed and read. The more general trend was nevertheless towards ever greater multiplication and interaction between media. From the early eighteenth century onwards, works of fiction and non-fiction alike were in much more overt and continuous dialogue with each other, and with their public, than ever before. In this new universe of communication, being publicly reviewed, excerpted, copied, commented on, parodied, criticized, praised and discussed was not secondary to the message of the work itself: it was an inextricable part of what was communicated to the audience. The popular success of any major work, whether *A Harlot's Progress* or *Pamela*, was henceforth always as much a mass media event as an artistic triumph.[11]

This also multiplied its possible meanings. Until the end of the seventeenth century, the consumption and interpretation of texts and images had always been a much more private and restricted process. Indeed, with the partial exception of political and religious controversies, we generally only know about people's reactions to new publications through private correspondence and the occasional marginal annotation in a book. There were no broader, permanent, public networks through which ordinary people could exchange cultural opinions. The media revolution changed this irrevocably. From the eighteenth century onwards, interpretations of any widely noticed publication were immediately made visible, magnified, and communicated to the general public through a dense network of ancillary media.

The result was a much wider, more permanent, and more self-conscious reading public than had existed before. Yet this was a virtual community, rather than a tangible one. Indeed, the explosion of newspapers, pamphlets, and novels may actually (as some contemporary moralists worried) have increased the extent to which men and women formed their opinions through solitary reading and in smaller groups, rather than from older, more general sources of authority.[12] It certainly encouraged the expression of a greater multiplicity of views than ever before. What, then, were the main features of this expansion and democratization of the media? How exactly did

Her Funeral properly attended

See the last Stage of Worldly matters
Of Whores, Rakes, Lap dogs, Stars & Garters
Alas! now dead She'll please no more
Who liv'd so oft to please before.

Th' Assembly well her Fun'ral suits,
And Scutcheon also none disputes,
To close the Scene (but don't you blab it)
A Painter's in the Parsons hat.

See the last Stage of worldly matters
Of Whores, Rakes, Lap Dogs, Garters;
Alas! now dead, shall please no more,
Who liv'd so oft to please before.

Her FUNERAL PROPERLY ATTENDED

The Assembly Well her Fun'ral suits,
And Scutcheon also none disputes;
To close the Scene (but dont you blab it)
A Painter in the Parsons Habit.

Her *Progress* Run, the certain End you See,
What Harlots, Empresses and Queens must be.

Her Burial the Funeral Pomp of a Harlot in Triumph

24–27. A few of the many unauthorized plagiaries of *A Harlot's Progress*: it was through the ubiquity of copies like these that Hogarth's compositions became so generally familiar.

28. William Hogarth, *A Rake's Progress* (1735): Scene 1: The young man comes into his inheritance.

it alter the nature of public opinion, and the boundary between public and private affairs?

SEXUAL CELEBRITY

The best way into these questions is through one of the most striking novelties of eighteenth-century culture: a growing public fascination with the lives of low-born whores. Around 1700 this would have been unimaginable. Even in London, few prostitutes ever became famous enough to be widely known or written about. By the end of the century, however, even as ever-greater stress came to be placed on the sexual passivity of respectable women, a whole culture of celebrity had grown up around their most immoral counterparts. Their actions were routinely reported in newspapers and magazines, their personalities analysed in pamphlets and poems, their portraits painted,

29. Scene 3: The would-be rake (at left, having his pocket picked),
in the company of whores.

engraved, and caricatured. So ubiquitous did this type of material become that a few decades later it gave rise to a new term, 'pornography', literally meaning the description of harlots.[1]

Some earlier cultures had shown unusual interest in promiscuous women. In Renaissance Italy many courtesans had achieved considerable fame and literary renown. The same was true of the leading *geisha* of pre-modern Japan. English observers were themselves particularly struck by the status of harlots in classical times, for their prominence appeared to prefigure the celebrity of immoral women in contemporary society, and to illustrate the untold wealth and power that they might accrue. It thus became fashionable in the later eighteenth century to refer to prostitutes as 'Paphians', 'Cyprians', and 'Cythereans', evoking the ancient worship of Venus (or 'Cytheria') on Cyprus and its city of Paphos, or to talk of a present-day 'Thaïs', 'Laïs', or 'Phryne', in comparison with the famous *hetaerae* of ancient Greece (see plate 12).[2]

30. This plagiary of the *Rake's Progress*, available in colour as well as black and white, was one of several immediately offered for sale by the leading printseller Thomas Bowles and his associates.

There were also various domestic precedents. Already in the middle ages particular interest had attached to women, such as royal mistresses, whose unchastity appeared to invert the natural order. The Reformation further politicized the issue of sexual morality and its social consequences. By the seventeenth century, as we have seen, immorality amongst the governing classes, and especially at court, had the potential to attract a great deal of attention in the world at large, whilst adultery lower down the social scale was also capable of provoking considerable publicity within its own sphere. Finally there was a growing literary interest in prostitution. Elizabethan and Jacobean drama is full of fictional bawds and whores. In the same period, cheap pamphlet biographies of recently executed criminals also became a popular genre, providing supposedly truthful narratives of real-life rogues and harlots.[3]

Yet in almost all these cases the interest was incidental and its tone hostile. It was not until the Restoration that notoriously immoral women began to be referred to regularly in print during their own lifetime, and in terms that were less severe.[4] In the 1660s, the public fame of bawds such as Damaris Page, Priscilla Fotheringham, and

HE AND HIS DRUNKEN COMPANIONS RAISE A RIOT IN COVENT GARDEN

31. Some of Bowles's sets included this extra scene, which
extended Hogarth's original narrative.

Madam Cresswell was such that their names were used in political
invective as well as to peddle salacious literature. By the 1670s and
1680s, Mrs Cresswell (the first procuress to merit entry in the *Dictionary of National Biography*) was renowned enough to be casually
referred to in plays, ballads, and pamphlets, and to be pictured as one
of the sights of the capital in Marcellus Laroon's much reprinted
Cryes of the City of London, first published in 1687.[5]

By the end of the seventeenth century there had thus begun to
emerge a new kind of sexual celebrity, characterized by sustained
public interest in the vices of low as well as high-born women. Yet
several key ingredients were still lacking. The sexual gossip of the day
was comparatively exclusive, and most of it was not published but
transmitted only through speech and manuscript. In September 1660,
for example, Pepys was told how the famous procuress Lady Bennett,
being hired by a man to get a pretty salesgirl to sleep with him, had
achieved it 'by counterfeiting to fall into a swoon upon the sight of
her in her shop, became acquainted with her and at last got her ends

32. The images of *A Rake's Progress* were endlessly copied and re-used: in cheaper sets, like this one,

33. . . . . as stand-alone engravings,

34. . . . to illustrate books,

35. . . . even to wrap tobacco.

36. Mrs Cresswell: The first bawd famous enough to be
pictured as one of the sights of London.

of her'. Like other news of rape, seduction, and bawdry, it was
recorded in his diary but never made it into print. Even verse satires,
the kind of contemporary writing most focused on topical sexual gossip, were only just beginning to circulate at all widely, and their
production and availability fluctuated considerably. Moreover, the
fame of individual prostitutes, compared with that of brothel-keepers,
remained insubstantial and fleeting. They are sometimes referred to in
poems, pamphlets, and private papers, but almost nothing tangible is
recorded about any such woman, unless she happened to become the
mistress of a great man, or appeared on stage. Finally, writing as yet
played a negligible part in creating or maintaining sexual celebrity: it
merely reflected it. Both in printed and in manuscript accounts of
notorious bawds and whores, the women themselves remain obscure

or obviously imaginary, their main role being to heighten the writer's own titillating or satirical message.[6]

Just a few decades later the picture was strikingly different. As well as a continued interest in fictional harlots, there developed a remarkable vogue for purportedly factual narratives about real women. In 1723, the downfall of the courtesan Sarah Prydden, better known as Sally Salisbury, provoked a string of biographical publications. An illustrated broadsheet summarized her *Effigies, Parentage, Education, Life, Merry-Pranks and Conversation*. The book-length *Genuine History of Mrs Sarah Prydden* was soon reprinted and extended into *Authentick Memoirs of the Life, Intrigues and Adventures of the Celebrated Sally Salisbury*, which ran to two further editions and was translated into Dutch and German in the same year. Soon afterwards there appeared a *Compleat History of the Life, Intrigues and Death of that Celebrated Lady of Pleasure, Sally Salisbury*. Pamphlets about her were published in Dublin as well as London, and memoirs of her life were also one of the selling points of *The Town Spy*, printed in Gloucester in 1725, sold in Bristol, Worcester, Hereford, Ross, Cirencester, Devizes, Cardiff, Monmouth, and Northampton, and distributed even further afield by travelling pedlars. Even fifty years later her name was still current in popular ballads. Other notorious contemporaries of Mrs Prydden were commemorated in such works as *The Life of the Late Celebrated Mrs Elizabeth Wisebourn, vulgarly call'd Mother Wybourn*, which went through three editions in 1721, *The History of the Life and Intrigues of that Celebrated Courtezan, and Posture-Mistress, Eliz. Mann, alias Boyle, alias Sample, commonly call'd The Royal Soveraign* (1724), *The Velvet Coffee-Woman: Or, the Life, Gallantries and Amours of the Late Famous Mrs. Anne Rochford* (1728), *The Life and Intrigues of the Late Celebrated Mrs Mary Parrimore, the Tall Milliner of 'Change Alley* (1729), and *The Life and Character of Moll King, late Mistress of King's Coffee-House*, which appeared in 1747. All this was still before 1750. In the second half of the century such individual histories became ubiquitous, and were even joined by collective biographies of leading courtesans and brothel-keepers.[7]

A similar trend is observable in the case of pictures of immoral women. Private paintings of lovers and mistresses had been made long before 1700, and they became increasingly common thereafter, in line

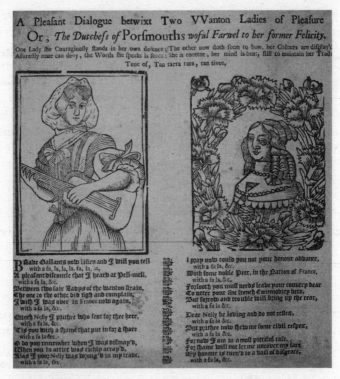

37. A cheap ballad of 1685, purporting to show the likenesses of Charles II's rival mistresses, the Duchess of Portsmouth and Nell Gwyn (in fact, both woodcuts reused existing, generic images).

with the general explosion of portraiture in eighteenth-century England. The rise of a more general interest in the appearance of famous harlots was new, and is apparent from the increasing mass-production of their prints for public sale.[8]

At first it was only royal courtesans who were commemorated in this way. In the later seventeenth century, images of Charles II's mistresses appear to have been tremendously popular. Cheapest of all were the crude woodcuts of them that adorned penny ballads. Much more numerous and realistic were separate engraved and mezzotint portraits, whose purpose was to provide a true likeness of the sitter. These retailed, in various sizes, for sixpence upwards. At least a dozen different ones were issued of the Duchess of Portsmouth before 1700. Some fourteen different contemporary prints survive of Nell Gwyn in various poses; and fifteen at least of Barbara Villiers, Duchess of Cleveland. Even pictures of lesser mistresses, such as Mary Davis and Peg Hughes, were popular enough to be regularly reissued (see illustrations 10, 11, 37, 38; and plates 13 and 14).[9]

This fashion continued in the eighteenth century, although the deferential tone of straightforward portraits was now increasingly challenged by satirical pictures of royal and aristocratic whores. In the reign of

38. A mass-market print from the 1670s of Mary Davis, another of Charles II's mistresses.

SOLOMON in his Glory.
Geo. II.

Come let us take our Fill of Love untill the Morning let us Solace our selves
with Love: For the Good Man is not at Home. He is gone a Long Journey,
He hath taken a Bag of Money with him & will come home at the Day Appointed.
Queen Caroline died Dec. 1737.   Proverbs 7. 18. 19. 20.   19 Jan! 1738
Publish'd According to Act of Parliment Dec. 19. 1703

39. A 1738 satire on George II and his mistress, Lady Yarmouth.

George II, both the king's own mistress, Lady Yarmouth, and the Prince
of Wales's, Anne Vane, were the butt of much visual comedy. Under
the uxorious George III, the focus shifted to women associated with
leading courtiers, such as the Prince of Wales and the Duke of Grafton,
whose premiership in 1769 provoked a flurry of prints of his lover,
Nancy Parsons. By the end of the eighteenth century it had become the
norm for such liaisons to be subjected to incessant and savage caricature (see illustrations 39 to 42, and plate 15).[10]

Images of less exalted courtesans first began to circulate publicly in
the first half of the eighteenth century. Several of the biographies of

THE PRINCE AND PRINCESS OF WALES.

40. The Prince of Wales with his new wife – and, in the background,
his discarded mistress and bastard son (1736).

Sally Salisbury included portraits. There was also an immediate market for high quality separate three-quarter and half-length mezzotints of her (see illustrations 43 and 44). Such was the interest in this new genre that as early as 1747 a guide to collecting prints recommended setting aside a whole volume for 'the portraits of women, both ancient

Miss Nancy Parsons.

41. Nancy Parsons, companion of the Duke of Grafton, Prime Minister from 1768 to 1770 – until she left him for another, much younger duke.

and modern, who were either imperfect, mad, or prostitutes'. But it was in the 1750s and 1760s that pictures of famous harlots really became popular. In the space of just five or six years, perhaps as many as a dozen different prints were published of the much-adored Kitty Fisher (see illustration 45 and plates 16 to 18). By 1765, a visitor to London noted that prints of celebrated ladies of pleasure were both extraordinarily cheap ('a few guineas will buy a whole seraglio') and were issued in huge editions, of three or four thousand at a time. In the following year, the catalogue of just one London print-seller included dozens of images of well-known courtesans, in a variety of formats. Large mezzotint portraits of 'the most celebrated beauties of the present time', chaste as well as unchaste, cost a shilling each. Smaller mezzotints of many of the same women were available for sixpence. Cheapest of all were tiny prints made to fit inside gentlemen's watch cases and snuff-boxes, the mass-produced equivalent of portrait miniatures. For threepence, or sixpence 'neatly coloured', a

42. A satire on the morals of the Prime Minister, his wife, and his mistress, published in the magazine *The Political Register* in February 1769.

The Celebrated Mrs Sally Salisbury

43. One of several mezzotint prints of the courtesan
Sally Salisbury produced around 1723.

man could carry his favourite harlot around with him in perfect privacy, gazing upon her whenever he felt like it (see illustration 45).[11]

The poses and symbolism of these representations often hinted at sexual availability. Yet even the most apparently demure print served several purposes. It spread knowledge of a woman's appearance, it enhanced her fame, and it allowed thousands of viewers to feel familiar, even possessive, towards her. As a commentator remarked in 1779, the most celebrated courtesans were now so well known, 'and their persons are so perfectly described at the print-shops', that they needed no introduction.* The same sense of celebrity and familiarity,

---

* Although the high-minded Lord Hardwicke liked to tell the story of how, confronted with a nude double-portrait of Fanny Murray and Kitty Fisher, he had, to its owner's astonishment, been able to express 'his perfect ignorance' of who the subjects were: Richard Cooksey, *Essay on the Life and Character of John Lord Somers* (Worcester, 1791), 102–3.

44. A cheap, mass-market broadsheet, including a woodcut
of the same image of Sally Salisbury.

sometimes leading to contempt, is also apparent from the 1750s onwards in the emergence of satirical representations of notorious whores.[12]

The growing renown of leading courtesans was also reflected in a whole variety of other ways. Their likenesses were circulated not just in prints and paintings but also in miniatures and medallions. Their sayings and doings were reported in newspapers, discussed in letters, and collected in books. Long before the sandwich had been invented, Fanny Murray was already legendary for having clapped a twenty-pound banknote between two slices of bread and consumed it, to show her disdain for the meanness of the sum.* Inevitably such fame infiltrated contemporary literature too. Already in the 1720s the poet Henry Carey was much annoyed to find that his chaste and innocent ballad 'Sally in our Alley', which depicted 'love in the lowest class of

* By 1763 the same story (by now involving a hundred-pound note) had come to be retailed of her rival, Kitty Fisher: Giacomo Casanova, *Memoirs of My Life*, transl. Willard R. Trask, 12 vols (1970), ix. 308.

45. A tiny engraving of the courtesan Kitty Fisher, made to be
carried around inside a pocket watch (*c.* 1759).

human life', had come to be regarded as an ode to Sally Salisbury. Half
a century later, her life-story remained a staple of travelling puppet-
shows, on a par with Dick Whittington and his Cat. Her successors
were referred to in countless plays, verses, and essays. Their names
were appropriated for everything from songs and tunes to items of fur-
niture. Even homosexual prostitutes used them. Their influence was
also apparent in fashion, so that reputable women were said to copy
'the Kitty Fisher style', or to appear in a 'Fanny Murray cap'. It even
introduced a new practice in the naming of racehorses, which before
1700 had rarely been called after individuals of any kind, let alone
scandalous ones. In the 1730s, several thoroughbreds called 'Sally
Salisbury' competed at meetings across the country. In later decades,
well-known competitors and broodmares in England and North America included 'Fanny Murray', 'Kitty Fisher', and 'Nancy Dawson'.[13]*

---

* At some point such names, like those of famous fictional characters, even came to
be given to pet dogs, such as the favourite Jack Russell terriers of the High Court judge
Sir Christopher French QC (1925–2003), who were called Lucy Lockett, Polly Pea-
chum, Roderick Random, Matthew Bramble, and Kitty Fisher: *The Daily Telegraph*,
27 March 2003.

Today the celebrity associated with sexual scandal is undoubtedly greater and more ubiquitous than ever before. Pornography of various kinds has become a major global industry. Across the western world, countless people achieve fame by publicizing their sexual exploits or revealing those of others. Publishers and broadcasters cater to an apparently insatiable public interest in the salacious details of people's private lives: the fascination with sex and fame is an inescapable fact of our culture. Because it is most forcefully perpetuated by comparatively recent inventions such as photo-magazines, television, and the internet, we tend to think of this as a quintessentially contemporary phenomenon. In fact, the foundations of this modern obsession were laid in the eighteenth century.

THE EXPLOSION OF PRINT

Its most obvious cause was an immense growth in printed media. Already by 1700 the population of London was markedly more literate than that of the rest of the country. Most men and women in the capital could read and write, including the bulk of servants and apprentices. Ever since the invention of printing, however, the publication and circulation of all kinds of information had been inhibited in various ways. The most overt were official licensing and censorship, through which successive governments tried, albeit never with complete success, to prevent and suppress the expression of heterodox views. In consequence, most of what appeared in print was already constrained by self-censorship and by the relative formality of the medium.[1]

The main alternative means of disseminating ideas in writing was through the circulation of manuscripts. Up to the end of the seventeenth century such 'scribal publication' remained extremely important, especially for material thought unfit to print. It offered much greater freedom of language and subject-matter, which is why most salacious material (bawdy and obscene verses, sexual satires, and erotic writings) circulated in this format. Script was also much more restricted in its audience, for the number of copies made was usually comparatively small, and many authors and transmitters of texts consciously limited their readership. Even the most widely circulated manuscripts

46. This broadside ballad about Fanny Murray probably sold for a penny. The woodcut portrait is a copy of one of the many engraved prints of her.

tended to remain the preserve of a social elite, largely unknown and inaccessible to the mass of the reading public.[2]

Since the invention of printing, censorship had broken down only on two occasions of political crisis: during the Civil War and again in the early 1680s. At both times a flood of material poured off the presses until licensing was re-imposed. In 1695, however, following the semi-accidental lapse of the Licensing Act, it came to be abandoned for good. The result was that the eighteenth century saw an unprecedented rise in the number and variety of books and pamphlets published, as well as a marked expansion in their freedom of expression. We know of about 800 different titles issued in 1677, for example; but by the end of the eighteenth century it was not unusual for there to be upwards of 8,000 publications in a single year. Around 1670 only about two dozen printing houses in London, Oxford, Cambridge, and York were authorized to print anything; by 1800 there were hundreds of printers and publishers, at least one in almost every town in England. There was a corresponding explosion in the number and spread of booksellers. Finally, publications of all kinds were also accessible to a mass audience in entirely new ways: through circulating and subscription libraries, book clubs, and coffee-houses.[3]

Especially important in creating a new intellectual climate was the spectacular rise of the periodical press. Before 1600 there were no newspapers; even in 1695, they remained few in number, narrow in scope, short-lived, and limited in distribution. Yet already by 1716 so many new titles had entered circulation that Dudley Ryder's diary refers in passing to at least a dozen of them. A modern list of the 'principal' London papers in 1752 runs to twenty daily, tri-weekly, bi-weekly, weekly, fortnightly, and monthly publications, not counting many lesser journals and magazines. By 1765 there were already, in addition to newspapers, over seventy-five metropolitan periodicals, many of them with very large circulations. Many of these papers were read far beyond the capital, whilst the provinces were served in addition by dozens of local journals.[4]

The combined readership of these various media was equally prodigious. When he started the *Spectator*, Joseph Addison calculated that, though he normally printed only 3,000 copies, each issue reached around 60,000 men and women every day, by being passed on privately, read aloud, and circulated in clubs and coffee-houses – so that 'if I allow twenty readers to every paper, which I look upon as a modest computation, I may reckon about three-score thousand disciples in London and Westminster'. In later years, when the paper was at its height, it was said 'that 20,000 [copies] were sometimes sold in a day'. In addition, it was increasingly common for the same items of news and opinion, the same letters and essays, the same stories and ideas, to be endlessly reused. Most popular journals were collected and reprinted in volume form at least once, ensuring that their contents remained in circulation long after the date on which they had first appeared. By the middle of the century, newspapers also incessantly reprinted, extracted, recycled, and plagiarized each other's contents from day to day.[5]

This enormous increase in the quantity and availability of printed publications transformed the nature of public communication. It allowed events and opinions to be publicized much more widely than before. New forms of print now made generally available material of a kind that had previously circulated only orally or in manuscript. News, gossip, and information were transmitted with ever greater speed and frequency. The scale on which they circulated was also infinitely amplified: by the 1750s, especially in the capital, even the most obscure men and women avidly consumed newspapers. That was precisely the reason, explained Samuel Johnson in his own paper, that the common people of England were the best informed in the world: 'this superiority we undoubtedly owe to the rivulets of intelligence, which are continually trickling among us, which every one may catch, and of which every one partakes'.[6] Without these developments, the extraordinary celebrity of eighteenth-century courtesans would plainly not have been possible.

Yet although the proliferation of new media was an important contributory factor, it cannot be a sufficient explanation. Already in the early seventeenth century engraved portraits of famous men and women had been tremendously popular – the fact that images of courtesans became fashionable a hundred years later testifies less to the emergence of a new medium than of a new attitude. The same is true of other forms of publicity. Even in the reign of Charles II it had been possible for the scandalous sex-life of a low-born woman to be widely publicized. Between 1663 and 1673, the serial bigamist Mary Carleton was the subject of dozens of biographical and autobiographical narratives, memoirs, plays, and pamphlets. Portraits of her were engraved and published alongside her works. She even appeared on stage, starring as herself, in a dramatized interpretation of her story.[7] In many respects Mrs Carleton's public persona, and its literary appropriation, prefigures that of the scandalous women of the mid-eighteenth century: and yet it stands as a lone exception before 1700. The deeper question is therefore why in the eighteenth century print and publicity, as well as expanding in scope, came increasingly to be used in new ways.

This transformation was so complex that it can only be understood as the product of several interrelated changes in the social and intellectual environment – in the character of public opinion; in the means and terms of debate; in assumptions about private and public life; and in the nature of fame and celebrity.

The first great change was that the availability of novel forms of communication helped to create a different attitude towards public opinion. Whereas in previous times the idea of directly appealing to popular judgement had generally been regarded with suspicion by writers, artists, and politicians, their Georgian successors grew to be highly self-conscious about their relationship to the broader public and their dependence upon its support. Instead of denouncing 'common' or 'vulgar' views as low and misguided, it now became increasingly fashionable to measure, shape, and defer to 'public opinion' – a new phrase, whose coinage in the first half of the eighteenth century reflects the change of sentiment. It remained perfectly possible for theorists, critics, and statesmen to denounce popular views as misguided; or to distinguish between refined and uneducated assessments; or to disdain popularity altogether – but the burgeoning importance of public opinion was undeniable. As Dr Johnson, a keen student of the subject, advised, 'there always lies an appeal from domestic criticism to a higher judicature, and the public, which is never corrupted, nor often deceived, is to pass the last sentence upon literary claims'.[8]

This development has been much studied by historians of politics, philosophy, and the arts.[9] But it is, if anything, even more relevant to the subject of this book. In literature and politics the effect of new genres and modes of communication can be traced back at least to the early seventeenth century; by contrast, in the case of attitudes to sexual behaviour, the power of print as an agent of public opinion developed much later and more suddenly. It was only in the early eighteenth century that there emerged a culture in which sexual matters could be continuously and publicly discussed by a mass audience. The rise of the periodical press ensured that social information was much more freely, continuously, and voluminously available, that it was endlessly copied and commented on from paper to paper, and that it was shared by much more open and substantial communities of readers than ever before. In this way there became established for the first time a set of permanent mass media for the circulation and discussion of news and opinion.

The use of pamphlets likewise burgeoned. The seventeenth century had already been a great age of pamphleteering, especially on political and religious topics. The controversialist Edward Stephens, whom we encountered in Chapter 1, put forth almost a hundred different tracts between 1689 and 1706, and he was a distinctly minor writer: doubtless other seventeenth-century authors were more prolific still. By 1750, though, pamphlet publication had come to address a far wider range of subjects, and to be much more easily accessible even to humble authors, than had generally been the case fifty years earlier. By the middle of the eighteenth century the evolution of the periodical and pamphlet press had together made it possible for almost any literate person who wished to disseminate information or opinion to address a large audience quickly, easily, and anonymously.

The new media also actively encouraged their readers to interact with them, and thus to take part in public discussion. It was not new for writers to address their audience directly, or for books and pamphlets to provoke printed rejoinders. However, the proliferation of newspapers and journals brought about something altogether different. Most of these publications depended heavily on unsolicited correspondence, verses, essays, advertisements, and announcements, sent in, often anonymously, by ordinary readers. In this way the public and its views gradually became much more visible and assertive than they had ever been before. What is more, exposure to the popular press itself inescapably instructed readers in the new opportunities and conventions of publicity. The prominence given to readers' responses to topical issues, the constant dialogue between correspondents, and the general, unremitting stream of public consciousness broadcast in papers, pamphlets, and magazines made concrete the sense of belonging to a large, active, and opinionated community of discussants.

This was no mere illusion, for already in the 1710s the editors of popular papers received many more letters than they could print. Unfortunately most submissions to newspapers and magazines were unsigned or pseudonymous, so that it will never be possible to determine where they came from. However, some sense of the opportunities available by the second half of the century is provided by the record of James Boswell's writings between 1758 and 1794. Even though very incomplete, this includes many hundreds of anonymous letters, essays, reviews, verses, epigrams, comments, announcements, reports, and other contributions, originally appearing in more than twenty different papers and widely reprinted in others. Boswell was obviously a gentleman and an increasingly practised writer, but humbler men and women, too, came to be acutely aware of the potential power of the press to advertise their opinions. By the middle of the eighteenth century it was common even for criminals, suicides, and convicts facing execution to take pains over the publication of their thoughts in pamphlets and newspapers. 'There was never a time', remarked Dr Johnson in 1753, 'in which men of all degrees of ability, of every kind of education, of every profession and employment, were posting with ardour so general to the press': it had become a signal characteristic of the age.[10]

THE MANIPULATION OF PUBLICITY

The popular press and its social counterparts, such as debating clubs and coffee-houses, were not merely the means of discussion: their practices also altered the very terms of debate. The new types of exchange created novel ways of thinking about morality. This was the second way in which the new media affected sexual sensibilities.[1]

For a start, a far greater diversity of views than ever before emerged into print. The early periodical press did much to create this new openness, by encouraging correspondence and providing advice on the problems of love and lust. Although conduct books and casuistical literature had been around for a long time, it had never previously been possible for men and women of all social classes, in their thousands, to seek help by writing anonymously to a newspaper and having their query published and answered in print, for all the world to see.[2]

This sudden innovation was the brainchild of the publisher John Dunton, whose hugely successful bi-weekly question-and-answer journal, the *Athenian Mercury* (1691–7), was the first English periodical to capture a popular audience. From the outset, the most common topics about which its readers sought advice were love, marriage, and sexual ethics. What was the propriety of unmarried cohabitation? What morals should one attribute to a woman who dressed indecently? Was innocent friendship ever possible between a man and a woman? Why were prostitutes generally barren? Was it wrong to masturbate? Could one conceive at first intercourse? Might adultery ever be justified? None of these questions was new, but never before had they been so popularly and publicly debated. So great was the volume of such correspondence that it spawned a monthly special issue to deal with the backlog, and then a separate spin-off publication, the *Ladies Mercury* (1693). The format and focus of Dunton's publication in turn inspired many notable successors, including Defoe's *Review* (1704–13), the *British Apollo* (1708–11), the *Tatler* (1709–11), the *Spectator* (1711–14), and the *Gentleman's Magazine*, founded in 1731.[3]

In addition to publicizing, and attempting to solve, moral dilemmas presented by their readers, eighteenth-century periodicals set themselves up to be much more general arbiters and communicators of social norms, which they expounded in essays, verses, and general reflections. By mid-century such aspirations had become a common feature of popular journalism. The growing popularity of periodicals thus created a new and widely read type of authority on questions of conduct. In the eyes of contemporaries there was no necessary contradiction with older sources of guidance. As one remarked, the Bible remained the fount of all moral knowledge; whereas the *Spectator* simply 'taught me a more easy and agreeable manner of practising virtue'. In fact, as has rightly been pointed out, there was a considerable divergence between the moral philosophy of early eighteenth-century advice literature and what had come before. Its motive was much more often to entertain as well as to instruct. Its basis was also different. Although it commonly invoked scripture to buttress its arguments, divine law was no longer automatically the primary criterion. Instead, virtuous behaviour now tended to be defined in secular terms: it followed reason, civility, and the dictates of human nature.[4] Finally, it is likely that the very form of popular journalism contributed to the idea that moral judgements might be essentially subjective. It was not just the growing volume of newspapers, magazines, and pamphlets that brought about a greater multiplicity and inconsistency of views, but also the fact that these media intrinsically depended on fomenting discussion, provoking questions and comments, contradicting one another, and competing for public attention.

Another consequence of these new conditions was the rise in the eighteenth century of what we might call 'media events': cases whose public discussion was so intense that it took on a momentum and a significance of its own. Many such episodes were inspired by some form of sexual controversy. In turn, they inevitably served to highlight contrasting views about sexuality. Even in the seventeenth century some scandalous incidents had provoked considerable comment. In the 1610s, the Overbury affair spawned a flurry of broadsides, pamphlets and poems, in addition to a large body of scribal material. Similar interest surrounded the trial of the Earl of Castlehaven in 1631 for abetting rape and committing sodomy, the divorce proceedings of the Duke and Duchess of Norfolk in the 1690s, and a string of other cases involving sexual impropriety. By the mid eighteenth century the novelty was not just that such episodes were much more numerous, nor even that the amount of printed commentary, and its circulation, was vastly greater.[5] It was that public involvement through the press was now so commonplace that it could itself become part of the course of events. The combination of frequent and competitive news reporting, and the availability of countless avenues for public intervention, meant that public scandals now almost always inspired endless printed debate between observers and interested parties, even as events were still unfolding.

In the case of sexual celebrities even the most apparently trivial incident could be amplified a hundredfold. When in March 1759 Kitty Fisher was thrown off her horse whilst riding in St James's Park, it inspired months of public comment, songs, verses, pictures, pamphlets, and entire books (see illustrations 47 to 49). The most common focal point, though, was a trial. After all, a court case contained all the ingredients for a ready-made public debate: different sides offering irreconcilable stories, personalities to dissect, the expectation of scandalous facts, the certainty of a final denouement, and the possibility of punishment, ruin, and even death for the defeated party. It was in the 1760s that the term '*cause célèbre*' first came to be used in English, and several of the earliest examples of the phenomenon are still so described today.[6] There was the case in 1753–4 of the young maid Elizabeth Canning, who claimed to have been abducted and held captive for several weeks in a bawdy house, but whose detractors were convinced, as Voltaire put it, that she was simply 'une petite friponne', who had got herself pregnant and had disappeared to cover up the fact. Even greater publicity surrounded the trials in 1775 of the bigamous Elizabeth Chudleigh, Duchess of Kingston, and of the courtesan Mary Rudd, her lover Daniel Perreau, and his twin brother Robert. Four years later, the murder of Martha Ray, mistress of the Earl of Sandwich, by a young, love-struck clergyman, likewise provoked endless comment and speculation. So overwhelming was the public discussion of such cases that the legal proceedings themselves, and their capacity to establish truth and justice, came to appear almost secondary to the trial by media that was conducted in print.[7]

The same dynamics shaped countless other now obscure and forgotten incidents of eighteenth-century sexual scandal. Take the case of Ann Sharp, alias Bell. In October 1760 it was widely reported in the London papers that a young gentlewoman had recently been seduced into a bagnio in mysterious circumstances, sexually assaulted, and mortally wounded. The truth of these rumours was equivocal. Even when the body was specially exhumed and examined, the inquest concluded that there had been no foul play. Yet the story refused to die, for it appeared to contain all the ingredients of the worst kind of seduction narrative: the happy daughter of a reputable family in the country, first ruined by a passing army officer; then, moving to

47. One of the prints devoted to Kitty Fisher's 'merry accident'
in March 1759.

London, gradually degraded into ever meaner forms of prostitution;
then, when down on her luck, sought out, abused, abandoned, and
destroyed by an upper-class rake who lacked any shred of humanity
or contrition. As a consequence, the lives, 'adventures', and characters
of Ann Sharp and William Sutton, her supposed assailant, were loudly
and endlessly debated in print: by correspondents to newspapers, in
editorials, in poetry, and in a steady stream of factual and fictional
accounts issued by interested and disinterested parties. Such was the
intensity of public comment that even the coroner and the chief magistrate, John Fielding, were forced to take out public advertisements in
the papers in defence of their conduct. In this way, the general perception of the case increasingly turned upon the motives and contributions
of rival commentators, rather than upon the evidence per se. By the
time that Sutton was brought to trial and acquitted of murder, four
and a half months later, the judicial verdict was largely irrelevant, for
many observers had long since made up their minds. 'To be tried by

HORSE and A W A Y to St.
JAMES'S PARK,
OR, a Trip for the Noontide Air

Who Rides Faſteſt, Miſs *KITTY FISHER*, or her
GAY GALLANT.

WALKING in the Park on Monday laſt, and enjoying the vernal air, and the warm beams of the returning ſun; the day, the company, and the gladneſs that appeared on every countenance, touched the ſprings of life, and gave me a ſatisfaction that cannot be well expreſt; it naturely ariſes in the heart, when we ſee not only ourly our kind, but all nature enjoying the benign influences of Heaven.

Whilſt I was there, the following accident alarmed me, and had like to have put an end to the pleaſure of the walk, and I own ſent me home rather chagrin'd.

Two young ladies, attended each with her officer, and ſervant, were returning from Hyde Park, where they had been airing on horſe back; one of the Laides was in a black riding-habit, and mounted on a horſe ſingularly marked they flung down the Green Park in an eaſy canter; but they no ſooner entered within the pails of St. James's, but the Lady in black loſt her ſeat, ſhrieked out, and came tumbling on the ground: — Numbers flew to her Relief; her diſtreſs and genteel Appearence awakened our curioſity and pity; —— Servants and the Chair were immediately called.

Upon our coming up, we found it to be the celebrated Miſs K - - - y F—r: her military attendant had raiſed her from the Ground. -- The Nymph was in tears, but rather from Apprehenſions of her Danger than the ſenſe of Pain; for whether it was owing to any thing her Heroe had ſaid, or from finding the danger over, ſhe, with a prity childiſhneſs, ſtopped the torrent tears, and burſt into a fit of Laughing. -- A ſuperb Chair ſonn arrived, -- ſhe flung herſelf into it, and away ſhe ſwung through a Crowd of Gentlemen and Ladies, who by this time were come up.

A ſort of a murmer was heard: but one Gentleman louder than the reſt, ſpoke up, and though what he ſaid was a little interlarded with a flower of rhetorick too common, but what might well be ſpared; yet the ſentiment was honeſt, and the reprimand ſuch as deſerv'd – D—n my B—d, ſays he, (raiſing the point of his Oaken plant, and beating it down again with ſome earneſtneſs) if this is not too much, who the D—l would be modeſt, when they may Live in this ſtate by turning. Why 'tis enough to debauch half the Women in London.

Written and Printed at Strawberry Hill

48. This handbill was one of several publications rushed out in March 1759 to capitalize on popular interest in Kitty Fisher's 'fall'.

Fun upon Fun, or the first and second part of Miss Kitty Fishers Merry-thought. No Joke like a True Joke. Come, who'l Fish in my Fishpond?

49. This documentary print by Paul Sandby shows a family of ballad-sellers in 1760 hawking copies of other (now lost) publications about Kitty Fisher. To attract attention, and in tribute to her name, the man is carrying them around attached to the end of a fishing rod: 'Come, who'll fish in my fishpond?', he cries.

the public,' as one of Miss Bell's partisans urged, had come to be almost more desirable than to be tried at law.[8]

The final notable feature of enlightened print culture was that it presented novel opportunities for the manipulation of public opinion. This may seem an ironic development. Indeed, Professor Jürgen Habermas, the most influential modern theorist of the subject, tells us that exactly the opposite is true. The emergence of a new type of public sphere in early eighteenth-century England, he argues, allowed the educated classes for the first time to engage in 'rational-critical debate' about literary and political issues, free of censorship, commercial pressures, or political partisanship. It was only in the nineteenth and twentieth centuries that this independent critical spirit was destroyed by the commercialization of the mass media, and the rise of advertising, public relations, and other modern tools of manipulation.[9]

Even in the eighteenth century, however, it was not unusual for publicity to be carefully managed and manufactured. The reports of news and gossip that appeared in the press were often produced and sold to papers by professional hack writers. The letters and comments supposedly sent in by ordinary readers were commonly re-written, and sometimes wholly made up. Some editors took payment for publishing or suppressing particular items of news; others were entirely in the pay of particular politicians – as were many of the leading writers of the day.[10]

This was also the period in which advertising and book reviewing first became important and ubiquitous promotional tools. Both lent themselves to underhand methods for marketing books, goods, performances, people, and causes. Advertisements masquerading as news or correspondence could disingenuously alert readers to events and publications; whilst notices and reviews that were in reality little more than meretricious plugs disguised themselves as objective recommendations. Amongst the wide variety of 'news' inserted for payment in one London newspaper in the spring of 1744, at exactly the same rate as normal advertisements, were spurious commendations of 'a bowling green, a play, a good fishing lake, and the knighting of Thomas Rider, esquire, of Kent'. It was to describe the rise of such tactics that the term 'puff' took on new meanings in the second quarter of the eighteenth century. In 1732 the *London Magazine* described it as 'a cant word for the applause that writers and book-sellers give their own books etc, to promote their sale'. Chesterfield similarly thought it a 'low' word – but used it repeatedly himself. Pretty soon it became a popular fictional epithet. A letter from 'John Puff Esq.' is prefaced to Henry Fielding's 1741 spoof, *Shamela*. In Samuel Foote's comedy *Taste* (1752), a 'Mr Puff' helps to palm off worthless objects as valuable works of art; in his *The Patron* (1764) the same name is given to a mercenary bookseller. Similar Mr Puffs appear in Susanna Centlivre's *The Election* of 1749 (a printer) and R. B. Sheridan's 1779 play *The Critic* ('a gentleman well known in the theatrical world').[11]

Exactly the same means that served to communicate and amplify public opinion were thus commonly employed to deceive and control it. The further development of the mass media in the nineteenth and twentieth centuries greatly expanded the audience susceptible to such techniques. From the outset, however, the manipulation of publicity was a natural, intrinsic by-product of the commodification and influence of printed news and opinion. Even today it is startling to realize quite how shameless eighteenth-century tactics could be. Popular newspapers sometimes found themselves faced by rival publications that had overnight adopted exactly the same title, date, and numbering, in order to trick the public. The common custom of anonymous and pseudonymous publication and reviewing allowed authors surreptitiously to insert, in one pamphlet or paper, trailers and testimonials for another. Writers could clandestinely plug their own books, as well as employing the puffing services of their friends. Jonas Hanway penned an enthusiastic notice of his three-volume *Advice from a Farmer to his Daughter* (1770), and asked Elizabeth Montagu to submit it as her own. John Cleland secretly reviewed his own work, and so did many other writers. Mary Rudd described one of her own publications, anonymously, as 'one of the most spirited, and at the same time the most elegant and temperate compositions' to have appeared in recent times. Although 'this may be regarded as a puff for the book', she concluded, 'it is however different from all other puffs in one respect – it is *literally true*'. Boswell not only repeatedly and prolifically reviewed his own public appearances and literary works ('a book of true genius', 'the production of no ordinary genius', etc.), he even prefaced one of his own anonymous pamphlets with a dedicatory address to himself.[12]

To illustrate the growing potential of the media to influence ideas, connect people, and motivate actions we have only to compare the methods adopted by Thomas Bray and Jonas Hanway, the two most energetic social reformers of their day. When in the 1690s Bray sought to establish a penitential hospital for prostitutes, he simply circulated manuscript copies of his plan to a handful of well-wishers, and canvassed acquaintances privately for their support. There were no regular newspapers or journals through which he could easily have advertised his idea to a broader public, nor did he seek to hold his proposals up to indiscriminate scrutiny by publishing them in pamphlet form. Instead, he personally approached a few key individuals and tried to gain their assistance. Even at the end of the seventeenth century this was an entirely conventional way of proceeding. It was precisely how, shortly afterwards, Bray succeeded in founding the Society for Promoting Christian Knowledge, perhaps the most successful charity of its time, as well as the Society for the Propagation of the Gospel, which similarly came into being without any recourse to the public at large.[13]

To Jonas Hanway, half a century later, such reticence would have been inconceivable. He, too, was a master of covert networking and of the personal appeal. Such was his attention to detail that, when prospective donors were given literature about the Magdalen House, it came bound in specially designed covers that showed penitents crying out 'O Save Me, Save Me' – ensuring that the volume's message was broadcast even if it was left unopened. However, Hanway also took for granted the need to appeal to a more general audience, and to exploit the power of print. Publication, he explained, was even more effective than public meetings. It allowed one's message to be delivered without interruption, distraction, or contradiction; and it gave people time to digest and ponder the merits of a case. What is more, although 'there are many who have not, and many more who think they have not, leisure to read . . . even these pin their faith chiefly on the report of those who criticise books': so that eliciting favourable notices was crucial too. His approach was therefore to flood the media with positive impressions, repeating himself over and over again, in order to get the message across as widely and insistently as possible: publishing and re-publishing, often anonymously, the same sentences and sentiments in the form of plans, letters, reviews, comments, plugs, trailers, and advertisements. All the while he strenuously kept up the disguise of a disinterested, impartial bystander. In truth, as Frances Burney noted, he was 'addicted' to newspapers. Yet to his audience Hanway presented himself as an aloof observer, drawn into the fray only by the exceptional merits of the case. 'As I have but little time to read', he suggested disingenuously, in one of his innumerable puffs for the Magdalen House, 'what I write myself is the more genuine'.[14]*

Hanway's methods testify to the transformation of public communication that had taken place over the previous fifty years. Even minor contributions to any debate were henceforth routinely and immediately magnified, duplicated, and circulated throughout the city, creating a range and depth of comment that would formerly have been unimaginable. Pamphlets, newspapers, literary journals, and ordinary readers rushed to comment on any popular topic. Yet, despite appearances, such discussion was never entirely spontaneous and free. At every stage it was now possible, as publicists like Hanway did so masterfully, to instigate, fan, provoke, influence, exploit, and direct the flow of public opinion towards one's own purposes.

PRIVATE AND PUBLIC AFFAIRS

The eighteenth century thus saw the birth of a new type of media culture, in which both private affairs and personal opinions came to be given unprecedented publicity. This development fuelled the freer

---

* Not to be outdone, his rival John Fielding exploited his powers as a magistrate to publicize his own scheme. First he instigated a series of raids on brothels; then, in the manner of a press conference, he interrogated each arrested prostitute in front of a large, invited audience, and had the results published in the papers – 'in order to shew the public in general, and the worthy subscribers to the Asylum or House of Refuge for deserted girls in particular, the great necessity of such a provision, and the great good this charity may produce'.[15]

public discussion of sexual matters, facilitated the celebrity of immoral women, and provided novel opportunities for the manipulation of public opinion. What is striking is that the same tendencies can be found in the fiction of the period, as well as in many other genres of contemporary writing. This points to the third major source of novel attitudes towards sex – a profound change in how men and women conceived of personal identity and its public significance.

At one level, this involved a transition away from the traditional view that character was primarily to be determined from a person's actions, and towards the presumption that the key lay in somehow uncovering their innermost feelings and private transactions. The more naturally inaccessible to others, the more potentially revealing such personal information might be. As the literary critic Hugh Blair explained, it was not just appropriate for a biographer to record his subject's intimate life, but essential: for 'it is from private life, from familiar, domestic, and seemingly trivial occurrences, that we often receive most light into the real character'. Dr Johnson agreed: the deepest insight came from biographers who 'lead the thoughts into domestic privacies, and display the minute details of daily life, where exterior appendages are cast aside'. It was for similar reasons that Jean-Jacques Rousseau in his autobiography (first published in 1782) was to lay great weight upon his sexual feelings and actions. 'If there be a [single] circumstance in my life, which describes my nature,' he announced at the beginning of one such confession, 'it is that which I am going to relate ... Whoever you may be who are desirous of knowing a man, have the courage to read the two or three following pages, and you will become fully acquainted with J. J. Rousseau.'[1] In this growing stress on the primacy of private sentiments the foundation was laid for one of the most basic assumptions of modern sexual attitudes. Instead of thinking that someone's sexual conduct merely reflected his or her general temperament, the idea was eventually to take hold that everyone had an essential inner sexuality, which itself shaped their outward personality.

Another manifestation of the changing outlook was that in many areas of intellectual endeavour the notion was advanced that truth lay not in the general and the universal but in the individual and the particular. This tendency derived from the popularization of philosophical trends that had been started in the mid-seventeenth century by Descartes, Hobbes, and Locke, and were consolidated by their successors after 1700. Instead of proceeding on the basis of inherited assumptions and supposedly innate ideas, it gradually came to be the logical ideal to accept nothing on trust and to rely solely on one's personal observation of the facts. The empirical scrutiny of specifics accordingly became much more important, for it was no longer merely a means of confirming universal truths, but an end in itself, the cornerstone of real knowledge.

As literary critics have long appreciated, there are remarkable parallels between these trends in philosophy and aesthetics and the simultaneous rise of fictional realism. The early-eighteenth-century novel, too, introduced into literature a new and influential way of describing reality, one which aimed at authenticity through particularity, whose characters were supposed to be indistinguishable from real people, and whose truth was seen to be inextricable from its verisimilitude. The same change of emphasis can be observed much more widely, not just in newspapers and other new forms of journalism, but in social description generally.[2]

Throughout the seventeenth century, as in earlier times, whoredom had been conventionally epitomized in the stock characters of 'a whore', 'a bawd', 'a town miss', and so on. When writers described particular sinners, they likewise focused on their correspondence to universal norms, rather than their individuality. Even in John Dunton's *Night-Walker* of the 1690s, which in many respects was in the vanguard of journalistic realism, the harlots and rakes are all essentially anonymous figures. To have emphasized their particularity would have been to diminish their universality, and their paradigmatic quality.[3] In the eighteenth century the position came to be reversed: now the addition of personal detail served only to heighten the apparent truth of a narrative. It is this new desire to personalize social phenomena that helps to explain, for example, why mid eighteenth-century sexual charities were so keen to publish the letters and stories of individual penitents; and, equally, why there was such interest in the supposed histories and memoirs of impenitent whores. Nowadays we are so used to this way of thinking that it seems scarcely remarkable. It is largely by learning about particular examples that we tend to accumulate our knowledge about, say, adultery, rape, or marital breakdown, and the more detail we have of specific instances the better we feel we understand the phenomenon as a whole. Yet it was only in the course of the eighteenth century that it became normal to treat individual stories in this way.

This development was evidently only gradual and far from comprehensive. All analysis of social and sexual relations depends to some degree on generic and impersonal archetypes. The older tradition of discussing whores and rakes in terms of abstract personifications continued throughout the eighteenth century, as did the use of symbolic names in literature, and of satirical stereotypes in prints.[4] Nor was the interest in particular life stories entirely new. The point is rather that there was a decisive shift of emphasis. Although many seventeenth-century writings on immorality had been packed with illustrative examples of harlots and whoremongers, much greater authority was always accorded to classical and biblical instances than to present-day exemplars. It was only after 1700 that it became common to rely mainly or exclusively on modern paradigms. In addition, whether real or made up, such personal narratives were now invested with a more immediate significance. Rather than interpreting the lives of individuals as simply confirming patterns of behaviour that were laid down by divine and natural laws, eighteenth-century descriptions of particular persons were increasingly inclined, even when seeking to establish general conclusions, to emphasize the individuality of the subject.

For all these reasons, the period after 1700 saw a growing interest in publishing the stories and materials of private life. Much of the originality and appeal of the first novels lay not just in their purported realism but in the supposed disclosure of confidential accounts and secret writings. Daniel Defoe's *Moll Flanders*, of 1722, described itself as a true 'private history', an autobiographical narrative 'written from her own memorandums' by the heroine. A similar format characterized Defoe's *Robinson Crusoe* (1719), *Colonel Jack* (1722) and *Roxana, the Fortunate Mistress* (1724), as well as countless later stories billed as autobiographies, memoirs, or histories. Accounts of real-life whores were part of this trend. Their similarity to new forms of fiction was noted as early as 1723 by the Lincolnshire poet and novelist Jane Barker, who observed that the most fashionable histories of the age were those of 'Robinson Crusoe, and Moll Flanders; Colonel Jack, and Sally Salisbury'.[5]

There was also an overlap with the increasing vogue for *romans à clef* which supposedly laid bare the sexual intrigues of notable contemporaries, especially politicians. This was not an entirely new type of writing. Veiled descriptions of recent court scandals had formed part of the elaborate plot of Lady Mary Wroth's *Urania*, printed in 1621. In the mid 1680s, Aphra Behn published several instalments of *Love Letters from a Nobleman to his Sister*, supposedly the correspondence of the Whig conspirator Lord Grey of Warke and his sister-in-law, Lady Henrietta Berkeley, whose adulterous and incestuous elopement had caused a great stir. However, it was only after the Glorious Revolution, as part of the growing freedom of party political satire, that the genre became properly established in English. Now there appeared numerous retrospective Whig accounts of the 'secret history' and sexual corruption of the recent Stuarts; whilst Tory writers mounted a string of acerbic attacks on past and present Whig personalities, led by Delarivier Manley's notorious 'secret histories' and 'secret memoirs'.[6]

Letters, another type of private writing, also came to be publicized in novel ways. There were obvious classical precedents for epistolary fiction and for the circulation of private correspondence. In the sixteenth century, humanists and reformers, like many later scholars and activists, communicated their message through letters that were meant to be widely publicized; so too did princes and bishops. In the seventeenth century knowledge of political events was spread through newsletters, and it became a common conceit to print polemical tracts in the form of 'a letter from' one personage to another. Only in the eighteenth century, though, did there develop a substantial market for the publishing of personal letters, real or otherwise, as a means of access to the private life of others. We have noted already the dependence of contemporary newspapers and magazines upon correspondence to and from their readers. Telling a story by printing a character's intimate communications also became a favourite tool of novelists, especially when describing love and lust. Nearly a fifth of all the fiction produced in the eighteenth century, it has been estimated, used some kind of epistolary technique.[7]

Above all, there was an immense new appetite for biographies of real people. The eighteenth century was the first age of biographical dictionaries, of regular obituaries, of collected letters, and of published memoirs on a large scale. 'No species of writing seems more worthy of cultivation than biography,' explained Dr Johnson in 1750, 'since none can be more delightful or more useful, none can more certainly enchain the heart by irresistible interest, or more widely diffuse instruction to every diversity of condition.' Even the most ordinary lives, 'not distinguished by any striking or wonderful vicissitudes', were worth relating in print, for in learning about others we inevitably learn about ourselves: 'we are all prompted by the same motives, all deceived by the same fallacies, all animated by hope, obstructed by danger, entangled by desire, and seduced by pleasure'. Not everybody would have agreed with Johnson's analysis of human nature. Some readers, biographers, and autobiographers preferred to dwell rather upon the oddity and uniqueness of personality. But the net result was the same. By 1800, the lives of a much broader spectrum of people were thought to be worthy of public interest than had been the case a hundred years earlier, and reading about the private affairs of the dead and the living, and collecting their portraits, had become something of a national pastime.[8]

FAME AND FORTUNE

The expanding scope of biography brings us to the final indication of shifting attitudes towards sex and publicity in this period: the growing fame of types of people previously regarded as disreputable. Traditionally, biography had served a moral purpose. The lives of saints, martyrs, rulers, divines, and other worthies were valuable as exemplars of virtue, whilst those of tyrants and murderers conventionally warned of the snares of sin and the providence of God. In the eighteenth century these remained important motives. But the heightened value now placed on individuality and personality, together with the other developments we have surveyed, also helped to create the first age of celebrity.

'Celebrity' is a slippery concept to define. The word 'celebrate' in its various forms was very old. As early as the fourteenth century we find Chaucer describing Hercules as 'celebrable for his hard travaile'; and by the seventeenth century it was established practice to write of people as 'celebrate', or 'celebrated', in the sense of famous or renowned. The sense of 'celebrate' as actually *making* someone well-known appeared at around the same time, and grew in importance during the nineteenth and twentieth centuries. Nowadays, as a consequence, 'celebrity' usually means a peculiar, lesser kind of fame, which is limited in three main ways. The first is that it is an essentially personal type of renown, as distinct from the reputation that comes to people who hold a notable office, such as monarchs, or are associated with some conspicuous achievement. The second is that celebrity is intrinsically fleeting, though it can be remarkably long-lived. Thirdly, and in consequence, it is especially dependent upon regular publicity. It was in the eighteenth century, as the opportunities for such exposure multiplied, that this particular form of ephemeral, media-dependent fame first became a widespread phenomenon.[1]

Its origins can be traced back to the earliest days of professional writing for publication, in the late sixteenth and early seventeenth century. This was the period in which it first became possible to make a living as a hack writer, churning out tracts and pamphlets for public sale, and there were soon authors who succumbed to the temptation of advancing their books by promoting themselves. According to the *Oxford Dictionary of National Biography*, we should think of the Elizabethan pamphleteer Robert Greene (1558–92) as 'England's first celebrity author'; whilst the most recent biographer of John Taylor 'the Water-Poet' (1578–1653) describes him as 'the first modern "personality", skilfully manipulating the media and "famous for being famous".'[2] When the first professional women writers appeared on the scene, a hundred years later, they were often the objects, willingly or not, of even greater interest in their personal lives. (This was particularly so when, as in the case of Aphra Behn, Delarivier Manley, and Eliza Haywood, their private affairs were rumoured to be as full of sexual intrigue as their writings.) As the means of publicity expanded, and writers became more dependent upon commercial success, personal celebrity became an ever more important feature of the English literary world.

After 1700 the same focus on personalities also came to characterize the public perception of other, even less reputable, professions. In the early eighteenth century there developed a new fascination with the lives and exploits of highwaymen and other apparently romantic criminals. In the 1720s, Jonathan Wild and Jack Sheppard inspired scores of ballads, sermons, plays, and satires. The notoriety of such figures was one of the inspirations for John Gay's phenomenally successful *Beggar's Opera* (1728), which itself did much to further the cult of the glamorous criminal. By 1700 there was already a long tradition of writing about notorious criminals, but it was only in the eighteenth century that many of them became renowned in their own lifetime, that their portraits were published as cheap prints, and that their biographies became celebratory as well as didactic.[3]

An even closer connection can be drawn between the growing fame of whores and of actresses, who had first appeared publicly on the English stage at the Restoration. The overlap between their roles was obvious. 'Indeed most stage-players are courtesans,' says one character in an early play by Margaret Cavendish; 'And most courtesans are good actors,' replies another. As we have seen, from the 1660s onwards actresses were on constant public display in London. Their personalities were the subject of great public interest, and they often facilitated such intimacy by addressing the audience in their own voice, in specially written prologues and epilogues. It was also well known that many of them led scandalous lives, offstage as well as on. Several of the period's leading mistresses, from Nell Gwyn to Dorothy Jordan, started out in the theatre. In many respects the contemporary celebrity of actresses was far greater than that of whores and bawds. But it is significant that it emerged at about the same time; that it took similar forms, from portrait prints to hack biographies; and that it was strongly fixated on their sexual behaviour.[4]

SELF-PROMOTION AND EXPLOITATION

The rising popularity of courtesans was therefore part of a whole series of interrelated developments in eighteenth-century society. It was the product of new attitudes to fame and notoriety, of novel forms of writing, of changing attitudes towards public opinion, and of shifting assumptions about personal identity. It also epitomized the emergence of a new type of mass media, in which private affairs and personal opinions were publicized on a previously unthinkable scale. Its lasting significance can be interpreted in two contrasting ways.

The first is to highlight the artificiality of material that celebrated immoral women. A lot of it – whether memoirs, or anecdotes, or portraits – was designed, at least superficially, to look truthful. Yet if we look closer it is equally evident that most of it was made up, by male writers and publishers. As with all biography, one attraction seems to have been the promise of authenticity, the revelation of private information and secrets about well-known people. So tempting are the style and format of many made-up accounts, and so scarce other sources, that many modern historians, and even the *Oxford Dictionary of National Biography*, have tended to treat them as essentially true.[1] We should also remember, though, that eighteenth-century readers loved ambiguity about fact and fiction. Whether or not particular stories were accurate was ultimately not necessarily important: their purpose was to entertain and to instruct. From this perspective, most writing about courtesans was no different, in form and function, from contemporary fiction. It can tell us quite a lot about eighteenth-century culture, but very little about the women it purported to describe. As much as it reflected and amplified their fame, it also distorted and abused it, projecting onto them, without their consent, other people's lies and fantasies.

Yet reputation in any society is not just a matter of public perception and projection. It also depends on one's own actions. The other way to interpret the publicity surrounding infamous women in the eighteenth century is therefore to recognize their own complicity in it. Many of them cultivated their own celebrity, indeed broadcast it loudly. Much of this was done through personal appearance, word of mouth, and manuscript correspondence within the circles of fashionable society. However, leading courtesans also actively promoted themselves, in print, to a much wider public audience.

One way they did this was through the publication of authorized prints, in which they collaborated with some of the leading artists, engravers, and publishers of the period. We can date the point at which this practice took off with remarkable precision. In the last week of March 1759, the courtesan Kitty Fisher took out a news-paper advertisement, deploring the constant exploitation of her persona by base 'little scribblers' and print-sellers, who foisted spuri-ous writings and images of her upon the public (it is printed at the head of this chapter). A few days later, she went to see the most suc-cessful painter of her day, Joshua Reynolds, who immediately set to work crafting more appealing images of her, for conversion into mass-market prints. It was the beginning of a long and fruitful partnership, for no one was more adept than Reynolds at the creation and manipu-lation of visual celebrity. From then on, he painted major portraits of the leading *demi-mondaines* of the time, exhibited them prom-inently, and got them published as cheap prints in all shapes and sizes. Like other portraitists who took up the practice, he was simultan-eously boosting his own public profile, and fuelling the celebrity of his sitters, to their mutual benefit (see plates 16 to 18, and illustra-tion 45).[2]

This was also the age in which scandalous women first published real autobiographies and vindications of their own behaviour. Such writings served a variety of purposes. They allowed the author to present a favourable picture of herself to the world, and to name and shame her enemies. They earned her money from eager readers and booksellers. Most lucrative of all was the practice of blackmailing for-mer lovers and clients, by threatening to publish their names and letters. This was one of the central aims of the serialized *Apology* of the courtesan Teresia Constantia Phillips, which was a runaway best-seller when it started appearing in 1748. In the same year were published the first two volumes of the *Memoirs* of Laetitia Pilkington, denounced by her estranged husband as 'an incorrigible prostitute'. By 1800 the genre had become well established. When Margaret Leeson, the most fashionable prostitute and brothel-keeper of eighteenth-century Dublin, found herself down on her luck in the 1790s, it was thus obvious to her what to do. Like any modern celebrity seeking to capitalize on her moment of fame, she began publishing her memoirs. In three volumes, over several years and several hundreds of pages, she told all, drawing on her extensive private papers, accounts, and cor-respondence. It was a heady brew. There was the inevitable narrative of her own seduction into unchastity and courtesanship, with vignettes of her many keepers; the even fuller story of her life as a madam to some of the richest and most powerful men in the kingdom; copious tales of high jinks in high society; letters from her lovers; histories of all the famous prostitutes she had known; and endless details of sexual commerce and scandal (see illustration 50). No wonder the work was 'bought up with the greatest avidity'.[3]

This development overlapped with the growing use of sexual histories as political weapons. There was obviously a long history of discrediting political opponents by associating them with sexual scandal: the tactic itself was not new in the eighteenth century. But three things were. Mass opinion was now increasingly acknowledged to be a legitimate, important, and inescapable arena of political debate. This was an idea that can already be glimpsed in the revolutions of 1649 and 1688; a hundred years later it had advanced exponentially. The second change was the incomparably greater power of publicity. In previous centuries most politico-sexual satire had been transmitted only orally or in brief, ephemeral, manuscript lampoons and libels. Now there had grown up entire genres of permanent, widely circulated public print devoted to the exposition of sexual scandal. Fictional memoirs, newspapers, titillating magazines, and satirical prints – all of them were regularly used, overtly or surreptitiously, to undermine politicians by associating them with particular courtesans or general immorality.

The final novelty was the increasing use of sexual satire for radical political purposes: not just to attack particular individuals, or even to condemn a particularly licentious court, but to agitate against the whole corrupt system of aristocracy and monarchy. From the 1760s onwards, French writers based in London put out an extraordinary stream of slander and pornography directed against the French church and government. Some of them were motivated more by greed than by principle, but the effect of their writings was the same. As Robert Darnton and other historians of eighteenth-century France have skilfully revealed, this flood of scandalous material helped shape French public opinion and seriously undermined the legitimacy of royal government, both before and after 1789. By the 1790s, English writers and publishers were increasingly adopting the same tactics in their

MEMOIRS

OF

MRS. MARGARET LEESON.

WRITTEN BY HERSELF;

AND

INTERSPERSED WITH SEVERAL INTERESTING AND
AMUSING ANECDOTES,

OF SOME OF THE MOST STRIKING

CHARACTERS

OF

GREAT-BRITAIN AND IRELAND,

VOL. II.

Then will I grant thee all thy soul's desire ;
All that may charm thine ear, and please thy sight :
All that thy thought can frame or wish require
To steep thy ravish'd senses in delight.
The sumptuous feast, entranc'd with music's sound,
Fittest to tune the melting soul to Love :
Rich odours, breathing choicest sweets around ;
The fragrant Bow'r, cool Fountain, shady Grove :
Fresh Flowers, to strew thy Couch, and crown thy Head ;
Joy shall attend thy steps, and Ease shall smooth thy bed ;
What pleasures, vain mistaken wretch are thine !
(Virtue with scorn reply'd)
Draining the copious Bowl, ere thirst require ;
Feasting ere hunger to the feast invite :
Whose tasteless Joys anticipate desire
When Luxury supply'd with appetite.

JUDGMENT OF HERCULES.

DUBLIN:

PRINTED FOR THE AUTHORESS,
AND SOLD BY THE PRINCIPAL BOOKSELLERS.

M,DCC,XCV.

50. The title page of the second volume of Margaret Leeson's sensational
memoirs, 'printed for the authoress' in 1795.

appeals to a mass audience. In the radical underworld of late Georgian London, the publication of anti-clerical and anti-aristocratic pornography came to be closely intertwined with the advocacy of democratic and revolutionary politics.[4]

Most extraordinary of all was the huge campaign of sexual muckraking, blackmail, extortion, and scandalous publicity orchestrated by, for, and against George IV's estranged wife, Queen Caroline, between 1806 (when he was still prince regent) and 1821 (when she died). He was a notorious rake; she was plausibly alleged to have taken lovers of her own. Their antagonism became a battle for public opinion that provoked hundreds of thousands of middle- and working-class men and women into serious political demonstrations and agitation across the land. It was waged in every medium of print, by every class of politician, from the king and queen themselves down to the lowliest Grub Street hacks (see plate 19).

Queen Caroline was in an exceptional position, and she always maintained her innocence. Yet by 1800 the media revolution had made it possible even for avowedly immoral, low-born women to manipulate their sexual power to previously unheard-of political and commercial effect. In no former age, for example, would a royal mistress have dreamed of challenging monarchical authority or of exposing sexual scandals to a mass public. Now this was exactly what happened, repeatedly. In 1781, the actress, author, and feminist Mary Robinson, who also happened to be one of the most celebrated courtesans of her day, publicly threatened to publish the letters of her former lover, the Prince of Wales – until she was granted a 'reward' of £5,000 and an annuity for life. In 1806, when the Duke of York cast off his mistress, Mary Anne Clarke, without an adequate financial settlement, she likewise threatened to publish details of their affair. Then, when it became public knowledge that she had been at the centre of a ring of bribery and corruption, trafficking in the duke's patronage over army, church, and civil service positions, she colluded in several ghost-written pamphlets excoriating the royal family. Finally, she had printed 18,000 copies of a sensational memoir, complete with the duke's love-letters to her. Her reward was a gigantic pay-off from the government (a lump sum of £10,000, and large annuities for life for her and her daughter), in return for the suppression of this dangerous text (see plate 20). The great courtesan Harriette Wilson went further still, maximizing her profits through a combination of extortion and titillation. First she announced the imminent appearance of her memoirs, which caused consternation amongst her innumerable former lovers, not least the king. Next she wrote privately to each man, threatening to expose him unless he immediately sent her hundreds of pounds. This tactic alone netted her several thousand pounds. Then her advance publicity advertised the names of those clients who were included in the book. Finally, the work was published, in instalments, to overwhelming success, bringing her many thousands more. In its first year alone it ran to thirty-one editions, in addition to innumerable pirated, plagiarized, and spurious versions (see plate 21).[5]

The eighteenth century thus saw the rise not just of novel forms of communication and new attitudes towards publicity, but also of a new type of immoral female celebrity. Such women did not shy away from scandal: they revelled in it. When James Boswell first met his future mistress, Mary Rudd, in 1776, she was already notorious, and proud of it. 'Oh Sir,' she cried when he introduced himself, 'pray sit down – I have often heard of you, we are *both characters* – pray Sir, sit down.' This self-consciousness, the awareness of being a character in the public gaze, was a key ingredient in the culture of celebrity. It fuelled the careers of successful prostitutes as it did those of female writers and performers. Such public assertiveness was never the preserve of more than a small minority of sexually independent women. It was widely deplored by conservative commentators. In the course of the nineteenth century it was to come under sustained attack. Nevertheless, its emergence after 1700 marked a watershed in the perception, and the self-presentation, of female sexuality.[6]

CELEBRATING SEX

By the end of the eighteenth century, a new openness about sex had transformed the culture of the English-speaking world. A whole range of sexual ideas and practices, within and without marriage, was now discussed, celebrated, and indulged more publicly than ever before.

From our own perspective it is easy to see the limits of this new tolerance. For an unmarried woman to conceive a child out of wedlock remained a social disaster that could ruin her life. For two men to have sex with each other was even more dangerous. It was primarily the heterosexual libido of white, propertied men that was celebrated – that was, after all, where power and cultural influence were concentrated in this society. Nonetheless, as we have seen, the acceptance of sex as natural, pleasurable, and empowering, was to be found in other circles too.[1]

Much more striking than its limitations is the contrast between the new frankness of the eighteenth century and the culture of discipline that had dominated English society up until that point. Gone was almost the entire formal machinery of sexual policing by the church and state. Gone, too, was the intellectual and social environment that had sustained it. The public discussion of sex was now vastly greater in scale and complexity; it was no longer tightly controlled by a male clerical and social elite; and it no longer overwhelmingly communicated the message that sex outside marriage was dangerous and wrong. On the contrary, by 1800 this presumption was constantly being denied, implicitly and explicitly, in a huge variety of new media. The result was a wholly new universe of communication, in which ideas about sex were shaped in radically different ways. This was a seismic shift. It was also primarily an urban phenomenon, one that was led by developments in London. Even in the cities of the far-away North American colonies, it was the capital's culture that was the dominant influence.[2] The principles of sexual discipline retained great authority throughout the nineteenth and twentieth centuries, as we shall see in the Epilogue: but they never again held such dominant sway. Henceforth, it was rather the tension between restraint and hedonism that was to determine the sexual culture of the English-speaking world.

The effects were remarkable. By 1800, it had become common for members of the aristocracy and gentry to live much more openly than ever before in unmarried and adulterous relationships. At various points in the later eighteenth century this was true of the Prime Minister, the Lord Chancellor, the Foreign Secretary, the First Lord of the Admiralty, the Duke of York, the Prince of Wales, and countless other notable men and women. Several of the Founding Fathers of the United States, including Franklin, Burr, Jefferson, and Hamilton, shared the same outlook.[3] It was an ethos that would have been inconceivable to the Pilgrim Fathers and their English counterparts.

Sexual pleasure was now also increasingly celebrated communally, in special masculine clubs. One of its most vigorous proponents, the politician Sir Francis Dashwood, founded several libertine societies. At the centre of his estate he built a Temple to Venus, landscaped to resemble a gigantic vagina – his was the company for which John Wilkes in 1763 was to print his infamous erotic poem, the *Essay on Woman*. Even more remarkable was a much humbler club called 'the Beggar's Benison', which from the 1730s onwards spread from the east coast of Scotland to Edinburgh, Glasgow, and as far afield as St Petersburg in Russia. Its members met regularly to drink, talk about sex, exchange bawdy jokes and songs, and read pornography. They paid young women to strip and display themselves naked. Their central purpose was to compare penises and masturbate in front of one another, singly and together, in elaborate rites of phallic celebration. The club's membership was a cross-section of respectable, middle-aged, propertied society: clergymen, noblemen, gentlemen, lawyers, army officers, customs men, merchants, craftsmen, and academics. Even though most of its records and artefacts have been lost, there still survives a remarkable collection of the club's ritual objects, adorned with texts and images celebrating sexual freedom – medals, seals, sashes, diplomas, punch bowls, phallic wine glasses, a specially embellished Bible, and a round pewter platter with various obscene decorations, upon which members collectively ejaculated (see plate 22).[4]

The late eighteenth and early nineteenth century also became the great age of the English courtesan. These women, the heirs of Kitty Fisher and Fanny Murray, were not mere mistresses but independent sexual entrepreneurs, whose fame and fortune sometimes rivalled that of their male companions. Nancy Parsons, the daughter of a tailor, was successively the lover of the Duke of Grafton and the Duke of Dorset, then married the Viscount Maynard, and finally, in her early fifties and with Lord Maynard's consent, became the companion of the teenaged Duke of Bedford. Grace Dalrymple Elliott, after being divorced by her husband for adultery with an Irish peer, became the longtime mistress of the Earl of Cholmondeley, and the sometime lover of various French noblemen, as well as of the Prince of Wales. Her illegitimate daughter married into the peerage. Countless others achieved greater or lesser renown.[5]

Especially in London and other towns, there grew up a huge material and cultural industry devoted to sexual pleasure. Prostitution became ever more visible and extensive. Bagnios and other places of assignation advertised openly, as did men and women seeking marital or sexual adventure. Sexual disease and sexual health were publicly debated. Newspapers incessantly discussed sexual scandals and personalities: several even devoted themselves entirely to sexual gossip and titillation. Overtly erotic pictures and writings also became more

Miss Roberts sitting naked in L.ᵈ Grosvenors lap at the Hotel in Leicester Fields.

51. One of the illustrations to the seven-volume *Trials for Adultery* (1779–80), which avidly chronicled the sexual peccadilloes of divorcing aristocrats.

52–55. The celebration of gentlemanly sexual freedom: two engravings from an illustrated edition of John Cleland's pornographic novel, *Memoirs of a Woman of Pleasure* (1766), and two of the many erotic prints produced by Thomas Rowlandson around 1800.

Carnival at Venice.

widely available. Before the later seventeenth century, pornographic writing had been largely confined to Latin, Greek, Italian and French texts; much of it circulated only in manuscript; all of it was produced and consumed fairly clandestinely. In the later eighteenth century, however, there developed a flourishing trade in English erotica. Though the publishing of obscenity remained illegal, pornography was now much more common and easily available. By the turn of the century, it was possible even for schoolgirls and rural clergymen to obtain commercially produced erotic books and illustrations of 'naked men and women in carnal connection with each other; in different situations, standing, lying, sitting, all of the most indecent kind' (see illustrations 52 to 55).[6] All this reflected a new appreciation of sex as the modern, enlightened, natural, rational pleasure par excellence. It also was a consequence of the media revolution. The changes it had inaugurated, and the infinite opportunities it provided for the publicization and celebration of sex, were here to stay.

Epilogue: Modern Cultures of Sex – from the Victorians to the Twenty-first Century

How we perceive the past, what we see in it and what we ignore, depends on our current perspective. Anyone who has looked back over their own life at various points will appreciate that. It is equally true of historical writing: the past looks different to different historians and at different times. This book grew out of my attempt to understand the profound chasm between our present attitudes to sex and those that prevailed for most of western history. In describing this change I have highlighted the themes and the time-frame that seemed to me most evidently important, and concentrated on the views of the educated middling and upper classes of the period. This was not a democratic world: its public culture was disproportionately shaped and controlled by these dominant social groups. Yet, as I have tried to show, it was also an increasingly open and pluralist society, in which sexual attitudes were far from uniform.

Other scholars and scientists take different perspectives. Some would lay greater stress on the limits of sexual discipline before the eighteenth century, or on its continued strength thereafter, or on variations between sexes, classes, and regions. Others assert that the most fundamental aspects of sexual behaviour are neurologically hardwired into our brains, so that studying the history of sexual attitudes doesn't reveal anything significant. But that is like saying that politics is always about the pursuit of power, without trying to understand how government evolved from tribal conflict to parliamentary democracy, or why even today it takes such different forms around the world.

How we view the past equally shapes how we see the present. The argument of this book has been that the origin of modern western attitudes to sex lies in the great intellectual and social revolutions of the eighteenth century. For well over a thousand years, from the early middle ages to the seventeenth century, the enforcement of ever-stricter public discipline over sexual behaviour was a central preoccupation of every Christian community across the globe – yet by 1800 this had been replaced by a fundamentally different outlook. This radical transformation laid the ground for the sexual culture of the Victorians, of the twentieth century, and of our own day.

The most basic modern novelty was a perennial indeterminacy about the limits of sexual freedom. In place of a relatively coherent, authoritative world view that had endured for centuries, the Enlightenment left a much greater confusion and plurality of moral perspectives, with irresolvable tensions between them. That has been part of our modern condition ever since. So, too, have been the growth of sexual liberty; the increasing dominance of urban ways of living and discussing sex; the presumption that men are naturally more sexually active and women more passive; an enduring association between morality and class; and our endlessly fluctuating obsessions with 'natural' and 'unnatural' behaviour, pornography and celebrity, and the distinction between the 'public' and the 'private'. These have been the dominant themes of nineteenth- and twentieth-century sexual culture. Only by looking back at the transition from the pre-modern to the modern world can we properly understand where they came from.

REPRESSION AND CONTROL

To explore their development after 1800 in detail would require a comprehensive description of the whole period: for, as was the case in preceding centuries, the evolution of sexual attitudes reflected the changing characteristics of the culture in general. My aim here is more modest. Histories of modern sexuality rarely consider the world before 1800, whilst their characterizations of the nineteenth and twentieth centuries vary widely – one authoritative recent account of Victorian mores argues for the sensuality of nineteenth-century private life, whilst another stresses its general 'anti-sensualism'.[1] The intention of these concluding pages is simply to explain how some of the most obvious characteristics and contradictions of the modern sexual world grew out of the developments described in this book.

At a basic level, attitudes after 1800 evolved in two contrasting ways. On the one hand we can trace continued, or even tightened, social control over various forms of sexual behaviour. Though the machinery of public punishment had been largely abandoned, its ideals were not. In part, as we have seen, this was inherent in new, enlightened ways of thinking, which did not discard the distinction between permissible and impermissible sex, but merely redefined it. In the eighteenth century, the growth of 'natural' sexual freedom for middle- and upper-class heterosexual men went hand in hand with the sharper proscription of what was defined as 'unnatural' or socially objectionable behaviour. In the nineteenth century, as scientific ways of describing sexuality took on new-found authority, they were likewise mainly used to argue for the undesirability of female lust, same-sex behaviour, or sexual licence amongst the lower classes. Similar ideals of 'social purity' were central to feminist and other progressive ideologies long into the twentieth century. Modern ways of thinking did not necessarily lead to greater liberty, at least not for everyone.

In any case, not everyone believed in them equally. The decades around 1800 also saw a fierce backlash against the perceived excesses of Enlightenment principles and practices. There were many reasons for this, which went much deeper than a simple distaste of permissiveness. The most obvious cause was the ongoing political crisis of the age, which began with the loss of Britain's North American colonies, continued through the terrifying cataclysm of the French Revolution, and culminated in the British ancien régime's desperate wars for survival against the forces of radicalism, both at home and abroad. Equally unsettling were the unprecedented demographic and economic changes of the period: a further colossal surge in the population (from about five million in 1700 to almost twenty million by the 1850s), and a huge expansion of the industrial and commercial economy, of urban living, and of mass poverty.

Against this backdrop of apparent national decline and social upheaval, the importance of religious faith and of social conservatism came to be widely reaffirmed: only by going back to basics would the nation find its way again. This outlook was part of the inspiration for the great religious revivals that swept the period, both in England and in North America, and for the intellectual Counter-Enlightenment. Christian and conservative observers often saw the spread of sexual freedom as the central manifestation of a broader cultural malaise, and the reassertion of moral discipline as the most urgent task in national regeneration. 'It is impossible to find a more apt description of a corrupt, profligate, and vicious age', urged the loyalist writer John Bowles in 1800, than one which palliated sex outside marriage: but 'such a description is unfortunately applicable to the present times; and a stronger proof cannot exist of extreme and general depravity'. Amongst the common people, warned the panic-mongering *Anti-Jacobin Review* around the same time,

this species of profligacy, so detestable in itself, and so pernicious in its consequences, both to the individuals, and to the community at large, has increased of late years, especially in the metropolis, to an extent that is almost incredible. Adultery and concubinage in the lower classes of society are unhappily most prevalent, and culprits of this description so rarely attend worship, and so seldom become objects of legal punishment, that little hopes of reformation remain. – Yet how can we expect a nation to flourish where the people are so abandoned![2]

Already in the middle of the eighteenth century such views had animated the early Methodist movement: its founder, John Wesley, was one of the chief supporters of the revived London Society for Reformation of Manners in the 1750s and 1760s. From the 1780s onwards, as the evangelical revival took hold within the Church of England itself, it inspired a much more powerful, broadly based, and long-lasting campaign for national moral reform. Along with the abolition of the slave trade, this was the life-long mission of its great leader, William Wilberforce, a campaign to which he felt he had been called by divine providence. 'God Almighty has set before me two great objects, the suppression of the slave trade and the reformation of manners,' he recorded in his diary in 1787, soon after his spiritual awakening: he set to work immediately, and never looked back. Out of this tide of reaction were born philanthropic efforts to re-educate the lower orders, such as the Sunday school movement (which began in the

1780s), more punitive initiatives such as the Society for the Suppression of Vice (1802), and unceasing attacks on the prevalence of upper-class debauchery. Underpinning it all was a flood of propaganda reasserting orthodox Christian values and propriety, such as the enormous quantities of edifying penny-pamphlets produced for the Religious Tract Society by the movement's chief publicist, Hannah More.[3]

Have you looked at Mary Wollstonecraft's *Vindication of the Rights of Woman*? Horace Walpole mischievously asked Mrs More in 1792. Certainly not, she replied: 'there is something fantastic and absurd in the very title'. But when she did read Wollstonecraft's posthumous novel, *Maria* (1798), she exploded in anger at its message that contemporary marriage laws were unjust and 'that adultery is justifiable'. 'Let us take comfort,' she advised her readers, 'these atrocious principles are not yet adopted into common practice ... Clear and strongly marked distinctions between right and wrong still subsist' – it was everybody's duty to uphold them. This was the context that spawned the deeply conservative and massively influential writings on population of the clergyman Robert Malthus. In the eyes of most orthodox and governmental observers his theories seemed to provide scientific, incontrovertible proof that without 'moral restraint' (i.e. the confining of sex within marriage) demographic catastrophe and national decline would inevitably ensue.

The cumulative effect of all these currents can be clearly seen in the changing moral tone of late eighteenth- and nineteenth-century Anglo-American society. By the 1820s, most commentators agreed that public manners had become more decorous in recent decades, and sexual vice more restrained (though they disagreed on whether it had been merely pushed underground, or really reduced). In 1837, Queen Victoria's ascent and example were seen as confirming this trend, rather than inaugurating a new age. And many historians would now concur that this 'Victorian' avowal of strict boundaries on sexual freedom, and the repression of various forms of sensuality, lasted well beyond 1901 – indeed, that it was a dominant feature of western sexual culture until the 1960s. So pervasive did this outlook become that it gradually affected sexual relations even within marriage. Between 1800 and 1920, for example, rates of childbirth in most western countries plummeted by fifty per cent or more. This was a permanent change, and it appears to have been brought about not principally by any innovation in birth control, but by the mass adoption of techniques of sexual restraint within settled relationships – abstinence, limits on intercourse, the use of coitus interruptus. (It was only towards the middle of the twentieth century that the balance began to shift towards the artificial methods of contraception that are now the norm, and which have allowed for greater sexual freedom without a revival of the birth rate.)[4]

A vital component in this re-emphasis on discipline was the relative desexualization of women. This book has tried to explain the eighteenth-century origins of this remarkable trend: but it reached its fullest development in the nineteenth and twentieth centuries. For women of all classes, sexual ignorance and passivity came increasingly to be valued as essential components of respectable femininity and heterosexual love. This was not just a male ideal: most women themselves deeply internalized it, and policed it in others. Nor did it apply only to virgins. As is vividly apparent from recent oral histories of twentieth-century sex, it remained the norm even when women became sexually active within marriage – and this, too, was a pattern that persisted well into the later twentieth century. Men, by contrast, were expected to take the initiative, to be sexually knowledgeable, and to understand that nice women would not necessarily enjoy sex very much.[5]* Publicly, this double standard was expressed everywhere, in the most blatant terms. It was not until 1991 that English law formally recognized the concept of rape within marriage.

Just as important, especially in the English context, was the further development of social double standards. Regulating, controlling, and forcibly improving the sexual mores of the working classes became in the nineteenth century, and into the twentieth, an immense fixation for many middle- and upper-class politicians, commentators, and social reformers. Like gender (and, especially in colonial contexts,

---

* As the feminist sexual reformer Janet Chance put it in 1931, 'In spite of all the talk about sex experience, in spite of all the apparent equality of outlook amongst the younger generation, passion in England remains a lopsided affair. The men, more or less, for their part, know what can be. The women, for their part, often do not': *The Cost of English Morals* (1931), 36.

race), class became a crucial marker of sexual otherness, which could be powerfully attractive as well as repellent. We can see this effect in countless private lives. It fuelled the fascination of innumerable propertied men and women with the lives and characters of prostitutes; it informed the sexual voyeurism of Victorian and Edwardian social investigators more generally; and it pervaded the everyday interactions of women and men throughout urban life. In one of the best-documented London examples, the gentleman civil servant Arthur Munby (1828–1910) spent his life sexually obsessing over, and documenting, the tension between the conventional feminine ideals of his day and the bodies of the strong, dirty, disfigured, working-class women who populated the city. He endlessly watched, interviewed, sketched, photographed, described, and catalogued them, titillated by the contrast between his power and their degradation. For decades he courted one particular menial servant, Hannah Cullwick; eventually they were married secretly. But until her death in 1909 she lived with him, and without him, as his servant, as a working woman – acting out for him, and for the world, over and over again, their private and public rituals of female, lower-class, submission, innocence, and bodily objectification.[6]

The same fascinations, and cross-class dynamics of wealth and power, fuelled same-sex affairs between men. Whether cruising in a crowded shopping street or in the privacy of a Turkish bath, for many better-off men the thrill of a clandestine liaison with some 'rough trade' was clearly heightened by the frisson of social transgression. In 1953, one of the patrician characters of *The Heart in Exile*, a sympathetic and best-selling novel about homosexual life in London, looked back wistfully on this apparently disappearing culture. 'People like us have less money now', he complained, 'the working class no longer respects us as they did' – whereas previously, young working-class men

were yours for the asking . . . Boys accepted us because we were class . . . they liked us because, unlike women, we didn't cost them money. I suppose we made a fuss of them, which their girls didn't. Anyhow, today they can afford women, and if they don't want women they have plenty of money for other amusements.

'We don't like people like ourselves', explained another, 'we don't want anybody who shares our standards. I mean educated, middle class and so on. In fact, we want the very opposite. We want the primitive, the uneducated, the tough.'

Heterosexual attitudes to same-sex behaviour were just as deeply inflected by presumptions about class. As doctors, lawyers, and criminologists struggled to understand homosexual desire, they tended to distinguish between the apparently more loving and 'natural' passions of mature, respectable men, and the perverted promiscuous practices supposedly more common amongst working-class queers – which, as a handbook on the *Psychological Treatment of Crime* explained with distaste in 1949, simply combined 'primitive sexual interests with an interest towards all forms of sexual activity'.[7]

Similar double standards characterized attitudes towards heterosexual prostitution. This was a prime enabler of sexual freedom for bourgeois men, yet perpetuated the depravation of lower-class women: small wonder that its class basis provoked such strong feelings on all sides. Equally telling was the character of nineteenth- and early twentieth-century censorship. The Victorians and their successors put considerable efforts into limiting the public availability of sexually explicit materials. To a certain extent it proved possible to push sexual imagery, writing, and information underground, and to police its availability. Yet this did not prevent ever-greater quantities of pornography from being clandestinely produced and circulated. Many gentlemen amassed huge collections of it: the main concern was simply to keep immoral materials away from women and from the masses. In 1960, when Penguin Books was prosecuted for publishing D. H. Lawrence's novel *Lady Chatterley's Lover*, this outlook was echoed in the opening speech of the lead prosecutor, J. M. G. Griffith-Jones (of Eton, Cambridge, and the Coldstream Guards). After he lost the trial, his remarks were to be held up by more liberal commentators as notoriously ill-judged; yet in earlier decades they would have been wholly unexceptional. Naturally, Griffith-Jones stressed, in this modern day and age it would be wrong to 'approach this matter in any priggish, high-minded, super-correct, mid-Victorian manner'. Nonetheless, the essential test for the jury was

to ask yourselves the question, when you have read it through, would you approve of your young sons, young daughters – because girls can read as well as boys – reading this book? Is it a book that you would have lying around in your own house? Is it a book that you would even wish your wife or your servants to read?*[8]

The subject of Lawrence's book, written in the later 1920s, was itself of course a testament to the great English obsession with sex and class.

The final key feature of modern boundaries on sexual freedom was the growing frequency and harshness with which homosexual men were persecuted, both legally and socially. This was once more a development that had its origins in the eighteenth century, but took on even greater prominence after 1800. It was, again, especially marked in England. Throughout the nineteenth century, there were hundreds of prosecutions and convictions per year for sodomy and homosexual indecency. Until the 1830s Englishmen were regularly executed for 'buggery': between 1810 and 1835, forty-six men were judicially killed for this crime. Thousands more were publicly humiliated in the pillory, or sentenced to jail for their unnatural perversions. Oscar Wilde's imprisonment at hard labour for two years in 1895 is only the best-known example. Even more remarkable than this Victorian severity is that, in numerical terms at least, it was vastly outstripped by the huge twentieth-century increase in legal persecution of homosexual behaviour. At the time of Wilde's trial, such incidents amounted to about 5 per cent of all trials for crimes against a person; by the later 1950s, the figure had increased to over 20 per cent – in other words, thousands of prosecutions per year. The same dramatic surge took place in other European countries and across the United States. To curb homosexuality, perhaps even to exterminate it, was for many decades a prominent concern of public policy.[9] There was far less overt anxiety about lesbian sex, which had never even fallen under any criminal law. Yet it is telling that, all the same, even its mere discussion in public was regarded as a threat to morality. In 1921, a proposal to criminalize sex between women was rejected in parliament partly because it was felt undesirable to draw the practices

* At an earlier trial of another purportedly obscene novel, he had asked the jurors if they'd be willing at Christmas to distribute the book 'as presents to the girls in the office – and if not, why not?'

of 'an extremely small minority' of women to the attention of the vast majority 'who have never heard of this at all'. Likewise, when in 1928 Radclyffe Hall's novel *The Well of Loneliness* tried to advocate tolerance for female 'inverts', its message was summarily deemed 'obscene' and 'unnatural', and the book banned.[10]

At the root of this collective nineteenth- and twentieth-century concern to restrict supposedly unnatural sexual practices was an important development in how such behaviour was conceived. Rather than as sinful actions, they were increasingly likely to be viewed as the marks of a deviant personality, whose origins (whether in nature or nurture) now became the focus of intense debate. The typology of 'natural' and 'unnatural' behaviour thus came to be mapped on to a medicalized pathology of character-types – the homosexual 'invert', the 'nymphomaniac', the 'criminal woman', and so on. As we have seen, this approach had its origins in the Enlightenment desire to understand human nature in new, scientific ways; but it grew increasingly elaborate and powerful in subsequent centuries, as medicine and biology became ever more authoritative determinants of what was sexually and socially 'natural'. (This was one of the chief insights of Michel Foucault's *History of Sexuality* (1976), the most influential late twentieth-century study of the subject.) Here was born our essentially modern way of thinking in terms of sexual identities, rather than sexual acts, and our obsession with labelling others and ourselves accordingly.[11]

Even after 1800, therefore, sexuality continued to be policed in a variety of important ways. Though the machinery of public punishment had been largely abandoned as far as sex between men and women was concerned, it was directed with increasing practical and symbolic force at 'unnatural' behaviour. More generally, the ideals of sexual restraint, newly reinforced, had a profound impact on mainstream attitudes and behaviour. Yet there were several crucial differences between the sexual regimes of the modern and the premodern worlds. As we have seen, there was now always in sexual matters a question over the exact boundaries between the public and the private domain. Overt policing was also a low priority for the major institutions of government: modern ways of enforcing discipline were much more diffuse and fragmented. All in all, the norms of

sexual discipline were far less hegemonic than before, and in continual and growing tension with alternative lifestyles and attitudes.

The result was a sexual culture riven by, indeed dependent on, a
whole series of contradictions and hypocrisies – this is sometimes
called the 'Victorian compromise', though its essential features lasted
into the later twentieth century. It was one in which, at one level, sexual matters were being continually dissected, discussed, and publicized;
and, at another level, were supposed to be hidden away from sight. It
was a culture in which what was normal and permissible behaviour
and knowledge varied strongly according to class and sex – and in
which the transgression of those boundaries consequently became
highly sexualized. It was equally one that, in its quest to shore up
moral norms, attempted to draw the boundaries between the public
and the private with ever greater rigour, so that exactly the same
behaviour could be treated according to widely different standards,
depending on its exposure. As the political history of the nineteenth
and twentieth centuries abundantly illustrates, sex outside marriage
by men was generally silently tolerated – yet if their conduct became
public it was to be fiercely condemned.*

This combination of paradoxes explains the variety of scholarly views
on the essential character of Victorian and early twentieth-century
sexual culture. It is easy to find well-off men who revelled in sexual
freedom; not hard to notice the huge population of prostitutes. On
such grounds, some early (and male) historians of Victorian sexuality
were keen to highlight its erotic aspects. More recent and feminist
scholars by contrast have tended to reaffirm the endless ways in which
women in this society, and to a lesser extent men too, were indoctrin-
ated in the repression of sexual desire.[12] Take again Arthur Munby
and Hannah Cullwick. Almost everything about Munby's outlook on
women was, actually or potentially, sexualized. He thought about

---

* This was the state of affairs that the impeccably patrician Prime Minister, Harold
Macmillan (1894–1986), grew up taking for granted, and whose apparent breakdown
from the 1960s onwards left him bewildered. As he recalled at the very end of his life,
'in the old days you could be absolutely sure that you could go to a restaurant with
your wife and not see a man that you knew having lunch with a tart. It was all kept
separate, but this does not seem to happen these days': Alastair Horne, *Macmillan
1957–1986* (1989), 495.

their bodies constantly. The two of them kissed: they saw each other naked. Yet in half a century together they never seem to have had intercourse. Theirs was undoubtedly a highly unusual relationship: yet there is no better illustration of the Victorian tension between sexual obsession and restraint.

LIBERTY AND EQUALITY

I have concentrated on the English case; but similar trends can be traced after 1800, at least in outline, in other western European and English-speaking societies. Conversely, one way of characterizing what has happened in the western world since the 1960s would be to say that the Victorian compromise has increasingly broken down. The social importance of marriage has declined spectacularly. Divorce rates have soared. Casual sex is now more commonplace than ever. The mass use of artificial contraception has divorced sex and pleasure more completely than ever before from pregnancy and procreation. As we have seen, the ultimate origins of this greater liberty lay in the social and intellectual revolutions of the Enlightenment. So the other important theme in nineteenth- and twentieth-century attitudes was the gradual expansion of sexual freedom, in theory and in practice. The experience of the last fifty years should be seen not as a sharp break with the past, but as an acceleration of these on-going trends, and their increasing expansion into the mainstream of sexual culture.[1]

Male libertine culture continued to flourish and develop throughout the Regency period and the Victorian and Edwardian ages. Modern city life provided heterosexual men with endless opportunities for casual sex; prostitution expanded further all through the nineteenth and into the twentieth century. By 1900, easily accessible homosexual subcultures had likewise spread to every port and city across the westernized world. (As Graham Robb puts it, 'Tchaikovsky could travel all over Europe and always be sure of finding someone to have sex with'.) As for women, from the 1920s onwards contemporaries were in no doubt (and subsequent historians have tended to agree) that they were living through the beginnings of a new era, in which urban lifestyles were increasingly associated with liberty for both sexes. The birth of the 'new woman' in the early twentieth century was the point at which mainstream feminism, and norms of femininity more generally, began to develop gradually away from their traditional fixation upon strict pre-marital chastity.[2]

This slow but steady decline in the sexual double standard was but one symptom of a larger intellectual shift between the nineteenth and the twentieth century: the steady rise, and eventual triumph, of equality as the guiding principle in ethical and political affairs. One of the foundations of the Victorian compromise had been that rights and norms should differentiate between social groups (whether by race, class, sex, or sexual orientation), for their own good and that of the wider community. Already in the nineteenth century this presumption had been challenged by feminists, socialists, and other progressives, but it was only in the course of the last century that it was seriously weakened, and ultimately overturned, by the opposite principle: that, legally and morally, all human beings deserve equal respect. Nowadays we have come to take this idea utterly for granted. So far has it advanced in recent decades that the sexual rights of individuals are now commonly presumed to be more tangible, and ultimately perhaps even more important, than any notion of public morality or the public good. Even fifty years ago such a consensus would have been unthinkable.

Equally important in bringing about these changes has been the ongoing evolution of ideas about the public and the private. As this book has shown, it was in the eighteenth century that this distinction took on a key role in defining the sphere of sexual freedom. In general terms, 'private' behaviour was by definition beyond the scope of legal and communal sanction. On the other hand, whenever actions were perceived to be unnatural, or detrimental to others or to the community, they remained a matter of legitimate public concern, even if carried out in secret. Thus the boundary between the two was never fixed, but dependent upon the balance of power, opinion, and circumstance. In essence, the rights of women and of homosexuals to sexual privacy were but weakly asserted in the eighteenth century; advanced somewhat in practice in the nineteenth century; but only became widely accepted and legally established in the course of the twentieth and twenty-first centuries. The history of this development contains a remarkable irony. As we have seen, the idea of the right to sexual privacy originally developed out of arguments for the inviolability of religious conscience. Yet nowadays it has expanded so far that traditionalist Christians have been reduced to arguing that their religious freedom is being infringed by the equal rights accorded to homosexual men and women, or by the provision of contraception and abortion. In the modern world, the right to express one's sexual instincts has come to be seen as more important even than spiritual conscience.[3]

Yet sex is not just more private than ever before: it is also more public. The gradual expansion of the sphere of sexual privacy has taken place alongside a continued and growing interest in the public discussion of sex. The media revolution that began in the eighteenth century did not stop in 1800: the scope and speed of public communication, and its fascination with sexual affairs, continued to develop. Since the 1960s, once again, these trends have further accelerated. Especially notable have been the continued falling away of censorship and personal inhibition, and the recent rise of the internet, which together have further complicated the relationship between the public and the private. Indeed, the great paradox of our times seems to be that, as a culture, we increasingly assert the essential privateness of sex and sexuality as far as the public realm of the state and the law are concerned, yet simultaneously seem to have a growing desire to expose the most intimate details of our lives to the broadest possible public gaze. This is a considerably different balance between the private and the public than the Victorians upheld, and it has shattered one of the key components of their compromise. The essential tension, as we have seen, goes back to the Enlightenment.

How far, then, have we really come? We like to think of social change in terms of linear progress: that, too, is a legacy of the Enlightenment. Yet this predisposes us to historical short-sightedness – we easily forget how contingent our present state is, that the past is littered with alternative paths not taken, that even within the last few generations the boundaries of the right to sexual privacy have been continually challenged and redrawn. Both in law and in social practice, the widespread acceptance of sexual freedom for women and for unmarried persons is a comparatively novel development. Even today, across the English-speaking world, the provision of contraception and of abortion remains highly contested, as does the issue of prostitution.

Though it is is variably defined, and often extends to relationships that are not obviously harmful, incest between consenting adults is permitted in some states but elsewhere remains a crime. Divergence of opinion about the limits of sexual freedom remains one of the most contentious cultural issues of our time.

Above all, despite the growing intellectual purchase of ideas of privacy and equality, the extension of homosexual freedom has proved persistently contentious. After homosexual sex in private for men over twenty-one was legalized in Britain in 1967, there was a sharp *rise* in prosecutions for 'public' homosexual cruising: it was not the principle of gay sex, but its confinement out of sight, that the enforcement of the new law was intended to promote. As recently as the later 1980s, the United States Supreme Court affirmed that even private, consensual sex between men was intrinsically immoral and punishable, whilst the government of the United Kingdom made it illegal for any local authority to do anything that might 'promote homosexuality' or the teaching in schools of 'the acceptability of homosexuality as a pretended family relationship' – laws which in both cases were not finally overturned until 2003.[4] Despite numerous and ongoing challenges, discrimination against same-sex relations persists, not just in respect of marriage, but equally when it comes to the criminalization of unacceptable forms of behaviour. In the United Kingdom it is now legal for a man to brand his wife on the buttocks with a red-hot iron during sex, but not for men, privately and willingly, to engage in equivalent kinds of sadomasochist ritual – a judgement upheld both by the House of Lords and by the European Court of Human Rights.[5] Small wonder that many academics and activists nowadays dismiss the distinction between public and private acts as an ideological construct that obscures the broader hegemony throughout society of particular, mainly 'heteronormative', presumptions and policies.[6]

Over the past fifty years the balance between liberty and repression, equality and inequity, individual rights and communal morality, has therefore been constantly shifting. Though their form keeps evolving, questions of sexual morality, private and public, constantly recur: right now, in various ways, they threaten a crisis within the worldwide Catholic church, are tearing apart the global community of Anglican churches, and continue to stir up great passions in American politics. Yet all these disagreements have taken shape within essentially new parameters, based on the modern ways of living and thinking that first emerged in the eighteenth century. What is more, the ideals of the Enlightenment are ever more firmly entrenched: the basic idea that sex between consenting adults, irrespective of their sex, sexual orientation, or marital status, is protected by a constitutional right to privacy is now, though still controversial, enshrined in the fundamental law of the United Kingdom, the European Union, and the United States.[7]

The ultimate legacy of the Enlightenment has thus been far from straightforward, and its consequences are still unfolding. Yet in retrospect it is easy to see that it marked the point at which the sexual culture of the west diverged onto a completely new trajectory. If anything, the characteristics of that culture – its individualism, its explicitness, its permissiveness, the equal status claimed by women and by homosexuals – have become more distinctive in recent decades, even as the world has grown smaller. They have also been widely influential: just as western feminism has had an impact across the globe, so too have western concepts of sexual freedom.[8]

In some parts of the world sexual ideals and practices reminiscent of pre-modern Europe nevertheless continue to be upheld. Men and (especially) women remain at risk of public prosecution for having sex outside marriage. Often, the word of God is supposed to justify this. As Ayatollah Khomeini famously affirmed in 1979, the execution of prostitutes, adulterers, and homosexuals was as justified in a moral society as the amputation of gangrenous flesh. In several Islamic countries, imprisonment, flogging, and execution by hanging or even by stoning continue to be imposed on men and women convicted of extra-marital or homosexual relations.[9] Even more widespread and deep-rooted is the extra-legal persecution of men and women for such matters. These are the same practices that sustained western culture for most of its history. They rest on very similar foundations – the theocratic authority of holy texts and holy men, intolerance of religious and social pluralism, fear of sexual freedom, the belief that men alone should govern. How they help maintain patriarchal social order is obvious: so too is their cost to human happiness. How durable they will prove to be in the rest of the world remains to be seen.

Notes

The spelling and punctuation of quotations has been modernized where necessary. The main purpose of the notes is to identify the sources of citations in the text, and to point to useful secondary reading on important themes. To save space I have shortened titles and omitted places of publication, except for works published outside London before 1900. The *Oxford English Dictionary* (*OED*), *Oxford Dictionary of National Biography* (*ODNB*), and *Proceedings of the Old Bailey* (*OBP*) are cited from their online editions (www.oed.com, www.odnb.com, www.oldbaileyonline.org). Full details of other sources are given at their first citation in every section.

PROLOGUE: THE CULTURE OF DISCIPLINE

1. Westminster City Archives, WCB 1. 150–51.
2. Lawrence Stone, *The Family, Sex and Marriage in England, 1500–1800* (1977), quoting 648; Keith Thomas, 'The Puritans and Adultery', in Donald Pennington and Keith Thomas (eds), *Puritans and Revolutionaries* (1978), 282. For fuller discussion see Faramerz Dabhoiwala, 'Lust and Liberty', *Past and Present* 207 (2010), and the references given there.

The Medieval Background

1. *English Historical Documents c. 500–1042*, ed. Dorothy Whitelocke (2nd edn, 1996), pt 11. The surviving records of Anglo-Saxon lawsuits also show fornication to have been commonly prosecuted: Patrick Wormald, *The Making of English Law* (1999), 160. The broader European and near-eastern context is brilliantly surveyed in James A. Brundage, *Law, Sex, and Christian Society in Medieval Europe* (1987), chs 1–4.
2. Brundage, *Law, Sex*, quoting 3; Exodus 20.14; Leviticus 20.10–18; Deuteronomy 5.18, 22.22–9.
3. Augustine, *Confessions*, 8. 7. 17; *Letters*, no. 6*. Cf. Peter Brown, *The Body and Society* (1988).

4. Much primary and secondary material on this subject is conveniently collected at www.anglo-saxon.net.

5. Margaret Clunies Ross, 'Concubinage in Anglo-Saxon England', *Past and Present* 108 (1985).

6. Brundage, *Law, Sex*; Eve Levin, *Sex and Society in the World of the Orthodox Slavs, 900–1700* (1989); R. H. Helmholz, *The Oxford History of the Laws of England*, vol. 1 (2004). Cf. R. I. Moore, *The Formation of a Persecuting Society* (1987); Christopher N. L. Brooke, *The Medieval Idea of Marriage* (1989).

7. William Hale Hale, *A Series of Precedents and Proceedings in Criminal Causes* (1847); Richard M. Wunderli, *London Church Courts and Society on the Eve of the Reformation* (1981); Brundage, *Law, Sex*, 481, 545; Andrew John Finch, 'Sexual Morality and Canon Law', *Journal of Medieval History* 20 (1994).

8. See e.g. London Metropolitan Archives, Acc. 518/80 (1519); M. Spufford, 'Puritanism and Social Control?', in Anthony Fletcher and John Stevenson (eds), *Order and Disorder in Early Modern England* (1985); Marjorie Keniston McIntosh, *Controlling Misbehavior in England, 1370–1600* (1998), 69–74, 115–16 (quoted); Wunderli, *London Church Courts*, ch. iv; Ruth Mazo Karras, *Common Women* (1996); Martin Ingram, 'Reformation of Manners in Early Modern England', in Paul Griffiths *et al.* (eds), *The Experience of Authority in Early Modern England* (1996), 58–65, 79, his 'Regulating Sex in Pre-Reformation London', in G. W. Bernard and S. J. Gunn (eds), *Authority and Consent in Tudor England* (2002), and his 'Shame and Pain', in Simon Devereaux and Paul Griffiths (eds), *Penal Practice and Culture, 1500–1900* (2004), esp. 44–6; Shannon McSheffrey, *Marriage, Sex, and Civic Culture in Late Medieval London* (2006), chs 6–7; Frank Rexroth, *Deviance and Power in Late Medieval London* (2007), esp. ch. 4.

9. Brundage, *Law, Sex*, 305, 517; *Certayne Sermons, or Homelies, Appoynted by the Kynges Maiestie* (1547), sig. [S iv^r]. Cf. Lawrence Stone, *The Crisis of the Aristocracy, 1558–1641* (1965), 662–3; Faramerz Dabhoiwala, 'The Construction of Honour, Reputation and Status', *Transactions of the Royal Historical Society* 6 (1996).

10. See Brundage, *Law, Sex*, e.g. 187, 206–7, 245, 297–9, 303, 305–6, 341–2, 429, 444–6, 459–60, 517; Pierre J. Payer, *The Bridling of Desire* (1993), 182, 195 n. 2, 258 n. 6; Peter Biller, *The Measure of Multitude* (2000), 40–57.

11. Martin Ingram, 'Spousals Litigation in the English Ecclesiastical Courts, *c.* 1350–1640', in R. B. Outhwaite (ed.), *Marriage and Society* (1981); Lawrence Stone, *Road to Divorce* (1990), 52–8, 67–70.

12. Ptolemy of Lucca, *On the Government of Rulers*, transl. James M. Blythe (1997), 254; Jacques Rossiaud, *Medieval Prostitution*, transl. Lydia G. Cochrane (1988), 80–81.

Reformed Morality

1. John Ramsay, *A Sermon Preach'd to the Protestants of Ireland* (3rd edn, Dublin, 1713), 6.

2. See e.g. Helen L. Parish, '"By this mark you shall know him"', *Studies in Church History* 33 (1997).

3. P. D. L. Avis, 'Moses and the Magistrate', *Journal of Ecclesiastical History* 26 (1975); James A. Brundage, *Law, Sex, and Christian Society in Medieval Europe* (1987), 558 n. 35.

4. See e.g. Leah Lydia Otis, *Prostitution in Medieval Society* (1985), pt 1; Lyndal Roper, *The Holy Household* (1989); James R. Farr, *Authority and Sexuality in Early Modern Burgundy* (1995); Michael Rocke, 'Gender and Sexual Culture in Renaissance Italy', in Judith C. Brown and Robert C. Davis (eds), *Gender and Society in Renaissance Italy* (1998); Ulinka Rublack, *The Crimes of Women in Early Modern Germany* (1999), ch. 4; Merry E. Wiesner-Hanks, *Christianity and Sexuality in the Early Modern World* (2000); Philip F. Riley, *A Lust for Virtue* (2001); Margo Todd, *The Culture of Protestantism in Early Modern Scotland* (2002), esp. ch. 3; Diarmaid McCulloch, *Reformation* (2003), ch. 16; Tessa Storey, *Carnal Commerce in Counter-Reformation Rome* (2008), esp. Conclusion.

5. Ruth Mazo Karras, *Common Women* (1996), esp. ch. 2 and p. 82.

6. *Tudor Church Reform*, ed. Gerald Bray (Church of England Record Society, 2000), 264-7; Keith Thomas, 'The Puritans and Adultery', in Donald Pennington and Keith Thomas (eds), *Puritans and Revolutionaries* (1978), 273-4.

7. Phillip Stubbes, *The Anatomie of Abuses* (1583), sig. H6^r; Avis, 'Moses and the Magistrate'; Thomas, 'Puritans and Adultery'; Ronald B. Bond, '"Dark Deeds Darkly Answered"', *Sixteenth-Century Journal* 16 (1985).

8. See e.g. Lawrence Stone, *The Crisis of the Aristocracy, 1558-1641* (1965), 662-3; Johanna Rickman, *Love, Lust, and License in Early Modern England* (2008); Alastair Bellany, *The Politics of Court Scandal* (2002); Cynthia B. Herrup, *A House in Gross Disorder* (1999).

9. Martin Ingram, *Church Courts, Sex and Marriage in England, 1570-1640* (1987), pt 2; R. H. Helmholz, 'Harboring Sexual Offenders', *Journal of British Studies* 37 (1998); F. Douglas Price, 'Gloucester Diocese under Bishop Hooper, 1551-3', *Transactions of the Bristol and Gloucestershire Archaeological Society* 60 (1938).

10. *English Historical Documents, 1485-1558*, ed. C. H. Williams (1967), 986; Patrick Collinson, *The Religion of Protestants* (1982), 158-9; Muriel C. McClendon, *The Quiet Reformation* (1999), 216, 219-21. Cf. *A Statement of the Mode of Proceeding . . . in the Royal Court of Jersey* (Jersey, '1789', i.e. 1790), 13-14; and, for religious and jurisdictional disputes over how to proceed, Patrick Collinson, *The Elizabethan Puritan Movement* (1967), 182-8, 204-5, and Elliot Rose, *Cases of Conscience* (1975), 158-68.

11. For this paragraph and the next see John Stow, *A Survey of the Cities of London and Westminster*, ed. John Strype, 6 bks (1720), i. 258; Ian W. Archer, *The Pursuit of Stability* (1991), ch. 6 (quoting 250-51); Martin Ingram, 'Regulating Sex in Pre-Reformation London', in G. W. Bernard and S. J. Gunn (eds), *Authority and Consent in Tudor England* (2002), and his 'Shame and Pain', in Simon Devereaux and Paul Griffiths (eds), *Penal Practice and Culture, 1500-1900* (2004);

McClendon, *Quiet Reformation*, 222–3; Joanna Innes, 'Prisons for the Poor', in Francis Snyder and Douglas Hay (eds), *Labour, Law, and Crime* (1987); Faramerz Dabhoiwala, 'Summary Justice in Early Modern London', *English Historical Review* 121 (2006); Paul Griffiths, *Lost Londons* (2008).

Power and Punishment

1. Patricia Crawford, *Blood, Bodies and Families in Early Modern England* (2004), 66; *The School of Venus* (1680), second dialogue: printed in Bradford K. Mudge, *When Flesh Becomes Word* (2004), 33. In February 1668, Pepys had purchased a copy of the French original, *L'escolle des filles* ('the most bawdy, lewd book that ever I saw'); read it furtively ('not amiss for a sober man once to read over to inform himself in the villainy of the world ... [it] doth me no wrong to read for information sake'); masturbated to it; 'and after I had done it, I burned it, that it might not be among my books to my shame': *The Diary of Samuel Pepys*, ed. Robert Latham and William Matthews, 11 vols (1970–83), ix. 21–2, 57–9.

2. *Two Elizabethan Women*, ed. Alison D. Wall (Wiltshire Record Society, 1983), introduction, 37–8 (quoted); Alison Wall, 'The Feud and Shakespeare's *Romeo and Juliet*', *Sydney Studies in English* 5 (1979–80) and her 'For Love, Money, or Politics?', *Historical Journal* 38 (1995).

3. Anne Kugler, *Errant Plagiary* (2002), 60; G. R. Quaife, *Wanton Wenches and Wayward Wives* (1979), 149 (quoted), 156–8; Randolph Trumbach, *Sex and the Gender Revolution* (1998), 400.

4. *ODNB*, Translators of the Authorized Version of the Bible; Bethlem Royal Hospital Archives, Beckenham, Kent: BCB 3, fol. 1ᵛ; Quaife, *Wanton Wenches*, 183; Keith Thomas, 'The Puritans and Adultery', in Donald Pennington and Keith Thomas (eds), *Puritans and Revolutionaries* (1978), 261.

5. Keith Wrightson, *English Society, 1580–1680* (1982), 85; Quaife, *Wanton Wenches*, 61–2; Martin Ingram, *Church Courts, Sex and Marriage in England 1570–1640* (1987), 229–30 (quoted), 267–8.

6. Faramerz Dabhoiwala, 'The Pattern of Sexual Immorality', in Paul Griffiths and Mark S. R. Jenner (eds), *Londinopolis* (2000); Ingram, *Church Courts*, ch. 4.

7. Thomas, 'Puritans and Adultery', 267.

8. For further details see e.g. L. R. Poos, 'Sex, Lies, and the Church Courts', *Journal of Interdisciplinary History* 25 (1995); Roger Thompson, *Sex in Middlesex* (1986); Ingram, *Church Courts*; Faramerz Dabhoiwala, 'Sex, Social Relations, and the Law', in Michael J. Braddick and John Walter, *Negotiating Power* (2001).

9. H[enry] C[onsett], *The Practice of the Spiritual or Ecclesiastical Courts* (1685), 386 (quoted), 396; Ingram, *Church Courts*, 51–2, 248–50, 331–4, and references given there.

10. Michael Dalton, *The Countrey Justice* (6th edn, 1635), 88, 189.

11. London Metropolitan Archives, COL/CA/01/01/014 (Repertory 13), fols 292ᵛ–293ʳ (quoted in Martin Ingram, 'Shame and Pain', in Simon Devereaux and

Paul Griffiths (eds), *Penal Practice and Culture, 1500–1900* (2004), 55); *Diary of Samuel Pepys*, vii. 240. It was occasionally argued that constables and watchmen could simply commit to prison overnight anyone they found on their nightly rounds, even if 'they be not suspicious': see e.g. W[illiam] Shepherd, *A Sure Guide for His Majesties Justices of Peace* (1669 edn), 412.

12. *Certayne Sermons, or Homelies, Appoynted by the Kynges Maiestie* (1547), sig. Tiiᵛ. For introductions to these themes see e.g. Laura Gowing, *Domestic Dangers* (1996); Bernard Capp, 'The Double Standard Revisited', *Past and Present* 162 (1999) and his *When Gossips Meet* (2003); Martin Ingram, 'Law, Litigants and the Construction of "Honour"', in Peter Coss (ed.), *The Moral World of the Law* (2000); David Turner, 'Nothing is So Secret', in Tim Hitchcock and Michele Cohen (eds), *English Masculinities 1660–1800* (1999); Alastair Bellany, *The Politics of Court Scandal* (2002); Christine Peters, *Women in Early Modern Britain, 1450–1640* (2004), ch. 3; Johanna Rickman, *Love, Lust, and License in Early Modern England* (2008); www.earlystuartlibels.net.

13. London Metropolitan Archives, DL/C/147, fol. 344[a]ᵛ (1696).

14. Quaife, *Wanton Wenches*, 201; Adam Fox, *Oral and Literate Culture in England 1500–1700* (2000), ch. 6 (quoting 303). For other examples see Martin Ingram, 'Ridings, Rough Music and Mocking Rhymes in Early Modern England', in Barry Reay (ed.), *Popular Culture in Seventeenth-Century England* (1985), and the references given in note 12 above.

15. [Daniel Defoe], *Conjugal Lewdness* (1727), quoting 84–6.

The Foundations of Sexual Discipline

1. Margaret Cavendish, *Political Writings*, ed. Susan James (2003), quoting 185.

2. See e.g. Paul Griffiths, *Youth and Authority* (1996), esp. ch. 7; Julia Merritt, *The Social World of Early Modern Westminster* (2005), ch. 7; Lena Cowen Orlin, *Locating Privacy in Tudor London* (2007).

3. See e.g. *Seventeenth-Century Economic Documents*, ed. Joan Thirsk and J. P. Cooper (1972), quoting 759; Keith Wrightson and David Levine, *Poverty and Piety in an English Village* (1979), quoting 80, 133; Keith Wrightson, *English Society 1580–1680* (1982), quoting 78; Martin Ingram, *Church Courts, Sex and Marriage in England, 1570–1640* (1987), 130–31; Lawrence Stone, *Uncertain Unions* (1992), 83–92; Steve Hindle, 'The Problem of Pauper Marriage', *Transactions of the Royal Historical Society* 8 (1998), quoting 85, and his 'Hierarchy and Community in the Elizabethan Parish', *Historical Journal* 42 (1999); Edgar J. McManus, *Law and Liberty in Early New England* (1993); Richard Godbeer, *Sexual Revolution in Early America* (2002), pt 1. For medieval precedents cf. e.g. Eleanor Searle *et al.*, 'Seigneurial Control of Women's Marriage', *Past and Present* 82 (1979) and 99 (1983); Judith M. Bennett, 'Writing Fornication', *Transactions of the Royal Historical Society* 13 (2003).

4. For this paragraph and the next, see e.g. G. R. Quaife, *Wanton Wenches and*

Wayward Wives (1979), chs 3–4, 9–10; Ingram, *Church Courts*, 158–9, 261–3 (quoted); Angus McLaren, *A History of Contraception* (1990), ch. 5; Laura Gowing, *Common Bodies* (2003), chs 4–6.

5. Quaife, *Wanton Wenches*, 64, 71.

6. Frank Rexroth, *Deviance and Power in Late Medieval London* (2007), 152.

7. Invaluable guides to this subject are Mark Goldie, 'The Theory of Religious Intolerance in Restoration England', in Ole Peter Grell *et al.* (eds), *From Persecution to Toleration* (1991); John Coffey, *Persecution and Toleration in Protestant England, 1558–1689* (2000); Alexandra Walsham, *Charitable Hatred* (2006). Cf. R. I. Moore, *The Formation of a Persecuting Society* (1987), esp. 61–5, 100–101.

8. *The Judgment of the Learned and Pious St Augustine* (1670), 3. Cf. A. M., *The Reformed Gentleman* (1693), sig. A3ʳ–A4ʳ; [Josiah Woodward], *An Account of the Societies for Reformation of Manners* (1699), 81–3.

9. Edmund Cressy, *Spiritual Directions for Hospitals, Houses of Correction, and Prisons* (1675), 28–41 (quoting 35); Richard Cooke, *A White Sheete* (1629), 36–7; John Disney, *An Essay upon the Execution of the Laws* (2nd edn, 1710), 40–42.

10. *Letters*, no. 185. Cf. William Prynne, *The Sword of Christian Magistracy Supported* (1647), 13–14; [Samuel Johnson], *A Letter from a Freeholder* [1688], 8.

11. William Clagett, *Seventeen Sermons* (1689), 43–4; James Knight, *A Sermon Preached to the Societies for Reformation of Manners* (1733), 9.

12. E.g. Leviticus 20.5. Cf. Samuel Mather, *A Testimony from the Scripture* [Cambridge, Mass., 1671?], 14; [Charles Leslie], *A Letter of Advice to a Friend* (1696), 9. How far the eroticization of Christ's body was compatible with strict monogamy and community control of sexuality is illustrated by the practice of the eighteenth-century Moravian church, in Pennsylvania and elsewhere: Craig D. Atwood, 'Sleeping in the Arms of Christ', *Journal of the History of Sexuality* 8 (1997).

13. [Robert Bolton], *An Answer to the Question* (1755), 43; *Reasons Humbly Offered to the Members of Both Houses of Parliament, For Passing the Bill against Vice and Immorality* [1699], 3; 'Mary Smith', *Observations on Seduction* (2nd edn, 1808), vii.

14. For typical examples, see O[liver] O[rmerod], *The Picture of a Puritane* (1605), sig. M, and his *The Picture of a Papist* (1606), 1st pagination 39–40, 61, 64, 69–70, 75–6, 197–9, 2nd pagination 34–7; Thomas Herbert, *A Relation of Some Yeares Travaile* (1634), 99, 154, 158; George Sandys, *A Relation of a Journey* (1615), 53; *A Description of the Sect called the Familie of Love* (1641), 3; *False Prophets Discovered* (1642); Daniel Featley, *The Dippers Dipt* (1645), 202–3, 209–10; E[phraim] Pagitt, *Heresiography* (2nd edn, 1645), 5–6, 10, 13, 27, 33, 88–9, 93, 142, 153; Thomas Edwards, *Gangraena* (1646), ii. 145, iii. 185–190; Alexander Ross, *ΠΑΝΣΕΒΙΑ: or, A View of all Religions in the World* (2nd edn, 1655), e.g. i. 63–5, 119, 361–6, 380–88; [Henrick van Haestens], *Apocalypsis*, trans. J[ohn] D[avies], (2nd edn, 1658), e.g. 9–10, 18, 59, 67; *Pyrotechnica Loyolana* (1667), 65, 69–72; [David Clarkson], *The Practical Divinity of the Papists* (1676), 337–60; *A True History of the Lives of the Popes of Rome* (1679), 10–14;

[Gilbert Crokatt and John Monroe], *The Scotch Presbyterian Eloquence* (1697), 6–7; John Edwards, *A Free Discourse Concerning Truth and Error* (1701), 137–8, 405–6; Christopher W. Marsh, *The Family of Love in English Society, 1550–1630* (1994), 66, 205–13; Ann Hughes, *Gangraena and the Struggle for the English Revolution* (2004), 74, 89–91, 101–2, 110, 113–14, 117); John Spurr, *The Restoration Church of England, 1646–1689* (1991), 234–7, 251–3, 269–70; John Marshall, *John Locke, Toleration and Early Enlightenment Culture* (2006), 218–22, 247–52, 259, 453–61; Peter Marshall, 'John Calvin and the English Catholics', *Historical Journal* 53 (2010).

15. Richard Baxter, *A Holy Commonwealth* (1659), 204.

16. Richard Capel, *Tentations* (1633), 97, 107, 308–9. Cf. Thomas Edwards, *The Casting Down of the Last and Strongest Hold of Satan* (1647), sig. A3. The general context is beautifully elucidated by David Wootton, 'The Fear of God in Early Modern Political Theory', *Historical Papers/Communications historiques* 18 (1983).

17. John Bunyan, *The Holy War* (1682), 13–25, 29–32, 222, 226.

18. James A. Brundage, *Law, Sex, and Christian Society in Medieval Europe* (1987), 15–17 summarizes the relevant passages (as well as noting important exceptions).

19. *The Folger Library Edition of The Works of Richard Hooker*, ed. W. Speed Hill et al., 7 vols (1977–98), iii. 321; Baxter, *Holy Commonwealth*, 212; John Disney, *A Second Essay upon the Execution of the Laws* (1710), 119–20, 123–5, 128, 155–9.

CHAPTER 1: THE DECLINE AND FALL OF PUBLIC PUNISHMENT

The Drive towards Perfection

1. *Tudor Church Reform*, ed. Gerald Bray (Church of England Record Society, 2000), 277.

2. P. E. H. Hair, 'Bridal Pregnancy', *Population Studies* 20 (1966) and 24 (1970). *Constitutions, and Canons Ecclesiastical* (1633), canon 109; Martin Ingram, *Church Courts, Sex and Marriage in England, 1570–1640* (1987), esp. chs 7–9; R. H. Helmholz, 'Harboring Sexual Offenders', *Journal of British Studies* 37 (1998); Bernard Capp, 'The Double Standard Revisited', *Past and Present* 162 (1999); Jason McElligott, 'The Politics of Sexual Libel', *Huntington Library Quarterly* 67 (2004).

3. *Calendar of State Papers, Domestic 1634–5* (1864), 325; Samuel R. Gardiner, *History of England*, 10 vols (1905 edn), viii. 144–6; Roland G. Usher, *The Rise and Fall of the High Commission* (1913); Winfield E. Ohlson, 'Adultery: A Review', *Boston University Law Review* 17 (1937), 349 and references given there; Kevin Sharpe, *The Personal Rule of Charles I* (1992), 379–83.

4. See e.g. Martin Ingram, 'Ridings, Rough Music and Mocking Rhymes in Early Modern England', in Barry Reay (ed.), *Popular Culture in Seventeenth-Century England* (1985); Adam Fox, *Oral and Literate Culture in England 1500–1700* (2000), ch. 6; Alastair Bellany, *The Politics of Court Scandal* (2002); Johanna Rickman, *Love, Lust, and License in Early Modern England* (2008); www. earlystuartlibels.net.

5. Keith Thomas, 'The Puritans and Adultery', in Donald Pennington and Keith Thomas (eds), *Puritans and Revolutionaries* (1978), 264.

6. John Cotton, *An Abstract of the Lawes of New England* (1641), 11; *Reports of Cases in the Courts of Star Chamber and High Commission*, ed. Samuel Rawson Gardiner (Camden Society, 1886), 201–2; Thomas, 'Puritans and Adultery', 268–72; Julian Goodare, *The Government of Scotland, 1560–1625* (2004), 207.

7. See Martin Ingram, 'Puritans and the Church Courts, 1560–1640', in Christopher Durston and Jacqueline Eales (eds), *The Culture of English Puritanism* (1996).

8. Joan Kent, 'Attitudes of Members of the House of Commons to the Regulation of "Personal Conduct" in Late Elizabethan and Early Stuart England', *Bulletin of the Institute for Historical Research* 46 (1973); Thomas, 'Puritans and Adultery', 273–4. Cf. Arthur Cleveland, 'Indictments for Adultery and Incest before 1650', *Law Quarterly Review* 29 (1913).

9. 7 James I c. 4; 21 James I c. 27; Keith Wrightson, 'Infanticide in Earlier Seventeenth-Century England', *Local Population Studies* 15 (1975).

10. David Underdown, *Fire from Heaven* (1992), 106–8; Keith Wrightson and David Levine, *Poverty and Piety in an English Village* (1979), 132–4.

11. *Colonial Origins of the American Constitution*, ed. Donald S. Lutz (1998), item 46 (Fundamental Articles of New Haven, 4 June 1639); Thomas, 'Puritans and Adultery', 271–2; Richard J. Ross, 'Puritan Godly Discipline in Comparative Perspective', *American Historical Review* 113 (2008).

12. Ohlson, 'Adultery', 352–68; Edmund S. Morgan, 'The Puritans and Sex', *New England Quarterly* 15 (1942); Richard Godbeer, *Sexual Revolution in Early America* (2002), 103.

13. *The Journal of John Winthrop*, ed. Richard S. Dunn *et al.* (1996), 500–502. Cf. e.g. Robert Foulkes, *An Alarme for Sinners* (1679). For contemporary punishments of sexual offenders in Plymouth colony (public whipping, shaming processions, being permanently marked by badges on one's clothes or branding on the skin), see Martha L. Finch, *Dissenting Bodies* (2010), 122–35.

Triumph and Failure

1. *The Constitutional Documents of the Puritan Revolution, 1625–1660*, ed. Samuel Rawson Gardiner (3rd edn, 1906), 142, 188; *Acts and Ordinances of the Interregnum, 1642–1660*, ed. C. H. Firth and R. S. Rait, 3 vols (1911), ii. 387–9;

Keith Thomas, 'The Puritans and Adultery', in Donald Pennington and Keith Thomas (eds), *Puritans and Revolutionaries* (1978).

2. Devon Record Office, Exeter: QS/1/9, 4 Apr. 1654 (I am most grateful to the Senior Archivist, Mrs Susan Laithwaite, for her help with this record); *Mercurius Politicus*, 26 June–3 July 1656; F. A. Inderwick, *The Interregnum* (1891), 34–8; Thomas, 'Puritans and Adultery', 258, n. 4; F. D. Dow, *Cromwellian Scotland* (1979), 178; Stephen K. Roberts, *Recovery and Restoration in an English County* (1985), 200–201.

3. Bernard Capp, 'Republican Reformation', in Helen Berry and Elizabeth Foyster (eds), *The Family in Early Modern England* (2007) (in the original record her name is transcribed as 'Frotheringham'); *ODNB*, Damaris Page; Bernard Capp, 'Bigamous Marriage in Early Modern England', *Historical Journal* 52 (2009).

4. London Metropolitan Archives: Westminster Quarter Sessions and Middlesex Quarter Sessions records sampled for 1653; The National Archives, Public Record Office: King's Bench records sampled for 1651, 1653, 1654; Luke Owen Pike, *A History of Crime in England*, 2 vols (1873), ii. 183, 627–8; Thomas, 'Puritans and Adultery', 280; Keith Wrightson, 'The Nadir of English Illegitimacy in the Seventeenth Century', in Peter Laslett *et al.* (eds), *Bastardy and its Comparative History* (1980); Roberts, *Recovery and Restoration*, 198–208; Christopher Durston, *Cromwell's Major-Generals* (2001), 156; Capp, 'Republican Reformation'.

5. *A True and Perfect List of the Names of those Prisoners in Newgate* (1652), 6.

6. *Middlesex County Records*, ed. John Cordy Jeaffreson, 4 vols (1886–92), iii. 294–5; Capp, 'Republican Reformation', 50, 53; E. P. Thompson, *Customs in Common* (1991), 478–9; Samuel R. Gardiner, *History of the Great Civil War*, 4 vols (1904 edn), ii. 252; Inderwick, *Interregnum*, 38–9; *ODNB*, Edmund Chillenden; *Calendar of State Papers, Venetian 1655–1656* (1930), 309. For the regime's forcible transportation of Irish girls and boys on similar grounds, see *A Collection of the State Papers of John Thurloe*, 7 vols (1742), iv. 191, 198; *Calendar of State Papers, Colonial* (1860–), i. 428–32.

7. For the illegitimacy figures and their interpretation, see Peter Laslett and Karla Oosterveen, 'Long-Term Trends in Bastardy in England', *Population Studies* 27 (1973); Wrightson, 'Nadir of English Illegitimacy'. Cf. Derek Hirst, 'The Failure of Godly Rule in the English Republic', *Past and Present* 132 (1991).

8. The topic remains under-researched, though the publication of current work by Martin Ingram and Eleanor Fox is eagerly awaited. Meanwhile see Martin Ingram, 'Law, Litigants and the Construction of "Honour"', in Peter Coss (ed.), *The Moral World of the Law* (2000), 154; Paul Griffiths, *Lost Londons* (2008), 201–9.

9. See London Metropolitan Archives, DL/C/55, 328–9, 625–6 (London Consistory Court, Office Side, 1661–1706); R. B. Outhwaite, *The Rise and Fall of the English Ecclesiastical Courts, 1500–1860* (2006); Andrew Thomson, 'Church Discipline', *History* 91 (2006).

10. Faramerz Dabhoiwala, 'Sex, Social Relations, and the Law', in Michael J. Brad-

dick and John Walter, *Negotiating Power* (2001), 91–2; John Miller, *Cities Divided* (2007), 73.

11. See e.g. *The Book of the General Laws and Libertyes Concerning the Inhabitants of the Massachusets* (Cambridge, Mass., 1660), 8, 33; *Severall Laws and Orders Made at the General Courts* (1665), 1; [Thomas Wood], *A New Institute of the Imperial or Civil Law* (1704), 264; Isabel V. Hull, *Sexuality, State, and Civil Society in Germany, 1700–1815* (1996), 65, 72–5, 78–9.

12. *Some Proposals Offered to Publick Consideration, before the Opening of Parliament* (1685), 2; *Journals of the House of Commons* (1802–), viii. 630 (4 Oct. 1666); ix. 592–3, 687 (12 Apr. 1679, 23 Dec. 1680); *A Letter to a Member of Parliament with Two Discourses Enclosed* (1675), 5–6. Cf. *A Proclamation against Vicious, Debauch'd, and Prophane Persons* (30 May 1660); *By the Maior* (23 Dec. 1672); *By the Mayor* (17 Nov. 1676); *By the Mayor* (31 Jan. 1679); *By the Mayor* (29 Nov. 1679); *By the King, a Proclamation* (29 June 1688); *Vertue's Triumph at the Suppression of Vice* (1688), 5–8.

13. See e.g. *The Poor-Whores Petition. To the most Splendid, Illustrious, Serene and Eminent Lady of Pleasure, the Countess of Castlemayne* (1668); Bodleian Library, Oxford, MS Don. b. 8, *passim*; *The Gracious Answer of the most Illustrious Lady of Pleasure, the Countess of Castlem----- To the Poor-Whores Petition* (1668); Tim Harris, 'The Bawdy House Riots of 1668', *Historical Journal* 29 (1986); *Articles of High-Treason and other High-Crimes and Misdemeanors against the Dutches of Portsmouth* [c. 1680]; *A Satyr* (first line, 'His Holiness Has Three Grand Friends') [c. 1680]; *Middlesex County Records*, ed. Jeaffreson, iv. 34–5; *The Poor Whores Complaint to the Apprentices of London* (1672); *A Word of Advice to the Two New Sheriffs of London* (1682); *The Informers Lecture* (1682); *The Diary of Samuel Pepys*, ed. Robert Latham and William Matthews, 11 vols (1970–83), ii. 156; iii. 60, 302–3; iv. 30; v. 56–61, 96; vi. 127, 210, 248, 276–7; vii. 29, 159, 297–8, 323, 325–6, 349–50, 400, 426; viii. 8, 286–9, 354–5, 361–2, 365, 366, 377–8; ix. 19–20; *The Diary of John Evelyn*, ed. E. S. de Beer, 6 vols (1955), iii. 316, 403, 464, 465–6, 505, 569, 573; iv. 85, 269, 331, 398; *Burnet's History of My Own Time*, ed. Osmund Airy, 2 vols (Oxford, 1897–1900), i. 453; John Spurr, *The Restoration Church of England, 1646–1689* (1991), 248.

God's Revolution

1. On these themes see esp. Eamon Duffy, 'Primitive Christianity Revived', *Studies in Church History* 14 (1977); Tina Isaacs, 'The Anglican Hierarchy and the Reformation of Manners 1688–1738', *Journal of Ecclesiastical History* 30 (1982); Donna T. Andrew, *Philanthropy and Police* (1989); Lee Davison *et al.* (eds), *Stilling the Grumbling Hive* (1992), esp. chs 5–7; Craig Rose, 'Providence, Protestant Union and Godly Reformation in the 1690s', *Transactions of the Royal Histor-*

ical Society 3 (1993); John Walsh *et al.* (eds), *The Church of England c. 1689-c. 1833* (1993), chs 5, 7; Tony Claydon, *William III and the Godly Revolution* (1996).

2. G. Meriton, *Immorality, Debauchery, and Profaneness* (1698), 105; John Bellers, *Essays About the Poor* (1699), 16. Cf. *Reasons Humbly Offered to the Members of Both Houses of Parliament, For Passing the Bill against Vice and Immorality* [1699], 1.

3. See e.g. [Edward Stephens], *A Specimen of a Declaration against Debauchery, Tendered to the Consideration of His Highness the Prince of Orange, and of the Present Convention of the Nation* [1689]; [idem], *A Caveat against Flattery* (1689), 28-32, 35-6; [idem], *The True English Government* (1689), 7-8; [idem], *Of Humiliation* [1689], 4-6; Claydon, *William III and the Godly Revolution*, 49-50, 57.

4. [William III], *His Majesties Letter to the Lord Bishop of London* [1690], 4. In some places, such as the diocese of Coventry and Lichfield, there was consequently a temporary surge in church court activity against adultery and fornication: Laura Gowing, *Common Bodies* (2003), 180.

5. *An Act for the more Effectual Restraining and Suppressing of Divers Notorious Sins, and Reformation of the Manners of the People of this Nation* (appended to [Edward Stephens], *A Plain Relation of a Late Action at Sea* (1690)), 5-7. Cf. *Some Modest Reflections Upon Mr Stephens's late Book* (1691), 1, 26; [W. Jones], *Ecclesia Reviviscens* (1691), 9; Eveline Cruickshanks *et al.* (eds), *The History of Parliament: The House of Commons 1690-1715*, 5 vols (2002), iv. 231. The same presumption of guilt in cases of adultery and fornication was the norm in continental civil law, and had also been advocated during the 1650s, as a means of strengthening the Adultery Act: [Thomas Wood], *A New Institute of the Imperial or Civil Law* (1704), 261-2; D[aniel] T[aylor], *Certain Queries* (1651), 9-10.

6. Narcissus Luttrell, *A Brief Historical Relation of State Affairs*, 6 vols (Oxford, 1857), iv. 349, 354-5; [John] Oldmixon, *The History of England* (1735), 175. Cf. *An Abstract of the Laws Already in Force against Profaneness, Immorality & Blasphemy . . . with the Laws and Ordinances . . . from 1640 to 1656* (1698), and [Daniel Defoe], *The Poor Man's Plea* (1698), 30 (whose reference to branding, transportation, or hanging for adultery and fornication perhaps reflects current proposals in parliament). At some point during the bill's amendment the clauses against sexual immorality were dropped, and ultimately it passed as the 1698 Blasphemy Act (9 William III c. 35): *Journals of the House of Commons* (1802-), xii. 132, 134, 142, 147, 151, 154-5, 160, 168-9, 176-7, 183, 258, 269, 276, 280, 284-5, 295.

7. 'A Bill for the more effectual Suppressing of Vice and Immorality', Lambeth Palace Library, London, MS 640, 497-9; 'Debates in the House of Commons 1697-1699', ed. D. W. Hayton, in *Camden Miscellany* 29 (1987), 373-5; *Journals of the House of Commons*, xii. 368, 387, 401-2, 466, 468-9, 484, 494; Luttrell, *Brief Historical Relation*, iv. 468, 471-2, 478, 481; Historical Manuscripts Commission,

The Manuscripts of His Grace the Duke of Portland, 10 vols (1891–1931), iii. 602; *Reasons Humbly Offered to the Members*; [Thomas Bray], *Reasons for the Passing of the Bill for the more Effectual Suppressing of Vice & Immorality* (2 edns, 1699); 'A True Narrative or Memorial Representing the Rise, Progress and Issue of Dr Bray's Missionary Undertaking' (1705), University of Maryland Archives, Thomas Bray Collection, Box 30, fol. 24ᵛ. For poetic allusions, see [Samuel Garth], *The Dispensary* (1699), 73; [Edward Ward], *The Weekly Comedy* 2 (10–17 May 1699); [Daniel Defoe], 'An Encomium upon a Parliament' (1699), lines 76–85, printed in *Poems on Affairs of State*, ed. George deF. Lord *et al.*, 7 vols (1963–75), vi. 56.

8. Garnet V. Portus, *Caritas Anglicana* (1912), 125n (quoted); *The Parliamentary Diary of Sir Richard Cocks, 1698–1702*, ed. D. W. Hayton (1996), xxxi, 9–10; *Conjugium Languens* (1700), 19, 24–6; *Journals of the House of Commons*, xvi. 532, 536, 544; *A Chapter in English Church History*, ed. Edmund McClure (1888), 319; Thomas Bray, *For God, or for Satan* (1709), 28; *The Third Charge of Whitlocke Bulstrode* (1723), 10–11; David Hayton, 'Moral Reform and Country Politics in the Late Seventeenth-Century House of Commons', *Past and Present* 128 (1990).

9. See e.g. *Acts and Laws . . . Of the Province of the Massachusetts-Bay* (1724), 11, 70; *Acts and Laws . . . of Connecticut* (Boston, 1702), 4, 63–4; Winfield E. Ohlson, 'Adultery: A Review', *Boston University Law Review* 17 (1937), 356–68; Jonathan I. Israel, *The Dutch Republic* (1995), 690–99; Luttrell, *Brief Historical Relation*, ii. 81, 120; *A Collection of all the Acts . . . relating to the Clergy and Ecclesiastical Affairs within the Kingdom of Scotland* (1693), 25 (quoted); *Acts of the Parliaments of Scotland, 1124–1707*, 12 vols ([Edinburgh], 1814–75), ii. 539; iii. 25–6, 213; vi (pt 2), 152–3; vii. 310–11; viii. 99; ix. 198, 327–8, 387–8; x. 65, 67, 279 (quoted). Cf. *A Collection of Some Acts of the General Assembly of the Church of Scotland . . . for Suppressing of Vice* (Edinburgh, 1714); *The Acts of the Town Council of . . . Edinburgh, for Suppressing of Vice . . . made since the Happy Revolution* (Edinburgh, 1742), 105–9, 121–5, 143–5.

10. *Journals of the House of Commons*, xii. 368, 387, 401–2, 466, 468–9, 484, 494; Luttrell, *Brief Historical Relation*, iv. 468, 471–2, 478, 481; *Manuscripts of His Grace the Duke of Portland*, iii. 602; Henry Horwitz, *Parliament, Policy and Politics in the Reign of William III* (1977), 256 (quoted).

11. Faramerz Dabhoiwala, 'Sex, Social Relations, and the Law', in Michael J. Braddick and John Walter, *Negotiating Power* (2001), 92; *Reformation and Revival in Eighteenth-Century Bristol*, ed. Jonathan Barry and Kenneth Morgan (Bristol Record Society, 1994), 22–3; *A Help to a National Reformation* (1700), sig. [C4ʳ] (quoted). Cf. F. W., *A Letter to a Bishop from a Minister of his Diocess* (1691), 15–16; [Josiah Woodward], *An Account of the Societies for Reformation of Manners* (1699), 2–3; John Disney, *A Second Essay upon the Execution of the Laws* (1710), preface; *A Representation of the State of the Societies for Reformation of Manners* (1715), 4–5.

12. Richard [Smalbroke], *Reformation Necessary to Prevent our Ruine* (1728), quot-

ing 21; Saunders Welch, *A Proposal to Render Effectual a Plan* (1758), quoting 8; Thomas Wood, *An Institute of the Laws of England* (1720), 686; Henry Fielding, *A Charge Delivered to the Grand Jury ... of Westminster* (1749), 44-5, 48-50, and his *The Covent-Garden Journal* [1752], ed. Bertrand A. Goldgar (1988), nos 67-8; [Samuel Glasse], *The Magistrate's Assistant* (Gloucester, 1784), 179.

13. London Metropolitan Archives, CLA/004/01/02/005 (Lord Mayor's Charge Book), 16 Sept., 23 Dec. 1730; *A Complete Collection of State-Trials* [ed. Sollom Emlyn], 6 vols (2nd edn, 1730), quoting vol. 1, p. ix and note n; *A Report of all the Cases Determined by Sir John Holt* (1738), 598; *Hansard's Parliamentary Debates* 147 (1857), 1854; Brian P. Levack, 'The Prosecution of Sexual Crimes in Early Eighteenth-Century Scotland', *Scottish Historical Review* 89 (2010).

Societies of Virtue

1. Stephen Pritchard, *The History of Deal* (Deal, 1864), quoting 159; Garnet V. Portus, *Caritas Anglicana* (1912); Dudley W. R. Bahlman, *The Moral Revolution of 1688* (1957); A. G. Craig, 'The Movement for the Reformation of Manners, 1688-1715' (University of Edinburgh Ph.D. thesis, 1980).

2. *A Chapter in English Church History*, ed. Edmund McClure (1888), quoting 350; [Josiah Woodward], *An Account of the Societies for Reformation of Manners* (1699), 23-6; [idem], *An Account of the Progress of the Reformation of Manners* (14th edn, 1706), 3-18; Portus, *Caritas Anglicana*, 125-7, 141-55; Bahlman, *Moral Revolution*, 38-9; T. C. Barnard, 'Reforming Irish Manners: The Religious Societies in Dublin during the 1690s', *Historical Journal* 35 (1992); *Reformation and Revival in Eighteenth-Century Bristol*, ed. Jonathan Barry and Kenneth Morgan (Bristol Record Society, 1994). Although usually explicitly modelled on the metropolitan societies, and guided by their published propaganda, these various rural, provincial, and overseas societies evidently differed from them in important respects. Only the Dublin and Bristol groups have yet been studied in any detail: the others warrant further investigation.

3. See Faramerz Dabhoiwala, 'Sex and Societies for Moral Reform, 1688-1800', *Journal of British Studies* 46 (2007), which includes further details about the subjects discussed in the remainder of this chapter; Robert B. Shoemaker, *Prosecution and Punishment* (1991), ch. 9, and his 'Reforming the City', in Lee Davison *et al.* (eds), *Stilling the Grumbling Hive* (1992).

4. *Dictionary of National Biography* (1885-1901), Thomas Tenison; *The Diary of John Evelyn*, ed. E. S. de Beer, 6 vols (1955), v. 7-8; Henri and Barbara van der Zee, *William and Mary* (1973), 387-8; Bahlman, *Moral Revolution*, 23-7; London Metropolitan Archives [hereafter 'LMA'], MJ/SP/1689/08/10; *By the Mayor* (19 Nov. 1689) (quoted); Bethlem Royal Hospital Archives, Beckenham, Kent: BCB 16; *Antimoixeia: Or, the Honest and Joynt-Design of the*

Tower Hamblets for the General Suppression of Bawdy-Houses (18 June 1691)
(quoted).

5. For this paragraph and the account that follows see esp.:

a) General sources: Edinburgh University Library, MS Laing III. 394 (quoting 465–
6); Bodleian Library, Oxford, MSS Rawlinson D. 129 and D. 1396–1404; *Anti-moixeia*; [Edward Stephens], *An Admonition to the Magistrates of England*
[1689]; [idem], *The Beginning and Progress of a Needful and Hopeful Reformation* (1691); [idem], *A Seasonable and Necessary Admonition* [1701]; [Edward
Fowler], *A Vindication of an Undertaking of Certain Gentlemen* (1692); *Proposals for a National Reformation of Manners* (1694); Josiah Woodward, *An
Earnest Admonition to All* (1697); [idem], *An Account of the Rise and Progress
of the Religious Societies* (1698); [idem], *Account of the Societies*.

b) The societies' annual *Black Lists*, 1693–1708. The first *Black Roll*, of sexual
offenders prosecuted by the society in 1693 (with a supplement for January
1694), was printed in *Proposals for a National Reformation*, 34–5. This list of
names was very erratically arranged and contained many errors, duplications,
and omissions, as appears from comparison with the legal records. The *Black
Lists* that followed were much more carefully produced accounts. The first (published in 1696) listed offenders punished during 1695, though no copy of it now
survives. Within a few years these broadsheets included precise figures for recidivists, as well as the grand total since Christmas 1695. The extant editions are: *A
Black List* (1698); *A Sixth Black List* [1701]; *A Seventh Black List* (1702); *The
Eighth Black List* (1703); *The Tenth Black List* (1705); *The Eleventh Black List*
(1706); *The Thirteenth Black List* (1708).

c) The societies' annual *Accounts* of prosecutions, 1708–38: the figures presented in
these are reproduced in Portus, *Caritas Anglicana*, appendix V (though the 1724
figure for keeping bawdy and disorderly houses should be 29; and the total number in 1728 was 778).

6. John Disney, *A Second Essay upon the Execution of the Laws* (1710), 48; *Anti-moixeia*.

7. See e.g. *A Short Disswasive from the Sin of Uncleanness* (1701); *Some Considerations Offered to such Unhappy Persons as are Guilty of ... Uncleanness*
(1701); [Josiah Woodward], *A Rebuke to the Sin of Uncleanness* (1704); *The
Fourteenth Account of the Progress made in Suppressing Prophaneness and
Debauchery* (1709); Disney, *Second Essay*, 207–9; [John Dunton], *The Night-Walker*, i/4 (1697), sig. [A3ʳ]; [Woodward], *Account of the Societies*, 48, 139
(quoted); *Proposals for a National Reformation*, 18–20 (quoted); *Acts of the
Parliaments of Scotland*, 1124–1707, 12 vols ([Edinburgh] 1814–75), ix. 327–8;
By the Queen, a Proclamation for the Encouragement of Piety and Virtue (18
Aug. 1708) (quoted). Cf. *An Act for the more Effectual Restraining and Suppressing of Divers Notorious Sins, and Reformation of the Manners of the People of
this Nation* (appended to [Edward Stephens], *A Plain Relation of a Late Action
at Sea* (1690)), 7; Julian Goodare, *The Government of Scotland, 1560–1625*
(2004), 209–10.

8. LMA, CLA/047/LJ/01: City of London Sessions Files and Minute Books, SF 391, 392, 393, 394, 395, 396, 397, 398; SM 63–4; CLA/047/LJ/13: City of London Sessions Papers, grand jury presentments of Jan. 1693, July 1693, Oct. 1694, Jan. 1695; The National Archives, Public Record Office: KB 10/7; KB 29/352.

9. See e.g. *Proposals for a National Reformation*, 2–3, 24; [Edmund Gibson], *The Bishop of London's Pastoral Letter* (1728), 2; [Dunton], *Night-Walker*, ii/1 (1697), 28; Josiah Woodward, *The Duty of Compassion* (1697), vii–viii; [idem], *Account of the Societies*, 21–3; Thomas Bray, *For God, or for Satan* (1709), 26–9; *The Fifteenth Account of the Progress Made towards Suppressing Prophaneness and Debauchery* (1710) (quoted); *The Two and Twentieth Account* [1717], quoting 1; LMA, CLA/047/LJ/01: City of London Sessions Files and Minute Books SF 552, 556; SM 79 (1713); William Simpson, *The Great Benefit of a Good Example* (1738), 16–17, 19–21.

10. In 1693 there were approximately 1,150 prosecutions of bawdy houses, prostitutes, and their clients across the metropolis, whilst the *Black Roll* for that year includes about three hundred names: these calculations are derived from *Proposals for a National Reformation*, 34–5; *A Psalm of Thanksgiving, to be Sung by the Children of Christ's Hospital* (1694); Bethlem Royal Hospital Archives, Beckenham, Kent: BCB 16. 215–310; LMA, CLA/047/LJ/01: City of London Sessions Files and Minute Books, SF 391–8; SM 63–4; Middlesex and Westminster Sessions, MJ/SR/1808, 1810, 1813, 1815, 1818, 1820, 1823, 1825; MJ/SBB/502–9; MJ/SBP/8, Jan.–Dec. 1693; WJ/SR/1807, 1812, 1817, 1822, 1826; The National Archives, Public Record Office: KB 10/7 (Easter 1693–Trinity 1694); KB 29/352. The figures for 1703 are estimated from the *Black Lists* for 1702 and 1704; *A Psalm of Thanksgiving to be Sung by the Children of Christ's Hospital* [1704]; John Stow, *A Survey of the Cities of London and Westminster*, ed. John Strype, 6 books (1720), i. 202; Bethlem Royal Hospital Archives, Beckenham, Kent: BCB 18. 128–88; LMA, CLA/075/01/007: Minutes of the Court of the President and Governors for the Poor of the City of London; SF 472, 476; MJ/SR/2005, 2016; MJ/SBP/9, Jan.–Dec. 1703; WJ/SR/2008, 2013, 2018, 2023, 2363, 2368; KB 10/10 (Hilary 1703); KB 10/11 (Easter–Michaelmas 1703). For sodomy prosecutions see Randolph Trumbach, 'London's Sodomites', *Journal of Social History* 11 (1977); Craig, 'Movement for the Reformation of Manners', 162–77; Alan Bray, *Homosexuality in Renaissance England* (1982), ch. 4; Rictor Norton, *Mother Clap's Molly House* (1992), chs 2–8.

From Amateurs to Professionals

1. See e.g. Margaret R. Hunt, *The Middling Sort* (1996), 114; T. C. Curtis and W. A. Speck, 'The Societies for the Reformation of Manners', *Literature and History* 3 (1976), 60.

2. [Josiah Woodward], *An Account of the Societies for Reformation of Manners* (1699), quoting 11 (his earliest account, written in 1696, spoke of 'about sixty

persons': idem, *An Earnest Admonition to All* (1697), 173); Edinburgh University Library, MS Laing III. 394: 447-71, 509-10; *Proposals for a National Reformation of Manners* (1694), 24-[25]. The constitution of the original initiative had been very similar: *Antimoixeia: Or, the Honest and Joynt-Design of the Tower Hamblets for the General Suppression of Bawdy-Houses* (18 June 1691). In addition to those described below, notable examples were James Jenkins (1692-5); James Cooper (c. 1694-7); Richard Hemmings, Thomas Jackson, John Holdway, and John Beggarly (1698-9 onwards); Jonathan Wright (c. 1704-16); Philip Cholmondely (c. 1709 onwards); and Edward Vaughan (c. 1720-23).

3. Edinburgh University Library, MS Laing III. 394: 49-57, 307-22, 447-64, 507-10; Woodward, *Earnest Admonition*, 175-6; [idem], *An Account of the Rise and Progress of the Religious Societies* (1698), 76-7 (quoted), 93; A. G. Craig, 'The Movement for the Reformation of Manners, 1688-1715' (University of Edinburgh Ph.D. thesis, 1980), 31-4. Cf. *Reformation and Revival in Eighteenth-Century Bristol*, ed. Jonathan Barry and Kenneth Morgan (Bristol Record Society, 1994), esp. 31.

4. Leon Radzinowicz, *A History of English Criminal Law*, 5 vols (1948-86), quoting ii. 14 (which cites W. E. H. Lecky, *A History of England in the Eighteenth Century* (1921 edn), iii. 33); Paul Langford, *A Polite and Commercial People: England 1727-1783* (1989), quoting 128. For traditional policing see e.g. Bethlem Royal Hospital Archives, Beckenham, Kent: BCB 12. 180-366; 14. 191-272; London Metropolitan Archives [hereafter 'LMA'], CLA/047/LJ/01: City of London Sessions Files and Minute Books, SF 206, 207, 211, 288, 292, 347, 351; Westminster Sessions, WJ/SR/1593, 1599, 1602, 1605, 1703, 1708, 1713, 1718; The National Archives, Public Record Office: KB 9/918, indictment 24; KB 9/919, indictment 28; KB 9/920, indictment 66. For the societies' efforts, see e.g. Robert B. Shoemaker, *Prosecution and Punishment* (1991), 262-5, 267-70; Edinburgh University Library, MS Laing III. 394: 424-5; Bodleian Library, Oxford, MSS Rawlinson D. 1396-1404. For disincentives (and the arguments deployed to try to overcome them) see esp. John Disney, *A Second Essay upon the Execution of the Laws* (1710).

5. Edinburgh University Library, MS Laing III. 394: 365, 368; LMA, CLA/047/LJ/01: City of London Sessions File SF 441, recognizance 73 (Apr. 1699); Bodleian Library, Oxford, MSS Rawlinson D. 1397, 1401; Thomas Bray, *The Good Fight of Faith* (1709), 2, 15-16 (quoted).

6. *Antimoixeia*; The National Archives, Public Record Office, KB 10/7 (Easter 1693), certiorari 18; LMA, MJ/SR/1820, prosecution recognizance 43; MJ/SR/1827, indictments 20, 45; MJ/SR/1829, indictment 4; MJ/SR/1837, recognizance 183; *The Proceedings of . . . the Old-Bayley* (18-20 Apr. 1694), 4; *Journals of the House of Commons* (1802-), xi. 246, 308 (Feb., Apr. 1695); *Middlesex County Records: Calendar of the Sessions Books 1689 to 1709*, ed. W. J. Hardy (1905), 105, 308, 310.

NOTES TO PAGES 63-5

7. Rewse's activities can be traced in the records cited at note 10 in the previous section, and also e.g. in Edinburgh University Library, MS Laing III. 394: 233–40, 366, 509–10; Bethlem Royal Hospital Archives, Beckenham, Kent, BCB 16. 327, 329, 333, 357, 358, 385, 420, 452, 453, 454, 456; BCB 17. 2; LMA, CLA/047/LJ/01: City of London Sessions Files and Minute Books, SF 399, 401, 402, 404, 405, 406, 407, 410, 411; CLA/047/LJ/13: City of London Sessions Papers, May 1697 (deposition of Sir Edward Clarke) and Feb. 1700 (deposition of Bodenham Rewse); DL/C/156, fols 237–8; DL/C/199, fol. 373; DL/C/255, fols 366–83 (1715); Guildhall Library, London, MS 9173/57, 'Rewse'; MS 9174/44, 'Rewse' (1725); *Calendar of Treasury Books* (1696–7, 227; 1697–1702, 523; 1704–5, 417); Tim Wales, 'Thief-takers and their Clients in Later Stuart London', in Paul Griffiths and Mark S. R. Jenner (eds), *Londinopolis* (2000); J. M. Beattie, *Policing and Punishment in London 1660–1750* (2001), 237–46.

8. For this paragraph and the next, see Faramerz Dabhoiwala, 'Sex, Social Relations, and the Law', in Michael J. Braddick and John Walter, *Negotiating Power* (2001), 94–7; Beattie, *Policing and Punishment*, chs 3–4, 8; Elaine A. Reynolds, *Before the Bobbies* (1998), chs 1–3; Norma Landau, 'The Trading Justice's Trade', in her (ed.) *Law, Crime and English Society, 1660–1830* (2002).

9. For the practical consequences, see Stanley Dana Nash, 'Social Attitudes towards Prostitution in London from 1752 to 1829' (New York University Ph.D. thesis, 1980), 45–52; Tony Henderson, *Disorderly Women in Eighteenth-Century London* (1999).

10. *The Vices of the Cities of London and Westminster* (Dublin, 1751), 14–15; John Brewer, 'The Wilkites and the Law, 1763–74', in John Brewer and John Styles (eds), *An Ungovernable People* (1980), 170; Joanna Innes, *Inferior Politics* (2009), chs 5, 7; M. J. D. Roberts, *Making English Morals* (2004). As these studies elucidate, the presumptions and priorities of later eighteenth- and nineteenth-century moral reformers were often significantly different. As far as sexual indecency was concerned, for example, the prosecution of obscene literature took on a new prominence in the later eighteenth century, whilst less importance was attached to punishing prostitutes. Nevertheless, the example of the original reform societies continued to serve as an inspiration to later activists, even as late as the 1880s: see e.g. John Wesley, *A Sermon Preached before the Society for Reformation of Manners* [1763], 5; Innes, *Inferior Politics*, 190–2; Roberts, *Making English Morals*, 255.

11. Peter Clark, *British Clubs and Societies 1580–1800* (2000), 67, 102–3, 434–5; Beattie, *Policing and Punishment*, 376–83, 401–23, and the literature cited there. For the general trend see esp. Douglas Hay and Francis Snyder (eds), *Policing and Prosecution in Britain 1750–1850* (1989); Christopher W. Brooks, *Lawyers, Litigation and English Society since 1450* (1998), esp. chs 3–4; W. A. Champion, 'Recourse to the Law and the Meaning of the Great Litigation Decline, 1650–1750', in Christopher Brooks and Michael Lobban (eds), *Communities and Courts in Britain 1150–1900* (1997); Craig Muldrew, *The Economy of Obliga-*

tion (1998), ch. 8; Robert B. Shoemaker, *The London Mob* (2004), chs 4, 8; David Lemmings (ed.), *The British and their Laws in the Eighteenth Century* (2005).

Hierarchy and Hypocrisy

1. W[illiam] Yonger, *Iudahs Penance*, in *The Nurses Bosome* (1617), quoting 54; *The Athenian Mercury*, 3/7 (18 Aug. 1691); John Shower, *A Sermon Preach'd to the Societies for Reformation* (1698), quoting 4. Cf. [Josiah Woodward], *An Account of the Societies for Reformation of Manners* (1699), 45; John Disney, *An Essay upon the Execution of the Laws* (2nd edn, 1710), 125–7.

2. Mainly, it seems, in cases of profanity: see e.g. Edinburgh University Library, MS Laing III. 394: 197–202; Narcissus Luttrell, *A Brief Historical Relation of State Affairs*, 6 vols (Oxford, 1857), ii. 346; Historical Manuscripts Commission, *The Manuscripts of His Grace the Duke of Portland*, 10 vols (1891–1931), iii. 472; Stephen Pritchard, *The History of Deal* (Deal, 1864), 161; Dudley W. R. Bahlman, *The Moral Revolution of 1688* (1957), 22; *Reformation and Revival in Eighteenth-Century Bristol*, ed. Jonathan Barry and Kenneth Morgan (Bristol Record Society, 1994), 20–21.

3. Shower, *Sermon Preach'd to the Societies*, quoting 23–4; [Daniel Defoe], *The Poor Man's Plea* (1698), quoting sig. [A], 6; [idem], *Reformation of Manners* (1702); [idem], *More Reformation* (1703); Charles Eaton Birch, 'Defoe and the Edinburgh Society for the Reformation of Manners', *Review of English Studies* 16 (1940). When he joined the Edinburgh society in 1707, Defoe was described as a current member of 'the Societies for Reformation in England': ibid., 307.

4. Francis [Hare], *A Sermon Preached to the Societies for Reformation* (1731), 23–4; John Fielding, *A Charge Delivered to the Grand Jury, at … Westminster … April 6th, 1763* (1763), 11; M. J. D. Roberts, 'The Society for the Suppression of Vice and its early Critics, 1802–1812', *Historical Journal* 26 (1983), 171, 173. Cf. *The Daily Gazetteer*, 9 Jan. 1740; M. J. D. Roberts, *Making English Morals* (2004), 50–51; Stanley Dana Nash, 'Social Attitudes towards Prostitution in London from 1752 to 1829' (New York University Ph.D. thesis, 1980), 138–9, 388. Outrage at the apparent impunity of aristocratic adulterers did, however, form part of the background to the unsuccessful adultery bills of the late eighteenth and early nineteenth centuries: Donna T. Andrew, '"Adultery à-la-Mode"', *History* 82 (1997).

5. Leon Radzinowicz, *A History of English Criminal Law*, 5 vols (1948–86), ii. 138–55; M. W. Beresford, 'The Common Informer', *Economic History Review* 10 (1957), quoting 221; Mark Goldie, 'The Hilton Gang and the Purge of London in the 1680s', in Howard Nenner (ed.), *Politics and the Political Imagination in Later Stuart Britain* (1997). Cf. Brian Harrison, 'State Intervention and Moral Reform in Nineteenth-century England', in *Pressure from Without in Early Victorian England*, ed. Patricia Hollis (1974).

6. Daniel Chadwick, *A Sermon Preached at ... Nottingham to the Society for Reformation of Manners* (1698), 22–3; *The Fourteenth Account of the Progress made in Suppressing Prophaneness and Debauchery* (1709); Edmund [Gibson], *A Sermon Preached to the Societies for Reformation* [1724], 14; [Edward Ward], *The London Spy Compleat* (1703), 362, 366; [Jonathan Swift], *A Project for the Advancement of Religion* (1709), 37–8, 44 (quoted). Cf. *The Invisible-Observator* (1705), 7–8; John Disney, *A Second Essay upon the Execution of the Laws* (1710), esp. 60–72 and his *Essay*, 103–9, which is notable also for its equivocal denial that the London societies relied on informers who 'make a trade of it, by being rewarded for their informations, if not directly hired to inform'.

7. Mary Pix, *The Different Widows: or, Intrigue All-A-Mode* [1703], Act IV; George Farquhar, *The Constant Couple* (1700), Act II; Thomas Baker, *An Act at Oxford* (1704), Act I, scene 1; Act V, scene 2. Cf. [idem], *The Humour of the Age* (1701); Benjamine Griffin, *Love in a Sack* (1715); Christopher Bullock, *The Per-juror* (1717); Henry Fielding, *Rape upon Rape* (1730), Acts II and IV.

8. [Ward], *London Spy*, 361; Roberts, 'Society for the Suppression of Vice', 169–71; cf. Shower, *Sermon Preach'd to the Societies*, 23.

Crimes and Punishments

1. Josiah Woodward, *A Sermon Preach'd ... at the Funeral of Mr. John Cooper* (1702); Thomas Bray, *The Good Fight of Faith* (1709); James Peller Malcolm, *Anecdotes of the Manners and Customs of London during the Eighteenth Century* (1808), 258, 277–8; *London Chronicle*, 22 Oct. 1757.

2. Narcissus Luttrell, *A Brief Historical Relation of State Affairs*, 6 vols (Oxford, 1857), vi. 437, 463, 510, 514; Robert, Lord Raymond, *Reports of Cases* (1743), 1296–1303; *The Tryals of Jeremy Tooley, William Arch, and John Clauson* (1732), quoting 18–19; *A Report of all the Cases Determined by Sir John Holt* (1738), 485–92 (quoting 489, 491); Robert B. Shoemaker, *Prosecution and Punishment* (1991), 263–5.

3. *Letters Illustrative of the Reign of William III*, ed. G. P. R. James, 3 vols (1841), ii. 133–4. For the general developments cf. Cynthia Herrup, *The Common Peace* (1987) and Barbara Shapiro, *'Beyond Reasonable Doubt' and 'Probable Cause'* (1991); and see Faramerz Dabhoiwala, 'Summary Justice in Early Modern London', *English Historical Review* 121 (2006), 797–8, and references given there.

4. See Anna Clark, *Women's Silence, Men's Violence* (1987), 121–3, and her *The Struggle for the Breeches* (1995), 51–2; Tony Henderson, *Disorderly Women in Eighteenth-Century London* (1999), 115–40.

5. London Metropolitan Archives, CLA/004/01/02/005: Lord Mayor's Charge Book, 1729–30; CLA/005/01/001–003: Guildhall Justice Room Minute Books, 1752, 1761–2; Henry Fielding, *The Covent-Garden Journal* [1752], ed. Bertrand A. Goldgar (1988), 436; Martin C. and Ruthe R. Battestin, *Henry Fielding* (1989), 709; Malcolm, *Anecdotes*, 116; Stanley Dana Nash, 'Social Attitudes

towards Prostitution in London from 1752 to 1829' (New York University Ph.D. thesis, 1980), 21–6; Henderson, *Disorderly Women*, 114.

6. 3 George IV c. 40 (1822); 5 George IV c. 83 (1824); 27 and 28 Victoria c. 85 (1864); 29 and 30 Victoria c. 96 (1866); 32 and 33 Victoria c. 86 (1869); Judith R. Walkowitz, *Prostitution and Victorian Society* (1980).

7. Prosecutions in the 1670s estimated from London Metropolitan Archives, CLA/047/LJ/01: City of London Sessions Files and Minute Books, SF 206–7, 211; SM 36–8; Middlesex and Westminster Sessions, MJ/SR/1402, 1413; WJ/SR/1405, 1415; MJ and WJ/SBB/275, 277, 282–3; MJ/SBP/6; WJ/SBP/1; The National Archives, Public Record Office, KB 9/918–20. Later estimates based on analysis of SF 472, 476, 552, 556, 632, 636, 729, 733, 830, 833; SM 72, 73, 79, 90, 102, 115; MJ/SBP/9, 11, 12, 14, 15; MJ/SR/2630, 2640, 2641, 2894, 2905; WJ/SR/2008, 2018, 2207, 2216, 2401, 2411, 2632, 2643, 2896, 2907; KB 10/10, 10/11, 10/15, 10/18, 10/22, 10/23, 10/28, 10/29, 15/23; Saunders Welch, *Observations on the Office of Constable* (1754), 8, 30–32. Prosecutions in 1748 traced through KB 10/28 (Hilary 1748), presentments 32, 39; KB 10/28 (Easter 1748), presentments 39, 43; KB 10/28 (Trinity 1748), presentments 64, 66, 67, certiorari 6; KB 10/29 (Michaelmas 1748), presentments 53, 54, certioraris 10, 11; KB 15/23. Obtaining convictions was not necessarily, of course, the only aim of legal action – but their total absence is nevertheless striking.

8. See e.g. [John Cleland], *The Case of the Unfortunate Bosavern Penlez* (1749); Peter Linebaugh, 'The Tyburn Riot against the Surgeons', in Douglas Hay *et al.* (eds), *Albion's Fatal Tree* (1975), 89–100; Nicholas Rogers, 'Confronting the Crime Wave', in Lee Davison *et al.* (eds), *Stilling the Grumbling Hive* (1992).

9. 25 George II c. 36, deemed 'useful and beneficial' and made perpetual by 28 George II c. 19 (1755); Saunders Welch, *An Essay on the Office of Constable* (1758), quoting 32–3. Prosecutions estimated from London Metropolitan Archives, CLA/047/LJ/01: City of London Sessions Files and Minute Books, SF 909, 913; SM 125; Middlesex and Westminster Sessions, MJ/SR/3073, 3081; MJ/SBB/1147; MJ/SBP/16; WJ/SR/3074, 3083; The National Archives, Public Record Office: KB 10/32 (1758); KB 15/24. For Welch's actions, see MJ/SR/3073, prosecution recognizance 19, recognizance 83; MJ/SR/3081, recognizances 69, 70, 103; WJ/SR/3074, prosecution recognizance of Sarah Smart, recognizances 28, 29, 36; WJ/SR/3083, prosecution recognizances of Samuel Williams, Margaret Read, recognizances 12, 18, 19, 20, 30, 31, 109, 110; *London Chronicle*, 30 Jun., 15 Jul., 9 Dec., 26 Dec. 1758. Cf. Nash, 'Social Attitudes', 56–84.

10. *A Sermon Preached before the former Societies for Reformation of Manners* ... *Whereunto is Subjoined, A Declaration from the Present Society* (1760), 34–6; George Downing, *A Sermon Preached before the Society for Reformation of Manners* (1760), 27–8, 34–5; Samuel Chandler, *The Original and Reason of the Institution of the Sabbath* (1761), [75] (ms. correction to the copy in the British Library, pressmark 225.a.25); John Wesley, *A Sermon Preached before the Society for Reformation of Manners* [1763], 6–11, 27–8, 31; *Gentleman's Magazine*,

23 Feb. 1763; John Conder, *A Sermon Preached before the Society for the Reformation of Manners* (1763), 30; Moses Browne, *The Causes that Obstruct the Progress of Reformation* (1765), 29–31; *An Extract of the Rev. Mr. John Wesley's Journal ... 1762, to ... 1763* (Bristol, 1768), 102 (4 Nov. 1764); *An Extract of the Rev. Mr. John Wesley's Journal ... 1765, to ... 1768* (Bristol, 1771), 28–9 (2 Feb. 1766); George Wilson, *Reports of Cases* (1770), 160–62; Joanna Innes, *Inferior Politics* (2009), ch. 7.

11. Arthur Bedford, *A Sermon Preached to the Societies for Reformation* (1734), quoting 18; *Cases Determined by Sir John Holt*, 406–7; Raymond, *Reports*, 562, 699, 1197; Sir John Strange, *Reports of Adjudged Cases* (1755), 882; Thomas Leach, *Modern Reports*, 12 vols (5th edn, 1793–6), v. 415–6. Cf. Faramerz Dabhoiwala, 'Sex, Social Relations, and the Law', in Michael J. Braddick and John Walter, *Negotiating Power* (2001), 90; Heather Shore, '"The Reckoning"', *Social History* 34 (2009).

12. J. M. Beattie, *Crime and the Courts in England, 1660–1800* (1986), 278–9, 356–76, his 'Scales of Justice', *Law and History Review* 9 (1991) and his *Policing and Punishment in London 1660–1750* (2001), 393–401; John H. Langbein, *The Origins of Adversary Criminal Trial* (2003), chs 3–5; Shoemaker, *Prosecution and Punishment*, 264. The rising involvement of defense lawyers was especially notable, and has been mainly studied, in respect of felony trials, where before the early eighteenth century most defendants had no right to legal representation in court. Although their employment in cases of sexual crime and other misdemeanours had a longer history, it appears to have undergone a similar expansion at this time.

13. Sir James Burrow, *Reports of Cases*, 5 vols (1766–80), v. 2684–6; Robert Holloway, *The Rat-Trap* [1773], 70–74; Nash, 'Social Attitudes', 31; *The Trial of Lord Dungarvan* (1791).

14. Isaac [Maddox], *The Love of Our Country Recommended* (1737), 9–10; M. J. D. Roberts, 'The Society for the Suppression of Vice and its early Critics, 1802–1812', *Historical Journal* 26 (1983), 169–70. As a result of these trends there were also recurrent proposals to punish brothel-keeping summarily (a measure finally introduced by the 1885 Criminal Law Amendment Act): John Fielding, *Extracts from such of the Penal Laws, as Particularly Relate to the Peace and Good Order of this Metropolis* (new edn, 1762), 67; Malcolm, *Anecdotes*, 122; Henderson, *Disorderly Women*, 101–2.

The End of Legal Discipline

1. Leon Radzinowicz, *A History of English Criminal Law*, 5 vols (1948–86), iii. 193–203; Lawrence Stone, *Road to Divorce* (1990), 257, 287–8, 335–9, 380–3; Donna T. Andrew, '"Adultery à-la-Mode"', *History* 82 (1997). Cf. *The Evils of Adultery and Prostitution* (1792), 65–70.

2. See e.g. *The Justicing Notebook (1750–64) of Edmund Tew*, ed. Gwenda Morgan

and Peter Rushton (Surtees Society, 2000); Stone, *Road to Divorce*, 81–95, 231–300.

CHAPTER 2: THE RISE OF SEXUAL FREEDOM
Religious and Moral Toleration

1. John Shower, *A Sermon Preach'd to the Societies for Reformation of Manners* (1698), 12. Cf. *A Reply to an Answer to the City-Minister's Letter* (1688), 8–9; Edmund Calamy, *A Defence of Moderate Non-Conformity*, 3 vols (1703–5), ii. 29–30; [John Toland], *The Memorial of the State of England* (1705), 43, 85; John Disney, *A Second Essay upon the Execution of the Laws* (1710), 110–13. A version of this chapter was first published (as 'Lust and Liberty') in *Past and Present* 207 (2010).

2. [John Locke], *A Letter Concerning Toleration* [transl. William Popple] (1689), 7–8.

3. [John Locke], *A Third Letter for Toleration* (1692), 238.

4. Thomas Long, *The Letter for Toleration Decipher'd* (1689), 4; [Jonas Proast], *A Third Letter Concerning Toleration* (1691), 13.

5. Jeremy Taylor, Θεολογία Ἐκλεκτική (1647), 11–12; *Acts and Ordinances of the Interregnum, 1642–1660*, ed. C. H. Firth and R. S. Rait, 3 vols (1911), i. 1133–6, ii. 409–12; *Long Parliament-Work* (1659), 2; J[ohn] M[ilton], *A Treatise of Civil Power in Ecclesiastical Causes* (1659), 17 (citing the 1650 Blasphemy Act); J[ohn] M[ilton], *Of True Religion, Haeresie, Schism, Toleration* (1673), 16. Cf. the equivocal treatment of this issue in John Milton, *Areopagitica* (1644), 5–6, 12–14, 17–18, 37.

6. *The Works of John Milton*, ed. Frank Allen Patterson *et al.*, 18 vols (1931–8), quoting viii. 9; *The Writings of William Walwyn*, ed. Jack R. McMichael and Barbara Taft (1989), 57–8, 163–4, 239–41 (quoting 239); [Roger Williams], *The Bloudy Tenent, of Persecution* (1644), 87; [Sir Henry Vane the younger], *Zeal Examined* (1652), 34; cf. Blair Worden, *Literature and Politics in Cromwellian England* (2007), 165–6, 186–7; John Coffey, 'Puritanism and Liberty Revisited', *Historical Journal* 41 (1998), esp. 975–7.

7. See e.g. Christopher Hill, *Milton and the English Revolution* (1977), 130–33, 226; Gordon Campbell and Thomas N. Corns, *John Milton* (2008), 164–9; Thomas Edwards, *Gangraena* (1646), i. 34, ii. 10–12; *Diary of Thomas Burton*, ed. John Towill Rutt, 4 vols (1828), i. 24; *The Leveller Tracts 1647–1653*, ed. William Haller and Godfrey Davies (1944), quoting 215–19; *Writings of William Walwyn*, 358, 387, 407–8; *The Works of Gerrard Winstanley*, ed. George H. Sabine (1941), 185, 366–7, 399–403, 526.

8. See esp. Rachel Weil, 'Sometimes a Sceptre Is Only a Sceptre', in Lynn Hunt (ed.), *The Invention of Pornography* (1993).

9. [Locke], *Letter Concerning Toleration*, 20–21, 41; cf. ibid., 36; John Locke, *An*

Essay Concerning Toleration and Other Writings, ed. J. R. Milton and Philip Milton (2006), 280–84.

10. [Locke], *Third Letter for Toleration*, 283; cf. [John Locke], *A Second Letter Concerning Toleration* (1690), 5; Locke, *Essay Concerning Toleration*, ed. Milton and Milton, 302.

11. Cf. Jeremy Waldron 'Locke: Toleration and the Rationality of Persecution', in Susan Mendus (ed.), *Justifying Toleration* (1988).

Freedom and Conscience

1. See e.g. Francis [Hare], *A Sermon Preached to the Societies for Reformation of Manners* (1731), quoting 44; Robert Drew, *A Sermon Preached to the Societies for Reformation of Manners* (1735), 17–18.

2. See e.g. Ole Peter Grell *et al.* (eds), *From Persecution to Toleration* (1991).

3. See *The Heaven-Drivers* (1701); Faramerz Dabhoiwala, 'Sex and Societies for Moral Reform, 1688–1800', *Journal of British Studies* 46 (2007), and references given there.

4. William Bisset, *Plain English* (1704), 27; [John] Dennis, *Gibraltar* (1705), Act III, scene 4; [Susanna Centlivre], *Love's Contrivance* (1703), Act II, scene 1; Arthur Bedford, *The Evil and Danger of Stage-Plays* (Bristol, 1706), 122. Cf. *The Spectator*, ed. Donald F. Bond, 5 vols (1965), no. 298; *Hell-Gates Open to all Men* (1751), 129.

5. Cf. Keith Thomas, 'Cases of Conscience in Seventeenth-Century England', in John Morrill *et al.* (eds), *Public Duty and Private Conscience in Seventeenth-Century England* (1993), 49–56; Christopher Hill, *Milton and the English Revolution* (1977), 126–7; Norman Jones, *God and the Moneylenders* (1989), 34–8, 149–63, 174, 197, 201–4.

6. *The Rambler*, no. 23 (5 June 1750); Thomas Hobbes, *Leviathan* (1651), 168. Cf. J. A. Passmore, 'Locke and the Ethics of Belief', *Proceedings of the British Academy* 64 (1978); John Kilcullen, *Sincerity and Truth* (1988); Mark Goldie, 'The Theory of Religious Intolerance in Restoration England', in Ole Peter Grell *et al.* (eds), *From Persecution to Toleration* (1991), 353–8.

7. See e.g. Thomas Cole, *A Godly and Frvtefvll Sermon* (1553), sigs Cii–iiii; George Huntston Williams, *The Radical Reformation* (3rd edn, 1992), chs 13, 20; Otthein Rammstedt, *Sekte und soziale Bewegung* (1966), 95–100; Philip McNair, 'Ochino's Apology', *History* 60 (1975), quoting 364; Hill, *Milton*, 75; James M. Stayer, 'Vielweiberei als "innerweltliche Askese"', *Mennonitische Geschichtsblätter* 37 (1980); John F. Davis, *Heresy and Reformation in the South-East of England, 1520–1559* (1983), 147; Anne Hudson, *The Premature Reformation* (1988), 141, 292, 385; Bob Scribner, 'Practical Utopias', *Comparative Studies in Society and History* 36 (1994), 745–52; Lyndal Roper, *Oedipus and the Devil* (1994), ch. 4; J. Patrick Hornbeck II, 'Theories of Sexuality in English "Lollardy"', *Journal of Ecclesiastical History* 60 (2009), 38–40. For medieval prece-

dents, see e.g. Roland Hissette, *Enquête sur les 219 Articles Condamnés à Paris le 7 Mars 1277* (1977), 294–300.

8. Christopher W. Marsh, *The Family of Love in English Society, 1550–1630* (1994), 20–24, 42; Geoffrey F. Nuttall, *The Holy Spirit in Puritan Faith and Experience* (1946); Christopher Hill, *The World Turned Upside Down* (1975 edn); Leo Damrosch, *The Sorrows of the Quaker Jesus* (1996); David R. Como, *Blown by the Spirit* (2004).

9. Bodleian Library, Oxford, MS Rawlinson d. 399, fol. 196ʳ, printed in Como, *Blown by the Spirit*, 482; Robert Towne, *The Assertion of Grace* ([1644]; written in 1632), quoting 47; *Diary of Thomas Burton*, ed. John Towill Rutt, 4 vols (1828), quoting i. 46; Robert Towne, *The Re-assertion of Grace* (1654); *ODNB*. Cf. *Reports of Cases in the Courts of Star Chamber and High Commission*, ed. Samuel Rawson Gardiner (Camden Society, 1886), 270–1; Jacob Bauthumley, *The Light and Dark Sides of God* (1650), 31–42; Abiezer Coppe, *A Remonstrance* (1651), 1, 4; Abiezer Coppe, *Copp's Return* (1651), 4, 13–14, 19–20.

10. L[aurence] C[larkson], *A Single Eye* [1650], 10, 12, 14. After his conversion to the sect of John Reeve and Lodowicke Muggleton he vehemently repudiated sexual antinomianism, whilst affirming his previous practice of it: Laur[ence] Claxton [i.e. Clarkson], *Look About You* (1659), 91–9 and his *The Lost Sheep Found* (1660), 22, 25–31, 37. For earlier examples of sectarian practice, see Folger Shakespeare Library, MS V. a. 399, fol. 19ᵛ; Keith Thomas, 'Women and the Civil War Sects', *Past and Present* 13 (1958), 49–50; Hill, *Milton*, 124, 131–2; Michael P. Winship, *Making Heretics* (2002), 154–5; Como, *Blown by the Spirit*, 404, 479–81; and for eighteenth-century equivalents cf. *The Works of John Wesley*, ed. Frank Baker *et al.* (1980–), xx. 117–18, 320 (23 Mar. 1746, 10 Apr. 1750).

11. *The Clarke Papers*, ed. C. H. Firth, 4 vols (Camden Society, 1891–1901), ii. 102; C. H. Firth, *Cromwell's Army* (1962 edn), 399; and the examples cited in Keith Thomas, 'The Puritans and Adultery', in Donald Pennington and Keith Thomas (eds), *Puritans and Revolutionaries* (1978), 278.

12. Edward Stokes, *The Wiltshire Rant* (1652) (quoting 4, 12, 51, 53); 'Abraham Lawmind', *The Juries Right* (1654). Cf. [Clarkson], *Look About You*, 92.

13. See J. C. Davis, *Fear, Myth and History* (1986), and the debate about it in *Past and Present* 117 (1987), 129 (1990), 140 (1993).

14. Pierre Bayle, *A Philosophical Commentary* (1708), 293–7, 303–6, 353–4 (the case was the famous one of Bertrande, the wife of Martin Guerre, for which see Natalie Zemon Davis, *The Return of Martin Guerre* (1983)). Cf. also Samuel Pufendorf, *The Law of Nature and Nations*, transl. Basil Kennet[t] *et al.* (5th edn, 1749), 2nd pagination, 32.

15. Thus wilful adulterers were to be treated as culpable 'disturbers of the public tranquillity', whilst if anyone claimed spiritual indulgence 'to preach up sodomy, adultery, and murder as actions praise-worthy and holy', these would be 'circumstances in which the magistrate regards not the plea of conscience': Bayle, *Philosophical Commentary*, 307–10, 486. But see also David Wootton, 'Pierre Bayle,

Libertine?', in M. A. Stewart (ed.), *Studies in Seventeenth-Century European Philosophy* (1997).

16. Bisset, *Plain English*, 28.

17. Richard [Smalbroke], *Reformation Necessary* (1728), quoting 40; Drew, *Sermon Preached to the Societies*, 8-10; *The Tatler*, ed. Donald F. Bond, 3 vols (1987), no. 14; David M. Turner, *Fashioning Adultery* (2002), ch. 2.

18. See Boyd Hilton, 'The Role of Providence in Evangelical Social Thought', in Derek Beales and Geoffrey Best (eds), *History, Society and the Churches* (1985); David Hume, *Essays Moral, Political, and Literary*, ed. Eugene F. Miller (1987), quoting 581-2 ('Of Suicide'); *A Sermon Preached before the Former Societies for Reformation* (1760), quoting 36; Moses Browne, *The Causes that Obstruct the Progress of Reformation* (1765), quoting 32. For the diminished role of providential fear in the attitudes of later eighteenth- and nineteenth-century activists, cf. Malcolm Gaskill, 'The Displacement of Providence', *Continuity and Change* 11 (1996); M. J. D. Roberts, *Making English Morals* (2004); Joanna Innes, *Inferior Politics* (2009), ch. 5.

19. P. D. L. Avis, 'Moses and the Magistrate', *Journal of Ecclesiastical History* 26 (1975), quoting 1; Wilfred R. Prest, 'The Art of Law and the Law of God', in Pennington and Thomas (eds), *Puritans and Revolutionaries*, 94-102; Thomas, 'Puritans and Adultery', 269-70; A. M., *The Reformed Gentleman* (1693), quoting 56.

20. Richard Fiddes, *Theologia Practica* (1720), 84. Cf. William Bisset, *More Plain English* (1704), 42-4; John Tillotson, *A Sermon Preach'd before the Queen* (1690); *Boswell: The Ominous Years, 1774-1776*, ed. Charles Ryskamp and Frederick A. Pottle (1963), 139, 199-200, 322; Philip C. Almond, *Heaven and Hell in Enlightenment England* (1994), ch. 5.

21. *A Modest Defence of Chastity* (1726), 73 (quoted); John Johnson, *Reasons why Vice ought to be Punish'd* (1708), 16; *Boswell's Life of Johnson*, ed. George Birkbeck Hill and L. F. Powell, 6 vols (1934-50), iii. 346.

Moral Laws and Moral Truths

1. Andrew Willet, *An Harmonie Upon the Second Booke of Samuel* (1614), 74; cf. his *Hexapla in Exodum* (1608), 396-8, and *Hexapla in Leviticum* (1631), 501-3.

2. *The Clarke Papers*, ed. C. H. Firth, 4 vols (Camden Society, 1891-1901), ii. 130. For the conventional argument that Christ in fact had strengthened the law, see e.g. Samuel Walker, *Reformation of Manners Promoted by Argument* (1711), 173-85.

3. John Turner, *Boaz and Ruth* (1685), quoting 53; J. Turner, *A Discourse on Fornication* (1698), quoting 2; [Charles Leslie], *A Letter of Advice to a Friend* (1696), quoting 5 and title page; *The Third Charge of Whitlocke Bulstrode Esq.* (1723), 11-18; *A Treatise Concerning Adultery and Divorce* (1700); 'Castamore', *Conjugium Languens* (1700), 27-8; John Locke, *A Paraphrase and Notes on the Epis-*

tles of St Paul, ed. Arthur W. Wainwright, 2 vols (1987), ii. 652; [Daniel Defoe], *Conjugal Lewdness* (1727), 123-4.

4. *The True State of the Case of John Butler* (1697); *Concubinage and Poligamy Disprov'd* (1698); J[ohn] B[utler], *Explanatory Notes on a Mendacious Libel* (1698). Cf. *The Genuine and Uncommon Will of a Clergyman lately Deceas'd* (1750).

5. Burnet to Philip van Limborch (undated: late 1698–early 1699), as translated and printed in T. E. S. Clarke and H. C. Foxcroft, *A Life of Gilbert Burnet* (1907), 348; Lawrence Stone, *Road to Divorce* (1990), 313–20; David M. Turner, 'Secret and Immodest Curiosities?', in Harald E. Braun and Edward Vallance (eds), *Contexts of Conscience in Early Modern Europe* (2004), 137–50.

6. Michel de Montaigne, *The Essayes*, transl. John Florio (1603), bk I, ch. xxii ('Of Custome'); Julius Caesar, *De Bello Gallico*, bk v; *A Collection of Voyages and Travels*, 4 vols (1704), i. 456; *The Philosophical Works of the Late Right Honourable Henry St John, Lord Viscount Bolingbroke*, 5 vols (1754), v. 179. Cf. Pierre Charron, *Of Wisdome*, transl. Samson Lennard [1608?], bk II, ch. viii; John Locke, *An Essay Concerning Human Understanding*, ed. Peter H. Nidditch (1975), I. iii. 9; Samuel Pufendorf, *The Law of Nature and Nations*, transl. Basil Kennet[t] *et al.* (5th edn, 1749), II. iii. viii.

7. Turner, *Discourse on Fornication*, 27. Cf. *Clarke Papers*, ii. 110; Walker, *Reformation*, 176.

8. [John Locke], *The Reasonableness of Christianity* (1695), 265, 271, 274; John Locke, *Essays on the Law of Nature*, ed. W. von Leyden (1954), 140–41, 160–79 (quoting 177). Cf. his 'Of Ethics in General', printed in Lord King, *The Life of John Locke*, 2 vols (1830 edn), ii. 129–33; Thomas Halyburton, *Natural Religion Insufficient* (Edinburgh, 1714), iv. 92–3.

9. [Locke], *Reasonableness of Christianity*, 279–81. For Locke's views on these themes see further Locke, *Essays on the Law of Nature*, *passim*; Locke, *Essay Concerning Human Understanding*, II. xxviii. 4–16; IV. iii. 18–20; IV. xviii–xix; John Locke, *The Reasonableness of Christianity*, ed. John C. Higgins-Biddle (1999), xv–cxv; *The Correspondence of John Locke*, ed. E. S. de Beer, 8 vols (1976–89), iv. 110–13; John Marshall, *John Locke* (1994), 51–2, 57–62, 71–2, 365, 376–83.

10. *Table-Talk: Being the Discourses of John Selden* (1689), 30–31. Cf. Locke, *Essays on the Law of Nature*, 72–3.

11. John Turner, *Two Discourses* (1682), 12; cf. Selden, *Table-Talk*, 50. On these developments see esp. John Spurr, '"Rational Religion" in Restoration England', *Journal of the History of Ideas* 49 (1988); J. A. I. Champion, *The Pillars of Priestcraft Shaken* (1992), 207–22; Isabel Rivers, *Reason, Grace and Sentiment*, 2 vols (1991–2000).

12. *The Writings of William Walwyn*, ed. Jack R. McMichael and Barbara Taft (1989), 109; Pierre Bayle, *A Philosophical Commentary* (1708), 55, 57; David Hume, *Essays Moral, Political, and Literary*, ed. Eugene F. Miller (1987), 588n ('Of Suicide'). Cf. [Anthony Collins], *A Discourse of Free-Thinking* (1713),

12–15; [Mathew Tindal], *An Essay Concerning the Power of the Magistrate* (1697), 106.

13. Christopher Hill, *The World Turned Upside Down* (1975 edn), 183.

Natural Law and Natural Ethics

1. Thomas Palmer, *An Essay of the Meanes How to Make our Travailes* (1606), 97; cf. Jeremy Taylor, *Ductor Dubitantium*, 2 vols (1660), i. 231.

2. John Maynard, *The Law of God Ratified* (1674), 76; Richard Baxter, *A Holy Commonwealth* (1659), 214, 246. Cf. Thomas Hobbes, *The Elements of Law*, ed. Ferdinand Tönnies (1889), 2. 10. 7; Thomas Hobbes, *Leviathan* (1651), 282; *The Clarke Papers*, ed. C. H. Firth, 4 vols (Camden Society, 1891–1901), ii. 127–30; John Locke, *Essays on the Law of Nature*, ed. W. von Leyden (1954), 196–203; Locke, *Two Treatises of Government*, ed. Peter Laslett (2nd edn, 1967), I. 59.

3. William Perkins, *A Discourse of Conscience* ([Cambridge], 1596), 17–20; *The Second Replie of Thomas Cartwright* ([Heidelberg], 1575), cii–ciii; Keith Thomas, 'The Puritans and Adultery', in Donald Pennington and Keith Thomas (eds), *Puritans and Revolutionaries* (1978), 268–72.

4. See e.g. John Turner, *Two Discourses* (1682), 22–9; Anthony Holbrook, *A Letter to the Author of Christianity as Old as the Creation* (1731), 4–6, 13–14; William Paley, *The Principles of Moral and Political Philosophy* (1785), 243–5, 249, 254–5, 269, 273.

5. [William Wollaston], *The Religion of Nature Delineated* (1724), 180. Cf. Charles-Louis de Secondat, Baron de Montesquieu, *The Spirit of Laws*, 2 vols (1750), i. 369.

6. Joseph Butler, *The Analogy of Religion* (1736), 317–19; Richard Fiddes, *Practical Discourses* (1712), 92–4; Francis Hutcheson, *A System of Moral Philosophy*, 2 vols (1755), i. 87–88, ii. 151–3; Richard Price, *A Review of the Principal Questions and Difficulties in Morals* (1758), 232–4, 261–2; [Joseph Priestley], *Considerations for the Use of Young Men* [1778 edn], 6–8, 23; T. R. Malthus, *An Essay on the Principle of Population* (1798), 19.

7. Cf. John Gill, *The Moral Nature and Fitness of Things Considered* (1738), 43–4; [Priestley], *Considerations*, 22.

8. Hutcheson, *System of Moral Philosophy*, ii. 162–3. Pre- and extra-marital concubinage in certain circumstances were defended outright by Emanuel Swedenborg, *The Delights of Wisdom* (1794), 421–4, 428–37 ['473']. Neither this question nor the inference was new: similar views had been advanced on biblical grounds by several sixteenth- and seventeenth-century commentators.

9. Adam Smith, *The Theory of Moral Sentiments*, ed. D. D. Raphael and A. L. Macfie (1976), I. ii. 1. 2–3; VII. iv. 21; Anthony Ashley Cooper, Earl of Shaftesbury, *Characteristics of Men, Manners, Opinions, Times*, ed. Lawrence E. Klein (1999),

221–2 (*Inquiry*, II. ii. 2); Brian Cowan, 'Reasonable Ecstasies', *Journal of British Studies* 37 (1998).

10. See e.g. *The Petty Papers*, ed. the Marquis of Lansdowne, 2 vols (1927), ii. 47–58; T. R. Malthus, *An Essay on the Principle of Population* [edns of 1803–26], ed. Patricia James, 2 vols (1989), quoting i. 19 n. 6. Cf. Butler, *Analogy of Religion*, 318; Holbrook, *Letter*, 15; Samuel Pufendorf, *The Law of Nature and Nations*, transl. Basil Kennet[t] *et al.* (5th edn, 1749), 2nd pagination, 134–5 n. 4.

11. University of Edinburgh Library, MS La. II. 620^{12}, printed in Norah Smith, 'Robert Wallace's "Of Venery"', *Texas Studies in Literature and Language* 15 (1973). For further examples see *Boswell's Life of Johnson*, ed. George Birkbeck Hill and L. F. Powell, 6 vols (1934–50), ii. 472–3; Faramerz Dabhoiwala, 'The Construction of Honour, Reputation and Status', *Transactions of the Royal Historical Society* 6 (1996), 206.

12. *The Yale Edition of Horace Walpole's Correspondence*, ed. W. S. Lewis *et al.*, 48 vols (1937–83), xv. 143; cf. Samuel Richardson, *Pamela; or, Virtue Rewarded* [1740], ed. Thomas Keymer and Alice Wakely (2001), 134–5; *Priest-Craft and Lust* (1743).

13. Though a few did face accusations of adultery: see *ODNB*, Richard Curteys, Robert Horne, John Thornborough, John Atherton.

14. *Boswell on the Grand Tour: Germany and Switzerland 1764*, ed. Frederick A. Pottle (1964), 235–6. His favoured status with the royal family, and his incessantly flirtatious and provocative conversation with female courtiers, were later documented by the novelist and diarist Frances Burney, who referred to him as 'Mr Turbulent': *Diary and Letters of Madame D'Arblay*, ed. [Charlotte Barrett], 7 vols (1842–6), vols iii and iv.

15. Bodleian Library, Oxford, MS Locke b. 4, fol. 99$^{r–v}$. See William Lorimer, *Two Discourses* (1713), v–vii; Thomas Halyburton, *Natural Religion Insufficient* (Edinburgh, 1714), 119–23; Michael Hunter, '"Aikenhead the Atheist"', in Michael Hunter and David Wootton (eds), *Atheism from the Reformation to the Enlightenment* (1992).

16. *The Diary of Dudley Ryder, 1715–1716*, ed. William Matthews (1939), 103–4, 178; [Daniel Defoe], *Conjugal Lewdness* (1727), 123–4; [Francis Hutcheson], *An Inquiry into the Original of Our Ideas of Beauty and Virtue* (1725), 188. Cf. [John Dunton], *The Night-Walker*, i/2 (1696), 1–10.

17. Thomas Hobbes, *Philosophicall Rudiments* [transl. Charles Cotton] (1651), 100–102, 217–19 (*De Cive* vi. 16, xiv. 9–10). Cf. Thomas Hobbes, *The Correspondence*, ed. Noel Malcolm, 2 vols (1994), i. 401; [Anthony Collins], *A Letter to the Reverend Dr Rogers* (1727), 46–7; Mark Goldie, 'The Reception of Hobbes', in J. H. Burns with Mark Goldie (eds), *The Cambridge History of Political Thought 1450–1700* (1991), 606–10; Jon Parkin, 'Hobbism in the later 1660s', *Historical Journal* 42 (1999). Similar claims were made by Grotius, who held that 'copulations without marriage' were not forbidden by nature, only by God (Hugo Grotius, *Of the Law of Warre and Peace* (1655), 356); Selden, who deduced that though natural law proscribed incest and 'unlawful intercourse'

(such as adultery, copulation between men, and bestiality), it permitted polygamy and voluntary divorce (John Selden, *De Iure Naturali & Gentium* (1640), bk v; cf. Eivion Owen, 'Milton and Selden on Divorce', *Studies in Philology* 43 (1946)); and Pufendorf, who was amongst those who doubted whether polygamy contravened natural law (*Law of Nature*, 2nd pagination, 574–7).

18. *The Reports and Arguments of . . . Sir John Vaughan* (1677), 221. Cf. Jason P. Rosenblatt, *Renaissance England's Chief Rabbi* (2006), ch. 10.

19. Alexandre Matheron, 'Spinoza et la Sexualité', *Giornale Critico della Filosofia Italiana* 8 (1977); Richard Tuck, *Natural Rights Theories* (1979), 141–2; Jonathan I. Israel, *Radical Enlightenment* (2001), 86–8.

20. John Locke, *An Essay Concerning Toleration and Other Writings*, ed. J. R. Milton and Philip Milton (2006), 391 ('Virtus'); cf. ibid., 276, 289; John Locke, *A Paraphrase and Notes on the Epistles of St Paul*, ed. Arthur W. Wainwright, 2 vols (1987), i. 186–96; idem, *Political Essays*, ed. Mark Goldie (1997), 256.

21. [William Lawrence], *Marriage by the Morall Law of God Vindicated* (1680), quoting 101–2; [William Lawrence], *The Right of Primogeniture* (1681); Mark Knights, *Politics and Opinion in Crisis, 1678–81* (1994), 162; Mark Goldie, 'Contextualizing Dryden's Absalom', in Donna B. Hamilton and Richard Strier (eds), *Religion, Literature, and Politics in Post-Reformation England* (1996). Cf. J[ohn] D[onne], *Poems* (1650), 388–90 (Elegy XVIII); Thomas Randolph, *Poems* (Oxford, 1638), [126]–128; [Francis Osborne], *Advice to a Son* (Oxford, [1655]), 50–52; George Etherege, *She Wou'd if She Cou'd* (1668), Act I, scene 1; [Aphra Behn], *Love-Letters between a Noble-Man and his Sister* (1684), 331–7.

22. *The Provok'd Wife* (1697), 34 [Act III, scene 1]. Cf. Margaret Cavendish, Marchioness of Newcastle, *Playes* (1662), 334, 349–50 ['The Unnatural Tragedy', Act II, scene 12; Act IV, scene 25]; *The Correspondence of John Locke,* ed. E. S. de Beer, 8 vols (1976–89), iv. 101–2; Εἰκών Βασιλική Δεύτερα (1694), 131–41; Tullio Gregory, 'Pierre Charron's "Scandalous Book"', in Hunter and Wootton (eds), *Atheism*.

23. Pierre Bayle, *An Historical and Critical Dictionary*, 4 vols (1710), iii. 1671. Cf. Thomas Stanley, *The History of Philosophy*, 3 vols (1655–60), iii/pt 4. 23–4.

24. G. S. Rousseau, 'The Sorrows of Priapus', in G. S. Rousseau and Roy Porter, *Sexual Underworlds of the Enlightenment* (1987); Pat Moloney, 'Savages in the Scottish Enlightenment's History of Desire', *Journal of the History of Sexuality* 14 (2005); Brian Young, 'Gibbon and Sex', *Textual Practice* 11 (1997).

25. Thomas Franklin Mayo, *Epicurus in England (1650–1725)* (1934); Howard Jones, *The Epicurean Tradition* (1989), ch. 8; Matthew Niblett, 'Man, Morals and Matter', in Neven Leddy and Avi S. Lifschitz (eds), *Epicurus in the Enlightenment* (2009). Cf. Jonathan Sheehan, 'Sacred and Profane', *Past and Present* 192 (2006).

26. *Burnet's History of My Own Time*, ed. Osmund Airy, 2 vols (Oxford, 1897–1900), i. 166–8; Gilbert Burnet, *Some Passages of the Life and Death of the Right Honourable John Earl of Rochester* (1680), citing 36, 38–9, 52, 54, 70–73, 100–101; *The Complete Poems of John Wilmot, Earl of Rochester*, ed. David M.

Vieth (1968), 35, 98, 101; Sarah Ellenzweig, 'The Faith of Unbelief', *Journal of British Studies* 44 (2005). For a scintillating theatrical exposition of such views, see Thomas Shadwell, *The Libertine* (1676); for interpretations of their role in contemporary drama, Dale Underwood, *Etherege and the Seventeenth-Century Comedy of Manners* (1957); Maximilian E. Novak, *William Congreve* (1971), 41-51; Robert D. Hume, 'The Myth of the Rake in "Restoration" Comedy', *Studies in the Literary Imagination* 10 (1977); Harold Weber, *The Restoration Rake-Hero* (1986); Warren Chernaik, *Sexual Freedom in Restoration Literature* (1995); for the broader context, Anna Bryson, *From Courtesy to Civility* (1998), ch. 7.

27. [Daniel Defoe], *An Essay upon Projects* (1697), 248; [Charles Leslie], *A Letter of Advice to a Friend* (1696), 3; J. Turner, *A Discourse on Fornication* (1698), 52; Richard Capel, *Tentations* (1633), 262-4; John Edwards, *Some Thoughts Concerning the Several Causes and Occasions of Atheism* (1695), 38-42; [Henry Compton], *The Bishop of London's Charge to the Clergy of his Diocese* (1696), 12; John Spurr, *The Restoration Church of England, 1646-1689* (1991), ch. 5.

28. *The Character of a Town-Gallant* (1675), 7. Cf. *An Answer to the Satyr against Mankind* [1675?]; Bryson, *From Courtesy to Civility*, 257-9.

29. Cf. Knud Haakonssen, *Natural Law and Moral Philosophy* (1996).

30. Samuel Richardson, *Clarissa, or The History of a Young Lady* [1747-8], ed. Angus Ross (1985), letter 254; Henry Fielding, *Tom Jones* (1749), bk v, ch. v. Cf. ibid., bk XVIII, ch. viii; [idem], *The History of the Adventures of Joseph Andrews*, 2 vols (1742), vol. ii, bk iii, ch. iii; [John Cleland], *Memoirs of a Woman of Pleasure*, vol. ii (1749), 11-12.

31. [Matthew Tindal], *Christianity as Old as the Creation* (1730), 119, 345-6. Cf. John Sainsbury, *John Wilkes* (2006), ch. 4.

32. [Alberto Radicati], *Christianity Set in a True Light* (1730), 19; [Alberto Radicati], *A Phliosophical [sic] Dissertation upon Death* (1732), 28, 81-3; Albert[o] Radicati], Count de Passeran, *Twelve Discourses* (1734), 26-52 (quoting 40, 45).

33. Bernard Mandeville, *The Fable of the Bees*, ed. F. B. Kaye, 2 vols (1924), i. 41-51, 142-6 (quoting 48, 144); 'Gideon Archer' [i.e. Peter Annet], *Social Bliss Considered* (1749), quoting iii-iv; *An Essay on Crimes and Punishments* (1767), 127-30.

34. David Hume, *Essays Moral, Political, and Literary*, ed. Eugene F. Miller (1987), 131 ('Of the Rise and Progress of the Arts and Sciences'); idem, *A Treatise of Human Nature*, ed. David Fate Norton and Mary J. Norton (2000), 2. 2. 11. 2, 3.2.12.4. In Hume's view, justice, fidelity, and allegiance were similarly 'artificial': his point was not that these were not proper virtues, but that their origins lay in historical and social conventions, rather than in human nature. Cf. Pierre Bayle, *Miscellaneous Reflections*, 2 vols (1708), ii. 330-34.

35. David Hume, *An Enquiry Concerning the Principles of Morals*, ed. Tom L. Beauchamp (1998), quoting Dialogue 36; Hume, *Essays*, ed. Miller, 181-90 ('Of Polygamy and Divorces'), 272 ('Of Refinement in the Arts'); Ernest Campbell Mossner, *The Life of David Hume* (1954), 327-8.

36. Cf. [Paul-Henry Thiry, baron d'Holbach], *The System of Nature*, transl. William Hodgson, 4 vols (1797), iv. 465-6.

37. See Michael Macdonald and Terence R. Murphy, *Sleepless Souls* (1990), ch. 5.

38. See e.g. Arthur Bedford, *A Serious Remonstrance* (1719), 159-61; cf. William Shakespeare, *Othello*, Act III, scene 3.

39. Hume, *Enquiry Concerning . . . Morals*, quoting 4.18, Dialogue 32; Hume, *Treatise*, 3.2.2.4. Cf. Christopher J. Berry, 'Lusty Women and Loose Imagination', *History of Political Thought* 24 (2003), 419-21.

40. N. A. M. Rodger, *The Insatiable Earl* (1993), 80; *Letters to the Duke of Portland* (1794), 30-31; *Boswell in Search of a Wife, 1766-1769*, ed. Frank Brady and Frederick A. Pottle (1957), 158. For illuminating case studies, see Anna Clark, *Scandal* (2004); Sainsbury, *John Wilkes*.

41. See *The Collected Works of John Stuart Mill*, ed. J. M. Robson *et al.*, 33 vols (1963-91), xviii. 296-7 [*On Liberty*, ch. v]; xxvii. 664 (quoted) [Diary, 26 Mar. 1854]; *Report of Royal Commission upon the Administration and Operation of the Contagious Diseases Acts*, 2 vols (1871), ii. 728-35; and, for Mill's own anti-sensualist preferences, Susan Mendus and Jane Rendall (eds), *Sexuality and Subordination* (1989), ch. 5. Cf. W. C. Coupland, *The Principle of Individual Liberty, How Far Applicable to the Relations of the Sexes* [1880].

Private Vices, Public Benefits

1. William Bisset, *Plain English* (1704), 13; *Reasons Humbly Offered . . . for Passing the Bill against Vice and Immorality* [1699], 3.

2. *The Athenian Mercury*, ii. 23 (17 Aug. 1691); University of Edinburgh Library, MS Laing III. 545, fol. 147ʳ (commonplace book of Robert Kirk). Cf. [Francis Osborne], *Politicall Reflections upon the Government of the Turks* (1656), 81-2; *The Third Volume of Letters Writ by a Turkish Spy* (1691), 189-93 (bk II, letter xvi).

3. John Potter, *Archæologiæ Græcæ*, 2 vols (1st edn Oxford, 1697-9; ten further editions, 1706-95), quoting bk IV, ch. xii; [Daniel Defoe?], *Some Considerations upon Street-Walkers* [1726], 4-5, 9-15; [Matthew Tindal], *An Address to the Inhabiants [sic] of the Two Great Cities* (1728), 9; *The Religious, Rational, and Moral Conduct of Matthew Tindal* (1735), 59; 'Luke Ogle', *The Natural Secret History of Both Sexes* (1740), 77-9; [Jonas Hanway], *A Plan for Establishing a Charity-House* (1758), xi-xii.

4. Saunders Welch, *A Proposal to Render Effectual a Plan* (1758), quoting 19; *A Congratulatory Epistle from a Reformed Rake* [1758], quoting 22; 'Gideon Archer' [i.e. Peter Annet], *Social Bliss Considered* (1749), 79-96; [John Cleland], *The Case of the Unfortunate Bosavern Penlez* (1749), 6; *An Essay on Modern Gallantry* [c. 1750], 32-8; *The Covent-Garden Journal* [1752], ed. Bertrand A. Goldgar (1988), no. 50; William Dodd, *An Account of the Rise, Progress, and Present State of the Magdalen Charity* (1761), [i]; John Fielding, *Extracts from*

such of the Penal Laws, as particularly relate to the Peace and Good Order of this Metropolis (new edn, 1762), 67; Considerations on the ... Present Excess of Public Charities (1763), 16–17; Boswell: The Ominous Years, 1774–1776, ed. Charles Ryskamp and Frederick A. Pottle (1963), 316.

5. See e.g. The Gentleman and Lady's Palladium (1751), 16; ibid. (1752), 21; Reflections Arising from the Immorality of the Present Age (1756), 50–63; Lloyds Evening Post, 25 Jan. 1759; London Chronicle, 9 Apr. 1759; Memoirs of the Bedford Coffee-House (1763), 31–4; Robert Holloway, The Rat-Trap [1773], 52–5; P[atrick] Colquhoun, A Treatise on the Police of the Metropolis (6th edn, 1800), 337, 341, 628–9.

6. Randolph Trumbach, 'London's Sodomites', Journal of Social History 11 (1977); Alan Bray, Homosexuality in Renaissance England (1982), ch. 4; Rictor Norton, Mother Clap's Molly House (1992), chs 2–6.

7. David Ogg, England in the Reign of Charles II (1984 edn), 254; J. D. Davies, Gentlemen and Tarpaulins (1991), 67; J. R. Jones, The Anglo-Dutch Wars of the Seventeenth Century (1996), 59; John Brewer, The Sinews of Power (1989), 30. Even higher estimates for the years between 1739 and 1763 are provided by Stephen Conway, 'The Mobilization of Manpower for Britain's Mid-Eighteenth-Century Wars', Historical Research 77 (2004).

8. Bernard Mandeville, The Fable of the Bees, ed. F. B. Kaye, 2 vols (1924), quoting i. 95–6, 100; 'A Layman' [i.e. Bernard Mandeville], A Modest Defence of Publick Stews (1724), quoting i, xi–xii; 'John Wickliffe' [i.e. Henry Hatsell?], Remarks upon Two Late Presentments (1729), 1–4; Richard I. Cook, '"The Great Leviathan of Leachery"', in Irwin Primer (ed.), Mandeville Studies (1975); W. A. Speck, 'Bernard Mandeville and the Middlesex Grand Jury', Eighteenth-Century Studies 11 (1978); Irwin Primer, Bernard Mandeville's 'A Modest Defence of Publick Stews' (2006).

9. See e.g. Mandeville, Fable, ed. Kaye, ii. 386–438, 453; M. M. Goldsmith, 'Regulating Anew the Moral and Political Sentiments of Mankind', Journal of the History of Ideas 49 (1988); John Robertson, The Case for the Enlightenment (2005), ch. 6; and, for casual references, Edward [Chandler], A Sermon Preached to the Societies for Reformation (1724 [i.e. 1725]), 18–21; A Modest Defence of Publick Stews ... Answer'd (1725); A Conference about Whoring (1725), republished in a revised and augmented version as A Modest Defence of Chastity (1726, printed at London and Northampton, for book-sellers there and in Harborough, Coventry, Chesham, and Tring); Samuel Ryder, The Charge to the Grand-Jury of the City and Liberty of Westminster (1726), 9; [Edmund Gibson], The Bishop of London's Pastoral Letter (1728), 2; The Presentment of the Grand-Jury for the County of Middlesex (1728), 3–4; A Vindication of the Bishop of London's Pastoral Letter (1729), 2, 6–8; The Weekly Miscellany, 2 vols (2nd edn, 1738), i. 205; C[harles] Mosley, The Tar's Triumph (etching, 1749).

10. Mandeville, Fable, ed. Kaye, i. 355–6. For his general philosophy, see esp. M. M. Goldsmith, Private Vices, Public Benefits (1985); E. J. Hundert, The Enlightenment's 'Fable' (1994). For his indebtedness to Bayle, cf. Bayle, Miscellaneous

Reflections, ii. 334–6; Mandeville, *Fable*, ed. Kaye, i. 98–100; E. D. James, 'Faith, Sincerity and Morality', in Primer (ed.), *Mandeville Studies*; David Wootton, 'Pierre Bayle, Libertine?', in M. A. Stewart (ed.), *Studies in Seventeenth-Century European Philosophy* (1997), 209–16.

11. Richard [Smalbroke], *Reformation Necessary* (1728), 19; John Disney, *A View of Ancient Laws, against Immorality and Profaneness* (Cambridge, 1729), sig. a2ᵛ; Samuel Richardson, *Clarissa, or The History of a Young Lady* [1747–8], ed. Angus Ross (1985), letter 246; *The Rules, Orders and Regulations of the Magdalen House* (2nd edn, 1759), 3; cf. James Hallifax, *A Sermon Preached in the Chapel of the Asylum for Female Orphans* (1766), 11.

12. *Gentleman's Magazine*, xvii. 563 (Dec. 1747).

13. See e.g. John Sekora, *Luxury* (1977), 110–15; Louis Dumont, *From Mandeville to Marx* (1977); Neil McKendrick *et al.*, *The Birth of a Consumer Society* (1982), 15–19, 51–3; Hundert, *Enlightenment's 'Fable'*; Pierre Force, *Self-Interest Before Adam Smith* (2003); Nicholas Phillipson, *Adam Smith* (2010).

14. [Annet], *Social Bliss*, 82; Hugo Arnot, *A Collection of Celebrated Criminal Trials in Scotland* (Edinburgh, 1785), 310.

15. See e.g. Linda Levy Peck, *Consuming Splendor* (2005); Paul Slack, 'The Politics of Consumption and England's Happiness in the Later Seventeenth Century', *English Historical Review* 122 (2007); Keith Thomas, *The Ends of Life* (2009), ch. 4.

16. M. J. D. Roberts, *Making English Morals* (2004), 25; William Wilberforce, *A Practical View of the Prevailing Religious System* (1797), 372.

Liberty Bounded and Extended

1. Soame Jenyns, *A Free Inquiry into the Nature and Origin of Evil* (1757), 46; 'Gideon Archer' [i.e. Peter Annet], *Social Bliss Considered* (1749), vi. Cf. the earlier views of John Hall, *Of Government and Obedience* (1654), 14; and, more generally, Roy Porter and Marie Mulvey Roberts (eds), *Pleasure in the Eighteenth Century* (1996).

2. *Boswell: Laird of Auchinleck 1778–1782*, ed. Joseph W. Reed and Frederick A. Pottle (1977), 114; [Mathew Bacon *et al.*], *A New Abridgment of the Law*, 5 vols (1736–66), iv. 569; University College London, MSS of Jeremy Bentham, lxxiv. 34 (in French).

3. *Boswell's Life of Johnson*, ed. George Birkbeck Hill and L. F. Powell, 6 vols (1934–50), iii. 17–18. But for Johnson's own indiscretions, and his wife's agreement that 'I might lie with as many women as I pleased, provided I *loved* her alone', see ibid., iii. 406; iv. 395–8.

4. For this theme see Michael Mason, *The Making of Victorian Sexual Attitudes* (1994) and his *The Making of Victorian Sexuality* (1994); for the general backlash, e.g. Maurice J. Quinlan, *Victorian Prelude* (1941); Ford K. Brown, *Fathers*

of the Victorians (1961); Eric Trudgill, *Madonnas and Magdalens* (1976); Boyd Hilton, *The Age of Atonement* (1988), 73–85.

5. See e.g. [Francis Hutcheson], *An Inquiry into the Original of Our Ideas of Beauty and Virtue* (1725), 182–90; P[eter] Annet, *Judging for Ourselves* (1739), 11; Richard Price, *A Review of the Principal Questions and Difficulties in Morals* (1758), 289–306.

6. For the additional interplay, in colonial settings, of racial ideas, see e.g. Kirsten Fischer, *Suspect Relations* (2002); Philippa Levine, *Prostitution, Race, and Politics* (2003); Durba Ghosh, *Sex and the Family in Colonial India* (2006); Peggy Pascoe, *What Comes Naturally* (2009), ch. 1.

7. Anna Clark, *The Struggle for the Breeches* (1995), ch. 4; Kathryn Gleadle, *British Women in the Nineteenth Century* (2001), 39–41, 123–4 (but cf. also ibid., 130–32); Leonore Davidoff and Catherine Hall, *Family Fortunes* (1987), 110, 401–2; Donna Andrew, '"Adultery à-la-Mode"', *History* 82 (1997); Frank Mort, *Dangerous Sexualities* (2nd edn, 2000), pt 1.

8. Adam Smith, *An Inquiry into the Nature and Causes of the Wealth of Nations*, ed. R. H. Campbell, A. S. Skinner, and W. B. Todd (1976), v. i. g. 10. But cf. Percy Bysshe Shelley, *A Philosophical View of Reform*, ed. T. W. Rolleston (1920), 51–4.

9. *A Treatise of Human Nature*, ed. David Fate Norton and Mary J. Norton (2000), quoting 3.2.12; Gilbert Burnet, *Some Passages of the Life and Death of the Right Honourable John Earl of Rochester* (1680), quoting 110; Aphra Behn, *Poems upon Several Occasions* (1684), esp. 'The Golden Age'. Cf. David Hume, *An Enquiry Concerning the Principles of Morals*, ed. Tom L. Beauchamp (1998), 4.5–4.7, 6.14; Charles-Louis de Secondat, Baron de Montesquieu, *The Spirit of Laws*, 2 vols (1750), ii. 198–9; T. R. Malthus, *An Essay on the Principle of Population* [edns of 1803–26], ed. Patricia James, 2 vols (1989), 200–203; Annette C. Baier, 'Good Men's Women', *Hume Studies* 5 (1979); Christine Battersby, 'An Enquiry Concerning the Humean Woman', *Philosophy* 56 (1981); Christopher J. Berry, 'Lusty Women and Loose Imagination', *History of Political Thought* 24 (2003). For many further examples, see Geoffrey May, *Social Control of Sex Expression* (1930), 4–6, 11–13, 47–8, 128–30; Keith Thomas, 'The Double Standard', *Journal of the History of Ideas* 20 (1959); Margaret R. Sommerville, *Sex and Subjection* (1995), 146–50; for the alternative argument, that it was 'natural' for women to be modest and chaste, see Thomas Reid, *Practical Ethics*, ed. Knud Haakonssen (1990), 219–22.

10. William Alexander, *The History of Women*, 2 vols (1779), quoting ii. 221. Cf. the acute analysis of Catharine Macaulay Graham, *Letters on Education* (1790), 220–21; and the chapters by Barbara Taylor, Vivien Jones, and John Robertson in Sarah Knott and Barbara Taylor (eds), *Women, Gender and Enlightenment* (2005).

11. *Boswell's Life of Johnson*, ii. 55–6; iii. 406–7; v. 209; cf. ibid., ii. 457; iii. 349–50.

12. [Tobias Smollett], *The Adventures of Peregrine Pickle* (1751), ch. lxviii (quoted); ibid. (2nd edn, 1758), v–xi; *ODNB*, Frances Anne Vane. Cf. Vic Gatrell, *City of*

Laughter (2006), ch. 12; Matthew J. Kinservik, *Sex, Scandal, and Celebrity in Late Eighteenth-Century England* (2007).

13. *Boswell's Life of Johnson*, iii. 25 (quoted); *Boswell in Search of a Wife, 1766–1769*, ed. Frank Brady and Frederick A. Pottle (1957), 26; *Boswell: The Ominous Years, 1774–1776*, ed. Charles Ryskamp and Frederick A. Pottle (1963), 320–21; Frederick A. Pottle, *James Boswell: The Earlier Years 1740–1769* (1966), 5 (quoted), 78–9; National Archives of Scotland, MS CC8/5/13, quoting p. 93. Cf. *Boswell in Holland, 1763–1764*, ed. Frederick A. Pottle (1952), 304.

14. [Henry Home, Lord Kames], *Sketches of the History of Man*, 2 vols (Edinburgh, 1774), bk I, sketch 6 (quoting 203); idem, *Loose Hints Upon Education* (Edinburgh, 1781), section VIII; *Boswell: The Applause of the Jury, 1782–1785*, ed. Irma S. Lustig and Frederick A. Pottle (1981), 26–8.

15. See e.g. Arthur Bedford, *A Serious Remonstrance* (1719), 192–9; Kathleen Wilson, 'The Female Rake', in Peter Cryle and Lisa O'Connell (eds), *Libertine Enlightenment* (2004); Sarah Lloyd, 'Amour in the Shrubbery', *Eighteenth-Century Studies* 39 (2006); Gatrell, *City of Laughter*, ch. 11; P[atrick] Colquhoun, *A Treatise on the Police of the Metropolis* (6th edn, 1800), 340.

16. James Fitzjames Stephen, *Liberty, Equality, Fraternity* [2nd edn, 1874], ed. Stuart D. Warner (1993), ch. 4 (quoting 105–6). Cf. Henry Sidgwick, *The Methods of Ethics* (7th edn, 1907), III. ix. 2–3, III. xi. 7–9.

17. *Report from His Majesty's Commissioners for inquiring into the Administration and Practical Operation of the Poor Laws* (1834), 92–9, 195–8. As one of the commissioners' correspondents observed, the effect of the new regime would be to create the same, perhaps unjust but nevertheless desirable, situation amongst the labouring population as amongst the higher and middle classes, whereby men were pardoned and women damned for unchastity (ibid., Appendix C, 394c). Though there was considerable resentment and agitation against the sexual presumptions and consequences of the New Poor Law, on the whole this tended to reinforce rather than challenge conventional moral norms: see U. R. Q. Henriques, 'Bastardy and the New Poor Law', *Past and Present* 37 (1967); Clark, *Struggle for the Breeches*, ch. 10; Lisa Forman Cody, 'The Politics of Illegitimacy in an Age of Reform', *Journal of Women's History* 11 (2000).

18. *The Journals and Miscellaneous Notebooks of Ralph Waldo Emerson*, ed. William H. Gilman *et al.*, 16 vols (1960–82), x. 551; *Report of Royal Commission upon the Administration and Operation of the Contagious Diseases Acts*, 2 vols (1871), i. 17; Levine, *Prostitution, Race, and Politics*, 265; cf. Thomas, 'Double Standard', and Mary Lyndon Shanley, *Feminism, Marriage, and the Law in Victorian England* (1989).

19. *The Collected Works of John Stuart Mill*, ed. J. M. Robson *et al.*, 33 vols (1963–91), xxvii. 664; Judith R. Walkowitz, *Prostitution and Victorian Society* (1980), 130; Christabel Pankhurst, *The Great Scourge and How to End It* (1913), 17.

20. Lawrence Stone, *Road to Divorce* (1990), 348–50. Amongst its early eighteenth-century advocates was Lady Mary Wortley Montagu, who, apparently inspired

by the Septennial Act of 1716 (which mandated regular parliamentary elections), seriously argued for a parallel statute to ensure 'that married people should have the liberty of declaring every seventh year whether they choose to continue their state together or not': Robert Halsband, *The Life of Lady Mary Wortley Montagu* (1956), 121–2.

21. William Godwin, *An Enquiry Concerning Political Justice* (1793), bk VIII, ch. vi (quoting 849–51) (cf. 2nd edn, 1796, ii. 498–503; 3rd edn, 1798, ii. 507–11); Mary Wollstonecraft, *The Wrongs of Woman* [1798], esp. ch. xvii, in *The Works of Mary Wollstonecraft*, ed. Janet Todd and Marilyn Butler, 7 vols (1989), vol. 1; William Godwin, *Memoirs of the Author of A Vindication of the Rights of Woman* (1798), chs vii–ix (quoting 103, 114, 154–5).

22. M. L. Bush, *What Is Love? Richard Carlile's Philosophy of Sex* (1998), quoting 62, 70, 147–8, 161; Thomas Holcroft, *Anna St Ives* (1792), esp. letter lxxxii; Richard Payne Knight, *The Progress of Civil Society* (1796), bk III, lines 101–73; Percy Bysshe Shelley, *Queen Mab* (1813), esp. note to v. 189; William Thompson, *Appeal of One Half the Human Race* (1825), esp. 199–202; idem, *Practical Directions* [1830], 232–48; *Works of John Stuart Mill*, x. 310–12; xvii. 1751; xxi. 39–49, 99, 281–98, 375–7, 392; B. Sprague Allen, 'William Godwin's Influence on John Thelwall', *Publications of the Modern Language Association of America* 37 (1922), 680–81; Marilyn Butler, *Peacock Displayed* (1979), 8–11, 104–9, 238–9, 302, and her *Romantics, Rebels and Reactionaries* (1981), 129–37; Iain McCalman, 'Females, Feminism and Free Love', *Labour History* 38 (1980); Barbara Taylor, *Eve and the New Jerusalem* (1983), 32–48, 53–5, 166–8, 173–4, 183–5, 190–216; William St Clair, *The Godwins and the Shelleys* (1989), 96–8, 165–73, 321–2, 338, 355–66, 371–6, 403, 414–22, 497–503; Dolores Dooley, *Equality in Community* (1996); Barbara Taylor, *Mary Wollstonecraft and the Feminist Imagination* (2003), 125 and ch. 6; Kathryn Gleadle, *Radical Writing on Women, 1800–1850* (2002), chs 6–8; *ODNB*, Sophia Catherine Chichester, Marian Evans [*pseud.* George Eliot], Thornton Leigh Hunt, George Henry Lewes, William James Linton, Edward John Trelawny.

23. T. Bell [i.e. John Roberton or Alexander Walker?], *Kalogynomia* (1821), ch. iv (quoting 279, 289; an expanded version of this text was included in Alexander Walker, *Woman Physiologically Considered* (2nd edn, 1840)); Robert Dale Owen, *Moral Physiology* (2nd edn, New York, 1831), 16–17, 43–53; Angus McLaren, *Birth Control in Nineteenth-Century England* (1978). Cf. *Loyola: A Novel* (1784), 220–30.

24. [James Lawrence], *An Essay on the Nair System of Gallantry and Inheritance* [*c.* 1793–9], quoting 14, 16, 32; James Lawrence, *The Empire of the Nairs; or, the Rights of Women*, 4 vols (1811); Jane Rendall, *The Origins of Modern Feminism* (1985), 221–2; *ODNB*. For the German context see Volker Hoffmann, 'Elisa und Robert', in Karl Richter and Jörg Schönert (eds), *Klassik und Moderne* (1983); Isabel V. Hull, *Sexuality, State, and Civil Society in Germany, 1700–1815* (1996), chs 6–7; for his influence in England, Walter Graham, 'Shelley and the Empire of the Nairs', *Publications of the Modern Language Association of*

America 40 (1925); St Clair, *The Godwins and the Shelleys*, 263–4, 338, 341, 357, 471, 544 n. 23; Bush, *What Is Love?*, 35, 43.

25. Shelley, *Queen Mab*, 145, 151 (note to v. 189); *The Clairmont Correspondence*, ed. Marion Kingston Stocking, 2 vols (1995), i. 314–15 (Clairmont was almost certainly illegitimate herself, as was Allegra, her daughter with Lord Byron); Celia Morris Eckhardt, *Fanny Wright* (1984); Lawrence Foster, *Religion and Sexuality* (1981), ch. III; for an English example see Taylor, *Eve and the New Jerusalem*, 252–7.

26. [George Drysdale], *The Elements of Social Science; or, Physical, Sexual and Natural Religion* (4th edn, 1861), quoting 369–70. Helpful introductions to these subjects are provided by Hal D. Sears, *The Sex Radicals* (1977); John D'Emilio and Estelle B. Freedman, *Intimate Matters* (1988), chs 6–7, 10–11; John C. Spurlock, *Free Love* (1988); Joanne E. Passet, *Sex Radicals and the Quest for Women's Equality* (2003); Sandra Ellen Schroer, *State of 'The Union'* (2005); J. Miriam Benn, *The Predicaments of Love* (1992); Sheila Rowbotham, *A New World for Women* (1977); Sheila Rowbotham and Jeffrey Weeks, *Socialism and the New Life* (1977); Mason, *Making of Victorian Sexual Attitudes*; Lucy Bland, *Banishing the Beast* (1995), here quoting 156; Lesley A. Hall, '"Disinterested Enthusiasm for Sexual Misconduct"', *Journal of Contemporary History* 30 (1995); Ivan Crozier, '"All the World's a Stage"', *Journal of the History of Sexuality* 12 (2003); *ODNB*, Janet Chance, Jane Hume Clapperton, Sylvia Pankhurst, Dora Winifred Russell, Herbert George Wells, Amber Blanco White, Rose Lillian Witcop.

Thinking the Unthinkable

1. For literary echoes of this theme see e.g. [John] Dennis, *The Stage Defended* (1726), 19–20; *A New Atalantis* (2nd edn, 1758), i–iii; [Charles Churchill], *The Times* (1764). My use of the term 'sodomy' is restricted to acts between men (or between men and youths).

2. The essential starting-point for seventeenth- and eighteenth-century England remains Alan Bray, *Homosexuality in Renaissance England* (1982), chs 3–4, to whose insights I am, like all subsequent scholars, greatly indebted. Much valuable information is also contained in several articles by Randolph Trumbach (see his *Sex and the Gender Revolution* (1998), 432–4, notes 1–5, 12); Arthur N. Gilbert, 'Buggery and the British Navy', *Journal of Social History* 10 (1976); Antony E. Simpson, 'Masculinity and Control' (New York University Ph.D. thesis, 1984), chs viii–ix; Rictor Norton, *Mother Clap's Molly House* (1992); Peter Bartlett, 'Sodomites in the Pillory in Eighteenth-Century London', *Social & Legal Studies*, 6 (1997); Netta Murray Goldsmith, *The Worst of Crimes* (1998); Matt Cook (ed.), *A Gay History of Britain* (2007). Developments after 1800 are analysed in H. G. Cocks, *Nameless Offences* (2003); Matt Cook, *London and the Culture of Homosexuality, 1885–1914* (2003); Matt Houlbrook, *Queer London* (2005). Two outstanding studies provide an invaluable comparative perspective: Michael

Rocke, *Forbidden Friendships* (1996) and Theo van der Meer, *Sodoms Zaad in Nederland* (1995).

3. J[ohn] D[onne], *Poems* (1633), quoting 38; Richard Godbeer, '"Love Raptures"', *New England Quarterly* 68 (1995), quoting 368; Tom Webster, '"Kiss me with the kisses of his mouth"', in Tom Betteridge (ed.), *Sodomy in Early Modern Europe* (2002); Bruce R. Smith, *Homosexual Desire in Shakespeare's England* (1991); Eve Kosofsky Sedgwick, *Between Men* (1985); Bray, *Homosexuality*, chs 1–3, his 'Homosexuality and the Signs of Male Friendship in Elizabethan England', *History Workshop Journal* 29 (1990), and his *The Friend* (2003); George E. Haggerty, *Men in Love* (1999); Alastair Bellany, *The Politics of Court Scandal* (2002), 254–61; Laura Gowing *et al.* (eds), *Love, Friendship and Faith in Europe, 1300–1800* (2005); Keith Thomas, *The Ends of Life* (2009), ch. 6.

4. *Select Trials ... at the Sessions-House in the Old-Bailey*, 2 vols (1734–5), i. 84; London Metropolitan Archives [hereafter 'LMA'], MJ/SP/1698/12/24: information of William Minton, 7 Nov. 1698; cf. ibid., MJ/SP/1698/12/21–3. (Despite much scholarly interest in Rigby's trial, these documents have not been noticed before. The account of the case printed by order of the court after Rigby's conviction reproduced much of Minton's statement, but omitted amongst other details his 'most blasphemous words': *An Account of the Proceedings Against Capt. Edward Rigby* (1698)); British Library, Harleian MS 6848, fols 185–6, printed in C. F. Tucker Brooke, *The Life of Marlowe* (1930), 99.

5. LMA, MJ/SP/1698/12/24 (the first allusion may have been to Louis XIII; the second was to Peter the Great and his favourite, Alexander Menshikov, who had recently visited England together. Rigby, a naval officer, claimed himself to have seen 'the Czar through a hole att sea actually lye with the said Prince Alexander'); [Tobias Smollett], *The Adventures of Roderick Random* (1748), ch. li. Cf. *A Genuine Narrative of ... James Dalton* (1728), 43; *The Tryal of John Cather* (2nd edn, Dublin, 1751), 8; *A Genuine Narrative of the Conspiracy, by Kather* [1751], 10–11.

6. The text of this work is now known only from the lengthy excerpts quoted in the indictment of its printer, John Purser: The National Archives, Public Record Office, KB 10/29 (Easter 1750), indictment 65 [hereafter 'Purser indictment']. A transcript with an introduction by Hal Gladfelder, 'In Search of Lost Texts', is printed in *Eighteenth-Century Life* 31 (2007).

7. The National Archives, Public Record Office, KB 1/10/5, affidavit of Hugh Morgan (6 May 1751), quoted in Gladfelder, 'Lost Texts', 27 (as 'Petronius, Arbiter, and Aretine'). Cf. also the telling sentiments in [Thomas] Cannon, *Apollo; a Poem* (1744); and see Whitney Davis, 'Homoerotic Art Collection from 1750 to 1920', *Art History* 24 (2001), for the broader circulation of such knowledge and its material artefacts in English and European intellectual circles.

8. *Select Trials*, i. 84 (quoted), ii. 193–8, 210–11 (quoted; italics in original). For a similar outburst see *OBP* t17181205-24: trial of John Bowes and Hugh Ryly, 5 Dec. 1718.

9. LMA, CLA/047/LJ/13/1696 (City Sessions Papers 3 March 1696, information of John Jones). Cf. ibid., City Sessions Papers 16 June 1699 (information of Joseph Thomas).

10. Rix quoted in H. G. Cocks, 'Safeguarding Civility', *Past and Present* 190 (2006), 131; Purser indictment (quoted); LMA, MJ/SP/1698/12/24; [Smollett], *Roderick Random*, ch. li.

11. [Smollett], *Roderick Random*, ch. li; Purser indictment. Contemporary Chinese attitudes towards same-sex relations, and western consciousness of them, are surveyed in Louis Crompton, *Homosexuality and Civilization* (2003), ch. 8.

12. Yale Lewis Walpole Library, MS CHW 69, fols 9–10 (1740). It is striking that even the most well-informed and sensitive modern scholars to have cited this material mistake it for a dialogue between two men, missing the references to passion between women: Hannah Smith and Stephen Taylor, 'Hephaestion and Alexander', *English Historical Review* 124 (2009), 298.

13. Anna Clark, 'Anne Lister's Construction of Lesbian Identity', *Journal of the History of Sexuality* 7 (1996), quoting 35–6, 39; Clara Tuite, 'The Byronic Woman', in Gillian Russell and Clara Tuite (eds), *Romantic Sociability* (2002). Important insights into female same-sex relations and their perception in this period are also provided by Lillian Faderman, *Surpassing the Love of Men* (1981); Simpson, 'Masculinity and Control', 364–75; *I Know My Own Heart: The Diaries of Anne Lister*, ed. Helena Whitbread (1988); *No Priest but Love: The Journals of Anne Lister*, ed. Helena Whitbread (1992); Betty T. Bennett, *Mary Diana Dods* (1991); Emma Donoghue, *Passions Between Women* (1993); Betty Rizzo, *Companions Without Vows* (1994), ch. 9; Patricia Crawford and Sara Mendelson, 'Sexual Identities in Early Modern England', *Gender and History* 7 (1995); Jill Liddington, *Female Fortune* (1998); Elizabeth Susan Wahl, *Invisible Relations* (1999); Harriette Andreadis, *Sappho in Early Modern England* (2001); Valerie Traub, *The Renaissance of Lesbianism in Early Modern England* (2002); Fraser Easton, 'Gender's Two Bodies', *Past and Present* 180 (2003); Bray, *The Friend*, ch. 6; Martha Vicinus, *Intimate Friends* (2004); Sharon Marcus, *Between Women* (2007); Molly McClain, 'Love, Friendship, and Power', *Journal of British Studies* 47 (2008).

14. To the evidence provided by William Henry Hart in *Notes and Queries*, 2nd series, 8 (1859), 65–6, and Gladfelder, 'Lost Texts', should be added [Thomas] Cannon, *A Treatise on Charity. To which is prefix'd, the Author's Retraction* (1753), here quoting 9; Thomas Cannon, *A Close View of Death and it's [sic] Subsequent Immortalities* (1760), here quoting 303; *ODNB*, Robert Cannon. Later in life, though Cannon returned to society, he maintained his prejudice against the 'false and hollow' freethinking of his youth, finding solace instead in constant rereading of Milton and of Edward Young's *Night Thoughts*: see *The Life of Thomas Holcroft*, ed. William Hazlitt, rev. Elbridge Colby, 2 vols (1925), i. 208–11.

15. Though the connections between Bentham's writings and existing ideas about sexual freedom have not previously been appreciated, my understanding of his manuscripts was aided immeasurably by the excerpts printed and discussed in

Jeremy Bentham, *Theory of Legislation*, ed. C. K. Ogden (1931), 473–97; Louis Crompton, 'Jeremy Bentham's Essay on "Paederasty"', *Journal of Homosexuality* 3 (1978) and 4 (1978); Louis Crompton, *Byron and Greek Love* (1985); Lea Campos Boralevi, *Bentham and the Oppressed* (1984). Dates of composition are given in A. Taylor Milne, *Catalogue of the Manuscripts of Jeremy Bentham* (2nd edn, 1962).

16. University College London, MSS of Jeremy Bentham [hereafter cited as 'Bentham MSS'], lxxii. 202; lxxiv. 14, 103; cf. ibid. 49, 75–82, 108–10.

17. Bentham MSS, lxxii. 202; clxi. 444–6; Cf. Cannon's comparison of the two kinds of intercourse: Purser indictment.

18. Bentham MSS, lxxii. 187–8; lxxiii. 100; lxxiv. 24; clxi. 411–33, 462–74.

19. Bentham MSS, clxi. 454–74 (quoting 458, 462).

20. Bentham MSS, lxviii. 10 (quoted); lxxiv. 37, 81, 83, 104 (quoted); clxi. 19, 141 (quoted), 143, 187, 189, 338–443 (quoting 362), 487 (quoted); 'Gamaliel Smith' [i.e. Jeremy Bentham], *Not Paul, but Jesus* (1823), 393–94; Jeremy Bentham, *A Comment on the Commentaries*, ed. J. H. Burns and H. L. A. Hart (1977), 23–8. Indeed, argued Bentham, all the Apostles save Paul had taken the same view, as had several early Christian sects: Bentham MSS, clxi. 338, 387, 434–43. Cf. the aspersions of [Paul-Henry Thiry, baron d'Holbach], *Ecce Homo!* [trans. George Houston] (1799), 58, 139–40, 144–5.

21. Bentham MSS, lxxiv. 169; clxi. 338 (quoted), 371, 384–410, 475–502 (quoting 497, 501).

22. Bentham MSS, lxxii. 188, 191, 195, 196, 197, 201, 203, 204; lxxiii. 100.

23. Bentham MSS, lxviii. 12–13; lxxii. 187–9, 201–3; lxxiv. 3, 6 (quoted), 25, 41, 80, 120, 175–8. For the particular parallel in Bentham's mind between the persecution of religious and of sexual 'nonconformity', see e.g. lxxii. 187–8; lxxiii. 90–100; lxxiv. 1–25, 168, 186–7. For his more general animosity towards all religion (including what he saw as the fraudulent, contemptible teachings of Jesus), see *The Correspondence of Jeremy Bentham*, ed. J. H. Burns *et al.* (1968–), xi. 282–3, 308, 360; James Steintrager, 'Language and Politics', *Bentham Newsletter* 4 (1980); James E. Crimmins, *Secular Utilitarianism* (1990).

24. Bentham MSS, lxxii. 191–3, 201; lxxiv. 5–7, 10, 15–16, 73–4, 86–7. Cf. *The Works of Jeremy Bentham*, ed. John Bowring, 11 vols (Edinburgh, 1843), i. 175; Jeremy Bentham, *Introduction to the Principles of Morals and Legislation*, ed. J. H. Burns and H. L. A. Hart (1970), 159, 281–93.

25. Bentham MSS, lxxii. 191–3 (quoting 192–3); lxxiii. 94–6; lxxiv. 69, 138–46; clxi. 16. Nor was it true of those who took the passive role in sodomy, as was sometimes supposed: lxxii. 193–4; lxxiv. 146.

26. Bentham MSS, lxviii. 14; lxxii. 68, 189, 194–5; lxxiii. 92, 97, 99; lxxiv. 123–33, 136; clxi. 17–18, 276–83; Campos Boralevi, *Bentham and the Oppressed*, 44–52.

27. Bentham MSS, lxxii. 189, 195–200 (quoting 195); lxxiv. 147–59, 197–9; clxi. 16, 284–8. And though this danger might theoretically arise in societies with absolute sexual liberty, the example of Polynesia seemed to show that in practice it did not: lxxii. 196–7; lxxiv. 156.

28. Bentham MSS, lxxii. 189; lxxiii. 92 (quoted), 94. Though he deplored the punishment of consensual sodomy, Bentham did twice, very briefly, consider the question of maintaining some penalty, to assuage social disgust towards the practice (for, 'how void so ever of support on any just grounds, popular discontent is not the less an evil'). His first thought was of banishment, or a fine payable to the London Foundling Hospital. Later he conceived of a purely symbolic statute – requiring for a conviction two witnesses not concerned in the act, which would have rendered it unenforceable in practice: lxxiv. 4; clxi. 18.

29. Bentham MSS, lxx. 271; lxxii. 204 (quoted); lxxiv. 34, 141–2, 145, 195, 206; the origin and development of this phobia is magisterially surveyed in Thomas W. Laqueur, *Solitary Sex* (2003).

30. No ill effects: see Bentham MSS, lxxiv. 123–33, 140, 188–96; clxi. 17–18, 309–22. Should not be termed 'unnatural': see Bentham MSS, lxxii. 197; lxxiv. 31, 32, 89–93; Crompton, *Byron and Greek Love*, 262–4. Natural: see Bentham MSS, lxxii. 199–200; lxxiii. 91. For the sexual sense as equivalent to the other senses, see Bentham MSS, lxxiv. 49–61, 160–61; clxi. 292–8.

31. Bentham MSS, lxxii. 191, 204 (quoted); lxxiv. 9, 189, 206–11; clxi. 17. (Though occasionally he categorized adultery and polygamy, more conventionally, as actions 'productive of mischief' (lxxiv. 35–6, 72; *Introduction to the Principles of Morals*, 256–7); and once, in an early note, alluded in similar terms to homosexual acts (xcvi. 197).)

32. Bentham MSS, lxxiv. 77 (quoted), 132–7, 190–91; 200–203, 214–22 (quoting 219); clxi. 6–14 (quoting 6), 18 (quoted), 190 (quoted), 336–7; *Jeremy Bentham's Economic Writings*, ed. W. Stark, 3 vols (1952–4), iii. 362; Norman E. Himes, 'Jeremy Bentham and the Genesis of English Neo-Malthusianism', *Economic History* 3 (1936). For his remarkable notes on sexual techniques, variations, tastes, and aids, see Bentham MSS, lxxiv. 33–4.

33. See Bentham MSS, lxxiv. 4; clxi. 1–19; Crompton, *Byron and Greek Love*, 269–74; and for other indications in the manuscripts of intended publication in various forms, Campos Boralevi, *Bentham and the Oppressed*, 63, 67–8, 79 n. 194; Bentham, *Comment*, xxxiii–xxxvi. The place of these published and unpublished materials within Bentham's general critique of Christianity is considered in Crimmins, *Secular Utilitarianism*, chs 7–9.

34. See e.g. Bentham MSS, lxxii. 68, 188; lxxiv. 4–5, 21, 23, 38, 71, 168, 200; clxi. 14.

35. Bentham MSS, lxxii. 188 (quoted); lxxiv. 220–22; British Library, Additional MS 33551, pp. 327–8, printed in Mary P. Mack, *Jeremy Bentham* (1962), 213.

36. Bentham MSS, lxx. 183; *Correspondence of Jeremy Bentham*, ii. 302–3, 324; vii. 574; ix. 22–3; *Dictionary of National Biography* (1885–1901), James Mill, Francis Place; *The Collected Works of John Stuart Mill*, ed. J. M. Robson *et al.*, 33 vols (1963–91), x. 413–17; xviii. 255 (quoted; and cf. *The Complete Works of Harriet Taylor Mill*, ed. Jo Ellen Jacobs and Pamela Harms Payne (1998), 225–6); Campos Boralevi, *Bentham and the Oppressed*, 68–9.

37. Bentham MSS, lxxiv. 3 (quoted); *Notes and Queries*, 1st ser., vii. 66–7 (1853);

12th ser., v. 143–4 (1919); *Don Leon* (1866 edn); Louis Crompton, '*Don Leon*, Byron, and Homosexual Law Reform', *Journal of Homosexuality* 8 (1983). Cf. H. G. Cocks, 'Making the Sodomite Speak', *Gender and History* 18 (2006).

Enlightened Attitudes

1. For suggestive examples see Willem Elias, 'Het Spinozistisch Erotisme van Adriaan Beverland', *Tijdschrift voor de Studie van de Verlichting* 2 (1974); Margaret C. Jacob, *The Radical Enlightenment* (1981), 228–30; R. de Smet, *Hadrianus Beverlandus* (1988); Theo van der Meer, *Sodoms Zaad in Nederland* (1988), esp. ch. vi; Nicholas Davidson, 'Theology, Nature and the Law', in Trevor Dean and K. J. P. Lowe (eds), *Crime, Society and the Law in Renaissance Italy* (1994) and his 'Sodomy in Early Modern Venice', in Tom Betteridge (ed.), *Sodomy in Early Modern Europe* (2002); Isabel V. Hull, *Sexuality, State, and Civil Society in Germany, 1700–1815* (1996); Jonathan I. Israel, *Radical Enlightenment* (2001), 86–9, 94–6, 630–31, 674, 676 and his *Enlightenment Contested* (2006), 366, 579–89, 601–2, 809–10; Edward Muir, *The Culture Wars of the Late Renaissance* (2007).

2. In this case particularly by French and Dutch trends. Examples of the latter include the diffusion of Beverland's works in English circles, as is evident from the catalogues of early eighteenth-century private libraries; and the unidentified 'book on Sodomy' sent by Samuel to Jeremy Bentham from Rotterdam in 1779 (*The Correspondence of Jeremy Bentham*, ed. J. H. Burns *et al.* (1968–), ii. 324), at an early stage of his thinking on the subject – this must have been [Abraham Perrenot], *Bedenkingen over het Straffen van Zekere Schandelyke Misdaad* (Amsterdam, etc., 1777), whose arguments on biblical, historical, and rational grounds adumbrated some of Bentham's own views. For English influences upon continental thought see e.g. Norman L. Torrey, *Voltaire and the English Deists* (1930); and, more generally, Israel, *Radical Enlightenment* and *Enlightenment Contested*.

3. I thus disagree with the arguments put forward on this point by Israel, *Radical Enlightenment* and *Enlightenment Contested*: cf. Anthony J. La Vopa, 'A New Intellectual History?', *Historical Journal* 52 (2009).

4. [Francis Hutcheson], *An Inquiry into the Original of Our Ideas of Beauty and Virtue* (1725), 182–90.

5. For modern interpretations of some of these issues, see e.g. *Report of the Committee on Homosexual Offences and Prostitution* (1957); Graham Hughes, 'Morals and the Criminal Law', *Yale Law Journal* 71 (1962); H. L. A. Hart, *Law, Liberty and Morality* (1963); H. L. A. Hart, 'Social Solidarity and the Enforcement of Morality', *University of Chicago Law Review* 35 (1967); H. L. A. Hart, 'Between Utility and Rights', *Columbia Law Review* 79 (1979); Patrick Devlin, *The Enforcement of Morals* (1965); Ronald Dworkin, *Taking Rights Seriously* (1977), chs 10–13; Tony Honoré, *Sex Law* (1978); Ruth Gavison, 'Privacy and

the Limits of Law', *Yale Law Journal* 89 (1980); Anne B. Goldstein, 'History, Homosexuality, and Political Values', *Yale Law Journal* 97 (1988); Joel Feinberg, *The Moral Limits of the Criminal Law*, 4 vols (1984–8); Robert P. George, *Making Men Moral* (1993); John Finnis, 'The Good of Marriage and the Morality of Sexual Relations', *American Journal of Jurisprudence* 42 (1997); A. P. Simester and Andrew von Hirsch, 'Rethinking the Offence Principle', *Legal Theory* 8 (2002); Andrew Bainham and Belinda Brooks-Gordon, 'Reforming the Law on Sexual Offences', in Belinda Brooks-Gordon *et al.* (eds), *Sexuality Repositioned* (2004); Gerald Dworkin, 'Moral Paternalism', *Law and Philosophy* 24 (2005); Nicholas Bamforth and David A. J. Richards, *Patriarchal Religion, Sexuality, and Gender* (2008); Martha C. Nussbaum, *From Disgust to Humanity* (2010). In the United States the question of how far sexual freedom extended *historically* has also been fiercely debated in recent decades, as part of legal battles over what protection the Constitution should afford to equivalent behaviours in the present.

CHAPTER 3: THE CULT OF SEDUCTION

1. [Robert Gould], *Love Given O're* (1682), quoting 5.
2. For convenient overviews see e.g. Anne Carson, 'Putting Her in Her Place', in David Halperin *et al.* (eds), *Before Sexuality* (1990); Sarah B. Pomeroy, *Goddesses, Whores, Wives, and Slaves* (1995 edn); James A. Brundage, *Law, Sex, and Society in Medieval Europe* (1987); Alcuin Blamires *et al.* (eds), *Woman Defamed and Woman Defended* (1992); Ian Maclean, *The Renaissance Notion of Woman* (1980); Margaret R. Sommerville, *Sex and Subjection* (1995); Anthony Fletcher, *Gender, Sex and Subordination in England 1500–1800* (1995), chs 3–4; Merry E. Wiesner-Hanks, *Christianity and Sexuality in the Early Modern World* (2000).
3. *The Diary of Samuel Pepys*, ed. Robert Latham and William Matthews, 11 vols (1970–83), v. 17 (16 Jan. 1664); Universiteitsbibliotheek Leiden, MS BPL 1325, fol. 149^r; Frances Harris, *Transformations of Love* (2003), 256.
4. Ian Watt, *The Rise of the Novel* (1957), quoting 160–62. On the emergence of these themes see the brilliant pioneering essays by Patricia Meyer Spacks, '"Ev'ry Woman is at Heart a Rake"', *Eighteenth-Century Studies* 8 (1974) and Nancy F. Cott, 'Passionlessness', *Signs* 4 (1978); many good examples are given in Madeleine Blondel, *Images de la femme dans le roman anglais de 1740 à 1771* (1976) and A. D. Harvey, *Sex in Georgian England* (1994), chs 2–3.

Scientific Explanations?

1. Though for stimulating treatments of related issues see e.g. Edmund Leites, *The Puritan Conscience and Modern Sexuality* (1986); Harold M. Weber, *The Restoration Rake-Hero* (1986); Ruth Perry, 'Colonizing the Breast', *Journal of the History of Sexuality* 2 (1991).

2. Thomas Laqueur, *Making Sex* (1990).

3. Ibid., quoting 11, 20, 23 (italics in original). Though Laqueur's argument has been much criticized, no alternative explanation has been advanced: for representative examples, see Tim Hitchcock, *English Sexualities, 1700-1800* (1997), 111; Robert B. Shoemaker, *Gender in English Society, 1650-1850* (1998), ch. 3; Elizabeth Foyster, *Manhood in Early Modern England* (1999), 212-13; Karen Harvey, 'The Century of Sex?', *Historical Journal* 45 (2002). The fullest recent description of the general shift can be found in Anthony Fletcher, *Gender, Sex and Subordination in England 1500-1800* (1995), esp. ch. 19 – though even this sensitive and insightful account ultimately explains it only as the 'impact of bio-medical discourses and the development of a romantic notion of womanhood' (392).

The Rise of the Libertine

1. *Certayne Sermons, or Homelies, Appoynted by the Kynges Maiestie* (1547), sig. Uii; Dorothy Leigh, *The Mothers Blessing* (1616), 33; Judith M. Bennett, 'Writing Fornication', *Transactions of the Royal Historical Society* 13 (2003), 146-7; James Durham, *A Practical Exposition of the X Commandments* (1675), 355; Richard Baxter, *A Christian Directory* (1673), 395.

2. For this and the following paragraphs see esp. Bernard Capp, *When Gossips Meet* (2003), chs 4, 6 (here quoting 227); Laura Gowing, *Common Bodies* (2003), chs 2, 3. Cf. G. R. Quaife, *Wanton Wenches and Wayward Wives* (1979), *passim*; Steve Hindle, 'The Shaming of Margaret Knowlsey', *Continuity and Change* 9 (1994); Garthine Walker, 'Re-reading Rape and Sexual Violence in Early Modern England', *Gender and History* 10 (1998).

3. *The Diary of Samuel Pepys*, ed. Robert Latham and William Mathews, 11 vols (1970-83) v. 37, 322, 351; vi. 20, 40; Arthur Bryant, *Samuel Pepys*, 3 vols (1933-8), iii. 166-7, 386. For the element of female barter, acceptance, and complicity within this male-dominated social and sexual context, cf. Faramerz Dabhoiwala, 'The Pattern of Sexual Immorality', in Paul Griffiths and Mark S. R. Jenner (eds), *Londinopolis* (2000).

4. See esp. Gowing, *Common Bodies*, quoting 61; Anna Clark, *Women's Silence, Men's Violence* (1987); Antony E. Simpson, 'Vulnerability and the Age of Female Consent', in G. S. Rousseau and Roy Porter (eds), *Sexual Underworlds of the Enlightenment* (1987); Randolph Trumbach, *Sex and the Gender Revolution* (1998), esp. ch. 7; Tim Meldrum, *Domestic Service and Gender 1660-1750* (2000), ch. 4; Martin Ingram, 'Child Sexual Abuse in Early Modern England', in Michael J. Braddick and John Walter, *Negotiating Power* (2001); Capp, *When Gossips Meet*, ch. 4; Anthony Fletcher, *Gender, Sex and Subordination in England 1500-1800* (1995), 93-4, and the literature cited there.

5. [Henry Fielding], *Ovid's Art of Love Paraphrased* (1747), quoting 31, 39, 75, 77; Ian Donaldson, *The Rapes of Lucretia* (1982), ch. 5; A. D. Harvey, *Sex in*

Georgian England (1994), ch. 4; Simon Dickie, 'Fielding's Rape Jokes', *Review of English Studies* 61 (2010).

6. See e.g. *Dives and Pauper*, ed. Priscilla Heath Barnum (Early English Text Society, 1976–2004), i. 2. 67–71; [John Milton], *An Apology against a Pamphlet* (1642), 18; Cynthia B. Herrup, *A House in Gross Disorder* (1999); Simon Blackburn, *Lust* (2004), chs 3–4; Christine Peters, *Women in Early Modern Britain, 1450–1640* (2004), ch. 3.

7. *The Complete Poems of John Wilmot, Earl of Rochester*, ed. David M. Vieth (1968), quoting 48, 60–61; Harold Love, *English Clandestine Satire 1660–1702* (2004), 61–2 and ch. 6 (quoting 213); John Harold Wilson, *Court Satires of the Restoration* (1976), *passim*; Buchanan Sharp, 'Popular Political Opinion in England 1660–1685', *History of European Ideas* 10 (1989); Rachel Weil, 'Sometimes a Sceptre is Only a Sceptre', in Lynn Hunt (ed.), *The Invention of Pornography* (1993); Anna Bryson, *From Courtesy to Civility* (1998), ch. 7; George Southcombe and Grant Tapsell, *Restoration Politics, Religion and Culture* (2010), 150–60.

8. Capp, *When Gossips Meet*, 145.

9. For typical examples, see *A Brief Collection of some Memorandums* (1689), 3; *Athenian Mercury*, ii/13 (1691), question 3; [John Dunton], *The Night-Walker* i/1 (1696), preface; *God's Judgements against Whoring* (1697), 45; J[ean] Gailhard, *Four Tracts* (1699), 2.

10. [Jonathan Swift], *A Project for the Advancement of Religion* (1709), 10–11; *The Guardian*, no. 45 (2 May 1713).

11. *Defoe's Review*, ed. Arthur Wellesley Secord, 9 vols (1938), iii. 132 (5 Nov. 1706) (cf [Daniel Defoe], *Conjugal Lewdness* (1727), 288–9; *Marriage Promoted* (1690), 27); Henry Fielding, *The Covent-Garden Journal* [1752], ed. Bertrand A. Goldgar (1988), quoting nos 20 and 57; *Critical Remarks on Sir Charles Grandison* (1754), 31.

12. Robert Holloway, *The Rat-Trap* [1773], 56–7; Edward Barry, *Theological … Essays* [1790?], 75; *Advice to Unmarried Women* (1791), 33; William Dodd, *An Account of the Rise, Progress and Present State of the Magdalen Charity* (1761), preface; *Reflections Arising from the Immorality of the Present Age* (1756), 45.

Rakes and Harlots

1. Francis Bacon, *New Atlantis*, published with his *Sylva Sylvarum* (1627), quoting 27; Ruth Mazo Karras, *Common Women* (1996); Anne M. Haselkorn, *Prostitution in Elizabethan and Jacobean Comedy* (1983).

2. [John Dunton], *The Night-Walker* (1696–7), quoting i/3, sig. [A3r]; i/4, p. 22; ii/3, p. 13; ii/4, sig. [A3v]; cf. ibid., i/1, sigs A2ʳ–Bʳ; *Account of the Societies for Reformation of Manners*, 93–7; A. M., *The Reformed Gentleman* (1693); [John Dunton], *The Hazard of a Death-Bed-Repentance* (1708).

3. *The Spectator*, ed. Donald F. Bond, 5 vols (1965), esp. nos 182 (quoted), 190

(quoted), 208, 266 (quoted), 274, 276, 528; *Original and Genuine Letters sent to the Tatler and Spectator*, 2 vols (1725), i. 54.

4. 'Capt. Johnson', *The History of . . . Eliz. Mann* (1724), quoting iv–v, 43–5; [Daniel Defoe?], *Some Considerations upon Street-Walkers* [1726], quoting 8; *Spectator*, ed. Bond, quoting no. 266; cf. also *Defoe's Review*, ed. Arthur Wellesley Secord, 9 vols (1938), ix. [84] (6 Jan. 1713); Joseph [Wilcocks], *The Righteous Magistrate* (1723), 13.

5. *The 'Prentice's Tragedy* [1700?]; *An Excellent Ballad of George Barnwell* (various edns); George Lillo, *The London Merchant* (1731), quoting Act I, scene 2 and Act IV, scene 2; *ODNB*, George Lillo.

6. Henry Fielding, *The Covent-Garden Journal* [1752], ed. Bertrand A. Goldgar (1988), 393, 415 (cf. also 400–401); William Dodd, *A Sermon on St Matthew* (1759), 12; Robert Holloway, *The Rat-Trap* [1773], 57–8. Cf. *The Holy Penitent* (1740), 3; Edward Cobden, *A Persuasive to Chastity* (1749); *Gentleman's Magazine*, xix. 125–7 (Mar. 1749).

7. *The Adventurer*, nos 86, 134–6 (1753–4); *The Rambler*, nos 170–71 (1751); [William Dodd], *The Sisters*, 2 vols (1754); Elizabeth Inchbald, *Nature and Art*, 2 vols (1796); *Innocence Betrayed, or the Perjured Lover*, quoting Penrith edn [*c.* 1800], 3–5.

8. *The New Oxford Book of Eighteenth-Century Verse*, ed. Roger Lonsdale (1984), 683.

9. [John Cleland], *Memoirs of a Woman of Pleasure*, 2 vols (1749) and his *The Case of the Unfortunate Bosavern Penlez* (1749), quoting 13; cf. Ruth Bernard Yeazell, *Fictions of Modesty* (1991), ch. 7, and, for nineteenth-century examples, Eric Trudgill, *Madonnas and Magdalens* (1976), ch. 11.

10. Faramerz Dabhoiwala, 'The Pattern of Sexual Immorality', in Paul Griffiths and Mark S. R. Jenner (eds), *Londinopolis* (2000), quoting 97; *OBP* t17300704-40; Tanya Evans, *'Unfortunate Objects': Lone Mothers in Eighteenth-Century London* (2005).

11. See e.g. Evans, *'Unfortunate Objects'*; *OED*, 'unfortunate'; *OBP*, 'unfortunate' and 'misfortunate'.

Feminine Perspectives

1. Excellent introductions to the broader context include Jane Rendall, *The Origins of Modern Feminism* (1985); Sarah Knott and Barbara Taylor (eds), *Women, Gender and Enlightenment* (2005); Karen O'Brien, *Women and Enlightenment in Eighteenth-Century Britain* (2009).

2. For the themes of this and the following paragraphs see esp. David Roberts, *The Ladies: Female Patronage of Restoration Drama* (1989); Elizabeth Howe, *The First English Actresses* (1992); Derek Hughes, *English Drama 1660–1700* (1996) and his 'Rape on the Restoration Stage', *The Eighteenth Century* 46 (2005). For the common treatment of rape as a metaphor for religious martyrdom and political

tyranny in earlier literature, see esp. Ian Donaldson, *The Rapes of Lucretia* (1982); Anna Swärdh, *Rape and Religion in English Renaissance Literature* (2003).

3. Quoting Act I, scene 3; Act II, scene 1.

4. Nicholas Rowe, *The Fair Penitent* (1703), quoting Act I, scene 2; Act II, scene 1; Act III, scene 1; Act V, scene 1; Epilogue; idem, *The Tragedy of Jane Shore* (1714), quoting Act I, scene 2; Maria M. Scott, *Re-Presenting 'Jane' Shore* (2005).

5. Thomas Otway, *The Orphan* (1680), Act I, final scene; Act III, scene 1. Cf. Susan Staves, *Players' Scepters* (1979), esp. ch. 5; Hughes, *English Drama*, esp. ch. 1.

6. For introductions to the themes of the following paragraphs, see e.g. Katharine M. Rogers, *Feminism in Eighteenth-Century England* (1982); Jane Spencer, *The Rise of the Woman Novelist* (1988); Jacqueline Pearson, *The Prostituted Muse* (1988); Cheryl Turner, *Living by the Pen* (1992); Ros Ballaster, *Seductive Forms* (1992); Elizabeth Eger (ed.), *Women, Writing and the Public Sphere, 1730–1830* (2001); Norma Clarke, *The Rise and Fall of the Woman of Letters* (2004); Susan Staves, *A Literary History of Women's Writing in Britain, 1660–1789* (2006); Sarah Apetrei, *Women, Feminism and Religion in Early Enlightenment England* (2010).

7. [Aphra Behn], *The Revenge* (1680), quoting Act II, scene 2; [Sarah Fyge], *The Female Advocate* (1686), quoting 4, 10–11, 21.

8. Samuel Richardson, *Clarissa, or The History of a Young Lady* [1747–8], ed. Angus Ross (1985), quoting preface; Jane Austen, *Northanger Abbey* (1818), quoting ch. 5. On the definition and evolution of the genre see esp. Ian Watt, *The Rise of the Novel* (1957), ch. 1; Michael McKeon, *The Origins of the English Novel 1600–1740* (1987); J. Paul Hunter, *Before Novels: The Cultural Contexts of Eighteenth-Century English Fiction* (1990); Brean S. Hammond, *Professional Imaginative Writing in England, 1670–1740* (1997); William B. Warner, *Licensing Entertainment* (1998).

9. Delarivier Manley, *New Atalantis* [1709], ed. Ros Ballaster (1991), quoting 45; Spencer, *Rise of the Woman Novelist*, ch. 4.

10. Mary Astell, *Some Reflections upon Marriage* (1700), quoting 65, 68, 74–5; [Margaret Cavendish], Duchess of Newcastle, *The Convent of Pleasure*, Act I, scene 2, in her *Plays Never Before Printed* (1668); [Damaris Masham], *Occasional Thoughts* (1705), 154–6; [John Taylor], *The Womens Sharpe Revenge* (1640), 7–9, 119–20, 130–37. Cf. Thomas Killigrew, *Comedies and Tragedies* (1664), 339, 396–7 (*Thomaso*, part I, Act II, scene 4; part II, Act I, scene 5).

11. See e.g. Alcuin Blamires, *The Case for Women in Medieval Culture* (1997), 38, 47–8, 132, 135, 138–42, 153–7; the fascinating discussion in *Dives and Pauper*, ed. Priscilla Heath Barnum, 2 vols (Early English Text Society, 1976–2004), i. 2. 71–95; and, most famously, the prologue of Chaucer's Wife of Bath (*The Complete Works of Geoffrey Chaucer*, ed. Walter W. Skeat (1957 edn), 573–4).

12. In addition to the works cited in note 6 above, cf. e.g. Kathryn Shevelow, *Women and Print Culture* (1989); Helen Berry, *Gender, Society and Print Culture in Late-Stuart England* (2003); Susan E. Whyman, *The Pen and the People* (2009).

13. *The London Journal*, no. 359 (11 June 1726). The discovery of the woman's body

had previously been widely reported: see e.g. *Daily Post*, no. 2088 (3 June 1726). Even if the letter was spurious, or edited for publication, its form and content illustrate how distinctive and pervasive the conventions of such narratives had become, already by the mid 1720s.

14. *The Rambler*, no. 18 (1750).

Novel Attitudes

1. For its popularity, and its deeper sexual and political resonances, see e.g. Susan Staves, 'British Seduced Maidens', *Eighteenth-Century Studies* 14 (1980–81); Anna Clark, 'The Politics of Seduction in English Popular Culture, 1748–1848', in Jean Radford (ed.), *The Progress of Romance* (1986); Tiffany Potter, 'Genre and Cultural Disruption', *English Studies in Canada* 29 (2003); Katherine Binhammer, *The Seduction Narrative in Britain, 1747–1800* (2009); Toni Bowers, *Force or Fraud: British Seduction Stories and the Problem of Resistance 1660–1760* (2011); and the works cited in note 7 below.

2. [Samuel Richardson], *Letters Written to and for Particular Friends* (1741; but begun before *Pamela*, and one of the inspirations for it), quoting 30, 94, 131, 179, 182, 200–201; *The Correspondence of Samuel Richardson*, ed. Anna Laetitia Barbauld, 6 vols (1804), iv. 292–3.

3. T. C. Duncan Eaves and Ben D. Kimpel, *Samuel Richardson* (1971), 87–8; *London Journal* (6 Apr. 1723), 3; Westminster Public Library, E.2576, no. 103 (1724), cited in Randolph Trumbach, 'Modern Prostitution and Gender in *Fanny Hill*', in G. S. Rousseau and Roy Porter, *Sexual Underworlds of the Enlightenment* (1987), 76; *The Proceedings at the Sessions of the Peace . . . against Francis Charteris, Esq.* (1730), quoting 4.

4. [Richardson], *Letters Written to . . . Friends*, 79–84.

5. Samuel Richardson, *Pamela; or, Virtue Rewarded* [1740], ed. Thomas Keymer and Alice Wakely (2001), quoting 108, 110, 134–5, 137.

6. Ibid., 213; Samuel Richardson, *Clarissa, or The History of a Young Lady* [1747–8], ed. Angus Ross (1985), quoting the list of characters.

7. See e.g. Robert Palfrey Utter and Gwendolyn Bridges Needham, *Pamela's Daughters* (1936); Eaves and Kimpel, *Richardson*, ch. xxiv; Margaret Anne Doody, *A Natural Passion* (1974), ch. xiv; Rita Goldberg, *Sex and Enlightenment* (1984); Ruth Perry, 'Clarissa's Daughters', *Women's Writing* 1 (1994); Rodney Hessinger, '"Insidious Murderers of Female Innocence"', in Merril D. Smith, *Sex and Sexuality in Early America* (1998); Thomas Keymer and Peter Sabor, *Pamela in the Marketplace* (2005).

8. *Fragment of a Novel written by Jane Austen*, ed. R. W. Chapman (1925), ch. 8. It is worth remembering that *Sir Charles Grandison* was Austen's favourite novel.

9. *Boswell in Extremes, 1776–1778*, ed. Charles McC. Weis and Frederick A. Pottle (1970), 180; cf. Yale Lewis Walpole Library, Hanbury Williams MSS, vol. 68, fol. 74ʳ (1745); Richardson, *Clarissa*, ed. Ross, letter 115.

10. 'Courtney Melmoth' [i.e. Samuel Jackson Pratt], *The Pupil of Pleasure*, 2 vols (1776), quoting i. 2; *Byron's Letters and Journals*, ed. Leslie A. Marchand, 13 vols (1973–94), iii. 108 (1813).

11. See e.g. Peter Sabor, 'Richardson, Henry Fielding, and Sarah Fielding', in Thomas Keymer and Jon Mee (eds), *The Cambridge Companion to English Literature 1740–1830* (2004); Eaves and Kimpel, *Richardson*, 302; *Boswell's Life of Johnson*, ed. George Birkbeck Hill and L. F. Powell, 6 vols (1934–50), ii. 495 (quoted).

12. Henry Fielding, *Tom Jones* (1749), quoting bk XIV, ch. iv; Cf. William Park, 'Fielding and Richardson', *Publications of the Modern Language Association of America* 81 (1966); Eaves and Kimpel, *Richardson*, 134, 297, 303–5; *The Correspondence of Henry and Sarah Fielding*, ed. Martin C. Battestin and Clive T. Probyn (1993), 70–1.

13. Henry Fielding, *Amelia* (1751), bk I, chs 6–9 (quoting ch. 8).

14. Ibid., quoting bk VII, chs 7 and 9.

15. See e.g. *Selected Letters of Samuel Richardson*, ed. John Carroll (1964), 141, 272–5; Eaves and Kimpel, *Richardson*, 366, 370 (quoted); *Correspondence of Samuel Richardson*, ed. Barbauld, iii. 7–10.

16. *Correspondence of Samuel Richardson*, ed. Barbauld, quoting vi. 42–4, 62–6, 75; [Francis Plummer], *A Candid Examination of the History of Sir Charles Grandison* (3rd edn, 1755), quoting 49. Cf. *The Spectator*, ed. Donald F. Bond, 5 vols (1965), no. 154; Eaves and Kimpel, *Richardson*, 322, 354, 369, 375; Samuel Richardson, *The History of Sir Charles Grandison* [1753–4], ed. Jocelyn Harris, 3 vols (1972), 'A Concluding Note by the Editor'; [Joseph Priestley], *Considerations for the Use of Young Men* [1778], 20–22.

17. Mark Philp, *Godwin's Political Justice* (1986), 177 n. 5; *ODNB*, (John) Bellenden Ker; cf. Anthony Fletcher, *Gender, Sex and Subordination in England 1500–1800* (1995), 342–6.

CHAPTER 4: THE NEW WORLD OF MEN AND WOMEN
Politeness and Sensibility

1. See e.g. John Dwyer, *Virtuous Discourse* (1987), esp. ch. 5; Michele Cohen, *Fashioning Masculinity* (1996); Philip Carter, *Men and the Emergence of Polite Society* (2001); Ingrid H. Tague, *Women of Quality* (2002); Sarah Apetrei, *Women, Feminism and Religion in Early Enlightenment England* (2010).

2. John Millar, *The Origin of the Distinction of Ranks* (1779), quoting 104–5; David Hume, *Essays Moral, Political, and Literary*, ed. Eugene F. Miller (1987), 131; Karen O'Brien, *Women and Enlightenment in Eighteenth-Century Britain* (2009), ch. 3; *The Works of Mary Wollstonecraft*, ed. Janet Todd and Marilyn Butler, 7 vols (1989), quoting v. 124–5.

3. Christopher Wren, *Parentalia* (1750), 261; Carolyn C. Lougee, *Le Paradis des Femmes* (1976); Ian Maclean, *Woman Triumphant* (1977); Anna Bryson, *From*

Courtesy to Civility (1998), 126–8; Siep Stuurman, 'The Deconstruction of Gender', in Sarah Knott and Barbara Taylor (eds), *Women, Gender and Enlightenment* (2005).

4. [William Ramesey], *The Gentlemans Companion* (1672), 9–10.

5. *The Spectator*, ed. Donald F. Bond, 5 vols (1965), nos 57, 433.

6. Benjamin Rand, *The Life, Unpublished Letters, and Philosophical Regimen of Anthony, Earl of Shaftesbury* (1900), 337; [James Forrester], *The Polite Philosopher* (1734), 49; 'Simon Wagstaff' [i.e. Jonathan Swift], *A Complete Collection of Genteel and Ingenious Conversation* (1738), xxix–xxx; Hume, *Essays*, ed. Miller, 134 ('Of the Rise and Progress of the Arts and Sciences').

7. *Spectator*, ed. Bond, nos 433–4; William Alexander, *The History of Women*, 2 vols (1779), i. 103. For many other examples, see Mary Catherine Moran, ' "The Commerce of the Sexes" ', in Frank Trentmann (ed.), *Paradoxes of Civil Society* (2000); Silvia Sebastiani, ' "Race", Women and Progress in the Scottish Enlightenment', in Knott and Taylor (eds), *Women, Gender*; O'Brien, *Women and Enlightenment*, esp. ch. 2.

8. *Byron's Letters and Journals*, ed. Leslie A. Marchand, 13 vols (1973–94), iii. 109; *Selected Letters of Samuel Richardson*, ed. John Carroll (1964), 82, 189; [Samuel Richardson], *Letters Written to and for Particular Friends* (1741), 94; Samuel Richardson, *Clarissa, or The History of a Young Lady* [1747–8], ed. Angus Ross (1985), Preface (quoted), letter 499. Cf. *Critical Remarks on Sir Charles Grandison* (1754), 16; Sarah Pennington, *An Unfortunate Mother's Advice to her Absent Daughters* (1761), 97.

9. Quoting Samuel Richardson, *Pamela; or, Virtue Rewarded* [1740], ed. Thomas Keymer and Alice Wakely (2001), 6, 408.

10. Hume, *Essays*, ed. Miller, 134; John Brown, *On the Female Character and Education* (1765), 15. Cf. Ingrid H. Tague, 'Love, Honor, and Obedience', *Journal of British Studies* 40 (2001), 87–9.

11. *Spectator*, ed. Bond, no. 156; 'Anne Frances Randall' [i.e. Mary Robinson], *A Letter to the Women of England* (1799), 76; Hannah More, *Strictures on the Modern System of Female Education*, 2 vols (1799), i. 27–8; *The Complete Letters of Lady Mary Wortley Montagu*, ed. Robert Halsband, 3 vols (1965–7), i. 35; *The Guardian*, no. 45 (2 May 1713). Useful introductions to the prescriptive literature are Fenela Ann Childs, 'Prescriptions for Manners in English Courtesy Literature, 1690–1760, and their Social Implications' (University of Oxford D. Phil. thesis, 1984) and Vivien Jones, *Women in the Eighteenth Century* (1990).

12. An 1803 trial report, quoted in Lawrence Stone, *Road to Divorce* (1990), 290. Cf. e.g. Janet Todd, *Sensibility* (1986); John Mullan, *Sentiment and Sociability* (1988), ch. 5; G. J. Barker-Benfield, *The Culture of Sensibility* (1992); Carter, *Men and the Emergence of Polite Society*, chs 2–3.

13. John Brown, *On the Female Character and Education* (1765), quoting 7, 10; William Hazeland, *A Sermon Preached in the Chapel of the Asylum* (1761), 4; for Rousseau and English thought see e.g. Ruth Bernard Yeazell, *Fictions of Modesty* (1991), ch. 2; Barbara Taylor, *Mary Wollstonecraft and the Feminist Imagination* (2003).

14. [Mary Hays], *Appeal to the Men of Great Britain in Behalf of Women* (1798), 234; *Works of Mary Wollstonecraft*, ed. Todd and Butler, v. 77, 195; Lucy Aikin, *Epistles on Women* (1810), 63.

15. *Works of Mary Wollstonecraft*, ed. Todd and Butler, v. 77, 208 (cf. ibid., 196, 209–10, 265, but also Mary Poovey, *The Proper Lady and the Woman Writer* (1984), ch. 2); [Hays], *Appeal*, 231–2; Gina Luria Walker, 'Mary Hays (1759–1843)', in Knott and Taylor (eds), *Women, Gender*; Vivien Jones, '"The Tyranny of the Passions"', in Sally Ledger *et al.* (eds), *Political Gender* (1994). An outstandingly perceptive treatment of these themes is Taylor, *Mary Wollstonecraft*.

Nature and Nurture

1. [William Ramesey], *The Gentlemans Companion* (1672), 13.

2. Alexander Pope, *Of the Characters of Women: An Epistle To a Lady* (1735), line 216.

3. Samuel Richardson, *Clarissa, or The History of a Young Lady* [1747–8], ed. Angus Ross (1985), letter 165; cf. Marlene LeGates, 'The Cult of Womanhood in Eighteenth-Century Thought', *Eighteenth-Century Studies* 10 (1976); Mary Poovey, *The Proper Lady and the Woman Writer* (1984).

4. See esp. the brilliant analyses of Vivien Jones, 'The Seductions of Conduct', in Roy Porter and Marie Mulvey Roberts (eds), *Pleasure in the Eighteenth Century* (1996) and Ruth Bernard Yeazell, *Fictions of Modesty* (1991).

5. Daniel Defoe, *The Fortunes and Misfortunes of the Famous Moll Flanders* [1722], ed. David Blewett (1989), quoting 56–7, 61, 65.

6. Ibid., quoting 39, 63–4.

7. [John Locke], *Some Thoughts Concerning Education* (1693), § 1.

8. 'Philogamus', *The Present State of Matrimony* (1739), 17–18; Samuel Richardson, *Pamela; or, Virtue Rewarded* [1740], ed. Thomas Keymer and Alice Wakely (2001), quoting 242 (cf 443–4); Richardson, *Clarissa*, ed. Ross, quoting letter 157.1 and conclusion.

9. *Advice to Unmarried Women* (1791), 36–7. Cf. Robert Holloway, *The Rat-Trap* [1773], 97.

10. *Innocence Betrayed, or the Perjured Lover* [c. 1800], quoting [2]; Francis Kelly Maxwell, *A Sermon Preached at Different Churches* (1763), quoting 14; *London Chronicle*, 1 Feb. 1759; Beilby Porteus, *A Sermon Preached in the Chapel of the Asylum* [1773], 14–17, 19–20.

11. Henry Fielding, *The Covent-Garden Journal* [1752], ed. Bertrand A. Goldgar (1988), no. 66 (italics in original); cf. *The Centinel*, no. 36 (30 July 1757).

12. Catharine Macaulay Graham, *Letters on Education* (1790), 218–19. For the ubiquity of this idea across the ideological spectrum cf. e.g. Hannah More, *Strictures on the Modern System of Female Education*, 2 vols (1799); William Thompson, *Appeal of One Half the Human Race* (1825); Vivien Jones, 'Advice and Enlightenment', in Sarah Knott and Barbara Taylor (eds), *Women, Gender and Enlightenment* (2005).

13. Augustine, *City of God*, bk 1, ch. 28; *The Centinel*, no. 36 (30 July 1757); Holloway, *Rat-Trap*, 89.

14. 'Anne Frances Randall' [i.e. Mary Robinson], *A Letter to the Women of England* (1799), quoting 77 and 7–8; Macaulay Graham, *Letters on Education*, 212; [Mary Hays], *Appeal to the Men of Great Britain in Behalf of Women* (1798), 235–7; cf. John Gregory, *A Father's Legacy* (1774), 34; [Jane Warton], *Letters Addressed to Two Young Married Ladies* (Dublin, 1782), 23–4; [Mary] Robinson, *The Natural Daughter*, 2 vols (1799); *The Victim* (1800), 50–52; Julie Shaffer, 'Ruined Women and Illegitimate Daughters', in Katharine Kittredge (ed.), *Lewd and Notorious* (2003).

15. [Hays], *Appeal*, 235; William Paley, *The Principles of Moral and Political Philosophy* (1785), 252 (italics in original); University College London, MSS of Jeremy Bentham, lxxii. 207, 210. Cf. George Mackenzie, *The Laws and Customes of Scotland* (1678), 168; [Henry Fielding], *Rape upon Rape* (1730), Act I, scene 10; idem, *Covent-Garden Journal*, ed. Goldgar, no. 57; [Robert Bolton], *An Answer to the Question* (1755), 37–8.

16. [Samuel Richardson], *Letters and Passages Restored from the Original Manuscripts of the History of Clarissa* (1751), 59 (from a passage added to letter 152 from the third edition onwards). For typical reiterations of these age-old tropes, see e.g. Richard Allestree, *The Ladies Calling* (Oxford, 1673), pt 1, section 1; Hugh Kelly, *Memoirs of a Magdalen*, 2 vols (1767); *An Address to the Guardian Society* (1817), 10–16; Lucia Zedner, *Women, Crime and Custody in Victorian England* (1991), esp. 40–41, 48–50, 80–82.

17. Paley, *Principles*, 252; 'A Layman' [i.e. Bernard Mandeville], *A Modest Defence of Publick Stews* (1724), 45–7; *A Collection of Miscellany Letters, Selected out of Mist's Weekly Journal*, 4 vols (1722–7), iv. 235–6.

18. Richardson, *Pamela*, ed. Keymer and Wakely, quoting 383, 385, 394 (cf. e.g. 8, 35–6, 41, 53, 66, 71, 162, 164, 230, 292, 455); *Critical Remarks on Sir Charles Grandison* (1754), 35–6, 58 (quoted).

19. See esp. Leonore Davidoff and Catherine Hall, *Family Fortunes* (1987); Anna Clark, *The Struggle for the Breeches* (1995).

20. Elizabeth Blackwell, *The Human Element in Sex* (1884 edn), quoting 51. Cf. e.g. Jeffrey Weeks, *Sex, Politics and Society* (2nd edn, 1989); Frank Mort, *Dangerous Sexualities* (2nd edn, 2000); Thomas Laqueur, *Making Sex* (1990), ch. 6.

21. [Edward Long], *Candid Reflections* (1772), 48–9; John Trusler, *The London Adviser* (1786), 47–8; Lawrence Stone, *Road to Divorce* (1990), 89; *Critical Remarks on Sir Charles Grandison*, 27–33; *Boswell in Extremes, 1776–1778*, ed. Charles McC. Weis and Frederick A. Pottle (1970), 342–3.

22. *Boswell's Life of Johnson*, ed. George Birkbeck Hill and L. F. Powell, 6 vols (1934–50), iii. 353. For typical examples, see Adam Smith, *An Inquiry into the Nature and Causes of the Wealth of Nations*, ed. R. H. Campbell, A. S. Skinner, and W. B. Todd (1976), I. viii. 37–8; Paley, *Principles*, 275; T. R. Malthus, *An Essay on the Principle of Population* [edns of 1803–26], ed. Patricia James, 2 vols (1989), e.g.

ii. 113–14; *Address to the Guardian Society*, 18–20, 42–3; Stone, *Road to Divorce*, 256–9; Donna Andrew, '"Adultery à-la-Mode"', *History* 82 (1997).

Marriage and Money

1. T. R. Malthus, *An Essay on the Principle of Population* [edns of 1803–26], ed. Patricia James, 2 vols (1989), i. 250. The sexual dynamics of courtship, marriage, and divorce in this period are illustrated from different perspectives in Lawrence Stone, *Uncertain Unions* (1992) and *Broken Lives* (1993); Randolph Trumbach, *Sex and the Gender Revolution* (1998); Joanne Bailey, *Unquiet Lives* (2003); Amanda Vickery, *Behind Closed Doors* (2009).

2. Francis Bacon, *New Atlantis*, published with his *Sylva Sylvarum* (1627), quoting 27; Samuel Butler, *Satires and Miscellaneous Poetry and Prose*, ed. René Lamar (1928), quoting 218; Warren Chernaik, *Sexual Freedom in Restoration Literature* (1995), 189–91; P. F. Vernon, 'Marriage of Convenience and the Moral Code of Restoration Comedy', *Essays in Criticism* 12 (1962).

3. See e.g. *Marriage Promoted* (1690), 52; Sir William Temple, *Miscellanea: The Third Part* (1701), 79; *Female Grievances Debated* (2nd edn, 1707), 10–13, 154–8; *The Tatler*, ed. Donald F. Bond, 3 vols (1987), nos 198–9, 223; *The Spectator*, ed. Donald F. Bond, 5 vols (1965), nos 149, 199, 268, 437, 511 528; *The Guardian*, no. 123; C. J. Rawson, 'The Phrase "Legal Prostitution"', *Notes and Queries* 11 (1964).

4. Mary Astell, *Some Reflections Upon Marriage* (1700), quoting 36; Mark Knights, *The Devil in Disguise* (2011), ch. 4 (quoting 122); [Sarah Fyge], *The Female Advocate* (1686), quoting 18–19. Cf. *The New Oxford Book of Eighteenth-Century Verse*, ed. Roger Lonsdale (1984), 36–7; Ingrid H. Tague, 'Love, Honor, and Obedience', *Journal of British Studies* 40 (2001), 98–9; Anne Kugler, *Errant Plagiary* (2002).

5. Samuel Richardson, *Clarissa, or The History of a Young Lady* [1747–8], ed. Angus Ross (1985), letter 31; cf. e.g. [Samuel Richardson], *Letters Written to and for Particular Friends* (1741), *passim*; idem, *Pamela; or, Virtue Rewarded* [1740], ed. Thomas Keymer and Alice Wakely (2001), 444; idem, *The History of Sir Charles Grandison* [1753–4], ed. Jocelyn Harris, 3 vols (1972), i. 231–2; Christopher Hill, 'Clarissa Harlowe and her Times', in his *Puritanism and Revolution* (1958); *The Rambler*, nos 18, 35, 39, 45, 97 (by Richardson), 113, 115, 167 (1750–51).

6. *Boswell's Life of Johnson*, ed. George Birkbeck Hill and L. F. Powell, 6 vols (1934–50), iii. 165 (1772); cf. Thomas More, *Utopia* [1516], transl. Paul Turner (1961), 103; [Robert Bolton], *An Answer to the Question* (1755), 31.

7. [Joseph Priestley], *Considerations for the Use of Young Men* [1778], 6; Alysa Levene *et al.* (eds), *Illegitimacy in Britain, 1700–1920* (2005), 6, and the literature cited there.

8. See Alysa Levene, 'The Origins of the Children of the London Foundling Hospital', *Continuity and Change* 18 (2003), and the literature cited there; John Black, 'Who Were the Putative Fathers of Illegitimate Children in London, 1740–1810?', in Levene *et al.* (eds), *Illegitimacy in Britain* (I have used the data provided by this study, esp. Table 4.1, though unpersuaded by its conclusions. Its figures in any case only cover women who publicly sought poor relief, excluding all those impregnated women who were otherwise paid off, taken care of, or left to shift for themselves); Daniel Defoe, *The Fortunes and Misfortunes of the Famous Moll Flanders* [1722], ed. David Blewett (1989), quoting 63, 67, 70.

9. *The Autobiography and Correspondence of Mary Granville*, ed. Lady Llandover, 3 vols (1861), i. 240; *The Correspondence of Samuel Richardson*, ed. Anna Laetitia Barbauld, 6 vols (1804), iv. 212. Cf. *Considerations on the Fatal Effects to a Trading Nation* (1763), 40.

10. See e.g. Amy Louise Erickson, *Women and Property in Early Modern England* (1993); John Habakkuk, *Marriage, Debt and the Estates System* (1994); Susan E. Whyman, *Sociability and Power in Late-Stuart England* (1999), ch. 5.

11. 26 George II c. 33; *A Master-Key to the Rich Ladies Treasury* (1742); Roger Lee Brown, 'The Rise and Fall of the Fleet Marriages', in R. B. Outhwaite (ed.), *Marriage and Society* (1981); Peter Borsay, *The English Urban Renaissance* (1989), 243–8 (quoting 245); Lawrence Stone, *The Family, Sex and Marriage in England, 1500–1800* (1977), 316–17, and his *Road to Divorce* (1990), chs iv–v; Erickson, *Women and Property*, 230–36; R. B. Outhwaite, *Clandestine Marriage in England, 1500–1850* (1995); David Lemmings, 'Marriage and the Law in the Eighteenth Century', *Historical Journal* 39 (1996), here esp. 357–8. The most accurate reading of the Act's provisions is provided by Rebecca Probert, *Marriage Law and Practice in the Long Eighteenth Century* (2009).

12. Lemmings, 'Marriage and the Law', quoting 356; in addition to the literature cited in the previous note, see David Blewett, 'Changing Attitudes toward Marriage', *Huntington Library Quarterly* 44 (1981); Ingrid H. Tague, 'Love, Honor, and Obedience', *Journal of British Studies* 40 (2001).

13. Temple, *Miscellanea: The Third Part*, 77–82; *ODNB*, Robert Craggs Nugent; Thomas Short, *New Observations* (1750), 159; Henry Fielding, *The Covent-Garden Journal* [1752], ed. Bertrand A. Goldgar (1988), no. 50. Cf. e.g. [Priestley], *Considerations*, 9; James Edward Hamilton, *A Short Treatise on Polygamy* (Dublin, 1786), 16; Edward John Trelawny, *Adventures of a Younger Son* (1835 edn), 47–8; Paul Langford, *Public Life and the Propertied Englishman* (1991), 540–48; Donna Andrew, '"Adultery à-la-Mode"', *History* 82 (1997).

14. Rachel Weil, *Political Passions* (1999); Knights, *Devil in Disguise*, ch. 4; *Correspondence of Samuel Richardson*, ed. Barbauld, vi. 100–101 (quoted). Cf. e.g. *Selected Letters of Samuel Richardson*, ed. John Carroll (1964), 199–210; Henry Fielding, *Tom Jones* (1749), e.g. bk XVI, ch. viii; bk XVII, ch. viii; Short, *New Observations*, 164–5; *Critical Remarks on Sir Charles Grandison* (1754), 15; James Fordyce, *Sermons to Young Women*, 2 vols (1766), i. 151; William Buchan,

Domestic Medicine (3rd edn, 1774), 128n; James Cookson, *Thoughts on Polygamy* (1782), 21–2, 448–9; Edward Barry, *Theological . . . Essays* [1790?], 59, 61.

Punishing Seduction

1. J. H. Baker, *An Introduction to English Legal History* (4th edn, 2002), 456–7; Lawrence Stone, *Road to Divorce* (1990), 81–95, 231–301; James Oldham, *The Mansfield Manuscripts* (1992), 1050 n.6, 1245–1312. For parallel developments in Scotland and North America, cf. Leah Leneman, 'Seduction in Eighteenth- and Early Nineteenth-Century Scotland', *Scottish Historical Review* 78 (1999); Ruth H. Bloch, *Gender and Morality in Anglo-American Culture, 1650–1800* (2003), ch. 4. On the remarkable nineteenth-century popularity of these actions, and their survival into the later twentieth century, see Saskia Lettmaier, *Broken Engagements* (2010) and Stephen Cretney, *Family Law in the Twentieth Century* (2003), 155–7.

2. William Paley, *The Principles of Moral and Political Philosophy* (1785), 253; [Martin Madan], *Thelyphthora: or, a Treatise on Female Ruin*, 3 vols (1780–81), i. sig. A2ᵛ (italics in original). Cf. Robert Holloway, *The Rat-Trap* [1773], 59–64; Donna T. Andrew, *London Debating Societies, 1776–1799* (London Record Society, 1994), nos 663, 1108.

3. *ODNB*, William Murray, first Earl of Mansfield; University College London, MSS of Jeremy Bentham, lxxii. 207; [Patrick Colquhoun], *A Treatise on the Police of the Metropolis* (3rd edn, 1796), 242 (quoted), 255; cf. e.g. Delarivier Manley, *New Atalantis* [1709], ed. Ros Ballaster (1991), 228–9; Holloway, *Rat-Trap*, 61–4, 92, 97; 'Mary Smith', *Observations on Seduction* (2nd edn, 1808), 33; *Hints to the Public and the Legislature* (1811), 19–20, 54; *An Address to the Guardian Society* (1817), 44; Andrew, *London Debating Societies*, no. 917. For the parliamentary bills see Leon Radzinowicz, *A History of English Criminal Law*, 5 vols (1948–86), iii. 193–203; Stone, *Road to Divorce*, 257, 287–8, 335–9, 380–83; Donna Andrew, '"Adultery à-la-Mode"', *History* 82 (1997).

4. See e.g. *The Works of Mary Wollstonecraft*, ed. Janet Todd and Marilyn Butler, 7 vols (1989), quoting v. 139 (cf. ibid., 140, 209); *Tudor Church Reform*, ed. Gerald Bray (Church of England Record Society, 2000), 21; Bodleian Library, Firth b. 18 (88) (quoted); *The Works of Gerrard Winstanley*, ed. George H. Sabine (1941), 599; *Law Quibbles* (1724), 10–11; [Arthur Dobbs?], *Some Thoughts Concerning Government in General* (1728), 29–30; James Cookson, *Thoughts on Polygamy* (Winchester, 1782), 32–4, 96, 234–5, 434, 459–60; Edward Barry, *Theological . . . Essays* [1790?], 82–3; 'Smith', *Observations on Seduction*, 9; Andrew, *London Debating Societies*, nos 91, 378, 694, 1131, 1733, 1901, 2024, 2025.

5. Henry Fielding, *The Covent-Garden Journal* [1752], ed. Bertrand A. Goldgar (1988), 432; Martin C. and Ruthe R. Battestin, *Henry Fielding* (1989), 421–3; [Colquhoun], *Treatise on the Police*, 255; Stephen Robertson, 'Seduction, Sexual Violence, and Marriage', *Law and History Review* 24 (2006).

Polygamy and Population

1. In addition to the various examples cited in Chapter 2 above, see e.g. *Epistulae et Tractatus*, ed. Joannes Henricus Hessels, 3 vols (1889–97), iii. 2727–36, 2754 (I owe my knowledge of this case to the kindness of Catherine Wright); George Psalmanaazaar, *An Historical and Geographical Description of Formosa* (1704), 256; and, for the broader European context, John Cairncross, *After Polygamy was Made a Sin* (1974); Ursula Vogel, 'Political Philosophers and the Trouble with Polygamy', *History of Political Thought* 12 (1991).

2. Delarivier Manley, *New Atalantis* [1709], ed. Ros Ballaster (1991), viii–ix, 115–30, 222–9 (quoting 117–18); cf. Anne Kugler, *Errant Plagiary* (2002), 67–8, and Mark Knights, *The Devil in Disguise* (2011), ch. 4.

3. [Patrick Delany], *Reflections upon Polygamy* (1737; 2nd edn, 1739), quoting 1; Samuel Richardson, *Clarissa, or The History of a Young Lady* [1747–8], ed. Angus Ross (1985), letter 254; *The Correspondence of Samuel Richardson*, ed. Anna Laetitia Barbauld, 6 vols (1804), vi. 163, 190, 207–12, 216–20 (quoting 218); *Selected Letters of Samuel Richardson*, ed. John Carroll (1964), 252–3; Alfred Owen Aldridge, 'Polygamy and Deism', *Journal of English and Germanic Philology* 48 (1949).

4. *Boswell on the Grand Tour: Germany and Switzerland 1764*, ed. Frederick A. Pottle (1964), quoting 247–8; *Boswell for the Defence 1769–1774*, ed. William K. Wimsatt, Jr and Frederick A. Pottle (1959), 36–7; *Boswell: The Ominous Years, 1774–1776*, ed. Charles Ryskamp and Frederick A. Pottle (1963), 65, 74, 81–2, 88, 95, 283, 286–7, 294; *Boswell in Extremes, 1776–1778*, ed. Charles McC. Weis and Frederick A. Pottle (1970), 28, 53, 61, 107, 146, 188; *Boswell: The Applause of the Jury, 1782–1785*, ed. Irma S. Lustig and Frederick A. Pottle (1981), 190; Frank Brady, *James Boswell: The Later Years, 1769–1795* (1984), 113; *ODNB*, Westley Hall.

5. [Martin Madan], *Thelyphthora: or, a Treatise on Female Ruin*, 3 vols (1780–81), quoting ii. 73; John Smith, *Polygamy Indefensible* (1780), quoting 7; Donna T. Andrew, *London Debating Societies, 1776–1799* (London Record Society, 1994), nos 451, 648, 652, 654, 676, 690, 693, 694, 702, 755, 804, 1428, 1555, 1719.

6. See e.g. Peter Biller, *The Measure of Multitude* (2000), 40–42, 114; Margaret R. Sommerville, *Sex and Subjection* (1995), 151–66.

7. *Complete Prose Works of John Milton*, ed. D. M. Wolfe, 8 vols (1953–82), quoting vi. 356, 366 (*De Doctrina Christiana*); Leo Miller, *John Milton among the Polygamophiles* (1974); Christopher Hill, *Milton and the English Revolution* (1977), 136–9; Gordon Campbell et al., *Milton and the Manuscript of De Doctrina Christiana* (2007); Sarah Barber, *A Revolutionary Rogue* (2000), 82–4, 144–51; [Francis Osborne], *Advice to a Son* ('1656', i.e. 1655), quoting 49–51; [Bernardino Ochino], *A Dialogue of Polygamy* [transl. Thomas Pecke] (1657); *ODNB*, Francis Osborne, Thomas Pecke; *A Remedy for Uncleanness* (1658) (for Cromwell's reaction, see *Calendar of State Papers, Domestic 1658–9* (1885), 22 June 1658); Thomas Hobbes, *Leviathan* (1651), 113; [Conyers Middleton], *A*

Letter to Dr Waterland (1731), 8. Cf. Thomas Grantham, *A Marriage Sermon* (1641); J[ohn] Ovington, *Christian Chastity* (1712), 15. For Boswell's reading of Osborne's defence of polygamy, see *Boswell for the Defence*, ed. Wimsatt and Pottle, 147.

8. See esp. [Madan], *Thelyphthora*: 1st edn, i. sig. A2^r; 2nd edn (1781), i. xviii, 1–4, notes to 201–5.

9. *Cobbett's Parliamentary History of England*, 36 vols (1806–20), xv. 6; *The Diary of Dudley Ryder, 1715–1716*, ed. William Matthews (1939), 85. The prolific clergyman Dr John Free attacked the 1753 Marriage Act by putting forward a detailed proposal to make marriage a purely civil contract, which would allow consensual polygamy and divorce, agreeable to the laws of God, the felicity of men, and the good of the nation. This 'serio-comick satire', which drew on biblical arguments, political arithmetic, verse, and reason, was persuasive enough to be taken seriously by some contemporary reviewers: *Matrimony Made Easy* (2nd edn, 1764); *The St James's Magazine* iv. 291–2 (May 1764); *The Scots Magazine* xxvi. 392 (July 1764). His son, Edward Drax Free, was to become the most notoriously libertine clergyman of his day: R. B. Outhwaite, *Scandal in the Church* (1997).

10. Cairncross, *After Polygamy*, chs ii–iii; John Locke, *An Essay Concerning Toleration and Other Writings*, ed. J. R. Milton and Philip Milton (2006), 275–6, 289; idem, *Political Essays*, ed. Mark Goldie (1997), 255–6; idem, *Two Treatises of Government*, ed. Peter Laslett (2nd edn, 1967), II. 78–81; British Library, Additional MS 61360, fols 174–181 (a letter from Dr Dudley Loftus to the Earl of Shaftesbury, undated but probably written *c.* 1671; I am grateful to Mark Knights for drawing this document to my attention); *Two Dissertations Written by the Late Bishop Burnet* (1731); *Debates of the House of Commons*, ed. Anchitell Grey, 10 vols (1763), iv. 9–10; Basil Duke Henning (ed.), *The History of Parliament: The House of Commons, 1660–1690*, 3 vols (1983), iii. 7–10; *Burnet's History of My Own Time*, ed. Osmund Airy, 2 vols (Oxford, 1897–1900), i. 470–71. For the familiarity of English divines and academics around this time with the works of Johan Leyser, the foremost continental proponent of polygamy, see e.g. Samuel Fuller, *Ministerium Ecclesiae Anglicanae* ([Cambridge], 1679); for his impact on eighteenth-century debates, cf. [Delany], *Reflections upon Polygamy*, 26; James Cookson, *Thoughts on Polygamy* (1782), 2–3.

11. Biller, *Measure of Multitude*, ch. 5.

12. See e.g. D. V. Glass, *Numbering the People* (1973); Julian Hoppit, 'Political Arithmetic in Eighteenth-Century England', *Economic History Review* 49 (1996); Sylvana Tomaselli, 'Moral Philosophy and Population Questions in Eighteenth Century Europe', *Population and Development Review* 14 (supplement) (1988); Paul Slack, 'Measuring the National Wealth in Seventeenth-Century England', *Economic History Review* 57 (2004) and his 'Government and Information in Seventeenth-Century England', *Past and Present* 184 (2004); Joanna Innes, *Inferior Politics* (2009), ch. 4; Ted McCormick, *William Petty and the Ambitions of Political Arithmetic* (2009).

13. William Paley, *The Principles of Moral and Political Philosophy* (1785), 589.

14. *Conjugium Languens* (1700), 9; *Marriage Promoted* (1690), 18. For other representative examples, see John Graunt, *Natural and Political Observations* (1662), 46–52; [William Petty], *A Treatise of Taxes* (1662), 50; Carew Reynel, *The True English Interest* (1674), ch. 24; *Seventeenth-Century Economic Documents*, ed. Joan Thirsk and J. P. Cooper (1972), 777; Richard Fiddes, *A General Treatise of Morality* (1724), lxiv–lxviii; Delaney, *Reflections upon Polygamy*, preface to 2nd edn, dissertations I, VI, VII; *London Magazine* (1732), 461, (1746), 324–5, (1756), 538; Thomas Short, *New Observations* (1750), 73, 151–7, 280–82; [Caleb Fleming], *The Oeconomy of the Sexes* (1751), e.g. 50, 62; Robert Wallace, *A Dissertation on the Numbers of Mankind* (1753), 13, 83–7; Cookson, *Thoughts on Polygamy*, 56–7, 331–6, 421–3, 444–6; Paley, *Principles*, 262–4; Alfred Owen Aldridge, 'Population and Polygamy in Eighteenth-Century Thought', *Journal of the History of Medicine and Allied Sciences* 4 (1949). Cf. Charles-Louis de Secondat, Baron de Montesquieu, *The Spirit of Laws*, 2 vols (1750), i. 269, 358–69.

15. Short, *New Observations*, 159 (quoted); Lawrence Stone, *Road to Divorce* (1990), 126, 132–3 (quoting 132); R. B. Outhwaite, *Clandestine Marriage in England, 1500–1850* (1995), 88–91, 106–8, 113–20; [Madan], *Thelyphthora*, ii. 58–9. Cf. *Marriage Promoted*; Cookson, *Thoughts on Polygamy*, 446.

16. 6 & 7 William and Mary c. 6, extended until 1 August 1706 by 8 & 9 William III c. 20; Josiah Tucker, *A Brief Essay* (1749), 46–50 (quoting 49–50); Cookson, *Thoughts on Polygamy*, 427, 432 (quoted). Cf. e.g. *Marriage Promoted*; *Female Grievances Debated* (2nd edn, 1707), 159–62; *The Spectator*, ed. Donald F. Bond, 5 vols (1965), no. 528; [Arthur Dobbs?], *Some Thoughts Concerning Government in General* (1728), 28–9; Wallace, *Dissertation on the Numbers*, 93–5, 154–5; [L. J. Plumard de Dangeul], *Remarks on the Advantages and Disadvantages* (1754), 216–18; Andrew, *London Debating Societies*, nos 626, 643, 683, 771, 817, 871, 960, 961, 1061, 1276, 1719, 2117, 2161, 2199. Attitudes towards spinsters underwent a similar shift: Amy M. Froide, *Never Married* (2005), ch 6.

17. [Daniel Maclauchlan], *An Essay upon Improving and Adding to the Strength of Great-Britain and Ireland, by Fornication* (1735); cf. [Allan Ramsay], *An Address of Thanks from the Society of Rakes* (Edinburgh, 1735); *A Modest Apology for the Prevailing Practice of Adultery* (1773), 20.

18. See e.g. Biller, *Measure of Multitude*, 88; [Ochino], *Dialogue of Polygamy*, 53, 61, 86–7; *Remedy for Uncleanness*, quoting sig. A2ʳ⁻ᵛ; William Temple, *Observations upon the United Provinces* (1673), 14–17; *Debates*, ed. Grey, iv. 10; *Solon Secundus* (1695), quoting 11, 21; Ovington, *Christian Chastity*, 15; Bernard Mandeville, *The Fable of the Bees*, ed. F. B. Kaye, 2 vols (1924), i. 330–31; *The Philosophical Works of the Late Right Honourable Henry St John, Lord Viscount Bolingbroke*, 5 vols (1754), quoting v. 160–63. For polygamy in contemporary travel accounts, see esp. Felicity A. Nussbaum, *Torrid Zones* (1995), ch. 3.

19. *Boswell in Search of a Wife, 1766–1769*, ed. Frank Brady and Frederick A. Pottle (1957), 3 (quoted), 25–6, 50–52; Annette Gordon-Reed, *The Hemingses of Monticello* (2008), 281–3, 344–5; *Diary of Dudley Ryder*, 85; [Daniel Defoe], *Conju-*

gal Lewdness (1727), 123–4; [Samuel Johnson], *The Philosophic Mirrour* (Dublin, 1759), 228–35 (quoting 232); [Madan], *Thelyphthora*, quoting i. 40–41.

20. *Plan for a Free Community* (1789), v–vii, 30–31 (quoted).

21. Andrew, *London Debating Societies*, no. 1719; *Boswell: The Ominous Years*, ed. Ryskamp and Pottle, 88 (quoted), 109–10.

22. [Madan], *Thelyphthora*, i. 7; James Edward Hamilton, *A Short Treatise on Polygamy* (Dublin, 1786), 16. Polyandry, by contrast, was commonly dismissed as unnatural, unprocreative, and insubordinate: see e.g. [Ochino], *Dialogue of Polygamy*, 47–51; Gordon Campbell and Thomas N. Corns, *John Milton* (2008), 357; British Library, Additional MS 61360, fol. 176; Manley, *New Atalantis*, ed. Ballaster, 117; *Philosophical Works of . . . Bolingbroke*, v. 160–61; *Boswell: The Ominous Years*, ed. Ryskamp and Pottle, 88; [Madan], *Thelyphthora* (2nd edn), i. 195n, 276, 279; Cookson, *Thoughts on Polygamy*, 56; Sommerville, *Sex and Subjection*, 152–61, 169 n. 34.

23. British Library, Additional MS 61360, fols 175–8; *Boswell: The Ominous Years*, ed. Ryskamp and Pottle, 81–2 (italics in original).

24. *A Letter to the Rev Mr Madan* (1780), 74–5; John Smith, *Polygamy Indefensible* (1780), 6–7.

25. *Correspondence of Samuel Richardson*, ed. Barbauld, vi. 194; David Hume, *Essays Moral, Political, and Literary*, ed. Eugene F. Miller (1987), 184–7; [Joseph Priestley], *Considerations for the Use of Young Men* [1778], 12–13; *The Works of Mary Wollstonecraft*, ed. Janet Todd and Marilyn Butler, 7 vols (1989), v. 139.

26. Prince Hoare, *Memoirs of Granville Sharp, Esq.* (1820), 149–51.

27. [Patrick Colquhoun], *A Treatise on the Police of the Metropolis* (2nd edn, 1796), 278; *The Letters of Samuel Wesley*, ed. Philip Olleson (2001), quoting xxxiii; *Samuel Wesley (1766–1837): A Source Book*, ed. Michael Kassler and Philip Olleson (2001), esp. 144, 151, 155–8, 164, 276, 381–2, 388–9, 457, 549 (quoting 157–8, 457); Philip Olleson, *Samuel Wesley* (2003), 101–2, 153–4; *ODNB*; Miranda Seymour, *Mary Shelley* (2000), 419, 603–4 n. 11.

28. Marsha Keith Schuchard, *Why Mrs Blake Cried* (2006), quoting 2; Hamilton, *Short Treatise*, quoting [iii]–iv. Cf. his *Strictures on Primitive Christianity*, 2 vols (1790–92).

29. [John Miner], *Dr Miner's Defence* (Hartford, Conn., 1781); Leonard J. Arrington and Davis Bitton, *The Mormon Experience* (1979), esp. 70 (quoted), 195–9, 222–3; *Deseret News – Extra* (Salt Lake City, Utah, 14 Sept. 1852), 14–28 (quoting 25); John S. Tanner, 'Milton and the Early Mormon Defense of Polygamy', *Milton Quarterly* 21 (1987). Cf. S. E. Dwight, *The Hebrew Wife* (New York, 1836).

30. *The Collected Works of John Stuart Mill*, ed. J. M. Robson *et al.*, 33 vols (1963–91), quoting xviii. 260, 290 [*On Liberty*, chs iii and iv]. Cf. e.g. H. L. A. Hart, *Law, Liberty and Morality* (1963), 38–43; Sarah Barringer Gordon, ' "The Liberty of Self-Degradation" ', *Journal of American History* 83 (1996); Stephanie Forbes, ' "Why Just Have One?" ', *Houston Law Review* 39 (2003); Martin Guggenheim, 'Texas Polygamy', *Houston Law Review* 46 (2009).

Modern Principles

1. See esp. Karen Harvey, *Reading Sex in the Eighteenth Century* (2004); Sarah Toulalan, *Imagining Sex* (2007).

CHAPTER 5: THE ORIGINS OF WHITE SLAVERY
Prostitution and Philanthropy

1. Katherine Ludwig Jansen, *The Making of the Magdalen* (2000); *Reformation Biblical Drama in England*, ed. Paul Whitfield White (1992); *OED*; and, for the broader European context, Susan Haskins, *Mary Magdalene* (1993).

2. Richard Cooke, *A White Sheete, or a Warning for Whoremongers* (1629), 31, 36–7; Z[acheus] Isham, *A Sermon Preached before the Right Honourable the Lord-Mayor* (1700), 22; Thomas Lynford, *A Sermon Preached before the Right Honourable the Lord-Mayor* (1700), 23–4; Sir Edward Coke, *The Second Part of the Institutes* (1642), 734; cf. Robert Moss, *A Sermon Preach'd Before the Right Honourable the Lord Mayor* (1709), 14.

3. [Jonas Hanway], *A Plan for Establishing a Charity-House* (1758), xxv; [Bernard Mandeville], *A Modest Defence of Publick Stews* (1724), x–xi; [Edward Ward], *The London-Spy Compleat* (4th edn, 1709), pt VI.

4. Karpeles Manuscript Library, Santa Barbara, California: Thomas Bray, 'A General Plan of a Penitential Hospital for the Imploying and Reforming Lewd Women' [c. 1699]; *Journals of the House of Commons* (1802–), xxvi. 190 (23 Apr. 1751); Henry Fielding, *The Covent-Garden Journal* [1752], ed. Bertrand A. Goldgar (1988), no. 57 (cf. Henry Fielding, *An Enquiry into the Late Increase of Robbers* (1751), ed. Malvin R. Zirker (1988), 120–22); Letter from Saunders Welch to the Duke of Newcastle (1753), printed in *The London Chronicle*, 14–17 Jan. 1758.

5. Bray, 'General Plan of a Penitential Hospital'; Thomas Nelson, *An Address to Persons of Quality and Estate* (1715), 212–13 (first pagination).

6. See e.g. Leah Lydia Otis, *Prostitution in Medieval Society* (1985), 72–6; Ruth Mazo Karras, *Common Women* (1996), 82; Peter Biller, *The Measure of Multitude* (2000), 74–6; Sherrill Cohen, *The Evolution of Women's Asylums Since 1500* (1992), chs 1–6; Olwen H. Hufton, *The Poor of Eighteenth-Century France* (1974), 309–10; Colin Jones, 'Prostitution and the Ruling Class in Eighteenth-Century Montpellier', *History Workshop Journal* 6 (1978). For the problem of Catholic precedents, and for other interesting parallels, cf. Bridget Hill, 'A Refuge from Men: The Idea of a Protestant Nunnery', *Past and Present* 117 (1987).

7. See e.g. [Christopher] Johnson, *The History of . . . Eliz. Mann* (1724), v–vi; Jonas Hanway, *Letter V* (1758), 23; [idem], *Plan for Establishing a Charity-House*, quoting xxi; idem, *Letters Written Occasionally on the Customs of Foreign Nations in Regard to Harlots* (1761).

8. Stephen Macfarlane, 'Social Policy and the Poor in the Later Seventeenth Century', in A. L. Beier and Roger Finlay (eds), *London 1500–1700* (1986); Paul Slack, *Poverty and Policy in Tudor and Stuart England* (1988), 195–9; chapters by Mary E. Fissell and Tim Hitchcock in Lee Davison *et al.* (eds), *Stilling the Grumbling Hive* (1992).

9. Indispensable guides to the general subject are David Owen, *English Philanthropy 1660–1960* (1965); Donna T. Andrew, *Philanthropy and Police* (1989).

10. For other sexual charities in London, see e.g. *An Account of the Misericordia Hospital* (1780); *An Account of the Institution of the Lock Asylum* (1796); *An Account of the London Female Penitentiary* (1809); *Report of the Provisional Committee of the Guardian Society* (1816).

11. Martin Madan, *Every Man Our Neighbour* (1764 edn), 8; William Dodd, *An Account of the Rise, Progress, and Present State of the Magdalen Charity* (2nd edn, 1763), 110; William Dodd, *A Sermon on St. Matthew* (1759), 15.

12. [Daniel Defoe], *Augusta Triumphans* (1728), quoting 14 (cf. Ruth K. McClure, *Coram's Children* (1981), esp. chs 1–3); *An Account of the Proceedings of the Governors of the Lock-Hospital* (1749), quoting [1] (cf. the 1751 edn, and John [Gilbert], *A Sermon Preached before the ... Governors of the Several Hospitals* (1743), 19–20); [John Reynolds], *A Compassionate Address to the Christian World*, ed. [Martin] Madan (1767), quoting [iii]. For the Lock Hospital and Asylum, see Linda E. Merians (ed.), *The Secret Malady* (1996), esp. ch. 8; Kevin P. Siena, *Venereal Disease, Hospitals and the Urban Poor* (2004), esp. chs 5–6.

13. In addition to the references given in the following paragraphs, see London papers for the years 1749–60 (*Daily Advertiser, Public Advertiser, Gentleman's Magazine, London Chronicle, London Magazine, Lloyd's Evening Post*); *The Rambler*, no. 107 (1751); *The Vices of the Cities of London and Westminster* (1751), 21–7; 'M. Ludovicus' [i.e. John Campbell], *A Particular but Melancholy Account* (1752); *Reflections Arising from the Immorality of the Present Age* (1756), 47–50; [Hanway], *Plan for Establishing a Charity-House*, quoting v, and his *Letter V*; John Fielding, *A Plan of the Asylum* (1758), citing [23]; *The Yale Edition of Horace Walpole's Correspondence*, ed. W. S. Lewis *et al.*, 48 vols (1937–83), quoting ix. 217; Lockman quoted from a clipping in British Library pressmark C. 116. i. 4 (125); [Edward Ward *et al.*], *The Insinuating Bawd, and the Repenting Harlot ... Intended to Promote a Provision to be Made for such Unhappy Females* (1758); H. F. B. Compston, *The Magdalen Hospital* (1917); James Stephen Taylor, *Jonas Hanway* (1985), 76; *Dictionary of National Biography* (1885–1901), David Garrick; Archives of the Royal Society of Arts, London: Society Minutes, vol. 3; D. G. C. Allan and John L. Abbott (eds), *The Virtuoso Tribe of Arts and Sciences* (1992), ch. 2.

14. *Boswell's Life of Johnson*, ed. George Birkbeck Hill and L. F. Powell, 6 vols (1934–50), i. 223–4 n. 2 (quoted), 457; iv. 321–2 (quoted), 395–6; *Johnsonian Miscellanies*, ed. George Birkbeck Hill, 2 vols (1897), ii. 168–9, 326.

15. *Selected Letters of Samuel Richardson*, ed. John Carroll (1964), 114, 172 (quoted); *Correspondence of Samuel Richardson*, ed. Anna Laetitia Barbauld, 6

vols (1804), i. clv; iv. 212, 252, 254 (quoted), 266–70, 292–3; vi. 56, 108–9; [Samuel Richardson], *Letters and Passages Restored from the Original Manuscripts of the History of Clarissa* (1751), quoting 150 (from a letter newly added to the third edition); idem, *The History of Sir Charles Grandison* [1753–4], ed. Jocelyn Harris, 3 vols (1972), quoting i. 355, 364, 372, ii. 356; T. C. Duncan Eaves and Ben D. Kimpel, *Samuel Richardson* (1971), 463–5. Cf. Henry Brooke, *The Fool of Quality*, 5 vols (1766–70), iv. 260–63; Markman Ellis, *The Politics of Sensibility* (1996), 166–9.

16. John Fielding, *An Account of the Origin and Effects of a Police* (1758), quoting 55; idem, *A Plan for a Preservatory and Reformatory* (1758); idem, *A Plan of the Asylum* (1758); Saunders Welch, *Observations on the Office of Constable* (1754), 12; idem, *A Proposal to Render Effectual a Plan* (1758), quoting 57–8.

17. [Hanway], *Plan for Establishing a Charity-House*, quoting iv–v, xvi (italics in original), and *Letter V*; Robert Dingley, *Proposals for Establishing a Public Place of Reception* (1758); Taylor, *Jonas Hanway*.

18. Compston, *Magdalen Hospital*, 59–61, 191 (quoted).

19. [Hanway], *Plan for Establishing a Charity-House*, quoting xxvi, xxviii.

Penitence and Resurrection

1. William Dodd, *A Sermon on Zechariah* (1769), 3; *The Histories of Some of the Penitents in the Magdalen-House*, 2 vols (1760), i. xviii; William Dodd, *An Account of the Rise, Progress and Present State of the Magdalen Charity* (1761), 63.

2. Dodd, *Account of the Rise*, passim (quoting 41, 74n, 78); H. F. B. Compston, *The Magdalen Hospital* (1917), 182–3.

3. Dodd, *Account of the Rise* (4th edn, 1770), *33–*44; [Martin Madan], *An Account of the Death of F. S.* [1763], quoting 8 ('triumphant' was added to the title after the first edition); Compston, *Magdalen Hospital*, 144. Cf. *Account of the Death of E.– C.–* (Dublin, 1794).

4. Dodd, *Account of the Rise* (1761 edn), xxvi, xxviii, 63; *The Rules, Orders and Regulations, of the Magdalen House* (2nd edn, 1759), 7; *The Yale Edition of Horace Walpole's Correspondence*, ed. W. S. Lewis *et al.*, 48 vols (1937–83), ix. 273–4; [Edward Jerningham], *The Magdalens: An Elegy* (1763).

5. John Fielding, *An Account of the Origin and Effects of a Police* (1758), 49–50, 53; Mr Marchant, *Observations on Mr Fielding's Plan* (1758), 17; Jonas Hanway, *Letter V* (1758), 25; Dodd, *Account of the Rise* (1761 edn), xx, 16, 75, 76n; ibid. (1763 edn), 106; [Jonas Hanway], *Thoughts on the Plan* (2nd edn, 1759), 57n; *The Visitor*, ed. William Dodd, 2 vols (Dublin, 1768), i. 41.

6. *The Plan of the Magdalen House* (1758), 17; Dodd, *Account of the Rise* (1761 edn), passim (quoting 68–9, 92–3); ibid. (1770 edn), 410; [Hanway], *Thoughts on the Plan*, 4.

7. *The Rules, Orders and Regulations of the Magdalen House* (2nd edn, 1759), 7; Dodd, *Account of the Rise* (1763 edn), 130.

8. [Jonas Hanway], *A Plan for Establishing a Charity-House* (1758), xxiin, 30n; [idem], *Thoughts on the Plan*, 34; *The Rules and Regulations of the Magdalen-Charity* (1769), vi; William Hazeland, *A Sermon Preached in the Chapel of the Asylum* (1761), 11; *A Letter to the Public on an Important Subject* (Dublin, 1767), 7; Hanway, *Letter V*, 15; *Rules, Orders and Regulations*, 8; *Plan of the Magdalen House*, 38; Dodd, *Sermon on Zechariah*, 6. Cf. Saunders Welch, *A Proposal to Render Effectual a Plan* (1758), 13n; [David Stansfield], *Candid Remarks on Mr Hanway's Candid Historical Account* (2nd edn, 1760), 41.

9. Donna T. Andrew, *Philanthropy and Police* (1989), 149, 178, 179 n. 51.

Sex and Work

1. Karpeles Manuscript Library, Santa Barbara, California: Thomas Bray, 'A General Plan of a Penitential Hospital for the Imploying and Reforming Lewd Women' [*c.* 1699]; [Daniel Defoe?], *Some Considerations upon Street-Walkers* [1726], 6; [Jonas Hanway], *A Plan for Establishing a Charity-House* (1758), quoting 31; Archives of the Royal Society of Arts, London: Society Minutes vol. 3, quoting 42; Guard Books vol. 9, quoting item 83; Loose Archives (M)A2, fols 59–60; Hanway, *Letter V*, 14; *Gentleman's Magazine*, xxviii. 192–3 (Apr. 1758); D. G. C. Allan, '"Compassion and Horror in Every Humane Mind"', in D. G. C. Allan and John L. Abbott (eds), *The Virtuoso Tribe of Arts and Sciences* (1992).

2. R. Campbell, *The London Tradesman* (1747), 209. Cf. e.g. John Gay, *Trivia* (1716), bk III, lines 277–8; *Serious Thoughts on the Miseries of Seduction and Prostitution* (1783), 51–2; *Thoughts on Alleviating the Miseries attendant upon Common Prostitution* (1799), 28.

3. [John Dunton], *The Night-Walker* (1696–7), i/3, sig. [A3^{r-v}] (quoted); i/4, pp. 8–9, 17–18, 22; ii/1, pp. 3–4, 29–30; [Josiah Woodward], *A Rebuke to the Sin of Uncleanness* (1704 edn), quoting 21; *Directions and Prayers for the Use of the Patients in the Foul Wards* (1734), quoting 16–17; cf. *A Short Dissuasive from the Sin of Uncleanness* (1701); Isaac [Maddox], *The Love of our Country Recommended* (1737), 23; Edward Yardley, *Christ's Appearing* (1749), 20.

4. Bray, 'General Plan of a Penitential Hospital'; [Dunton], *Night-Walker*, ii/1, p. 30; ii/2, sig. [A4^{v}] (quoted); Josiah Woodward, *Sodom's Vices* (1697), 14–15; idem, *The Duty of Compassion* (1697), xii–xvi; *The Invisible-Observator* (1705), 8; Stephen Macfarlane, 'Social Policy and the Poor in the Later Seventeenth Century', in A. L. Beier and Roger Finlay (eds), *London 1500–1700* (1986); Paul Slack, *Poverty and Policy in Tudor and Stuart England* (1988), 195–200.

5. This and the following paragraphs draw esp. on Vivien Jones's incisive and illuminating 'Placing Jemima', *Women's Writing* 4 (1997), here quoting 218 n. 23. Cf. e.g. *Gentleman's Magazine* (Dec. 1795), 1078–9; Edward Barry, *Theological, Philosophical, and Moral Essays* [1790?], 70–72; *Remarks upon Seduction* (1799), 23; Donna T. Andrew, *Philanthropy and Police* (1989), 188.

6. Priscilla Wakefield, *Reflections on the Present Condition of the Female Sex* (1798), quoting 164; Mary Ann Radcliffe, *The Female Advocate* (1799), quoting 27.

7. See Mary Hays, *The Victim of Prejudice* (1799); *The Works of Mary Wollstonecraft*, ed. Janet Todd and Marilyn Butler, 7 vols (1989), quoting i. 120 (Todd and Butler print the last word as 'woman', but in the first edition of 1798, upon which they base their text, it is given as 'women'); Archives of the Royal Society of Arts, London: Guard Books vol. 9, quoting item 83; *The Histories of Some of the Penitents in the Magdalen-House*, 2 vols (1760), quoting i. vi; [L. J. Plumard de Dangeul], *Remarks on the Advantages and Disadvantages* (1754), 215.

8. *A Congratulatory Epistle from a Reformed Rake* [1758], quoting 44–5.

9. *The Vices of the Cities of London and Westminster* (1751), quoting 23 (apparently referring to a type of needle-work, rather than porcelain); *Gentleman's Magazine*, quoting xxi. 164 (Apr. 1751); Hanway, *Letter V*, 12–13, 24; [idem], *Plan for Establishing a Charity-House*, 32; J[oseph] Massie, *A Plan for the Establishment of Charity-Houses* (1758), 6–12.

10. [Hanway], *Plan for Establishing a Charity-House*, quoting 30n; John Fielding, *A Plan for a Preservatory and Reformatory* (1758), quoting 19–21; Archives of the Royal Society of Arts, London: Guard Books vol. 9, quoting item 83; Mr Marchant, *Observations on Mr Fielding's Plan* (1758), 7; *The Rules, Orders and Regulations, of the Magdalen House* (1760 edn), 20.

11. *Rules, Orders and Regulations*, 20; Fielding, *Plan for a Preservatory and Reformatory*, 20; H. F. B. Compston, *The Magdalen Hospital* (1917), 180; *An Account of the ... Asylum* (1763 edn), 20 (and identical accounts in later editions); Archives of the Shaftesbury Society, London: Minute Book of the Lambeth Asylum (1761–5).

Self-interest and Sexual Interest

1. See H. F. B. Compston, *The Magdalen Hospital* (1917), 35–8; James Stephen Taylor, *Jonas Hanway* (1985), chs v–vi; Donna T. Andrew, *Philanthropy and Police* (1989), esp. ch. 3. Cf. Ruth K. McClure, *Coram's Children* (1981), esp. 238 (chart 2).

2. Martin C. and Ruthe R. Battestin, *Henry Fielding* (1989), quoting 614; Compston, *Magdalen Hospital*, 34–5; Taylor, *Jonas Hanway*, 71, 73, 97–9, 126, 156; Saunders Welch, *A Proposal to Render Effectual a Plan* (1758), esp. 1–6, 36–8, 42.

3. *The Idler*, no. 4 (May 1758); *Considerations on the Fatal Effects to a Trading Nation* (1763), 17–18; Tobias Smollett, *The Adventures of Ferdinand Count Fathom*, 2 vols (1753), ii. ch. lii. Cf. Bernard Mandeville, *The Fable of the Bees*, ed. F. B. Kaye, 2 vols (1924), i. 261; Charles Johnstone, *Chrysal, or the Adventures of a Guinea*, 2 vols (1760), i. bk 2 and ii. bk 1; Edward Bayley, *A Sermon*

Preached on the Opening of the New Chapel of the Magdalen Asylum (Dublin, 1770), 59; Andrew, *Philanthropy and Police*, 86–7, 161.

4. See Compston, *Magdalen Hospital*, 61–4; Andrew, *Philanthropy and Police*, 71 n. 69; Martin Madan, *Every Man Our Neighbour* (1764 edn), 17; Gerald Howson, *The Macaroni Parson* (1973); Archives of the Shaftesbury Society, London: Minute Book of the Lambeth Asylum (1761–5); *An Account of the . . . Asylum* (1761), 7–9; *A State of the Asylum, as Far as it Relates to Mr Maxwell* [1782]; *Asylum Minutes* [1782].

5. Mandeville, *Fable*, ed. Kaye, i. 280; William Dodd, *A Sermon on St. Matthew* (1759), 15; Beilby Porteus, *A Sermon Preached in the Chapel of the Asylum* [1773], 9.

6. [Jonas Hanway], *A Plan for Establishing a Charity-House* (1758), 18 (though in fact when it opened the London Magdalen Hospital was to operate an open policy); *Account . . . of the Lock-Hospital* (1749), 2; *Account of the . . . Asylum*, 16.

7. *An Account of the Institution and Proceedings of the Guardians of the Asylum* (1782); Ford K. Brown, *Fathers of the Victorians* (1961), 73–4; Linda E. Merians (ed.), *The Secret Malady* (1996), esp. ch 8; Kevin P. Siena, *Venereal Disease, Hospitals and the Urban Poor* (2004), esp. chs 5–6.

8. *The Yale Edition of Horace Walpole's Correspondence*, ed. W. S. Lewis *et al.*, 48 vols (1937–83), ix. 273–4.

9. See e.g. *London Chronicle* 21 Apr. 1758; *The Visitor*, ed. William Dodd, 2 vols (Dublin, 1768), nos 8, 10, 53, 73–4; Dodd, *Sermon on St. Matthew*, 18; *Autobiography of the Rev. Dr Alexander Carlyle* (2nd edn, 1860), 503–4. Cf. Sarah Lloyd, '"Pleasure's Golden Bait"', *History Workshop Journal* 41 (1996).

10. See e.g. M. G. Jones, *The Charity School Movement* (1938), 58–61; Faramerz Dabhoiwala, 'Summary Justice in Early Modern London', *English Historical Review* 121 (2006), 801–2; Francis Kelly Maxwell, *A Sermon Preached at Different Churches and Chapels* (1763); Simon McVeigh, 'Music and the Lock Hospital in the 18th Century', *The Musical Times* 129 (1988); Nicholas Temperley, 'The Lock Hospital Chapel and Its Music', *Journal of the Royal Musical Association* 118 (1993) and his 'The Hymn Books of the Foundling and Magdalen Hospital Chapels', in David Hunter (ed.), *Music Publishing and Collecting* (1994). Cf. Sarah Lloyd, 'Pleasing Spectacles and Elegant Dinners', *Journal of British Studies* 41 (2002).

11. *London and its Environs Described*, 6 vols (1761), quoting iv. 224; William Dodd, *An Account of the Rise, Progress and Present State of the Magdalen Charity* (1761), quoting 110–11; *Walpole's Correspondence*, ed. Lewis, ix. 273–4; William Dodd, 'An Ode, occasioned by Lady N–d's being prevented by illness from coming to the chapel of the Magdalen House' and 'Verses occasioned by seeing the Countess of Hertford, in tears at the Magdalen House', in his *Poems* (1767), 148–52 (quoted), 168–70; *Considerations on the Fatal Effects to a Trading Nation* (1763), 15; Compston, *Magdalen Hospital*, 150–51; *Autobiography of the Rev. Dr Alexander Carlyle*, quoting 503.

Inside the Asylum

1. Unless otherwise noted all details and quotations in the account that follows are from Representative Church Body Library, Dublin: Magdalen Asylum Admissions Book 1 (1769–95), entries for 1767–79. My work on these materials was greatly facilitated by the generosity of Maria Luddy, whose *Prostitution and Irish Society, 1800–1940* (2007) is the best guide to the later history of the subject. For the functioning of other early British asylums for penitent prostitutes, see Stanley Dana Nash, 'Social Attitudes towards Prostitution in London from 1752 to 1829' (New York University Ph.D. thesis, 1980), chs iv–v; Kevin P. Siena, *Venereal Disease, Hospitals and the Urban Poor* (2004), ch. 5; and cf. Martin Madan, *Every Man Our Neighbour* (1764 edn), 4, 15–16.

2. William Dodd, *A Sermon on St Matthew* (1759), 11; *By-Laws and Regulations of the Magdalen Hospital* (1802), viii; Beatrice Bayley Butler, 'Lady Arbella Denny, 1707–1792', *Dublin Historical Record* 9 (1946–7), 13.

3. Cf. John Styles, *The Dress of the People* (2007), 63–9.

4. 'Rules and Regulations', 6–8, 15–18, appended to Edward Bayly, *A Sermon Preached on the Opening the Chapel of the Magdalen Asylum* (Dublin, [1768]); Richard Woodward, *A Sermon Preached Before the Vice-Patroness, Governesses and Guardians of the Asylum for Penitent Women* (Dublin, 1774), appendix.

5. Cf. *A Short Account of the Magdalen Hospital* (1807), 10.

6. See e.g. William [Newcombe], *A Sermon Preached at the Chapel in Leeson-Street* (Dublin, 1773), 14; Woodward, *Sermon Preached Before the Vice-Patroness*, quoting 18–20; Thomas Leland, *The Christian's Duty to Offenders* (Dublin, 1775), quoting 16; John Lever, *The Nature and Extent of Christian Love* (Dublin, 1778), 15–18; Nash, 'Social Attitudes', 279–83.

7. Leland, *Christian's Duty*, 7, 20.

8. Cf. the 1768 'Rules and Regulations', 6–8, and *Rules and Regulations for the Asylum of Penitent Females* (Dublin, 1796), 6–8.

9. Edward Bayly, *A Sermon Preached on the Opening of the New Chapel of the Magdalen Asylum* (Dublin, 1770), 70–74.

10. *Rules and Regulations for the Asylum*, 60.

11. Bayly, *Sermon Preached on the Opening of the New Chapel*, 75–6 (I have conjectured the authors based on information in the Admissions Book).

Chastity and Class

1. Jeffrey Weeks, *Sex, Politics and Society* (2nd edn, 1989), quoting 58; Michael Mason, *The Making of Victorian Sexuality* (1994), quoting 169.

2. P[atrick] Colquhoun, *A Treatise on the Police of the Metropolis* (6th edn, 1800), quoting 340; Michael Mason, *The Making of Victorian Sexual Attitudes* (1994), 73–103, 233–6 (quoting 101). Cf. [J. W.] D'Archenholz, *A Picture of England*, 2 vols (1789), ii. 89 ('London is said to contain fifty thousand prostitutes, without

reckoning kept mistresses'); Judith R. Walkowitz, *Prostitution and Victorian Society* (1980), ch. 2.

3. J[oseph] Massie, *A Plan for the Establishment of Charity-Houses* (1758), 2–4; [Jonas Hanway], *Thoughts on the Plan* (2nd edn, 1759), 12; William Hazeland, *A Sermon Preached in the Chapel of the Asylum* (1761; preached in 1760), 10.

4. Josiah Tucker, *A Brief Essay* (1749), quoting 21–2; John Fielding, *An Account of the Origin and Effects of a Police* (1758), quoting 44; Robert Dingley, *Proposals for Establishing a Public Place of Reception* (1758), 7; [Hanway], *Thoughts on the Plan*, 11–12; *Thoughts on the Misery of a Numerous Class of Females* (Dublin, 1794), 6; James Hallifax, *A Sermon Preached in the Chapel of the Asylum* (1766), quoting 14; Archives of the Shaftesbury Society, London: Minute Book of the Lambeth Asylum (1761–5), 7–10, 71–2, 74–5, 144–6; T. R. Malthus, *An Essay on the Principle of Population* [edns of 1803–26], ed. Patricia James, 2 vols (1989), quoting ii. 111–14.

5. Saunders Welch, *A Proposal to Render Effectual a Plan* (1758), 3–5; William Dodd, *An Account of the Rise, Progress, and Present State of the Magdalen Charity* (2nd edn, 1763), 122.

6. Henry Fielding, *The Covent-Garden Journal* [1752], ed. Bertrand A. Goldgar (1988), quoting 312 and n. 1; [Jean André Rouquet], *Lettres de Monsieur** (1746), quoting 4; *The Histories of Some of the Penitents in the Magdalen House*, 2 vols (1760); [Martin Madan], *An Account of the Death of F. S.* [1763], quoting 1; William Dodd, *An Account of the Rise, Progress and Present State of the Magdalen Charity* (4th edn, 1770), quoting *36; [Jonas Hanway], *A Plan for Establishing a Charity-House* (1758), xvii, 29–30 (quoting 29); idem, *Letter V* (1758), 9, 11, 14–15; Mr Marchant, *Observations on Mr Fielding's Plan* (1758), 8–9, 14–15.

7. *Gentleman's Magazine*, quoting xxvii. 366–7 (Aug. 1757); John Fielding, *A Plan for a Preservatory and Reformatory* (1758), 116–17; Massie, *Plan for the Establishment of Charity-Houses* (1758), 38–44. Cf. Jennie Batchelor, '"Industry in Distress"', *Eighteenth-Century Life* 28 (2004).

8. [Hanway], *Plan for Establishing a Charity-House*, 19–20; *The Plan of the Magdalen House for the Reception of Penitent Prostitutes* (1758), 15–16; William Dodd, *An Account of the Rise, Progress, and Present State of the Magdalen Charity* (1761), xii, 134; idem, *A Sermon on Zechariah* (1769), fold-out plan and explanation.

9. See e.g. Hanway, *Letter V*, 9, 14–15, 23; [idem], *Plan for Establishing a Charity-House*, viii; *An Address to the Guardian Society* (1817), 21.

10. Stanley Dana Nash, 'Social Attitudes towards Prostitution in London from 1752 to 1829' (New York University Ph.D. thesis, 1980), 244–5; *By-Laws and Regulations of the Magdalen Hospital* (1802), 39–43; *A Short Account of the Magdalen Hospital* (1807), 5–9.

11. *Address to the Guardian Society*, 10 (quoted); *The Evils of Adultery and Prostitution* (1792), 64; *An Account of the Institution of the Lock Asylum* (1796); *An Account of the London Female Penitentiary* (1809); *Report of the Provisional*

Committee of the Guardian Society (1816); Ford K. Brown, *Fathers of the Victorians* (1961), 15–16, 21–5; Nash, 'Social Attitudes', chs ii–v.

12. See e.g. the pioneering study by Nash, 'Social Attitudes'; Donna T. Andrew, *Philanthropy and Police* (1989), 187–94 (quoting 194); H. F. B. Compston, *The Magdalen Hospital* (1917), quoting 200; Frances Finnegan, *Poverty and Prostitution* (1979), ch. 6, and her *Do Penance or Perish* (2001); Maria Luddy, *Women and Philanthropy in Nineteenth-Century Ireland* (1985), ch. 4, and her *Prostitution and Irish Society, 1800–1940* (2007); and, for general attitudes to the immorality of poor women in nineteenth-century social and penal policy, Lucia Zedner, *Women, Crime and Custody in Victorian England* (1991).

Rescue and Reformation

1. See e.g. Robin Evans, *The Fabrication of Virtue* (1982); Stanley Nash, 'Prostitution and Charity', *Journal of Social History* 17 (1984); John Bender, *Imagining the Penitentiary* (1987); Sherrill Cohen, *The Evolution of Women's Asylums Since 1500* (1992), ch. 7; Miles Ogborn, *Spaces of Modernity* (1998), ch. 2.

2. *The Works of Mary Wollstonecraft*, ed. Janet Todd and Marilyn Butler, 7 vols (1989), quoting v. 140. Cf. *The Collected Works of John Stuart Mill*, ed. J. M. Robson *et al.*, 33 vols (1963–91), xvii. 1692–5, 1715; Vivien Jones, 'Placing Jemima', *Women's Writing* 4 (1997), 203.

3. *Thoughts on Means of Alleviating the Miseries Attendant on Common Prostitution* (1799), quoting 27; *An Address to the Guardian Society* (1817), quoting 17; and, for typical examples, *Boswell in Search of a Wife, 1766–1769*, ed. Frank Brady and Frederick A. Pottle (1957), 293; *Boswell for the Defence 1769–1774*, ed. William K. Wimsatt, Jr and Frederick A. Pottle (1959), 69; T. C. Duncan Eaves and Ben D. Kimpel, *Samuel Richardson* (1971), 225, 232; University College London, MSS of Jeremy Bentham, cvii. 100–106; Robert Holloway, *The Rat-Trap* [1773], 57; *The Works of John Wesley*, ed. Frank Baker *et al.* (1980–), xxv. 365 (14 Jan. 1734); *An Extract from the Reverend Mr John Wesley's Journal, from … 1746 to … 1759* (1754), 34–5 (22 Nov. 1747); John Wesley, *A Sermon Preached before the Society for Reformation of Manners* [1763], 10; Moses Browne, *The Causes that Obstruct the Progress of Reformation* (1765), 30–31; *ODNB*, Dorothy Ripley; *The Diary of Sylas Neville, 1767–1788*, ed. Basil Cozens-Hardy (1950), 44.

4. Eric Trudgill, *Madonnas and Magdalens* (1976), 282; *The Gladstone Diaries*, ed. M. R. D. Foot and H. C. G. Matthew, 14 vols (1968–94), *passim*, here quoting iv. 586 (20 Jan. 1854); *ODNB*, Angela Georgina Burdett-Coutts, Charles John Huffam Dickens, George Gissing, Catherine Gladstone.

5. For surveys, see e.g. *Address to the Guardian Society*, 6; H. F. B. Compston, *The Magdalen Hospital* (1917), 16; Edward J. Bristow, *Vice and Vigilance* (1977), quoting 70, and his *Prostitution and Prejudice* (1982); Judith R. Walkowitz,

Prostitution and Victorian Society (1980) and her *City of Dreadful Delight* (1992); Cohen, *Evolution of Women's Asylums*, chs 6–7; Paula Bartley, 'Preventing Prostitution', *Women's History Review* 7 (1998), quoting 45, and her *Prostitution: Prevention and Reform in England, 1860–1914* (2000).

6. See e.g. Frances Finnegan, *Do Penance or Perish* (2001).

CHAPTER 6: THE MEDIA AND THE MESSAGE

1. I am encouraged to see that some of the ideas developed in this chapter have also been taken up by the contributors to Clifford Siskin and William Warner (eds), *This is Enlightenment* (2010).

The Rise of Mass Culture

1. George Vertue, *Note Books*, 6 vols (Walpole Society, 1930–55), iii. 58; vi. 192.

2. John Ireland, *A Supplement to Hogarth Illustrated* (1798), 3, 27.

3. Ronald Paulson, *Hogarth's Harlot* (2003). In his eagerness to prove Hogarth's elevated originality, Paulson also downplays the striking parallels between his progresses and earlier foreign and indigenous prints about the life-cycles of rakes, harlots, and prodigal sons: see his *Hogarth's Graphic Works* (3rd edn, 1989) and *Hogarth*, 3 vols (1991–3), i. 256–7; ii. 20–21; and cf. Hilde Kurz, 'Italian Models of Hogarth's Picture Stories', *Journal of the Warburg and Courtauld Institutes* 15 (1952); David Kunzle, *The Early Comic Strip* (1973), esp. ch. 9.

4. Horace Walpole, *Anecdotes of Painting in England*, 4 vols (1765–71), iv. 76.

5. For this and the following point cf. Sophie Carter, *Purchasing Power* (2004), ch. 2.

6. Walpole, *Anecdotes*, iv. 76; 8 George II c. 13; [John Nichols *et al.*], *Biographical Anecdotes of William Hogarth* (1782), 32–3; Paulson, *Hogarth*, i. 309–14; but cf. Robert Etheridge Moore, *Hogarth's Literary Relationships* (1948); David Kunzle, 'Plagiaries-by-Memory of the *Rake's Progress*', *Journal of the Warburg and Courtauld Institutes* 29 (1966); Timothy Clayton, *The English Print 1688–1802* (1997), 81–90; and the tenor of David Bindman, *Hogarth and His Times* (1997).

7. Quotation from an advertisement by the printsellers Thomas and John Bowles, *London Evening Post*, 16 May 1732. The most comprehensive collection of copies and plagiaries after Hogarth's prints is in the still almost entirely unstudied collection in twenty-four volumes amassed by J. R. Joly, held at the Department of Paintings, Drawings and Prints, Fitzwilliam Museum, Cambridge [hereafter 'Joly Collection']: vols 10 and 11 include items relating to *A Harlot's Progress*. I am most grateful to Craig Hartley and Andrew Morris for facilitating my work on these materials. I am equally indebted to the staff of the British Museum's Department of Prints and Drawings (especially Sheila O'Connell) and of the

Yale Lewis Walpole Library (especially Joan Sussler), whose kindness over many years has greatly eased my exploration of their collections.

8. See e.g. *The Progress of a Harlot* (2 edns, 1732); *The Harlot's Progress* (at least 7 edns, 1732–53); 'Joseph Gay' [i.e. John Durant Breval], *The Harlot's Progress* (2 edns, 1739); Theophilus Cibber, *The Harlot's Progress* (1733); Henry Potter, *The Decoy: An Opera* (2 edns, 1733–44); *The Jew Decoy'd; or the Progress of a Harlot* (2 edns, 1733–5); *Daily Advertiser*, 29 Oct. 1746; *Gazetteer and New Daily Advertiser*, 2 June 1769; *The Diary of Sylas Neville, 1767–1788*, ed. Basil Cozens-Hardy (1950), 71; John Nichols and George Steevens, *The Genuine Works of William Hogarth* (2 vols, 1808–10), ii. 7; Lionel Cust, *Catalogue of the Collection of Fans and Fan-Leaves Presented to the British Museum by Lady Charlotte Schreiber* (1893), unmounted nos 151–5; Art Institute of Chicago, fan mount with scenes 4–6 of *A Harlot's Progress* (c. 1732–61), accession no. 1947.144; H. J. L. J. Massé, 'Some Notes on the Pewter', *Burlington Magazine* 3 (1903), 76; *The London Stage, 1660–1800*, 5 parts, ed. W. van Lennep *et al.* (1960–68), parts iii and iv; R. B. Beckett, *Hogarth* (1949), 68; *Secret Comment*, ed. Alan Saville (1997), 234, 241; Lars Tharp, *Hogarth's China* (1997), 39–40.

9. See also Richard Newton, *Progress of a Woman of Pleasure* (etching, 1796); Joly Collection, vol. 11; Ellen G. D'Oench, 'Prodigal Sons and Fair Penitents', *Art History* 13 (1990).

10. See Joly Collection, vols 12 and 13.

11. See Joly Collection, esp. vols 15 and 16; Tharp, *Hogarth's China*; Clayton, *English Print*, 81–3, 86, 88; William St Clair, *The Reading Nation in the Romantic Period* (2004). For excellent case studies, see William B. Warner, *Licensing Entertainment* (1998); Mark Hallett, *The Spectacle of Difference* (1999), esp. ch. 3, and his 'Manly Satire', in Bernadette Fort and Angela Rosenthal (eds), *The Other Hogarth* (2001); Thomas Keymer and Peter Sabor, *Pamela in the Marketplace* (2005).

12. Cf. e.g. Peter H. Pawlowicz, 'Reading Women', in Ann Bermingham and John Brewer (eds), *The Consumption of Culture, 1600–1800* (1995); Markman Ellis, *The Politics of Sensibility* (1996), 164–5; and, for a scintillating analysis of this and other related cultural changes of the period, John Brewer, *The Pleasures of the Imagination* (1997), esp. chs 3, 4, 11.

Sexual Celebrity

1. *OED*, 'pornographer', 'pornography'. The French equivalents must by then have been familiar, as Restif de la Bretonne's *Le Pornographe* (1769) was also available in London: Thomas Davies, *A Catalogue of very Curious and Valuable Books* [1770], 96; Thomas Payne, *A Catalogue of very Valuable Books, in Various Languages* (1796), 205–6; University College London, MSS of Jeremy Bentham, lxxvii. 194.

2. See e.g. Margaret F. Rosenthal, *The Honest Courtesan* (1992); Timothy Clark

et al. (eds), *The Dawn of the Floating World 1650–1765* (2001), cat. no. 25; *OED*, 'Cyprian', 'Cytherean', 'Paphian'; *Tom K---g's: or, The Paphian Grove* (1738); Samuel Richardson, *Letters and Passages Restored from the Original Manuscripts of the History of Clarissa* (1751), 203; [idem], *A Collection of the Moral and Instructive Sentiments ... Contained in the Histories of Pamela, Clarissa, and Sir Charles Grandison* (1755), 315, 318; *A New Atalantis* (2nd edn, 1758), 89; *Nocturnal Revels*, 2 vols (1779), *passim*; *The Modern Atalantis* (1784), 56; *Reynolds*, ed. Nicholas Penny (1986), 295–6.

3. Anne M. Haselkorn, *Prostitution in Elizabethan and Jacobean Comedy* (1983); A. V. Judges, *The Elizabethan Underworld* (1930).

4. For two early exceptions, the mid-sixteenth-century bawd Long Meg and her early Stuart counterpart Elizabeth Holland, see Bernard Capp, 'Long Meg of Westminster: A Mystery Solved', *Notes and Queries* 243 (1998); Nicholas Goodman, *Hollands Leaguer* (1632); Shackerley Marmion, *Hollands Leaguer* (1632); Henry Glapthorne, *The Hollander* (1635), sig. B^v.

5. See e.g. John Dryden, *Sir Martin Mar-All* (1668), Act IV, scene 1; William Wycherley, *The Plain Dealer* (1677), dedication; *The Criers and Hawkers of London*, ed. Sean Shesgreen (1990), plate 52; [James Caulfield?], *Blackguardiana* [1793?], s.v. 'A* / ABB'; *Dictionary of National Biography* (1885–1901), Madam Cresswell; *ODNB*, Madam Cresswell, Damaris Page, and references given there.

6. See *The Diary of Samuel Pepys*, ed. Robert Latham and William Matthews, 11 vols (London, 1970–83), quoting i. 250; John Harold Wilson, *Court Satires of the Restoration* (1976); Roger Thompson, *Unfit for Modest Ears* (1979), esp. ch. 5; Harold Love, *English Clandestine Satire 1660–1702* (2004); Melissa M. Mowry, *The Bawdy Politic in Stuart England, 1660–1714* (2004); Robert D. Hume, '"Satire" in the Reign of Charles II', *Modern Philology* 102 (2005).

7. For fiction, see e.g. *Look E're You Leap: or, A History of the Lives and Intrigues of Lewd Women* (10th edn [1720?]); *The Prostitutes of Quality; or Adultery a-la-mode* (1757); *Intrigue a-la-mode: or, The Covent-Garden Atalantis* (1767); for Sally Salisbury in later ballads, e.g. *The Bleach Yard's Garland* (Darlington, 1775); *The Muses' Delight* (Warrington, [1775?]); *The Case of Sally Salisbury* [1780]; *Sally Slisbury's Garland* (Liverpool, [1780?]); for other women cf. also *Tom K----g's*; *The Highlanders Salivated* (1746); *Covent Garden in Mourning* (1747); Helen Berry, 'Rethinking Politeness in Eighteenth-Century England', *Transactions of the Royal Historical Society* 18 (2001); for collective biographies see e.g. *The Humours of Fleet-Street and the Strand*, 2 vols [1749]; *Nocturnal Revels*, 2 vols (1779); *Harris's List of Covent Garden Ladies* (surviving edns of 1761, 1764, 1773, 1774, 1779, 1783, 1788, 1789, 1790, 1793); *Ranger's Impartial List of the Ladies of Pleasure* (Edinburgh, 1775).

8. Unless otherwise indicated, the analysis that follows is based on John Chaloner Smith, *British Mezzotinto Portraits*, 4 vols (1878–84); Charles E. Russell, *English Mezzotint Portraits and their States*, 2 vols (1926); Freeman O'Donoghue and Henry M. Hake, *Catalogue of Engraved British Portraits Preserved in the Department of Prints and Drawings in the British Museum*, 6 vols (1908–25); the col-

lections of print publishers' catalogues held at the British Museum and the Paul Mellon Centre for Studies in British Art (described in Antony Griffiths, 'A Checklist of Catalogues of British Print Publishers *c.*1650–1830', *Print Quarterly* 1 (1984)); and the collection of auction catalogues 1689–92 held at the British Library (pressmark 1402.g.1).

9. See also *Diary of Samuel Pepys*, vii. 359, 393; viii. 23, 206; Antony Griffiths, *The Print in Stuart Britain 1603–1689* (1998), ch. 9; Catherine MacLeod and Julia Marciari Alexander, *Painted Ladies* (2001), *passim*; Julia Marciari Alexander, 'Painting a Life', in Kevin Sharpe and Steven N. Zwicker, *Writing Lives* (2008); Michael Hunter (ed.), *Printed Images in Early Modern Britain* (2010), esp. ch. 15.

10. See e.g. Frederic George Stephens and M. Dorothy George, *Catalogue of Prints and Drawings in the British Museum: Division I: Political and Personal Satires*, 11 vols (1870–1954), vols 3–7 (for Anne Vane and Lady Yarmouth see e.g. nos 2270, 2348, 2350, 2450, 2451, 2464, 2454, 2453, 2495, 2578, 2606, 3018); *Love after Enjoyment* (1732); *Vanelia: or, the Amours of the Great* (6 edns, 1732); *The Humours of the Court* (2 edns, 1732); *Vanella in the Straw* (3 edns, 1732); *The Fair Concubine: or, the Secret History of the beautiful Vanella* (4 edns, 1732); *Authentick Memoirs of the Unfortunate Vanella* (1736); *Vanella: A Tragedy* (1736); *Vanella's Progress* (1736); *Vanella: or an elegy* (1736); Diana Donald, *The Age of Caricature* (1996), ch. 3; Cindy McCreery, 'Keeping up with the *Bon Ton*', in Hannah Barker and Elaine Chalus (eds), *Gender in Eighteenth-Century England* (1997); Cindy McCreery, *The Satirical Gaze* (2004), 153–67.

11. *Sculptura-Historico-Technica* (1747), quoting 72; [Ange Goudar], *The Chinese Spy*, 6 vols (1765), quoting vi. 208; *Robert Sayer's New and Enlarged Catalogue* [1766], 95–103.

12. *Nocturnal Revels*, quoting ii. 227; Stephens and George, *Catalogue of Prints*, e.g. nos 3180, 3215, 3567, 5204.

13. In general see e.g. Samuel Derrick, *Letters*, 2 vols (Dublin, 1767), ii. 8; Graham Reynolds, *English Portrait Miniatures* (rev. edn., 1988), 112; *The Centinel* 36 (30 July 1757); *The English Roscius* [1785?], 85; Horace Bleackley, *Ladies Fair and Frail* (1909); McCreery, *Satirical Gaze*, ch. 3; for Fanny Murray's sandwich, *The Yale Edition of Horace Walpole's Correspondence*, ed. W. S. Lewis, 48 vols (1937–83), ix. 80; *The Vis-à-vis of Berkley-Square* [1783], 11–12; for Sally Salisbury, H[enry] Carey, *Poems on Several Occasions* (3rd edn, 1729), 127–8; [Henry Man], *Mr Bentley, the Rural Philosopher*, 2 vols (1775), i. 210; for typical references to Fanny Murray see e.g. *The Modern Courtezan* [1750?]; [John Hill], *The Inspector*, 2 vols (1753), ii. 300; [Eliza Fowler Heywood], *The Invisible Spy*, 2 vols (1755), iii. 285; *Reflections Arising from the Immorality of the Present Age* (1756), 55; *British Worthies* (1758), 14n; [Edward Thompson], *The Meretriciad* (1761); *The Adulteress* (1773), v, vii; *The Works of the English Poets*, ed. Samuel Johnson, 58 vols (1779–80), liii. 185, 299; [Alexander Dalrymple], *The Poor Man's Friend* (1795), 12; for the appropriation of courtesans' names, e.g. *The Complete Letter–Writer* (4th edn, 1757), 216; [William Dodd], *The Sisters*, 2 vols

(1754), i. 75; [George Colman], *The Connoisseur*, 2 vols (1755–6), i. 280; 'Oddibus Funnybus', *A Collection of Original Comic Songs* [1765?], 27, 72–3; *OED*, 'Nancy Dawson', 'Rudd', 'Moll Peatley'; Robert Holloway, *The Phoenix of Sodom* (1813), 13; Iona and Peter Opie, *The Oxford Dictionary of Nursery Rhymes* (1973 edn), 279–80; Stella Tillyard, *Aristocrats* (1994), 155; for racehorses, John Cheny, *An Historical List of all Horse-Matches Run* (1731 edn), 133, 135; ibid. (1739 edn), 38; ibid. (1741 edn), 17; ibid. (1751 edn), 55; Reginald Heber, *An Historical List of Horse-Matches Run* (1760 edn), 39; ibid. (1764 edn), 77; ibid. (1766 edn), 45; ibid. (1767 edn), 36; B. Walker, *An Historical List of Horse-Matches* (1771), 44; W[illiam] Pick, *An Authentic Historical Racing Calendar* (York, [1785]), 47; James Weatherby, *Racing Calendar* (1775 edn), 137; ibid. (1795 edn), 33, 101, 170; Charles E. Trevathan, *The American Thoroughbred* (1905), 54–5.

The Explosion of Print

1. See e.g. David Cressy, *Literacy and the Social Order* (1980), 121, 128–9, 134–5, 147 (which measures the ability to sign one's name: reading skills were even more widespread); Sheila Lambert, 'State Control of the Press in Theory and Practice', in Robin Myers and Michael Harris (eds), *Censorship and the Control of Print* (1992); Cyndia Susan Clegg, *Press Censorship in Elizabethan England* (1997) and her *Press Censorship in Jacobean England* (2001) and *Press Censorship in Caroline England* (2008).

2. See esp. Arthur F. Marotti, *Manuscript, Print, and the English Renaissance Lyric* (1995), 75–82; Ian Frederick Moulton, *Before Pornography* (2000), esp. ch. 1; Harold Love, *Scribal Publication in Seventeenth-Century England* (1993) and his *English Clandestine Satire, 1660–1702* (2004); Adam Fox, *Oral and Literate Culture in England 1500–1700* (2000).

3. See esp. James Raven, *The Business of Books* (2007); Michael F. Suarez and Michael L. Turner (eds), *The Cambridge History of the Book in Britain: Volume V, 1695–1830* (2009).

4. For this paragraph and the next, see *The Diary of Dudley Ryder, 1715–1716*, ed. William Matthews (1939), index s.v. 'journals'; Henry Fielding, *The Covent-Garden Journal* [1752], ed. Bertrand A. Goldgar (1988), 13 n. 4; Frank Donoghue, *The Fame Machine* (1996), 3; R. B. Walker, 'The Newspaper Press in the Reign of William III', *Historical Journal* 17 (1974); Michael Harris, *London Newspapers in the Age of Walpole* (1987); Charles E. Clark, *The Public Prints* (1994); Joad Raymond (ed.), *News, Newspapers and Society in Early Modern England* (1999); Hannah Barker, *Newspapers, Politics and English Society, 1695–1855* (2000); Suarez and Turner (eds), *History of the Book*, pt IV. III.

5. *The Spectator*, ed. Donald F. Bond, 5 vols (1965), quoting i. xxvi and no. 10.

6. *The Idler*, no. 7 (27 May 1758).

7. See *The Diary of Samuel Pepys*, ed. Robert Latham and William Matthews, 11 vols (1970–83), iv. 163, 177; v. 124; Ernest Bernbaum, *The Mary Carleton Narratives, 1663–1673* (1914); C. F. Main, 'The German Princess', *Harvard Library Bulletin* 10 (1956); Hero Chalmers, '"The Person I am, or what they made me to be"', in Clare Brant and Diane Purkiss (eds), *Women, Texts and Histories 1575–1760* (1992) and her 'The Feminine Subject in Women's Printed Writings, 1653–1689' (University of Oxford D.Phil. thesis, 1993), 158–208.

8. *OED*, 'opinion'; John Brewer, *The Pleasures of the Imagination* (1997), 190–97; *The Rambler*, no. 23 (5 June 1750). Cf. [David Hume], *An Abstract of a Book Lately Published* (1740), preface.

9. For stimulating syntheses see e.g. David Zaret, *Origins of Democratic Culture* (2000); James Van Horn Melton, *The Rise of the Public in Enlightenment Europe* (2001); T. C. W. Blanning, *The Culture of Power and the Power of Culture* (2002); Peter Lake and Steve Pincus, *The Politics of the Public Sphere in Early Modern England* (2007); Jason Peacey (ed.), *The Print Culture of Parliament, 1600–1800* (2007); Brean S. Hammond, *Professional Imaginative Writing in England, 1670–1740* (1997); Brewer, *Pleasures*.

10. See e.g. *Spectator*, ed. Bond, esp. i. xxxvi–xliii; Robert Haig, *The Gazetteer, 1735–1797* (1960), 71–4; Harris, *London Newspapers*, 196–7; *The New Cambridge Bibliography of English Literature*, ed. George Watson (1971), columns 1218–1235; Michael Macdonald and Terence R. Murphy, *Sleepless Souls* (1990), 324–37; P. Linebaugh, 'The Ordinary of Newgate and his *Account*', in J. S. Cockburn, *Crime in England, 1550–1800* (1977); Caroline Gonda, 'Misses, Murderesses and Magdalens', in Elizabeth Eger *et al.* (eds), *Women, Writing, and the Public Sphere, 1700–1830* (2001); *The Adventurer*, no. 115 (11 Dec. 1753).

The Manipulation of Publicity

1. For new types of interaction and communication see, in addition to works cited in the previous section, e.g. Donna T. Andrew, 'Popular Culture and Public Debate', *Historical Journal* 39 (1996) and her *London Debating Societies, 1776–1799* (London Record Society, 1994); Peter Clark, *British Clubs and Societies 1580–1800* (2000); William St Clair, *The Reading Nation in the Romantic Period* (2004), esp. chs 1, 22; Brian Cowan, *The Social Life of Coffee* (2005).

2. For the older tradition, see Keith Thomas, 'Cases of Conscience in Seventeenth-Century England', in John Morrill *et al.* (eds), *Public Duty and Private Conscience in Seventeenth-Century England* (1993), and the literature cited there.

3. See esp. Gilbert D. McEwen, *The Oracle of the Coffee House* (1972); Stephen Parks, *John Dunton and the English Book Trade* (1976); Kathryn Shevelow, *Women and Print Culture* (1989); J. A. Downie and Thomas N. Corns (eds), *Telling People What to Think* (1993); Helen Berry, *Gender, Society and Print Culture in Late-Stuart England* (2003).

4. *The Spectator*, ed. Donald F. Bond, 5 vols (1965), introduction to vol. 1 (quoting i. lxxxvi); Thomas, 'Cases of Conscience'; David M. Turner, *Fashioning Adultery* (2002), ch. 2.

5. See Alastair Bellany, *The Politics of Court Scandal* (2002), esp. ch. 2; Cynthia B. Herrup, *A House in Gross Disorder* (1999); Rachel Weil, *Political Passions* (1999), ch. 5; Lawrence Stone, *Road to Divorce* (1990), 248–54, 313–22.

6. See esp. Marcia Pointon, 'The Lives of Kitty Fisher', *British Journal for Eighteenth-Century Studies* 27 (2004); *ODNB*, Catherine Maria Fischer; *OED*, 'cause célèbre'; cf. Sara Maza, *Private Lives and Public Affairs* (1993); Gary Kates, *Monsieur d'Eon is a Woman* (1995).

7. Monsieur de Voltaire, *Histoire d'Elizabeth Canning* (1762), quoting 5; Lillian Bueno McCue, 'Elizabeth Canning in Print', *University of Colorado Studies (Series B)*, 2 (1945); John Treherne, *The Canning Enigma* (1989); Judith Moore, *The Appearance of Truth* (1994); Donna T. Andrew and Randall McGowen, *The Perreaus and Mrs Rudd* (2001); John Brewer, *Sentimental Murder* (2004); Matthew J. Kinservik, *Sex, Scandal, and Celebrity in Late Eighteenth-Century England* (2007).

8. See e.g. *London Chronicle* viii. 353, 362, 386, 397, 430, 607, 630 (1760); 'One of the Jury', *The True and Whole Proceedings of the Coroner's Inquest ... of Ann Sharp* [1760]; 'A Lover of Justice', *An Answer to the Pamphlet wrote by the Juryman ... Touching the Death of Ann Sharp* [1760]; 'Heartfree', *A Most Circumstantial Account of that Unfortunate Young Lady, Miss Bell* (5 edns, 1760–61); *A Full Refutation of a Libellous Pamphlet, Entituled A Most Circumstantial Account of that Unfortunate Lady, Miss Bell* (1761); 'An Impartial By-Stander', *Remark upon the Trial of William Sutton* (1761); *OBP* 25 Feb. 1761 (reprinted in *Select Trials*, 4 vols (1764), vol. iv); *A Short View of the Remarkable Difference* [1761]; T[homas] Holland, *A Circumstantial Account, Relating to that Unfortunate Young Woman, Miss Anne Bell* [1761], quoting iii. For another case, cf. [Richard de Courcy], *Seduction* (1782); [idem], *The Seducer Convicted* (Shrewsbury, 1783); [Ralph Winwood], *Calumny* (1782); and, more generally, Robert B. Shoemaker, *The London Mob* (2004), ch. 9.

9. Jürgen Habermas, *The Structural Transformation of the Public Sphere*, transl. Thomas Burger (1989).

10. For this paragraph and the next two, see esp. Lucyle Werkmeister, *The London Daily Press 1772–1792* (1963); Michael Harris, *London Newspapers in the Age of Walpole* (1987); for further examples, [J. W.] D'Archenholz, *A Picture of England*, 2 vols (1789), ii. 65; *Spectator*, ed. Bond, i. xxxvi–xlii; Brewer, *Sentimental Murder*, 40–41, 155.

11. See e.g. A. Aspinall, 'Statistical Accounts of the London Newspapers in the Eighteenth Century', *English Historical Review* 63 (1948); R. B. Walker, 'Advertising in London Newspapers, 1650–1750', *Business History* 15 (1973), quoting 129–30; Frank Donoghue, *The Fame Machine* (1996); chapters by Harris, Ferdinand, and Mathison in Joad Raymond (ed.), *News, Newspapers and Society in Early Modern England* (1999); Antonia Forster, 'Review Journals and the Reading

Public', in Isabel Rivers (ed.), *Books and their Readers in Eighteenth-Century England: New Essays* (2001); *OED*, 'puff', 'puffer', 'puffery', 'puffing'; Thomas Keymer and Peter Sabor, *Pamela in the Marketplace* (2005), ch. 1.

12. See e.g. *The New Cambridge Bibliography of English Literature*, ed. George Watson (1971), e.g. columns 1223 (Boswell's review of his own *Reflections on the Late Alarming Bankruptcies* (1772)), 1329–30 (piracies of *Common Sense* and *All-Alive and Merry*); Werkmeister, *London Daily Press*, passim; [David Hume], *An Abstract of a Book Lately Published* (1740), preface; James Stephen Taylor, *Jonas Hanway* (1985), 136 (she declined); Roger Lonsdale, 'New Attributions to John Cleland', *Review of English Studies* 30 (1979), 271; Andrew and McGowen, *Perreaus and Mrs Rudd*, quoting 212 (italics in the original); *Boswell's London Journal 1762–1763*, ed. Frederick A. Pottle (1950), quoting 249 n. 2; [James Boswell], *An Ode to Tragedy* (1661 [i.e. 1761]); Frederick A. Pottle, *James Boswell: The Earlier Years 1740–1769* (1966), e.g. 331–4, 338, 425, 434 (quoting 332).

13. H. P. Thompson, *Thomas Bray* (1954).

14. See Taylor, *Jonas Hanway*; Donna T. Andrew, *Philanthropy and Police* (1989), esp. ch. 3; Christie's Auctioneers, King Street, London: sale 4852 (21 Oct. 1992), lot 164; [Jonas Hanway], *A Plan for Establishing a Charity-House* (1758), iii–iv; [idem], *Thoughts on the Plan* (2nd edn, 1759), quoting 5; idem, *Letter V* (1758), 27 (part of a 'postscript' added to editions published after 7 April 1758); *Diary and Letters of Madame D'Arblay*, ed. [Charlotte Barrett], 7 vols (1842–6), ii. 231.

15. See e.g. *The Public Advertiser*, no. 7338 (4 May 1758); John Fielding, *A Plan of the Asylum* (1758), 20–22. Cf. John Styles, 'Sir John Fielding and the Problem of Criminal Investigation', *Transactions of the Royal Historical Society* 33 (1983) and his 'Print and Policing', in Douglas Hay and Francis Snyder (eds), *Policing and Prosecution in Britain, 1750–1850* (1989).

Private and Public Affairs

1. Hugh Blair, *Lectures on Rhetoric and Belles Lettres*, 2 vols (1783; first delivered in the 1760s), ii. 287; *The Rambler*, no. 60 (13 Oct. 1750); *The Confessions of J. J. Rousseau . . . Part the Second*, 3 vols (1790), i. 99–100.

2. See esp. Ian Watt, *The Rise of the Novel* (1957), ch. 1; Lennard J. Davis, *Factual Fictions* (1983); Michael McKeon, *The Origins of the English Novel 1600–1740* (1987) and his *The Secret History of Domesticity* (2005); J. Paul Hunter, *Before Novels* (1990). Particularly influential accounts of the philosophical trajectory are Charles Taylor, *Sources of the Self* (1989); Jerrold Seigel, *The Idea of the Self* (2005); a useful historical overview is Roy Porter (ed.), *Rewriting the Self* (1997).

3. Though *The Night-Walker* does make some use of initials and elliptical dashes (e.g. 'C— G—') to describe persons and places. This practice, which suggested the

reader was penetrating a secret reality, was to become much more common in the eighteenth century.

4. Cf. Dror Wahrman, *The Making of the Modern Self* (2004), 182–5; Cindy McCreery, *The Satirical Gaze: Prints of Women in Late Eighteenth-Century England* (2004), ch. 2.

5. Daniel Defoe, *The Fortunes and Misfortunes of the Famous Moll Flanders* [1722], ed. David Blewett (1989), quoting title page and Preface; Jane Barker, *A Patch-Work Screen for the Ladies* (1723), quoting iv.

6. Rosalind Ballaster, 'Manl(e)y Forms', in Clare Brant and Diane Purkiss (eds), *Women, Texts and Histories 1575–1760* (1992), and her *Seductive Forms* (1992); Robert Mayer, *History and the Early English Novel* (1997); Rebecca Bullard, *The Politics of Disclosure, 1674–1725* (2009).

7. David Randall, 'Epistolary Rhetoric, the Newspaper, and the Public Sphere', *Past and Present* 198 (2000); Robert Iliffe, 'Author-Mongering', in Ann Bermingham and John Brewer (eds), *The Consumption of Culture 1600–1800* (1995), citing 171; Susan E. Whyman, *The Pen and the People* (2009).

8. Quoting *The Rambler*, no. 60 (1750). See e.g. Donald A. Stauffer, *The Art of Biography in Eighteenth-Century England*, 2 vols (1941); Jane Rendall, '"A Short Account of My Unprofitable Life"', in Trev Lynn Broughton and Linda Anderson (eds), *Women's Lives/Women's Times* (1997); Isabel Rivers, 'Biographical Dictionaries', in her (ed.), *Books and their Readers in Eighteenth-Century England: New Essays* (2001); Keith Thomas, *Changing Conceptions of National Biography* (2005); and, for portraits, Antony Griffiths, 'Sir William Musgrave and British Biography', *The British Library Journal* 18 (1992); Marcia Pointon, *Hanging the Head* (1993), esp. chs ii–iii; Timothy Clayton, *The English Print 1688–1802* (1997), 57–62, 76–8, 183–5, 215–16, 244–5.

Fame and Fortune

1. *OED*, 'celebrable', 'celebrate', 'celebrated', 'celebration', 'celebrator', 'celebre', 'celebrious', 'celebrity', 'celebrous'. There is as yet no adequate general study of this important subject. For recent approaches to it by scholars of art and drama see Martin Postle (ed.), *Joshua Reynolds: The Creation of Celebrity* (2005); Tom Mole, *Romanticism and Celebrity Culture* (2009); the works cited in note 4 below; and, more generally, Leo Braudy, *The Frenzy of Renown* (1986); Fred Inglis, *A Short History of Celebrity* (2010).

2. *ODNB*, Robert Greene; Bernard Capp, *The World of John Taylor the Water-Poet 1578–1653* (1994), 196.

3. Gerald Howson, *Thief-taker General* (1970); Peter Linebaugh, *The London Hanged* (1991), ch. 1; William Eben Shultz, *Gay's Beggar's Opera* (1923); Robert R. Singleton, 'English Criminal Biography, 1651–1722', *Harvard Library Bulletin* 18 (1970); Michael Harris, 'Trials and Criminal Biographies' in Robin Myers and

Michael Harris, *Sale and Distribution of Books from 1700* (1982); Lincoln B. Faller, *Turned to Account* (1987).

4. *Plays written by the Thrice Noble, Illustrious and Excellent Princess, the Lady Marchioness of Newcastle* (1662), quoting 641. See Elizabeth Howe, *The First English Actresses* (1992); Sandra Richards, *The Rise of the English Actress* (1993); Kimberly Crouch, 'The Public Life of Actresses', in Hannah Barker and Elaine Chalus (eds), *Gender in Eighteenth-Century England* (1997); Philip E. Baruth (ed.), *Introducing Charlotte Charke* (1998); Robyn Asleson (ed.), *Notorious Muse* (2003); Cheryl Wanko, *Roles of Authority* (2003); Mary Luckhurst and Jane Moody (eds), *Theatre and Celebrity in Britain, 1660–2000* (2005); Gill Perry, *Spectacular Flirtations* (2007); Felicity Nussbaum, *Rival Queens* (2010).

Self-promotion and Exploitation

1. See e.g. Horace Bleackley, *Ladies Fair and Frail* (1909); *ODNB*, Frances Murray, Richard Nash.

2. See *The Public Advertiser* (24, 27, 29 Mar. 1759); Gordon Goodwin, *James McArdell* (1903), cat. nos 80, 184; *Reynolds*, ed. Nicholas Penny (1986), 22–3, 45, 193, 356; Martin Postle (ed.), *Joshua Reynolds: The Creation of Celebrity* (2005), 24, 26–31, 51–4, 181–91, 224–5, 236–7, 256–7; David Mannings and Martin Postle, *Sir Joshua Reynolds: A Complete Catalogue of his Paintings* (2000), cat. nos 498–9, 611–19, 1353–6; Martin Postle, '"Painted Women"', in Robyn Asleson (ed.), *Notorious Muse* (2003).

3. *An Apology for the Conduct of Mrs. Teresia Constantia Phillips*, 3 vols (1748–9); *Memoirs of Laetitia Pilkington*, ed. A. C. Elias, Jr (1997), quoting xl; [Frances Vane], 'Memoirs of a Lady of Quality', in Tobias Smollett, *The Adventures of Peregrine Pickle* (1751); *An Apology for the Life of George Anne Bellamy* (1785); *Memoirs of Mrs Margaret Leeson*, 3 vols (Dublin, 1795–7), quoting iii. 314; Felicity A. Nussbaum, *The Autobiographical Subject* (1989), ch. 8; Clare Brant, 'Speaking of Women', in Clare Brant and Diane Purkiss (eds), *Women, Texts and Histories 1575–1760* (1992); Lynda M. Thompson, *The 'Scandalous Memoirists'* (2000). Cf. Iain McCalman, *Radical Underworld* (1988), 41–2, 221–31; Julie Peakman, *Lascivious Bodies* (2004), 73–102.

4. For this and the following paragraphs, see esp. Robert Darnton, *The Forbidden Best-Sellers of Pre-Revolutionary France* (1996); Simon Burrows, *Blackmail, Scandal and Revolution* (2009) and his *A King's Ransom* (2010); McCalman, *Radical Underworld*; Jonathan Mee, 'Libertines and Radicals in the 1790s', in Peter Cryle and Lisa O'Connell (eds), *Libertine Enlightenment* (2004), and his '"A bold and free-spoken man"', in David Womersley (ed.), *'Cultures of Whiggism'* (2005); E. A. Smith, *A Queen on Trial* (1993); Anna Clark, *Scandal* (2004), chs 7–8.

5. *ODNB*, Mary Robinson, Mary Anne Clarke (which gives the sum as £7,000), Harriette Wilson; *Harriette Wilson's Memoirs*, ed. Lesley Blanch (2003 edn);

Frances Wilson, *The Courtesan's Revenge* (2003). For the different position and (often, considerable) power of Stuart royal mistresses, cf. Sonya Wynne, 'The Mistresses of Charles II and Restoration Court Politics', in Eveline Cruickshanks (ed.), *The Stuart Courts* (2000).

6. *Thraliana*, ed. Katharine C. Balderston (2nd edn, 1951), quoting 358-9 (italics in the original). Cf. Lisa O'Connell, 'Authorship and Libertine Celebrity', in Cryle and O'Connell (eds), *Libertine Enlightenment*; Claire Brock, '"Then Smile and Know Thyself Supremely Great"', *Women's Writing* 9 (2002).

Celebrating Sex

1. Cf. Roy Porter, 'Mixed Feelings', in Paul-Gabriel Boucé (ed.), *Sexuality in Eighteenth-Century Britain* (1982).

2. See e.g. Richard Godbeer, *Sexual Revolution in Early America* (2002), ch. 8.

3. *ODNB*, Augustus Henry FitzRoy, Edward Thurlow, Charles James Fox, John Montagu (fourth Earl of Sandwich), Prince Frederick (Duke of York and Albany), George IV; *American National Biography* (1999), Benjamin Franklin, Aaron Burr, Alexander Hamilton; Annette Gordon-Reed, *The Hemingses of Monticello* (2008).

4. Arthur H. Cash, *John Wilkes* (2006), 32-5; John Sainsbury, *John Wilkes* (2006), 101-12; *ODNB*, Franciscans [Monks of Medmenham]; David Stevenson, *The Beggar's Benison* (2001). Cf. R[ichard] P[ayne] Knight, *An Account of the Remains of the Worship of Priapus* (1786); Jason M. Kelly, 'Riots, Revelries, and Rumor', *Journal of British Studies* 45 (2006).

5. See *ODNB*, Anne Parsons, Grace Elliott, Mary Nesbitt, Ann Elliot, Elizabeth Armitstead, Gertrude Mahon; and the examples given in Horace Bleackley, *Ladies Fair and Frail* (1909); Katie Hickman, *Courtesans* (2003); Donna T. Andrew and Randall McGowen, *The Perreaus and Mrs Rudd* (2001), esp. 98-111.

6. See e.g. *London Courtship* [1759]; the clippings collected in Yale Lewis Walpole Library, Quarto 724.771N; *ODNB*, James Graham, and the references given there; Roy Porter, *English Society in the Eighteenth Century* (1982), 259-65; *Harris's List of Covent Garden Ladies*; *The Rambler's Magazine*; *The Ranger's Magazine*; *Town and Country Magazine*; David Foxon, *Libertine Literature in England, 1660-1745* (1965); Donald Thomas, *A Long Time Burning* (1969); Roger Thompson, *Unfit for Modest Ears* (1979); Peter Wagner, *Eros Revived* (1988); Lynn Hunt (ed.), *The Invention of Pornography* (1993); Ian Frederick Moulton, *Before Pornography* (2000); Bradford K. Mudge, *The Whore's Story* (2000) and his *When Flesh Becomes Word* (2004); James Grantham Turner, *Schooling Sex* (2003); Julie Peakman, *Mighty Lewd Books* (2003); Karen Harvey, *Reading Sex in the Eighteenth Century* (2004); Vic Gatrell, *City of Laughter* (2006), esp. pt III; Sarah Toulalan, *Imagining Sex* (2007); Malcolm Jones, *The Print in Early Modern England* (2010), esp. chs 6 and 10; Ford K. Brown, *Fathers of the Victorians* (1961), 428; R. B. Outhwaite, *Scandal in the Church* (1997), quoting 33.

EPILOGUE: MODERN CULTURES OF SEX – FROM THE
VICTORIANS TO THE TWENTY-FIRST CENTURY

Repression and Control

1. See Peter Gay, *The Bourgeois Experience: Victoria to Freud*, 5 vols (1984–98); Michael Mason, *The Making of Victorian Sexual Attitudes* (1994) and his *The Making of Victorian Sexuality* (1994); and cf. the roundtable discussion in *Journal of Victorian Studies* 1 (1996).

2. John Bowles, *Reflections on the Political and Moral State of Society* (1800), 135; *The Anti-Jacobin Review and Magazine* 12 (1802), 72.

3. For this paragraph and the next, see Robert Isaac Wilberforce and Samuel Wilberforce, *Life of William Wilberforce*, 5 vols (1838), quoting i. 149; *ODNB*, Mary Wollstonecraft; Hannah More, *Strictures on the Modern System of Female Education*, 2 vols (1799), quoting i. 45. Excellent surveys include Maurice J. Quinlan, *Victorian Prelude* (1941); Ford K. Brown, *Fathers of the Victorians* (1961); Eric Trudgill, *Madonnas and Magdalens* (1976); Boyd Hilton, *The Age of Atonement* (1988), Vic Gatrell, *City of Laughter* (2006), pt IV.

4. Simon Szreter, 'Victorian Britain, 1831–1963', *Journal of Victorian Culture* 1 (1996) and his *Fertility, Class and Gender in Britain, 1860–1940* (1996); Angus McLaren, *A History of Contraception* (1990), chs 6–7.

5. Hera Cook, *The Long Sexual Revolution* (2003); Kate Fisher, *Birth Control, Sex, and Marriage in Britain, 1918–1960* (2006); Simon Szreter and Kate Fisher, *Sex Before the Sexual Revolution: Intimate Life in England 1918–1963* (2010).

6. See esp. Jeffrey Weeks, *Sex, Politics and Society* (2nd edn, 1989); Anna Clark, *The Struggle for the Breeches* (1995); Judith R. Walkowitz, *Prostitution and Victorian Society* (1980) and her *City of Dreadful Delight* (1992); Barry Reay, *Watching Hannah* (2002), and the literature cited in these studies.

7. Matt Houlbrook, *Queer London* (2005), quoting 190, 197; Matt Houlbrook and Chris Waters, 'The Heart in Exile', *History Workshop Journal* 62 (2006), quoting 155, 162.

8. *ODNB*, (John) Mervyn Guthrie Griffith-Jones, *Lady Chatterley's Lover* trial (*act.* 1960).

9. Graham Robb, *Strangers* (2003), conveniently summarizes these facts; for further details see e.g. Richard Davenport-Hines, *Sex, Death and Punishment* (1990); H. G. Cocks, *Nameless Offences* (2003); Matt Cook, *London and the Culture of Homosexuality, 1885–1914* (2003); Houlbrook, *Queer London*; Margot Canaday, *The Straight State* (2009).

10. Lesley A. Hall, *Sex, Gender and Social Change in Britain since 1800* (2000), citing 102, 113–14.

11. This distinction has, of course, never been entirely clear-cut: for incisive remarks on its evolution see Anna Clark, *Desire: A History of European Sexuality* (2008). Amongst many stimulating studies of its broader origins and impact on

nineteenth-century social policy, see e.g. Lucia Zedner, *Women, Crime and Custody in Victorian England* (1991); Nicola Lacey, *Women, Crime, and Character* (2008).

12. Cf. e.g. Gay, *Bourgeois Experience*; Steven Marcus, *The Other Victorians* (1966); Ronald Pearsall, *The Worm in the Bud* (1969); Lesley A. Hall, *Hidden Anxieties: Male Sexuality, 1900–1950* (1991); Cook, *Long Sexual Revolution*; Szreter and Fisher, *Sex Before the Sexual Revolution*.

Liberty and Equality

1. See e.g. John D'Emilio and Estelle B. Freedman, *Intimate Matters* (1988); Brian Harrison, *Seeking a Role* (2009), chs 5, 9 and his *Finding a Role?* (2010), ch. 4; Frank Mort, *Capital Affairs* (2010).

2. See e.g. Graham Robb, *Strangers* (2003), quoting 157; Jeffrey Weeks, *Sex, Politics and Society* (2nd edn, 1989), ch. 11; *Outspoken Women*, ed. Lesley A. Hall (2005), ch. 3.

3. See e.g. William N. Eskridge, Jr, 'A Jurisprudence of "Coming Out"', *Yale Law Journal* 106 (1997); United Kingdom Parliamentary Joint Select Committee on Human Rights, *Legislative Scrutiny: Sexual Orientation Regulations* (Feb. 2007, HL Paper 58 / HC 350) and *Legislative Scrutiny: Equality Bill* (Nov. 2009, HL Paper 169 / HC 736).

4. Harrison, *Seeking a Role*, 510; *Bowers v. Hardwick* (1986) 478 *United States Supreme Court Reports* 186 (cf. 'Survey on the Constitutional Right to Privacy in the Context of Homosexual Activity', *University of Miami Law Review* 40 (1986)); Local Government Act 1988 (c. 9) (repealed in Scotland by the Ethical Standards in Public Life etc. (Scotland) Act 2000 (asp 7), and in the rest of the United Kingdom by the Local Government Act 2003 (c. 26)). Cf. Richard Davenport-Hines, *Sex, Death and Punishment* (1990), chs 8–9.

5. See Stephen Cretney, *Same Sex Relationships* (2006); Rosie Harding, 'Sir Mark Potter and the Protection of the Traditional Family', *Feminist Legal Studies* 15 (2007); Nicholas Bamforth, 'Same-sex Partnerships', *European Human Rights Law Review* (2007); *R. v. Wilson* (1996) 3 *Weekly Law Reports* 125; *R. v. Brown et al.* (1993) 2 *WLR* 556; *Laskey et al. v. United Kingdom* (1997) 24 *European Human Rights Reports* 39. Cf. Nicholas Bamforth, 'Sado-Masochism and Consent', *Criminal Law Review* (1994); Matthew Weait, 'Harm, Consent and the Limits of Privacy', *Feminist Legal Studies* 13 (2005).

6. See, amongst many other examples, Ryan Goodman, 'Beyond the Enforcement Principle', *California Law Review* 89 (2001); Carl F. Stychin, *Governing Sexuality* (2003); special issue of *McGill Law Journal* 49, no. 4 (2004); Robert Wintemute, 'Same-Sex Couples', *European Human Rights Law Review* (2006); and recent volumes of the journal *Law and Sexuality*. Cf. John Gardner, 'On the

NOTES TO PAGE 364

Grounds of Her Sex(uality)', *Oxford Journal of Legal Studies* 18 (1998); *X v. Y* (2004) *Industrial Cases Reports* 1138; *Pay v. Lancashire Probation Service* (2004) *Industrial Cases Reports* 187.

7. See the judgements, dissenting opinions, and precedents cited in *Dudgeon v. United Kingdom* (1981) 4 *European Human Rights Reports* 149; *A.D.T. v. United Kingdom* (2001) 31 *European Human Rights Reports* 33; *Lawrence et al. v. Texas* (2003) 539 *United States Supreme Court Reports* 558; N. A. Moreham, 'The Right to Respect for Private Life', *European Human Rights Law Review* (2008).

8. For the advance of similar principles in the jurisprudence of former colonies, see e.g. *Naz Foundation v. Delhi and Others* (2009) 4 *Law Reports of the Commonwealth* 838.

9. See e.g. Oriana Fallaci, 'An Interview with Khomeini', *The New York Times*, 7 Oct. 1979; *Iran: End Executions by Stoning* (Amnesty International report, Jan. 2008, www.amnesty.org); Janet Afary, *Sexual Politics in Modern Iran* (2009).

List of Illustrations

I. PICTURES IN THE TEXT

II. PLATES

Section 1

Index

For ease of use, many central themes are included under 'sexual discipline' and 'sexual freedom'. Biblical books and passages are listed under 'Bible'; legislation under 'laws, actual' and 'laws, proposed'. Works of art and literature are generally indexed under their creators. Persons with titles are listed under the name or title used in the text. Most sub-entries are arranged thematically and/or in the order in which they occur in the text.

America and American – *cont.*
  fiction 173
  transportation to 207
  laws against seduction 215
  polygamy 230–31
  emigration to 270
  sexual philanthropies 280–81
  influence of London 343
  religious revival 352
  persecution of homosexuality 357, 363
  sexual freedom 363–4
  Supreme Court 363
  politics 363–4
Amsterdam 111
Anabaptists 33, 88, 135
anatomy 143–4
Anglicans *see* Church of England:
  members of
Anglo-Saxons 5, 8–9
Anne, Queen 59
Annet, Peter 79, 117
Anti-Jacobin Review 352
antinomians 89–90
Aretino, Pietro 131
aristocrats
  Anglo-Saxon 9
  sexual laxity of 14, 22, 118, 166,
    343–5
  censured 14, 24, 41–2, 67, 210,
    339, 341
  see also gentlemen and gentry;
    upper classes
Aristotle 34
army, parliamentary 49–50
Ashley, Lord, first Earl of Shaftesbury
  220
Ashmore, Alice 147
Asia 104, 226, 231
Assyrians 5
Astell, Mary 167, 202
atheists 33, 82
Athenian Mercury 111, 320
Atticus, bishop of Constantinople 8
Aubin, Penelope 170
Augustine, St 7–8, 32, 196
Austen, Jane 166, 173–4
Axtell, Daniel 83

Babylon
  laws of 5
  whore of 12
bachelors 11, 193, 205, 223, 226, 250
Bacon, Francis 202
bagnios 322, 345
Bagwell, Mrs 146–7
Bagwell, William 146–7
bail 23, 42, 48
ballads 16, 25–6, 70, 299, 303–4, 311,
  314, 325, 336
Bangor (Caernarfonshire) 55
Bank of England 257
Banks, John 162
Barbados 50, 246
  see also West Indies
Barker, Jane 170, 322–3
Barker, Robert 18
bastards and bastardy
  incidence 41, 50, 120n, 204–5, 224
  concerns 13n, 15, 27–31, 85,
    119–21, 151
  laws 13, 49, 78
  punished 1, 14, 22, 25–6, 29–31,
    41, 44, 48–9, 122, 147
  extenuated 103, 107, 126–7, 214n
  of St Augustine 7
  and same-sex actions 132–3, 136
  and forced marriage 214
  and Foundling Hospital 222, 243–4
  see also children; concubinage and
    concubines; mothers, unmarried;
    pregnancy, illicit;
bawds and bawdry
  attacked 10, 37, 47–8, 53–4, 56–7,
    59, 74–5, 78, 154–5, 283
  depicted 284 (illus. 21), 290–91
    (illus. 22), 292 (illus. 23), 302
    (illus. 36)
  actions of 18, 160, 171, 175, 177,
    338–40
  blackmail of 63
  immunity of 59, 74–7
  fame of 298–9, 302–3, 338–40
  see also brothels; prostitutes and
    prostitution
bawdy houses *see* brothels